McGRAW-HILL PUBLICATIONS
IN SOCIOLOGY

Richard T. LaPiere, Consulting Editor

RURAL LIFE IN PROCESS

McGRAW-HILL PUBLICATIONS IN SOCIOLOGY

RICHARD T. LAPIERE, *Consulting Editor*

Baber—MARRIAGE AND THE FAMILY

Bowman—MARRIAGE FOR MODERNS

Cook—COMMUNITY BACKGROUNDS OF EDUCATION

House—THE DEVELOPMENT OF SOCIOLOGY

LaPiere—COLLECTIVE BEHAVIOR

LaPiere—SOCIOLOGY

Landis—RURAL LIFE IN PROCESS

Lumley—PRINCIPLES OF SOCIOLOGY

McCormick—ELEMENTARY SOCIAL STATISTICS

Mead—COOPERATION AND COMPETITION AMONG PRIMITIVE PEOPLES

Queen and Thomas—THE CITY

Reckless—CRIMINAL BEHAVIOR

Reckless and Smith—JUVENILE DELINQUENCY

Reuter and Hart—INTRODUCTION TO SOCIOLOGY

Reuter and Runner—THE FAMILY

Smith—POPULATION ANALYSIS

Thompson—POPULATION PROBLEMS

von Hentig—CRIME: CAUSES AND CONDITIONS

Young—INTERVIEWING IN SOCIAL WORK

Young—SOCIAL TREATMENT IN PROBATION AND DELINQUENCY

The late Edward B. Reuter
was Consulting Editor of this
series from its inception in 1928
until his death in 1946.

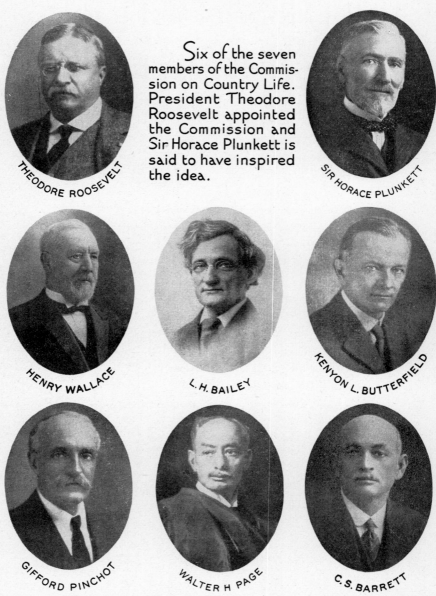

Six of the seven members of the Commission on Country Life. President Theodore Roosevelt appointed the Commission and Sir Horace Plunkett is said to have inspired the idea.

THEODORE ROOSEVELT

SIR HORACE PLUNKETT

HENRY WALLACE

L. H. BAILEY

KENYON L. BUTTERFIELD

GIFFORD PINCHOT

WALTER H PAGE

C. S. BARRETT

The appointment by Theodore Roosevelt of the Country Life Commission in 1907 "probably moved rural sociology ahead a generation." For a history of rural sociology, see Appendix.

RURAL LIFE
IN PROCESS

By PAUL H. LANDIS

Chairman, Division of Rural Sociology
Professor of Sociology
The State College of Washington

SECOND EDITION

NEW YORK   TORONTO   LONDON

McGRAW-HILL BOOK COMPANY, INC.

1948

RURAL LIFE IN PROCESS

THE MAPLE PRESS COMPANY, YORK, PA.

PREFACE TO THE SECOND EDITION

The usefulness of a textbook depends upon the timeliness of the factual material presented, as well as on the basic theory it contains, especially in the field of sociology where social experience quickly disturbs the trend of events. The basic theory of *Rural Life in Process* remains. Factual data have been brought up to date. Changes in public policy affecting rural life have been recognized, and new research has been taken into account. Chapters on population, farm labor, and welfare have had to be extensively reworked and others changed substantially to take into account new forces operating in rural life.

Special attention has been given to the expansion of the chapters on migration, since this phase of rural behavior is of increasing significance. During the past years, since the first edition appeared, special studies of the Bureau of the Census as well as those of individual workers and of the author have greatly increased our knowledge of rural migration and factors associated with it. Five chapters, including much new material, have replaced the four chapters in the first edition.

New data of objective studies on rural personality, rural youth, and rural culture have been introduced. The personality-forming process is the basic interest in this as in the first edition.

The author hopes that the book will continue to have a wide use in the classroom, not only to give students a specific picture of various phases of rural life but to build for them a perspective of rural society in a dynamic culture. The emphasis on rural life in a dynamic industrialized society continues, the general theme of the introductory chapter being the same as in the first section.

Appreciation is expressed to Carol Larson for revising the index.

Paul H. Landis

Pullman, Wash.
March, 1948

PREFACE TO THE FIRST EDITION

TODAY all of life is connected not only by the material devices that multiply contact and broaden experience but also by the interactive processes which these material devices facilitate. Rural society can be understood only when considered as a part of the total design of American life. Therefore, this book deals with rural society in its functional, processual, psychological, interactive aspects, viewing the rural drama in the cultural perspective of American civilization. In such an approach social facts and statistical findings, analyses of structure, and descriptions of organizational frameworks are used as data to reveal the more active, dynamic, living elements of rural association. Interest centers in the personality formation and adjustment of the individual, in alignments and realignments of social relationships within the rural group, in the functioning of institutions, in their lags and readjustments, and in the emergence of new problems in the life processes of the social group and the analysis of old problems as they are manifest in the new cultural scheme.

The phrase "in process" used in the title implies primarily the view maintained throughout that rural life is in a state of rapid transition. New patterns are at many points replacing the old. Everywhere in rural society one senses the "onward movement of life." Experience, institutions, and problems, every important aspect of personal and institutional life, are being modified by new social forces. Secondarily, but in a more specific sense, the phrase "in process" is used to suggest the emphasis on the social processes operative in rural life. The rural sociologist, like sociologists in other fields, begins his study with man and the environment. The purpose of his science is to show how raw human nature is formed by forces within the environment. Social processes are the interactive forces that shape and reshape the person in the environment and that also lead to the continual modification of the environment itself.

The first chapter is the keynote to the point of view developed in the book. The other two chapters of Part I deal with the basic structural patterns of the organization scheme in which rural society functions. Part II describes the environmental setting in which the personality of the rural person is formed, emphasis being placed on the more static aspects of the environmental mold. Part III launches more directly into the major interest of the book—processes operative in the functioning of a dynamic, highly mobile, modern rural society. Part IV considers the effectiveness of basic rural institutions in meeting the needs of the individual in this kind of society. Part V is a survey of problems as they appear in the light of the processes operative in the new rural environment. The final chapter is a summary of possible social implications of recent rural trends.

Sincere thanks are extended to colleagues at the State College of Washington who assisted in the development of the book by suggestions and criticisms: to Dr. Carl F. Reuss of the Division of Rural Sociology for many valuable suggestions on form and structure of the full manuscript; to Professor A. A. Smick of the Graduate School of Social Work for a critical reading of Chapters 26 and 27; to Professor Carl E. Dent of the Department of Sociology for reading and offering suggestions on Chapter 18; to Professor F. W. Clower of the Department of Economics for a critical reading of Chapter 22. Richard Wakefield read several chapters and shared in the development of certain ideas that have originated in our joint research in the farm labor and rural migration fields. H. D. McCullough of the Division of Extension and Industry, U.S. Department of the Interior, read the entire manuscript and made valuable suggestions. My brother, Judson T. Landis, sociologist at Southern Illinois Normal University, criticized several chapters in their initial stages. Mollie Hollreigh prepared the index. Acknowledgment is made in footnotes to journals that permitted the use of material which they had previously published.

PAUL H. LANDIS

PULLMAN, WASH.
July, 1940

CONTENTS

CONTENTS xiii

CONTENTS

PART IV. SOCIAL INSTITUTIONS IN A CHANGING CULTURE

PART V. EMERGING PROBLEMS OF A DYNAMIC SOCIETY

CONTENTS

The great rural interests are human interests, and good crops are of little value to the farmer unless they open the door to a kind of life on the farm.

—Theodore Roosevelt

I would that the rural youth could see in front of them the opportunity to build not an urban but a new rural civilization.

—O. E. Baker

In view of the ever-increasing control of social processes by urban standards and ideals, it is emphatically important to recognize the vital contributions of rural communities, always the primary sources of population and the guardians of the Holy Earth.

—Thomas J. Jones

Part I

THE STRUCTURE AND ORGANIZATION OF RURAL LIFE
IN THE UNITED STATES

IN THE beginning rural sociologists talked of the anatomy of the rural community and made studies of the skeletal structure. These were interesting, necessary, and important beginnings. But anatomy is important because it relates to function. Organization implies both structure and function. Even more important than the externals of organization are the life processes that operate within the framework of organization. Although interest in this book centers primarily in social experience, social process, and social function as these elements work themselves out in the formation of personality and social institutions, and in the creation of social problems, one must describe the stage on which the social drama is set.

CHAPTER 1

RURAL LIFE IN AN URBAN-INDUSTRIAL SOCIETY

THE INTERACTION OF CONTEMPORARY RURAL AND URBAN LIFE

ONCE rural life was relatively static, the ebb and flow of similar events grooving deeply into channels of custom; today rural life is dynamic, changing, a mixture of old traditions and new techniques. Contemporary rural culture contains many relics of the thinking of those ages when all societies changed slowly, but prominent in it also are evidences of the effects of a revolutionary age. Evidences of culture lag, of an emotional clinging to old culture traits, to fixed attitudes, to established patterns of life are apparent; but a desire for the mechanically new, the progressive, the efficient, the modern, the urbane, is manifest also.

Vast differences are to be found in the degree to which these conflicting elements exist in various sections of the country and in different localities. Rural life is not one culture but many cultures. Old folk cultures persist with remarkable integration in the isolated hinterlands; where farm and city are in close contact, as in urban-industrial areas, rural and urban cultures are much alike. Within a few miles of New York City with its seven million people one may find isolated areas in which simple folk cultures persist, but in areas in immediate contact with the great city one finds a metropolitan-minded farm populace which is closely tied in with urban life. Between these two extremes is the great mass of American farmers who have little in common with peasants of other nations or with the metropolitan population of this nation.

The nation's past is one of rural experience; its present is a blending of ruralism with urbanism, the latter holding the dominant place in the mechanized phases of experience and at the same time rapidly encroaching on the more psychological aspects of behavior, making deep inroads into the mores, customs, and traditions of rural people. The nation's future is, if present trends continue, to be one in which urban patterns may be expected to dominate even more. It is, of course, possible that the future trend may be toward a balance between metropolitan urbanism and progressive ruralism; it is possible that the rural life of tomorrow, by combining the better elements of the folk culture of rural society with selected phases of urban culture, may achieve a level of human adjustment that has been unparalleled in either rural or urban cultures of the past.

3

In the nation's recent history there has been a clash between patterns of the old folk cultures of rural society and the patterns of a highly dynamic urban-industrial civilization. In rural areas is the bigness of space; in urban areas, the bigness of man's creative power. In rural areas the slow-moving, slow-changing folkways which make for the adaptation of a stable people to a stable environment persist;[1] in the new metropolitan culture technical patterns are dominant, leading to rapidly changing adaptive technicways[2] which lack the guide of precedence and have only a short background of experience. In the society of yesterday with its slow and ineffective means of communication and transportation, there was a significant degree of self-sufficiency; in the new metropolis, rapid means of communication and transportation concentrate and in these nerve centers of the nation there have arisen groups with vested interests which employ communication and transportation devices in selling and distributing goods, and in creating new desires for goods on the manufacture and sale of which the metropolis itself subsists.

The old folk cultures of rural society achieved adaptation but lacked inventiveness; the new metropolitan culture specializes in inventiveness but often is lacking in adaptation. In the old rural order, which lacked much in the way of modern sophisticated specialized personality types, there was fairly perfect adjustment because life was relatively stable, simple, and sure; in the new metropolis social adjustment is a perpetual problem; nervous strain, personal tensions, blighted hopes, frustrations, diversity of patterns, and problems of choice constantly disturb the individual.

In the old rural order self-sufficiency was achieved by long hours of steady toil, by playing a shrewd hand against nature; in the newer economy men live by matching wits with men and with the market.[3] There is often little relationship between hours of toil or strenuousness of work and economic reward. In the older society one achieved ruggedness of character and a steadfastness of purpose, as well as status in the community, by vigorously attacking his natural environment and conquering it; in the newer cultural community a different set of social definitions prevails and status comes, not so much by conquering the nature environment, as by achieving success in a vocation accepted as being superior, or by acquiring great wealth through the manipulation of highly artificial social values. In the older rural economy there was

---

[1] This characterization of rural life has never been so true of farm life in America as of peasant cultures elsewhere, but it is true as compared to urban culture.

[2] This term is used by Howard W. Odum to describe behavior traits developed in man's adaptation to machine technology. See his "Notes on Technicways in Contemporary Society," *American Sociological Review*, vol. 2, pp. 336–346, June, 1937.

[3] Competitive capitalism which characterizes urban-industrial culture is at the base of this characteristic of modern civilization.

little competition for goods, power, or status; seldom did the farmer recognize himself as a competitor with his neighbor. In the new metropolitan economy competition has become a major process; races, social classes, individuals within the same profession, and those in different professions, all are engaged in a mighty competitive struggle, each recognizing that the rewards they seek, whether enviable jobs, much wealth, or social honors, are scarce and that only a few will attain them.

In the old rural order man lived so near nature that he himself acted in most phases of his behavior in a fairly natural manner— not that human beings ever live without the embellishments of culture, but there are striking differences in the number of these embellishments. In a highly civilized age embellishments deeply overlay much of natural behavior.

The rural sociologist, like the urban sociologist, is interested in the contemporary merging of the rural-agricultural and urban-industrial worlds as the two have been drawn together by the newer forces making for movement and contact. Generally speaking, the urban sociologist has been inclined to forget that urbanism in America has grown out of a rural heritage. This the rural sociologist must emphasize. It matters not from which angle one approaches the problem—it is from many viewpoints the same problem, that of urban-industrial civilization in a rural world or of rural civilization in an urban-industrial world. The problem is centered in the meeting and blending of the rural and the urban in our time and generation. At one end of the road in America today is the metropolis, the center of cultural diffusion in the modern world; at the other end in the distant hinterland, reached last by media for contact, one finds surviving elemental rural traits that have characterized peoples living under conditions of rural isolation throughout history. Most of farm life has left behind elemental traits in the field of material culture, and only those few rural areas that for some exceptional reason are still extremely isolated by geographical factors retain all the old rural mores intact. Most farmers in the United States are distributed somewhere along the scale between extreme ruralism and metropolitan urbanism.

This meeting and blending of rural-urban civilization only recently began. On a nationwide scale it has been in the process scarcely forty years. Or to view the problem from the urban angle, the city is so new in many parts of America that most of its inhabitants and many of its mores have a rural heritage only one or two generations removed—a heritage which is kept alive even today by the constant urbanward movement of youth.

The process of blending elements of rural and urban culture and the readjustment of the two to each other is almost certain to continue, for absolute geographical isolation in America is rapidly becoming a matter of history. Not that all areas are closely knit into the communicative scheme, but all areas are more closely knit than they have ever been before in this nation or in any other, and they are becoming more so each year as the tentacles of radio,[1] press, and the transportation system are extended into the rural hinterland.

The automobile, the airplane, and the railroad have not only increased mobility but also decreased the time-space distance between the metropolis and remote hinterlands. Year by year the continent shrinks in size and the time factor in the diffusion of information is reduced. There is scarcely such a thing as time in the radio flash; television, when perfected, will practically eliminate it in the diffusion of pictures and personalities; the wire photo, which is widely used in the press today and which was only recently made practical, has greatly reduced the time element in the graphic presentation of news. These new developments, and others as yet unforeseen, added to the telephone, telegraph, wireless, and similar devices, multiply enormously the possibilities of making spatial separation relatively meaningless. Therefore, the problem of the rural community's adjusting to an urban-industrial age and that of urban-industrial society's establishing relationships with rural society are and will continue to be prominent and of vital concern to all sociologists and certainly to all persons who would understand either rural or urban life.

THE URBAN FOCUS OF AMERICAN LIFE

An aerial view of the nation reveals a striking formation of its spatial patterns. There appear the highways for mobility—roads, railroads, air routes—and the paths of communication—telegraph wires, telephone lines, mail routes. In the remote rural districts the highways are narrow dirt roads, but all converge at points in the heart of the great metropolis. Approaching the city, the network of roads becomes a close-knit web; the traffic thickens as the routes converge and there is congestion in the city's center. This network is suggestive of the flow of goods and of men in American life. Of course, the picture is more complex than this; there are minor, intermediate, and major centers where highways focus and from which they disperse; and in the metropolis land routes meet the water on which ship lines of the world come and go with passengers and cargoes of goods for human use. In a like sense every small town is a center of dominance for a rural hinterland.

Such is the pattern of lines of travel, trade, communication, and contact. The metropolis is the nucleus of American material civilization. If one could trace the less tangible network of the social structure, he would find that the social organizations of national scope center in the metropolis also. The men

[1] A study of radio ownership of farm and nonfarm households in 1945 showed that 66 per cent of all farm households and 80 per cent of nonfarm households had radios, making a percentage for the rural population of 73. Lowest rates were in the farm South where 51 per cent had radios. *Attitudes of Rural People toward Radio Service*, U.S. Department of Agriculture, Washington, D. C., January, 1946.

who run the nation's presses, who control its newspapers, its books, its magazines, its schools, its churches, and its radios work in the city; the nation's
great cathedrals, its shrines, its most admired architecture, its most lavish
displays of wealth are found there; the nation's mechanical industries center
in and are controlled from the city. It is the seat of political power.

The metropolis, because it is located at the crossroads between continents
and at the converging point of the nation's nerve centers, is charged with
energy; in it innovations are quickly adopted and diffused. The new, spectacular, colorful metropolis has become the focus of attention; the comparatively
colorless, staid, prosaic rural community, in spite of its long past, in spite of its
fundamental nature in providing for human needs, fails to challenge the imag-

	Urban	Rural
1890	35.4%	64.6%
1900	40.0%	60.0%
1910	45.8%	54.2%
1920	51.4%	48.6%
1930	56.2%	43.8%
1940	56.7%	43.3%
1944	59.6%	40.4%

Per Cent of the Population of the United States Living in Urban and in Rural
Areas, 1890–1947

During the course of 50 years the nation changed from a predominately rural nation
to a predominately urban one. In 1890 almost two out of three of the population lived in
the open country and in hamlets, towns, and villages of less than 2,500 people. By 1947
only about two out of five persons of the nation's 142 million civilians lived in these rural
areas, approximately three out of five living in urban places (places of 2,500 people and
above).

ination as does the metropolis in an age when it is still new. But cities do not
make or maintain a nation; the rural hinterland beyond is basic in providing
food, raw materials, and social stability. And this rural hinterland in our time
is dynamic with change, pulsating with conflicting impulses of new social
forces.

THE URBANIZATION OF POPULATION

The trend of population in the industrialized Occident and in port cities
of the Orient[1] for well over a century has been toward urbanization. Census
data for the United States present a concrete picture of the increasing urbaniza-

[1] A. F. Weber, *The Growth of Cities in the Nineteenth Century*, Columbia Studies in
History, Economics, and Public Law, no. 29, Columbia University Press, New York, 1899.

tion of the United States. Estimates for 1944 show that only 40.4 per cent of the population was rural, that 59.6 per cent was urban. ("Rural" as defined by the census applies to open country or places of under 2,500 population.) The figure preceding traces the changes of recent decades. In 1890, 65 per cent of the people lived in rural communities. Now, in a nation of approximately 140 million people, less than a fifth are farmers (see table) From a traditionally rural-agricultural nation ours has become an urban-industrial one.

FARM POPULATION IN THE UNITED STATES, 1910–1946

Year	Number of Persons on Farms Jan. 1*
1910	32,076,960
1920	31,614,269
1925	30,830,000
1930	30,169,000
1935	31,800,907
1940	30,269,000
1946 (Jan.)	25,990,000
1947 (Jan.)	27,550,000

* *Farm Population Estimates*, U.S. Bureau of Agricultural Economics, and U.S. Census estimates, August, 1947.

The farm population reached an all-time high in 1910. There were fewer persons on farms in 1946 than during any period since 1910. In 1910 approximately 32 million of the total population of 92 million were farm population; in 1940 approximately 30 million of a total population of 130 million, in January, 1946, less than 26,000,000 of approximately 140,000,000. This represented the war-time low in farm population. By 1947 the return to farms had begun.

The population drift has been toward large centers and in consequence huge metropolises have come into positions of dominance.[1] The 1940 census reports 140 metropolitan communities in the nation, communities in which the central city had at least 50,000 population (see map 9). Population has concentrated on the deepwater front[2] of the nation, for it is on the ocean coasts, the Great Lakes front, and the Gulf shore, where water meets land,[3] that most of the great industrial centers have developed.

THE MEANING OF THE POPULATION SHIFT

The shift of population from rural to urban territory is indicative of a redistribution of occupations and of social interests as well as of people. It reflects a new emphasis in economic and social life. Commercial and industrial

[1] R. D. McKenzie, *The Metropolitan Community*, McGraw-Hill Book Company, Inc., New York, 1933.

[2] *Ibid.*

[3] C. H. Cooley advanced the view that cities tend to develop at breaks in transportation. See his *Sociological Theory and Social Research*, Henry Holt and Company, Inc., New York, 1930.

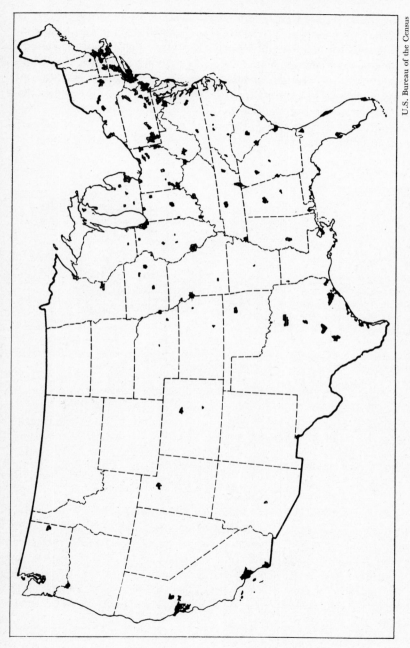

U.S. Bureau of the Census

The Nation's 140 Metropolitan Communities as of 1940

In the 140 metropolitan communities listed, each of which has at least 50,000 people in the central city, reside 48 per cent of the total people of the nation. From these nuclei of the national life emanate most of the influences making for change in the rural hinterland.

occupations are acting as magnets, drawing population from agricultural communities. This shift is reflected in the occupational trend (see figure). Agriculture now employs less than one-fifth of the gainfully employed of the nation; 70 years previously it engaged half of them. At the same time the proportions engaged in trade, transportation, industry, commerce, and allied occupations have greatly increased. Only in a society that has accumulated numerous techniques for the production of consumable goods can great numbers live apart from the soil. The shift of a majority of the population to urban residence and to nonagricultural vocations is suggestive of the highly inventive character

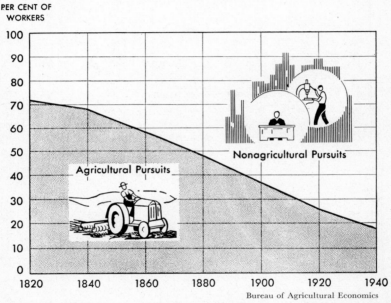

PER CENT OF WORKERS

Agricultural Pursuits

Nonagricultural Pursuits

Bureau of Agricultural Economics

In the year 1870, 53 of every 100 workers were engaged in agriculture, in 1940 less than one in 20, and during World War II perhaps only one in 15 to 18—evidence that nonagricultural occupations have come to play leading roles on the vocational stage.

of American civilization. While the industrial revolution has been in progress, the agricultural revolution has made great strides, hastening the decline in the proportion of, and the need for, farmers and at the same time making life apart from the soil possible for four-fifths of the gainfully employed of the nation. In 1787 the surplus food produced by 19 farmers was required to feed one city person. During recent years 19 farmers have been able to produce enough food for 56 nonfarm people in the United States and 10 people living abroad, a total of 66 people.[1]

[1] *Technological Trends and National Policy*, p. 99, National Resources Committee, Section on Agriculture, by S. H. McCrory, R. F. Hendrickson, and Committee, Washington, D. C., 1937.

The farm population is still the largest group dealing with primary processes. Farmers, like miners, lumbermen, fishermen, and hunters, perform the first step in production; they work with nature and exploit her resources. At the opposite extreme in the metropolis are found the highest degree of specialization and the highest development of the arts; there extremely intricate invented products are formed from basic raw materials. As the life of the nation has developed, numerous inventions have led to new manufacturing processes, all of them requiring an elaborate division of labor so that there has come to be centered in the metropolis a multiplicity of functions catering to numerous created human desires that are at the basis of the new standard of living.

IMPLICATIONS OF URBANIZATION TO SOCIAL LIFE

The urban majority in the population is indicative of major changes in social experience, social functions, and cultural structure. Great differences in population density have developed and are becoming greater each year. In the nation there are approximately 44 people per square mile, but in New York City the average is over 25,000 per square mile. At the other extreme, Beaverhead County, Montana, has an average of slightly more than one person per square mile. Obviously, patterns of social organization must differ also.

Problems in institutional organization and services as well as differences in attitudes and points of view are traceable to these differences in spatial distribution of our people. Consider the comparative difficulties of obtaining electric lights in New York City and in Beaverhead County, or sewer systems, or schools, or churches, or hospitals, or doctors and nurses. Consider the necessary differences in material culture, in attitudes, in such behavior traits as hospitality, in standards of living, in outlook on life, in daily routine, to mention but a few of the thousands of differences existing between areas in which people live at a density of one per square mile and areas in which they live 25,000 to the square mile. Human values and relationships are different in densely and in sparsely populated areas.

The simple and homely culture of the self-sufficient agricultural community is inadequate to sustain life and create comfort in areas where population congregates. As multitudes jostle together in congested quarters, the simple nonmaterial culture of the rural environment proves inadequate also for purposes of control; in place of custom, laws must be invented, protective devices increased, and restrictions multiplied. The trend urbanward necessarily means a trend toward a more intensive domestication of man.

The shift urbanward is indicative of the growing number of secondary, impersonal group relations and of the decline of elemental, primary group relations in contemporary society. The intimate, homely social virtues and vices of yesterday are being replaced by the impersonal, sophisticated, competitive patterns of an anonymous people; the simple, occupationally homogeneous society of yesterday is giving way to the highly complex and somewhat stratified society of a heterogenous occupational world. It is in this world of complex and dynamic relationships that a sociology of farm life must be built.

RURAL DEFINED

The U.S. Bureau of the Census classifies people living in the open country and in places of less than 2,500 population as rural. People living in cities and other incorporated places having 2,500 inhabitants or more are termed urban.[1] The census divides the rural population for the years 1920 to 1940 into "rural farm" and "rural nonfarm." The rural farm population consists of people living on farms; the rural nonfarm of all other rural people whether living in villages, hamlets, or open country. A "farm," as defined by the census, is a tract of three acres or more being farmed or a smaller tract yielding $250 worth of produce per year.

When one is dealing with social and psychological traits the arbitrary division point of the census is not always practical. Socially the rural area is one in which people live far enough apart spatially to reduce contacts to the point where they cultivate and appreciate intimate relationships with most of their neighbors. The environment wherein people talk about their neighbors and regulate them by observation and gossip does not always cease to exist in a place of 2,500 people, even though there are a few areas in the open country where it has already practically disappeared.

No clear-cut, universally applicable definition of the rural has ever been stated, nor can it be.[2] Definitions that provide a working basis for mutual understanding depend somewhat on the point of view and the trend of emphasis of an author.[3] This being the case, the reader will find the following elements entering into the definition of "rural" in this work: For statistical purposes rural consists of places with less than 2,500 people, unless otherwise noted. For

---

[1] An exception to this standard procedure is found in New Hampshire, Massachusetts, and Rhode Island, where "towns (townships) are classified as urban if they have more than 2,500 inhabitants and certain urban characteristics." A few large townships in other states are likewise classified as urban under a special rule of the census.

[2] A working definition of the city or of the urban is no less difficult to state than of the rural. For a condensed summary of points of view see Stuart A. Queen and Lewis F. Thomas, *The City*, pp. 3–9, McGraw-Hill Book Company, Inc., New York, 1939.

[3] The most exhaustive definition of "rural" and "urban" attempted in this country is that of P. A. Sorokin and C. C. Zimmerman. They differentiate the rural and urban worlds by occupation, environment, size of community, density of population, heterogeneity and homogeneity of population, social differentiation and stratification, mobility, and system of interaction, devoting 45 pages to the topic. Those interested in difficulties of definition, not only for rural sociology in this country but also for it in European countries, will do well to read their interesting account in *Principles of Rural-urban Sociology*, chap. 2, Henry Holt and Company, Inc., New York, 1929.

purposes of social-psychological analysis, rural consists of those areas in which a high degree of intimacy and informality characterizes relationships, the urban beginning at the ill-defined point where people assume impersonal attitudes toward each other. For purposes of economic-occupational analysis, farming is the central point of interest.

AN APPROACH TO RURAL SOCIOLOGY

Any text which tries to describe a field as comprehensive as that covered by rural sociology, a science which attempts to understand the social environment, social activities, and interactive processes of a major sector of the American population, must of necessity select a point of emphasis, for no one book can begin to cover with any degree of completeness all the important phases of the social experience of a group of people in as complex a social system, cultural structure, and institutional arrangement as exist in America.

In selecting a point of orientation one has several alternatives from which to choose, as a citation to certain authorities will demonstrate. In 1937 a group of leading rural sociologists began a study to learn the outstanding contributions of rural sociological research and to formulate a statement of what they believed to be the most fruitful field for research in the future. In their report, which was completed in 1938, they have the following to say with regard to the field of rural sociology:

Sociology is the description of the forms of human association, the factors influencing the origin, development, structure, and functioning of these various forms, and of their cultural products. Rural sociology is the study of these forms of association in the rural environment, and describes their differences from and relations to those of towns and cities. By "forms of association" are meant all describable types of human association, whether they be institutions, community or neighborhood organizations, cultural patterns, or trade or class organizations. By "the origin, development, and functioning of these forms" are meant the conditions under which, and the processes by which, different forms of human association have come into existence, tend to maintain their existence, and function in relation to their own life processes and the environment in which they exist.[1]

Obviously this statement is comprehensive and inclusive.

John M. Gillette, author of the first textbook in rural sociology, both in the organization of the latest edition of his book and in his definition of rural sociology emphasizes a more specialized theme. He believes that the central idea of rural sociology is the "results ensuing from the adjustment to the land," for such adjustment is "paramount in national and rural life, or at least of first-rate importance."[2]

[1] *The Field of Research in Rural Sociology*, prepared by a committee of the Rural Sociological Society and the Bureau of Agricultural Economics, p. 2, U.S. Department of Agriculture, Washington, D. C., October, 1938.

[2] *Rural Sociology*, 3d ed., The Macmillan Company, New York, 1936.

C. C. Zimmerman believes that the central concept of rural sociology is "the mechanisms and effects of urbanization and ruralization upon a population." He says, "We cannot go far wrong if we make urbanization or ruralization, its social mechanisms, causes and effects, the central point of discovery for a science of rural sociology."[1]

In line with Zimmerman's view, the writer considers that urbanization is a major force in rural society today and that the effects of urbanization in all its implications upon both urban and rural society should be a major interest of sociologists. That it should be the central interest of rural sociology may not be universally accepted, but those who have their fingers on the pulse of rural life will agree that it is one of the most important, if not the most important, centers of interest of rural sociological science.

Barnes suggests that urbanization of rural life virtually creates a new epoch in human history. He says,

The relative decline in the importance of rural life and the urbanization of that which lingers on certainly constitutes one of the major turning points in the cultural and institutional history of mankind. The reduction of rural life and institutions to a subordinate position in Western civilization has veritably introduced a new epoch in human history.[2]

By urbanization I suppose we mean primarily the tendency of life to become more formalized in its system of social control, more mechanized in its material aspects, more artificial in its environmental setting in that inventions become more prominent and nature phenomena less prominent, more impersonal in its social relationships in that social organization becomes more systematic and less spontaneous.

In emphasizing this urbanization process we must always keep in mind that the culture pattern of a nation is in a broad sense a unity. Influences that we call urban are a part and product of broader forces that dominate and color the American culture pattern, such as mechanization, industrialization, specialization, individualization, struggle for status induced by our open-class system, traits for which America has come to be known throughout the world. These forces tend to appear first and to be most prominent in the city. But change brought about by contact is never fully one-sided. No culture group ever does all the taking or all the giving. Rural life makes its contribution to the culture pattern and interactive processes of a dynamic society.

---

[1] "The Trend of Rural Sociology," *Trends in American Sociology*, chap. 5, pp. 254–255, ed. by George Lundberg, Read Bain, and Nels Anderson, Harper & Brothers, New York, 1929.

[2] Harry Elmer Barnes, *Society in Transition*, pp. 559–560, Prentice-Hall, Inc., New York, 1939.

QUESTIONS FOR REVIEW AND DISCUSSION

1. What influences have brought about the increased interaction between rural and urban areas in the United States?

2. Discuss communication as a factor in breaking down rural isolation.

3. Contrast the metropolis with the rural community as to the prominence of forces making for change.

4. In what sense does American life have its focus in the metropolis?

5. Show how basic economic and occupational interests have changed within the nation. How have these changes affected farming as an occupation?

6. Where does one find the greatest occupational specialization in American life?

7. Suggest how changes in population distribution of recent years have affected social experience.

8. Do the things of the city seem to have greater prestige in our culture than the things of the farm community? Explain.

9. Define the term "rural" as used by the sociologist.

10. What is to be the central theme of this book?

COLLATERAL READING

Gillette, J. M.: *Rural Sociology*, 3d ed., chap. 5, The Macmillan Company, New York, 1936.

McKenzie, R. D.: *The Metropolitan Community*, McGraw-Hill Book Company, Inc., New York, 1933.

Odum, Howard W.: "Notes on Technicways in Contemporary Society," *American Sociological Review*, vol. 2, pp. 336–346, June, 1937.

Recent Social Trends in the United States, chap. 10 (by J. H. Kolb and E. de S. Brunner), McGraw-Hill Book Company, Inc., New York, 1933.

Sanderson, Dwight: *Rural Sociology and Rural Social Organization*, chap. 2, John Wiley & Sons, Inc., New York, 1942.

Smith, T. Lynn: *The Sociology of Rural Life*, rev. ed. chap. 2, Harper & Brothers, New York, 1947.

Sorokin, P. A., C. C. Zimmerman, and C. J. Galpin: *A Systematic Source Book in Rural Sociology*, vol. 3, chap. 23, University of Minnesota Press, Minneapolis, 1932.

Weber, A. F.: *The Growth of Cities in the Nineteenth Century*, Columbia Studies in History, Economics, and Public Law, no. 29, Columbia University Press, New York, 1899.

Williams, J. M.: *The Expansion of Rural Life*, chap. 2, Alfred A. Knopf, Inc., New York, 1926.

CHAPTER 2

THE STRUCTURAL PATTERN OF RURAL SOCIETY

THE STRUCTURAL pattern of a society bears directly on the nature of its functions, the character of its relationships, the tasks of its institutions, the nature of the social processes that characterize its life, and the social problems that interfere with its operations. As a foundation for our study of rural society, it is necessary to outline its ground plan.

PATTERNS OF RURAL ORGANIZATION

Rural life, although not ordinarily organized according to a plan, may be described by four general types of dispersion (see figure): (1) the *farm village type*, with the farmers living in a village and cultivating the outlying fields; (2) the *nebulous farm type* with a part of the farmers living in the village and tilling the surrounding fields and others scattering beyond the village who live on isolated farms; (3) the *arranged isolated farm type* with people dwelling in systematic fashion on main roads which lead out from a central village or trade center; and (4) the *pure isolated farm type* with all farmers dispersed, living on their own tracts of land. In the case of the last two forms of rural organization the village population is a service group engaged largely in trade and the professions rather than in farming.

THE FARM VILLAGE AS A MODE OF LIFE

Historically, the farm village form of rural social organization has predominated[1] and, considering the world as a whole, still is foremost. With few exceptions, it is now the typical form of rural aggregate throughout the Orient, each village usually being located on an elevated spot surrounded by an earthen wall and existing in the midst of its fields as an isolated and self-sufficient social world. In many sections of Europe also, the agricultural village still characterizes settlement.[2]

[1] Because of its unique sociological significance, this type of community has been studied fairly extensively by rural sociologists. The late Dwight Sanderson in his study, *The Rural Community* (Ginn and Company, Boston, 1932), traced the development of the agricultural village as a primary type of association throughout the world. Walter A. Terpenning studied village and open-country neighborhoods, confining his attention chiefly to European nations (*Village and Open-country Neighborhoods*, D. Appleton-Century Company, Inc., New York, 1931). N. L. Sims emphasized especially the ancient agricultural community (*The Rural Community, Ancient and Modern*, Charles Scribner's Sons, New York, 1920).

[2] P. A. Sorokin, C. C. Zimmerman, and C. J. Galpin, *A Systematic Source Book in Rural Sociology*, vol. 1, chap 5, University of Minnesota Press, Minneapolis, 1930.

Although common throughout the world, farm villages are the exception in the United States. Early settlers in New England, partly, no doubt, for mutual protection but also in order to perpetuate the form of life to which they had been accustomed in England, constructed farm villages after the Old

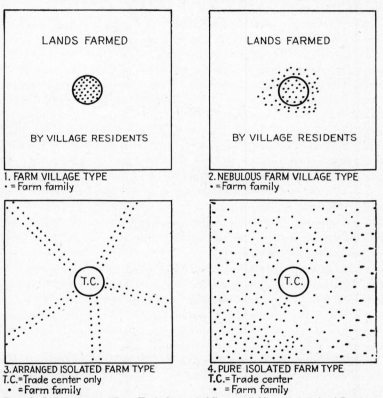

LANDS FARMED

BY VILLAGE RESIDENTS

1. FARM VILLAGE TYPE
• = Farm family

LANDS FARMED

BY VILLAGE RESIDENTS

2. NEBULOUS FARM VILLAGE TYPE
• = Farm family

3. ARRANGED ISOLATED FARM TYPE
T.C.=Trade center only
•   =Farm family

4. PURE ISOLATED FARM TYPE
T.C.= Trade center
•   = Farm family

From C. C. Zimmerman, "Farm Trade Centers in Minnesota," *Minnesota Agricultural Experiment Station Bulletin* 269.

FOUR MAJOR PATTERNS OF RURAL ORGANIZATION

Number 4, the pure isolated farm type, under which farmers live dispersed in unorganized fashion on their individual farms, using the town as a trade center, is almost universal in the United States, although number 1, under which farmers live in the village and go out to their fields, has characterized much of rural life throughout the world. The social implications of the pure isolated farm type of rural organization are numerous.

World plan. The three-field system for the rotation of crops, common pastures where the cattle were grazed, and a common wood lot where village families obtained their supply of winter fuel were characteristic. Some of these villages have persisted until the present time.[1] The Mormons in Utah settled in farm

[1] For a description of New England villages see N. L. Sims, *Elements of Rural Sociology*, rev. ed., chap. 3, The Thomas Y. Crowell Company, New York, 1934.

villages. This scheme of settlement, which was probably borrowed from the eastern part of the United States, proved to be especially well adapted to irrigated areas.[1] Today many Mormon communities are of the nebulous farm type, the individual choosing for himself whether he will remain in the village or locate on his outlying farm. The Amana Colony in Iowa, which was settled on a communistic basis, developed a farm village form of rural life. Members of the colony live today in seven villages, and from them work their 26,000 acres of land.[2] Many of the plantations in the Old South developed a system of organization comparable to a farm village, the laborers on the plantations being housed together in a small village within a short distance of the plantation home.[3]

With these exceptions and perhaps a few others, farm villages did not develop in the United States.[4]

The advantages of an agricultural village are numerous but depend somewhat upon the conditions of life of a people. It makes for a close-knit community unit by hindering the development of extreme individualism such as has characterized American farmers; in case a community faces danger, it provides common protection and always it increases the possibilities of mutual aid. Economies in providing institutional services and in establishing utilities on a cooperative basis are realized. The state of Utah had by 1920 a larger percentage of its farms equipped with electricity than had any other state in the Union.[5] In that state a rural social life has developed that is unique; the township does not exist as a functional unit but is used in property descriptions only. There is no isolation of farm and town; they are one in the sense that the farm is a part of the municipality. The village is a political, social, and economic entity; institutional participation is more extensive and socialization more complete than on the isolated farm.

On the other hand, as is illustrated by European village life, there develops an almost too close social integration in the farm village. A fairly self-sufficient village community easily becomes stagnant in that patterns of life are so completely impressed upon members that there is very little chance for variation or change;[3] community ideas and sentiment become firmly molded and limited in perspective.[7] Problems of sanitation arise where livestock are kept

---

[1] See Lowry Nelson, *A Social Survey of Escalante, Utah*, Brigham Young University Studies, no. 1, Provo, Utah, 1925; also his *Some Social and Economic Features of American Fork, Utah*, 1933.

[2] In 1932 the colony was incorporated as a capitalistic unit. However, the farm village plan of organization still persists.

[3] T. Lynn Smith in his "Farm Trade Centers in Louisiana, 1901–1931," describes life on certain plantations. *Louisiana State University Bulletin* 234, January, 1932.

[4] The nebulous farm type is so rare in America that it is not discussed.

[5] Lowry Nelson, *Some Social and Economic Features of American Fork, Utah*, p. 11.

[6] Dwight Sanderson, *op. cit.*, chap. 14.

[7] W. I. Thomas and Florian Znaniecki, *The Polish Peasant in Europe and America*, 5 vols., Chapman & Grimes, Inc., Boston, 1918–1920.

in the village and there is greater susceptibility to epidemics of disease than on the isolated farm.

In addition to the social disadvantages, numerous economic drawbacks exist for commercial agriculture. In a mechanized age, commercial agriculture calls for the farming of large areas, making impractical the agricultural village type of living as distances to fields and livestock would be great. Living on the farm has the added advantage of permitting the operator to give continuous attention to crops and livestock.

THE ARRANGED ISOLATED FARM TYPE

The arranged isolated farm type of rural life has developed in various sections of the world but is rarely found in the United States.[1] In certain areas of the lower Mississippi Valley early French settlements developed according to this plan. T. Lynn Smith[2] describes typica French parishes (counties) on the lower Mississippi (see figure, p. 20) where lland is divided into strips along the river, which once formed the transportation route. At the present time highways extend along the river with homes facing them; the land has been subdivided into strips so that all holdings continue to front on the river; all roads are built to conform to the location of the houses along the main water front. For miles along the river front the countryside has the appearance of one extended village street with all the houses and an occasional social institution—a school, a church, or a small trade center—alongside. Stores make deliveries daily to farm homes.

This form of life combines some of the advantages of the farm village with some of the advantages of the isolated farm type. Special services may be developed conveniently and contact with neighbors and with social institutions easily maintained; at the same time the individual lives on his land in close proximity to his livestock and crops.

THE PURE ISOLATED FARM TYPE

Throughout most sections of the United States the pure isolated farm type of settlement has developed. Such settlements are found in parts of all European countries but predominate in northern Europe, especially in the Baltic countries, Finland, and Scandinavia. The isolated settlement is not unknown even in parts of the Orient and is typical in England at the present time.[3]

As people moved westward it was difficult to maintain a close-knit group. The American nation was settled by a land-hungry lot whose eagerness to

[1] Parts of Canada settled by the French are of this type.

[2] *Op. cit.*, pp. 2–5; Vernon J. Parenton, "Notes on the Social Organization of a French Village in South Louisiana," *Social Forces*, pp. 76–77, October, 1938.

[3] For a concise discussion of the European situation see P. A. Sorokin, C. C. Zimmerman, and C. J. Galpin, *op. cit.*, pp. 267–273.

acquire land made them willing to make great social sacrifices. Land was more important than friends or associates and men were willing to take great risks in order to obtain it. Moreover, there developed in the westward movement the pioneer tradition of self-reliance. As the frontier continued to be pushed westward and the newly settled areas became more secure, land was

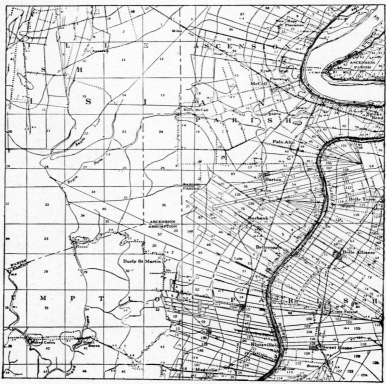

From T. Lynn Smith, *Farm Trade Centers in Louisiana*

AN EXAMPLE OF THE ARRANGED ISOLATED FARM TYPE (NUMBER 3) OF RURAL ORGANIZATION

This is a French settlement on the lower Mississippi in Louisiana where homes are located along the waterfront in systematic fashion and fields are narrow strips stretching back from the river. Today roads follow the river with the "arranged" pattern persisting. This is one of the few examples of such settlement to be found in the United States.

sold by the rugged individualists, who had braved the danger of the frontier to acquire it free, to the second wave of more home-loving families.[1] In many cases, however, even their stay was temporary.

A number of other psychological elements were involved in the breakdown

[1] See Thomas P. Abernathy, *From Frontier to Plantation in Tennessee*, University of North Carolina Press, Chapel Hill, 1932.

of group unity during the westward movement. The early settlers were a conglomerate lot representing many European nations. To build an agricultural village with an integrated social life requires a common tradition, a similarity of population stock, a homogeneity of nationality background; the mixed population elements found on the frontier in many instances provided no such foundation for unified agricultural settlements; pioneer life blended only temporarily creeds, classes, nationalities, and moral standards.

Added to these psychological factors were physical ones. The land survey system established by the Ordinance of 1787 resulted in the blocking off into squares of practically all of the land in the nation. This division was not conducive to close-knit settlements. Moreover, the country was new and lacking in established patterns which might indicate a desirable blueprint for social organization; roads had not been built and there were no institutions about which communities could be grouped. Later, as means of transportation developed, towns were located arbitrarily at points where goods could be picked up or left. Reinforcing the above influences were the homestead acts, designed to encourage settlement, which required a man to live on his land for a number of months or to cultivate or build upon it. Requirements varied somewhat with the various acts.

So much for history. Today, for the mass of American farmers who live under the pure isolated farm type of rural organization, the farm is the home. This fact is not only basic to an understanding of the general social structure of rural America but is also fundamental to an understanding of its economic, institutional, and psychological patterns. It is difficult under an isolated farm type of life to unify sentiment and achieve social action. A geographically isolated person tends to resist social pressure; in fact, until recently he was likely to have little contact with devices that would bring social pressure to bear upon him. There has generally been a paucity of social contact and of institutional relationships on the isolated farm. On the other hand the isolated farm has offered great economic advantages, in making possible the cultivation of large tracts of land. In America it paved the way for a machine revolution in agriculture such as the Old World has not experienced; it made it easier for the farmer to care for his livestock because he could be near it; it promoted family solidarity because the family on an isolated unit provides the chief social experience; it made for such economic prosperity that many of the handicaps of early isolation have been overcome by the extensive use of new means for contact and movement.

In other respects the social and economic costs of isolated settlement have been excessive. Living on the farm has led to an overemphasis on work. There are few social contacts to interfere with work and life is lived in the midst of tasks calling for action. The isolated farmer has paid an excessive cost for running water, sewage facilities, and electricity or has done without them because he could not afford the expense.[1] Rural institutions have been expensive, especially in the horse-and-buggy days, because the church, the school, and the government center had to be situated within driving distance if the farmer were to profit by their services. The one-room school, the little country church, the small county unit—all these were developed to serve the isolated farm. Unorganized isolated farm settlement has been expensive also from the standpoints of road building and upkeep. It has led to much futile conflict between town and country.[2]

THE NEIGHBORHOOD AS A PRIMARY SOCIAL UNIT IN THE PURE ISOLATED FARM TYPE OF RURAL ORGANIZATION

The most elemental social group beyond the family in the dispersed type of settlement is the neighborhood. In most communities the neighborhood arose primarily for purposes of self-help. It often sprang directly from the geographic locality, although it might center about an institution. The school, the church, the recreational group, or the store were creations of the neighborhood group, and these institutions helped to maintain over long periods of time a group consciousness.

Neighborhood boundaries were often irregular and indefinite, as is indicated by Taylor and Yoder's study of rural neighborhoods in Whitman County, Washington, which is typical of many studies in various states[3] (see figure). In spite of irregular boundaries people living in the neighborhoods had a consciousness of their extent and a name for the social unit. Of the 37 neighborhoods studied 11 were named for some individual; 11 for geographical phenomena—a flat, a hill, a river valley; six for wheat warehouses;[4] five for churches; two for stores; two for other factors. Union Flat, Oak Grove, Willow Creek, Long Tree, Bald Butte, and Badger Mountain, names such as one may find in any rural area, illustrate those obtained from nature phenomena. Such neighborhoods as Jones Neighborhood, Brown Neighborhood, Jackson Gulch, or Benjamin Creek are common and usually were named for an early settler. Pataha Flat, Penewawa Neighborhood, Wawawai Neighborhood, and Cowichee are Indian names. Fred School, Whelan Grange, U. B. Church, Baptist Church Neighborhood suggest institutions that have provided not only a name but also a focus for a neighborhood.

Classifying neighborhoods according to number of institutional bonds or

[1] In 1945 only 23 per cent of farm homes had water piped into the dwelling and only 44 per cent had electricity.

[2] See E. de S. Brunner, G. S. Hughes, and M. Patten, *American Agricultural Villages*, Doubleday & Company, Inc., New York, 1927, for examples of typical conflicts between small-town and farm groups.

[3] Edward Taylor and Fred R. Yoder, "Rural Social Organization in Whitman County," *Washington Agricultural Experiment Stations Bulletin* 203, June, 1926.

[4] The area covered by the study was devoted almost entirely to growing wheat.

interests, Taylor and Yoder found that in some cases there was more than one institutional center, whereas in others only one determined neighborhood consciousness. In some instances there was no institution at all, the locality determining group consciousness.[1] The school was a primary factor in 15

From Taylor and Yoder, "Rural Social Organization of Whitman County" *Washington Agricultural Experiment Stations Bulletin* 203, June, 1926.

NEIGHBORHOOD AREAS IN SOUTHEASTERN WHITMAN COUNTY, WASHINGTON

Throughout the nation, with its unorganized geographically isolated settlement patterns, neighborhoods arose spontaneously. Within these irregular areas scattered throughout the countryside a sense of primary group unity developed and social isolation disappeared.

of the 37 neighborhoods, the school and the grange together in three, the school and a warehouse in five, the church only in one, the school and church in four, the warehouse in three, a geographical factor only in three, and in one each a dance hall, a school and a post office, a grange and a warehouse.

[1] Edward Taylor and Fred R. Yoder, *op. cit.,* p. 16.

An interesting institution of the old neighborhood was the graveyard where families, lacking the lavish services of modern undertakers, buried their dead in simple style. These cemeteries, which were maintained by the neighborhood group, have all but disappeared except in remote mountainous sections. In many areas the graves have been plowed over and forgotten because American society has been too mobile for their maintenance.

The interest of the rural sociologist has centered upon the neighborhood as a natural group in the rural community,[1] for the neighborhood has characterized rural settlement throughout America, with the possible exception of areas in the Old South where it was hindered by the plantation system and by the system of social stratification.[2] The conflict of the black and white in the South has also encouraged this separation, resulting in the creation of two distinct neighborhood groups within the same locality.

In the open country of most sections the neighborhood early became the social unit, and in preautomobile days preserved some semblance of social activity in a rural world which otherwise would have been hopelessly stagnant. There is no doubt that the independent and democratic spirit of these rural neighborhoods has lent much to the democratic spirit of the nation, keeping alive a love of freedom and political autonomy and a hatred of centralized government and bureaucracy.

Since the coming of the automobile, many neighborhood groups have disappeared, some to reappear with new functions. Some neighborhoods lose certain functions and retain or gain others depending on social changes taking place in the locality. Neighborhoods in the vicinity of towns and villages are most likely to disintegrate, their functions being transferred to the town. Village-centered groups in certain areas are on the increase. Mutual intests, organizations, and institutions are playing a greater part in group formation than locality or tradition or just living together. Locality groups, however, tend to persist and to influence new forms of social organization.[3]

THE FARM TRADE CENTER IN THE RURAL SPATIAL PATTERN

Throughout the United States farm trade centers sprang up, linking isolated farmsteads with the commercial market beyond, and at the same time

[1] John H. Kolb, Rural Sociologist at the University of Wisconsin, has contributed extensively to the sociology of the open-country neighborhood in the United States. See his "Rural Primary Groups," *Wisconsin Agricultural Experiment Station Bulletin* 51, Madison, 1921; and his "Service Relations of Town and Country," *Wisconsin Agricultural Experiment Stations Bulletin* 58, Madison, 1923.

[2] C. C. Taylor, *Rural Sociology*, rev. ed., p. 559, Harper & Brothers, New York, 1933. See also Howard W. Odum, *Southern Regions of the United States*, pp. 97–99, University of North Carolina Press, Chapel Hill, 1936.

[3] This paragraph is based on findings of John H. Kolb and E. de S. Brunner. See their *A Study of Rural Society*, rev. and enlarged ed., pp. 64–66, Houghton Mifflin Company, Boston, 1940, or their *Rural Social Trends*, McGraw-Hill Book Company, Inc., New York, 1933.

serving as distributing points for goods which farmers needed. These trade centers also became service centers because, generally speaking, professional people and artisans—dentists, doctors, lawyers, teachers, ministers, blacksmiths, and mechanics—lived in the trade center rather than in the country side.

The open country has developed institutions of its own, notably the rural church and the rural school; nevertheless, as means of transportation have facilitated movement, the village has become a center for most institutional services, including recreation. Thus, the trade center bridges the gap between the rural neighborhood and the commercial, professional, recreational, and institutional organizations of the nation which have their focal point in the metropolis.

Farm trade centers ordinarily have less than 5,000 population and most of them are much smaller. They are located throughout agricultural districts and range in size from the crossroads store to the larger town which may draw trade from a wide hinterland. There are in the United States over 78,000 places with less than 2,500 population.[1] Of these, approximately 58,800 are places with less than 250 people and 19,200 are places with 250 to 2,500 population. Of all places with less than 2,500 population 13,288 were incorporated in 1940. In all places with under 2,500 there are living about 17,700,000 people or approximately 14 per cent of the nation's population. Of this group 4,000,000 live in places with less than 250 population, and almost 3,700,000 in places with 250 to 2,500 population.[1] The exact proportion of these places and of their resident populations which serve the farm population is not known.

In the early days farm trade centers needed to be located within a distance which could be covered by a team and wagon haul. Therefore, in more densely populated sections they usually were only eight or ten miles apart, although in more sparsely populated areas they were much more infrequent. As good roads and automobiles have multiplied, the very small hamlets have often disappeared, the farmer now going greater distances to market his produce and to obtain his merchandise. The small town has lost a number of its functions to the city which could handle them more effectively.[2] The trend of professional service has been the same, highly specialized practitioners locating

[1] For the best brief factual summary of data on number of unincorporated and incorporated places see Kolb and Brunner, *A Study of Rural Society*, 3d ed., chap. 13. For original studies of unincorporated places see C. Luther Fry, *American Villagers*, George H. Doran Co., 1926; Brunner and Smith, "Village Growth and Decline, 1930–1940," *Rural Sociology*, vol. 9, pp. 103–115, June, 1944; Douglas G. Marshall, "Hamlets and Villages in the United States: Their Place in the American Way of Life," *American Sociological Review*, vol. 11, pp. 159–165, April, 1946; Paul H. Landis, *The Number of Unincorporated Places in the United States and Their Estimated Populations*, Research Studies of the State College of Washington, vol. 6, pp. 160–188, December, 1938.

[2] See C. E. Lively, "Growth and Decline of Farm Trade Centers, 1905–1930," *Minnesota Agricultural Experiment Station Bulletin* 287, St. Paul, 1932; Paul H. Landis, "South Dakota Town-country Trade Relations, 1901–1931," *South Dakota Agricultural Experiment Station Bulletin* 274, Brookings, 1932.

in the large city. The farmer today can go greater distances to the metropolis to seek specialized consultation on health, medical, or financial problems.

All rural areas of the nation are supplied with trade centers which vary both in size and in the number and character of their mercantile, artisan, professional, and institutional services. Kolb has made the following fivefold classification of trade centers:[1] (1) the single-service type of trade center, which offers one service such as is performed by the general store, the rural church, or the rural school; (2) the limited or simple-service type, which has a relatively small service area and offers but a few services; (3) the semi-complete service type, which provides almost all the services that farm people need; (4) the complete or partially specialized type, which provides the farmer a choice of stores and has most of the social institutions that a community group would desire; (5) the urban or highly specialized type, which is prepared to satisfy a great range of interests and desires.

Without plan or creative design trade centers of the types outlined above are scattered throughout agricultural areas of the nation, their size and frequency depending upon the density of farm population and the prosperity of the region. Since the coming of the automobile overlapping zones of influence and division of function between small and large towns is characteristic, and most rural areas have within easy driving distance a choice of any one of a number of trade centers. Close at hand may be several small centers and at greater distances one or more urban centers. (See map for an example of spatial distribution.)

SOCIAL SIGNIFICANCE OF SEPARATION OF TOWN AND FARM

The artificial separation in America of the farm trade center from the open country by means of incorporation has led to a great number of petty conflicts and misunderstandings between town and country which probably would not have existed under a farm village economy.[2] Incorporation means separate existence of the town and exclusion of the farmer from town affairs and ordinarily from the regulation of town institutions. The open country is under the political supervision of the county—not of the town. The farmer often has been excluded from the associations of the townspeople, so that even though he came to the small town frequently on business he was in a real sense a stranger and an outsider.[3]

In what way American farm life, and in fact American civilization, would have been different had rural areas been settled on a different plan than the disorganized isolated farm plan one can only guess. That it would have been very different seems likely. The problems, processes, and institutions of rural

---

[1] J. H. Kolb, "Service Relations of Town and Country," *op. cit.*

[2] E. de S. Brunner, G. S. Hughes, and M. Patten, *op. cit.*

[3] Horace B. Hawthorn, *The Sociology of Rural Life*, pp. 421–422. D. Appleton-Century Company, Inc., New York, 1926.

life that are the focus of rural sociological interest would have also been different. In any case, an appreciation of the structural pattern and its possible implications to social life is important at a time when various government projects for planning new communities in irrigated sections are in the making.[1]

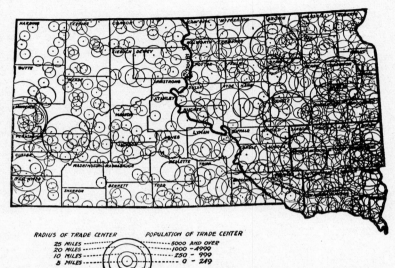

From Paul H. Landis, "The Growth and Decline of South Dakota Trade Centers, 1901–1933," *South Dakota Agricultural Experiment Station Bulletin* 279, Brookings, 1933.

A DIAGRAMMATIC SCHEME SHOWING SPATIAL DISTRIBUTION OF TRADE CENTERS OF VARYING SIZES

Throughout our nation of geographically isolated farms are scattered trade centers of varying sizes and capable of supplying needs of hinterland population to varying degrees. This map shows the location of all places in South Dakota and shows zones of overlapping influence based on the theoretical assumption that each center of a specified size extends its influence the specified distance. The more densely populated southeastern corner of the state has many trade centers; the western part of the state few and smaller trade centers. In parts of the state trade centers of less than 250 population actually serve extensive geographical areas.

CHANGED MEANING OF ISOLATED FARM SETTLEMENT

Once settlement on the isolated farm meant extreme isolation from both human contacts and the stimulating influences of social change. It no longer necessarily means either of these. It offers some handicaps to frequent direct contacts with others, but in communities that have all-weather roads these handicaps are not so serious as they once were. Although mail deliveries are less frequent than in the city they are made daily in most rural sections. Telephone and radio are about as effective in rural as in urban areas and about

[1] In the recent planning for the settlement of more than a million acres in the Columbia Basin to be irrigated by the Grand Coulee Dam rural sociologists had a major part. The arranged isolated farm type of settlement was recommended for large areas.

as readily obtained and as economically operated. Many of the momentous changes taking place in the farm community of today are in process because geographical isolation has so suddenly lost its social meaning, because in fact, living on the isolated farm is a different social experience now from what it was forty years ago.

QUESTIONS FOR REVIEW AND DISCUSSION

1. Name and define typical patterns of rural settlement.

2. Discuss advantages and disadvantages of the farm village; of the arranged isolated farm type.

3. What historical factors help explain the unorganized isolated settlement of farm lands in the United States?

4. Suggest possible social consequences to American life of settlement on the isolated farm.

5. What economic advantages and disadvantages are inherent in isolated settlement?

6. Show how the neighborhood came to be an important social unit in areas of isolated farm settlement.

7. What place did the farm trade center come to serve in a nation of isolated farms?

8. What has been the effect of changes in transportation upon rural organization as it affects the trade center?

9. Suggest possible social consequences of the separation of the trade center from its supporting rural territory.

10. Explain how new social forces have changed the meaning of the isolated disorganized pattern of rural organization.

COLLATERAL READING

Brunner, E. de S., G. Hughes, and M. Patten: *American Agricultural Villages*, Doubleday & Company, Inc., New York, 1927.

——— and T. Lynn Smith: "Village Growth and Decline, 1930–1940," *Rural Sociology*, vol. 9, pp. 103–115, June, 1944.

Douglass, H. Paul: *The Little Town*, The Macmillan Company, New York, 1927.

Kolb, J. H., and E. de S. Brunner: *A Study of Rural Society*, 3d ed., chap. 13, Houghton Mifflin Company, Boston, 1946.

——— and Douglas G. Marshall: "Neighborhood-community Relations in Rural Society," *Wisconsin Agricultural Experiment Station Bulletin* 154, Madison, November, 1944.

Landis, Paul H.: *The Number of Unincorporated Places in the United States and Their Estimated Populations*, Research Studies of the State College of Washington, vol. 6, pp. 160–188, December, 1938.

Marshall, Douglas: "Hamlets and Villages in the United States: Their Place in the American Way of Life," *American Sociological Review*, vol. 11, pp. 159–165, April, 1946.

Sanderson, Dwight: *The Rural Community*, Ginn and Company, Boston, 1932.

Sims, N. L.: *The Rural Community, Ancient and Modern*, Charles Scribner's Sons, New York, 1920.

Smith, T. Lynn: *The Sociology of Rural Life*, rev. ed., chap. 10, Harper & Brothers, New York, 1947.

Sorokin, P. A., C. C. Zimmerman, and C. J. Galpin: *A Systematic Source Book in Rural Sociology*, vol. 1, chap. 5, University of Minnesota Press, Minneapolis, 1930.

Terpenning, Walter A.: *Village and Open-Country Neighborhoods*, D. Appleton-Century Company, Inc., New York, 1931.

Williams, J. M.: *The Expansion of Rural Life*, chap. 15, Alfred A. Knopf, Inc., New York, 1926.

CHAPTER 3

THE STRUCTURE OF THE RURAL POPULATION

DIFFERENCES in biosocial characteristics of a population have a bearing not only on social organization but also on social interaction processes and on social institutions. Human society on its physical side is a purely biological group composed of human units of different characteristics and capacities. Since these units "are the raw materials of human life and social organization," it is important to consider the biosocial traits of the rural population and their possible importance to social life and to the interaction processes that dominate the rural setting. Most important of the biosocial traits are sex, age, race, and vitality.

SEX COMPOSITION AND MARRIAGE

Over many decades in the United States males have outnumbered females at birth by about 105.7 to 100. This excess of males at birth is offset by a higher death rate of males from infancy through every year of life so that by middle life the sex ratio of a given generation born is approximately equal and by old age women are in a substantial majority. This indicates clearly that both the birth and death rates are sex selective, but they work in opposite directions.

In the American population, however, the most significant sex-selective factor is migration which, in most sections of the country, draws from the rural community more young women than young men. In frontierlike rural states which still draw migrants, males move in in much larger numbers than females, as they did to the original frontier.

The more rural and frontierlike the community, the greater the tendency for the male sex to predominate. The state of Nevada, a semifrontier mining, lumbering, and cattle-raising state, had a higher male sex ratio than any other state in 1940 with 125.9 men for every 100 women. North Dakota, a state with a large proportion of its population living in the open country and in places of less than 2,500 people, had 109.5 males per 100 females. Massachusetts, the most urban state in the nation, had only 95 men per 100 women. In the deep South where distances of migration for youth who go to northern urban centers is great, and therefore hinders the migration of girls, the sex ratio is less extreme. Mississippi, the most rural state in 1940, had only 101.1 males per 100 females.

Throughout the nation the rural population is weighted with males as the table shows. The rural farm population in 1940 had 11.7 extra males per 100 females and the rural nonfarm population 3.7. The urban population was weighted with females, the deficiency of males being 4.5 per 100 females.

1940 data	Males per 100 females*	Per cent 15 years old and over married†	
		Male	Female
Rural farm..............................	111.7	58.3	66.3
Rural nonfarm..........................	103.7	62.7	64.5
Urban.................................	95.5	61.8	58.1
United States total......................	100.7	61.2	61.0

* *Population*, vol. 2, Table 1, p. 9, Bureau of the Census, U.S. Department of Commerce, Washington, D. C., 1945.

† *Population*, Series P-19, No. 2, Bureau of the Census, U.S. Department of Commerce, Washington, D. C., 1940.

One of the most obvious effects of an unbalanced sex ratio is its hindrance to mate-seeking and marriage. This shows up in the data at the right of the table above, which shows the proportion of each sex married in the various residential groups. In rural farm areas where there was an abundance of men it will be seen that 66.3 per cent of women 15 years old and over were married. This compares with 58.1 per cent in urban communities when men were scarce.

Men, on the other hand, find difficulty in getting a marriage partner in rural areas where women are scarce. Only 58.3 per cent of those 15 years of age and over were married. In urban areas, however, where women were plentiful, 61.8 per cent of men were married.

In the nation, the sex ratio has approximately balanced itself as immigration has declined to an insignificant point (immigrants are predominantly male), and in many of the states the differences in numbers of males and females has declined. But in the marriageable ages, where an unbalanced sex ratio is most significant, the situation is still critical.

The trend lines on the accompanying chart show the sex ratio of whites at various age periods for various residential groups. It will be seen that at ages 20 to 24, the most marriageable period in life, only the nonfarm population approached a balanced sex ratio. The rural farm population had an excess of 26 males; the urban population had a deficiency of 11 males per 100 females. In old age the difference in sex ratio in these two population groups was even greater, but this has much less social significance since it has no bearing on marriage and child bearing.

The chart tends to exaggerate the marriage problem produced by the unbalanced sex ratio in that it assumes that those of the same ages marry.

This is not the case. A man in about two cases out of three marries a woman younger than he. A man in the early twenties will usually marry a woman 2 to 3 years younger; one in the late twenties or early thirties one 6 years younger.[1] Since a proportion of any population dies in each year of life, there are fewer males in the marrying group than in the younger female group.

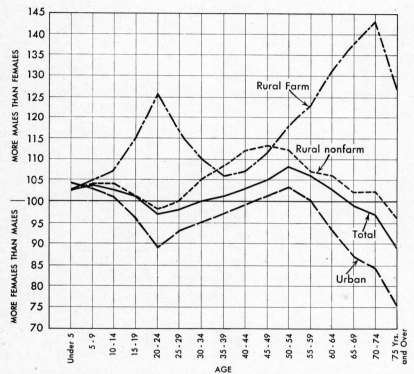

WHITE MALES PER 100 WHITE FEMALES FOR THE TOTAL, THE URBAN, THE RURAL NON-FARM, AND THE RURAL FARM POPULATION OF THE UNITED STATES BY AGE GROUPS, 1940.

Observe that the rural farm population has approximately 126 males per 100 females in the ages 20-24, the urban population only 89 males per 100 females in this age group.

To correct for this factor the table below is developed. It actually over-corrects somewhat since the lag in marriage is not quite as great on the average as the periods shown. Even then, however, the difference in the sex ratio is considerable.

[1] See James H. S. Bossard, "The Age Factor in Marriage: A Philadelphia Study, 1931," *American Journal of Sociology*, vol. 38, pp. 536–549, 1933. Also Paul Popenoe, "Where Are the Marriageable Men?" *Social Forces*, vol. 14, pp. 257–262, December, 1935.

RATIO OF MALES TO 100 FEMALES IN VARIOUS AGE CLASSES

Population	Ratio of males 25–34 to females 20–29	Ratio of males 25–29 to females 20–24	Ratio of males 30–34 to females 25–29
Total..........................	91.2	92.5	89.9
Urban..........................	87.7	89.3	86.1
Rural..........................	96.6	97.3	95.9
Rural nonfarm.................	96.1	97.7	94.4
Rural farm....................	97.3	96.9	97.7

The sex composition of the nonwhite races in the farm population was much less out of balance at the marriageable ages than for the white population

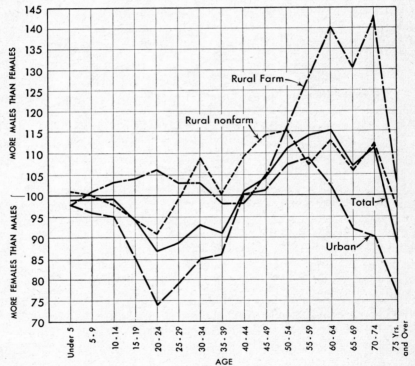

NONWHITE MALES PER 100 NONWHITE FEMALES FOR THE TOTAL, THE URBAN, THE RURAL NONFARM AND RURAL FARM POPULATION BY AGE GROUPS 1940

Observe the great deficiency of males in the urban group age 20 to 24. The ratio was only 74 males per 100 females this age.

(see chart) but was even more out of balance in nonfarm and urban areas. There were only about six more males than females in the rural farm population in the age group 20 to 24, but in the nonfarm group there were only 91 males per 100 females and in the urban population there were only 74 males per 100 females.

Since this population group is made up primarily of Negroes, the majority of whom are in rural areas of the South, it shows the tendency of Negro girls to concentrate in small towns and in cities where domestic, office or factory work offer occupational outlets.[1]

In addition to the effect of the sex ratio on mate-seeking and marriage, and consequently on the family, are possible effects on sex mores, social codes, social ritual and social institutions. The roughness and toughness of the male frontier and its peculiar social institutions—saloons, gambling haunts, legalized prostitutions—are part of America's western tradition. The disappearance of chivalry in the city where women are in the majority, their growing aggressiveness and rivalry in courtship, the girls' bachelor quarters with unchaperoned courtship, in place of the family parlor of rural society, are suggestive of tendency to redefine "proper" behavior in woman-dominated society.

AGE COMPOSITION AND SOCIAL ROLES

The social roles of any population are determined by the age makeup of the population. This factor also has a decided bearing on many other phases of interactional and institutional life.

The rural farm population, as compared to the national and especially as compared to the urban population, has a heavy excess of the young of all ages under 20, is low in proportion of people in the middle ages of life, 20 to 45, and is high in proportion of the aged. (These differences are graphically shown in the age-sex pyramids presented below.) The large proportion of children in the rural farm population is conspicuous as compared with the urban population. The most noticeable feature in the urban pyramid is the heavy proportion in the middle years of life. In the pyramid urban includes all places above 2,500 population. If one were to examine a pyramid of population of the large metropolis it would be found to bulge even more in the middle, showing the predominance of the people in the productive years of life, and to be cut off even more sharply at the base. Villages range between these two extremes, having more children than the city but less than the farm, and more in the productive ages than the farm group but less in the productive ages than the city group. In one respect, however, the village does not fall between the rural and urban. Generally speaking, villages in America contain a greater proportion of old

[1] T. Lynn Smith has called attention to the fact that in many Southern villages there are large excesses of females. See his "Some Aspects of Village Demography," *Social Forces,* vol. 20, pp. 15–25, October, 1941. See also his *The Sociology of Rural Life,* pp. 177–180, which shows that from Southern states more males than females move to Northern cities. Harper & Brothers, New York, 1940.

PROPORTION OF RURAL-FARM POPULATION IN EACH 5-YEAR AGE GROUP, UNITED STATES, 1930 AND 1940

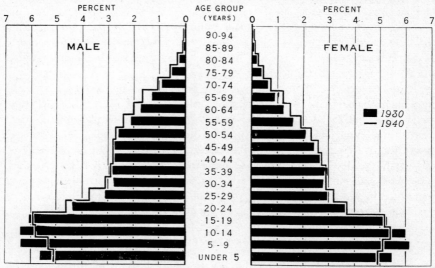

PROPORTION OF URBAN POPULATION IN EACH 5-YEAR AGE GROUP, UNITED STATES, 1930 AND 1940

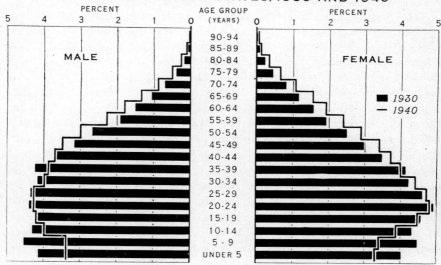

U.S. Bureau of Agricultural Economics

POPULATION PYRAMIDS COMPARING AGE AND SEX DISTRIBUTION OF RURAL FARM AND URBAN POPULATIONS OF THE UNITED STATES FOR 1930 AND 1940

The city has many in the productive years of life (20-45) whereas the farm is burdened with those of the dependent ages. (For an explanation of these facts study the charts in Chapter 12.)

people than either farm or city. Some villages, for example, those in the Middle Atlantic States, have a great excess of old people.[1] In many parts of the country the tendency of farm people to retire to town when their children are able to take over the farm or when they have saved sufficient funds to turn it over to a tenant probably accounts for this excess of the aged.

Data in the table are more specific in that they show differences in age composition of population for areas ranging from the most rural to the most urban. At the far extreme in high proportion of the population under 20 years of age is the farm group. Lowest in proportion of this age group are cities with 100,000 or more population. Less than a third (28.6 per cent) of the population of the large cities is in those dependent ages under 20, but four in ten (42.7 per cent) of the population of the farm communities is in this group. The most productive age from the standpoint of reproductive power and economic activity is the group 20 to 44. Here the farm population fares badly and the large city is most favored. The large city has 43 per cent of its people in this age classification, the farm population only 32.5 per cent. The group of most interest from the standpoint of old age pensions, hospitalization, and other problems of indigency, incapacity, and social inadequacy is that 65 years of age and over. Here the rural nonfarm population, probably because of the prominence of village population in the rural nonfarm group, has the highest proportion and the large city the smallest.

PERCENTAGE DISTRIBUTION OF THE WHITE POPULATION BY AGE FOR URBAN PLACES AND RURAL AREAS IN THE UNITED STATES, 1940*

Area	Age group					
	0 to 4	5 to 19	20 to 29	30 to 44	45 to 64	65 and over
Urban......................	6.7	23.4	18.1	23.8	21.2	6.8
Places of						
100,000 and over.........	6.3	22.3	18.2	24.8	21.9	6.5
10,000 to 100,000........	6.9	24.2	18.1	23.0	20.8	7.0
2,500 to 10,000..........	7.7	25.6	17.7	21.8	19.7	7.5
Rural......................	9.7	30.3	16.1	19.0	18.0	6.9
Farm......................	10.0	32.7	15.2	17.3	18.2	6.6
Nonfarm..................	9.7	18.6	17.1	21.0	17.9	7.3

* *Population*, Series P-10, No. 21, Bureau of the Census, U.S. Department of Commerce, Washington, D. C., 1943.

The larger the community the smaller the proportion of children in the dependent ages, the farm community having many children, the large city few. The large city has comparatively few of the aged but has a high proportion of people in the middle years of life.

[1] N. L. Sims, *Elements of Rural Sociology*, 3d ed., Fig. 35, p. 178, presents a population pyramid for Middle Atlantic villages. It shows that a relatively high proportion of the population is in the older groups. The Thomas Y. Crowell Company, New York, 1940.

The effect of age composition is interwoven in the warp and woof of rural society. The fact that rural society is predominantly made up of the young and the old shows up decidedly in the working population. Study for example the accompanying chart in which the National Resources Planning Board analyzed the age composition of the working population in various phases of the nation's economy.

Agriculture had an unusually high proportion of very young workers and an unusually high proportion of those above 60 years of age. In this respect no

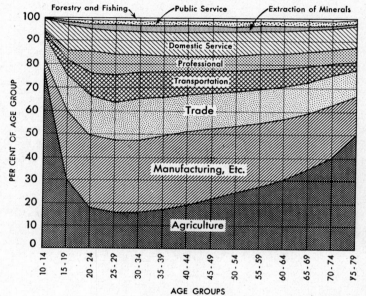

Redrawn from *The Structure of the American Economy*, p. 31, National Resources Planning Board.

AGE OF WORKERS IN THE VARIOUS OCCUPATIONS

Observe that workers in agriculture are predominately the young and the old.

other phase of the nation's economy is comparable. Manufacturing, by contrast, is carried on by those in the middle age of life. So also is trade and transportation.

It is clear that agriculture is being carried on predominantly by those outside the range of highest productive capacity. Levine, calculating the earning capacity of workers in terms of age, found that the maximum working capacity comes at the age of 40 and therefore gives this point an index of 100. Workers approach this maximum only during the period of from 35 to 45 years of age. At the age of 15 the index drops to 50; at the age of 74, it drops to 42.[1]

[1] N. P. Levine, "Statistical Study of the Economic and Sociological Significance of Population Age," *Journal of the American Statistical Association*, vol. 23, pp. 41 *ff.*, March, 1938.

The demand for and cost of school buildings, hospitals, housing, sanitary facilities, health programs, welfare services, and many other aspects of institutional activity are determined by the age composition of the population.[1] The rural community being heavily loaded with both the young and the old always has a relatively heavy burden of dependents as compared to the city. The city, having an abnormal proportion of those in the middle years of life, has more productive power and fewer people of dependent age.

Behavior norms are affected also by age composition. The presence of a large dependent group in the farm population may account, in part, for its greater number of domestic interests, and may also have a bearing on the conservation in rural areas of traditions and ethical standards. One who has incurred family responsibilities must pay more heed to his way of life than one who has only himself to consider. Perhaps one reason that isolated rural communities are antagonistic toward outsiders who come into the community with new ideas and set an example for unsanctioned behavior is that the innovators' conduct is believed to threaten the moral welfare of the young. Were it tolerated, all the teachings and traditions of the older generation would be endangered.

Associational life is affected. Age stratification is not prominent in rural society; children, youth, and adults associate more fully in rural than in urban America, not only in the home but also in public gatherings. In most rural communities, there is not the specialized talent necessary to permit diversified programs for all age groups, nor facilities to house large gatherings, nor means of conveyance; as a consequence, group meetings cater largely to the adult although many programs are designed for family rather than individual participation. In the city, on the other hand, most gatherings are by age groups and are designed primarily for individual rather than family membership.

In the rural community there is not only a high proportion of the old but there seems to be great respect for age, as American culture goes, although we nowhere revere age so much as do the Chinese[2] or so much as have peoples in many historic cultures. In the farm community especially the voice of experience carries weight; there youth respects the opinion of the old because so much of farming can be learned only by doing. The man who has lived long has observed the times and seasons and knows much that has not been written in books; he has seen the changes, the abnormal circumstances, and kaleidoscopic events of nature, and by virtue of living and working has accumulated knowledge that a younger person could not possibly have gained. Many techniques of industry can be learned most quickly and performed most

[1] See Frank Lorimer, *Suggested Procedure for Population Studies by State Planning Boards*, preliminary ed., National Resources Committee, Washington, D. C., July, 1938. Also *The Problems of a Changing Population*, National Resources Committee, Washington, D. C., 1938.

[2] In China the fifty-first birthday brings great rejoicing; the sixty-first and seventy-first bring progressive happiness; the eighty-first shows one to be specially favored by the gods.

effectively by a young person; youth in the urban community dazzles age with its speed and skills. The young person on the farm may excel in the mechanical aspects of agriculture, but not in the total activities of the average farm. In the rural community there is a disrespect for the judgments of youth because youth lacks experience. Only those who have lived and worked long can know thoroughly the intricate details that make up the life of a farmer.

From the standpoint of the happiness of the aged person, the farm and small town offer what is probably the most ideal situation in America for there the old find it possible to maintain a place in work activities—caring for the children, weeding the garden, feeding the chickens, acting as water boy in harvest, or doing chores. Most people become habituated to a certain amount of work during their lifetime and are discontented when they grow old if they must spend their time in perpetual pleasure-seeking or daydreaming. One of the tragedies of old age in an urban culture is the lack of a place for the aged in work affairs.[1]

Rural associational life also has a place for the old. The close contact of relatives in many rural communities gives the old folks a chance to visit back and forth. In some cases the spirit of neighborliness prevails to the extent that older people in the community who are beyond work years feel free to drop in on a neighbor at almost any time for a visit or to see the children.

Care of the aged is more likely to be considered a responsibility of the children in the country than in the city. Urban-industrial society with its intense economic competition, its limited space, its epicurean philosophy, and its extreme individuation has largely abandoned this concept of individual for one of social responsibility for the aged.[2] One must not overlook the fact that rural mores have weakened decidedly in this sphere also with the coming of social security, but not as much as have urban mores.[3]

The rural social group sometimes becomes overburdened with old people, as in some small towns where the character of social life is determined by retired farmers. In these towns youth find life unsatisfactory; the towns become known as "dead towns."[4] In open-country areas also, too often the conservative hand of the aged rules community affairs, blocking innovations

[1] One merit of the pension crusades of the depression years was that they furnished many aged, in the city especially, with a focus for their interests, displacing former emptiness. The psychological benefits may have been considerable. Work opportunities for the old during World War II also gave many a new interest in living.

[2] Arthur S. Y. Chen, "Social Significance of Old Age," *Sociology and Social Research*, vol. 23, pp. 519–527, July–August, 1939.

[3] Robert M. Dinkle, "Attitudes of Children Toward Supporting Aged Parents," *American Sociological Review*, vol. 9, pp. 370–379, August, 1944.

[4] E. de S. Brunner and I. Lorge suggest that adult education is one of the safeguards against an aging population as far as the nation is concerned. *Rural Trends in Depression Years*, p. 179, Columbia University Press, New York, 1937.

and the forces of progress. Where age dominates there is likely to be community conflict.[1]

KINSHIP, RACE, AND NATIVITY IN SOCIAL SOLIDARITY

Kinship has been the basis of many rural aggregates in the past, and remains so in more static societies. In long-settled communities of the United States, during the preautomobile days, kinship helped cement neighborhoods, for where there is little mobility young people tend to marry at home. The mobility of the last twenty years has broken into the large family circles that once dominated many neighborhoods, but it seems likely that more people of kin are still to be found living near each other in rural localities than in urban. They visit back and forth, share their joys and sorrows, and hope that in their old age their sons will take over their farms as they retire to an adjoining town. In some cases the son becomes the tenant on his father's farm and old and young live as neighbors. Parents are more likely to spend their last years with their children and grandparents also are a part of the family social group more often on the farm than in the city. Whole neighborhoods may be dominated by one or two or perhaps three large family groups.[2] In isolated mountain areas, especially, kinship groups accumulate in local areas,[3] thus adding emphasis to primary associations and intensifying the influence of the family group upon the child.[4] The city is made up to a greater extent of people who have migrated from towns, villages, and farms and who have little or no contact with relatives.

Many integrated neighborhoods have been built by nationality groups. In localities where two or more nationalities have settled together, there has often been conflict. Unique religious groups, fairly distinct agricultural practices, variations in work customs, in educational traditions, in recreational interests, and in neighborhood persistence, differences in thrift and frugality and in progressive tendencies, and many other such phenomena can be attributed to the presence of immigrant groups in many rural communities.

Race also has been a significant factor in the population structure and therefore in the social organization of biracial rural communities. Class lines not

[1] Bruce L. Melvin, "Age and Sex Distribution in Relation to Rural Behavior," *Publications of the American Sociological Society*, vol. 23, pp. 93–103, 1929.

[2] Bird T. Baldwin, *et al.*, in their Iowa study, pp. 57–58 (*Farm Children*, D. Appleton-Century Company, Inc., New York, 1930), found that in one community of 145 families, 73 per cent had near relatives, such as brothers, sisters, aunts, and uncles, living within a few miles of them, whereas others, in addition to such relatives, had parents living in towns close by. In another community they found that 73 per cent of the families had relatives living near by. Dwight Sanderson cites similar situations and considers them common in the rural neighborhod. *The Rural Community*, pp. 542–543, Ginn and Company, Boston, 1932.

[3] Feuds are sometimes explained by the clannish character of group life in isolated areas. See Dwight Sanderson, *op. cit.* also E. C. Branson, "Our Carolina Highlanders," in John Phelan's *Readings in Rural Sociology*, pp. 58–65, The Macmillan Company, New York, 1922.

[4] For a discussion of familistic traits in the rural South, see Chap. 11.

ordinarily found in the rural neighborhood have long prevailed in the deep South, where races have been set apart by social tradition. Partly because of a tradition of slavery, the sharecropper system, resembling the feudal system of serfs and lords, developed under and has remained confined chiefly to cotton culture. Because of the biracial system and the distinctive social and cultural characteristics that have developed about it, only those who live in the South and participate in its culture can fully understand all the implications of racial stratification to social organization.

Much more significant than race from the standpoint of numbers, social relationships, and cultural traditions have been nationality groups. Such democratic procecures as the town meeting and the township form of social organization, which emphasizes local autonomy, are in large part a result of the settlement of New England by English yeomanry. English country gentlemen went into the South and there resurrected in part the old manorial structure carried over in English society from the days of feudal estates.[1]

As the nation expanded many nationalities found a home on the land. The early migration of peoples from southern Germany into Pennsylvania occurred during the eighteenth century. An even greater migration came during the middle years of the nineteenth century (1836–1886, especially) from central and northern Germany into the North Central and West North Central states. Large numbers of Scandinavians also came during the nineteenth century to settle on new lands of the West North Central states. The great stream of southern Europeans that poured into the country between 1890 and 1910 went for the most part to urban industrial centers. In 1940, according to the census, only 3.6 per cent of the rural farm population was foreign-born white as compared to 13.4 per cent of the urban population.

As to the full effect of this blending of patterns of many nations with the agrarian patterns of this nation one can only speculate. Mores, social institutions, farming practices, associational life, culture patterns, and social organization have without doubt been affected in a measure as foreign groups have been gradually acculturated to the American way of life.[2]

QUESTIONS FOR REVIEW AND DISCUSSION

1. Indicate significant differences in sex ratios of rural and urban populations.
2. Summarize the social effects of an unbalanced sex ratio.
3. Summarize the differences one would expect to find in the proportion of people in the various age groups in open-country, small-town, and city populations.

[1] N. L. Sims, *op. cit.*, pp. 30–41; or his *The Rural Community, Ancient and Modern*, chap. 2, Charles Scribner's Sons, New York, 1920; J. H. Kolb and E. de S. Brunner, *A Study of Rural Society*, rev. and enlarged ed., chap. 8, Houghton Mifflin Company, Boston, 1940; Carl C. Taylor, *Rural Sociology*, rev. ed., pp. 47–53, Harper & Brothers, New York, 1933.
[2] John P. Johansen, "Immigrant Settlement and Social Organization in South Dakota," *South Dakota Agricultural Experiment Station Bulletin* 313, Brookings, 1937.

4. Point out important differences in associational life contributed to in part by the peculiar age composition of the farm population.

5. What significant facts about race and nationality that have affected farm life can you mention?

6. Are kinship groups more common in rural or in urban areas? Why?

Collateral Readings

Cox, Oliver C.: "Sex Ratios and Marital Status Among Negroes," *American Sociological Review*, vol. 5, pp. 937–947, December, 1940.

Helton, R.: "Old People, a Rising National Problem," *Harper's*, vol. 179, pp. 449–459, October, 1939.

Landis, Paul H.: *Population Problems*, chaps. 14–15, American Book Company, New York, 1943.

Popenoe, Paul: "Where Are the Marriageable Men?" *Social Forces*, vol. 14, pp. 257–262, December, 1935.

Smith, T. Lynn: "Some Aspects of Village Demography," *Social Forces*, vol. 20, pp. 15–25, October, 1941.

Thompson, Warren S.: *Population Problems*, 3d ed., pp. 98–100, 106–109, McGraw-Hill Book Company, Inc., New York, 1942.

Willcox, Walter F.: *Studies in American Demography*, chap. 8, Cornell University Press, Ithaca, N. Y., 1940.

Yerushalmy, J.: "The Age-sex Composition of the Population Resulting from Natality and Mortality Conditions," *The Milbank Memorial Fund Quarterly*, vol. 21, pp. 37–63, January, 1943.

CHAPTER 4

THE FERTILITY OF THE RURAL POPULATION

As NATIONS of the Western World have experienced or approached population decline, the rural population with its relatively high birth rate has come to play an increasingly important part in population policy. The United States, which is a generation or more away from a population decline, would have long ago experienced decline had it depended upon those in metropolitan communities to replace the nation's people.

The population of a nation grows as births outnumber deaths and as immigrants outnumber emigrants. Once the United States accepted large numbers of immigrants, but for more than two decades immigration has had little effect on population growth. It probably will have little effect in the future. The numbers of people in the future will, therefore, depend in large part upon the ratio of births to deaths. In this situation the rural population, and more especially the farm population, has an important place.

FACTS CONCERNING THE RURAL BIRTH RATE

Comparisons of the crude birth rates of rural and urban populations have little meaning because of marked differences in age and sex composition of rural

CHILDREN UNDER 5 PER 1,000 NATIVE WHITE WOMEN OF CHILD-BEARING AGES, FOR URBAN GROUPS AND RURAL AREAS IN THE UNITED STATES, 1920 TO 1946*

Area	1946	1940	1930	1920
Area as a whole................................	345	281	376	425
Urban:.......................................	293	219		
Cities of 100,000 and over......................	...	...	262	277
Cities of 25,000–100,000......................	...	...	301	316
Cities of 10,000–25,000.......................	...	...	328	347
Cities of 2,500–10,000........................	...	...	350	379
Rural:				
Farm..	477	409	529	596
Nonfarm......................................	407	345	463	496

* For the years 1920 and 1930 the census used ages 15 to 44 as the child-bearing period; for the two later periods, 15 to 49.

The larger the city the fewer the children born. The farm community produces almost a third more children per unit of women of child-bearing age than the metropolis.

and urban populations described in the preceding chapter. Married women in the child-bearing period of life are the only potential child bearers. Populations must therefore be compared on the basis of ratio of births to this particular age-sex group in the population rather than to the total population.

On a basis of age and sex composition the urban population should have a far higher number of births in ratio to total numbers since in the urban population the sex ratio is dominantly female and since the urban population has a much higher proportion of its population in the age period 20 to 45 than does the rural population. It is for this reason that population authorities have developed a basis for comparing fertility that takes into account age differences.

The table below shows the ratio of children under 5 per 1,000 women in the child-bearing age for the rural and urban population for two decades. These data make it strikingly clear that the larger the area the smaller the proportion of births in ratio to women of child-bearing ages.

CHILDREN UNDER 5 YEARS OF AGE PER 1,000 WOMEN 16 TO 44 IN THE UNITED STATES AND SELECTED STATES (WHITE POPULATION ONLY)*

Year	United States	Agricultural states	Semiindustrial states	Industrial states
1930	402	526	454	370
1920	489	629	534	458
1880	611	759	640	500
1840	835	966	773	697
1800	1,000	1,043	962	786

* P. K. Whelpton, "Industrial Development and Population Growth," *Social Forces*, vol. 6, p. 462, 1928. Data for 1930 from Warren S. Thompson, *Population Problems*, Table 38, p. 138.

Agricultural areas produce more children per unit of women of child-bearing age than do industrial or semiindustrial states. This has always been true and remains so today, even though the birth rate has been falling rapidly in agricultural as well as industrial states.

A special study of the ratio of women to children in agricultural states, semiindustrial states, and industrial states illustrates the fact that throughout the entire period of American history since 1880 the agricultural population has had a relatively high ratio of children to women of child-bearing age. Industrial states have had the lowest ratio of children to women of child-bearing age. In 1930 agricultural states had 526 children under 5 per 1,000 women of child-bearing age, or slightly more than one child for every two women. In industrial states there were only 370 children per 1,000 women of child-bearing age. Equally striking is the rapid decline in number of children under 5 in all classes. In 1800 there was an average of more than one child under 5 for every woman of child-bearing age in agricultural states as compared to about one for every two women in 1930.

A third series of data (bar chart), compares the ratio of children under 5 to women of child-bearing ages. It will be seen that the birth rate of farm groups is equaled only by that of laborers. The ratio of children to women in the ages compared is little more than half as high among business, professional, and white-collar workers as among farm families.

CHILDREN UNDER 5 YEARS OLD PER 1,000 NATIVE WHITE WOMEN OF AGES 15 TO 49 BY OCCUPATION, 1940

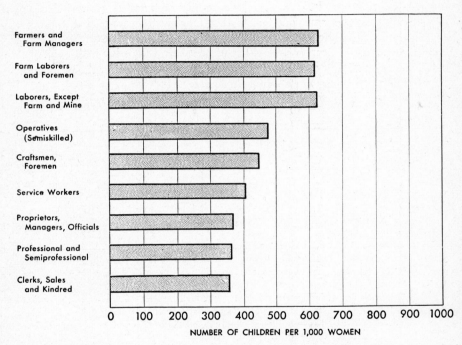

NUMBER OF CHILDREN PER 1,000 WOMEN

In the farm population the concentration of children per given unit of women of child-bearing age is not uniform throughout the nation as will be seen by studying the map which shows the ratio of children under 5 per 1,000 rural farm women in the child-bearing period. It will be observed that on the Northeastern seaboard and on the West Coast and the Great Lakes and Gulf Coast areas where metropolitan centers extend their influence into the hinterland and a high standard of living is characteristic, the ratio of children to women of child-bearing age drops below 600. In the mountainous regions of the Appalachian and Ozark areas, in the deep South, in the Spanish-American culture of New Mexico and Arizona, in the Mormon culture of Utah and in the northern Great Plains states, *i.e.*, the Dakotas, Montana, and in the foreign mining settlements of the upper peninsula of Michigan and northen Minne-

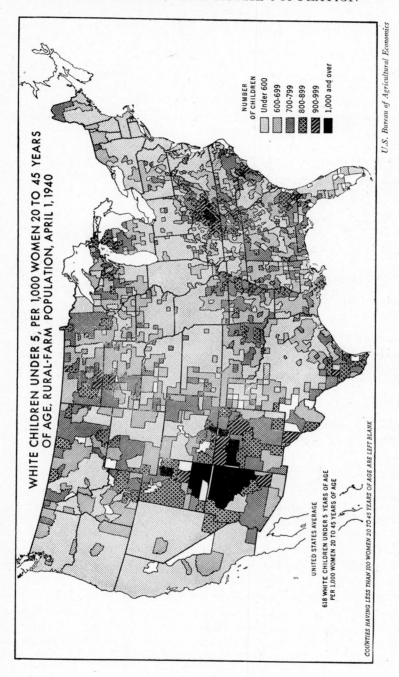

WHITE CHILDREN UNDER 5, PER 1,000 WOMEN 20 TO 45 YEARS
OF AGE, RURAL-FARM POPULATION, APRIL 1, 1940

NUMBER
OF CHILDREN

Under 600
600-699
700-799
800-899
900-999
1,000 and over

UNITED STATES AVERAGE

618 WHITE CHILDREN UNDER 5 YEARS OF AGE
PER 1,000 WOMEN 20 TO 45 YEARS OF AGE

COUNTIES HAVING LESS THAN 100 WOMEN 20 TO 45 YEARS OF AGE ARE LEFT BLANK

U.S. Bureau of Agricultural Economics

sota, a high ratio of children to women of child-bearing age is characteristic, in some cases running above 1,000, that is, an average of more than one child under 5 per woman of child-bearing age.

The differences in actual fertility of rural and urban populations and of groups living in the urbanized Northeast as compared to the cotton South are probably much greater than the figures show. Smith[1] believes that in many rural counties, especially in the South, a large proportion of births are not reported, citing as evidence the fact that the 1930 Census in some of these counties reported twice as many children under 1 year of age as had been reported born during the preceding year. In many rural areas, especially in the South, deliveries are made by midwives, some of them illiterate, instead of

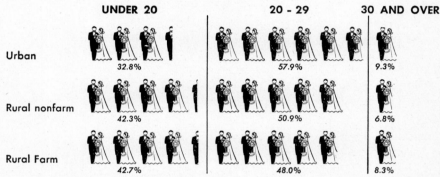

UNDER 20	20 - 29	30 AND OVER
Urban 32.8%	57.9%	9.3%
Rural nonfarm 42.3%	50.9%	6.8%
Rural Farm 42.7%	48.0%	8.3%

Data from *Population—Special Reports*, Series P-45, No. 7, U.S. Bureau of the Census, May 28, 1945.
EARLY MARRIAGE IS MORE COMMON IN RURAL THAN URBAN AREAS
Data are for 1940 and show the age at first marriage for American women.

physicians, so that registration of such births is hardly to be expected. Another source of error previous to 1935 was the practice of allocating births to place of birth rather than to place of residence. Since an increasing number of births in rural families are occurring in urban hospitals, this practice has been an important cause of error.

FACTORS IN THE DIFFERENTIAL RURAL-URBAN BIRTH RATES

Age of Marriage.—A birth rate reflects so fundamentally the cultural accumulations, social pressures, personal and family values, moral restraints, taboos and other factors in the life of a particular social group that one cannot hope to answer all questions regarding reasons for the differential birth rate.

Some of the more obvious differences in the rural-urban differential birth rate are, however, worth mentioning. Difference in age of marriage is an important factor. It is an established fact that the average couple in the rural community marries earlier than in the urban community (see chart absve.)

[1] T. Lynn Smith, *The Sociology of Rural Life*, pp. 134–135, Harper & Brothers, New York, 1940.

Not only is early marriage a rural trait, but differences are found within the farm group itself (see bar chart on next page). Farm laborers marry youngest, farm renters next, and farm owners latest.

Early marriage is associated with a high birth rate as is clearly shown in the second bar chart. Farm laborers marry youngest and have the highest proportion of births. All three farm groups shown have a high ratio of births. In all occupations early marriage is related to a high birth rate, but this is especially so among farm groups.

Comparative Sterility of Rural and Urban Marriages.—A special study by the census of the generation of wives which had just passed child-bearing age in 1940 showed that 14.7 per cent of marriages produced no children. Among urban wives 16.9 per cent produced no children, among rural nonfarm wives, 13.9 per cent, among rural farm wives, only 8.8 per cent.[1]

The differences in proportion of sterile marriages in the rural-urban population are probably not due to differences in fecundity, but to social factors. The older the person is at the time of marriage the greater likelihood of encountering difficulties in conception. This fact is suggested by the following data relative to age of marriage and sterility of the marriage.

AGE OF MARRIAGE AND PER CENT CHILDLESS BY OCCUPATIONS*

Age at marriage	Professional	Business	Skilled workers	Unskilled workers	Farm owners	Farm renters	Farm laborers
Under 20	10.2	7.4	5.4	3.1	4.6	2.6	2.8
20 to 24	11.2	10.7	10.4	6.3	7.6	5.5	4.9
25 to 29	15.6	16.3	16.3	14.2	12.9	8.0	10.6

* Frank W. Notestein, "The Differential Rate of Increase Among the Social Classes of the American Population," (The Milbank Memorial Fund), *Social Forces*, vol. 12, p. 28, October, 1933.

Late marriage cuts down the length of exposure to pregnancy during the fertile period of life. Psychological and sociological factors may also be important. For example, fears, real and imaginary, of greater difficulty in child-birth because of age are undoubtedly a factor.

The fact that rural women tend to marry considerably younger than those in other occupational groups is probably only a partial factor in explaining the fewer number of sterile unions. Another factor is the lower venereal disease and abortion rates in the farm population. Both venereal disease and abortion are accompanied by a high incidence of sterility.

Birth Control.—Another set of factors vital to the birth rate are the attitudes, taboos, values and behavior practices that center about sex behavior.

[1] "Women Classified by Number of Children Ever Born, 1940," Table 3, *Population—Special Reports*, Series P-44, No. 2, Feb. 10, 1944.

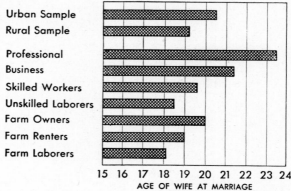

Notestein, Milbank Memorial Fund

MODAL AGE OF MARRIAGE FOR URBAN AND RURAL GIRLS AND FOR OCCUPATIONAL GROUPS BY OCCUPATION OF HUSBAND

Rural girls marry earlier than urban girls; farm laborers marry younger than any other occupational group.

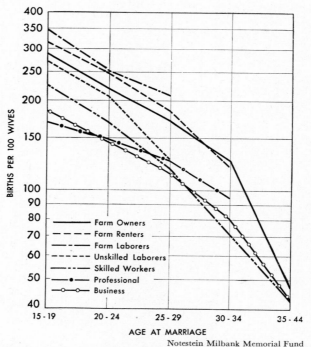

Notestein Milbank Memorial Fund

TOTAL BIRTHS PER 100 WIVES BY AGE OF MARRIAGE FOR SELECTED OCCUPATIONAL GROUPS

Data are for women under 45 of unbroken marriage unions for the year 1910. Each marriage group was standardized for duration of marriage.

Most important of these aspects of behavior is the attitude toward the practice of birth control. Other things being equal, no single fact is so deterministic of the size of a family.[1] Studies of the comparative practice of birth control in rural and urban areas indicate clearly that the farm population has more taboos against the practice of birth control, more handicaps to its practice because of a lack of bathroom facilities and, in fact, less frequently practices birth control.

It has been shown that the practice of birth control increases with the size of the city and with improved economic status.[2] Raymond Pearl's[3] study of birth control showed that birth control increases with the amount of education and economic privilege of the group under observation.

The Market Research Corporation[4] made an extensive study of contracep-

EXTENT TO WHICH BIRTH CONTROL IS PRACTICED BY THOSE RESIDING IN URBAN AND RURAL AREAS*

	Total urban		Over 100,000		100,000 and under		Rural	
	Number	Per cent	Number	Per cent	Number	Per cent	Number	Per cent
Do not practice............	424	17	256	16	168	19	138	29
Practice "simpler" methods only†..................	436	18	252	16	184	21	80	17
Practice other methods.....	1,569	65	1,056	68	513	60	256	54
Total respondents......	2,429	100	1,564	100	865	100	474	100

* John W. Riley and Matilda White, "The Use of Various Methods of Contraception," *American Sociological Review*, vol. 5, p. 894, December, 1940.

† "Simpler" methods comprise: *coitus interruptus*, safe period, and plain douche.

tive practices among women in the upper economic classes. The study was conducted through personal interviews by field investigators. The extent and nature of birth control practice among 2,429 women as found by this study is shown in the accompanying table, which also compares practices of the rural population with those in places of under 100,000 and those in places of over 100,000. It will be seen that almost twice as many rural women as urban women of this economic class did not practice birth control.

[1] Frank Lorimer and Frederick Osborn, *Dynamics of Population*, chap. 9, especially p. 279, The Macmillan Company, New York, 1934.

[2] John W. Riley and Matilda White, "The Use of Various Methods of Contraception," *American Sociological Review*, vol. 5, pp. 890–903, December, 1940. Also Lorimer and Osborn, *op. cit.*

[3] Raymond S. Pearl, *The Natural History of Population*, chaps. 4 and 5, especially pp. 203 ff., Oxford University Press, New York, 1939.

[4] Riley and White, *op. cit.*

Studies[1] of birth control in areas where birth control clinics were located show that the higher classes voluntarily seek advice of birth control clinics more than others. Few of the lower classes come except when sent by social workers. A study of birth control and attitudes toward sex in the deep South showed that although the prevailing attitudes of families was that they did not want more children, few employed contraceptive practices.[2] There was little discussion of sex problems between husbands and wives, in part because they had no scientific or objective terminology in which they could be discussed. Of 69 tenant-farm mothers questioned, only eight used contraceptives, in spite of the fact that 37 out of 42 expressed opinions favoring birth control. Vance[3] has characterized the attitude of the deep South as one of helpless resignation rather than of revolt and prudential control.

Even though there are many more unwanted births in rural areas than in cities, the practice of abortion is widespread in large cities, relatively infrequent in rural areas.[4]

Sex Behavior.—Added to the above factors, which assure less protection from conception of rural than of urban women, is the fact that the exposure of farm women to pregnancy is probably greater than that of any other large occupational class. Several studies suggest that farm couples engage in intercourse more frequently than those in other occupational groups. Pearl ranked three broad occupational classes with regard to frequency of coitus in the following order: farmers most frequent, merchants and bankers next, professional couples last.[5] The vigorous physical life of the farmer, the lack of diverting recreational interests and activities, the close association of husband and wife, and the persistence of the custom of using double beds may be partial explanations.

These various sociocultural influences that reflect in the values and behavior patterns of the rural and urban population would seem to be an adequate explanation for the fertility of the two groups without resort to an explanation in terms of difference in fecundity of the rural and urban populations.

Family Mores.—It has been implied in the previous discussion that factors other than purely biological ones explain the relatively high fertility of the rural population and especially of the farm population.

---

[1] Regine K. Stix, "Contraceptive Service in Three Areas," reprint from *The Milbank Memorial Fund Quarterly*, vol. 19, April and June, 1941.

[2] Margaret J. Hagood, *Mothers of the South*, pp. 122–125, University of North Carolina Press, Chapel Hill, 1939.

[3] Rupert B. Vance, "The Regional Approach to the Study of High Fertility," *The Milbank Memorial Fund Quarterly*, vol. 19, pp. 356–374, October, 1941.

[4] Lorimer and Osborn, *op. cit.*

[5] *The Biology of Population Growth*, chap. 8, Alfred A. Knopf, Inc., New York, 1925. Also Riley and White, *op. cit.;* also G. W. Beebe, *Contraception and Fertility in the Southern Appalachians*, pp. 62–64, The Williams & Wilkins Company, Baltimore, 1942.

The whole system of ideas and attitudes relative to the importance of family and children in the scheme of life has a vital bearing on the birth rate. In urban communities competition for status, the individualistic roles of women, and other such factors have long given both marriage and child bearing a low place in the scheme of urban values.

In urban communities children have little to do with social status or economic well-being, in fact, tend to detract from both. While one cannot argue that the child is the economic asset in the farm community that he once was, children still have a place in the status values, both social and economic, of the farm community and create fewer problems for parents than in towns and cities. The difficulties of rearing a family under urban conditions, the economic risks involved, provide logical justification for the decreasing interest of urban couples in children.

The greater stability of rural marriages gives the rural couple a greater sense of security than the average urban couple possesses. Their constant association and mutual endeavor provides bonds and continuity to family life such as is lacking in urban culture. Children have a more normal and natural place in the life plans of the couple.

Determining the scheme of values of any particular class or group in a population today is the amount of their education. There is abundant evidence to indicate that the more the education of a couple, the fewer children there will be.[1] This is true of all occupational classes. Throughout the United States the rural population has on the average considerably less education than the urban.[2]

THE DECLINE IN RURAL FERTILITY

The Committee on Population of the National Resources Planning Board, using the ratio of children under 5 years of age per 1,000 women 20 to 44 years of age, has traced the trend in fertility by different-sized communities for both native-born and foreign-born whites and Negroes for the period 1910–1930 (see the following table). The fertility of native whites declined 16 per cent; of the foreign-born whites, 30.2 per cent; of the Negro, 24.7 per cent. The most marked decline in the fertility of the native-born white group occurred in rural areas.

[1] "Fertility and Educational Level of Parents," *Statistical Bulletin*, Metropolitan Life Insurance Company, vol. 26, pp. 6–8, November, 1945; Paul H. Landis, "A Nation of Eighth Grade Sires," *Forum*, vol. 105, pp. 1–6, September, 1945; Paul H. Landis, "Education and the Birth Rate," *The Clearing House*, vol. 21, pp. 131–135, November, 1946; republished also in the *Education Forum*, vol. 12, pp. 19–21, February, 1947.

[2] Census data show that the median schooling of urban residence in 1940 was 8.7 years, of rural nonfarm 8.4, of rural farm 7.7. Of youth 24 years of age not attending school, the urban group had 11.7 years of schooling, the rural nonfarm 10.5 years, the farm only 8.7 years.

The major decline in fertility of urban areas came about before 1910.[1] The most marked decline in fertility of the foreign-born came in rural nonfarm areas, although the decline in metropolitan areas was almost as great. The greatest decline in fertility of Negroes was in small cities.

PERCENTAGE CHANGE IN FERTILITY BY NATIVITY AND RACE IN DIFFERENT-SIZED COMMUNITIES, FROM 1910 TO 1930*

Size of community	Native white	Foreign-born white	Negro
Total..	−16.0	−30.2	−24.7
Total rural.................................	−12.3	−26.7	− 3.6
Total urban................................	− 4.8	−28.1	− 2.7
100,000 or more population..................	− 3.7	−29.6	12.8
25,000 to 100,000 population................	− 1.3	−24.3	5.0
10,000 to 25,000 population.................	− 0.9	−20.0	− 5.1
2,500 to 10,000 population..................	− 4.9	−24.3	−17.1
Rural-nonfarm†..............................	− 5.3	−34.8	− 0.3
Rural-farm†.................................	− 8.4	−20.8	− 3.6

* From *The Problems of a Changing Population*, p. 127; based on changes in the number of children under 5 per 1,000 women 20 to 44 years of age. The number of children under 5 reported by the census was increased by the following factors to adjust for estimated underenumeration: White 1.05 in all cases; Negro 1.13 for the total United States, 1.11 in the North, 1.135 in the South, and 1.08 in the West. The ratios were standardized to the age distribution of women in the United States in 1930. Mexicans are not included with whites in 1930, but are included in 1920 and 1910, in accordance with census procedure. City and rural-urban groupings were made according to the population in the current census, except that the 1920 basis of rural-urban classification was used in 1910 for Maine, Vermont, and Connecticut.

† Change from 1920 to 1930.

RURAL FERTILITY AND NATIONAL POPULATION REPLACEMENT

The rural population and especially the farm population is responsible not only for population increase but also for replacement. This is made clear by recent studies which compare the net reproduction rates of the three residential

[1] W. F. Ogburn found that the greatest decline in size of families during the years 1900 to 1930 took place among professional classes. The declines were: professional, 10 per cent; proprietary, 6 per cent; clerical, 5 per cent; skilled and semiskilled, 3 per cent; unskilled, 1 per cent; farm owners, 1 per cent. Farm tenants' families increased 5 per cent in size; but when age groups were standardized, they were found in reality to have declined somewhat. Farm labor families, on the other hand, were found to have actually increased in average size when age groups were standardized. *Recent Social Trends in the United States*, p. 686, McGraw-Hill Book Company, Inc., New York, 1933.

groups. These rates calculate the extent to which the present generation is providing offspring to replace itself in the next generation. A net reproduction index of 100 is necessary for population replacement.

The urban population (in place of 2,500 and above) had a net reproduction rate of 74 in 1940, which indicates a potential decline of 26 per cent per generation (see table); in 1930, the net reproduction rate was 88. At the other extreme was the rural farm population, which had a net reproduction rate in 1940 of 144. The rural farm rate in 1930 was 159. The rural nonfarm group

NET REPRODUCTION RATES BY COLOR AND URBAN-RURAL RESIDENCE, FOR THE UNITED STATES, BY REGIONS: 1940 AND 1930*

(1940 data are estimates based on a preliminary tabulation of a 5 per cent cross section of the 1940 census returns)

Region and color	1940				1930			
	Total	Urban	Rural nonfarm	Rural farm	Total	Urban	Rural nonfarm	Rural farm
All classes								
United States........	96	74	114	144	111	88	132	159
North.............	87	74	109	133	103	90	128	150
South.............	111	75	118	150	127	86	138	165
West.............	95	75	120	138	101	80	129	155
White								
United States.......	94	74	114	140	111	90	133	159
North.............	87	74	109	133	104	91	128	150
South.............	110	76	120	145	132	92	145	169
West.............	94	76	119	134	99	79	128	151
Nonwhite								
United States........	107	74	114	160	110	75	119	156
North....	83	79	(†)	(†)	87	82	(†)	(†)
South.............	113	71	112	160	115	71	116	153
West.............	119	(†)	(†)	(†)	157	(†)	(†)	(†)

* U.S. Census, Population, series P-5, no. 13, Aug. 23, 1941.

† Rates not shown for those population groups which, in 1940, had fewer than 20,000 nonwhite females under 5 years old.

had a net reproduction rate of 114 in 1940 and of 132 in 1930. A detailed comparison of the net reproduction rates by urban, rural nonfarm and rural farm groups, both white and nonwhite, for the nation and its three major geographic divisions for 1930 and 1940, appears also. Marked differences between rural and urban groups were characteristic for all sections shown. Note that differences in rural and urban net reproduction rates were even greater for nonwhite races than for the whites.

The Committee on Population of the National Resources Planning Board has compared the replacement ratio of population in urban areas, rural non-farm areas, and rural farm areas by states, using 1930 data (see maps page 55).

It will be observed that the rural farm population in most states was at least 20 per cent above replacement, and in four states was more than 100 per cent above replacement, namely, Utah, Alabama, North Carolina, and West Virginia. In California and four of the smaller states on the Atlantic Coast it was less than 20 per cent above replacement.

The rural nonfarm population, which consists of village population and people living in the open country who are not engaged in farming, had over a replacement ratio in all the states, but in 13 states (five Far East, four Central, and four Far West) this ratio was less than 20 per cent above replacement. In two states it was more than 80 per cent above replacement, viz., Utah and West Virginia.

The urban population of 40 states was below the replacement ratio. The urban population of states on the West Coast was more than 20 per cent below, as was also that of New York, Illinois, Missouri, Colorado, Arizona, and Nevada. The urban population in eight scattered states was slightly above replacement ratio, but in none was it over 26 per cent above.

Even with high war birth rates for the period 1941 to 1946, net reproduction rates of the urban population were slightly below replacement, but those of the rural population rose far above the level of the preceding decade as is shown in the following:[1]

NET REPRODUCTION RATES, BY RESIDENCE, 1941 TO 1946

United States.. 120.2
Urban.. 97.6
Rural nonfarm.. 135.9
Rural farm... 192.8

It will be seen that rural farm net reproduction rates were almost twice the level required for replacement.

Hill and Marshall[2] studied population replacement in four Midwestern states (Minnesota, Wisconsin, Iowa and Illinois) in relation to various historic-socioeconomic variables such as period of settlement, economic position, nationality, religion, and urbanization and found that with long-time settlement, improvement in the level of living and general similarity to urban standards and values, the population approaches the point of mere population replace-

[1] "Differential Fertility," Series P-20, No. 8, U.S. Bureau of the Census, Washington, D.C., Dec. 31, 1947.
[2] George W. Hill and Douglas G. Marshall, "Reproduction and Replacement of Farm Population and Agricultural Policy," *Journal of Farm Economics*, vol. 29, pp. 457–474, May, 1947.

ment or even falls below that level. Only in those communities settled by immigrants which still maintain a relative degree of isolation and a low level of

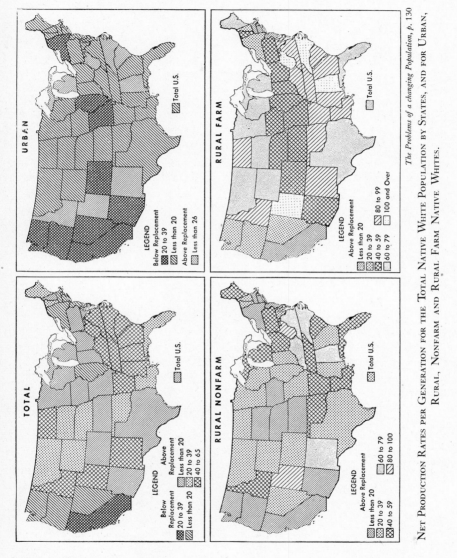

NET PRODUCTION RATES PER GENERATION FOR THE TOTAL NATIVE WHITE POPULATION BY STATES, AND FOR URBAN, RURAL, NONFARM AND RURAL FARM NATIVE WHITES.

The Problems of a changing Population, p. 130

living do high net reproduction rates persist. It is likely that their data are typical of most Northern states.

Applying their findings to the problem of further increase of the rural population, one is led to the conclusion that only in isolated population pockets such as mountainous areas, regions in the deep South, and other areas where lack of economic and educational privilege exist can one long expect the rural population to make a heavy contribution to the nation's population increase. To the extent that education, economic opportunity, and the privilege of contact and mobility affect these areas, their birth rates may be expected to drop toward the level of mere population replacement.

FARM POPULATION IN NATIONAL POPULATION POLICY

The United States has never had a well-defined population policy except in the field of immigration. In the future, however, it is possible that our nation, like western European nations, all of which are on the fringe of those urban-industrial influences which either have brought, or have threatened to bring about population decline, will give attention to the birth rate.

For more than a century certain European countries, notably France and Belgium, have tried to encourage population by various social measures.[1] The dictator countries prior to World War II developed elaborate population policies designed to increase numbers. Democratic Sweden had also developed comprehensive population policies. If America should ever consider population policy which centers about increasing numbers of births, it will have to be concerned with the rural population which has been the most fertile sector of the population.

If population policies should become concerned with welfare of children, as those in Sweden have, the health, nutrition and educational privileges of the rural population of the United States will of necessity become the focal point of interest. At many points throughout this book it will be shown that although the rural population produces children out of all proportion to its numbers, these children are at a disadvantage from the standpoint of health and medical care and educational privilege.

QUESTIONS FOR REVIEW AND DISCUSSION

1. What factors increase a nation's population?
2. Cite data proving that the rural birth rate is relatively high.
3. Compare various regions of the nation with regard to children per 1,000 women of child-bearing age.
4. What is meant by the term "differential birth rate"?
5. Show how age of marriage may be a factor in the differential birth rate of rural and urban populations.

[1] See such studies as D. V. Glass, *The Struggle for Population*, Clarendon Press, Oxford, 1936; Joseph J. Spengler, *France Faces Depopulation*, Duke University Press, Durham, N. C., 1938; G. F. McCleary, M.D., *Pre-war European Population Policies*, *The Milbank Memorial Fund Quarterly*, vol. 19, pp. 105–120, April, 1941.

For the best statement of Swedish population policy see Alva Myrdal, *Nation and Family*, Harper & Brothers, New York, 1941; also Gunnar Myrdal, *Population*, Harvard University Press, Cambridge, Mass., 1940.

6. Present facts showing that fewer rural than urban marriages are sterile.
7. How does birth control affect the differential rural-urban birth rate?
8. May different patterns of sex behavior be a factor?
9. Show how faulty mores might affect the differential birth rate.
10. Trace the decline in fertility.
11. Compare different residential groups with respect to net reproduction index.
12. Why must the farm population have an important place in national population policies?

COLLATERAL READING

Baker, O. E.: "The Effect of Recent Public Policies on the Future Population Prospect," *Rural Sociology*, vol. 2, pp. 123–142, June, 1937.

———, Ralph Borsodi and M. L. Wilson: *Agriculture in Modern Life*, part I (by O. E. Baker), Harper & Brothers, New York, 1939.

Beebe, G. W.: *Contraception and Fertility in the Southern Appalachians*, The Williams & Wilkins Co., Baltimore, 1942.

Landis, Paul H.: *Population Problems*, part II, and chap. 25, American Book Company, New York, 1943.

Lorimer, Frank, and Frederick Osborn; *Dynamics of Population*, chap. 9, The Macmillan Company, New York, 1934.

National Resources Committee: *The Problems of a Changing Population*, Washington, D. C., 1938.

Smith, T. Lynn: *The Sociology of Rural Life*, rev. ed., chaps. 10–13; 25–26, Harper & Brothers, New York, 1947.

Thompson, Warren S.: *Population Problems*, 3d ed., chaps. 25–26, McGraw-Hill Book Company, Inc., New York, 1942.

Vance, Rupert B.: "The Regional Approach to the Study of High Fertility," *The Milbank Memorial Fund Quarterly*, vol. 19, pp. 356–374, October, 1941.

Part II

SOCIAL EXPERIENCE AND PERSONALITY FORMATION

AT THE center of all sociological inquiry is the person behaving as a member of society. But habits, attitudes, values, the meaning that life has to the person, are very much the product of living in certain groups; personality is molded from the raw materials of biological heritage.

Entering into the experience of groups and of persons is the natural setting in which life is carried on. This setting affects associational life and social forms in a measure and also the culture pattern which is the die in which personality is cast. In the culture heritage is the group's storehouse of experience, its reserve of selected values earned through the race's long history of wasteful trial and error.

How does the natural setting of the rural group affect associational life and culture building? How do these combined factors affect personality, human performance, social quality? In what respects is the kind of rural world in which the farm child or youth of today grows to maturity shaping him appropriately for the kind of society in which he is likely to have to function as an adult? These are some of the questions to be discussed.

Emphasis in Part II is on the more static aspects of rural life for the motive is to learn the kind of traditional influences that have shaped and are shaping personality in the open-country setting of the United States. Part III turns to the more dynamic aspects of the rural setting. There, also, personality as affected by the social processes is the center of interest for, in studying the dynamic aspects of rural society, one sees the traditional patterns rocked by new forces, and group life and personality disturbed by them.

CHAPTER 5

NATURAL FACTORS IN FARM EXPERIENCE

MAN's natural environment consists of inanimate factors such as soil, climate, temperature, humidity, and natural forces and of animate objects such as microscopic life, parasites and insects, plants, forests, and larger animals.[1] Man belongs also in this sequence of nature, but a discussion of his biological traits as a factor in social experiences was given in the preceding chapter.

In what respect are natural-geographical factors which constitute one of man's environments, significant in shaping the personality, social life, and culture-building processes? More specifically, how do these natural factors affect farm life as compared to urban life in the nation at the present time?

THEORETICAL PREMISE

Huntington and Cushing, human geographers, state that:

All over the world, people of different places vary in appearance, dress, manners, and ideas. They eat different kinds of food, and enjoy different pleasures. They differ in the way they work and get a living, and in their government, education, and religion. . . . These differences . . . arise largely from differences in geographical surroundings, or physical environment to use a more technical term.[2]

Here we have positively expressed the view of the geographical determinist who believes that human activities are determined fairly completely by natural factors. Quite different is the view of sociologist and anthropologist, and of many human geographers, who believe that "man, who begins by acquiring just enough force to compel nature to supply his bare needs, himself becomes the greatest force of nature" because he has the capacity to build culture and thereby transform the natural habitat to suit his social needs. The Indian aborigines on this continent dwelt among the same natural factors that exist now, but the social life and culture of the American people of today bear little resemblance to those of any tribe of aborigines. The white man has the tools and the historic experience essential to developing, exploiting, and using not only the meager resources that the Indian employed, but many that were meaningless to him because he lived in a stone age culture. Many of the hazards of natural factors, *e.g.*, germs, pests, fire, and flood, which in his experience

[1] For an exhaustive classification of environments, see L. L. Bernard, "A Classification of Environments," *American Journal of Sociology*, vol. 31, pp. 318–322, November, 1925.

[2] Reprinted by permission from *Principles of Human Geography*, by Huntington and Cushing, published by John Wiley & Sons, Inc., New York, 1924.

Farm Security Administration (Lange)

THE NATURE ENVIRONMENT IS PROMINENT IN THE EXPERIENCE OF RURAL PEOPLE.

were catastrophic, have been brought under fairly effective control by the white man in the twentieth century.

In discussing the effect of natural factors on life in the United States and on the experience of the farmer in particular, it is recognized that the importance of nature forces is always relative to the state of development of man's civilization, and that there is no such thing as an absolute geographical determinism in the experience of civilized man.

NATURE FORCES AND SOCIAL GROUPINGS

Importance of Locality.—Farm life is unique as compared to urban living in that there is greater dependence upon immediate locality. As we have seen, local groupings have been prominent in rural society and have often been named for and outlined by some natural phenomena such as valley or hill, flat or stream. Association in the past was very much conditioned by these geographical barriers. As facilities for transportation have improved, these locality groupings have become less rigid, but rural association is still probably more subject to the influence of natural boundaries than is urban association. In the case of subsistence farming, economic dependence on immediate locality is of first importance. The urban man of necessity draws his subsistence from a territory that may cover two or more continents. To the extent that the farmer buys rather than raises his living, he has become free of immediate locality.

Influence of Nature Factors in Human Distribution.—Many naïve assumptions are made concerning the effect of such nature factors as land, moisture, climate, and germ hazards on the distribution of man over the surface of the earth, because of a failure to take cultural factors into account. Without culture man, like plants and animals, would be confined to areas where natural conditions were sufficiently favorable to permit him to survive. But the white man now lives fairly safely in the once malaria-plagued districts of Panama. The desert wastes of the Nile Valley, which never see rain, have been converted to irrigated gardens as has the desert waste of the Imperial Valley of California, and many similar areas. Man with a highly advanced civilization has conquered many natural factors and without doubt will in the future conquer many more.

With this qualification in mind, it is safe to say that within the limits of a given culture pattern, the distribution of the agricultural population is conditioned in large part by natural factors. Soil, rainfall (or water supply in case of irrigated areas), and climate are of first importance in the survival of man on the land, and influence vitally the number of people that can be supported with a given kind of agricultural practice. For example, Kolb and Brunner, taking carefully selected one-crop community areas, find the following differences in social phenomena:[1]

[1] *A Study of Rural Society*, rev. and enlarged ed., p. 211. By permission of Houghton Mifflin Company, Boston, 1940.

Crop area	Number of villages	Average area of community, square miles	Average country population	Persons per square mile
Corn....................	10	80.0	1640	20.5
Wheat...................	9	294.4	1908	6.5
Citrus..................	6	40.0	1443	31.1

The distribution of urban populations has become far removed from such simple nature factors. Urban life may exist in a desert, among mountains, or on infertile lands, but as a matter of fact it tends to be concentrated at breaks in transportation where goods change modes of transportation. The movement of the urban population tends to be not in quest of natural resources, but of artificial values. If there is an ecology of the city it must be in terms of artificial-cultural values, not of natural-geographical values.

NATURE FORCES AND CULTURE PATTERNS

Nature Factors in the Building of Urban and Rural Culture Patterns.—The city is a product of man's created wants, not of his essential needs; the city is a cultural entity, not a simple geographical or ecological entity in the natural sense; the city caters to tastes that man has invented, not to tastes that are inherent in his original nature; the city in many phases of its life reveals man to be not an animal but a civilized creature living on a highly sophisticated plane, a creature who has put the basic drives of life secondary. There many struggle not primarily for food, protection from the elements, or space in the biological sense; they struggle for a place in the social sun. Urban life is almost entirely artificial in the sense that it is man-made. The city is the house that Jack built. It could be destroyed and still the race would survive.

Many forces which man defies in urban culture, or which he carelessly disregards without harm, prove disastrous to those who win their livelihood from soil, plants, or animals. There is, therefore, a tendency among farm folk to regard nature as an active agent in their culture-building experience.

Nature Forces in the Adaptation of Culture Patterns.—Farming is so much dependent on soils, topography, climate, rainfall, and length of growing season that marked changes induced in the geographical habitat require changes in the manner of life of the people living there. Moreover, in the case of the migration of a rural population, marked revisions in techniques and practices are required if a new set of geographical circumstances are encountered. Urban life is so completely enmeshed in an artificial structure that culture patterns are modified chiefly in response to social demands and rarely to conform to changes in habitat. An industrial enterprise can be transferred from one coast to the other or from north to south, with no change in technique even though the natural

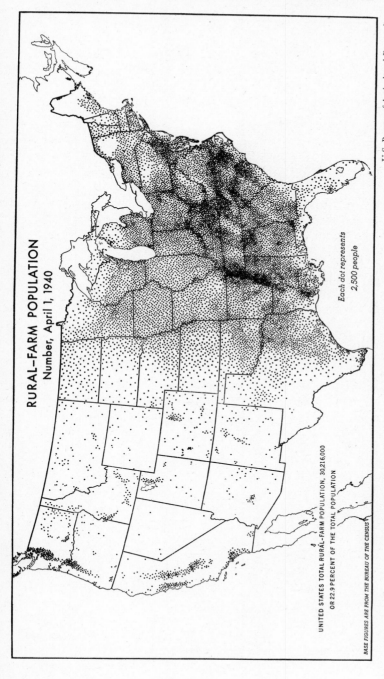

RURAL–FARM POPULATION
Number, April 1, 1940

Each dot represents
2,500 people

UNITED STATES TOTAL RURAL–FARM POPULATION, 30,216,000
OR 22.9 PERCENT OF THE TOTAL POPULATION

BASE FIGURES ARE FROM THE BUREAU OF THE CENSUS

U.S. Bureau of Agricultural Economics

Density of farm population varies greatly in different sections of the nation. The eastern half contains the majority of its farmers, whereas the western half, with its arid and semiarid plains and plateaus, and its mountain ranges, is sparsely settled. Most of the clusters of population in the Far West mark reclamation projects with irrigated lands.

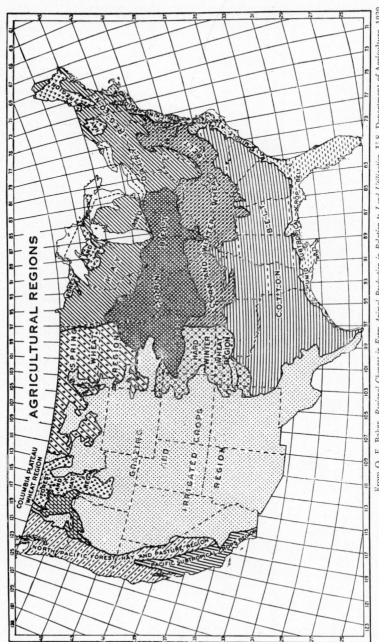

From O. E. Baker, *Regional Changes in Farm Animal Production in Relation to Land Utilization*, U.S. Department of Agriculture, 1929

MAJOR CROP REGIONS OF THE NATION

The culture pattern of the American people calls for specialized uses of the agricultural land. Where a few years ago a continent of rich and varied lands provided only a meager subsistance for scattered tribes of a Stone Age Culture, millions are fed today. Nature factors are much the same now as they were then, but cultural factors have changed their meaning.

setting may be much different. A farm enterprise must always be adapted to the immediate locality. Few agricultural techniques can become nation-wide in scope.

Nature Forces and the Inventive Process.—Since agricultural techniques are more directly adapted to nature factors than urban-industrial techniques, it would seem that the inventive process in the rural environment is likely to take the direction of making tools adaptable to working with nature forces, whereas in the city it takes the direction of making tools that aim at meeting demands growing out of artificially created needs. In a wind-blown area, a lister to hinder the shifting of the topsoil is a logical invention; in the city, a new device for directing the traffic. For this reason in part, urban inventions are likely to be more numerous, for change in human needs is more rapid in an artificial setting than in a setting where nature takes a fairly regular and predictable course.

NATURE FORCES IN PERSONALITY CONFIGURATIONS

The farmer as a partner with nature is influenced in a vital way by processes which operate throughout the natural world. Therefore, if one assumes that psychological traits, social outlook, philosophical values, and general personality patterns are in part a product of habits growing out of long-established relationships with environment factors, he must, if he would understand the farmer, come to a full appreciation of the importance of his contact with nature.[1]

Nature Experience and Life Philosophy.—One can only speculate as to the importance of close contact with nature as a factor in the formation of life philosophies of individuals; that there is a profound effect seems likely, since personality is made up in large part of past experiences as they are molded into configurations by human organisms possessing varying degrees of capacity to make use of experience. Baker has suggested certain possible effects of closeness to nature on attitudes, habits, and basic life philosophies. He says,

Deeper in my opinion than the differences between individualistic or laissez-faire economics and socialism, deeper even than the differences between capitalism and communism, are those between rural and urban attitudes toward life. The farmer tends to think in terms of plants and animals, of birth and growth and death. The city man, on the other hand, tends to think in terms of wheels and levers and machines, or of buying and selling. Whereas agriculture is founded on life processes, particularly as influenced by soil and weather and the laws of inheritance, urban occupations are founded on manufacturing and commerce, and the activities are mostly carried on indoors. To the city child milk is associated with a bottle, not with a cow; an apple comes from a box, not from a tree; and these early impressions influence, I believe, the ideas of later life.

[1] O. E. Baker, "Farming as a Life Work," p. 15, *U.S. Agricultural Extension Service Circular* 224, Washington, D. C., 1935.

As a consequence the farmer's philosophy of life is primarily organic, whereas the city man's philosophy usually is mechanistic. The farmer lives in a natural world, the city man in an artificial world. Because of his occupation the farmer's thoughts are largely biological, whereas the city man's thoughts are largely physical or economic . . .

Perhaps because of the open air and the contact with nature, perhaps because the farmer sees the stars at night and observes the progress of the seasons, perhaps also because of stronger family ties, farmers and farm women tend to think of the past and the future; city people, it seems to me, tend to think more about the present.[1]

Nature Forces in the Formation of Habit Patterns.—Matthews in a penetrating behavioristic study of personality in the mountain culture of the Appalachians describes the effect of daily life activities of the mountain farmer as experience and events are molded into personality patterns.

For simple folk the meanings of daily life flow in large measure from the logical and chronological continuums and climaxes, the sequence patterns of which may be compound (rather than complex) in any order. For instance, the harnessing of the team after breakfast on Monday morning makes a sojourn to the fields where logically continuous activity will take place till noontime and after noontime till evening, when the unharnessing of the team will lead up to the doing of small chores till supper or bedtime. The finishing of some or so much work furnished the immediate climax or point which was looked forward to, the point of sleep provided the closing of the paragraph or chapter. But in daily life evening looks forward to dawn, sleep to awakening. Monday night is the frontispage to Tuesday morning. And so throughout the week. By the same token in the simple life, the working week is the continuum that moves toward the Sabbath—a larger climax in the immediate daily round, and generally as well itself a unit in the succession of Sabbaths and Special Sabbaths in the Appalachian culture looking forward to the eternal Sabbath of the Soul.   The finishing of so much work in the fields on Monday was itself an event in the succeeding amounts of work to be done until the winter plowing should be finished; but the end of winter plowing was significant because it meant readiness for springtime planting. The end of planting looked toward the growing and cultivating season which itself looks toward maturity and harvest time. Harvest is then the grand climax in the annual activity. But harvest means abundance or leanness of subsistence until the next harvest. Any surplus is put away for rainy weather, for retirement from the active life, to help eke out a living in the feeble days of later age, or to give the children a start educationally or financially.[2]

The slower pace of rural as compared to urban people cannot be explained adequately by differences in intensity of economic competition, or in the speeded-up processes of urban mechanization. It is explained in part by the fact that the farmer has learned to scale his activities and to accommodate his movements to the slow- moving processes of nature. Patience and a degree of

[1] O. E. Baker, *ibid.*, p. 6.
[2] M. Taylor Matthews, *Experience-worlds of Mountain People*, pp. 42–43, Teachers College, Columbia University, New York, 1937.

stolidness become desirable qualities in those who must wait for a harvest. Habits are built to conform to the necessities of living in a setting where the natural processes of life, growth, disease, and death take their slow but certain course.

Nature Consciousness and the Sense of Security.—Nature forces come to play the role in the life of the farmer that the job plays in the life of the workingman. If the workingman's job is uncertain, he feels insecure as does the farmer when nature threatens his crops. The average farmer has little appreciation of the dread and suspense of the worker living from day to day with the job on which he depends for a livelihood for himself and family uncertain. He cannot fully understand that the security of thousands of wage earners rests primarily in the hands of employers, the whims of style, or the sporadic shifts in culture-building trends.[1] Neither can the average workingman in industry appreciate the following account of the experience of a Great Plains farmer:

Nothing discourages a farmer more than to watch his crops dry up when there is nothing he can do except to wait and hope for rain. One farmer said, "One hopes for rain out here so much that it hurts." Even when there is a single crop failure, the morale of the farmers is severely taxed. They become irritable and pessimistic and this is heightened when the drought continues for several years.

This attitude affects in turn the purchases of farmers. A local merchant said that when farmers came in to get coal during a dust storm they bought only a few hundred pounds, when they really needed at least a ton, and resented his suggestion of a larger quantity. An automobile salesman cited another instance. He had sold a new car to a farmer in the fall of 1936 but there was no written contract. A brief dust storm occurred before delivery, and the salesman had so much difficulty persuading the farmer to take the car, even though he had enough money to pay for it in cash, that it was a week before the transaction was completed.[2]

One who makes daily, even hourly, adjustments to nature factors cannot but be conscious of their importance and aware of their eternal presence. The city person is likely to be indoors most of the time and his contact with nature to be mediated by numerous cultural factors. Much of the farmer's work is out of doors and in direct contact with nature. Climatic factors, therefore, are uppermost in his consciousness. The weather is a constant topic of conversation, because it is important in the execution of his plans and the conditioning of his anxieties. Leisure depends upon the day's weather—"more rain more rest"; livestock are imperiled in a sudden storm; the outcome of the

[1] The Lynds' *Middletown*, Part 1, gives an account, through quoted statements, of the sense of insecurity felt by the city wage worker under the insecure conditions of factory work. See also E. Wright Bakke, *The Unemployed Man*, E. P. Dutton & Company, Inc., New York, 1934.

[2] A. D. Edwards, *Influence of Drought and Depression on a Rural Community; A Case Study in Haskell County, Kansas*, Social Research Report VII, Farm Security Administration, Washington, D. C., 1939.

crop hinges on the date of the first frost; a hailstorm the day before the harvest may beat down the year's wheat crop; windstorms may blow away the soil or a raging torrent cut gutters in the fields, carrying away tons of fertile soil. Even in irrigated areas the volume of water is dependent on the snowfall of the previous winter in the distant mountains and the farmer may lack water for his ditches when he needs it most. A rain may split the cherries or a freeze may ruin the apple crop. Any of a thousand pests and diseases attack crops and livestock, thereby threatening the families' livelihood.

The constant care of living, perishable things affects the philosophy of the farmer. He acquires a regard for nature which those who work in the urban factory seldom possess. Life processes are geared to the seasons; new seasons bring a new routine of work and a change in the flow of income and expenditures. A certain conservatism in facing the future is acquired. Much rural experience lies back of the old adage, "Don't count your chickens before they're hatched." To live happily, the farmer must resign himself to the fate nature holds in store. "Man proposes but God disposes."

Prominence of Nature Folklore in Rural Thought.—Taylor collected and classified 467 different signs and superstitions of farmers.[1] Over one-fourth of them had to do with climate and weather; plants, animals, climate, and weather, all taken together, accounted for well over one-half of those found among the farmers studied.

Superstitions concerning the effect of the moon on agricultural practices have been especially prominent. Weather signs are numerous.[2] Dr. Miles' *Almanac* with its weather signs had a circulation of 20 million copies in 1939 and, according to its publishers, went into four of every five American homes. There is no way of knowing the proportion of homes following the signs. Many no doubt consign the almanac immediately to the wastebasket.

The back page of the McKesson calendar contains "astrological information on farming and gardening," telling in which sign of the zodiac one should plant, prune, or pluck, dig potatoes, sterilize animals, set hens, turkeys, ducks, and geese, cut wood, graft trees, destroy weeds, and do a great number of other farm tasks. It also informs the reader that phases of the moon are related to successful agricultural practice, showing which crops should be planted in the first quarter, which in the second, and which in the third.[3]

In our scientific age it is probable that most farmers have begun to consider natural phenomena subject to predictable scientific laws; but many traditional

---

[1] C. C. Taylor, *Rural Sociology*, rev. ed., chap. 7, Harper & Brothers, New York, 1933.

[2] J. M. Williams, *Our Rural Heritage*, chap. 5, Alfred A. Knopf, Inc., New York, 1925. gives a full discussion of weather superstitions.

[3] Belief in the effect of the moon on garden plantings is still widespread. Let any who question this assertion talk with their local seedsman about the beliefs and practices of his customers.

attitudes persist, stock explanations of nature phenomena being given and the old beliefs and signs and cures of rural folklore being passed on year after year.

Nature Experience in Meeting the Luck Element.—The element of luck has been prominent in all human calculations. Among primitive peoples practices for dealing with it through magic, ritual, ceremony, fetishes, and charms exist. Some anthropologists once went so far as to assume that such practices were evidence that the primitive mind operates on a prelogical level. Further developments in the field of contemporary anthropology and cultural sociology have refuted these early theories,[1] it now being recognized that peoples in all times and places develop many nonrational techniques for controlling unpredictable phenomena in their environment and getting the best of chance.

The prominence of devices for dealing with luck in nature does not necessarily reflect the illogical character of the rural mind but instead the natural hazards that the farmer experiences. Although many of the devices may not be reasonable from the standpoint of contemporary scientific knowledge, they have served a purpose in making him feel that he was beginning to deal successfully with unknown elements. From the point of view of one who believes in them, they are logical.

Interestingly enough, although many of these nature superstitions have disappeared among city folk, one finds in their place techniques for dealing with new unpredictable elements.[2] Astrologists, numerologists, fortune tellers, and other such dealers in magic phenomena increased rapidly during the depression years of the early thirties when men had become desperate and past experience no longer seemed a safe guide. In war time these soothsayers were sought out even more diligently by city dwellers. The luck element for them has less to do with nature, more to do with the fortunes of love, social prestige and wealth.[3]

Nature Experience, One Key to Rural Personality.—The nature environment makes its imprint on the personalities of farm people just as definitely and permanently as do the factory and the machine on the urban worker. One who works day after day and year after year with cows and pigs, corn and cotton, soil and sunshine, plow and reaper, develops habits different from those of men who build buildings, make shoes, serve in the professions, or seek political honors. Farmers who in their quest for a livelihood match wits with drought and flood, frost and scorching wind, grasshopper and army worm, are likely to hold attitudes and life philosophies different from those of men who depend on the employer or the government for a salary check. Urbanites who work

[1] For a critical evaluation of various theories of primitive mentality see Franz Boas' *The Mind of Primitive Man*, especially chaps. 4 and 8, The Macmillan Company, New York, 1911.

[2] A. M. Tozzer, *Social Origins and Social Continuities*, pp. 225–229, The Macmillan Company, New York, 1926.

[3] Compare Robert Redfield, "Culture Changes in Yucatan," *American Anthropologist*, n.s., vol. 36, pp. 64–68, January–March, 1934.

inside can forget nature because they are surrounded by an invented world. Never can the farmer.

1. Distinguish between geographical determinism and a sociological view of the place of natural factors in human experience.

2. Show the degree to which farmers of today are dependent upon immediate locality as compared to farmers of the past.

3. Cite evidence showing that nature factors affect the distribution of farm population.

4. Are urban populations as directly affected in their distribution by nature factors?

5. Explain the statement, "There is a tendency among farm folk to regard nature as an active agent in their culture-building experience."

6. Why do nature forces affect the farmer more directly than they do the urbanite?

7. Show why nature factors must be taken into account more fully in adapting a farming than an industrial enterprise to a given place.

8. What effect do nature forces have on the inventive process in farming areas?

9. Suggest possible effects of nature influences on the personality and life philosophy of the farmer?

10. What are some of the possible effects of close association with nature on the habits of farm people?

11. Contrast farmers with industrial wage workers with regard to influences that threaten their sense of security.

12. Are farmers more given to belief in signs, luck, and superstititons than other groups in our society? Defend your answer.

13. Is the nature environment the most important one in which the farmer functions?

COLLATERAL READING

Gillette, J. M.: *Rural Sociology*, 3d ed., chap. 4, The Macmillan Company, New York, 1936.

Hawthorn, Horace B.: *The Sociology of Rural Life*, chaps. 8 and 14, D. Appleton-Century Company, Inc., New York, 1926.

Lively, C. E.: "Type of Agriculture as a Conditioning Factor in Community Organization," *Publications of the American Sociological Society*, vol. 23, pp. 35–50, 1929.

Taylor, C. C.: *Rural Sociology*, rev. ed., chap. 6, Harper & Brothers, New York, 1933.

Wallis, Wilson D.: *An Introduction to Sociology*, chap. 9, F. S. Crofts & Co., New York, 1930.

Williams, J. M.: *Our Rural Heritage*, chaps. 4 and 5, Alfred A. Knopf, Inc., New York, 1925.

CHAPTER 6

ASSOCIATIONAL LIFE IN THE RURAL SETTING

THE PSYCHOSOCIAL CHARACTER OF THE RURAL GROUP

In Chapter 3 we considered the biological characteristics of the rural group and their possible sociological implications. Of more direct importance to sociological study are social psychological characteristics. What in brief are the unique psychosocial characteristics of the rural group that carry over directly into associational life?

Primary Groups Characteristic.—Rural society, as has been inferred previously, is a society composed chiefly of primary groups; *i.e.*, of groups characterized by intimate, face-to-face association and cooperation.[1] Urban society is more largely one of secondary groups in which casual, competitive, impersonal relationships predominate.

Cumulative Association Predominates.—Sorokin, Zimmerman, and Galpin, using somewhat different terms to describe rural in contrast to urban experience, emphasize a very important point[2] other than that implied by the concept "primary group." They use the term *cumulative group* in referring to the situation in which the individual is bound to the group by multiple ties such as exist in the family or in the rural neighborhood and *functional association* in referring to the type of situation in which the individual has one or at most a very few attachments to a social group. In most societies in the past, especially where the farm village has characterized rural organization, association has been of a cumulative character, each individual being closely bound to the neighborhood and community group. In America, with its isolated farms and small-town business centers in which there is considerable stratification and specialization, rural society, though cumulative, has never been so much so as in many more basically agricultural societies. In the urban community, the individual is more inclined to belong almost entirely to functional groups.

TRADITIONAL PATTERNS OF RURAL ASSOCIATION

Neighborliness.—Although in some farm communities settlement was of such heterogeneous groups that there was little neighborliness,[3] in most com-

[1] Charles H. Cooley, *Social Organization*, pp. 23 *ff.*, Charles Scribner's Sons, New York, 1909.

[2] P. A. Sorokin, C. C. Zimmerman, and C. J. Galpin, *A Systematic Source Book in Rural Sociology*, vol. 1, pp. 307–321, University of Minnesota Press, Minneapolis, 1930.

[3] Carl F. Kraenzel, of Montana State College, feels that in certain areas of the West

munities there was a common feeling of sympathy, or perchance, in case of neighborhood conflict, of hatred. Life was rooted deeply, was intimate, personal, and full of meaning, was of the kind that man has experienced throughout most of his past as he has lived in the simple environment of the primary group. Neighborliness was exhibited in numerous situations—joint ownership of machinery and exchange of work, mutual helpfulness and democratic associations, informal social control and spontaneous, unplanned social organization characterizing relationships.

Intimacy of Institutional Relationships.—Open-country social institutions not only ministered to basic needs of a universal nature but developed many meaningful social by-products. The Christmas program in the rural school, the visiting and gossip session after service in the open-country church, the conversation incidental to the formal functions of the grange—these contacts were often more meaningful than the formal ones provided for by the institution and were in sharp contrast to urban social institutions which confine experience more rigidly to formal programs. For example, members of the church congregation in a secondary group file out after service without shaking hands and often with no exchange of greetings.

The auction sale in spring or fall has been an important economic institution in farming areas; it also served as a social function, for men gathered to talk, tell yarns, and exchange experience as well as to strike a bargain.

The party telephone line, ordinarily built and maintained by the neighborhood, has been of no small social importance in those rural neighborhoods where all receivers come down when anyone's phone rings. (On party lines all phones ring on each call but each person's ring is distinct, being composed of a different combination of long and short rings.) In sharp contrast is the modern telephone controlled by a nation-wide organization and so operated that it is difficult to know when to "listen in."

---

where economic motives were dominant in settlement, close-knit neighborhood primary groups are lacking. Commenting on the settlement of Montana and the exploitation of her resources he says, "All this was carried forward without the development of communities, and without much of community self-help ideas and institutions. Montana does have some strong communities, usually built on nationality groupings, where the commercialized phases of the economy are subordinated in considerable degree to community services, institutions, and ways of living that mean the ability 'to get along' when the economic phases of the situation begin to contract. Casual observation, without detailed analysis of factual data, shows that the 'community ideal' of settlement and social organization is not only less prevalent in Montana agriculture than in older settled portions of the nation, but it never was present to an important extent in many parts of the state. It should be remembered that modern rapid transportation and easy communication appeared almost simultaneously with agricultural settlement in Montana." "Farm Population Mobility in Selected Montana Communities," pp. 47–48, *Montana Agricultural Experiment Station Bulletin* 371, Bozeman, 1939.

Survivals of Traditional Neighborhood Association Patterns.—In most rural areas there are survivals of many of the older forms of neighborhood association which are in direct contrast to much of urban association. A girl writes, "In the city where I live when someone is sick one usually just says 'poor soul' and

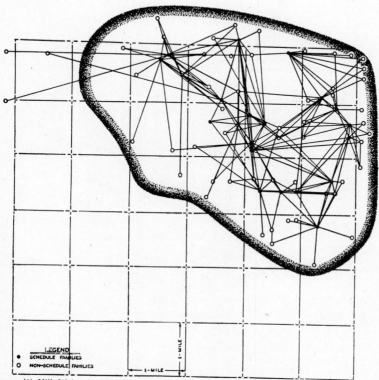

From George W. Hill, Walter Slocum, and Ruth O. Hill, "Man-land Adjustment," *Wisconsin Agricultural Experiment Station Research Bulletin* 134, Madison, 1938.

WORK EXCHANGE PATTERNS OF A CENTRAL WISCONSIN NEIGHBORHOOD

Garden Valley neighborhood, where work was exchange l with several neighbors. (Lines connect families that exchanged work in 1935. The blocks are a mile square.)

dismisses the matter, but in the rural neighborhood in which I have acquaintances if someone is ill, neighbors are glad to help in any way they can by doing chores, sitting up at a bedside, or performing other services."

A young man with an urban background visited a farm home for the first time in his life during a spring vacation in 1938. He gives his version of an incident that illustrates a trait in rural association:

Near the middle of the week, Adolf Mann phoned to say that he had a sick cow on his hands, and would Stanley come down and have a look at her. Adolf met us at the barn door and began immediately to explain in no uncertain language his diagnosis of the case. I wondered at the time why, if he knew what was wrong with her, he had called in Stanley, who didn't know but was inclined to agree with Adolf that it was not the "bloat" but some minor ailment. When he suggested a remedy, Adolf said, "I was thinkin' that was best, too." I thought in my urban way, "Here is a waste of

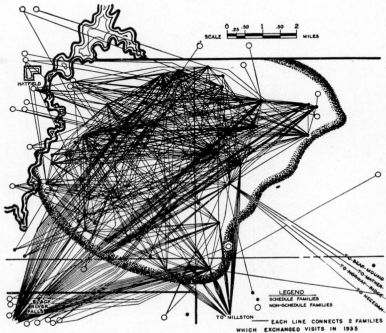

From George W. Hill, Walter Slocum, and Ruth O. Hill, "Man-land Adjustment," *Wisconsin Agricultural Experiment Station Research Bulletin* 134, Madison, 1938.

ASSOCIATION PATTERNS IN A CENTRAL WISCONSIN NEIGHBORHOOD
Komensky neighborhood, where families visited extensively within the neighborhood.

time." But somehow it wasn't. They had chatted amiably over unimportant things, the weather, the farm, the "missus," the kids. I can see now that all Adolf wanted was company. He had not seen Stanley, whom he liked, for four months. He hadn't, as city people do, asked for advice merely to hear someone agree with him. He wanted to renew an old friendship.

CHANGE IN TRADITIONAL ASSOCIATION PATTERNS

Even those who have lived in intimate contact with rural areas can scarcely appreciate the extensive changes that have come about during the last forty years in rural personalities, rural social processes, rural social institutions, and rural problems. In no phase of American society has change been more pervasive, has a transition in associational relationships been more pronounced.

A generation or two ago neighborhoods were intact, locality bonds were strong, often fortified by kinship relations. Common activities, a common life made for homogeneity of attitude and experience. The celebration of special days by members of the great family and by neighbors cemented local ties.

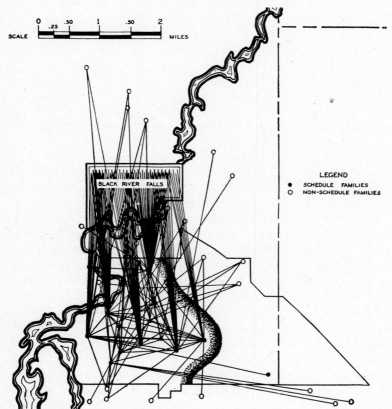

From George W. Hill, Walter Slocum, and Ruth O. Hill, "Man-land Adjustment," *Wisconsin Agricultural Experiment Station Research Bulletin* 134, Madison, 1938.

ASSOCIATION PATTERN IN ANOTHER CENTRAL WISCONSIN NEIGHBORHOOD

South Brockway neighborhood, where most visiting was with people in the neighboring town. (Lines connect families exchanging visits in 1935.)

Most activities having to do with business, entertainment, and social contacts were bounded by the neighborhood or the nearest trade center. The contacts of the average farm family were limited by a horse-and-buggy drive. Their circumscribed horizon excluded the world beyond the immediate locality. At that time there were no radio programs drawing the farmer into daily contact with events and activities of a world community; he scarcely recognized himself as being a vital part of a national or world economic order.

Fifty years ago to live on the isolated farm meant to be geographically isolated in a world consisting of neighbors of similar occupation and experience. Institutions were located either in the open country or in the adjoining trade center. Roads were dirt; movement was slow and difficult.

Then came the telephone, rural routes, rural free delivery, automobiles, surfaced roads, and radios and the old neighborhood in less than one generation was drawn from its isolation into direct contact with the stimulating, challenging influence of a dynamic, changing world culture, urban-focused, industry-driven, business-directed.

In 1900 practically no farms had automobiles; in 1910 comparatively few had them; by 1920 the automobile had almost replaced the horse and buggy. By 1930, 58 per cent of farms had automobiles and 13 per cent, motor trucks. In many prosperous rural sections almost every farm had at least one motor vehicle. In 1900 there were practically no surfaced highways; even in 1910 there were few all-weather roads. In 1920 all-weather roads were becoming common and by 1930 practically every neighborhood in the more progressive sections had at least one surfaced highway giving it year-round connections with the world at large. Farm-to-market roads are now not uncommon.

Came also a growth in mechanized farming and a consequent decrease in neighborhood interdependence. Came also greater freedom and leisure to use the conveniences made available by the new age—cheap newspapers, magazines, radios, cinemas, and the open highway. The rural community was in touch with the world and the isolation of the farm had lost its meaning.

Even more far-reaching changes began to appear in the psychological and social structure of the neighborhood. Educational achievement levels in the rural community suddenly changed from an eighth-grade training in the rural school to training in the consolidated high school. Many a rural community previous to 1910 had never sent a young person to high school or college, but by 1920 most of them were sending a select few to high school and by 1930 many rural neighborhoods were sending more than half of their young people to town high schools. The rural neighborhood thus became town-focused in its institutional life. In many cases local churches boarded up their doors and local schools were closed. When this occurred neighborhood life practically disappeared as a new but less intimate community group developed around a town or open-country consolidated school.

In the realm of behavior the tentacles of the city were extended out so that new patterns of the dynamic metropolis began to permeate even the outposts of rural civilization. Vacation trips, luxury goods, commercial recreation, and other such patterns of urban origin fascinated the farm youth and enticed the more progressive farm adults. So the rural neighborhood rapidly came to participate in a measure in a new society, and as it did so the bounds of experience outreached the neighborhood, local controls giving way to new interests acquired from contacts outside.

In the new scheme of social relationships the local trade center changed in meaning. Once the hamlet, small village, and town could depend upon the patronage of the immediate countryside.[1] But roads and automobiles gave farmers new freedom in the realm of trade and markets as in other things, and despite slogans designed to build loyalty to the home town, farmers, given the automobile and the open road, began to exercise choice. The old general store at the crossroads no longer satisfied when a longer trip could be made in much less time than it once took to drive to the crossroads. Between 1900 and 1920 thousands of general stores closed, many hamlets losing every business enterprise they possessed. In place of the old general store in surviving hamlets came the gasoline filling station. In all towns came a growth in specialization. The smaller town and village stores turned to providing necessary articles in which the farm populace demanded little choice, whereas enterprises supplying specialized items like furniture, jewelry, and ready-to-wear garments disappeared from the small town. Farmers preferred the store in the large town or city which could carry a better stock of goods and thus meet the newly created needs which the growing standard of living in the farm community demanded.

Then the highly urbanized department store and branches of famous mail-order houses began to locate in focal trade centers in the rural hinterland, so that the old general store with its many items of few varieties was replaced by the urban department store with departments much like those of the old general store but more adequately stocked.

So also with the marketing of produce, the farmer with his car or with his truck began to ignore the local market, produce station, and shipping yard, for a short morning drive could take him 25, 50, or even 100 miles away to a large market center. Thus he enjoyed freedom from a middleman, could market promptly, and sell in small lots.

With these newer trends in trade and business small towns, villages, and

[1] For detailed analyses of changes in the farm trade center, see such studies as C. C. Zimmerman, "Farm Trade Centers in Minnesota, 1905–1929," *Minnesota Agricultural Experiment Station Bulletin* 269, St. Paul, 1930; J. H. Kolb, "Service Relations of Town and Country," *Wisconsin Agricultural Experiment Station Bulletin* 58, Madison, 1923; C. R. Hoffer, "A Study of Town Country Relationships," *Michigan Agricultural Experiment Station Special Bulletin* 181, East Lansing, 1928; J. F. Page, "Relations of Town and Country Interests in Garfield County Oklahoma," *Oklahoma Agricultural Experiment Station Bulletin* 194, Norman, 1930; H. B. Price and C. R. Hoffer, "Services of Rural Trade Centers in Distribution of Farm Supplies," *Minnesota Agricultural Experiment Station Bulletin* 249, St. Paul, 1928; Paul H. Landis, "South Dakota Town-country Trade Relations, 1901–1931," *South Dakota Agricultural Experiment Station Bulletin* 274, Brookings, 1932.

hamlets not only lost some of their earlier meaning in the scheme of local organization, but many of them actually went out of existence.[1] These trends hastened other trends involving the farmer's relationships to service needs in the professional field. There was less need for a doctor in the local hamlet and

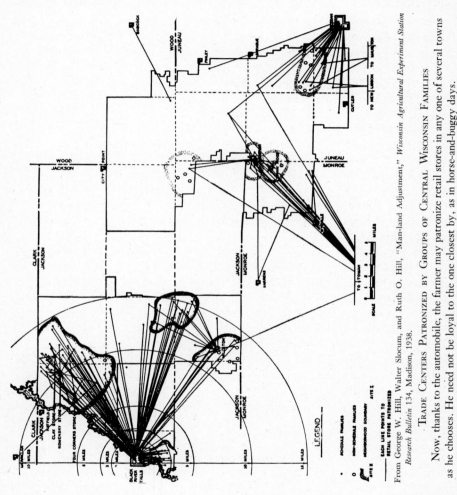

From George W. Hill, Walter Slocum, and Ruth O. Hill, "Man-land Adjustment," *Wisconsin Agricultural Experiment Station Research Bulletin* 134, Madison, 1938.

TRADE CENTERS PATRONIZED BY GROUPS OF CENTRAL WISCONSIN FAMILIES

Now, thanks to the automobile, the farmer may patronize retail stores in any one of several towns as he chooses. He need not be loyal to the one closest by, as in horse-and-buggy days.

less support for one because, with greater freedom of movement, farm people could choose their physician from among many in the city and could go to see him rather than expecting him to come to them. So also it was with dental service, legal advice, and religious and recreational expression. The old neces-

[1] The following studies present evidence on this point: C. E. Lively, "Growth and Decline of Farm Trade Centers, 1905–1930," *Minnesota Agricultural Experiment Station*

sary orientation of life about the neighborhood, the local town, and open-country institutions no longer existed. The automobile had undermined the foundations of the old system of social organization, providing the necessary groundwork for a new type of associational relationships.

How far has this transition in local experience gone? What is its meaning to rural life today and to rural society of tomorrow?

THE TREND OF RURAL ASSOCIATIONAL LIFE

Kolb, studying neighborhoods in Wisconsin, demonstrated that the general tendency of association, with the coming of the automobile, has been to shift from a locality to a common-interest basis. In 1920 he found most of the neighborhoods studied intact.[1] Later (1931), he restudied the same area (Dane County) and found that neighborhood lines were tending to break down somewhat and that people were organizing on a larger basis and in terms of some particular interest which they held in common and less in terms of locality, although locality and living near one another continued to play a part.[2]

Neighborhood groups are no longer the important organization units. Grouping arrangements are along new lines. These groups are more largely determined by the interests, the deliberate intent, the purposive action of people, than by locality relations. Locality groups have lateral or geographic dimensions. Interest groups have perpendicular or psychocultural dimensions. Locality groups depend upon *common* life, proximity, residence in a recognized physical area. Interest groups depend upon polarity, promotion, *special* concerns, leadership, deliberate effort. This polarity implies fields of magnetic influence. When thus released from locality restrictions certain people are attracted to certain of these poles of interest.[3]

These new interest groups may center in organizations having to do with recreation, better farming methods, better marketing, school, young people, health, social welfare, home improvement, church, the Farm Bureau, or any

---

Bulletin 287, St. Paul, 1932; T. Lynn Smith, "Farm Trade Centers in Louisiana, 1901–1931," *Louisiana Agricultural Experiment Station Bulletin* 234, University, 1933; Paul H. Landis, "The Growth and Decline of South Dakota Trade Centers, 1901–1933," *South Dakota Agricultural Experiment Station Bulletin* 279, Brookings, 1933; and his "Washington Farm Trade Centers, 1900–1935," *Washington Agricultural Experiment Station Bulletins* 360, Pullman, 1938.

[1] J. H. Kolb, "Rural Primary Groups," *University of Wisconsin Agricultural Experiment Station Bulletin* 51, Madison, 1921.

[2] J. H. Kolb, "Trends in Country Neighborhoods," *Wisconsin Agricultural Experiment Station Bulletin* 120, Madison, 1933.

[3] J. H. Kolb and A. F. Wileden, "Special Interest Groups in Rural Society," *Wisconsin Agricultural Experiment Station Research Bulletin* 84, Madison, December, 1927.

one of a number of organizations operative in rural areas.[1] Of course, many locality groups remain with their common life, and often influences of the old groupings are projected onto new social organizations.

Several generalizations can be made regarding the contemporary trends of rural groups. Locality groups have tended to disappear first in the vicinity of towns and to persist in isolated areas.[2] In general, the more numerous the bonds of the neighborhood the longer it maintains its integration. An educational institution provides an important bond. Many neighborhoods which were once the strongholds of homogeneous foreign-born nationality groups have disintegrated as the groups have assimilated American culture. The neighborhood tends to remain intact longest in the area inhabited by a homogeneous religious group.[3]

A significant aspect of the shift to interest groups has been the marked tendency for the new groups to center in towns and villages. Farm life in many areas has become, in part, town-centered, certain farm institutions and activities focusing there.[4] In communities where this shift has occurred life has taken ón a broader character, although experience is still for the most part of an intimate character.

Kolb and Brunner conclude that regardless of the villageward trend of farm life, "the farmer is giving up the open-country social organizations established during the last century only when it appears advantageous for him to do so."[5] In their study of 140 village-centered communities, where one would expect change to be far more pervasive than in the average farming area, they find that of 513 old rural neighborhoods centering about these villages, less than one in five disintegrated between 1924 and 1930.[6] Similar findings are reported for the same areas for the period 1930–1936.[7] In 1924, there were 513 neighborhoods centered about these 140 villages; in 1930, 429; in 1936, 328.[8] Since neighborhoods are showing such persistence in village-centered areas, one can safely assume that throughout farming areas the primary group is still basic in social experience.

C. C. Zimmerman in his *The Changing Community* concludes that although

---

[1] For an extensive classification of interests about which rural groups center, see J. H. Kolb and E. de S. Brunner, *A Study of Rural Society*, rev. and enlarged ed., chap. 6, Houghton Mifflin Company, Boston, 1940.

[2] Neighborhood ties in Wisconsin were found to break first in areas where population was most dense, cars most numerous, and improved roads most common. *Ibid.*, p. 65.

[3] *Ibid.*, pp. 56–59.

[4] E. de S. Brunner and I. Lorge, *Rural Trends in Depression Years*, pp. 83–84. Columbia University Press, New York, 1937.

[5] *Recent Social Trends in the United States*, p. 508, McGraw-Hill Book Company, Inc., New York, 1933.

[6] *Ibid.*

[7] E. de S. Brunner and I. Lorge, *op. cit.*, Table 30, p. 94.

[8] *Ibid.*

CHAPTER 7

TRADITIONAL CULTURE PATTERNS

THE TERM "culture" as used by sociologists and anthropologists refers not to special refinement that sets the elite or privileged classes apart, but to the mode of life of a people, their civilization. Culture so defined embraces everything that is artificial in man's experience—the things he has made as contrasted to the things which are natural—and includes not only material objects produced by invention but traditions and customs, religious and philosophical systems, morals and laws—everything in the way of behavior patterns that are passed on from generation to generation through training. It is in this sense that the term "culture" is used here, interest being confined primarily to a study of the culture of rural America, contrasting it at points with that of the city.

Major culture patterns throughout this nation and, for that matter throughout Western Europe also, are alike but within the major patterns there are many minor variations. We speak of the North and the South, the East and the West, meaning to suggest not merely geographical differences but unique cultural configurations within the national culture. Equally fundamental and significant are the basic underlying differences between urban and rural culture patterns. Just what elements constitute the differences in all cases it is not possible to tell, and yet all who have known both city and farm community intimately know that they exist. Many tangible differences in material culture are obvious, but the more important and more subtle differences in non-material culture, folkways, mores, customs, social usage, and so forth, which have most to do with the formation of personality are not so readily located or analyzed. Nonetheless much of this chapter on these more subjective aspects, attention, for the most part, being directed toward a study of those elements of rural culture which seem to be important to an understanding of rural social experience and personality conditioning. Emphasis is on what still appear to be basic traits, many of which are in the process of change as farm and city have come closer together. A discussion of more dynamic aspects of rural culture is reserved for Chapter 19.

RELATIVE SIMPLICITY OF THE MATERIAL CULTURE

One need not travel far through the countryside to appreciate that the man-made is less prominent there than in the city. Architecture in home, church, and school is more simple and less ornate. Tools and machinery are for the most part those which can be operated by one man, and the most complicated of them usually require only two or three men. This remains true in spite of the fact that mechanization of agriculture has been extensive, and that new and more efficient machines have come into use.[1] One of the most complex of farm machines is the grain combine, but this machine and the tractor which draws it can be operated with from two to six men. The entire crew required to harvest 50 acres of grain, around 2,000 bushels, in a 10-hour day, may not exceed five or six men. By far the larger part of the work is still that of one man and his tools.

There is little of the complexity that characterizes the urban setting generally or the urban factory in particular. Take the matter of time precision alone. Time clocks, whistles, and bells telling one when to begin or to stop work and transportation devices geared to the minute are hardly suited to the experience of one working with nature. The farmer sets his own pace, working against nature but not against time. He often must scale his activities to the rising and setting of the sun and he may awaken daily by the alarm clock, but he is not forced to begin work exactly at 8 A.M. and stop at 5 P.M., or to begin at 7 A.M. and quit at 4 P.M.,[2] and has little sympathy with urban advocates of daylight-saving plans or similar tinkerings of man with the course of time or nature.

PROMINENCE OF CUSTOMARY FOLKWAYS

For more than 20 years the attention of sociologists has been focused on change and for a much longer period contemporary culture has been characterized by rapidity of change. Not only has material culture been revolutionized, but many of man's life habits and philosophies have been transformed. Balancing somewhat this picture of change is the age-old tendency of numerous rural customs to persist generation after generation relatively unmodified.

Rural culture conserves custom even in an age of extensive change. In spite of the development in machine agriculture there are thousands of things on the farm learned only by experience and example. The planting of seeds, the cultivating of plants, the care of animals, the treatment of animal diseases, the storing of crops, the building of fences, the upkeep of property are proce-

---

[1] The per capita output of farm labor doubled during the period 1870 to 1920. C. C. Taylor, *Rural Sociology*, rev. ed., p. 4, Harper & Brothers, New York, 1933.

[2] In some respects the country man often keeps a more regular schedule than the town man. For example, meals in the country may be served at more regular hours than meals in the town for meals in the city are a family affair. Many meals in the city are taken individually at restaurants or elsewhere outside the home and the individual eats more or less when he chooses. Livestock on the farm are usually fed on a fairly regular schedule. No doubt there are other exceptions to the proposition that there has been a more prominent development of the punctuality complex in the city than on the farm, but these exceptions do not invalidate the general tendency of the city to be more precise in the measurement of time.

dures that are passed on by tradition. Even though aspects of farming and of farm management have been scientifically investigated by college agricultural experiment stations, the U.S. Department of Agriculture, and other agencies engaged in agricultural research, much of farm practice has never been made the subject of scientific research or experimentation and is, therefore, based on the lessons of experience. The Federal government, recognizing the inability of the family-farm enterprise to conduct research, institute change, and make needed inventions, has subsidized research in agriculture more than in other fields.

Even when scientific conclusions are known, procedures may still follow tradition. New ideas and new practices diffuse less rapidly in the family-farm enterprise than in the centralized, large-scale, institutional structure of the urban enterprise. Similarly, rural codes, behavior practices, life philosophies, and political theories of long standing persist in spite of effective agencies of communication, in part because the established practices of the farm community require no new rationalizations to support them.

EMPHASIS ON THE PRACTICAL

Rural culture tends to emphasize the practical and necessary and to disregard the ornamental and comfortable. Traditionally, the farmer builds a good barn before he builds a new house and buys a pickup truck before a pleasure car. As Hughie Call expresses it, "sheep come first."[1] Before her marriage to a Montana woolgrower she had lived all her life in a Southern city. To learn that on the sheep ranch she was less important than sheep and that the whole of life must be ordered to see that the sheep are cared for was a new experience. "If you have an idea that you are more important than sheep, a sheep ranch is no place for you."

Cash in most farm homes is limited; year after year money must be spent for interest, tools, upkeep of machinery, care of livestock, and other things essential to earning a livelihood and to building a lifetime enterprise. On the farm such sacrifices may extend over many years, until the patterns and attitudes they require become life habits and philosophies, the wife and husband alike are taking for granted that "sheep come first." After years of deprivation the family may reach a place where comforts might well come first, but well-established habits forbid.

Because of the farmer's emphasis on the practical, farm journals still find it necessary to appeal to utility, economy, usefulness, and price, to a greater extent than magazines which go almost exclusively to the urban public. Urban magazines are more likely to stress artistic design, beauty, comfort, and

[1] "Sheep Come First," *Saturday Evening Post*, Mar. 27, 1937; condensed in the *Reader's Digest*, pp. 100–104, August, 1937.

pleasure.[1] Advertising in the journals that go almost exclusively to farm people emphasizes the institutional, business aspects of living whereas urban magazines in contrast emphasize personal effects. Much more prominent in urban than in farm magazines are advertisements dealing with beauty aids, automobile gadgets, and amusements.[2]

The average farm home is more modestly furnished than the urban home of equal income, as many studies of consumption tendencies in rural as compared to urban homes demonstrate. For example, the average expenditure of 137 farm families in Virginia for furnishings was $24, or 1.4 per cent of the budget; for 140 city families $78, or 3.0 per cent of the budget.[3] There seems to be less intense competition for status by means of conspicuous display in the farm than in the city home.

The rural index of living is low compared to the urban, as measured not only by furnishings, but also by such common conveniences as running water, bathtubs, central heating, electrical lighting, and the use of electrical devices. Greater cost in rural areas is a factor, but differences in values is also an important one. For a graphic picture of the rural living index, study the map which shows that few counties of the nation have a high level of living, many have a very low index.

THE PRACTICAL VS. THE ARTISTIC

In fiction and on the screen the farmer is at times depicted as a man with a vivid appreciation of the beauties of nature or of the miraculous qualities of the soil. Actually those who have lived and worked among farmers know that such attitudes rarely if every exist. The practical almost entirely overshadows the artistic in the lives of most; there is little in rural culture as such to encourage artistic observation.

In an attempt to get some measure of the relative weight of the practical and artistic in rural and urban culture, as it affects personality values, 882 girls[4] in the State College of Washington in 1942 were given the Allport-Vernon scale "A Study of Values."[5] The results of this test, as they apply to

---

[1] This conclusion is based chiefly on correspondence with editors and staff members of the Pacific Northwest Farm Trio, which publishes *The Idaho Farmer, The Washington Farmer* and *The Oregon Farmer;* of *Capper's Farmer, The Farmer's Wife,* and the *Country Gentleman.*

[2] These findings are clearly indicated in a study made by Fred Winkler as a seminar project in rural sociology in 1939. The study contrasts the display of advertising in one 1938 issue each of 12 farm magazines and 12 nonfarm magazines.

[3] *Rural-urban Standards of Living,* Institute Monograph 6, University of Virginia, Charlottesville, 1929.

[4] Few young men were in college during the war period and the group in college would not have been representative of young men's attitudes generally, therefore, only young women were included.

[5] Published by Houghton Mifflin Company, Boston.

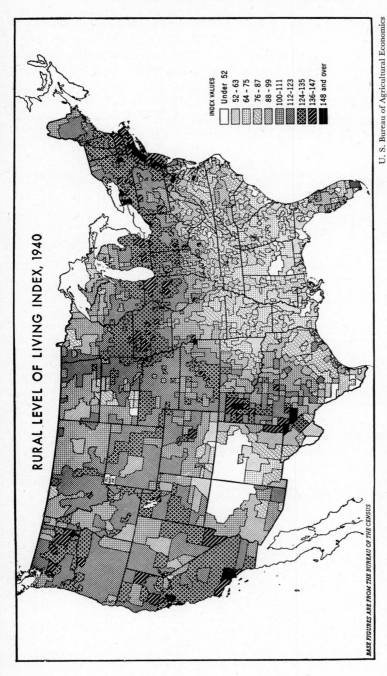

RURAL LEVEL OF LIVING INDEX, 1940

INDEX VALUES

Under 52
52 - 63
64 - 75
76 - 87
88 - 99
100-111
112-123
124-135
136-147
148 and over

BASE FIGURES ARE FROM THE BUREAU OF THE CENSUS

U. S. Bureau of Agricultural Economics

The rural index is a weighting of combined farm and nonfarm indexes. The rural farm index takes into account per cent with gross income of over $600 and per cent with 1936 or later model cars. The rural nonfarm index takes into account per cent of dwellings with running water and per cent with mechanical refrigeration. Both indexes take into account median years schooling of persons 25 years of age and over, radios in dwelling, and rooms per person in occupied dwellings.

aesthetic and economic values, are shown in the two charts. The consistent and marked difference in the ratings of the three groups is immediately apparent. The farm group leans heavily toward the practical end of the aesthetic values scale, with a low proportion having high aesthetic ratings. On the eco-

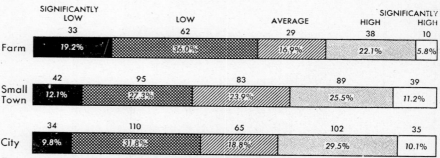

From Landis, *Washington Agricultural Experiment Station*. Findings are statistically significant, as measured by the analysis-of-variance test.

Aesthetic Values of Farm, Small-town, and City Girls

Marked differences in aesthetic values of farm, small-town, and city girls are shown by these comparisons of the Allport-Vernon Scale of Values. The scale is based on the assumption that personalities are distinguished by their values or evaluative attitudes. The above shows clearly that young farm women lean toward the artistic much less than young women in towns and cities. The study compares 882 girls registered at the State College of Washington during the spring of 1942.

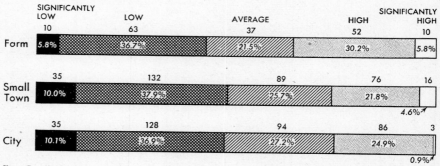

From Landis, *Washington Agricultural Experiment Station*. Findings are statistically significant, as measured by the analysis-of-variance test.

Economic Values of Farm, Small-town, and City Girls

A high rating on economic values indicates undue emphasis of young farm women on the practical and useful. In this trait young farm women rated high compared to town and city groups. (Same scale and sample as the preceding chart.)

nomic values scale they rate high. The city group is at the other extreme, with the small-town group falling generally between.

PROMINENCE OF THRIFT MORES

Although the proverbial thrift patterns of the farmer have been affected by social changes necessitating the purchase of labor-saving devices, by the new urban pattern of installment buying, and many other factors, there still survive in many sections the traditional frugal habits of the rural culture pattern.[1] In the background is the long tradition of the laying up of foodstores for winter and of seed gathering for the next season, which has tended to heighten respect for the value of commodities.[2] The fact that the majority of rural people are responsible for the training and upbringing of children may also make for greater thrift than exists in the metropolis.

Thrift has survival value in the farm enterprise. As farming is a long-time venture, one gets ahead by a gradual but slow accumulation of experience and goods.

The greatest stimulus to thrift is felt when one's present savings will plainly lighten future labor. The farmer pinches now so that next year a windmill may relieve his aching arms, or the horse fork take the strain off his shoulders. Moreover, his saving is expended under his eyes, just where it will do the most good, and no paltry 6 per cent is his reward. The tiles he lays through his slough may pay for themselves in three years; so likewise, the new barn, the improved dairy herd, or the self-binder. On the other hand, the typical city dweller rents his savings to someone else and takes the reward of his abstinence not in a vivid personal experience, but in an annual 4 per cent from a savings bank or in 6 per cent from some remote company whose directors he does not know and whose business he has never seen and would not understand.[3]

NONMERCENARY CHARACTER OF NEIGHBORHOOD EXCHANGE

Farmers have long been accustomed to the exchange of work, which was usually made without a strict keeping of time. But in exchanging work with a tractor, standard rates per acre are established and settlement is made on a cash basis, because of the cash outlay for fuel. Back of the traditional practice was the long-standing custom of the farmer of putting no value upon his own individual work and little value upon the work of a team. (It has been customary in many communities for a farmer to furnish his team or not in exchanging work according to the wishes of the neighbor.)

In rare cases even today farm youths hire out to work on a farm without making any bargain beforehand as to the rate of pay or hours and conditions of work. Usually such work involves long hours, depending upon the season and the nature of the work; it is assumed that the hired man or girl will keep whatever hours the farmer and his family keep. (The above applies only to

[1] J. M. Williams, in discussing the proverbial thrift of the farmer, cites his well-known fear of the poorhouse. *Our Rural Heritage*, chap. 11, Alfred A. Knopf, Inc., New York, 1925.

[2] Bernard believes that farmers are frugal because until recently most of their income has been on a commodity rather than a cash basis. "A Theory of Social Attitudes," *American Journal of Sociology*, p. 648, March, 1917.

[3] E. A. Ross, *Principles of Sociology*, p. 28, New York, 1920. By permission of the D. Appleton-Century Company.

the worker who lives with the family. There are many hired laborers in agriculture who work by the hour or even on a piece-work basis.)

There is not so much danger of exploitation in a situation of this sort as one might expect. In areas where a neighborhood consciousness still persists, the farmer ordinarily does not wish to risk paying less than the going wage for fear of gossip and ostracism. People who have the reputation of paying low wages are usually known throughout the community and avoided by local job seekers. Even the seasonal workers who wait in small towns to be contacted by farmers seeking help often learn about the various employers in the community before accepting a job. In this situation, as in many others in primary or semiprimary groups, there is no external force compelling one to conform to custom but more subtle pressures act with equal or even greater effectiveness.

These inexact patterns are in part a carryover of the barter economy which characterized much of rural exchange in the past and which still persists in certain situations. Today most small-town stores will accept goods in trade in preference to buying them; if a produce buyer is paying 22 cents a dozen for eggs, the storekeeper will offer 23 or 24 cents in trade in order to draw business to his store.

Many contracts entered into by the farmer are by word of mouth with no written agreement to bind the contracting parties. The Farm Security Administration reported that 80 per cent of all farm leases consist of nothing more than verbal agreement.[1]

ABSENCE OF ELABORATE CULTURE INVOLVING SOCIAL USAGE

Rural culture with few exceptions has never specialized in etiquette and manners. The one principal exception in America was the group of aristocratic rural families in the ante-bellum South. Generally speaking, farm people expect less of human nature in the way of embellishments than certain other groups; leisure, social stratification, and similar elements in a culture are required to give value to social ritual. Rural people usually have neither the time nor the patience to devote to ceremony. Moreover, since rural life is ordinarily lived in a primary group, social ritual would serve little purpose. Superficialities are unnecessary in a situation in which everyone knows everyone else. Because the rural culture pattern demands little in the way of sophistication, the person developing under it lacks this trait.

Farmers are often accused of lacking sociability; certainly aloofness does not seem to characterize the individual growing up in isolation. But this supposed lack of sociability may be rather a lack of means of social expression. The individual in the rural primary group is not resistant to sociability as such.

---

[1] *The Flexible Farm Lease*, leaflet by the U.S. Department of Agriculture, Washington, D. C. (undated, but 1938 or 1939).

He is sociable in the primary-group setting where he feels at home and understands the modes of social expression, but in strange groups he appears antisocial or nonsocial and is unable to fit into the social ritual or to express himself. But despite an external crudeness rural people usually possess a genuine courtesy such as often does not characterize urban relations smoothly oiled by social graces. This frank, homely, friendly spirit of rural culture is a product of the natural setting in which the rural man lives and works. Here is sociality unhindered by a restraining consciousness of propriety, a naturalness of contact which characterizes family and other primary group relations, in which intimacy rather than etiquette guides behavior.

Deeply imbedded in rural mores of the past has been the custom of hospitality toward the stranger. The extent to which this trait has survived depends a great deal on the degree of isolation; for instance, workers checking on wheat allotments reported that they were almost always asked to stay for dinner in isolated areas but not in areas located near towns. In studying drought migrants in the state of Washington, research workers found that those located in areas in the immediate vicinity of a city had no time for night conferences, whereas those living in isolated districts welcomed night calls and seemed reluctant to have the interviewer leave, even prolonging the visit if possible. This observation is verified by canvassers in rural and urban communities. The more rural the area the easier it is to gain entrance to the home.

Practical considerations help explain the hospitality of rural culture. Housing space is more adequate; a reserve food supply usually is on hand in the cellar and pantry. In the city, since groceries are all bought with cash, people are conscious of their cost. On some farms a substantial part of the food is produced and consumed without the idea of cost being considered. In the city there are numerous eating places where the stranger can conveniently buy his meals; in more isolated rural sections there are none. In part, however, hospitality represents the carry-over of tradition from an age of isolated living when the family welcomed the stranger and was compensated by the social experience of talking with one from the outside.

ABBREVIATED SPEECH PATTERNS

The language of farm people has been simple, practical, and often abbreviated. Colloquialisms are primarily rural; old forms of speech persist in isolated areas;[1] the rural character in fiction employs crude forms of speech; farm journals usually do not contain the elaborate forms of rhetorical expression that are found in sophisticated magazines read by the upper strata of the urban community.

[1] James Raine, *Land of the Saddle Bags* (Missionary Education Movement, 1924), gives many examples of the persistence of old English compound words in the isolated Appalachian highland culture.

A lack of language development was noted by Baldwin, Fillmore, and Hadley in their study of farm children in Iowa communities.[1] They found that on those intelligence tests demanding a knowledge of language rural children rated much lower than children in urban schools and also that rural children in one-room schools did more poorly than children in consolidated schools. With regard to speech habits they found that many farm children spoke indistinctly or carelessly, making frequent use of provincial words and pronunciations.[2] The authors conclude that the training of rural children in correct habits of speech is generally neglected because neither the school nor the home is much concerned. The one-room school is not organized to give more than passing attention to speech habits and there are few other corrective influences in the rural environment.

The grammar, rhetoric, and literary skill of the average student in the agricultural colleges of this country are notoriously bad. This is due in part to the poor foundation in grammar and English received in rural schools, but also in part to faulty language habits which the rural child acquires from contact with the abbreviated, practical vocabulary of adults in his community. Since a generation of better educated parents is now taking over activities in many farm communities, speech difficulties are likely to disappear and, in fact, already have in many progressive sections. Consolidated schools, where they have developed, are also effecting improvements in speech habits. The radio too is having its effect in improving speech in all areas.

RIGID MORAL STANDARDS

The rigidity of rural moral standards is traditional. Morality is considered absolute (final) rather than relative (subject to circumstances), whereas the general tendency of the present time is to look upon moral codes as being subject to particular conditions, circumstances, times, and places. This rigid conception of morality reflects in attitudes toward the Bible, which farmers have been inclined to interpret literally. It is in the rural community that the greatest resistance toward such concepts as evolution and relativity are found; the Scopes evolution trial could have taken place only in a rural Tennessee, never in an urban Rhode Island.[3] It could not now take place in many rural areas.

The rural family is much more conservative than the urban in its moral values, especially as they apply to family life. Birth control makes its inroads last among rural families and the lowest economic strata of the city. Voluntary sterilization, abortion, and similar practices encounter more opposition and

[1] Bird T. Baldwin, *et al.*, *Farm Children*, pp. 243–247, D. Appleton-Century Company, Inc., New York, 1930.

[2] *Ibid.*, chap. 16.

[3] The rural South is often referred to as the "Bible belt." For a popular account of the extensive sale of Bibles there, read T. H. Alexander, "High Pressure in the Bible Belt," *Reader's Digest*, pp. 37–41, January, 1937.

inertia in rural than in urban areas. Judging by divorce statistics, marriage is held more sacred in rural than in urban communities. Undoubtedly a study of attitudes toward divorce would show that the rural family is more conservative than the urban.[1]

A survey in 1934 by *Farm and Fireside*[2] studied the attitudes of farm people on certain nonlegal moral issues during that year and compared the results with rural reactions on moral issues covered by law in 1930. The 1930 vote was interpreted by the magazine as indicating that, although four-fifths were old-fashioned or strict in their moral reactions, urban influences were gradually battering down the old-time rustic virtues. However, even in 1930 well over one-half of the group, or 67 per cent, thought that doctors should be allowed to give birth-control information to young married couples. In 1934, the study indicated an even greater trend toward leniency in moral standards.

Illegitimate births are more frequent in rural than in urban areas. Data for 1934 are typical of past conditions in the United States. In that year there were 41.5 illegitimate births reported per 1,000 total births in rural areas (places of less than 10,000 people) as compared to 31.1 per 1,000 in cities of 10,000 population and over.[3] This differential, however, does not necessarily reflect a difference in morality. The use of contraceptives and the practice of abortion hide illegitimate conception in the city; the rural community conceals illegitimate conception by marriage where marriage can be arranged. Baldwin and his colleagues in their study of communities in rural Iowa, by comparing birth records and marriage certificates, learned that a number of births occurred within a few months after marriage, suggesting the tendency of community pressure to force marriage in cases of illegitimate conception.[4] In checking the records of girls to whom illegitimate children were born, they found that all these girls with the exception of one ultimately married.

Lister and Kirkpatrick in a study of a sample of over 13,000 Maryland youths, compared the attitudes and habits of farm, village, town, and city youth with regard to drinking. They found comparatively little difference in the attitudes of farm boys and those of other groups, but found a marked resistance to drinking on the part of farm girls, 32 per cent of them being opposed to drinking as compared to 15.5 per cent of city girls.[5] Duvall and Motz,[6]

---

[1] For a critical summary of various types of evidence on the problem of rural morals, see P. A. Sorokin, *et al.*, *A Systematic Source Book in Rural Sociology*, vol. 2, pp. 266–342, University of Minnesota Press, Minneapolis, 1931.

[2] R. Lord, "Backbone Relaxes," *New Republic*, vol. 78, pp. 175–177, Mar. 28, 1934.

[3] *Birth, Stillbirth, and Infant Mortality Statistics*, pp. 14–15, U.S. Bureau of the Census, 1934.

[4] Bird T. Baldwin, *et al.*, *op. cit.*, p. 146.

[5] J. J. Lister and E. L. Kirkpatrick, *Rural Youth Speak*, p. 83, American Youth Commission, Washington, D. C., Feb. 1, 1939.

[6] Evelyn Millis Duvall and Annabelle Bener Motz, "Are Country Girls so Different?" *Rural Sociology*, vol. 10, pp. 263–274, September, 1945.

comparing 403 native-born, single girls 14 to 24 years of age in rural and urban areas of the Middle West, found that urban girls smoke and drink more often than do rural girls. They also found that rural girls had more strict religious training in the home and attended church considerably more.

The White House Conference on Child Health and Protection in studying the home environment of children reports that faith in old moralities is more evident in rural than in urban families.[1]

Roger William Riis[2] describes an automobile trip throughout the United States on which he and his secretary used an old car that was in perfect condition. He found that the majority of repair men would gyp the automobile user, especially the woman user, but marked differences in the honesty of urban and small-town garage owners were reported. The investigators were taken for suckers and treated accordingly by 63 per cent of garages.

Places of less than 10,000 inhabitants were found safer for motorists than places of over 10,000. The most honest place of all was the crossroads repair shop in the small hamlet. The investigators concluded that, as a rule, the small struggling garage, with the owner himself at work in overalls, gives a squarer deal than the large and prosperous one.

The farm community, like other areas, is composed of people of differing moral stripe. However, it does seem that rural folk are guided in the main by a more strict moral code than prevails among urban folk.

The rural neighborhood rarely offers more than than one or two levels of opinion upon the conduct of its members. Usually it applies a single standard sound enough but mediocre. Individuals with a strong bent either upward or downward chafe under unstimulating self-complacent neighborhood opinion and migrate in quest of countenancers, models, and appreciators. The city, on the other hand, offers circles which differ immensely in their standards of right and of excellence. At every stage of descent into the pit one finds cronies, while one will hardly rise so far into the empyrean as to find himself without comrades. In the city, therefore, one's possibilities whether for good or for evil more fully develop. Angel or devil, hero or sneak, doer or loafer, miser or spendthrift, sage or fool—each more fully attains the limit of his nature than he is likely to do in the rural community.[3]

THE EMERGENCE OF CONFLICTING CULTURAL VALUES

Such values as work, family, land, and security have provided a focus for life's energies under traditional rural culture patterns. Such core interests have

[1] Subcommittee report appearing in *The Adolescent in the Family*, pp. 158–179, the White House Conference on Child Health and Protection.

[2] Roger William Riis, "The Repair Man Will Gyp You if You Don't Watch Out," *Reader's Digest*, pp. 1 ff., July, 1941.

[3] E. A. Ross, *Principles of Sociology*, pp. 28–29, New York, 1920. By permission of the D. Appleton-Century Company.

furnished goals for personality, determining personality configurations as well as neighborhood culture patterns. At the basis of much of farm culture still these essential values remain. But experience widens, contacts between rural and urban culture patterns become more numerous, and these basic rural values become modified and in many cases there is conflict between the old values and the new.

Take, for instance, the matter of work. In the past, farm interests were very much work-centered; they still are to a considerable extent.[1] Until quite recently the leisure-pleasure complex of the city found little place in the farm community. Work was not only held to be a virtue, but distinction achieved in work by being the first in the field in the morning, by putting on the biggest load of hay, by cutting the most grain in a day, by planting the straightest row of corn, brought status. Work tended to be an end in itself whereas in the urban community it tends to be a means to remote ends.

These work mores had their origin in necessity. On the farm there was always work to be done. The farmer was a proprietor of his own enterprise and therefore did not limit his work to certain hours. He lived on his land and so was always in the midst of work that needed to be done.

In direct contrast is the pleasure-seeking motive which has become a part of the life philosophy of the more favored classes of the city and increasingly of all classes, for even the proletariat emulates the luxury economy of those of the social strata above and tries to participate in it. Increasingly as farm youth have contacted town and urban school systems, they have absorbed the pleasure-seeking philosophy and, having done so, cease to find the enjoyment and spiritual strength in work that their parents claimed to find. At this point there is a clash which often leads to a separation between the old generation and the new.

This same clash of interest shows up in the development of recreational patterns. In the city these patterns have expanded as part of a philosophy of escape, an expression of a desire to forget a real world that has grown unpleasant, as a means of finding satisfaction for those who, in working for others, find no pleasure in work as an antidote for forced leisure or idleness, as an escape from frayed nerves, failure, frustration, and other such factors.

As yet recreation patterns have expanded much less rapidly in the country. Farm youth often fail to recognize the essential differences between rural and urban needs and many come to crave the thrills of urban recreation and to desire the leisure and luxury upon which commercialized recreation is predi-

[1] J. J. Lister and E. L. Kirkpatrick find that the average workday for both young men and young women between the ages of 16 and 24 years is considerably longer on the farm than in village, town, or city. Their data deal with 13,528 farm and village, town and city youths in Maryland. *Rural Youth Speak*, p. 40, American Youth Commission, Washington, D. C., 1939.

cated. But once youth start participating, it is only another generation until adults participate, so that there has been a gradual encroachment by urban leisure-pleasure recreation patterns into the field of rural values.

Closely akin to work as a supreme value in rural culture has been land ownership. Tangible property has had deep meaning and land has been the ultimate material value. "Farmers raise more corn, to feed more hogs, to buy more land." Not stocks and bonds, life insurance and annuities, chiefly, but land has been the end goal in ownership. In the urban community the desire to own immobile, tangible assets has declined,[1] but the farmer has wanted land. His security was in the land, not in endowments or social security plans, industrial or unemployment insurance,[2] retirement plans or annuities, but in land; other kinds of property were considered less safe. Investment in land has brought the farmer those satisfactions which the urbanite has sought through conspicuous consumption of consumable goods such as will let the world know that he is keeping ahead of the Joneses.

But even this value has come into question, partly because of economic forces, partly no doubt because of a breadth of contact and a clash of new desires. With the decline in the importance of land as a life goal[3] has gone a part of the old security that motivated the life of the farmer. He still probably does not accumulate debt through installment buying of luxury goods, clothes, and objects for conspicuous display to the extent that urban classes do, and probably more often acquires debt in the purchase of real estate than do other classes,[4] but his life is tending in this direction.

[1] See L. Wirth, "Urbanism as a Way of Life," *American Journal of Sociology*, vol. 44, pp. 1–24, July, 1938. Also, W. F. Ogburn's discussion of the decline of economic functions in the urban home, *Recent Social Trends in the United States*, vol. 1, pp. 664–672, McGraw-Hill Book Company, Inc., New York, 1933. See also the McKenzie footnote below.

[2] Wilson Gee and William H. Stauffer, in studying a group of Virginia families, find that only 1.9 per cent of farm families' incomes as compared to 6.1 per cent of urban families' incomes was spent for life insurance. *Rural-urban Standards of Living*, Institute Monograph 6, University of Virginia, Charlottesville, 1929.

C. C. Zimmerman finds that 71.6 per cent of Minnesota farmers' investments concerned land ownership, 6 per cent insurance, and 22.4 per cent all other kinds of investments. Urban investments are diversified. "Incomes and Expenditures of Minnesota Farm and City Families, 1927–1928," pp. 10, 26–28, *Minnesota Agricultural Experiment Station Bulletin 255*, St. Paul, 1929.

[3] C. C. Zimmerman finds that the primary competition in the family budget of the farm family is between investments centered around the tradition of land ownership and the increased consumption of material goods. *Ibid.*, pp. 8–10.

[4] McKenzie summarizes data showing that in the 14 largest cities in the nation, all with over 500,000 population, permits for multiple dwellings increased from 34 per cent to 64.4 per cent of the total number of building permits issued. Not only has the proportion of multiple dwellings increased in the larger cities but it has increased in all cities. The larger cities, however, show the greatest increase. This trend reflects a decline in interest in home ownership in the city. *Recent Social Trends in the United States*, vol. 1, pp. 474–477.

There is some evidence that the new desire for luxury goods is directly related to the level of education. Nelson and Burt, in a study in rural Utah,[1] found that the more educated the family the greater the number of material possessions, such as running water system, power washing machine, automobile, and other items making for more convenient and luxurious living. They concluded that schooling intensifies wants for utilities, so that the tendency is to purchase them even if it means mortgaging the future income.

M. L. Wilson, Director of the United States Extension Service, has cited a growing feeling of economic insecurity among farm as well as among city people.[2] He believes that farmers do not feel secure in the possession of their farms as was once the case, nor do they feel safe from the hazards of old age, many of them realizing that they are implicated in social forces wholly beyond their control.

Pollard shows that people in Grainger County, a rural county in a mountainous area in Tennessee, spend almost as much for automobiles as for food or clothing. The estimated annual expenditure for automobiles in the county is $120,000; for clothing, $140,000; for food, $155,000. Commenting on these expenditures, he concludes,

It is, perhaps, in this item of automobile expense that we find the explanation of the more serious effect of the depression upon the rural population of America when compared with similar population in Europe. This expenditure is almost as great as that for such traditionally primal needs as food and clothing.[3]

Here one sees new cultural values entering farm life in America, values which enrich life but at the same time increase its hazards. The boasted security of farming is in part a myth. Security has vanished in a measure on the family farm even though many cling to it still as a fundamental value. Here, as at many points, new values intrude, modifying and, in certain instances, replacing traditional culture patterns.

INCREASING IMPORTANCE OF PECUNIARY VALUES

In a highly advanced civilization economic factors come to control the destiny of human beings in many noneconomic realms. The operation of pecuniary factors in nonpecuniary realms has been most prominent in urban

[1] Lowry Nelson and N. I. Burt, "Influence of Formal Schooling on Consumptive Tendencies in Two Rural Communities," *Publications of the American Sociological Society*, vol. 23, pp. 255–260, October, 1929.

[2] M. L. Wilson, "Whither Rural America?" p. 11, address before the annual meeting of the Christian Rural Fellowship in New York, N. Y., Dec. 2, 1938.

[3] A. L. Pollard, "What a Country Trade Balance through Agricultural-industrial Companionship Will Mean," p. 2, excerpt from the *Proceedings of the Third Conference on Companionship of Agriculture and Industry*, held at the University of Tennessee, November, 1933.

culture, but now in rural culture also the pecuniary element looms large in many phases of experience; in fact, social status, health, leisure and recreation, group contacts, personal freedom, and numerous other fundamental values are so closely identified with economic factors in our time that all people are finding their lives hemmed in increasingly by these forces. With the relative breakdown of rural isolation, extension of the range of rural contacts, and enrichment of desires in rural areas owing to the great number of material values to which farm people are exposed in an age of rapid diffusion, the farmer's realizations, like those of other groups, have come to be limited increasingly by his means. As farm life has become associated with a cash-competitive market economy, economic forces are playing an even greater part in determining the functioning of farm people in their social order. One effect of a rising standard of living has been the creation of artificial needs that cannot be satisfied on the average farm. The farmer expects financial rewards for his work and, failing to obtain them, feels frustrated, resentful, and bitter toward the economic order, just as do many of the unsuccessful in other occupations. With the creation of new desires for goods and services, the old struggle for subsistence and the old satisfaction that mere subsistence brought disappear, and many of the supposed virtues of a simple life lose their meaning.

Whether the average American farm can provide an automobile, a high school education for the children, stylish clothing for the women, and leisure time for their display is yet to be seen. But this much is certain, the farmer is rapidly adopting sufficient values of a cash-competitive, luxury-pleasure economy to continue to desire these things and to expect them of life. If he is of the old school and knows from past experience that he cannot have them, his children are likely to pursue a militant educational policy in trying to change his mind and likely as not they succeed in changing his conservative practices if not his convictions.

Summarizing, there persist in farm life many traditional culture patterns built up through ages of usage. Prominent among them are customary folkways, emphasis upon the practical as compared to the ornamental, prominence of thrift, a nonmercenary philosophy as it applies to work exchange, simplicity of social ritual, abbreviated speech patterns, and rigid moral standards. But mingled with these traditional values which have predominated in rural folk cultures are new interests borrowed from the more leisure-pleasure-seeking urban culture based on more intense competition for consumable goods and for status. There is a growing desire on the part of certain groups in rural society to participate in the pleasure-leisure-luxury economy of the better classes of urban society. These new cultural values create new needs and project new problems into the rural scene. They help determine the measure to which the old means for maintenance, recreation, and social expression, and the old standards of living meet or fail to meet life's needs as they are redefined.

1. Define culture. Distinguish material from nonmaterial culture.

2. How does farm culture compare with industrial culture with regard to complexity of material traits?

3. Explain why customary and traditional practices tend to persist in agriculture.

4. Cite evidence for the view that the farm community emphasizes the practical and the necessary.

5. Compare farm with town and city homes in regard to possession of necessities or conveniences such as radio, telephone, running water, and automobile.

6. Compare rural and urban youth with regard to artistic and economic values.

7. Explain the prominence of thrift mores among farmers.

8. Show how primary-group living protects one under a system of nonmercenary, noncontractual exchange.

9. Explain why elaborate social ritual is not required for primary-group association.

10. Show how rural hospitality may be a survival of a previous period in our national history.

11. What evidence can you cite illustrating abbreviated speech patterns of farm people? Are these patterns being modified? If so, by what influences?

12. Discuss moral standards of farmers as a group.

13. What basic values of rural culture are being challenged by diffusion of urban culture patterns to rural areas?

14. Explain the effect of expanding pecuniary values on rural needs and their satisfaction.

COLLATERAL READING

Baker, O. E., Ralph Borsodi, and M. L. Wilson: *Agriculture in Modern Life*, chap. 14 (by M. L. Wilson), Harper & Brothers, New York, 1939.

Duvall, Evelyn Millis, and Annabelle Bender Motz: "Are Country Girls So Different?" *Rural Sociology*, vol. 10, pp. 263–274, September, 1945.

Plant, James S.: *Personality and the Cultural Pattern*, The Commonwealth Fund, New York, 1937.

Riis, Roger W.: "The Repair Man Will Gyp You," *Reader's Digest*, vol. 39, pp. 1–6, July, 1941.

Sims, N. L.: *Elements of Rural Sociology*, 3d ed., chaps. 15–18, The Thomas Y. Crowell Company, New York, 1940.

————: *The Problem of Social Change*, The Thomas Y. Crowell Company, New York, 1939.

Sorokin, P. A., C. C. Zimmerman, and C. J. Galpin: *A Systematic Source Book in Rural Sociology*, vol. 2, chap. 14, University of Minnesota Press, Minneapolis, 1931.

Williams, J. M.: *Our Rural Heritage*, chap. 6, Alfred A. Knopf, Inc., New York, 1925.

CHAPTER 8

RURAL FUNCTIONS AND SOCIAL QUALITY

RURAL sociological literature contains much argument as to the relative mental capacity of rural and urban population stock. Early research was stimulated by the feeling that the quality of the rural population was becoming a threat to the national welfare. E. A. Ross popularized this point of view in his discussion of the migration urbanward from certain farming areas, suggesting that many farm communities resembled fished-out ponds with chiefly bullheads and suckers left.[1] A considerable volume of statistical literature investigating whether or not folk of better quality have left the farm has accumulated, intelligence tests having been used as the measuring device in numerous cases.

APPROPRIATE DEFINITIONS OF QUALITY

In dealing with plants and animals one can establish definite criteria by which quality can be measured; in dealing with human beings one has no such specific criteria. Appropriate definitions of social quality can seldom be divorced from social functions, the relative importance of which depends on group definitions and community circumstances. They reflect the culture of a people at a given time in history and border on the subjective-emotional rather than on the objective-scientific.

It is true that one can measure the human being for some traits by a fairly objective standard. Physical type, health, physical vigor—these characteristics primarily of an animal nature can be evaluated;[2] but man does not rate socially because of such traits; instead his status is set by social traits that are determined in large part in our society by functions performed. Who is to say whether a banker is superior to a preacher, a farmer to an urban laborer, a secretary to a housewife, a president to a justice of the Supreme Court? Which are held in higher esteem depends upon a number of factors of cultural and sociological import which may have little or no relationship to biological capacity as such.

---

[1] E. A. Ross, *Principles of Sociology*, pp. 24–27, D. Appleton-Century Company, Inc., New York, 1920.

[2] For an extensive discussion of vital qualities of rural and urban peoples and for a survey of quantitative evidence, see P. A. Sorokin and C. C. Zimmerman, *Principles of Rural-urban Sociology*, part 2, Henry Holt and Company, Inc., New York, 1929.

SOCIAL TYPES AND SOCIAL FUNCTIONS

In our society we assume that one who performs a function which is considered unique, superior, or difficult has greater mental capacity than one who performs tasks that are less difficult and less important to economic life. It is for this reason in part that those who compare rural and urban social types reach the hasty conclusion that the rural type is inferior in mentol capacity and general ability. Because some urban persons play more flashy roles in the social system, urbanites are assumed to be superior.

There is no certain correlation between social status and personal quality, between success as measured by contemporary standards and innate capacity, and no necessary relationship between occupation and intellectual capacity. It is true that in an open-class system specialized occupations tend to be selected by those possessing fairly specific mental and personality traits, but many people who pass for dullards do so because of the role they play in the social system and not because they lack a spark of genius. Even a competitive open-class society is not always fair in its selections; there are many circumstances that may keep a person of superior ability from rising to the pinnacle of the social pyramid and acquiring respect, admiration, and public recognition.

STATUS AS A FACTOR IN OCCUPATIONAL SELECTION

Because high status comes from performing unique and specialized functions rather than performing tasks that require little training, skill, or ability, farmers and common laborers, domestics, and the great mass of unskilled workers, as well as workers in forests and mines, acquire little social recognition.

The vocations that bring status in our time because of their distinctive social functions are (1) those requiring special skills with tools—craftsmen, specialists, doctors, engineers, architects, and builders being typical in this group, (2) those requiring special skill in manipulating symbols (statisticians, mathematicians), words (journalists, authors, lecturers), and money (bankers insurance men), and (3) those requiring an aptitude for handling people—teachers, lawyers, salesmen, politicians, in fact, any leaders of men being included in this group.

Farming, like housekeeping, though basic to the national economy is one of those occupations in which almost anyone can function. It is logical to expect that a large number of people with little ambition or ability gravitate toward this relatively uncompetitive mode of life.

ABILITY AND SOCIAL FUNCTION AS REFLECTED IN OCCUPATIONAL DIFFERENCES

In our society there is a relationship between ability and social function, and therefore status, although it is never a fixed relationship. Every occupation is somewhat selective, each tending to draw people who are interested in and have the capacity for functioning in it. This is to be expected in a society that erects no barriers of tradition to anyone's entering any vocation he chooses. Considerable evidence demonstrates a relationship between ability and occupation. Terman's famous work, *Genetic Studies of Genius*, is typical of the findings of many studies. Five hundred sixty fathers of child geniuses were grouped into occupational classes. In the area studied, 2.9 per cent of the population were in the professional group; yet 29.1 per cent of the gifted children's fathers were in this group. At the other extreme was the industrial group, which composed 57.7 per cent of the total population but contributed only 20.2 per cent of the gifted children. Ranking the four groups into which the fathers were classified, Terman found that the professional group produced 1,003 per cent of its normal quota of gifted children; the public-service group (public officials, postmen, military men), 137 per cent; the commercial group, 128 per cent; but the industrial group, only 35 per cent. It seems likely that the opportunity factor has to some extent affected these genius scores; yet the results cannot be set aside on the basis of differences in opportunity alone.

EXACT MEASURES OF INNATE ABILITY

Is there any way to isolate innate ability from the role the individual plays in the social system? Is capacity separate from social experience? Few problems have received more attention from sociologists, educators, and psychologists. In its early days the intelligence test was heralded as a tool for isolating and measuring biological capacity apart from social experience, it being generally assumed that the test proved conclusively the extent of the individual's native endowments. Few sociologists ever accepted this view and today practically none of the advocates of intelligence testing hold that test scores are measures of innate ability alone but, instead, of innate ability as affected by experience. The general tendency is to establish norms for each educational level so that the experience factor may be equalized as far as possible in interpreting the scores.

Intelligence test scores of rural and urban children have made possible a number of interesting comparisons. With few exceptions urban children have achieved higher scores;[1] this may mean little more than that the tests have been built on the experience background of the urban rather than of the rural child and have been standardized on urban groups. The rural sociologist feels that it is just as important to equalize the informal environmental experience as

[1] P. A. Sorokin, C. C. Zimmerman, and C. J. Galpin, *A Systematic Source Book in Rural Sociology*, vol. 3, pp. 266–281, summarizes the results of 65 studies employing intelligence tests in comparing rural and urban children; with few exceptions the urban children excelled in the scores. University of Minnesota, Minneapolis, 1932.

it is to equalize the formal educational factor; *i.e.*, years of schooling.[1] It has been found that when information tests are standardized for rural children, urban children are retarded about a year. Rural children are retarded when given tests standardized for the city.[2]

Baldwin and his coworkers, studying the intelligence of grade school children on farms in Iowa,[3] found that the one-room school children were at a decided disadvantage in tests having to do with effective use of language. In performance tests, however, they did equally as well as pupils in multiple-room schools, no inabilities in motor control or coordination being observed. All the farm children lacked speed. It was decided that the experience factor was primarily responsible for the differences in the children.

The Army Alpha Test used in the World War placed farmers seventh from the bottom in intelligence in a list of 74 occupational classes drafted for service.[4] The question of the selective factor immediately arises. Were the farmers drafted for the World War typical or atypical? The fact that successful farmers were exempted from the draft in order to raise wheat and other food-stuffs to feed the Allies may mean that the drafted farm group was of lower mentality.

That farm people have almost universally placed lower than urban groups in intelligence testing may be of some significance but interpretations must be carefully qualified, for intelligence tests as ordinarily used are not a safe method of arriving at an index of population quality.

One study[5] classifies 2,423 former high school students by occupation and relates these occupations to their I. Q. as determined while in school. Farmers are relatively numerous in the group with an I. Q. below 95, and under represented in the group with an I. Q. above 105. Of the ten occupational groups listed they rank ninth.[6] The scores of those people living in rural territory but holding nonagricultural jobs, such as professional and clerical workers, sales-people, skilled workers, and housewives, on the average are lower than the scores of urban persons in comparable occupations. The evidence of this study

[1] In this connection see the following studies: Myra E. Shimberg, *An Investigation into the Validity of Norms with Special Reference to Urban and Rural Groups*, Archives of Psychology, no. 104, 1929; and J. N. Shaler, "A Study of Mind-set in Rural and City School Children," *Journal of Educational Psychology*, vol. 21, pp. 256–258, 1930.

[2] James L. Mursell, *The Psychology of Secondary-school Teaching*, p. 317, W. W. Norton & Company, Inc., New York, 1939.

[3] Bird T. Baldwin, *et al.*, *Farm Children*, pp. 248–300, D. Appleton-Century Company, Inc., New York, 1930.

[4] For a graphic summary, see N. L. Sims, *Elements of Rural Sociology*, rev. ed., p. 260, The Thomas Y. Crowell Company, New York, 1934.

[5] Carroll D. Clark and Noel P. Gist, "Intelligence as a Factor in Occupational Choice," *American Sociological Review*, pp. 683–694, October, 1938.

[6] *Ibid.*, Table 2, p. 688.

suggests that the city selects those who are somewhat superior in traits measured by the intelligence tests. The authors conclude on this point:

So far as they may be safely interpreted, the results indicate that the cities are drawing a marked preponderance of those having superior ratings in the teachers and housewives categories. In all other classes the workers of rural residence made a better showing than might have been anticipated on *a priori* grounds. Since cities are centers of dominance exercising executive controls and organizing specialized functions in major spheres of economic activity, thus enabling them to offer greater scope for vocational development and more lucrative compensation, it seems natural that they should maintain considerable advantage in the competition for workers of superior intelligence in most vocations which are both urban and rural.[1]

A comparison of college groups—rural-farm, rural-nonfarm, and urban— showed marked differences in ability and performance of the three groups.[2] Both rural groups were more highly selected in terms of having attained a high rank in their high school graduating classes, but the urban students, in spite of an average lower rank in their high school classes, did much better on the college psychological test[3] than the other groups, the farm group ranking lowest.

In terms of actual college performance no significant differences were found in the total grade-point averages of rural and urban groups. The rural farm students showed a consistent tendency to rank slightly lower than the rural nonfarm and urban students during the first college semester. But the rural farm students showed the greatest improvement in scholastic per- formance, as indicated by differences between the first semester and total college grade-point average. When persistence was introduced as a measure of college success, the rural farm students achieved significantly greater success than did urban students. Proportionately fewer rural farm students dropped out during the first college year (see chart), and a larger proportion persisted to graduation. Of both rural farm and rural nonfarm groups, 38.6 per cent per- sisted to graduation; of the urban students only 33.5 per cent obtained degrees. The greater tendency of urban students to transfer to other schools may explain the differences at graduation time in part but hardly the greater mortality during the early semesters in school.

The *effective intelligence* of rural students, as measured by their ability to make satisfactory scholastic adjustments, was apparently as high as that of

[1] Carroll D. Clark and Noel P. Gist, *op. cit.*, p. 694. By permission of the American Sociological Society.

[2] Data were for 1,097 freshmen who entered the State College of Washington without previous college experience. They were followed through until 1941. From Raymond W. Hatch and Paul H. Landis, "Social Heritage as a Factor in College Achievement," *Research Studies of the State College of Washington*, vol. 10, pp. 215–272, December, 1942.

[3] The test used was the American Council on Education Psychological Examination for College Freshmen prepared by L. L. Thurstone and T. G. Thurstone.

urban students. This would seem to be a more valid basis for drawing rural-urban comparisons than performance on psychological tests.

In the college situation the farm youth seemed to have the advantage of somewhat earlier maturity and a greater singleness of purpose. He less often participated in intercollegiate athletics, was less often a member of a social fraternity or sorority, and had a lower social-participation score. The urban students were more successful in terms of the noncurricular activities of the college campus.

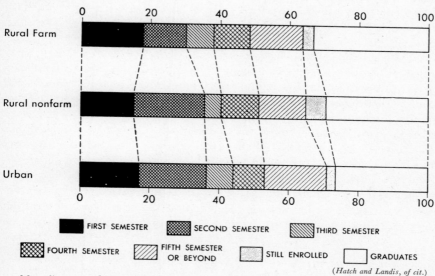

(Hatch and Landis, of cit.)

Mortality rates for successive semesters, and total mortality rates for rural farm, rural nonfarm, and urban students. Data are for 1,097 college youth.

It seems likely that differences in the interests and performance of the rural and urban groups reflect in large part the values that predominate in rural and urban areas. Urban experience, with its multiple contacts, leads one to appreciate the values of leadership and to know the importance of learning to manipulate other persons. The more isolated farm youth sticks more strictly to the business of pursuing a classroom education.

LEADERSHIP TRAITS AS INDICES OF SOCIAL QUALITY

Success and prestige as indicated by occupational achievement are often considered adequate measures of social quality. *Who's Who in America* is the principal American volume listing people outstanding distinction in various spheres of activity. A number of studies[1] which center around this and similar

[1] For typical studies on rural-urban distribution of leaders listed in *Who's Who in America*, *American Men of Science*, and similar rating volumes, see J. M. Cattell, "The Dis-

volumes show that people of rural birth and rural training generally do not contribute their proportionate share to the nation's leaders. The rural sociologist is inclined to discount this fact somewhat because these volumes select leaders who perform functions that are considered outstanding in American life. These, as we have intimated, are more often urban than rural functions.

Sorokin, Zimmerman, and others present data[1] on a sample of 2,171 farmer leaders who were given at least 12 lines in the 1925 *Rus*.[2] (*Rus*, a volume comparable to *Who's Who*, registers living rural leaders.) They find that the farm community produces a greater relative share of agricultural leaders than the city. In 1880 about 40 per cent of the population was on farms; this group produced 64.5 per cent of the farmer leaders of 1925.

Thaden, basing his conclusions on a study of 1,957 males listed in the 1930 edition of *Rus*, reports that a relatively high percentage of men listed as leaders in agriculture have been country-reared.[3] Of the men 71.3 per cent were reared entirely on the farm and another 12.2 per cent were reared in part on the farm, making a total of 83.5 per cent who had some farm background. At the time of birth of the average member of this group only 57 per cent of the nation's population lived on farms or in other rural territory. He concludes that farm rearing is conducive to the attainment of prominence in agriculture and agricultural science.

His study of 357 women listed in *Rus* shows that only 48.0 per cent were farm-reared and 11.9 per cent were reared in the farm and village or farm and city, making a total of 59.9 per cent who were reared wholly or partly on

---

tribution of American Men of Science," *Science*, vol. 24, pp. 658–665, and vol. 32, pp. 633–648; also his *American Men of Science*, 2d ed., pp. 555, 568, and 3d ed., p. 784; G. R. Davies, "A Statistical Study of the Influence of Environment," *Quarterly Journal*, University of North Dakota, vol. 4, pp. 212–236; S. Nearing, "Younger Generation of American Genius," *Scientific Monthly*, vol. 2, pp. 51–52; S. S. Visher, "A Study of Place of Birth," *American Journal of Sociology*, vol. 30, p. 552.

[1] "Farmer Leaders in the United States," *Social Forces*, vol. 7, pp. 33–45, September, 1928.

[2] The character of *Rus* is shown by the following quotation from the introductory statement, "Rus is intended to be a register of rural leadership, in the persons of living men and women. It aims to include those persons who are prominently engaged in rural work, and in whom the public has reason to be interested, as farmers, teachers, investigators, business men, lecturers, ministers, farm, county, and home demonstration agents, authors, editors, and the leading personalities in the administrative, commercial, cooperative, organizational, political and public-service fields as they directly influence agriculture and country life. It is not intended to include persons because they are good farmers but only as they are charged with public interest. Staffs of colleges of agriculture and of experiment stations have been included above the rank of instructor or its equivalent, in case the title indicates that the person is engaged in the agricultural side of the work."

[3] J. F. Thaden, "Characteristics of Persons Listed in *Rus*," *Rural Sociology*, vol. 2, pp. 429–443, December, 1937.

farms. The majority of women in *Rus* are home economists. He concludes that leadership in this field does not presuppose a rural background.

Do rural peoples make a substantial contribution to urban leadership? All of the studies of men of distinction previously cited[1] show that a number of rural people do acquire distinction in urban leadership. Lott in a study of rural contribution to urban leadership in the rural state of Montana, in which he analyzes data on leaders in the ministry, in university and college teaching, in public schooling, editorship, public administration, banking, business, and clerical work, concludes:

Fifty-eight per cent of the leaders were reared in rural districts as compared with our 75 per cent who were rural-born. On the basis of the available data, the rural-reared have attained to the ranks of leaders in about their proportionate share. The farm-reared attained high rank more frequently than the village and city-reared.[2]

It has been adequately demonstrated that rural peoples contribute heavily to urban leadership in certain vocations in spite of their lack of city background. Gee, studying the origin of persons listed in *Leaders of Education*, which was published in 1932, finds that 61 per cent of the leaders were rural-born.[3] At the time when the average educational leader was born, 71.4 per cent of the nation's population was rural, but 75 per cent of all educational leaders hold positions in urban educational institutions, indicating that many of those with a rural background find a place of distinction in the educational profession in the city. He suggests two hypothetical explanations: (1) that urban youths are attracted to high-salaried positions in the business and commercial world and therefore avoid teaching and educational administration; and (2) that the rural environment develops traits that especially fit an individual for leadership in the educational field.

A PRACTICAL VIEW OF RURAL-URBAN INTELLIGENCE

The important thing from the viewpoint of those who work among rural people is not the capacity of the rural mind but the way it is trained to act. True, capacity is related to action, in that it determines the quality and kind of action, but opportunity is a much more important factor. If one of two minds of equal capacity is placed in the metropolis and the other on an isolated home-stead, they become for all practical social purposes different minds. In any community, rural or urban, there is more mental capacity at hand than is being used and what is mistaken at first for stoicism and dullness in rural personality may prove to be a conservative shrewdness born of experience. Speed, vocabu-

[1] Refer again to footnote 1, p. 107.

[2] Elmo H. Lott, "Rural Contributions to Urban Leadership in Montana," *Montana State Agricultural Experiment Station Bulletin* 262, p. 42, Bozeman, 1932.

[3] Wilson Gee, "Rural-urban Origins of Leaders in Education," *Rural Sociology*, vol. 2, pp. 402–408, December, 1937.

lary, and sharp or dull wits may be markedly affected by experience. Each environment calls for the exercise of different capacities. The urban environment may encourage alertness, for alertness has survival value in the city; but steady, persistent plodding may be equally important in the rural environment.

PATHOLOGICAL CONDITIONS AS INDICES OF SOCIAL QUALITY

Often the comparative number of socially undesirable types in a community is employed as an index of population quality. Such data do provide a fairly tangible basis for comparison provided they are properly interpreted. Certain comparisons between rural and urban population can be made with a fair degree of reliability.

Mental Disease.—The rate of mental disease is socially significant. The Bureau of the Census in 1923 analyzed data on commitments to institutions for mental disease for 1910 and 1920 in terms of proportion of commitments from rural and urban areas. These data for first admissions to hospitals for mental disease show that in 1910 the commitment rate per 100,000 urban population was 86; per 100,000 rural population, 41.1. The rate in 1920 was 78.8 for the urban population and 41.1 for the rural.[1] Data for 1933 show a commitment rate per 100,000 urban males of 106 and per 100,000 rural males of 60.7. The rate for urban females was 75.8; for rural females, 41.2.[2]

One cannot, however, accept these figures at face value. Mental disease affects adults. Rural areas have a comparatively high proportion of children, which fact affects the rate of commitment.[3] Even more important in accounting for the difference in rates is the fact that in urban communities where living space is limited, where competition is intense, and where people constantly struggle for social status, there is do doubt a greater tendency to have the mentally ill committed to institutions. It is probable, however, that none of these factors wholly explains the difference in rates.

Recent studies suggest that there is a close correlation between the occurrence of schizophrenia (dementia praecox), the most common of mental diseases, and one which is frequently considered functional, *i.e.*, produced by experience, and certain areas in the great city, the disease tending to be con-

[1] *Patients in Hospitals for Mental Diseases*, 1923, p. 14, Department of Commerce, Bureau of the Census, Washington, D. C.

[2] *Patients in Hospitals for Mental Diseases*, 1933, pp. 48–49, Department of Commerce, Bureau of the Census, Washington, D. C.

[3] J. M. Gillette, summarizing census data by age groups for the year 1922, finds that marked differences appear in favor of the sanity of the rural population for all ages and for both sexes. *Rural Sociology*, 3d ed., p. 342, Fig. 28, The Macmillan Company, New York, 1936.

centrated in areas of disorganization.[1] In the results reported, there is a strong suggestion that certain disintegrated areas of the city put abnormal strain on personality. If such is not the case, these areas must select persons who break easily under stress.

Other social factors help explain the higher urban rates. The foreign-born are found in much larger proportion in urban than in rural populations and there is a higher rate of mental disease among them than among the native-born.[2] General paresis, produced by syphilis, is more frequent in the city, probably because prostitution, at least in America, is confined largely to the metropolis, where sex mores seem to be more lax than in rural or small-town areas. Thus, high rates of insanity may be explained in part by conditions which the city itself produces.

Feeble-mindedness.—The rate of commitment of feeble-minded to institutions from year to year is about twice as high for urban as for rural areas, the average rate being about 80 to 85 per 100,000 population for the city, and about 40 to 45 for the country. The situation differs considerably, however, from section to section, a few rural sections having a higher rate of commitment than the average urban rate.[3]

Rural families are less likely than urban to send feeble-minded members to institutions. One of the striking bits of evidence on this point is that although the rates of commitment of imbeciles for urban and rural areas are approximately equal, the commitment rate of morons in the country is much lower than in the city. The logical inference is that rural communities more often allow their moron group to run at large.[4] In the less competitive economic and social system of the farm community, morons have a better chance to achieve adjustment, thus lessening the need for institutionalization. It is likely, too, that the rural family is more prone to shelter its weak members than the urban. The rural family can more easily provide tasks for the able-bodied moron than can the urban family.

That many writers assume feeble-mindedness to be more common in the

[1] Robert E. L. Faris, "Cultural Isolation and the Schizophrenic Personality," *American Journal of Sociology*, vol. 40, pp. 155–164, September, 1934. H. Warren Dunham, "The Ecology of the Functional Psychoses in Chicago," *American Sociological Review*, vol. 2, pp. 467–479, August, 1937.

[2] For example, of those admitted to hospitals for the insane in 1910, the rate for foreign-born was 116.3 per 100,000 total foreign-born in the population; for native-born, 57.9 per 100,000 native-born in the population. Data for New York State are summarized by age groups and for males and females by H. M. Pollock and B. Malzberg, in "Expectation of Mental Disease," *Mental Hygiene*, vol. 13, p. 138, 1929. For all ages and both sexes the rates for the foreign-born are considerably higher than for the native-born.

[3] *Feeble-minded and Epileptics in Institutions.* These reports are published annually by the U.S. Bureau of the Census.

[4] For a summary of evidence, see P. A. Sorokin, C. C. Zimmerman, and C. J. Galpin, *op. cit.*, vol. 3, p. 240.

rural community than in the urban may be due to the fact that in the migration of rural people to the city the feeble-minded tend to remain on the farm. The point is one of controversy and there is no conclusive evidence, but it seems plausible that the proportion of feeble-minded at large in the rural community is greater than in the city.[1] Both logical and statistical reasons for this last assumption may be offered. The population of the rural community contains a relatively high percentage of children and youth; feeble-mindedness is a defect due to heredity or arrested development and, therefore, present at birth or before maturity; death rates among the mentally defective are excessive; of 1,000 normal females, for example, about 809 will survive to 20 years of age, but of an equal number of morons only about 685 will survice to the age of 20 years, of imbeciles only 338, and of idiots only 193.[2] The city population, because it consists largely of adults should, therefore, have fewer feeble-minded.

During the First World War, 1.5 per cent of urban draftees and 3.9 per cent of rural draftees were rejected because of "mental defectiveness."[3] Age groups were comparable. It is possible that selective factors might have operated to increase the proportion of feeble-minded in the rural sample but it is doubtful whether any such factor fully explains the difference. Evidence, therefore, points toward the conclusion that rural areas have a higher percentage of mentally defective at large.

Suicide.—Suicide rates are much higher in the city than in the country and, of course, are much higher in some areas in the city than in others. The prevalence of suicide often reflects the amount of stress and social disorganization existing in a community and the amount of unhappiness and misery faced by members in their social adjustment. Rates for the U.S. Registration Area show the following suicides per 100,000 population for 1940.[4]

Size of place	Suicides per 100,000	Age-adjusted rates
Rural...........................	12.0	12.9
2,500 to 10,000.....................	15.1	14.8
10,000 to 100,000..................	15.6	14.9
100,000 or more....................	16.8	15.6

One must take into account age distribution in interpreting suicide data. Most people who take their own lives are over 20 years of age. There are

[1] *Ibid.*

[2] Based on data for Massachusetts as presented in a study by Dr. Neil A. Dayton, *et al.*, "Mortality and Expectation of Life in Mental Deficiency in Massachusetts—Analysis of a Fourteen-year Period, 1912–1930," *New England Journal of Medicine*, vol. 206, nos. 11 and 12, pp. 555–570, 616–631, Mar. 17 and 24, 1932.

[3] See N. L. Sims, *op. cit.*

[4] Bases on data from *Vital Statistics*, part 2, 1940.

more people of this age in the city, which automatically raises the urban crude rate somewhat, although in the country and small town the proportion of aged is higher than in the city which compensates in part. But even where these differences are standardized as they have been done in the right column of the table above, more suicide is found in the city.[1]

Leading students of suicide find a relationship between social isolation and suicide.[2] It has already been suggested that neighborliness finds its deepest expression in the rural community, that rural ties are intimate and binding, that rural people feel themselves an intricate part of the social scheme. Social isolation more often occurs in anonymous areas of the large city where population is dense and where there are many but very superficial contacts. Studies of people in the rooming-house area of the city[3] indicate that they may live with only a thin wall between them and others and yet be desperately lonely and socially isolated. A part of the high urban suicide and insanity rates may be explained by the influx of rural persons to the city, many of whom no doubt break under the stress of urban adjustment.[4]

Leading studies of suicide relate it historically to periods of social decadence and in contemporary societies to urban areas where social disorganization is characteristic and where social ties have been broken.[5] Cavan states succinctly the differential influences in rural and urban suicide rates:

Rural areas . . . have settled ways of living, established moral codes, a narrow range of interests, but fairly adequate ways of caring for the interests they have. There are few newcomers, few transients, only a small degree of mobility, and consequently little disturbance to the rigid social control of the family, neighborhood, and institutions. People do not commit suicide without a cause, and in the rural areas there is less of the disturbance to accustomed way of living, which constitutes a major cause of personal disorganization in urban centers.[6]

The explanations of suicide given here take into account only individualized suicide such as is common in the United States and in most European countries. Customary suicide might not show the same distribution; e.g., hara-kiri, face-saving suicide in Japan, may have no relation to social disorganization or

---

[1] This has been found true for other nations also. See P. A. Sorokin, C. C. Zimmerman, and C. J. Galpin, op. cit., vol. 3, pp. 116–118.

[2] E. Durkheim, Le Suicide, Paris, 1887.

[3] H. W. Zorbaugh, The Gold Coast and the Slum, The University of Chicago Press, Chicago, 1929.

[4] Niles Carpenter discusses this probability. See his The Sociology of City Life, pp. 334–337, Longmans, Green and Company, New York, 1931.

[5] Ruth S. Cavan, Suicide, University of Chicago Press, Chicago, 1928. C. F., Schmid, Suicides in Seattle, 1914–1925, An Ecological and Behavioristic Study, University of Washington Press, Seattle, 1928; C. F. Schmid, "Suicide in Minneapolis, Minnesota, 1928–1932," American Journal of Sociology, vol. 39, pp. 30–48, July, 1933.

[6] Ruth S. Cavan, Suicide, p. 54. By permission of the University of Chicago Press.

to social isolation. In the Netherlands the rural suicide rate actually exceeds the urban, probably because under the Dutch farming system, the aged find themselves a burden and often resort to suicide.[1]

Juvenile Delinquency.—Although official figures on the extent of juvenile delinquency for rural and urban populations are not available, there is abundant inferential and some statistical evidence showing that juvenile delinquency is much more prominent in the city than in rural areas. The close-knit neighborhood and family groups of the rural community are not conducive to the development of deliquent gangs; rather they create a situation in which it is difficult for the child to form established habits of delinquent behavior, numerous and effective controls keeping him in line. On the other hand, in the congested slum areas of the great city juvenile delinquency seems to be the characteristic pattern of life. Shaw and others in studying the slum areas of Chicago found that in the loop district as high as 37 per cent of the boys in certain areas were brought before juvenile agencies in a period of 1 year.[2] Thrasher studying gangs in Chicago located 1,313 gangs, many of them practicing delinquency as an established way of life. These gangs were concentrated in areas of social disintegration near the city's center.[3]

It is unfair in some respects even to compare urban and rural areas in this regard because delinquency is so much a matter of social definition. Much behavior that would be considered delinquent in the city would not be so considered in rural areas.

Certain characteristics of juvenile delinquency in rural areas have been studied.[4] Smith found that tiers of counties in Kansas lying at a distance from the city have lower delinquency rates than those lying adjacent.[5]

Studies of adult crime, although not entirely conclusive, show that urban communities more than rural communities stimulate criminality.[6] Since crime careers often begin early in life, this fact would seem to suggest that delinquency is less prevalent in rural areas. The rural community provides work to occupy the time of its young; the town or city youth, because he lacks work and other outlets for energy, is often restless and hungry for excitement.

[1] See S. Gorgas, "Suicide in the Netherlands," *American Journal of Sociology*, vol. 37, pp. 697–710, March, 1932.

[2] Clifford Shaw, "Correlation of Rate of Juvenile Delinquency with Certain Indices of Community Organization and Disorganization," *Publications of the American Sociological Society*, vol. 22, pp. 174–179, 1928.

[3] Frederic Thrasher, *The Gang*, University of Chicago Press, Chicago, 1927.

[4] K. H. Clayborn, *Juvenile Delinquency in Rural New York*, pp. 21–25, U. S. Children's Bureau Publication, no. 32, 1917.

[5] Mapheus Smith, "Tier Counties and Delinquency in Kansas," *Rural Sociology*, vol. 2, pp. 310–322, September, 1937.

[6] Thorsten Sellin, "Research Memorandum on Crime in the Depression," chap. 3, Social Science Research Council, *Bulletin* 27, 1937.

This same restless spirit, however, may be found also in rural communities where life appears drab and fundamentally uninteresting.

Criminality.—Crime rates are much higher for cities than for farming communities[1] and would be even higher if one compensated for the fact that the city has a larger proportion of its population in the early adult years, when criminal activities are most often engaged in.[2] It is frequently suggested that the migration of rural criminals to the city may help to explain the high crime rates there. This is possible but hard to demonstrate. Undoubtedly many small-town or rural youths who have developed criminal tendencies go to the city in search of a better field of operation.

Second-generation immigrants are more numerous in the city than in the country, and crime rates are higher among them than among other groups. Interestingly enough, however, second-generation immigrants do not seem to have an abnormally high crime rate in rural areas.[3]

Racketeering and organized crime are acknowledged as being products of the great metropolis. Criminal hideouts are for the most part located there; the racketeer thrives on the business enterprises existing there; crimes against property naturally are committed in the city because it is there that one finds mobile property that can most easily be seized. In farming areas wealth accumulates slowly; the thief must confine his activities chiefly to stealing property that is bulky, such as cattle, chickens, hogs, or grain, is hard to dispose of, and brings relatively small returns. It is more lucrative to rob a bank in a town or city, to establish a racket and collect fat commissions, or to organize a vice ring and live in luxury on the proceeds.

Even in the field of minor law violations city people commit many more offenses than rural. The urbanite lives in a world of law and is much more likely to encounter legal restrictions in his common everyday activities than the farmer. Farm communities are not legal minded and maintain few law-enforcement agencies.

Vice.—Vice, which in our nation consists largely of prostitution, gambling, and illicit traffic in drugs and liquor, has existed for the most part in the city. In fact, prostitution for years has been confined almost entirely to large cities and to frontier towns in lumbering and mining regions. Similarly, gambling rings operate in the large city. The great liquor rings of prohibition days were organized in the metropolis and drug peddling is and always has been confined chiefly to the city. The available data on venereal disease sug-

---

[1] *Ibid.*

[2] Males in the age group 19 to 24 have the highest rate of commitment to prison of any age group. All years from 19 to 29 have a high commitment rate. See *Statistical Abstract of the United States* (1935), p. 75, for characteristic evidence.

[3] Donald R. Taft, "Nationality and Crime," *American Sociological Review*, p. 75, October, 1936.

gest that prostitution is more prevalent in the city.[1] Since prostitution often is closely identified with organized crime, it would be expected to center chiefly in the metropolis where organized crime flourishes.

Summarizing, exact measures of many aspects of social quality are lacking. It is erroneous to consider social function as reflecting native capacity, for although a relationship between the two exists, it is never a fixed or rigid one. The tendency of our society is to accept as superior social types that perform unique functions. Rating volumes, such as *Who's Who*, in their selection of notables, choose according to current cultural values and, therefore, list few rural people, for rural people ordinarily do not perform unique functions. Leadership in rural life, in rural educational institutions, in rural business enterprises, and even in urban education shows that a rural background is not a liability for certain kinds of special functions, and may even be an asset for them. Intelligence tests, although they usually show results favorable to the urban child, are so constructed as to give him the initial advantage. Farm experience may select the less alert or may slow the pace of those who participate in rural life, whereas the city may make for alertness. In any case, rural people do not seem to equal in test performance people in comparable vocations living in the city.

The practical problem is that of meeting the rural mind on the level of its interests and utilizing its forces to best advantage. There is no lack of capacity on the farm, even though there may be fewer geniuses than in the metropolis.

As to pathological indices of social quality, the city seems to have more insanity, more suicide, and more delinquency, vice, and crime than the country. The rural community seems to have more feeble-minded at large in the population, although no information is available on the proportion of the feeble-minded born in rural and in urban areas.

DECREASING IMPORTANCE OF THE PROBLEM OF RURAL SOCIAL QUALITY

The extreme emphasis sociologists once placed on the problem of quality of rural population stock as affected by selective migration and by the conditioning influences of an isolated rural environment is rightly shifting to more important topics. Tangible measures, as has been indicated, leave little doubt that certain qualitative differences exist. There is still, however, much confusion of thought and much contradictory evidence on such matters as general differences in rural and urban intelligence. Intelligence undoubtedly varies from community to community and from one social class to another. A gross comparison of intelligence of the farm occupational group with all urban occu-

---

[1] Syphilis rates are generally highest in large cities and lowest in rural districts. Among rural Negroes in the South the syphilis rate is high. See Thomas Parran's, "No Defense for Any of Us," *Survey Graphic*, vol. 27, pp. 197–202, April, 1938.

pational groups en masse is on the face of it absurd and meaningless. Undoubtedly the city draws a high proportion of people of genius because of certain functions which are of necessity performed in the city under our system of social organization. But the country often shares in the benefits of intelligent urban leadership. As to the various forms of pathology which appear most often in the urban community, the city, no doubt, contains influences that lead to an exaggeration of such traits, but many migrants from the rural community add to pathological conditions of the city. Rural migrants unprepared for the complexities of urban living, faced with the stress and strain of personal adjustment, make good candidates for suicide, delinquency, nervous and mental disease.

Differences in quality that may have existed in the past tend to become less striking as rural and urban experience become more alike under the influences of communication and contact so prominent in modern society. To the extent that differences in social quality are the product of experience, they are likely to decrease as rural and urban areas becomes increasingly similar.

QUESTIONS FOR REVIEW AND DISCUSSION

1. What factors complicate the exact definition of social quality?
2. What do social roles affect evaluations of personal worth?
3. Is high social status necessarily associated with superior ability? Defend your position.
4. What classes of occupations bring prestige in our culture? Is farming among them? Does this have any bearing on the listing of farmers in such volumes as *Who's Who?*
5. Is there any evidence to demonstrate that the different occupations select people of differing degrees of ability?
6. Discuss the weaknesses of the intelligence test as a test of innate ability. As ordinarily used, is it an exact measure of differences in mental ability of rural and urban classes? Explain.
7. Is there any evidence indicating that the city selects a superior mental type?
8. In what field of leadership do people with a farm background seem to achieve success?
9. How do rural and urban populations compare in proportion of (a) insane, (b) feeble-minded, (c) suicide cases, (d) juvenile delinquents, (e) criminals, (f) persons given to vice?
10. Explain how the farm community may contribute to pathological groups in the city.

COLLATERAL READING

Baldwin, Bird T., Eva A. Fillmore, and Lora Hadley: *Farm Children*, chaps. 13–16, D. Appleton-Century Company, Inc., New York, 1930.

Chapman, Stanley H.: "The Minister: Professional Man of the Church," *Social Forces*, vol. 23, pp. 202–206, December, 1944.

Clark, C. D., and N. P. Gist: "Intelligence as a Factor in Occupational Choice," *American Sociological Review*, pp. 683–694, October, 1938.

Gee, Wilson: "Rural-urban Origins of Leaders in Education," *Rural Sociology*, vol. 2, pp. 402–408, December, 1937.

Gillette, J. M.: *Rural Sociology*, 3d ed., chap. 17, The Macmillan Company, New York, 1936.

Hatch, Raymond W., and Paul H. Landis: "Social Heritage as a Factor in College Achievement," *Research Studies of the State College of Washington*, vol. 10, pp. 215–272, December, 1942.

Lott, Elmo H.: "Rural Contributions to Urban Leadership in Montana," *Montana Agricultural Experiment Station Bulletin* 262, Bozeman, 1932.

Sims, N. L.: *Elements of Rural Sociology*, 3d ed., chap. 9, The Thomas Y. Crowell Company, New York, 1940.

Smith, T. Lynn: *The Sociology of Rural Life*, rev. ed. chap. 6, Harper & Brothers, New York, 1947.

Sorokin, P. A., and C. C. Zimmerman: *Principles of Rural-urban Sociology*, chaps, 11 and 12, Henry Holt and Company, Inc., New York, 1929.

———, ———, and C. J. Galpin: *A Systematic Source Book in Rural Sociology*, vol. 2, pp. 266–342, and vol. 3, chaps. 19 and 20, University of Minnesota Press, Minneapolis, 1931 and 1932 respectively.

Thaden, J. F.: "Characteristics of Persons Listed in *Rus*," *Rural Sociology*, vol. 2, pp. 429–443, December, 1937.

CHAPTER 9

PERSONALITY TRAITS AND FARM EXPERIENCE

HEREDITARY differences of infinite variety, plus environmental stimuli as diverse as is human experience, make for a variety of individual differences. Every personality is a distinct social unit, with a configuration of physical, psychological, and emotional traits all its own. Yet there exists the other incontestable fact that all people, both by hereditary endowment and by experience, are very much alike in fundamental characteristics.

Much has been made of hereditary variation by students of individual differences and of race differences by biologists, psychologists, sociologists, and anthropologists, and ventures at grouping individuals into a few major classes on the basis of personality traits have frequently been attempted. Equally active have been those who believe that human types can be grouped on the basis of social selection and environmental conditioning. Urban and rural sociologists fall in this latter group who believe that personalities can be classified and if not adequately, at least helpfully, described on the basis of characteristics that develop in response to a given set of environmental circumstances. As a consequence, most urban sociologists have listed type classes of urban personalities and rural sociologists have named mental, emotional, and attitudinal traits which they felt that farmers possessed. In addition to these more scientific attempts at understanding general personality and psychological traits, are works of fiction, art, and literature which carve out in bold relief some one or more traits that authors believe to be outstanding in the rural person.[1] More formal means of study are the various scales that measure emotional, informational, and intellectual traits of groups and classes. The results of these more exact measures are discussed in other chapters. Here, interest is confined to the more subjective evaluations of the personality of the farmer.

Since all men possess much of the same original hereditary capacity and since everywhere conditioning influences of the environment are somewhat

---

[1] P. A. Sorokin and C. C. Zimmerman, *Principles of Rural-urban Sociology*, chap. 14 (Henry Holt and Company, Inc., New York, 1929), employ three sources of information in studying the psychosocial traits of farmers and peasants: (1) stories, novels, poems, poetry, and literature, (2) statements, songs, stories, and letters of farmers and peasants, and (3) investigations of social scientists. After an exhaustive review of data from these sources they conclude that such sources give some insight and valuable suggestions as to the mind and character of the rural class, but yield very little final proof of what is typical of the rural mind.

the same, it would be expected that any group or class would possess most of the personality traits of any other. If this is taken into account, it is not surprising that those who have characterized rural personality have attributed to the farmer a great range of traits. The list which follows suggests the variety of personality traits that are said to characterize farmers.[1]

Farmers are supposed to be conservative, individualistic, superstitious, fatalistic, to possess stability, to lack cooperative qualities, to be of a magical turn of mind, mystical in outlook, to be religious, dogmatic, prejudiced, straitlaced in morals, stern and just, patient, stolid, introspective, versatile, impressionistic, suspicious, to possess much common sense, to be of sound and adequate judgment, to be independent in forming judgments, to possess deep convictions, to be meditative, to have fixed purposes, to have endurance, to be immune to radicalism, to have peace of mind, to practice simplicity, to feel aversion for fads and show, to practice thrift and frugality, to assume responsibility readily, to have initiative, to be resourceful, frank, hospitable, sympathetic, to lack socialization, to be characterized by hardiness, to be pessimistic, to brood over injuries. They are supposed to be emotionally intensive, highly suggestible, shy, sentimental, to lean toward the emotional in religious expression, to be conformists, to lack idealism, to love nature, to have a developed artistic sense, to like gossip, to be moody, to be given to resignation, to have a tendency to be discouraged, to be orthodox in religion, to be introverted, silent, to think and speak directly, to be democratic, to lean toward "fogyism," to be unprogressive, realistic, intolerant, naïve, skeptical, serious, clannish, economical, complaining, honest, stubborn, easygoing, reticent, gullible, trustworthy, conventional, tenacious, nonmercenary, unselfish, neighborly, friendly, wholesome, and narrow-minded.

The list probably could be greatly extended if one consulted a greater variety of sources. Of all the traits listed above, fatalism, conservatism, individualism, and superstition are most often mentioned.

The late Charles H. Cooley, sociologist, upon observing a group of Michigan farmers at a Fourth of July celebration some years ago, gave his reaction as a town dweller, describing them as being characterized by uncouthness and a slight imbecility.[2] They were dressed in any old way, seemed

---

[1] The most important sources for lists of traits developed by rural sociologists are: C. C. Taylor, *Rural Sociology*, rev. ed., chap. 7, Harper & Brothers, New York, 1933; L. L. Bernard, "Theory of Social Attitudes," *American Journal of Sociology*, pp. 648 ff., March, 1917; E. R. Groves, *The Rural Mind and Social Welfare*, University of Chicago Press, Chicago, 1922; N. L. Sims, *Elements of Rural Sociology*, rev. ed., chap. 11, The Thomas Y. Crowell Company, New York, 1933; A. W. Hayes, *Rural Sociology*, pp. 167–174, Longmans, Green and Company, New York, 1929; J. M. Williams, *Our Rural Heritage*, Alfred A. Knopf, Inc., New York, 1925.

[2] Charles H. Cooley, *Life and the Student*, pp. 50–51, Alfred A. Knopf, Inc., New York, 1927.

vacant and purposeless, naïve and lacking in social discipline; many could have been stage types. But on reflecting, he concluded that they were good people, self-respecting, proud, honest, more intelligent than they appeared; that they came from good stock even though their level of ability may have been lowered somewhat by migration to towns; that they seemed to lack, however, some of the vitality of the crowd of foreign urbanites he had previously viewed at Revere Beach near Boston. Farmers, he concludes, are characterized by a more naïve individuality, "the individuality of isolation as contrasted with the organic and sophisticated individuality" of townspeople.

E. A. Ross, observer of many rural cultures of the world, concludes:

The world over, the psychology of city people is notably different from that of country people. The urban type lives on surfaces, life being so crowded with impressions that there is little energy left for reflection. Compare the sights and sounds which hail one in the street with those one meets in the country lane. Compare the big headlines, chromatic print, dramatic posters, and palpitant lights which must be used in order to reach the city mind with the meek announcement posted at the crossroad. The former measures the intensity of the competition to arrest attention. The things the urbanite noticingly looks at or listens to in a day are generally many times more numerous than those that impinge on the farmer's mind. As a result, one country dweller sinks into stagnation, the machinery of his rusty mind moving slowly and only in response to a strong stimulus. The mind of another grinds on itself mulling over his narrow personal experience, his little stock of inherited dogmas, his scanty fund of scrappy uncoordinated information gleaned from his weekly newspaper. Another mind wrestles futilely with passages from the prophet Daniel or the Book of Revelation because it is quite without the equipment for interpreting them. Finally there is the farmer of trained mind who, furnished by his schooling with orderly knowledge and supplied with trustworthy current data, by his own reflections works out sound principles.[1]

The importance of broad rural-urban personality differences cannot be overlooked even though specific criteria of many subjective differences are lacking. Impressionistic observations, although they lead to controversy even among sociological authorities, are not without value to the student. In much of everyday life, reactions to persons are necessarily in terms of general impressions and most of our social adjustments are based on them.

Two general principles must be kept in mind at all times in studying personality traits. First, personality traits always reflect past experience. If the farmer possesses characteristics that are unique, they are in considerable part the result of his experience with the nature environment, rural society, and rural culture, the factors discussed in earlier chapters. Second, in discussing psychological traits one can only aim at describing approximate norms; since

[1] E. A. Ross, *Principles of Sociology*, p. 27, New York, 1920. By permission of D. Appleton-Century Company, Inc.

differences in personality are a matter of the degree to which various traits have been developed, those traits most developed determine personality configuration.

THE EXPERIENCE WORLD AND PSYCHOLOGICAL PROCESSES

Sorokin and Zimmerman, instead of cataloguing psychological traits as such, analyze psychological processes in terms of environmental experience.[1] The gist of their analysis is this: The farmer's life is characterized by direct experience, *i.e.*, experience obtained through immediate contact with objects, events, or human beings; the life of the urban person contains a wide variety of indirect experience obtained through such media as newspapers and moving pictures. Because of the limited amount of indirect knowledge which the farmer possesses, he is easily misled outside the field of his immediate experience. Logic of the farmer-peasant group, therefore, is likely to be sound in dealing with phenomena of direct experience but unsound in dealing with phenomena of indirect experience. Because the farmer-peasant class has more direct knowledge than the urban classes their "mental luggage" is more stable than that of urban groups, which is based on inadequate and overdeveloped indirect experience. The farmer-peasant group is more concerned about things in the immediate occupational world than about urban phenomena. This probably slows down mental velocity. In character the farmer-peasant class is less "soft" and "feminized" than the mass of the city population and more "stern and austere or puritanic." Farmer-peasants have virulence, patience, and endurance developed by the requirements of their work. Rural imagination is likely to deal with different subject matter from that dealt with by urban imagination, because of different environmental experience.

RURAL PERSONALITY TYPES

In popular parlance we hear much of special farm types—rancher, cowboy, cattleman, sheepman, herder, fruitgrower, orange grower, hop grower, general farmer, fruit farmer, fur farmer, truck farmer—designations growing out of differences in kind of agriculture practiced but often implying significant personality traits. Other terms are even more suggestive—"hick," "hayseed," "hillbilly," "mountaineer," "poor white," "jig," "rubber tramp," "pea picker," "hop picker," "automobile gypsy," "Oakies," "Arkies," "dude rancher," "rural aristocrat," and other labels indicating that there are in rural life recognized social types. These terms are about as close as one can come to accurate description of personality types in the absence of exact data. In localities where they are employed they suggest fairly definite stereotypes that immediately catalogue an individual.

[1] *Op. cit.*, chap. 13.

PSYCHOLOGICAL TRAITS OF FARM PEOPLE

Personality traits of farm people throughout the nation depend to a great extent upon the type and size of farm, the condition of roads, the number and type of social institutions and voluntary social organizations in the community, and the frequency of contact with an urban market.[1] The cotton farmer on the Southern plantation has a background of long tradition, as also has the share-cropper on his small tract of land; psychological traits of Southern farmers are in certain respects unique. The densely settled, irrigated districts of the Far West, with small farms and intensive crops, are characterized by another pattern of life. The wheat farmer who operates a large ranch entirely by machines, hiring for a short season sufficient labor to harvest his crop, no doubt possesses behavior traits distinctly his own; the truck farmer in the hinterland of the large metropolis who deals in perishable produce and contacts the urban market daily is likely to be urbane in characteristics, life philosophy, and habit patterns; the backwoods farmer of the Appalachian or Ozark regions or of isolated areas of the Rocky Mountains is also a rural social type. There is probably as much difference between the psychological traits of an Ozark mountaineer and those of a California orange grower as between the traits of a resident of the slums of Chicago and a Gold Coast millionaire, for the social roles of the two rural types are as different as those of the two urban types. Although many of the traits of the typical farmer are to be found in extreme form among those in isolated mountain regions and many urban traits recently acquired by the average farmer are found in highly developed form in the cosmopolitan-minded truck farmer of the metropolitan fringe, our interest must be confined to the great mass of American farmers who live on individually operated family farms scattered throughout all regions of the nation.

But even when the field is thus delimited, characterization of an occupational group scattered over a continent of varied regional culture patterns, geographical phenomena, and social traits, by specific psychological categories is certain to be more or less speculative and opinionated. Admittedly the following characterization is based for the most part on the author's observations and reading and is, therefore, subject to the weaknesses of any other subjective material. The traits mentioned are more typical of farmers than of city folks whom the author has known intimately. They may be more or less important than others which might be included, but are at least worthy of consideration by those interested in understanding farm people. That these traits are less prominent now than a generation ago is presupposed.

Ambivalence toward the Urban.—Ambivalence implies an alternating love and aversion for persons or objects. Such a state of mind, in which opposing

[1] C. E. Lively, "Type of Agriculture as a Conditioning Factor in Community Organization," *Publications of the American Sociological Society*, vol. 23, October, 1929.

emotions are experienced simultaneously, seems to characterize the thought patterns of many country people with respect to urban values. The farmer dislikes the patterns of life of the city but sometimes wishes he could follow them; he fears much that the city holds but frequently is highly pleased if his child can find a niche in urban life; he condemns the town man's ways, his use of leisure time, his pleasure-seeking motives, but dreams of the day when he can retire to a town or city. Despite his dislike of change, his skepticism of the new, his suspicion of city patterns, he envies the urban man his mode of life. At the center of personal dislike is the banker who employs exacting business methods in an environment where many transactions are verbal on a man-to-man friendship basis, rather than contractual;[1] but even here one finds a secret admiration for a man who coldheartedly hews the line.

Inferiority Feeling.—Often the farm person possesses an intense feeling of inferiority because of his lack of social graces. As long as he stays in the environment to which he is habituated, he is at ease, because he has mastered it; but in facing townspeople the farmer from an isolated rural community may feel awkward.

Feelings of inferiority are prominent among farm children who attend town school and usually grow out of unfavorable comparisons of themselves with town children. The fact that urban children seem accommodated and know their way around the new world into which the farm child is thrust helps to feed his sense of inferiority. In some cases his introduction to town may have been accompanied by the ridicule of urban children who observed peculiarities in his habits, beliefs, speech, manner, or dress. The following account by a college student of her childhood experience well illustrates the point:

When my parents discussed consolidating with the town school, we girls were very excited. To us that was just perfect—to be able to attend "town school." Our school was consolidated, and we rode to school every day in the school bus a total distance of 50 miles. To keep us warm Mother made us wear long underwear and high-top shoes. We felt so inferior to our schoolmates who wore anklets and low shoes a good share of the winter. My father had us get the mail and, because his mail was important, he made a canvas bag in which to carry it that rolled up and fastened by a strap. It was about a foot and a half long and very clumsy looking. We felt embarrassed carrying it, but my parents, thinking it was the only safe thing to do, made us carry it every day. All of this helped to build up an inferiority complex that I haven't until recently been able to conquer.

Sometimes the feeling of inferiority grows out of the fact that the farm child, if he comes from an isolated environment, has not learned to wear suitable clothes or is not able to afford them. In the farm community even women do not concern themselves with dress to the extent they do in the town

[1] Refer again to Chap. 7, p. 91.

and city. The rural girl's clothes may not be particularly well adapted to the needs of her age and play group and, even if they are fairly suitable, the mother and daughter may lack the artistic sense which is so easily developed in the city where people are exceedingly fashion-conscious. Fashions represent differences in emphasis in rural and urban culture patterns.

The farmer, because he is not habituated to shifts in the style of his own garments, which consist mostly of working clothes, can hardly be expected to pay much attention to fashion in buying children's clothing. It may be also that farm parents do not appreciate as fully as urban parents the effect of psychological experiences in the play group upon the personality of the child. Many a practical-minded farmer has forgotten that a child wearing different clothes from those of his classmates is likely to be made the object of their jibes, suffering hurts that are difficult to heal and that may even lead him to withdraw from social participation. Parents of the more prosperous urban classes are accommodated to frequent changes in fashion; they buy new clothes primarily for fashion rather than for wearing qualities and generally apply the same principle in buying clothing for their children. Realizing that if all the other boys are wearing high boots, their child likewise needs to wear them if the family is to keep face, they are willing to throw away the old shoes in order that their child and the family may be in vogue and not bear the stigma of being considered peculiar.

Lack of money with which to buy new clothes often produces feelings of inferiority among the poor of all classes but probably such feelings appear more often in the farm family than in the city family when financial resources would permit it to be otherwise. In our time appearance becomes of increasing importance to farm children as they mingle with town children in consolidated schools; as a consequence farm families are becoming more style conscious and less conspicuously different in dress.

The economically disadvantageous position of farmers as a class is no doubt a vital factor in their feelings of inferiority. For example, Stott,[1] studying 270 farm young people in small-town high schools in Lancaster County, Nebraska, found that favorable economic status is an advantage in personality adjustment. He concludes:

. . . material prosperity is of some importance to the psychological well-being of farm people, both parents and children. The effects of this factor may come about in any of a variety of ways. It is quite likely, for example, that young folks in some instances are affected directly in their development by the relative lack of cultural advantages in the home. In other instances a sense of insecurity might develop from the economic failure of the family, or a feeling of social inferiority might arise from an unfavorable relative economic level. It is also probable that youngsters often are

[1] Leland H. Stott, "Family Prosperity in Relation to the Psychological Adjustments of Farm Folk," *Rural Sociology*, vol. 10, pp. 256–263, September, 1945.

affected indirectly through their parents' reactions, attitudes, and adjustments to unsuccessful farming operations, financial difficulties and relatively poor living conditions. An economically poor farm family situation need not necessarily result in personal maladjustments in family members, but apparently it might operate as an unfavorable factor. Likewise, farm family prosperity can by no means insure the optimum psychological adjustments within families, but it definitely may be regarded as one condition conducive to such a desirable outcome.

Rank within agriculture is also no doubt often a factor in producing inferiority. There is little doubt that in many sections of the South the cropper, and in the West the migratory farm laborer, have good reason to feel inferior, for they are in fact given an inferior rating by the communities in which they work. Even in the Middle West, where there is comparatively little feeling of status and rank, Stott[1] found that children of farm laborers ranked lower than other groups in social adjustment scores. This probably reflects in part feelings of social inadequacy.

Introversion.—The concepts of introversion, ambiversion, and extroversion describe emotional tendencies of individuals. The introverted person lives within himself, is unexpressive, has only a few intimate friends, is suspicious of strangers, enjoys solitude, meditation, and daydreaming; the extroverted person seeks association, expresses social feelings and emotions freely, is hearty toward strangers, makes new acquaintances easily; the ambivert lies between these two extremes.

It seems logical to expect, and observation verifies the conclusion, that rural people on the whole develop somewhat introverted personalities. Temperamental traits are to some extent innate and there are many farmers who by native endowment are extroverted, whereas many urban people are introverted; on the other hand, tests of the degree of expression of emotional tendencies of preschool children indicate that introversion and extroversion are qualities that can be cultivated.[2] One who lives in isolation develops introverted traits; one who lives in constant contact with others develops extroverted traits. The rural environment is conducive to meditation and daydreaming.[3] The one thing the farmer detests most in his city cousin is his extroverted characteristics, his tendency to be aggressive, talkative, and forward, as compared to his own tendency to be reticent, bashful, and reserved.

An objective measure of social traits in a three-fold classification is shown in the chart. It will be seen that the Bell Adjustment Inventory shows marked

[1] Leland H. Stott, "Some Environmental Factors in Relation to the Personality Adjustments of Rural Children," *Rural Sociology*, vol. 10, pp. 394–403, December, 1945.

[2] Leslie Ray Marston, *The Emotions of Young Children*, p. 94, University of Iowa Studies, Iowa City, 1925.

[3] J. M. Williams, *op. cit.*, pp. 171–173.

differences in social traits of farm, small-town and city groups for the sample of young women studied. A much higher proportion of rural young women than of urban young women are retiring; a much lower proportion are aggressive. Small-town girls fall between the farm and urban extremes.

Conservatism.—Conservatism is one of the traits most frequently attributed to the farm person. Only in rare instances is he accused of radicalism. Radicalism often is the product of suppression; conservatism of self-direction. Thwarted groups in urban-industrial activities feel the impulse to revolt because they are under the domination of a boss or supervisor. Many of these individuals placed in a position of leadership or one permitting self-direction, such as that of the average farmer, would become conservative.

Conservatism may grow out of the fact that the farmer works for himself. The urban worker, directed by an employer, must adapt his behavior to the

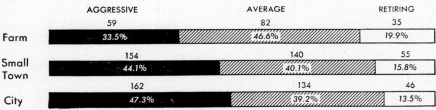

Paul H. Landis, Washington Agricultural Experiment Station.

SOCIAL ADJUSTMENT OF FARM, SMALL-TOWN AND CITY GIRLS

The Bell ratings show that young college women with a farm background tend to be retiring rather than aggressive compared to town and city youth. Ratings are for 882 young women at the State College of Washington in 1942 and are statistically significant as measured by the analysis-of-variance test. (Figures above bars indicate number of cases.)

conditions of work imposed upon him. Frequently he must discard old methods and beliefs. But in the farmer's game there are fewer rules imposed from above and he can, if he chooses, persist unhindered in following proverbial beliefs and practices.

The farmer tends to be conservative in his expenditures in part because he has to wait long for returns and plan far ahead in financial matters. Moreover, his income for any given year is always uncertain. He has to learn to keep a reserve and to await the outcome of the crop. Involved in farm income are not only changes in market price which are a factor in city income also, but in addition, the factor of natural hazards which may affect yield or destroy the crop entirely. To the generalization that farmers are conservative in financial matters as in other fields, there are spectacular exceptions, however. Some wheat farmers are notorious gamblers, throwing caution to the winds, mortgaging everything they own for new combines, new cars, or a new quarter section of land. Activities of certain farm groups indicate that liberal and even radical political action is possible among farmers.[1]

Provincial Outlook.—Lack of contact breeds provincialism; one is interested in that which is far away only as he understands it. The farmer at times is so absorbed in his own activities that he does not take the time to learn of distant events or to develop sympathy for programs and philanthropies lying in the larger world beyond his own community. This narrowness may be interpreted as selfishness or the manifestation of greediness; actually it is due to circumscribed experience. The limited nature of much of farm experience is suggested by Hawthorn:

Every task meets the farmer's individuality and personality. Every post, shock of hay, or "critter" reflects his personal touch. All depends on himself; there is no extra shift. No one sets a pace, a standard for his day's work, or issues orders. The farmer is his own boss, capitalist, pacesetter, and business manager. He is the worker who toils to execute plans. The farm seems aloof from the economic tentacles of an outside world of markets, prices, demands, and supplies, and so his salvation seems to lie inside his fence lines; he has no business outside of it; nobody else has any business inside of it. He and his family seem to be a self-sufficing unit, that, like a cell, can be isolated without the stoppage of its vitality and life. The entire industrial and financial machinery of the outside world could stop, but still he could go on, for he has the basic needs of existence. The farmer works and thinks alone without the mental stimulus or interference of others. A set of factors of this character will tend to develop the latent ego of the most dependent individuals. The farmer, not excepting the renter, is an undertaker of ventures and an entrepreneur, who must not only shoulder the responsibility of his own decisions, but must abide by the vagaries of weather and markets. To endure the strain of such anxieties, he must develop an almost blind confidence in himself and his luck.[2]

Neuberger, an author living in Portland, Ore., describing some of the people in the isolated part of the great hinterland of his city,[3] suggests that the person living at the outposts encounters public opinion in a very different fashion from the person in the metropolis. The hinterland resident may get his newspaper a week late after a long trek to some remote post office.

At a grange meeting in an isolated region he observes the tan, rugged countenances and calloused hands of people who are accustomed to work in the open; their dress is somewhat out of style and few of the women wear high-heeled pumps; old-fashioned gold watch chains dangle across the vests of most of the men, although the lumberjack in blue denim shirt may have a dollar

---

[1] The Farmer Labor movement in Minnesota, the Nonpartisan League in the spring-wheat area, and the Farmer's Holiday movement are examples.

[2] Horace B. Hawthorn, *The Sociology of Rural Life*, p. 255, D. Appleton-Century Company, Inc., New York, 1926.

[3] Richard Neuberger, *Our Promised Land*, pp. 362–372, The Macmillan Company, New York, 1939.

timepiece fastened to his suspenders with a big blanket pin. Visiting with friends whom they have not seen since the previous county-wide grange meeting three months before, the attention of these people focuses chiefly on things of immediate concern—the weather, the crops, the influx of drought refugees, the lumber industry. It is the first time many of them have left their farms and ranches for several weeks; stirring developments in this nation and abroad are discussed, argued about, and wondered about but usually with a local application. One farmer remarks that he doesn't think the common people in Japan care anything about what their army is doing in China and proves it by saying that his little Japanese neighbor, who raises tomatoes, "ain't got anything against the Chinaman."

On the basis of these and other observations Neuberger concludes that hinterland opinions do not necessarily fit into the general compartments of public thought. People in the outposts have minimum contact with the influences of propaganda; their opinions are more independently formed than are those of city people.

The radio in the farm home extends the scope of the family's contacts and, therefore, of its interests. Modern farmers sometimes have broader interests and more information than the lower working classes of the city, although rarely are they so well informed as the white collar and professional classes. Many farmers, even when they have little time to read, give their attention chiefly to substantial reading matter.[1]

The life that a farmer lives makes it unimportant that he hear the latest news broadcast, or that he view social questions from all angles, or that he quickly embrace the fad of the moment. It is the more sophisticated classes in urban society who feel that they must buy the latest extra, follow the latest craze, read the most recent best seller, know by name the great singers and actors, and speak fluently of the latest gestures of foreign dictators. These are part of the urban person's stock in trade, devices by which he attains the respect of others and shows that he is in gear with the social life of the world community. Such things have less meaning to the average farmer, for in his world he is not judged by knowledge of the latest happenings in the politico-social world, but rather by the effectiveness with which he executes his everyday tasks.

Positive Philosophy.—Farm people are less open to doubt concerning even those matters about which they have only superficial knowledge than people living in more complex environments; dogmatism, fatalism, adherence to

[1] For comparisons of reading matter in farm and town homes see E. L. Morgan and M. W. Sneed, "The Activities of Rural Young People in Missouri," pp. 37*ff.*, *Missouri Agricultural Experiment Station Bulletin* 269, Columbia, 1937; C. E. Lively and I. J. Miller, "Rural Young People 16 to 24 Years of Age," pp. 14–15, *Ohio Experiment Station Bulletin* 73, Columbus, 1934.

convention, stolidness are all traits mentioned by students of rural life as characterizing farm people.[1] In contrast, urban groups are more likely to possess a questioning attitude, to express frequent doubts, to be cynical, versatile, alert.

The farmer thinks long and deeply about matters of concern to him; his opinions are fortified during long hours of brooding while he is engaged in physical work. Constant physical activity develops stolidness and interferes with extensive reading and the reception of new ideas.

Farmers are prone to pass judgment on very complex issues by simple and positive conclusions. Complicated economic issues may be blamed on big business, the political party in power, or the tariff, in utter disregard of the numerous factors that enter into any such issues; many farmers are able to present a simple, direct, concise solution to almost any social problem of which they have a talking knowledge. In this respect they solve the problems of the universe in barbershop style, the same problems which authorities on economics, sociology, history, or social policy are unable fully to understand.

This tendency of the farmer to pass positive judgment on matters about which he knows little has been demonstrated again and again in his reaction to farm programs and tariff policies. As Hawthorn expresses it, the farmer's interests and fancies push out along one line without the checks and balances of the opinions of others.[2] The farmer notes the discrepancy between the price he receives for a hide and what he pays for shoes, between the price he receives for wheat and what he pays for bread, between the price he receives for cotton and what he pays for clothes, and immediately concludes, because he has little appreciation of the numerous processes involved in the movement, manufacture, and distribution of goods from the raw product to the finished goods, that all the world is trying to "slick" him. It is true that many times there is an unjust difference between the price of raw materials and the price of manufactured goods,[3] but of the many complicated social and economic factors involved the farmer usually has no conception. In many farm communities the Lord, the weather, and the middleman are still blamed by the people for most of their troubles.

Tolerance within the Limits of Local Patterns and Intolerance toward Out-group Values.—The farmer, being accustomed to restricted patterns, may be less tolerant than the urban person of patterns that differ from his own, and therefore may receive less quickly into his fellowship the person who is different.

---

[1] See C. C. Taylor, *op. cit.*, pp., 137–141, for a list of psychological traits of farmers mentioned by various authors.

[2] H. B. Hawthorn, *op. cit.*, pp. 42–43.

[3] The Federal Trade Commission has implied that "industrial and commercial corporations" dealing with agricultural products are "unduly enriching themselves at the expense of the agricultural population." *Agricultural Income Inquiry*, part I, p. 39, U.S. Government Printing Office, Washington, D. C., 1938.

The urbanite, because he lives in a setting of many different small cultural worlds, is more likely to learn to tolerate and accept people with approaches to life different from his own, and even to respect them when they challenge his own set of values. The urban person's tolerance, however, does not necessarily indicate greater democracy, but more likely a lack of interest in other people. He views other ways of life impersonally, tolerating them because he considers them to be none of his concern. The farm person is tolerant within the sphere of his mores, but usually his mores are so restrictive as to exclude radically different out-group values, since in the primary group to tolerate innovations is to invite disintegration of the local mores.

Fatalism versus Social Manipulation.—The idea of engaging in social manipulation rather than resigning oneself to circumstances seems to be less developed among farmers than among many other occupational groups. Necessary submission to many forces in the nature environment lends to the view that no amount of wishing or tinkering will effect a desired change. In contrast is the view, highly developed among certain groups in the city and to some extent among all urban people, that one can "fix" things if he knows the right people and pulls the right strings. The urban person has this belief because he lives in a world where the forces in operation are human forces; he deals with social laws and human personalities, not with nature; his experience with politics and his knowledge of the way institutions and social organizations are run lead him to believe the "right" people must be approached if he is to obtain the thing he wants. Therefore, he concentrates on knowing the "right" people rather than on submitting to overmastering forces as the farmer often must. A relative in the personnel department or other "pull" from the inside may be much more important in obtaining a job than any personal qualities of the applicant.[1] A union membership may bring greater rewards from the employer than years of diligent conscientious effort.

It is possible that the resignation of the farmer carries over into many phases of the farm problem. The Agricultural Adjustment Administration in some of its far-reaching legislation may have done more than any other single influence to make the farmer realize that his universe is capable of being manipulated and that the social environment is more important to his economic success than the geographical.

Man has become more rational because he lives in the mechanized city, where he must at all times maintain a degree of rational control if he is to survive.[2] Certainly the city has made man rational in the sense of making him

---

[1] A study of youth in San Francisco shows that over 40 per cent received jobs with the aid of parents, relatives, or friends. In the reported difficulties in obtaining employment, lack of "pull" was the third most important difficulty mentioned. "Lack of experience" was first; "union restrictions," second. Data from a confidential preliminary report.

[2] Robert E. Park, writing on "Magic, Mentality, and City Life," in *The City*, by Park, Burgess, *et al.*, p. 130, University of Chicago Press, Chicago, 1925.

aware that conscious manipulation may determine the outcome of his efforts. The traditional farmer is habituated to an individual rather than a social approach to his problems, to resignation rather than defiant manipulation. The new farmer is gradually learning that in social manipulation there is power.

TRADITIONAL PERSONALITY PATTERNS AND THE NEW SOCIAL ENVIRONMENT

It seems likely that the marked differences in personality traits of farm people and those of other occupations will continue to decrease as differences in social roles are lessened. Since personality is a product of experience and since the experience of farm people is becoming more like that of other social and occupational classes, the molding process that goes on within the new rural social scheme will naturally tend to change many of the traditional habit patterns that have been prominent in the orientation of the personality of farm people. The old rugged individualism of isolation, the old introversion that came from spending a great deal of time alone, the provincial outlook that was determined by a narrow experience horizon, the old suspicion of the urban which developed because the farmer was far from the urban and had little contact with it, the old conservatism that grew from the fact that the farmer lived directly from the land he operated rather than from cash income, and the old positive philosophy that was as much a product of the lack of reading and reception of new ideas as of conviction are becoming and will continue to become less pronounced.

QUESTIONS FOR REVIEW AND DISCUSSION

1. What characteristics of human nature make it difficult to differentiate traits of one occupational group or social class from those of any other?
2. Are personality traits of farmers generally considered to be different from those of other groups?
3. Explain how experience affects personality formation.
4. Is there any one rural type that characterizes all farmers of the nation?
5. Explain the farmer's ambivalent reaction toward the city.
6. What influences enter into the development of inferiority feelings among farm children? of introverted tendencies?
7. What factors in the farmer's experience might make for conservatism?
8. What factors in rural society make it unnecessary for the farmer to be as cosmopolitan in interest and up-to-date in information as certain urban classes?
9. Explain how isolation and lack of information may lead to dogmatic, positive attitudes.
10. In what realm is the farmer tolerant? intolerant?
11. How does the farming class compare with urban groups in skill at social manipulation?
12. Indicate the effects of the new rural social environment on personality configurations.

COLLATERAL READING

Bernard, L. L.: "A Theory of Rural Attitudes," *American Journal of Sociology*, pp. 648 *ff.*, March, 1917.

————: "Research Problems in the Psychology of Rural Life," *Journal of Social Forces*, vol. 37 pp. 446–458, March, 1925.

Hawthorn, Horace B.: *The Sociology of Rural Life*, chap. 10, D. Appleton-Century Company, Inc., New York, 1926.

Katz, D. and R. L. Schanck: *Social Psychology*, chaps. 17 and 18, John Wiley & Sons, Inc., New York, 1938.

Kolb, J. H., and E. de S. Brunner: *A Study of Rural Society*, 3d ed., chap. 5, Houghton Mifflin Company, Boston, 1946.

Sims, N. L.: *Elements of Rural Sociology*, rev. ed., chap. 16, The Thomas Y. Crowell Company, New York, 1940.

Sorokin, P. A., and C. C. Zimmerman: *Principles of Rural-urban Sociology*, chap. 13, Henry Holt and Company, Inc., New York, 1929.

Stott, Leland H.: "Family Prosperity in Relation to Psychological Adjustments of Farm Folk," *Rural Sociology*, vol. 10, pp. 256–263, September, 1945.

————: "Some Environmental Factors in Relation to the Personality Adjustments of Rural Children, "*Rural Sociology*, vol. 10, pp. 394–403, December, 1945.

Taylor, C. C.: *Rural Sociology*. rev. ed., chap. 7, Harper & Brothers, New York, 1933.

Williams, J. M.: *Our Rural Heritage*, chap. 23, Alfred A. Knopf, Inc., New York, 1925.

CHAPTER 10

ADVANTAGES AND DISADVANTAGES OF RURAL SOCIALIZATION

SOCIOLOGICAL PRINCIPLES APPLICABLE TO RURAL SOCIALIZATION

EVERY person at birth encounters an imposing world of group patterns which he will adopt as his manner of life. The social group thus has power to build attitudes and habits which in themselves will constitute the basis for the individual's social behavior. One who is placed in a restricted social group will have imprinted indelibly on his personality the patterns of this group, whereas one who contacts many groups will acquire a diversity of patterns; but, however simple or complex the social environment, there will be present in the world of the child social definitions adequate for meeting most life situations arising in the immediate environment.[1]

In considering the advantages and disadvantages of the farm child's experience as a factor in the development of his personality and in shaping him for the world in which he is to live, it must be recognized that no group situation is ever ideal and that few individuals are perfectly prepared for life. The human being is remarkably adaptable and has the capacity to make radical personality changes.

THE SOCIALIZATION OF THE FARM CHILD

Many personality patterns become relatively fixed early in life, being deeply ingrained in the preschool age.[2] In all sections of society these early years are spent under the influence of the family. The complete dominance of family patterns in the experience of the child lasts longer on the farm than in the town or the city, and habits become more deeply fixed; consequently, the problem of interpreting the outside world in terms different from those of the immediate family is more difficult for the farm than for the urban child.[3]

In extremely isolated rural areas family ideas about religion, politics,

---

[1] For W. I. Thomas' classic discussion of the group's definition of situations, see his *The Unadjusted Girl*, pp. 41–44, Little, Brown & Company, Boston, 1923.

[2] John B. Watson, *Psychological Care of Infant and Child*, W. W. Norton & Company, Inc., New York, 1928.

[3] S. M. and B. C. Gruenberg, "Education of Children for Family Life," *Annals of the American Academy of Political and Social Science*, vol. 160, pp. 205–215. Also see Lawrence K. Frank, "Social Change and the Family," *Annals of the American Academy of Political and Social Science*, vol. 160, pp. 94–102.

vocations, and life in general are likely to be perpetuated with relatively few changes from generation to generation. Neighborhood isolation produces homogeneity. The more isolated a people the more certain may one be that the prevailing values will dominate all their interests and activities; if intellectual achievements are not respected, intellectual development is sought only by the daring or ambitious; if simplicity is characteristic, personality develops without sophistication, the established customs and traditions forming the life outline. In some communities undue respect for material objects has been ingrained through long periods of struggle for survival; in others an appreciation of spiritual things supersedes problems of economic security; in still others cultural traits of foreign origin are maintained by a purposeful isolation and aloofness. In the rural community the ambitious individual is circumscribed by the knowledge, information, and social experience to which the community limits him. Many farm communities do not provide a live atmosphere for mental stimulation and only as the individual contacts neighborhoods beyond his own does he obtain visions of new interests and new possibilities.

The child, absorbing the family and neighborhood patterns, which often are similar, may form an idealistic concept of human nature. Because of his submergence in the social framework that bounds him, he seldom sees the way others live and hence acquires little information concerning other groups and classes of society. In many rural primary groups he may never see certain perverse elements of human nature expressed; in others he may see little aside from the sordid. In a dynamic society the pervasive conditioning influences of the primary group at most characterize only a limited period in life— childhood and early youth. The chief difference between conditioning in urban society and in the more progressive portions of rural society consists in the fact that the rural child's experience is limited during a longer period in early life.

Factual data on the conditioning of the farm child are not extensive. Two studies are of special significance, one by Baldwin and his colleagues working in the Iowa Child Welfare Research Station at the University of Iowa;[1] the other by the White House Conference on Child Health and Protection.[2]

Most of the field work for the Baldwin study was done in the middle twenties (1923–1927), but many of the influences characterizing that decade still exist in the numerous rural sections where one-room rural schools persist.[3] Many of the farm children were found to be extremely shy.[4] Schoolteachers commented upon the fact that some children upon entering the first grade would

[1] Results are published in Bird T. Baldwin, *et al.*, *Farm Children*, D. Appleton-Century Company, Inc., New York, 1930.

[2] *The Adolescent in the Family*, D. Appleton-Century Company, Inc., New York, 1934.

[3] There are still approximately 100,000 one-room schools in the nation.

[4] Bird T. Baldwin, *et al.*, *op cit.*, p. 121.

not speak for several days.[1] Visitors in rural homes were often avoided by the children, who crawled under the table or hid behind the door or even ran out of the house. The authors conclude that "perhaps the outstanding characteristic of children in the one-roomed school is their aloofness." In comparing two different communities, they observe that the more restricted the environment, the more likely is the child to conform to the patterns of his elders; the fewer the influenes from the outside the more likely is he to conform to the patterns of the locality group.[2]

The attitudes of parents toward their children and the nature of their attempts at guidance were found to be of fundamental importance.[3] Some farm parents expressed little interest in the school even though their children attended, did not consider it necessary to give their children advantages, required them to work hard at an early age and to walk long distances to school even in inclement weather. Some even opposed the serving of hot lunches at school, and a few refused to buy their children needed school supplies. Many were in the habit of opposing anything progressive in the community, even such organizations as had constructive programs; they would not permit their children to participate in the sale of tuberculosis stamps because they assumed that there must be graft hidden somewhere. Some opposed organizations generally on the principle that their programs would cause an increase in taxes even though no such connection was evident. Of those who wanted to give their children opportunities according to their conception of the best, many had no idea of what the best was; some felt that an eighth-grade education was ample, since that was more schooling than they themselves had had. In several families the accumulation of property was the major goal to the exclusion of all other interests. In the main, parents with the above attitudes were of foreign birth or were second-generation immigrants; usually the father dominated the family.

In the one-room school district the children had no contact beyond their immediate community. Parents in some of these localities, the authors suggest, may have felt that they were doing much for their children, when in reality they were doing little to prepare them for the larger social experience of the life outside, because they themselves had no insight into manners of life different from their own and no experience with methods used by outside groups.

In contrast, another community is described in which education is valued above work, in which spiritual values are placed above the materialistic.

---

[1] Back of this behavior may have been the home training of the child which required that he be seen and not heard. This idea was prominent in patriarchially dominated foreign settlements of the last generation, and to a lesser extent in all farm homes.

[2] Bird T. Baldwin, *et al.*, *op cit.*, p. 48.

[3] *Ibid.*, pp. 44–46.

Here, as in many communities, there were rural parents who constantly strove to keep in touch with important social changes, who borrowed much from people of other rural areas or of town and city, who were interested in giving their children opportunities far beyond those they themselves had had, and who favored the progressive development of rural institutions.

The report of the White House Conference on Child Health and Protection,[1] which deals with home activities in the education of the child, is of special significance in that it is concerned with some of the more intangible effects of family training. Although, like others in the field, the study leaves much to be learned, it points out certain important aspects of the situation. The gist of the findings is as follows:

The farm child spends much of his spare time with his parents or under their supervision, the home and farm environment being his chief playground; most of his evenings are spent at home; he has tasks about the home in a much higher proportion of cases than do urban children, and he associates with his parents both in leisure time and at work. Reading and studying rather than group activities occupy his evenings.

The report states that a somewhat higher percentage of urban than of farm children have scores indicating good personality adjustment. The urban child learns the skills necessary for urban living and the farm child learns the skills necessary for farm living. Considering the drift of population from country to city, the committee suggests that one should deplore the lack of education for urban living among farm adolescents rather than the lessened home activities of urban children.

Two pursuits of children that seem to be distinctly urban are going to the movies and taking walks. The one activity that is distinctly rural is reading. All other recreational activities that are favorites among country children are also favorites among city children.

This report challenges the widely held idea that the farm family is more united than the urban on the basis of findings to the effect that farm children are more inclined to criticize their parents than are urban children. The authors suggest that perhaps it is the too close association between parent and child which results in antagonism, or that perhaps there are other influences in farm life which tend to alienate parent and child. Possibly too much work in which the parent is the taskmaster causes conflict in the farm home. The fact that parental education and child study groups in the urban community have made for more intelligent parenthood may also explain in part the differential in urban and rural family harmony.

With regard to the problem of family tensions, W. G. Mather and Mildred

[1] *The Adolescent in the Family*. On pp. 158–179 is a subcommittee report developed under the chairmanship of Ernest W. Burgess, sociologist, entitled "Family Activities, Celebrations, and Recreations."

B. Thurow report that there is more tension between father and children in rural homes than in urban homes, although there is less tension between the mother and the children in the rural family. Children are most satisfied with their family life in the large city. Farm families rank second with small-town families revealing the least satisfactory parent-child relationships.[1]

Leland H. Stott has reported the results of an extensive study of 325 high school boys and 370 high school girls from farm homes in Nebraska.[2] The group ranged from 11 to 22 years of age. He makes no comparison between farm children and those from town and city, but relates certain family characteristics making for successful personal development. The following are found to be highly important to the adjustment of the farm child: attitude of welcome on the part of the parent toward the child's friends in the home, having good times together in the home as a family group, infrequent punishment of the child, a minimum of nervousness on the part of the parents, display of affection between parent and child, having nothing in the behavior of the parent which the child particularly dislikes.

ADVANTAGES OF SOCIALIZATION IN THE RURAL SETTING

Mature Realism.—Rural living and farming in particular are of such a nature that child and adult are together much of the time. The farm child, unlike the city child who is on the outside of the everyday activities of adults, participates in a realistic world of workday affairs. Through such association he absorbs much practical information and develops a mature point of view.

The farm child is initiated early into the work world of the adult, having chores to do and at a fairly early age helping with regular work.[3] Of recent years school has seriously interfered with his practical work experience; but if the school encroaches on home duties, by encouraging too many extracurricular activities or demanding too much homework, farm parents are likely to protest.

[1] From an unpublished doctor's thesis by W. G. Mather, Jr., "A Statistical Analysis of Family Relations Based on Students' Autobiographies," reported in Dwight Sanderson, "Rural Family," *Journal of Home Economics*, vol. 29, pp. 223–228, April, 1937. See also Mildred B. Thurow, "A Study of Selected Factors in Family Life as Described in Autobiographies," *Cornell Agricultural Experiment Station Memoir* 171, Ithaca, 1935.

[2] Leland H. Stott, "The Relation of Certain Factors in Farm Family Life to Personality Development in Adolescents," *Nebraska Agricultural Experiment Station Bulletin* 106, Lincoln, 1938.

[3] Many studies have shown that farm children and youths work much more than town and city children. For type studies, see E. Gardner and C. E. Legg, *Leisure-time Activities of Rural Children in Selected Areas of West Virginia*, U.S. Children's Bureau, Publication no. 208; E. L. Morgan and M. W. Sneed, "The Activities of Rural Young People in Missouri," Table 9, *Missouri Agricultural Experiment Station Bulletin* 269, Columbia, 1937; and Mildred B. Thurow, "Interests, Activities, and Problems of Rural Young Folk," Table 10, *Cornell Agriculture Experiment Station Bulletin* 617, Ithaca, 1934.

Farm Security Administration (Rothstein)

INITIATION TO THE WORK WORLD

The farm child develops a mature realism, for he knows life as adults live it. He serves a natural apprenticeship to farming and also to adulthood.

In direct contrast is the experience of the town and city child who has so much leisure that the school must carry on elaborate time-consuming extracurricular activities to help keep him out of mischief. Parents for the lack of real chores may invent them, but more often leave it to the child to find entertainment in park or playground or on the street when not occupied by school activities.

The value of the discipline of work during childhood and youth has been challenged in recent years. Modern educational philosophy and urban training have stressed the pleasure more than the duty principle in pedagogy. An extreme emphasis upon pleasure, however, may entirely unfit the child for adjustment to adult life.[1] The emphasis on pleasure motivation in phases of urban experience may make it difficult for the young adult to shoulder responsibility. On the other hand, childhood on the farm is sometimes sacrificed too much in adult interests. In some homes work becomes almost a religion, the child's formal education being sacrificed to work. The farm child serves an apprenticeship to farming which is invaluable if he later becomes a farmer.[2] In urban occupations the child has no natural apprenticeship to his father's vocation and, as a substitute, vocational schools have been developed.

The White House Conference report raises a doubt as to the helpfulness of the close application of the farm child to duties about the home from the viewpoint of harmonious family relationships,[3] suggesting that there is a lack of evidence of valuable results from the performing of numerous home tasks. The common assumption is that these duties develop cooperativeness and unselfishness and a feeling of family unity, but the report hints that a detailed study might show that tasks extraneous to the child's interest carried out unwillingly and under compulsion may be an undesirable influence in the family situation.

Even though this may be true, one needs to know the full implications of disciplinary influences during childhood to life adjustments in the period when the youth is freed from parental domination and enters life on his own responsibility. The other extreme, of allowing too much freedom, may be equally undesirable. For example, Margaret Mead, in discussing the experience of the Manus child in New Guinea, presents an interesting bit of evidence to the effect that the child who grows up where childhood is made supremely pleasant, where adults try to see that the child is always happy, makes the

---

[1] According to the psychoanalysts, the hysterical personality is due in part to pampering in infancy. Hysteria is a return of the adult to the infantile period when he had affection showered upon him, making him the center of attention. John B. Watson no doubt had this in mind in cautioning against too much emotional indulgence on the part of the parent in training the young child. *Op. cit.*, chap. 3.

[2] See Dwight Sanderson, *op. cit.*, vol. 29, pp. 223–228, for further discussion of this point.

[3] *The Adolescent in the Family*, pp. 158–178.

transition to adult life with great difficulty.[1] The event of initiation into adult responsibilities is looked upon with deep sorrow by the Manus child. He never again in his lifetime will recover the joy of living that he loses with the passing of childhood. Childhood is his golden age.

There is no doubt a happy mean as far as the balance between work and play is concerned, but whether rural or urban society more nearly attains it is, in the light of meager evidence, debatable.

Limited Social Participation.—In an age of constant stimulation, highly developed extracurricular activities in the school, and extensive club participation among adults, there is undoubtedly some advantage in the limited social experience of the rural child. Baldwin and his colleagues, studying the activities of children in one-room schools, find that their lives are less hurried than the lives of children in large communities.[2] The one-room school introduces the child to few outside activities; even the consolidated school has difficulty in carrying on an extracurricular program because the rural child has chores to do at home and finds it difficult to set aside practice periods for glee club, orchestra, band, football, or basketball. Busses start for home promptly at the close of the school day. Town children feel that home duties which interfere with their participation in activities at school are unjust, whereas farm children on the whole do not appear to question the priority of home responsibility, but seem to enjoy much more than town children their privilege of participation in extracurricular activities when given the opportunity. Even when the farm child does participate in outside school programs he usually participates in only one at a time; he cannot spare the time for more.

The study shows, on the other hand, that organizational activities of children and youth in the small town sometimes tend toward too great profusion, especially during adolescence when elaborate extracurricular schedules fill up their time. The town child frequently is so overloaded with extracurricular work that he has little time for home activities, and so overstimulated that he loses much of the sheer joy of social participation, becoming weary of many things because of an overenrichment of experience.

Equanimity.—There is a smoothness in the flow of events in many rural environments that remains relatively undisturbed by the influences of mechanical change which has a stabilizing effect upon the child, developing in him a sense of smugness and of certainty regarding the universe in which he lives. Children need security in order to develop confidence and assurance.

The farm child, if he lives on the same farm throughout childhood, develops firm attachments to familiar things on the farmstead—trees, stream, woods. People who move often have no landmarks, few objects meaning a

[1] Margaret Mead, *Growing Up in New Guinea*, William Morrow & Company, Inc., New York, 1930.

[2] *Op. cit.*, pp. 152–154.

great deal to them. To the mobile child the new may involve certain elements of wonder, but he has seen too many things and acquired too much superficial information to form anything but shallow attachments. Detachment from fixed objects characterizes the children of the highly mobile farm laborer and the mobile farm tenant, as well as the children in mobile urban families.

Ordinarily the farm child, like the farm adult, feels little of the nervous tension experienced by children of many urban groups. The mental strain of schoolwork is balanced by daily physical labor and there is little time or opportunity to become bookish.

Discipline of Nature Forces.—Since the rural world is primarily geographical and organic rather than cultural, the forces of nature play an important part in the conditioning of the rural child. The weather, the seasons, the open spaces, the water, the wind, and the heavens are a vital part of his experience, and he learns their meaning as they affect his physical comfort and the economic welfare of the family.

The regularity and implacability of the laws of nature in the environment of the rural child discipline him as man-made laws could never do. He observes the futility of man's efforts in the face of drought, storm, and flood hail and wind; he learns that damage to or destruction of the crop is one of those things that man cannot help; he sees life close up—sex, reproduction, growth, sicknesses, death, basic biological realities which urban culture veils from the child. He faces life on this level frankly and maturely as a matter of course. Overseriousness may result, but a certain amount of such realism is the essence of maturity and must be learned if one would functon as a psychologically mature person in adult life.

Training in Personal Self-sufficiency and Resourcefulness.—Baldwin and his coworkers,[1] in studying the play equipment of children in rural communities in Iowa, found it to be more meager than that of town children in families of similar or even poorer financial status. The writers express the view that, since farm children are not surrounded with manufactured toys and ready-made pleasures, they have more opportunity than the urban child for the development of imagination. Many of the farm children were found to enjoy make-believe games such as keeping house or playing Indians. Most of them had pets with ample room to keep them, and seemed to enjoy the expansive rural environment where there were trees to climb, meadows in which to roam, and livestock to tend. The authors conclude that farm children need fewer toys than town and city children and do not seem to feel the need for the constant companionship of other children which most urban children learn to expect early in life.[2]

[1] *Op. cit.*, pp. 135, 150–155.

[2] For a discussion of the play world of the urban child, see Joseph K. Folsom, *The Family*, pp. 209–210, John Wiley & Sons, Inc., New York, 1934.

The one-room rural school, although lacking many of the merits of the better multiple-room educational institutions of today, has probably contributed to the resourcefulness of the farm child. When a teacher has eight grades to teach with some forty or fifty classes a day there is no time for supervised study and little time for personal direction. From the first grade on, the child must depend upon himself in considerable part, providing his own "busy work" and study plans.

DISADVANTAGES OF RURAL SOCIALIZATION TO PERSONALITY IN A DYNAMIC AGE

The effect of a given social experience on personality can be evaluated only in terms of ultimate adjustment, involving a consideration of the kind of world in which the individual is going to live. In many respects (certain of which have just been discussed) the farm environment is ideal from the standpoint of desirable childhood experience. The most desirable adjustment in childhood, however, may not be the most desirable when early experience is evaluated in terms of its implications to adult life. Even from this viewpoint, rural conditioning has, as we have seen, certain assets, but let us also consider its liabilities. In what kind of world is the farm youth of today going to live? Is rural life preparing him for that kind of world?

Too Limited Social Experience.—One does not have to survey extensively the literature dealing with farm youth or that dealing with adult family life on the farm to be convinced that the social experience of a substantial part of our farm population is so limited as to make it questionable whether the farm child and adolescent are being adequately prepared for situations faced by the average adult of today. Farm people ordinarily belong to few social organizations as compared to village, town, and city people, and function in fewer social situations.[1]

Spatial contacts are limited. Thurow, studying the interests and activities of rural girls in New York state between the ages of 16 and 24 years, found that during the preceding five years 34 per cent had not taken a trip of fifty miles within the state and 60 per cent had not taken a trip of this distance outside the state.[2] Morgan and Sneed, studying high school youths in Missouri, found that 25 per cent of 965 farm youths had not traveled outside the state.[3] Village youth had traveled more widely.

[1] For a sample study see J. J. Lister and E. L. Kirkpatrick, *Rural Youth Speak*, Fig. 4, American Youth Commission, Washington, D. C., 1939. E. de S. Brunner and I. Lorge, *Rural Trends in Depression Years*, pp. 274 *ff.*, Columbia University Press, New York, 1938, find that rural women today are participating in the social life of village-centered communities much more extensively than men, the tendency of newer organizations being to include more women than men.

[2] Mildred B. Thurow, "A Study of Selected Factors in Family Life as Described in Autobiographies," *op. cit.*, p. 31.

[3] E. L. Morgan and M. W. Sneed, *op. cit.*, p. 42.

The amount of contact the individual has affects his social adjustments. As would be expected, farm youth often feel ill at ease among people of their own

PRINCIPAL LEISURE-TIME ACTIVITIES OF WHITE FARM YOUTH ACCORDING TO SEX*

Male		Female	
Activity	Per cent	Activity	Per cent
Sports†	24.1	Reading	38.1
Loafing	19.2	Handicrafts	18.9
Reading	14.4	Movies	9.2
Movies	11.0	Dancing‡	9.0
Dancing‡	11.0	Loafing	7.2
Team games	7.7	Sports†	6.4
Hobbies	4.7	Radio§	3.0
Radio§	2.4	Team games	1.3
Quiet games	0.8	Quiet games	0.3
Other	4.7	Other	6.6
Total	100.0	Total	100.0
Number of youths	1,174		955

* Howard M. Bell, *Youth Tell Their Story*, p. 164, American Council on Education, Washington, D. C., 1938.

† Individual sports such as swimming, tennis, golf.

‡ Dancing and dating.

§ Listening to the radio.

TOO LIMITED SOCIAL PARTICIPATION CHARACTERIZES THE LEISURE-TIME ACTIVITIES OF FARM YOUTH

The concentration on individual rather than group activities is striking. The study compares farm youths with other groups and finds less social participation among the farm youths of Maryland than those of towns, villages, and cities. More than 13,000 youths ages 16 to 24 were interviewed. The author concludes, "The reason for this unfortunate concentration upon individual types of recreation in farm areas is not in any lack of enthusiasm of farm youth for group recreational activities . . . these farm youths are keenly conscious of the paucity of community facilities for social recreation. They take their fun alone or in pairs, not because they prefer it, but because it is so often the only thing to do."

Maryland is a highly urbanized and densely populated state. If this condition exists there it is likely that social participation of farm youth in most of the nation is even more limited.

age. The Thurow study touches on this point. Of the girls interviewed it was found that a much higher percentage of the farm and nonfarm girls than of the village girls felt ill at ease when among their contemporaries.[1]

[1] Mildred B. Thurow, "Interests, Activities, and Problems of Rural Young Folk," *Cornell Agricultural Experment Station Bulletin* 617, Ithaca, N. Y. 1934, p. 43, finds that 14.8 per cent of farm girls, 17.4 per cent of nonfarm girls, and 6.4 per cent of village girls reported that they never felt at ease in their own age group.

A considerable proportion of rural youth eventually find a place in urban vocations; some of the most remote and isolated areas feed the highest percentage of their youth to the large city. Under such circumstances it seems probable that the socializing processes as they operate in more isolated rural communities are a handicap and that many rural children experience extreme culture shock in the transition to urban culture. A person who has spent his childhood and youth exclusively in intimate primary groups is likely to have little appreciation of relationships in an impersonal secondary group. For this reason he is hindered in functioning in large cooperative undertakings and in working with others in joint enterprises. The eccentricity and selfishness of which he is sometimes accused are frequently a result of his lack of understanding of the character of broader group relationships rather than of any desire to be obstinate or selfish. It would seem desirable that considerable attention be given to the improvement of the social experience of rural children especially in more isolated areas.

Social experience is enriched through consolidated schools[1] and through youth organizations like the 4-H Club and the Future Farmers of America, and personality traits are developed which provide a foundation for adjustment to the secondary group. Much personality conflict could be avoided if all farm youths had experience in such organizations.[2]

W. I. Thomas, in his study, *The Unadjusted Girl*, shows that, in leaving the primary group to seek larger opportunities elsewhere, youth become detached from the family and community and in the transition often lose their old loyalty to former standards. Entering a more complex environment where new behavior definitions exist, personality disorganization may ensue; revolt may take place; self-centered desires may find expression; the old system of life may even be repudiated in the haste to find a place in the new.

Inflexibility of Personality.—Educators often cite as one of the chief aims of education, the preparing of the child for a world of social change in which he must make adjustments with facility. Certainly some preparation for change is imperative in the modern world. An urban child, passing from one group to another, may develop something of a culture consciousness, an awareness that groups differ in their manner of life; he may absorb the patterns of more than one group and face the necessity of adjusting his personal outlook to all of them. No doubt he suffers more personality conflict than the farm child of limited experience, but even so when the time comes for him to leave the

---

[1] Consolidated schools probably are the chief hope for a broader basis for conditioning the rural child. Dwight Sanderson suggests that they are also the hope for the focus of the new community life. See his "Criteria of Rural Community Formation," *Rural Sociology*, vol. 3, pp. 373–384, December, 1938.

[2] See Weber H. Peterson, "An Appraisal of 4-H Club Benefits," *Rural Sociology*, vol. 3, pp. 303–308, September, 1938.

family group he likely is better prepared to face the diversity of experience that awaits him.

Children in the farm community usually grow up with a well-defined sense of right and wrong and acquire a knowledge of the way people should behave; urban children often do not have such definite moral ideas. Sometimes the country child reared too strictly is moved to revolt later in life, occasionally with disastrous consequences. When family and neighborhood pressures are relaxed, he may engage in extreme forms of behavior.

The weakness of the urban environment, in contrast, is that it so hinders the development of definite patterns that none may be formed. Because the child experiences so much diversity, he is unable to organize a system of life for himself. If born in a slum environment where gang patterns predominate, where family patterns are weak, and where neighborhood controls are absent, he is as likely to acquire the patterns of the gang as those of the family, church, or school.

A TEST OF EFFECTIVE SOCIALIZATION

A pragmatic test of socialization influences, of their effectiveness or lack of it, comes when the individual faces life situations on his own. Most people encounter these situations first during the adolescent period when they begin to shift from the family group to membership in higher educational institutions or occupational groups. How well do farm youth meet these problems as compared to youth from other sectors in our society? This is a pertinent question, for in its answer lies the core of the rural youth problem as well as the test of the effectiveness of the socialization experiences by which the personality of the farm child is built. At various points later in this book, aspects of the youth problem are presented and answers sought.[1] The problem is one that requires more extensive study and thought than have yet been given to it.

The ultimate effects of rural socialization on adult adjustment are unknown. Difficult adjustments in childhood and youth may strengthen character and build confidence. Even feelings of inferiority, though painful at the time they are experienced, may lead to compensation; that is, overreaction in an attempt to gain recognition, driving individuals to greater achievement than that attained by those who never sense inferiority.[2]

It seems logical to conclude that although a completely ideal situation for socializing personality cannot be visualized, it is to be found neither in the isolated farm neighborhood nor in the cosmopolitan community. There are

[1] Chap. 26 deals extensively with many aspects of the youth problem.

[2] This is according to Alfred Adler's "individual psychology." For a brief popular statement of his views, see *The Science of Living*, Greenberg: Publisher, Inc., New York. 1929.

undoubtedly many rural communities at the present time which, because of enriched experience made possible by consolidated schools, effective social organizations, and numerous contacts with town and city, offer a nearly ideal environment for the formation of personality. Many farm communities, however, face the necessity of providing a broader experience base for the building of personality in order that the child may be better prepared to function in the varied relationships of a dynamic social order. Herein lies a challenge to the wide-awake rural leader who has sufficient foresight to help youth stake out future goals and prepare for them, but who at the same time has sufficient appreciation of values inherent in rural culture to retain many of them rather than debunking them in a wholesale fashion.

QUESTIONS FOR REVIEW AND DISCUSSION

1. Explain the part of group experience in the formation of personality.

2. Explain why the degree of isolation of the farm family tends to determine the importance of the family in molding personality.

3. Summarize the important findings of the Baldwin study on socializing influences most effective in the experience of the farm child.

4. What did the White House Conference Report show with regard to differences in social experience of farm and city children?

5. What factors in rural life tend to develop a "mature realism" in the child?

6. Can one be sure that successful adjustment in childhood will prepare one for successful adjustment in youth and adult life? Explain.

7. What are some of the advantages of limited social participation?

8. Is a changing environment or a stable one more conducive to developing a sense of security and assurance in the child?

9. Explain why nature forces have an important disciplinary effect on the farm child.

10. Do you think that close association with life, death, birth, and other natural influences is an advantage or a disadvantage to the child?

11. What factors in the rural one-room school environment are conductive to the development of resourcefulness? in the play environment of the farm child?

12. Cite evidence showing that the social participation of the farm child and youth may be too limited for normal personality development.

13. Which environment, rural or urban, seems to prepare the child better for living in a changing world?

14. What is the final test of effective socialization? What environment or environments seem to meet this test most adequately?

COLLATERAL READING

Baldwin, Bird T., Eva A. Fillmore, and Lora Hadley: *Farm Children*, D. Appleton-Century Company, Inc., New York, 1930.

Hoffer, C. R.: *Introduction to Rural Sociology*, rev. ed., chaps. 5 and 6, Farrar & Rinehart, Inc., New York, 1934.

Landis, Paul H.: *Adolescence and Youth: The Process of Maturing*, McGraw-Hill Book Company, Inc., New York, 1945.

Sanderson, Dwight: "Rural Family," *Journal of Home Economics*, vol. 29, pp. 223–228, April, 1937.

Stott, Leland H.: "The Relation of Certain Factors in the Farm Family Life to Personality Development in Adolescence," *Nebraska Agricultural Experiment Station Bulletin* 106, Lincoln, 1938.

Thurow, Mildred B.: "A Study of Selected Factors in Family Life as Described in Autobiographies," *Cornell Agricultural Experiment Station Memoir* 171, Ithaca, 1935.

White House Conference on Child Health and Protection: *The Adolescent in the Family*, pp. 8–29, 158–178, D. Appleton-Century Company, Inc., New York, 1934.

Part III

INTERACTION PROCESSES OF A DYNAMIC SOCIETY

THAT MAN is a time-binding creature is well demonstrated by the chapters of Part II. At many angles we have seen the past projecting itself into the present. Both social group and person have continuity of experience, which may be disturbed by new experience and modified by it; but persist it will, making itself a part of the future.

In static societies the persistence of influence of the past in the social group and in the personality of the individual is an asset, for present and past are so much alike that the past always has a pertinent meaning. In a dynamic society the past is necessary and often convenient, but if the rate of change becomes rapid, if movement of persons becomes frequent, it is at many points a liability. The old group experience may not fit well into aspects of the new culture pattern; lag and maladjustment may result. The personality of the individual may be shocked repeatedly as change or movement take him into new situations where experience conflicts with his past.

Interaction processes of our society are greatly speeded up. Dynamic forces stir the rural setting. Movement, change, and multiple contacts predominate in the experience of the farm community; conflict and adjustment in the social experience of the person. The blending of past and present, the mixing of the traditional rural with the urbanlike modern rural, are the order of the day.

CHAPTER 11

ISOLATION, CONTACT, AND THE INTERACTIVE PROCESSES

THE CONCEPT OF ISOLATION AND ITS APPLICATION TO RURAL AMERICA

THOSE who live in the group adopt and retain its ways; those who live apart become eccentric and peculiar as though of a different tribe or race, strange and mysterious persons. "He who is unable to live in society, or has no need to because he is sufficient unto himself, must be either a beast or a God."[1] Historically, geographical isolation has played a major part in the life of peoples and of nations; mountains, rivers, seas, deserts, and oceans have been impassable barriers to many, as they are today among primitives in parts of the world.

The *geographical isolation* of the American farmer is, as we have seen, a basic factor in social organization (see Chapter 2). He is separated spatially from his fellows, and to this extent is out of touch with them. Isolation may grow out of *cultural difference*. In rural areas cultural isolation usually accompanies geographical isolation. Among migrating groups such as have populated both urban and rural areas in the United States, isolated clusters of people of distinct national cultures have been characteristic. *Racial isolation*, due to difference in racial stock, has in certain areas been an important factor in keeping groups apart and in perpetuating social and cultural differences. There is an *isolation by social definition*. The urbanite has expressed his separateness by dubbing the farmer a "hayseed." The rural man likewise has coined the term "city dude" to set apart his urban cousin. In some rural areas the line between sheepmen and cattlemen has been sharply drawn; many a cattle rancher has called a sheep rancher "the scum of the earth." Finally, there is a *protective isolation* coming from congested living, which consists in deliberately remaining anonymous in order to retain a degree of privacy while living in close quarters. This voluntary, protective isolation exists in the rooming houses and apartment houses of the city, where people live with only thin walls between them. It is seldom found in rural life.

Three of the types of isolation outlined above have been of sufficient importance in American rural life to deserve special attention—geographical

[1] Aristotle's *Politics*, translated by Benjamin Jowett, pp. 29–30, Clarendon Press, Oxford.

isolation, cultural isolation, and isolation based on ethnic differences.[1] The first has been adequately discussed in preceding chapters.

CULTURAL ISOLATION

Distinctness of culture because of difference in religion or nationality background has been especially important as a factor in producing isolation in America. In all large cities isolated "cultural islands" have developed—Little Sicilies, Little Italies, Little Bohemias, Little Austrias, Deutschlands, Little Hollands, and other areas of distinct foreign cultures. In the rural community, likewise, similar areas have formed, some by design and others more or less by accident. Migrating peoples, in locating on the frontier, often moved in in groups—families, neighborhood groups, national or religious groups—and settled in colonies. This has had its effect on the ethos of particular rural communities and on their social forms and manner of life. In some German-American settlements residents are extremely thrifty and inclined to over-value work, some even valuing work above their children's education. Their thrift is manifest in the ownership of land, livestock, and tools, which are often acquired at the expense of leisure and personal development. Other communities are highly progressive because of a national ethos which calls for education and enlightenment, and place these values first.[2]

Some rural colonies have maintained a voluntary isolation because of peculiar customs which they wish to preserve. The Hutterites, the Mennonites, the Ikronians, the Oneida group, and the Amana Society are examples. The Amana Society may be used as a type. This group of German origin migrated to the United States in 1842, settling first in Erie County, New York, and later, as land became scarce, moving to its present location in Iowa, where it acquired a tract of 26,000 acres of farm land. Here the members were able to perpetuate not only their religion but also their communistic philosophy and German customs. In Iowa they developed a fairly self-sufficient, communistic economy but eventually began to center their efforts on the weaving of woolen cloth. Entering the commercial market, the society became famous for the manufacture of the Amana woolen blanket. It survived with remarkable success as a communistic venture in a capitalistic order until the advent of the automobile and paved highway. But as numerous curious spectators from the outside appeared on the scene, youths in the colony began to assimilate new ideas. Then too, the selling of woolen goods had placed the colony on a commercial footing; it was operating on the one hand as a communistic order

[1] Chap. 18 is given to social differentiation, which is the process involved in isolation by social definition.

[2] For a contrast of German-American and Danish-Holland-Quaker communities in Iowa see Bird T. Baldwin, *et al.*, *Farm Children*, chaps. 2 and 3, D. Appleton-Century Company, Inc., New York, 1930.

which divided its goods equally among its members, and on the other, as a capitalistic unit competing in the open market with other manufactured goods. These combined influences led the colony in 1932 to disband as a communistic society and to incorporate as a capitalistic corporation, each worker being given shares on the basis of the number of years he had worked in the community, his returns thereafter to be in interest on the shares which he owned and in wages for work which he performed. Had the Amana colony been established in an isolated mountain region, it undoubtedly could have perpetuated its cultural differences for a much longer time.

The effect of the cultural factor in isolating a people and hindering their assimilation of outside culture, *i.e.*, their acculturation, is well illustrated by the French Acadians. Smith and Parenton studying their culture in Louisiana describe not only the resistance of this group to outside cultures, but its power to assimilate outsiders whose culture is less integrated.

Settled at long last in a peaceful abode—Spanish Louisiana—the Acadians began in earnest to transform their new habitat into a second *Acadie*, in customs as well as in all phases of their culture. In the course of time original French and Spanish settlers began marrying Acadian maidens. From 1820 on, various Anglo-Saxon elements settled along the bayous of south Louisiana and a number of them also married Acadian girls. Now, the offspring resulting from these marriages were, in practically all instances, thoroughly indoctrinated with the culture of their Acadian mother in language, religious beliefs, amusements, food habits, as well as various other forms of social interactions indigenous to this group. So thorough was this process of cultural inculcation, assimilation, and absorption of all the extraneous human element that came among them that two generations usually sufficed for Irish, named McCarthy, O'Brien, Hanks, and Collins; Germans, named Chutz, Foltz, Zweig, and Hymel; English, named Jewell and White; to become thoroughly acculturated as Acadians. Today, many of these people have lost entirely the knowledge of their original stock, and claim to be pure descendants of the original Acadians who settled Louisiana . . .

. . . .

In summary, the harsh and cruel fate experienced by the homeless Acadian unfortunates—forcefully strewn, and segregated without regard to family ties, from Massachusetts to Georgia; and reduced to abject poverty and a most miserable existence—so reacted on the entire *Gestalt* of this group as to make them cling all the more tenaciously to their mode of living, irrespective of consequences, so bitter had been their experience under a different culture. Unyielding in their own culture, it appears to the writers that the most important factors in their acculturation of others have been: (1) the intermarriage of the Acadian and the French maidens with the males who constituted the bulk of the newcomers; (2) the dominance of the Acadian mother in all matters pertaining to the child, the mothers' thorough inculcation of the offspring with all phases of Acadian culture; (3) the tremendous influence and control of the French Catholic priest over his parishioners; and (4) the *esprit de corps* of the French-speaking people which engendered imitation. Finally, (5) the way of life of these people, animated with *la joie de vivre*, is—as expressed in the saying of a recently acultured Anglo-Saxon member—"easy to catch, and once caught, who . . . wants to change?"[1]

In less extreme form, culture groups have been important in other parts of rural America. Members of German communities, for example, have for a time spoken chiefly the language of the fatherland, parents going so far as to punish children for speaking English; church services in the German language have persisted until the second or third generation came to their majority and assumed control. Often neighborhoods have been divided by having been settled by two or more nationality groups with distinct cultures.

In most parts of rural America, as in the city, unique culture groups are yielding to the influence of forces of Americanization.

THE RACIAL FACTOR IN ISOLATION

These Sabines (of rural Louisiana) are considered locally as a hybrid of three races; *i.e.*, Indians, Negroes, and whites, with the three racial elements predominating in the order named.

Rejected by the white society and unwilling to fraternize with the Negroes, the Sabines stand aloof—an endogamous group—suspended, so to speak, between two social worlds, reflecting in their lives the tragedy of a people doomed to racial isolation.[2]

Usually where two races inhabit a common environment, whether urban or rural, there is a tendency for artificial marks of distinction to appear and social devices are created for keeping the races at arm's length. The most prominent development of this character in America was the plantation-slave society of the deep South, where a system of social stratification developed leading to an artificial separation of the races. Stratification found expression in numerous customs defining the situations in which the races could have contact, and also in discriminatory legislation such as antiintermarriage laws, segregation ordinances, and voting restrictions.

On the frontier the Indian and the white clashed, and there was considerable bloodshed before the Indian was dispossessed of his lands; once subdued, he caused little further trouble. Because the Indian's was a stone-age, hunting culture, he has never offered competition in agriculture or in industry and his isolation from the white has been of no particular significance to American agriculture.

On the West Coast the Oriental created a rural problem which led to isolation and also to discrimination. State laws restricting ownership of land by Japanese and national legislation putting severe limitations on immigration have been passed, but in spite of these restrictions Orientals found a place in

[1] T. Lynn Smith and Vernon J. Parenton, "Acculturation among the Louisiana French," *American Journal of Sociology*, vol. 44, pp. 355–364, November, 1938. By permission of the University of Chicago Press.

[2] *Ibid.*, p. 363. By permission of the University of Chicago Press.

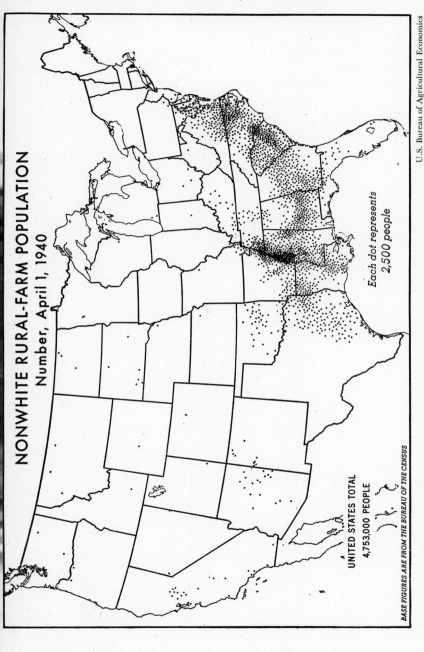

NONWHITE RURAL-FARM POPULATION
Number, April 1, 1940

Each dot represents 2,500 people

UNITED STATES TOTAL
4,753,000 PEOPLE

BASE FIGURES ARE FROM THE BUREAU OF THE CENSUS

U.S. Bureau of Agricultural Economics

The nonwhite rural farm population is concentrated in the southwestern part of the United States. Here most of the 4,502,300 Negro farmers of the 12,865,518 Negroes in the nation dwell. The sprinkling of nonwhite groups in the West is made up primarily of Orientals and Indians.

truck gardening in the hinterland of many coast cities. During World War II, smoldering prejudices were awakened by Army action, which led to undemocratic and unjust treatment of Japanese citizens.

ISOLATION AS A PSYCHOLOGICAL EXPERIENCE

We have discussed various forms of isolation, considering the factors that reduce contact. The nature of the contact experience is also important. Contacts may be intimate or extremely superficial. Generally speaking, the more intimate the contact, the more meaningful it is and the more satisfying. As has been pointed out previously, human nature is nourished in the primary group, where intimate contact is characteristic, the human being long conditioned by this kind of influence coming to demand it and to feel at a loss without it. Few people can be happy apart from intimate contacts. The problem of *social-psychological isolation* is fundamental to an understanding of isolation in rural as compared to urban America.

The feeling of being alone in the world, of being unnoticed and uncared for by others, *i.e.*, social-psychological isolation, has little relationship to spatial distance.[1] It may be experienced in the dense crowd as readily as on an isolated island, being determined chiefly by the character of social participation, rather than by spatial separation; in fact, a certain amount of spatial separation may add to the meaning of social contacts and thus actually decrease the sense of social isolation. Much has been said about the incidence of mental disease in rural life due to isolation, and many have wasted sympathy on rural people because of their supposed loneliness. Actually, isolation of a social-psychological sort is more prominent in the congested metropolis than on the American farm or in the small town.

In rural society much association demands a more complete participation than in the city; thus rural life is conducive to the development of close friendships and to the expression of intimate confidences. Geographical distance does not necessarily breed a consciousness of aloneness, especially in a close-knit family group. True, neighbors may be few and far apart, but contacts with them are usually intimate and meaningful.

Most urban association is in terms of specialized interests so that the whole personality is seldom involved: many everyday contacts in the city are either meaningless or irritating. One cannot read Zorbaugh's description of the world of furnished rooms in Chicago without being impressed by the social-psychological isolation that may exist in a congested urban area where people live in

---

[1] The term "social distance" has been used by certain writers, notably Robert E. Park and Emory S. Bogardus, to distinguish between geographical separation and social-psychological separation, social distance being their term for the social-psychological separation of individuals or groups.

close spatial contact. He characterizes the social experience of a part of this environment:

The rooming-house world is in no sense a social world, a set of group relationships through which the person's wishes are realized. In this situation of mobility and anonymity, rather, social distances are set up, and the person is isolated. His social contacts are more or less completely cut off. His wishes are thwarted; he finds in the rooming house neither security, response, nor recognition. His physical impulses are curbed. He is restless, and he is lonely.[1]

Hayner describes the social experience of the urban hotel dweller, who has many contacts but who lives in a world of social isolation:

In the metropolitan hotel the guest is only a number. His mark of identification is a key and his relation to the host is completely depersonalized. His status, in so far as he has any, is almost entirely a matter of outward appearance and "front." The bellboy and waiter judge a guest largely by the size of tip he is likely to yield. Even the barbers look at him in a cold, hungry, calculating way. The personal hospitable relation between landlord and guest in the inns and taverns of the past has been replaced by impersonality and standardized correctness. The huge hostelries of our great cities have all the comforts and luxuries that science can devise; but they have lost, as have many other institutions, the friendly individuality of an earlier day.

The modern hotel dweller is characteristically detached in his interests from the place in which he sleeps. Although physically near the other guests, he is socially distant. He meets his neighbors, perhaps, but does not know them. One may be ill and die without producing a ripple on the surface of the common life. One loses his identity as if a numbered patient in a hospital or a criminal in a prison.

But the human being is like a vine. He is made to have attachments and to tie onto things. If the tendrils are broken it is a great loss. Hotel dwellers have, to a large extent, broken these attachments, not only to things and to places, but to other people. They are free, it is true; but they are often restless and unhappy.[2]

Joseph F. Nelson, rector of St. James Church in Philadelphia, on reading thousands of letters from readers of his newspaper feature, "Everyday Living," suggests that human beings are never so much alone as in the "crowded loneliness of the great cities."[3]

One should not imply that there are no rural communities today in which there is such extreme physical isolation that little chance for contact with other human beings exists, but that such are few in rural America and are becoming scarcer each year. However, the same influences which make for

[1] H. W. Zorbaugh, *The Gold Coast and the Slum*, p. 82, Chicago, 1929. By permission of the University of Chicago Press.

[2] Norman S. Hayner, "Hotel Life and Personality," *American Journal of Sociology*, vol. 33, pp. 784–795, March, 1928. Appears also in Ernest W. Burgess, *Personality and the Social Group*, pp. 113–114, University of Chicago Press, Chicago, 1929.

[3] "The Minister's Mail," *Reader's Digest*, pp. 80–81, October, 1938. Condensed from the *Atlantic Monthly*, November, 1937.

superficiality of contact in the urban environment are affecting the more fluid rural areas so that it is doubtful whether the close neighborhood friendships and the exchange of mutual confidences are so extensive in rural communities as they have been in the past.[1]

FAMILISTIC TRAITS AS FACTORS IN ISOLATION AND CONTACT

In many stable rural communities, and to some extent in all of them, the great family still constitutes a unit for contact and association. Relatives gather for holidays; the men hunt or visit; the women cook and analyze their men and describe in detail the families' work and health; young and old associate; traditions and experiences of the families are reiterated. Neighborhood and community customs in connection with the celebration of special days persist year after year. Although migration of youth from the farm has broken heavily into family circles, many great-family occasions still constitute a high light in the experience of children and adults, providing topics of conversation from one meeting to the next. For those members with least contact, especially the small children and the very old, they are the main goal of anticipation through several months of the year. The families learn on these occasions what the others have been doing during the preceding year, see the new babies, observe the increase in stature of the adolescents, admire the youngster who has just entered high school, and comfort each other concerning the child who has gone to the city or college and been lost to the primary group. In such associations firm attachments between even distant relatives are formed; a community of interest is maintained and restraint is exercised over the individual by family custom. As one youth expresses it in describing gatherings of his relatives, "being an intimate part of a clan gives a feeling of having roots somewhere."

Many urban dwellers, though having corresponding interests, are unable to express them, for there are few large family gatherings in the city. It is not unusual, if one talks long enough to a clerk in a department store, for instance, to find that he has a son who is achieving distinction in the university. If you draw him out he may tell with pride of the unique achievements of his son and of the sacrifices he is making to see that he finishes college; but this same man finds few people who are willing to listen to his story and those who do are likely to be bored with it.

The same influences, which have wrought great changes in the urban family in a similar manner, have broken down to some extent the cohesion of the rural kinship group. The chief factor in this trend has been the migration

[1] See E. de S. Brunner and I. Lorge, *Rural Trends in Depression Years*, pp. 284 *ff*., Columbia University Press, New York, 1938.

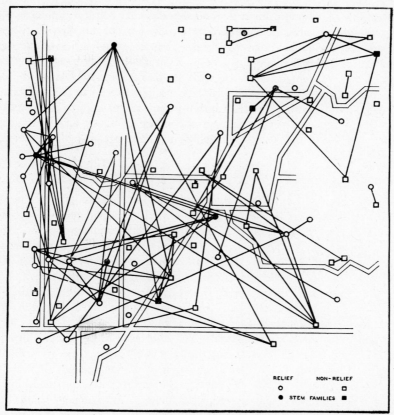

George W. Hill, Wisconsin Agricultural Experiment Station

FAMILISM IN THE NEIGHBORHOOD LIMITS CONTACT AND MAKES FOR THE TRANSMISSION OF IN-GROUP PATTERNS

(Fifty-six of eighty neighborhood families in this Wisconsin area came from ten "stem" families. Each symbol represents the location of a family. Connecting lines indicate families that visited each other.)

Familistic lines still influence neighborhood associations in northern Wisconsin and influence not only many associational relationships but also such behavior patterns as relief acceptance. Of the 40 relief cases in the neighborhood, 30 were branches of the four stem (parent) families. One of these stem families produced four of the second-generation and 11 of the third-generation families. All of these second- and 10 of these third-generation family groups were on relief. In this same neighborhood, six stem nonrelief families account for 26 of the 40 nonrelief branch families.

of rural youth to the city and the participation of rural families in town and city functions.

Such change has not been without its advantages. Too close unity of the kinship group is undesirable, for the same cohesions that make for close psychological ties also make for a degree of social and cultural aloofness. The family which maintains the closest ties often, because of this very fact, builds up a wall of isolation from outside groups.[1] Branson, commenting on the social experience of isolated mountain people, suggests that there may be such a complete lack of contact under extreme forms of familistic orders that the members of the family lack neighborhood consciousness.[2] The fact that loyalty is confined almost entirely to the kinship group, rather than to the neighborhood, no doubt helps to explain the prevalence of feuds among mountain families. Branson is inclined to explain high homicide rates in isolated mountain areas on this basis.

INDIVIDUATION AS A FACTOR IN SOCIAL ISOLATION

It is necessary to emphasize two kinds of individualism. First is an individualism produced by lack of contact, the kind of individualism fostered on the open-country homestead in America in an environment where "a man carries himself out to his logical conclusions; he becomes a concentrated essence of himself."[3] Cooley called it an *individualism of isolation*.[4] The other kind Cooley labeled *functional individualism*. This is an individualism of choice and comes from participating in a diversified social world. It is functional in the sense that it has a useful place in a society of specialized groups, for it represents the development of special capacities.[5]

Urban living develops functional types, the trend of personality development taking more directions in urban than in rural society. Ideas or sentiments once shared with relatives or friends die as urban living and the job shape the personality in line with narrow vocational interests; casual friendships are developed in recreation and leisure-time pursuits; long-time visits with old friends no longer compatible become embarrassing because of difference in interests.

In rural society occupation and social function both leave character relatively unchanged; old friends can meet on a common basis and be sure they retain common interests; relatives can talk for hours with mutual satisfaction about their common problems, most of which center in farming, rearing children, and making ends meet. Personalities are discussed—the exploiting merchant, the new tenant on the farm across the way, delinquencies of the neighbor's boy, and accidents, even minor ones, are of great importance

[1] See H. B. Hawthorn, *The Sociology of Rural Life*, p. 328, D. Appleton-Century Company, Inc., New York, 1926.

[2] E. C. Branson, "Our Carolina Highlanders," adapted and reprinted in John Phelan, *Readings in Rural Sociology*, pp. 58–65, The Macmillan Company, New York, 1922.

[3] R. L. Hartt in "A New England Hill Town," *Atlantic Monthly*, pp. 561–574, April, 1899.

[4] Charles H. Cooley, *Social Organization*, pp. 93–94, Charles Scribner's Sons, New York, 1909.

[5] *Ibid.*

because everybody knows everybody else; every courtship becomes a topic of conversation when neighbors meet or relatives visit.[1] The most commonplace conversation may be rich with emotional content because people are talking about the world in which they live and function; the homely events, which would seem dead and dry to people from another community and especially to people from an urban environment, to the home folks are full of color and sentiment.

This intimate kind of experience is often absent in the visits of people in the urban community because they may lack mutual interests; without a common topic of conversation, their visits become merely calls, which become brief as they become urbanized. In many cases callers are happy to find the occupant away so they may discharge their obligation with an engraved card.

The influence of a growing functional individualism which has proceeded so far in the city has not been without its effect on rural association. The farm youth who goes to the city to enter a vocation acquires new friends, new habits, a new philosophy of life. When he returns home, he is struck with the fact that he has few things in common with the family and neighborhood; he awakens to the realization that he has become a person with very specialized interests. The old topics of conversation no longer appeal to him and the things in which he is interested are outside the realm of experience of his old friends. Finding himself out of step he concludes that rural folk are old-fashioned, narrow, prejudiced, that most of their talk is idle chatter about things of no consequence. His visits home become less frequent and the common meeting ground of mutual interests on which intimate ties must necessarily be based gradually disintegrates.

Hamlin Garland in his story, "Up the Coolly,"[2] describes the conflict of two brothers growing out of the individuating effect of urban experience on one of them. One brother has remained on the home farm; the other has gone to the city and become prosperous and successful. The great differences in economic prosperity and outlook on life of the brothers are in vivid contrast: the one on the farm is stolid, hard, morose, resentful of the other, discouraged by economic hardship; the one from the city is sophisticated, prosperous, carefree, and egotistical. Their only common bond is their mother.

SOCIAL INTERACTIVE PROCESSES AND SOCIAL CHANGE

Social processes in the community are to be understood chiefly in terms of the interactive forces that characterize its life. The degrees of isolation, contact, and movement are factors underlying all other interactive processes and bearing directly upon them, whether one is considering social change, accommodation, differentiation, stratification, cultural change, or social control.

[1] The writer has known young men who, since the coming of the automobile, choose to go with girls from a distant rural area or village to avoid the gossip that comes from going with a local girl.

[2] Published in *Main Traveled Roads*.

The following chapters deal with the major interactive processes that seem to characterize the American rural community both in its intragroup relations and in its relations with outside groups, especially with the city. One factor in the major interactive processes in America is mobility, for America is a nation with an unusual degree of freedom of movement both in the horizontal and vertical sense. Partly for this reason it is a nation with comparatively little social stratification, one in which accommodation of the individual to the social system is difficult; one in which social change is pervasive and in which certain interactive processes are speeded up. Similarly, it is a highly inventive social order in which rapid cultural change is characteristic. Because of extensive movement and rapid change, its problems of social control are in many respects unique and challenging, it being extremely difficult to achieve the desired balance between social discipline and individual freedom.

Although this chapter has discussed the interactive processes of isolation and contact in their possible effect on the individual as a social creature, these processes bear also on social change. The problem of social change as it grows out of the total interactive picture is one of much broader scope and hence demands more extensive treatment. The following chapters, dealing with various aspects of mobility, differentiation, stratification, and accommodation, analyze the major factors in interactive processes by which social change occurs. The chapter on social control deals with phases of the interactive processes by which regulation and stability are realized.

QUESTIONS FOR REVIEW AND DISCUSSION

1. Discuss five factors producing isolation.
2. How does geographical isolation affect culture growth and personality formation?
3. What circumstances lead to the formation of distinct culture pockets within a nation? Describe one of these unique little cultural worlds in rural America.
4. Has the racial factor been important in producing isolation in rural America?
5. Is isolation as a psychological experience necessarily related to the above types of isolation? Explain.
6. Is psychosocial isolation more common in the metropolis or on the so-called isolated American farm? City proof.
7. Show how familistic tendencies reduce psychosocial isolation.
8. Differentiate an "individualism of isolation" from "functional individualism." Which is more prominent on the farm?
9. Show how the process of individuation may increase psychosocial isolation.

COLLATERAL READING

Cooley, Charles H.: *Social Organization*, part 2, Charles Scribner's Sons, New York, 1909.
Gillette, J. M.: *Rural Sociology*, 3d ed., chap. 16, The Macmillan Company, New York, 1936.
Hayner, Norman S.: "Hotel Life and Personality," *American Journal of Sociology*, vol. 33, pp. 784–794, March, 1928.
Taylor, C. C.: *Rural Sociology*, rev. ed., chap. 10, Harper & Brothers, New York, 1933.
Zorbaugh, Harvey W.: *The Gold Coast and the Slum*, chap. 4, University of Chicago Press, Chicago, 1929.

CHAPTER 12

MOBILITY AS A FACTOR IN RURAL PROCESS

HORIZONTAL AND VERTICAL MOBILITY DEFINED

MAN MOVES through both geographical and social space. With the improvement in the techniques of civilization, the pace, distance, and frequency of geographical movement have increased. More significant in some respects, though, is man's capacity to move through social space, both up and down.

In describing mobility Sorokin has employed the terms *horizontal mobility* and *vertical mobility*. By horizontal mobility he refers to change in geographical location (the phase of mobility ordinarily covered by the term migration) or social movement from occupation to occupation provided this movement is on the same general social plane; by vertical mobility he refers to the tendency to move up or down on the social scale from lower to higher or higher to lower classes.[1]

Some writers use the term "fluidity"[2] to refer to the movement of people back and forth from the same abode, such as the daily commutation of the suburban dweller to the city. In this discussion there is little need of the term; but "horizontal mobility" and "vertical mobility" are of great value in analyzing social processes operating in rural America.[3]

IMPORTANCE OF HORIZONTAL AND VERTICAL MOBILITY TO THE PROBLEM OF ACCOMMODATION

Movement of a person, whether through geographical or social space, is of fundamental importance because it is likely to have numerous psychological and sociological implications. Movement realigns social relationships, calls for a redefinition of social values, challenges the individual with new problems of adjustment.[4] Any change in location is stimulating, for it leads one to break old

[1] P. A. Sorokin, *Social Mobility*, Harper & Brothers, New York, 1927.

[2] Noel P. Gist and L. A. Halbert, *Urban Society*, p. 115, The Thomas Y. Crowell Company, New York, 1933. For a critical evaluation of the term, see R. E. Park's discussion in *Research in the Social Sciences*, Wilson Gee, ed., pp. 19–20, The Macmillan Company, New York, 1929.

[3] For an exhaustive discussion of forms of mobility, see C. E. Lively, "Spatial and Occupational Changes of Particular Significance to the Students of Population Mobility," *Social Forces*, vol. 15, pp. 351–355, March, 1937.

[4] For an extensive treatment of this topic see P. A. Sorokin, *op. cit.*, chap. 22. See also J. H. S. Bossard's discussion of social circulation in his *Social Change and Social Problems*, rev. ed., chaps. 5 and 6, Harper & Brothers, New York, 1938.

connections and to adopt new standards, releases him from old systems of social control, bringing new freedom, or perchance, introducing him to new forms of control. Movement increases problems of social adjustment in that it broadens experience, stimulates the intellect, and brings one into situations which test moral standards.[1] Mental strain may be so greatly increased that skepticism or cynicism develops, or if it becomes too great, nervous and mental disease may result. Social isolation may follow, the individual remaining as a stranger in the new social group.

The process of becoming adjusted to one's social situation is referred to as *accommodation*. When a person reaches a satisfactory state of adjustment, it is said that he has become accommodated, meaning that he feels at home in the situation in which he finds himself. Social accommodation has always been a major problem in America because of the migratory habits of its population. Adding to the strain of social adjustment consequent to rural migration has been that induced by the rapid change in social characteristics in rural America, conditioned first by the passing of the frontier and then by the rapid encroachment of forces of urbanization.

Not only when the individual moves in geographical space does he face the issue of social adjustment, but also when he moves vertically, for one who moves up and down the social scale must learn to live in different social groups. Horizontal and vertical mobility often occur at the same time. The individual may climb higher on the social ladder by virtue of horizontal mobility, or he may fall lower;[2] or he may find a social stratum which has the same status but different social forms. Any change in social space—whether by horizontal movement or by ascent or descent on the social ladder—that takes the individual beyond accustomed social forms and culture patterns creates for him a problem.

Horizontal mobility of a kind involving no radical change in geographical environment may, nevertheless, bring with it many problems of adjustment, such as learning to get along in situations surrounding a new job. Likewise, movement through geographical space of a kind involving no change in occupational and social level is likely to call for many social adjustments.

All of American life has been full of the various kinds of mobility described and few have escaped the adjustment processes consequent to movement. In an open-class system in which every door is left open to every man, it is almost inevitable that this will be so. Caste systems by their rigid method of stratification limit, and in their extreme forms prohibit, opportunity for vertical mobility and in so doing also slow down horizontal movement.[3] Our open-class

[1] See P. A. Sorokin, *op. cit.*

[2] The relationship between horizontal and vertical movements has been demonstrated by many studies. For a comprehensive summary of the problem see P. A. Sorokin, *op. cit.*

[3] A caste system is one in which social status is determined by heredity, as compared to an open-class system in which social status is determined in large part by individual achievement.

system, by permitting individuals to climb from one social class to another, encourages a struggle upward. Many in their effort to climb upward also move horizontally, thinking they will thereby obtain an advantage in social status. This horizontal movement may involve getting a new job in the same locality without a change in residence or may take one far from his native locality, even across the continent. Under a culture pattern of this sort problems of accommodation are certain to be prominent.

Though it would be difficult to substantiate the point by conclusive proof, it seems that problems of social accommodation in the United States are, and have been, more frequent among rural than among urban people. Not that rural people are more mobile than urban people in this country—the opposite is true—but adjustments called for in rural movement are likely to be more severe. No attempt is made to support this hypothesis at this point, and the importance of the problem of rural mobility does not rest upon it. The following inferential evidence of the greater consequence of mobility to rural than to urban peoples may, however, be offered: (1) From one- to two-thirds of the youth of most farm communities leave their homes for towns and cities, as will be later shown. Involved here is not only geographical movement but an attempt at vertical movement, which together, considering the limited experience background, are likely to be a supreme test of personality. Urban young people stay in the city where they are already more or less familiar with conditions. (2) We have come to a point in the United States where more than two of every five farmers are tenants; of the tenants about one in three move every year.[1] Movement from farm to farm probably involves more severe adjustments than moving from job to job in industry. Conditions of work on various farms are infinitely varied, as are soils and management practices. Urban jobs are very much standardized. The movement of the farm tenant, and owner alike, in cases where the owner moves, takes him into a group which is likely to be more or less primary in character. It is often difficult for the family and children to break into a new primary group. (3) Interregional farm-to-farm movement has been prominent in America as has the settlement on farms of immigrants from foreign nations. Both types of settlement are fraught with hazards to social and economic adjustment because of the diversity of customs, farming practices, and natural resources encountered. Industry throughout the nation is more standardized. (4) During the years since city and farm have been in close contact, the farm population has changed its technology and ideology more than the urban population, for borrowing from the city has been more extensive on the part of farm people than has borrowing from the farm been on the part of city people. People in the process of rapid assimilation of new culture traits experience more problems of social adjustment than those who are living in a culture pattern to which they are already accustomed. (5) The farm labor group is periodically one of the largest

[1] Chap. 27 deals with farm tenancy.

mobile occupational group in the nation, and one which is becoming increasingly composed of nomadic families. Their life is one of constant readjustment under the most adverse social and economic conditions. Many of them do not have the experiential background of mobility of the industrial worker, having once been farmers or croppers in stable communities. But enough of inferential proof. Each of these problems will be discussed in some detail in its proper place.

MOTIVATING FORCES IN MIGRATION AND THEIR BEARING ON THE ADJUSTMENT PROCESS—AN HYPOTHESIS

Although no broad generalization can encompass satisfactorily a phenomenon so extensive as human migration or classify motives into simple yet all-inclusive categories, the following tentative premises seem to throw some light on the problem of rural migration within our open-class society. Motives for migration, though they are many, can for the most part be subsumed under two major classifications: (1) attractions in new areas, (2) compulsive forces driving people from old areas.[1] A major motive in migration seems to be the hope of climbing vertically as a consequence of the horizontal move. Supplementing this major motive and sometimes contributing to it are many other motives—the glitter of new economic opportunities, the phantom of imagined novel experiences, the desire for greater security, the quest for better climate for the sake of more pleasant or more healthful living, the wish to go where relatives and friends have gone or are going.

Equally important in the history of migration, and often more so, have been those compulsive forces which drive a people from their habitat, sending them out to try the unknown. Few mature people with family responsibilities would uproot themselves except under strong compulsion. Ostracism from the community because of misdeeds, fear of apprehension by the law, persecution because of religious beliefs or other convictions, fear of hazardous natural circumstances, defeat by nature, humiliation in the face of neighbors or friends because of the loss of economic or social status, accumulated irritations from contact with neighbors, relatives, or friends, relief authorities, or other officials are illustrative of these compulsive forces.

In the case of movement because of the attractions of a new rural environment the motives for migration and for selection of the destination are usually the same. In the case of migration to avoid the social, economic, or natural hazards of the home community, the motives for leaving and those entering into the selection of the destination are not the same, although they are related. In the latter case men seek an area in which they can find safety from the law,

---

[1] For a more detailed classification of motives for farm migration see O. D. Duncan's tabular summary, p. 5 of "The Theory and Consequences of Mobility of Farm Population," *Experiment Station Circular* 88, Stillwater, Okla., May, 1940.

isolation from inquisitive neighbors, anonymity to permit turning over a new leaf, subsistence in a more safe natural habitat, or security in a less competitive one. Thus the man who must move seeks an environment where he can be free of the frustrating circumstances that troubled him in the old one.

Migrations motivated by the hope of increased socioeconomic status or other rewards uproot chiefly the young, footloose, and adventuresome, although even the youthful-minded old become epicures of mild or health-ful climates and move to find them. Migrations motivated by compulsives in the native environment uproot those of all ages—the young, the middle-aged, the old—the Bohemian and Philistine alike; even among these the young predominate.

Generally speaking, migrations between rural areas in America until quite recently have been motivated by forces of attraction, although compul-sive forces have often supplemented the attractive forces. However, modern interregional farm-to-farm migrations are motivated, and likely will continue to be, chiefly by compulsive forces. Movement to the city has been stimulated chiefly by a desire to increase socioeconomic status, that to the farm from the city, to increase security.

The validity of these premises probably cannot be fully demonstrated, but in this chapter and the four following ones, dealing with important phases of rural migration in our nation, evidence is produced in support of the proposition that when people move voluntarily they tend to direct their horizontal move-ment toward resources or values that they hope wll place them on a higher vertical plane, and that when people move because of compulsive forces they attempt to seek relief from frustrating circumstances even at the risk of lower-ing their position on the vertical plane.

It is assumed in the discussion which follows that there is a relationship between motivating forces in migration and problems of adjustment. People who move in quest of opportunity and status are in danger of experiencing great frustration if they fail in the struggle to attain them. They expect much of life, but realization is not always certain. Those who move under the moti-vating force of compulsive factors and who seek primarily security are often escaping from a situation of struggle and are hoping to enter a situation where conflict will be less intense and where life will be more satisfying, even though its rewards are meager. Whether or not these supplemental hypotheses can be adequately demonstrated, the importance of movement and contact to an understanding of problems of accommodation, differentiation, change, and control cannot be minimized.

MIGRATION AND POPULATION BALANCE

It has been implied in Chapter 3 that migration is a factor in disturbing the sex ratio and normal age distribution of a population. It is, in fact, the principle influence in the unbalanced sex ratios characteristic of the American population in most communities, and also explains for the most part communities with abnormal ratios of the young, the middle-aged, or the old.

The migration from farms to towns and cities varies greatly from section to section of the nation, but generally involves between one-fourth and one-half of farm youth. For the nation as a whole it has been estimated that approximately two-fifths of all persons between the ages of 10 and 19 who lived on farms in 1920 had moved off the farm by 1930. A lesser number, however, moved from farms during the thirties.[1] During the decade 1920–1930, the movement was relatively heavy from areas of submarginal land; during the depression period following, the major movement from cities was back to the poor land from which this group had come.[2] Also, during the depression there was a serious damming up of youth in these submarginal areas, especially in mountainous sections and in the South. Migration to cities has been especially heavy from the rural South and most excessive from the Appalachian and Ozark regions, where high rural birth rates have led to an abnormally high rate of population increase. This abundance of human resources combined with long years of misuse of natural resources has resulted in widespread poverty in rural homes in these areas.

It is estimated that one-third of those moving from farms to towns and cities during the decade 1920–1930, or about 2,000,000, were youths 15 to 25 years of age.[3] And this estimate is extremely conservative. Of migrating youth more girls than boys leave the farm.[4]

Hamilton, studying the departure of rural youth from their parental homes in Texas, found that young women left home about three years earlier than young men, that more women left home during the 18th year than at any other age, but that the rate of their departure continues to increase until the 20th year, after which it gradually falls off.[5] Of the young men the maximum number left home during the 21st year of life but their highest departure rate occurred in the 23rd year, after which the rate gradually declined. Rates of departure during the worst years of the depression (1931–1932) were very low but there was a significant increase in departures in 1933–1934. There was a marked rise in the rate of departure immediately following the First World War, when cotton and tobacco prices were high, and a sharp fall during the

[1] *Farm Population Estimates*, Bureau of Agricultural Economics, U.S. Department of Agriculture, Washington, D. C., 1940.

[2] Bruce L. Melvin and E. N. Smith, *Rural Youth: Their Situation and Prospects*, pp. 7 *ff.*, Works Progress Administration, Research Monograph XV, Washington, D. C., 1938.

[3] O. E. Baker, "The Outlook for Rural Youth," p. 4, *U.S. Department of Agriculture Extension Service Circular* 23, Washington, D. C., 1935.

[4] Bruce L. Melvin and E. N. Smith, *op. cit.*, pp. 13 *ff.*

[5] C. Horace Hamilton, "The Annual Rate of Departure of Rural Youths from Their Parental Homes," *Rural Sociology*, vol. 1, pp. 164–179, June, 1936.

postwar agricultural depression of 1921. Between the years 1929–1934 the rate of departure for relief families was significantly lower than for nonrelief families, whereas in good years the rate of departure for relief families was higher.

NET MIGRATION FROM THE RURAL-FARM POPULATION, 1930-40

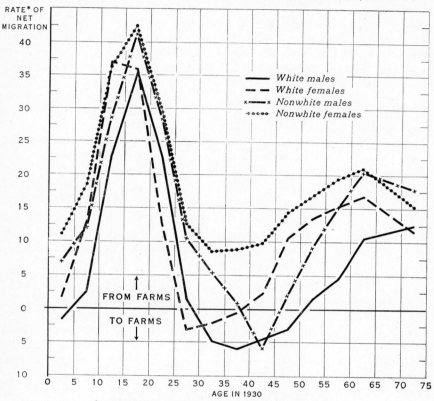

RATE* OF NET MIGRATION

White males
White females
Nonwhite males
Nonwhite females

FROM FARMS

TO FARMS

AGE IN 1930

* CHANGE DUE TO NET MIGRATION EXPRESSED AS A PERCENTAGE
OF SURVIVORS TO 1940 OF PERSONS LIVING IN 1930

Those aged 15 to 20 in 1930 accounted for most of the urbanward migration during the decade 1930 to 1940.

The age and sex selectivity of the migration from the rural farm population to towns and cities for the 1930–1940 decade is shown in the chart. This chart[1] summarizes clearly several important facts.

First, the rate of migration of nonwhite youth, chiefly Negroes, was considerably greater than of white youth. Second, in both white and nonwhite

[1] Eleanor H. Bernert, *Volume and Composition of Net Migration from the Rural Farm Population 1930–1940, for the United States, Major Geographical Divisions and States,* U.S. Department of Agriculture, Bureau of Agricultural Economics, January, 1944.

groups the migration rate of young women was considerably greater than for young men. Third, young women left farm areas at a younger age than did young men. Fourth, the highest rate of migration was among those who were 15 to 19 in 1930 and who were 25 to 29 by the end of the decade, in other words, who were somewhere in the age range of 15 to 30 years during the decade. At the peak age period the proportion migrating ranged from 35 to 43 persons per 100 in the particular age class.

In old age as in youth, the migration to cities of females is greater than of males. This is true for both whites and nonwhites. The largest net migration to farms takes place in the middle ages of life and is primarily a movement of males.

PROPORTION OF THE POPULATION IN VARIOUS AGE GROUPS IN THE SOUTH AND THE NORTHEAST

Age Group	Northeast	South
	Per cent	Per cent
Under 15...................................	22.0	29.6
15 to 24...................................	17.8	19.5
25 to 64...................................	53.0	45.4
65 and over................................	7.2	5.5

Interregional migration, from rural South to industrialized Northeast, is primarily responsible for the fact that the region which produces the most children has the smallest unit of working population in its total numbers, and also for the fact that the Northeast, which received migrants, has a relatively large working population.

Census data indicate[1] that the above selective pattern of migration is typical of that which took place in the preceeding decade, 1920–1930, when the numbers moving from rural areas to towns and cities was much greater than during the depression decade described in the chart.

The effect of the flow of population from the South, which, as we have seen, has a relatively high birth rate because it is dominantly rural and has, therefore, a population to export is strikingly illustrated in the accompanying table, which compares the age classes of the population with those of the Northeast, an industrial region that imports large numbers of youth, mainly from the South.

It will be seen that the Northeast has only 22 per cent of its population in the child group, the South 29.6 per cent. In the youth group (15 to 24), when migration begins, the South has only 19.5 per cent of its population, the Northeast 17.8 per cent, indicating clearly that the one region has been losing a substantial proportion of its youth, the other region gaining. In the produc-

[1] *Ibid.*

tive ages of life, 25 to 65, the Northeast has 53 per cent of its population, the South only 45.4, indicating that the industrial Northeast has continued to gain working population through migration.[1]

IMPORTANCE OF MIGRATION TO SOCIOECONOMIC BALANCE

The economic importance of the migrations described are perhaps most conclusively illustrated by data assembled by the Committee on Population of the National Resources Planning Board and presented in the map which shows

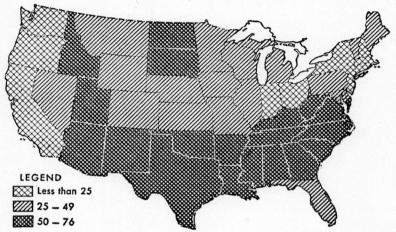

LEGEND

Less than 25

25 — 49

50 — 76

National Resources Planning Board

PER CENT INCREASE IN RURAL FARM POPULATION 1930 TO 1960 IF THERE WERE NO MIGRA-
TION ACROSS STATE LINES

Without a loss by migration, states offering least opportunity in agriculture would gain the most in numbers.

the extent to which the rural farm population would increase between 1930 and 1960 with no migration from farms. It is clear that the Southern, Southwestern, some Mountain states, and the Dakotas would increase from 50 to 76 per cent in population. Such an increase would be disastrous to the farm level of living if all the youth in these states had to be supported from farm income.

The period of World War II demonstrated the necessity for a highly mobile population to meet the demands of war industry. This period saw an interregional migration never before equaled in the nation and also brought an unprecedented shift in farm population to industrial centers, many of them far distant from the home community.[2]

[1] It is recognized that a differential death rate and immigration could account for the differences described, but in the generations discussed interregional migration was undoubtedly the major factor.

[2] See chart in the following chapter for data on interregional migration during the war period.

A mobile population adjusts quickly to cultural trends and is especially sensitive to changes in the economy.

On the other hand, migration falls far short of achieving an ideal socio-economic balance. Vance[1] points out that migration is highly effective in supplying the labor demands of the urban-industrial sector, but is "ineffective in draining rural problem areas of their population pressure," moreover there is much lost motion in American migration, much needless expense, much misdirection, innumerable problems of personal and social maladjustment. Vance[2] calculates that from 1920 to 1925 it took over 14,000,000 moves in both directions to realize a net movement to cities of 3,300,000; from 1925 to 1930 it took 18,000,000 to give a net movement of 2,900,000 and from 1930 to 1935, 13,000,000 total moves to give a net movement of 500,000. These data suggest that in depression periods especially much rural-urban migration proves fruitless.

Summarizing, movement both horizontal and vertical is fraught with many implications to personality and the social order. Much that is great in American civilization and in rural life in particular can be credited to the American tradition of permitting a man to satisfy his ambitions for migration or for social climbing. In such a tradition lies the essence of democracy and the power to populate a continent and exploit its resources; in it lie the potentialities for rapid readjustment and also for maladjustment; in it inhere problems of personal stress and strain, for human wants are insatiable and to fall short of attaining even too far-reaching goals may breed frustration. In the eternal striving and moving of our farm population, problems involving basic resources have their roots.[3] Depleted soil, poorly built and ramshackle houses and sheds strewn across a continent, betray the restless surge of a people who thought that maybe tomorrow they would move on—on to new lands, or to new honors which would require leaving the old acquisitions behind, or to new positions which would mean a change of habitat, or to the phantomlike city where men are supposed to realize their hearts' desires.

QUESTIONS FOR REVIEW AND DISCUSSION

1. Movement in society is two-dimensional. What terms have been used to describe both types of movement?

2. How does mobility relate to the process of social adjustment?

[1] Rupert B. Vance, "Research Memorandum on Population Redistribution Within the United States," *Social Science Research Council Bulletin* 42, p. 103, New York, 1938.

[2] *Ibid.*, p. 105.

[3] O. E. Baker, commenting on his experience in visiting European countries, notes the pride in ownership of many farmers who trace ownership within the family back many years, some as far as 300 to 500 years; one family back to the 11th century. On their lands there is little soil erosion and farm buildings are added to and maintained generation after generation. See his "Farming as a Life Work," *Extension Service Circular* 224, mimeographed, U.S. Department of Agriculture, Washington, D. C., 1935.

3. Explain the bearing of our open-class philosophy on both types of movement.

4. What reasons can you cite for thinking that problems of accommodation are more prominent among farm than urban people under conditions existing in American society?

5. Point out effects of migration on population balance; on socioeconomic balance.

6. What forces enter into the motivation of migrants? Suggest how motivation in migration may affect accommodation to the new environment.

7. Present evidence on the age and sex selectivity of migrants between town and country.

8. What effect does migration between regions have on age distribution of regional population? Relate this phenomenon to the birth rate.

9. What would happen if there were no migration from rural areas?

10. Present evidence suggesting that undirected migration is not a perfect form of population adjustment.

COLLATERAL READINGS

Bossard, J. H. S.: *Social Change and Social Problems*, rev. ed., chaps. 5–7, Harper & Brothers, New York, 1938.

Duncan, O. D.: "The Theory and Consequences of Mobility of Farm Population," *Oklahoma Experiment Station Circular* 88, Stillwater, Okla., May, 1940.

Landis, Paul H.: *Social Policies in the Making: A Dynamic View of Social Problems*, chap. 3, D. C. Heath and Company, Boston, 1947.

Sorokin, P. A.: *Social Mobility*, Harper & Brothers, New York, 1937.

———, C. C. Zimmerman and C. J. Galpin: *A Systematic Source Book in Rural Sociology*, vol. 1, chap. 8, University of Minnesota Press, Minneapolis, 1930.

CHAPTER 13

THE NATURE AND EXTENT OF RURAL MIGRATION

MAJOR MIGRATIONS IN AMERICAN RURAL LIFE

The movements of the American people, past and present, are important in the annals of rural society. This has always been a country of migrants from many lands, of a mixture of diverse elements, of ideals as well as nationalities, of various cultures as well as of different races. It was settled both by the virtuous and by criminals, for not only did the Colonies serve as a place of refuge for unwanted Christians, but also as a dumping ground for lawbreakers of England and Europe. Much of America's history, at least up to about 1890, is a story of man's quest for land; land brought people to the country and land hunger settled the West. There were times when gold occupied attention, but most of the gold seekers did not find riches and many, penniless, unable to return home, stayed to acquire land. The movement in quest of land was a steady and persistent stream flowing westward. Although less spectacular than the rush for gold it involved far greater numbers. Land brought hundreds of thousands of immigrants who spread out over the continent, settling on farms. Later immigrants sought unskilled positions in urban industry. Their movements are reflected in the composition of the rural and urban populations; the northern European groups which came first settled in rural areas of the Middle West; the southern European immigrants who came last settled primarily in Eastern industrial centers.

Immigration has largely ceased but migration has continued. The farm population today is more mobile than any other large farm group in the world. The first great internal movement in the United States, one which lasted for well over a century, was the movement westward, first from the Atlantic seaboard across the Appalachians and down the Ohio Valley and later on to the Mississippi Valley. The Middle West had not been well settled when gold discoveries supplied the incentive for further movement westward to the coast. A series of great migrations populated the West and led to the agricultural settlement of the country. "Go West, young man, go West!" is advice that was widely followed. In the West could be found the opportunity every man wanted. This philosophy pervaded American thought until the last decade of the nineteenth century, by which time most of the land suitable for agricultural purposes had been taken.

By 1900 there was actually some movement back toward the East. Land

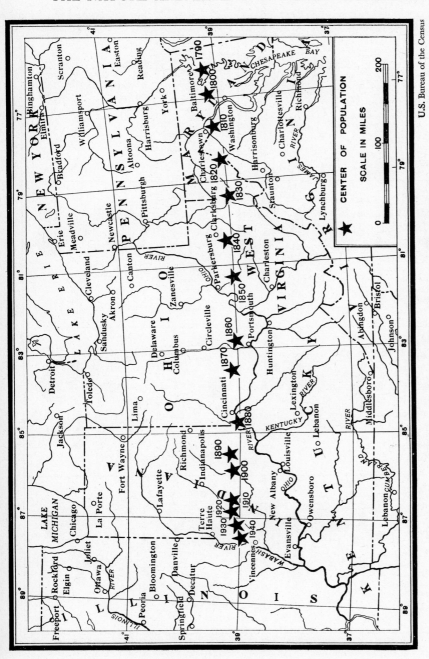

WESTWARD SHIFT OF CENTER OF POPULATION, 1790–1940

Symbolic of the drift of population westward in quest of opportunity is this westward shift of the population center of the nation during 150 years.

U.S. Bureau of the Census

NATIVE WHITE MIGRANTS BORN IN NEW YORK LIVING ELSEWHERE, 1870–1940

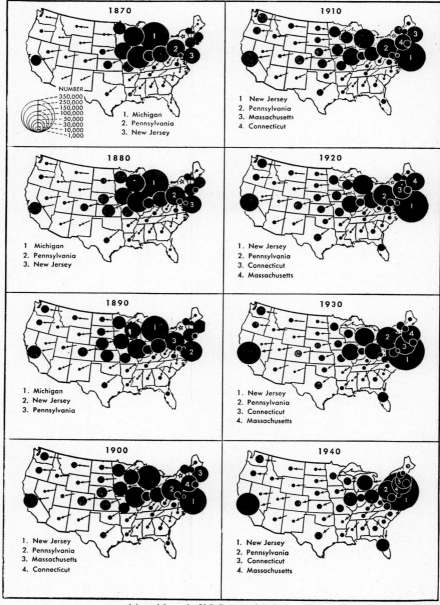

Adapted from the U.S. Bureau of Agricultural Economics with 1940 data added

Each succeeding census showed a heavier movement from New York westward and southward. As the years passed, the major migration tended to reach farther westward. This trend illustrates the historic movement toward the western frontier.

NATIVE WHITE MIGRANTS INTO NEW YORK FROM STATE OF BIRTH, 1870–1940

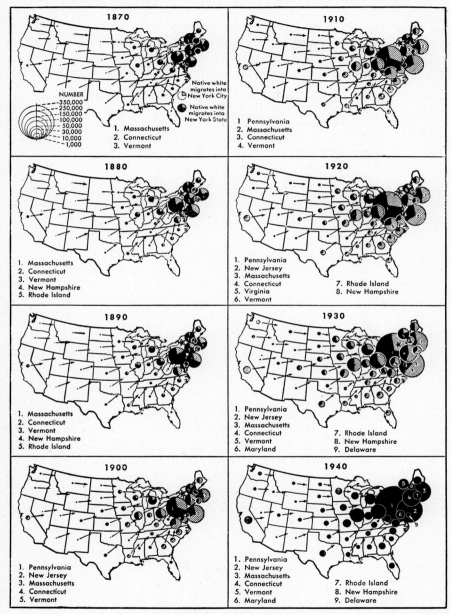

Adapted from U.S. Bureau of Agricultural Economics with 1940 data added

With the passing of years the magnetic power of New York State has extended over an increasing hinterland. By 1940 New Yorkers had been gathered in considerable numbers from every state. This is indicative of the urbanward migration characterizing this century.

prices had become so high in the Middle West that people began to turn back to abandoned farms where land was cheaper and poorer.[1] This movement was in part a reaction to the excess migration westward of 1850 to 1880 which almost depopulated New England towns and countryside. The counter movement, however, was never sufficient to compensate for population losses; in fact, New England towns do not now average half their population of 1870.[2]

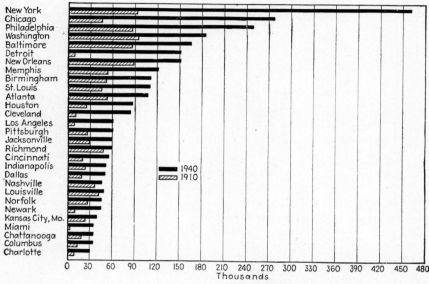

W. S. Thompson, *Population Problems*, 3d. ed., p. 133.

NEGRO POPULATION FOR 1940 AND 1910 IN CITIES HAVING 100,000 OR MORE INHABITANTS AND AT LEAST 30,000 NEGROES IN 1940

Indicative of the heavy migration of Negroes northward is the marked growth in Negro population of large urban-industrial centers, most of which are located in the North. This movement was more than a horizontal one; involved was the struggle of a race to climb upward.

About 1910 the migration cityward grew to major proportions, marking a radical change in ends sought. No longer was land the goal of the migrants; a place in the work world of the urban industrial structure had become the motivating force. Movement shifted toward areas where factories and urban commerce were developing. Since that time the major movement in this country has been from farm to town and city, from the open spaces toward the population centers on the deep water fringe of the continent.

Another significant rural migration, that of Negroes from the agricultural

[1] N. L. Sims, *Elements of Rural Sociology*, rev. ed., pp. 289–296, The Thomas Y. Crowell Company, New York, 1934, gives a brief discussion of this movement.
[2] *Ibid.*, p. 290.

South to Northern industrial cities, began during the First World War, when a million and a half Negroes from the cotton states moved to Northern industrial centers. In this movement was expressed more than the desire to capitalize on an unusual economic opportunity by a race that had been introduced to the nation under conditions of slavery and that, upon emancipation, had become near-serfs on the lands of the cotton states. There was offered to the Negro, in addition, a chance to escape his low-caste status, to cross the barriers of social stratification long fortified by custom in the South, to rise to a plane of equality in social and institutional associations, and to give his children a chance to escape the limitations of their racial heritage. This migration continued between the two world wars, and again became a major stream during World War II.

The drought depression period in the Great Plains, which was most critical during the years 1932, 1934, and 1936, the first year because of low prices and deficient rainfall, and the latter two because of unprecedented drought, provoked a mass movement of farm people out of the Plains to more favored areas, many going westward to the Mountain and Pacific Coast states. Thousands of dispossessed share croppers and farm laborers of the cotton states were also set adrift by the reduction of tillable acreages, by increased mechanization, and the growth of corporation farming. Considerable numbers moved to the Far West, thousands entering Arizona, California, and smaller numbers, the Pacific Northwest states.

World War II brought a mass migration westward, other regions losing more than a million net to the West (see table). The rural South had a net

CIVILIAN IN-MIGRANTS, OUT-MIGRANTS, AND NET MIGRATION FOR REGIONS: DECEMBER, 1941 TO MARCH, 1945*

	The North	The South	The West
In-migrants	1,240,000	780,000	1,560,000
Out-migrants	1,550,000	1,630,000	400,000
Net migration	−310,000	−850,000	+1,160,000

* "Civilian Migration in the United States: December, 1941, to March, 1945." *Population—Special Reports*, Sept. 2, 1945, Series P-S, No. 5, Bureau of the Census.

loss of 850,000 people. The North also had a net loss of 310,000 people. Much of this migration was of rural persons who, unable to find work opportunity that would justify migration during the depression decade, found it in expanding war industries. Scattered studies give evidence on this point, although the huge loss of farm population during the war period is sufficient evidence to demonstrate this fact. (Refer again to data in Chapter 1.) Spot studies in various parts of the nation add further evidence to the extent of this migration. For

INTERREGIONAL MIGRATION IN THE UNITED STATES

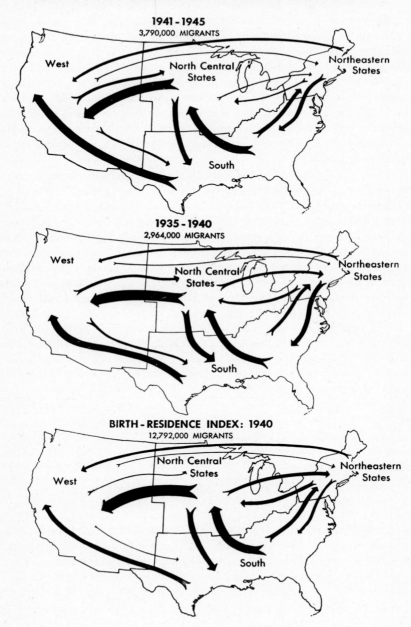

1941 - 1945
3,790,000 MIGRANTS

West

North Central States

Northeastern States

South

1935 - 1940
2,964,000 MIGRANTS

West

North Central States

Northeastern States

South

BIRTH - RESIDENCE INDEX: 1940
12,792,000 MIGRANTS

West

North Central States

Northeastern States

South

example, a study[1] of two rural counties in the state of Washington in the summer of 1942 showed that these rural counties had already lost 2.9 and 3.2 per cent respectively of their population to war industries.

A summary of interregional migration in the nation appears in the chart on page 180.[2] Interregional migration during the war period, the depression period preceding, and the further long-time period going back to the time of the birth of the present generation is shown. The predominant flow has been from South to North and from all areas of the country westward, especially from the South westward. The war period alone saw 3,790,000 persons cross these four great regional boundaries. The flow of population across regional boundaries was quite similar during the depression period (1935–1940), except that at that time the movement into the South was heavy, representing the return home of those who had gone to Northern cities during a more prosperous industrial period.

The birth and residence index (bottom map) compares the place of birth with the 1940 place of residence of the total population thereby giving an index of "lifetime mobility." It shows that the dominant movement of population is from the rural South to all other regions of the country, especially to the North Central states. It also shows a predominant movement of those from the Northwest states, undoubtedly those from the rural areas, to states westward, most of this movement being undoubtedly to West Coast cities.

RURAL-URBAN MIGRATION

By far the most significant movement during the present century has been that between farms and town and city; in fact, this movement has reached such amazing proportions that a more complete discussion of its characteristics is desirable (see figure). During the years 1920–1930, 2,542 counties lost rural population through migration; only 517 gained rural population through migration.[3]

During the decade 1910–1920, 6,500,000 more people moved to towns and cities from farms than moved to farms from towns and cities. During the agricultural depression of 1920–1922—the postwar depression—the cityward movement slackened; nevertheless, between 1920 and 1930, 6,300,000 more people moved from farms to towns and cities than moved to farms. During the worst of the depression (1930–1935), the preponderate movement was popularly assumed to be ruralward; actually, during most of those years, the migra-

[1] Paul H. Landis, "The Loss of Rural Manpower to War Industry by Migration," Series in Rural Population, No. 10, *Washington Agricultural Experiment Stations Bulletin* 427, January, 1943.

[2] Henry S. Shryock, Jr., and Hope Tisdale Eldridge, "Internal Migration in Peace and War," *American Sociological Review*, vol. 12, pp. 27–39, February, 1947.

[3] C. E. Lively and Conrad Taeuber, *Rural Migration in the United States*, Research Monograph XIX, Works Progress Administration, Washington, D. C., 1939.

Movement to and from Farms in the United States, 1920–1945
(Births and deaths not taken into account. Data for civilian migrants only)

Year	Persons arriving at farms from cities, towns, and villages	Persons leaving farms for cities, towns, and villages	Net movement from	
			Cities, towns, and villages to farms	Farms to cities, towns, and villages
1920	560,000	896,000	....	336,000
1921	759,000	1,323,000	....	564,000
1922	1,115,000	2,252,000	....	1,137,000
1923	1,355,000	2,162,000	....	807,000
1924	1,581,000	2,068,000	....	487,000
1925	1,336,000	2,038,000	....	702,000
1926	1,427,000	2,334,000	....	907,000
1927	1,705,000	2,162,000	....	457,000
1928	1,698,000	2,120,000	....	422,000
1929	1,604,000	2,081,000	....	477,000
1930	1,611,000	1,823,000	....	212,000
1931	1,546,000	1,566,000	....	.20,000
1932	1,777,000	1,511,000	266,000	
1933	944,000	1,225,000	....	281,000
1934	700,000	1,051,000	....	351,000
1935	825,000	1,211,000	....	386,000
1936	719,000	1,166,000	....	447,000
1937	872,000	1,160,000	....	288,000
1938	823,000	1,025,000	....	202,000
1939	805,000	1,063,000	....	258,000
1940	690,000	1,296,000	....	606,000
1941	814,000	1,960,000	....	1,146,000
1942	819,000	2,739,000	....	1,920,000
1943	994,000	1,982,000	....	988,000
1944	817,000	1,293,000	....	476,000
1945	1,684,000	1,081,000	603,000	....
1946	1,077,000	1,343,000	....	266,000
1920–1924	5,370,000	8,701,000	....	3,331,000
1925–1929	7,770,000	10,735,000	....	598,000
1930–1934	6,578,000	7,176,000	....	598,000
1935–1939	4,044,000	5,625,000	....	1,581,000
1940–1946	6,895,000	11,694,000	....	4,799,000

U.S. Bureau of Agricultural Economics, *Farm Population Estimates*

Movement from farms to towns and cities and from towns and cities to farms is a major migration phenomenon in the United States, involving millions of people. In times of indus-

tions were nearly balanced, almost as many moving toward farms as toward towns and cities. Only during the year 1932 was there a slight excess movement to farms. During the last half of the decade towns and cities made a net gain of over a million and a half in the exchange with farms. From 1932 to 1944 the preponderate movement was urbanward.

The first seven years of the forties saw an urbanward movement without precedent in American history—almost five million persons more moved to

MOVEMENT TO AND FROM FARMS, UNITED STATES, 1920-46*

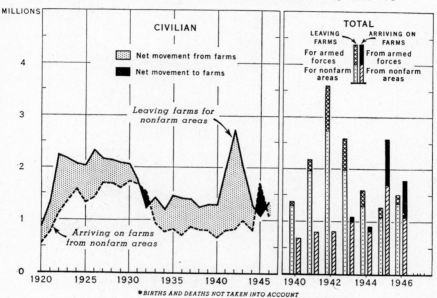

*BIRTHS AND DEATHS NOT TAKEN INTO ACCOUNT

U.S. Bureau of Agricultural Economics

towns and cities from farms than came to farms. In the year 1942, 2,739,000 civilians moved to towns and cities from farms, only 819,000 from towns and cities to farms. The year 1945 saw the postwar backwash to rural life. Thus, for the second time since 1920, the movement to farms was greater than that to towns and cities.

The net migration loss of farm population in various counties and in the various states for 1930–1940 are shown in the maps on pages 184–185.

---

trial prosperity the movement is accelerated; in times of depression retarded. Most years of the twenties saw more than two million persons leaving farms for towns and cities. The exchange of people between rural and urban areas was much less during the thirties than during the twenties, but was again at a high level during World War II. War's end brought a heavy migration ruralward.

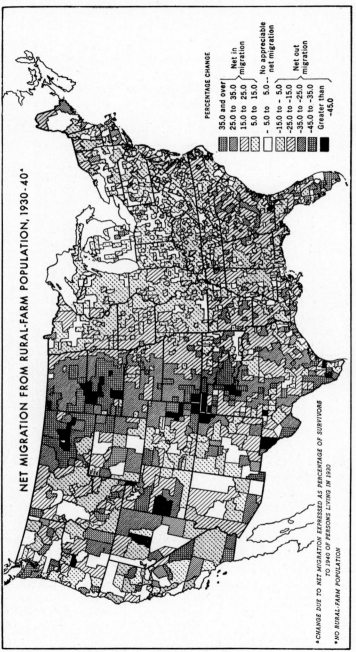

NET MIGRATION FROM RURAL-FARM POPULATION, 1930-40ᵃ

PERCENTAGE CHANGE

35.0 and over
25.0 to 35.0
15.0 to 25.0   Net in
5.0 to 15.0   migration
- 5.0 to   5.0 -- No appreciable
                    net migration
-15.0 to - 5.0
-25.0 to -15.0
-35.0 to -25.0   Net out
-45.0 to -35.0   migration
Greater than
-45.0

U.S. Bureau of Agricultural Economics

ᵃ CHANGE DUE TO NET MIGRATION EXPRESSED AS PERCENTAGE OF SURVIVORS
TO 1940 OF PERSONS LIVING IN 1930

* NO RURAL-FARM POPULATION

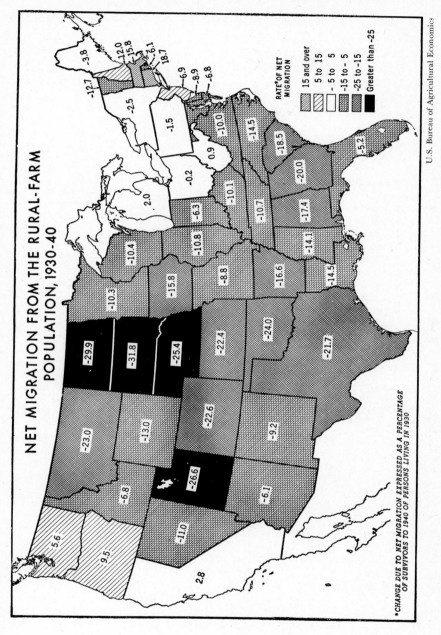

NET MIGRATION FROM THE RURAL-FARM
POPULATION, 1930-40

RATE*OF NET
MIGRATION

15 and over
5 to 15
- 5 to 5
-15 to - 5
-25 to -15
Greater than -25

*CHANGE DUE TO NET MIGRATION EXPRESSED AS A PERCENTAGE
OF SURVIVORS TO 1940 OF PERSONS LIVING IN 1930

U.S. Bureau of Agricultural Economics

It will be seen that during this decade the heaviest loss was in the Northern Plains states and Utah. The loss, however, was heavy in Southern and mountain states. Some gains were registered in the Northeast, but the heaviest gains were in the Pacific Northwest. California also made a net gain.

It must be remembered that this migration was only a third of that which took place between 1940 and 1945. Presumably outmigration was similarly from rural states with high birthrates.

QUESTIONS FOR REVIEW AND DISCUSSION

1. Outline the major migrations of the nation affecting rural areas or involving rural people.

2. In the migration of Negroes, what motivating factors were prominent?

3. Summarize the extent of the migration from farms to towns and cities and that to farms from towns and cities since 1910.

4. How have the various regions of the nation been affected by these migrations?

5. Characterize the movement to and from New York State by periods.

6. Discuss the drought migration.

7. How did the war migration affect the various regions? Were rural people involved in this movement?

8. Summarize data showing the extent of the migration between farms and towns and cities. How is this movement affected by economic conditions?

9. What particular states lost most heavily in the migration of farm population during the decade 1930 to 1940?

COLLATERAL READING

Brunner, E. de S.: *Immigrant Farmers and Their Children*, Doubleday & Company, Inc., New York, 1929.

Gillette, J. M.: *Rural Sociology*, 3d ed., chap. 13, The Macmillan Company, New York, 1936.

Johansen, John P.: "Immigrant Settlements and Social Organization in South Dakota," *South Dakota Agricultural Experiment Station Bulletin* 313, Brookings, 1937.

Kolb, J. H., and E. de S. Brunner: *A Study of Rural Society*, 3d ed., chap. 5, Houghton Mifflin Company, Boston, 1946.

Landis, Paul H.: *Population Problems*, chaps. 23–24, American Book Co., New York, 1943

Lively, C. E., and Conrad Taeuber: *Rural Migration in the United States*, Division of Social Research Monograph XIX, Works Progress Administration, Washington, 1939.

National Resources Planning Board: *Problems of a Changing Population*, chap. 3, Washington, D. C., 1938.

Sims, N. L.: *Elements of Rural Sociology*, 3d ed., chap. 10, The Thomas Y. Crowell Company, New York, 1940.

Smith, T. Lynn: *The Sociology of Rural Life*, rev. ed., chap. 23, Harper & Brothers, New York, 1947.

CHAPTER 14

MOTIVES FOR THE URBANWARD MIGRATION

CULTURAL COMPULSIVES IN FARM-TO-CITY MIGRATION

As A working hypothesis it may be assumed that the movement toward towns and cities is in general motivated by a desire to increase *economic* and *social status;* the counter movement to the farm by a desire for *security* and *subsistence.* The urban community, rightly or wrongly, has come to stand for the modern, forward-looking, and progressive; it is supposed to provide an arena for individual development, personal expansion, and a greater life of experience and expression. The city is regarded as the place of opportunity for the better things of life; the farm, as the place where life is most secure.

This fact or fiction, whichever it may be, of American thought is held strangely enough no more strongly by the urban man than by the rural man. The farmer who claims that he dislikes the city will at the same time educate his child for a white-collar job with the rationalization that "my John will not have to work hard all his life like I have." Even the farmer who wants his son to become a farmer also may be motivated by a desire to hand over the farm to him to manage so that he himself can retire to the town or city when he reaches 50—a confession to himself as well as to his son that he considers the urban environment superior. Overalls have for years been less popular than tweeds in spite of the fact that Uncle Sam still wears them. Our culture does not put a high value on rural life.[1] Herein lies a part of the city's magnetic power over rural youth.

---

[1] Schuler, studying attitudes of a large group of farm owners and tenants in North and South, presents interesting reactions of farmers toward farming as a vocation for their children. His questions and the answers received were:

"If you had your choice, what would you prefer to have a son do for a living?" Among Negro farmers, both owners and renters, the majority say they would rather have their sons choose occupations other than farming; among Southern white farmers, likewise, less than half of owners and renters would prefer their sons to be farmers. Northern farmers most often respond that they have no preference, *i.e.*, they say, "I would leave it up to him to decide for himself"; but of those specifying occupations, the majority prefer farming.

"If the informant expressed a preference for farming as the occupation desired for his son, he was asked whether he would prefer the son to be a farm owner. Overwhelming proportions, regardless of region or race, answer this question in the affirmative." Edgar A. Schuler, "The Status of American Farm Tenants," *Rural Sociology*, vol. 3, pp. 20–33, March, 1938.

How are these urban values built into farm attitudes? Many influences are at work in addition to those fostered by farm parents who put a premium on urban values. The city is considered a place of bright lights and leisure; the farm a place of prosaic work. In America we hold in special regard the man who works with his head instead of his hands, and work on the farm is primarily physical. Neither is there so little physical labor nor so much mental work in the city as many farm people erroneously assume.

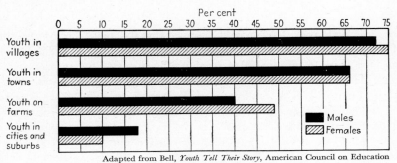

Adapted from Bell, *Youth Tell Their Story*, American Council on Education

Per Cent of Maryland Youth Dissatisfied with Where They Live

About three-fourths of young men and women living in villages (places under 2500) express dissatisfaction with living there, about 65 per cent of those in towns (places of 2500–25,000), about 40 per cent of young men and about 50 per cent of the young women on farms. Few young men and still fewer young women in cities and suburbs (places of 25,000 and over) report dissatisfaction with the place where they live. (Based on replies of 13,528 young people, ages 16–24, to the question. "If the opportunity for choice presented itself, where would you prefer to live?")

The author concludes, "Regardless of whether youth are living on farms, in villages, towns or cities, the greatest preference is shown for cities and the suburbs of metropolitan areas. . . . It would seem that the urbanization of our population is as yet an uncompleted trend. The 'back to the farm' movement may have a powerful appeal to harassed and depression-sick breadwinners, but it seems to have made very little impression on the younger generation."

Advertising flaunts before all classes the new and better product which almost invariably is urban in its origin and which first finds a place in urban usage; the ostentatious display of the more favored classes of the city creates the illusion that the city affords a better standard of living to the majority as measured by the consumption of economic goods. The rapid turnover of funds in the city makes it appear to the rural man who handles cash at infrequent intervals that the urban man rolls in wealth.

In visiting with town and city friends, the farm child is impressed by the better furniture and conveniences in the home, the wider scope of reading matter, the greater freedom of children and, because he is likely to measure success in terms of these manifestations, he is likely also to conclude that the urban community is the more desirable place to live.[1] When the urban youth returns from the city to the old home farm, the neighbors may comment about his sophisticated ways and his ridiculous mannerisms, but at the same time they look up to him as one who has made good and wish that their son or daughter might fare equally well. Secretly they wish their children to possess the poise and nicety of manner that come from a life of numerous social contacts.

Youths sometimes idealize the value of the urban world because of casual contacts which register a favorable impression. For example, the uniform and leather leggings of a highway engineer surveying near the home place may make an indelible impression upon the farm child, who for years afterward may dream of being an engineer. Contact on a vacation trip with a forest ranger may lead the farm child, because of his limited experience, to dream of a day when he can wear the brown-green uniform of the forest service, escort strangers through the park gates, and achieve something of the status that the ranger appeared to have. Even a hotel doorman or a theater usher, because of his flashy garments, may, to the unsophisticated farm child, embody an unusual degree of romance which conditions his desires in favor of urban vocations about which he knows little. Every one of these uniforms and personalities suggests to the farm youth urbanity, for his world is devoid of uniforms. In it the common garb is blue shirt and blue denim overalls.

The rural teacher, because he is usually trained and prejudiced in favor of the urban,[2] sees little that is fascinating in the rural environment; it is drab, colorless, dead. Pupils acquire these attitudes without being taught them directly. The very fact that the teacher goes to the city on week ends suggests to them that he likes city ways best.

Since the majority of textbooks are written by people with urban experience, their bias in favor of the city is almost sure to appear in their writing. Even when they do not idealize the city or condemn the farm, the picture they create of the city appears strange and fictitious and very appealing to those youth who are isolated in the commonplaces of the farm community. Often in the town school system social pressures are operative which shift the interests and ambitions of youth away from farming. A South Dakota college student, in his autobiography, tells of plowing corn at 10 years of age and of his pride in being able to do a day's work and in having neighbors and friends know about it. He traces the transformation in his attitudes and values on moving to town and entering town school:

[1] J. L. Hypes reports that superior physical equipment in the rural home seems to give the home more holding power over girls, but not over boys. "Physical Equipment of Homes in Relation to Their Residential Holding Power," *Journal of Home Economics*, vol. 29, pp. 397–404, June, 1937.

[2] Compare E. R. Groves, "Suggestion and City Drift," in John Phelan, *Readings in Rural Sociology*, pp. 172–175, The Macmillan Company, New York, 1922.

One of the first things I noticed at school was that my classmates delighted in making fun of farm boys. In order to become popular with the town boys, I began to fool myself into believing that the farm was an uninteresting place and that I did not like it. This brought me into conflict with my father who took me out to work on the farm every Saturday, hoping to keep me interested in it. But the work was drudgery for I had lost my former interest in it and was in constant fear that some of my new friends would hear that I worked on a farm and cease associating with me. Not until the last few years have I rid myself of this feeling, and I would probably still have the same attitude were it not for football. Learning that nearly all the good athletes in college kept in shape in the summer months by working on farms, I was able to enjoy farm work; however, I have no desire to become a farmer.

The moving picture often presents an unrealistic view of urban life. The farm youth in the dark of the theater may be led to dream of work in the city and of night-club life, or in the case of a girl, of life on the screen, or in a great department store, or in a "grand hotel." Comparatively few films idealize rural life; in fact, many are derogatory, depicting an exaggerated, ridiculously backward culture.[1] So also is it with the magazine and newspaper cartoon.

Movement in the quest of status is much more important in the life of the farm girl than of the boy. The girl who would stay on the farm must plan to marry and make a home, for there are almost no outlets for specialized feminine talents on the farm and few careers for women in the rural community. It is not that rural people are necessarily more conservative about the positions they will allow women to occupy, but that there are none there to be occupied except for temporary jobs at housework. If the farm girl aspires to a vocational career or to a name for herself, she must move urbanward; it is the town and city that offer positions to the tap dancer, the saleslady, the secretary, the telephone operator, the clerical worker, or the housemaid; in fact, to almost all white-collar workers, as well as practically all industrial laborers receiving wages.

Accumulated experience builds up the attitude in farm youth that the city possesses the outstanding values and that the farm is good enough only for those who can find no other outlet. There are some of the factors that have built and are building the frame of mind that makes the urban drift a major movement in America. Thousands of our educated rural youth look upon the farm as the lease desirable of alternatives;[2] even those who remain on the farm would like to "make a killing" and retire to a small town or city where they could educate their children and enjoy the luxuries and leisure that city life is supposed to afford.

[1] See Hugh Carter, "Broadway's Picture of Rural America," *Rural Sociology*, vol. 4, pp. 89–92, March, 1939, for a discussion of rural types on the screen.

[2] See Chap. 26 for data on vocational desires of farm youth.

EDUCATION AND MIGRATION

Education, with the breadth of understanding it gives of the larger world beyond the home community, undoubtedly is a major factor in migration and presumably might be related to distance of migration. A study[1] of the migration of 13,361 civilian youth between the ages of 18 and 24 indicates that there

PERCENTAGE DISTRIBUTION, BY DISTANCE OF MIGRATION AND AMOUNT OF EDUCATION, OF 6,590 WASHINGTON CIVILIAN YOUNG MEN

Amount of education, in years	4,132 men who remained in zone 1 (county of parental residence)	1,539 men who moved to zone 2 (other counties in Washington)	615 men who moved to zone 3 (475 miles from Washington)	178 men who moved to zone 4 (950 miles from Washington and southern Alaska and Yukon)	70 men who moved to zone 5 (1,400 miles from Washington)	56 men who moved to zone 6 (1,850 miles from Washington)	Total
5 to 8........	74.3*	10.1	9.9*	4.2*	0.9	0.6	100.0
9 to 11......	64.8*	22.9	9.0	2.2	0.6	0.5	100.0
12...........	62.2	25.4*	8.9	2.4	0.4	0.8	100.1
13 to 15......	51.2	28.8*	10.2*	3.9*	4.4*	1.5*	100.0
16 to 22......	41.1	32.6*	13.2*	3.1*	6.6*	3.5*	100.1
Percentage of all migrant men........	62.7	23.3	9.3	2.7	1.1	0.9	100.0

* The percentages that are marked with asterisks are those which are greater than would be expected, that is, those that are greater than the percentage that the column total is of the grand total.

is a relationship between schooling and migration and also between schooling and distance of migration. It was found that with an increase of education a corresponding increase came in the proportion of young people who left their home counties. Less than half as many youth with only elementary-school education as of those with 4 or more years of college left the home county. (See table.) It will be seen that 25.7 per cent of the young men with 5 to 8 years of schooling and 58.9 per cent of those with 16 to 22 years of schooling were living outside the county of their parental residence after an average of 5 years

[1] Katherine H. Day and Paul H. Landis, "Education and Distance of Migration of Youth," Scientific Paper No. 637, Washington Agricultural Experiment Stations, published in *The Elementary School Journal*, vol. 46, pp. 200–208, December, 1945.

out of school. Of the young women, 32.0 per cent with 5 to 8 years of schooling and 64.4 per cent of those with 16 to 22 years of schooling were living elsewhere. (See second table.)

This same study also shows that generally the more education the youth has, the greater the distance he is likely to migrate from the parental home.

PERCENTAGE DISTRIBUTION, BY DISTANCE OF MIGRATION AND AMOUNT OF EDUCATION, OF 6,771 WASHINGTON CIVILIAN YOUNG WOMEN

Amount of education, years	4,173 women who remained in zone 1 (county of parental residence)	2,019 women who moved to zone 2 (other counties in Washington)	385 women who moved to zone 3 (475 miles from Washington)	114 women who moved to zone 4 (950 miles from Washington and southern Alaska and Yukon)	67 women who moved to zone 5 (1,400 miles from Washington)	13 women who moved to zone 6 (1,850 miles from Washington)	Total
5 to 8........	68.0*	26.5	3.7	1.5	0.4	...	100.1
9 to 11......	63.9*	28.8	4.1	2.3*	0.8	0.1	100.0
12...........	63.3*	28.5	5.5	1.6	0.9	0.2	100.0
13 to 15......	53.2	34.8*	8.9*	0.8	1.9*	0.4*	100.0
16 to 22......	35.6	46.7*	11.9*	3.1*	1.9*	0.8*	100.0
Percentage of all migrant women.....	61.6	29.8	5.7	1.7	1.0	0.2	100.0

* The percentages that are marked with asterisks are those which are greater than would be expected, that is, those that are greater than the percentage that the column total is of the grand total.

The relationship was more striking for young men than women, as young women, regardless of the amount of education, were likely to remain in the home state.

This study does not break down the sample into urban and rural classifications but it seems likely that the rural group is no exception to the findings reported above. It is even possible that further study by residential classifications will show that education is a more deterministic factor in migration from the home area for rural than for urban youth. Other data, dealing with the educational selectivity of those leaving the rural community, reported later in this chapter, suggest that the more educated rural youth is the one who feels most strongly the pushes and pulls which lead to migration in quest of social and economic status.

A nation-wide study[1] of the relationship of mobility to education more recently reported, also found a consistent relationship between years of schooling completed and migration, with those having the most education being more mobile. Distance of migration was also related to education, those with most education moving the greater distances. Almost a third of the college graduates studied moved to a noncontiguous state, but of those who were noncollege, with less than five years schooling, only one-seventh moved. It is

PER CENT IN MOBILITY CLASS

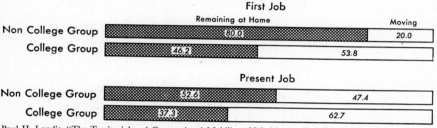

Paul H. Landis, "The Territorial and Occupational Mobility of Washington Youth," Washington Agricultural Experiment Stations Bulletin 449, July, 1944

At the time of obtaining their first jobs and after an average period of 5 years (present job), the college group was more mobile. The total sample included approximately 3,000 civilian young men in 1942.

reported that these differences hold true for both males and females and for persons in urban, rural nonfarm and rural farm areas.

A general summary of these results for the age group studied appears in the table on page 194.[2]

The relationship between education and migration is one which would be expected. Education stimulates ambition. Ambition makes it necessary for many, especially for those from open-country and small-town communities where the range of occupational choices is limited, to migrate if they are to find opportunity to exercise acquired skills and interests. As these young people enter the more competitive and specialized occupations, many are pushed farther up the educational ladder and, in turn, later migrate for the sake of occupational advancement.

ECONOMIC MOTIVES IN MIGRATION

The economic motive for youth moving to the city may originate in experience on the farm. They may be given few advantages there; they may even be

[1] Henry S. Shryock, Jr., and Hope Tisdale Eldridge, "Internal Migration in Peace and War," *American Sociological Review*, vol. 12, pp. 27–38, February, 1947.

[2] *Ibid.*, p. 34.

exploited by parents; they may develop resentment because of this and seek economic freedom at the first opportunity.

Lively and Miller report that 73 per cent of 300 farm young people studied in Ohio working in the home or on the home farm had no definite arrangement for economic return for their labor. Even of those not in school only 31 per cent of the males and 16 per cent of the females received cash according to any definite plan. They conclude regarding the group who were of legal age and no longer in school: "In most cases the young people were forced to be content

Years of school completed	Total	Non-migrants	Migrants			Immi-grants	Migration status not reported
			Total	Within a state	Between states		
Total	100.0	79.6	18.8	10.5	8.3	0.5	1.1
Grade school:							
Less than 5 years...	100.0	82.2	13.3	8.7	4.6	0.5	3.9
5 and 6 years......	100.0	85.0	13.6	8.3	5.3	0.3	1.1
7 and 8 years......	100.0	84.5	14.2	8.3	5.9	0.4	0.9
High school:							
1 to 3 years.......	100.0	81.1	17.7	10.2	7.5	0.4	0.8
College:							
4 years...........	100.0	77.6	21.1	11.5	9.5	0.5	0.8
1 to 3 years.......	100.0	69.0	29.5	15.5	14.1	0.6	0.9
4 or more years....	100.0	61.5	36.4	17.8	18.6	1.1	0.9

with subsistence plus whatever else the parents felt able to give, which frequently was nothing at all."[1] Smith-Hughes teachers report that they have considerable trouble in getting farm parents to cooperate on project work, the parents often pocketing the money from the sale of produce raised on school projects, thus discouraging the pupil.[2] Morgan and Sneed, in studying 1,294 farm young people in high school, found that almost three-fourths of them were dependent upon their parents for spending money.[3] Only about two-thirds of the nonfarm group were dependent on their families for spending money.

Regularity of wage appeals to the farm boy who has awaited the cash return from the harvest; shorter hours of work at established rates of pay also

[1] C. E. Lively and L. J. Miller, "Rural Young People, 16 to 24 Years of Age," pp. 6–7, *Ohio Agricultural Experiment Station Mimeograph Bulletin* 73, Columbus, 1934.

[2] Based on the comment of a Smith-Hughes teacher in one of the writer's rural sociology classes in 1938, who said this situation was frequently encountered by teachers whom he knew.

[3] E. L. Morgan and M. W. Sneed, "The Activities of Rural Young People in Missouri," p. 17, *Missouri Agricultural Experiment Station Bulletin* 269, Columbia, 1937.

seem important to him. These are found in the city (see table and pictographic chart). Having had no experience with paying bills, farm youth are likely to confuse the handling of money so conspicuous in the city with the possession of money. In many cases, the economic advantage of the city proves to be delusionary, fictitious, unreal, the youth having been impressed with the osten-

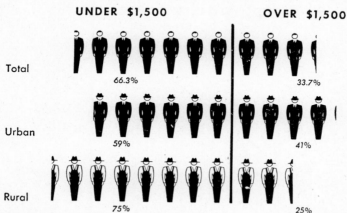

UNDER $1,500   **OVER $1,500**

Total 66.3%   33.7%

Urban 59%   41%

Rural 75%   25%

Data from "Educational Attainment by Wage or Salary Income: 1940," Series P-46, No. 5, U.S. Bureau of the Census, June 18, 1946

WAGE AND SALARY INCOME FOR RURAL NONFARM AND URBAN AREAS

A much higher proportion of workers in urban areas, as compared with rural nonfarm workers, realized incomes exceeding $1,500. (Data exclude those with $50 or more from sources other than wages or salaries.) Data are for annual income.

MEDIAN WEEKLY WAGES AND HOURS OF ALL EMPLOYED YOUTH BY LOCALITY OF RESIDENCE*

Locality of residence	Median weekly wages	Median weekly hours
City	$13.82	40.4
Town	13.51	42.7
Village	13.28	44.9
Farm	8.44	53.9
Total	12.46	43.4
Number of youths	6063	6621†

* Howard M. Bell, *Youth Tell Their Story*, p. 119, American Council on Education, Washington, D. C., 1938.

† Included are youths reporting hours but no income; also included in this table are 512 employed students.

ECONOMIC FACTORS IN THE URBAN PREFERENCE

Fewer hours and higher wages in the city are a factor in the drift of farm youth toward the city; long hours and low wages characterize farming as an occupation. This table represents the findings of a study of over 13,000 youths, aged 16 to 24, in Maryland.

tation of more prosperous city classes, while having overlooked the masses of urban workers with low incomes and periods of unemployment.

Beyond personal economic motives, compelling migration, are impersonal economic forces. We have discussed (Chapter 4) the differential fertility of the rural and urban populations. The farm has no room for its natural increase in an

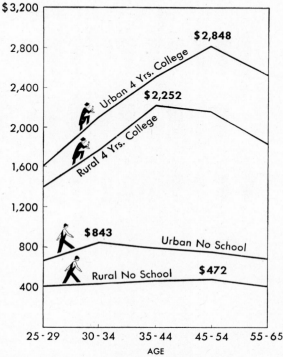

Data from "Educational Attainment by Wage or Salary Income: 1940," Series P-46, No. 5, U.S. Bureau of the Census, June 18, 1946

The Trained Can Climb Longer and Higher on the Income Ladder in the City

Data are for those whose income came almost wholly from wages or salaries (less than $50 from other sources), and are for the year 1939. Rural includes nonfarm only.

age of machine agriculture;[1] the city, periodically, has many vacant places, since it fails to reproduce itself.

Added to this are the capital requirements of commercial farming. Even the tenant in most sections must have money for the purchase of machinery and livestock. Once, the youth who started as a farm hand could gradually work into tenancy and then by thrift become an owner; but no longer can a farm laborer expect to become a tenant easily, and many tenants can never hope to become owners. Lively and Miller in a study of a group of youths

[1] For concrete data on farm replacement rates see Chap. 26.

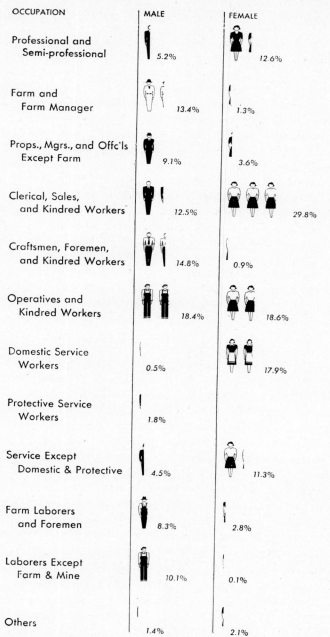

OCCUPATION	MALE	FEMALE
Professional and Semi-professional	5.2%	12.6%
Farm and Farm Manager	13.4%	1.3%
Props., Mgrs., and Offc'ls Except Farm	9.1%	3.6%
Clerical, Sales, and Kindred Workers	12.5%	29.8%
Craftsmen, Foremen, and Kindred Workers	14.8%	0.9%
Operatives and Kindred Workers	18.4%	18.6%
Domestic Service Workers	0.5%	17.9%
Protective Service Workers	1.8%	
Service Except Domestic & Protective	4.5%	11.3%
Farm Laborers and Foremen	8.3%	2.8%
Laborers Except Farm & Mine	10.1%	0.1%
Others	1.4%	2.1%

OPPORTUNITIES OF FARM GIRLS ARE IN URBAN OCCUPATIONS. MIGRATION FOR THEM IS NECESSARY

Data show major occupation groups of the experienced labor force, by employment status and sex, for the United States for 1939 and are from the U.S. Census.

living on farms in Ohio found that only 70 out of 247 expected to take charge of the home farm at some future date.[1]

Melvin and Smith observe that farm youths living on owner-operated, family-sized farms and members of one- or two-child families have good prospects of future security in that they may become owners through inheritance.[2] On the other hand, farm youths from large families, particularly in poor land areas, and children of tenants, share croppers, and farm laborers have no such future before them. They estimate that less than one-half of the youths in agricultural territory today can be placed on good commercial farms and that, the other half face one of two alternatives: (1) accepting a lower standard of living on the farm, or (2) going into nonagricultural occupations. The latter of course means migration. They suggest that untrained farm youth from the poorer homes are likely to find available in the city only the hardest, most menial, and most poorly paid work.[3]

Henry Wallace, commenting upon the surplus of youth in rural areas in times of industrial unemployment, stated in January, 1938: " . . . within the next two decades, approximately 7,000,000 farm youths will mature with virtually no prospect of finding land to farm or even steady employment as agricultural laborers."[4]

INDIVIDUALISTIC MOTIVES

In addition to economic factors there are various personal motives which enter into the movement from the farm. Sickness of middle-aged and older people sends them to the town where they can have better care or easier or less work, or work less subject to the whims of weather. The farm youth in poor health may be educated for a vocation requiring less strenuous physical exertion than farming. Sometimes parents take the attitude that their children are too good for the farm and should go to the city where there is a chance to exercise their talents. Frequently they hold that the farm is no place for a girl since what they consider eligible young men are lacking, or the girl of her own accord may become an urban-career seeker or look for better opportunities for marriage in the city.

While there are no doubt many who do increase their marriage prospects by urbanward migration, the young woman moving urbanward is taking herself from the area where men of marriageable age are plentiful and locating

[1] C. E. Lively and L. J. Miller, *op. cit.*, p. 6.

[2] Bruce L. Melvin and E. N. Smith, *Rural Youth: Their Situation and Prospects*, p. 124, Works Progress Administration Research Monograph XV, Washington, 1938. For a complete summary of this problem, see their chap. 2.

[3] *Ibid.*, p. xv.

[4] *Rural Relief Needs*, p. 8, from a press release covering the statement by Henry A. Wallace, then Secretary of Agriculture, before the Hearings of the Special Senate Committee to Investigate Unemployment and Relief, Jan. 11, 1938.

where there is the most severe competition for men of marriageable age, for we have seen (Chapter 3) that cities in general have a high proportion of young women in marriageable ages compared to young men. It is also known that cities deter and delay marriage of all groups, perhaps by at least 10 per cent.[1]

There is, however, the possibility that mobility, through the contacts it brings, may be a factor in increasing the marriage rate. A study[2] of several thousand migrations comparing the marriage rates of rural youth who remained in rural areas with those who moved cityward, and of urban youth who moved ruralward with those who remained in the city, shows that those who move are more often married. Since it is not known from this study whether the marriage took place before migration or after, the evidence is not conclusive as to whether migration as such increased prospects of marriage, although it is likely that it did since marriage itself is ordinarily a deterrent to migration.

Data are presented for young men under 26 years of age, and for young women under 23 years of age in the charts on page 200. It will be seen, in the case of young men, that the mobile groups have a much higher incidence of marriage. For young women moving from city to country the marriage rate is far higher than for those remaining in the city. The marriage rate for those moving from country to city is greater than for those remaining in the country, but differences are small. Differences in the marriage rates of those over 26 and 23 respectively (not shown on these charts) show the same relationship for young men, and for urban young women moving to the country, but rural young women over 26 in the city had a slightly lower marriage rate than those remaining in the country.

College girls report that they would not live on the farm unless they were guaranteed certain conveniences, chief among which are running water and electricity,[3] which suggests that many leave the farm to get away from undesirable conditions. Somewhat contradictory to these reactions, however, are the findings of Yoder and Smick who report that on the average the youths whom they studied in the state of Washington who left farms for town or city had better opportunities than those who remained at home, as measured by leisure time, books, and opportunity to participate in leisure-time activities.[4]

[1] W. F. Ogburn, *Recent Social Trends in the United States*, p. 681, McGraw-Hill Book Company, Inc., New York, 1933.

[2] Paul H. Landis, "Rural-urban Migration and the Marriage Rate—An Hypothesis," (Scientific Paper No. 661, Washington Agricultural Experiment Stations) published in *American Sociological Review*, vol. 11, pp. 155–158, April, 1946.

[3] This point is often illustrated in student papers submitted in rural sociology classes in answer to the question, "Would you return to the farm to live?"

[4] A. A. Smick and Fred R. Yoder, "A Study of Farm Migration in Selected Communities in the State of Washington," *Washington Agricultural Experiment Stations Bulletin* 233, Pullman, 1929.

A study by Cushing[1] of 955 unmarried girls at the State College of Washington and 147 at the Central Washington College of Education as to marriage preferences showed that, whereas 34 per cent of girls with farm experience only previous to coming to colleges would prefer to marry a farmer, only 14 per cent of those who had lived in both town and country, and only 6 per cent of those who had no farm experience would prefer to marry a farmer. By

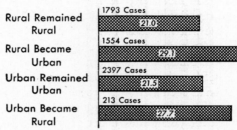

PER CENT OF YOUNG MEN UNDER 26 YEARS OF AGE MARRIED, BY RESIDENCE-MOBILITY CLASSIFICATION

Change in type of residential area is associated with a high marriage rate.

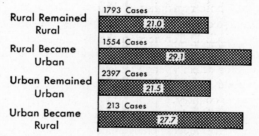

PER CENT OF YOUNG WOMEN UNDER 23 YEARS OF AGE MARRIED, BY RESIDENCE-MOBILITY CLASSIFICATION

As with young men, mobility is associated with a high marriage rate.

contrast the following per cents would prefer to marry a man who was going to enter the professions: 35 per cent of girls with farm experience only, 40 per cent of those who had lived in both town and country, and 60 per cent of those with no farm experience.

The Cushing study, however, indicates clearly that preference depends somewhat on the way the question is formulated. The proportions who "would be willing" to marry a farmer ranged from 71 per cent of those with no farm experience to 93 per cent of those with farm experience only. When the question was formulated, "Would you marry a farmer, other things being equal?" the proportions ranged from 81 per cent to 95 per cent. The study

[1] Hazel M. Cushing, "Marriage Preferences of College Women," *Washington Agricultural Experiment Stations Bulletin* 490, August, 1947.

was carried on during World War II when men were scarce, which may have made girls more willing to marry farmers than would be true at some other periods.

In favor of marrying a farmer, girls listed such factors as economic independence, enjoyment of farm life, and skills involved. Less frequently they mentioned the favorable environment for child rearing, family relationships, and health.

Most frequent objections to being a farm wife mentioned by those who had had farm experience were hard work and long hours. Those without farm experience seldom mentioned this handicap. Restricted social opportunities, isolation, and loneliness were mentioned by both those with and without farm experience as serious objections. Approximately 10 per cent felt that economic opportunities were not good on the farm and several thought that the farm was a disadvantageous place for rearing a child, particularly in opportunities for schooling. Fewer conveniences in the farm home were less often mentioned than some of the other difficulties.

Anderson's[1] study of attitudes of girls at Cornell University showed that they were, in general, slightly more favorable than unfavorable in their attitudes toward the rural environment as a place for health, income, social life, family life, recreation, and related factors. The study dealt with opinions and evaluations of rural life in the abstract, rather than asking girls specifically whether they would choose farm life for themselves if they had to make a choice between farm, town, and city. For this reason the results are not comparable in meaning to those of the studies previously cited.

Whether illusory or real in actual realization the marriage motive is prominent in much movement of young women from farm to town and city. While many are willing to marry farmers, the fact remains that great numbers, even of farm girls, have another preference, and plan to have their try for romance in the larger world beyond the farm neighborhood. If that fails they can always come back home. Some of the boys with whom they went to school will still be there.

QUESTIONS FOR REVIEW AND DISCUSSION

1. What cultural compulsives affect the farm-to-city movement?
2. Show how these compulsives affect motives of the farm youth.
3. Explain how differences in opportunity to acquire status and prestige in different sectors of American society affect mobility.
4. How does education affect migration?
5. What factors in the farming occupation act as compulsives in inducing cityward movement?

[1] W. A. Anderson, "A Study of the Values of Living and Working in the Rural Environment. Part II—The Opinions of Young Women University Students," *Cornell Agricultural Experiment Station Mimeographed Bulletin* 19, February, 1946.

6. What basic economic factors have a bearing on the urbanward drift? what basic population factors?

7. Explain why girls move urbanward in larger numbers than boys.

8. Show that migration may increase marriage prosperity.

9. Summarize attitudes of girls toward farm marriages and farm living.

COLLATERAL READING

Anderson, W. A.: "A Study of the Values of Living and Working in the Rural Environment. Part II. The Opinions of Young Women University Students," *Cornell Agricultural Experiment Station Mimeographed Bulletin* 19, February, 1946.

Carter, Hugh: "Broadway's Picture of Rural America," *Rural Sociology*, vol. 4, pp. 89–92, March, 1939.

Cushing, Hazel M.: "Farm Marriage Preferences of College Women," *Washington Agricultural Experiment Stations Bulletin*, 490, August, 1947.

Day, Katherine H., and Paul H. Landis: "Education and Distance of Migration of Youth," (Scientific Paper No. 637, Washington Agricultural Experiment Stations). Published in *The Elementary School Journal*, vol. 46, pp. 200–208, December, 1945.

Hypes, J. L.: "Physical Equipment of Homes in Relation to Their Residential Holding Power," *Journal of Home Economics*, vol. 29, pp. 397–404, June, 1937.

Landis, Paul H.: "Rural-urban Migration and the Marriage Rate—An Hypothesis," (Scientific Paper No. 661, Washington Agricultural Experiment Stations). Published in *American Sociological Review*, vol. 11, pp. 155–158, April, 1946.

————: *Social Policies in the Making: A Dynamic View of Social Problems*, chap. 3, D. C. Heath and Company, Boston, 1947.

Shryock, Henry S., Jr., and Hope Tisdale Eldridge: "Internal Migration in Peace and War," *American Sociological Review*, vol. 12, pp. 27–39, February, 1947.

CHAPTER 15

IMPLICATIONS OF THE URBANWARD MIGRATION

No PROBLEM has been more vital to farm people than the loss of their youth to the city. Is the best blood being drained away? Is the leadership of tomorrow's rural institutions being lost? Rural sociologists, realizing the importance of this problem, have made it a subject of extensive study. Yet it is a problem which may have no one answer, as conditions differ from one part of the country to another.

The migration of farm youth to the city also has implications to the city. This phase of the problem has not been as extensively studied but there is some evidence of its meaning to urban America.

COST OF URBANWARD MIGRATION TO THE FARM COMMUNITY

The Quality of Migrants.—Many of the costs of the farm exodus to the city cannot be adequately measured. Ross some years ago spoke with alarm concerning conditions in rural areas drained of their more capable youth.[1] Zimmerman, in studying migration in Minnesota, concluded that youths with the most and those with the least natural ability went to the city, whereas the average youth remained on the farm. This suggested that the city attracts both those with special talents and abilities and a great number of unambitious, pleasure-seeking ne'er-do-wells of little ability.[2] It may be the plodding, patient type to whom the farm appeals. No doubt many youths of average ability are not willing to fight their way in the city when they can achieve a mediocre success in the familiar environment of the farm.

The quality of migrants probably varies considerably with the community. Reuss, approaching the problem from this angle in a study[3] of a Virginia community which he compares with two similar studies, suggests that "environmental influences largely determine the qualitative character of migration and its effect upon the residual rural population." In all three types of rural areas, (1) adjacent to a small city, (2) affected by industrial development, and

[1] E. A. Ross, *Principles of Sociology*, pp. 24–27, D. Appleton-Century Company, Inc., New York, 1920.

[2] The findings of a series of these Minnesota studies by Zimmerman are summarized in P. A. Sorokin, C. C. Zimmerman, and C. J. Galpin, *A Systematic Source Book in Rural Sociology*, vol. 3, pp. 496–497, University of Minnesota Press, Minneapolis, 1932.

[3] Carl F. Reuss, "A Qualitative Study of Depopulation in a Remote Rural District: 1900–1930," *Rural Sociology*, vol. 2, pp. 66–75, March, 1937.

(3) remote from both city and industry, there was found to be a heavy depletion of the upper class. Differences were found in the middle and lower classes. In the area of industrial development, the heaviest migration from farms occurred in the lower class and there was a net gain by inward migration of 15 per cent in the middle-class membership; in the area remote from both city and industry, there was a considerable net loss in the middle class and a 12 per cent net increase in the lower class; in the area adjacent to the small city, each class suffered loss through urbanward migration, the upper class proportionately the most, the lower class the least.

McCormick, studying the comparative intelligence of rural and urban college youth, takes a sample of 200 freshmen students and tries to correlate grades with urbaneness, holding constant the factors of amount of time given to study the student's age. He concludes that:

. . . the rural students, with little more effort, equal the scholastic achievement of the urban students in the East Central Oklahoma Teachers College. It is the unanimous opinion of Oklahoma educators that the preparatory training of the rural students is much inferior to that of the urban students. A careful inquiry failed to establish a probability that the rural college students are more highly selected in mental ability than are the urban college students. In the face of these results, it may be said that this investigation gives no support to the theory of rural mental inferioritv in the population of east central Oklahoma.[1]

Gessner,[2] studying migrants from a rural school district in New York, found that a larger proportion of those remaining in the district were in the lowest quartile of their school class.

Gist and his colleagues studied[3] the selective processes involved in the migration of 5,464 persons who had attended high schools in rural communities in Missouri between 1920 and 1930, using school grades as an index of "superiority" and "inferiority." They checked selectivity by size of communities receiving migrants and by distance of migration. Their evidence indicates that those with better scholastic ratings tend to go to rural nonfarm and urban areas. Comparatively little difference was observed in the scholastic ranking of those going to small towns, small cities, and intermediate-sized cities, although each of these places drew a higher level of scholastic ability than remained in the farm community. Cities over 50,000 drew on the average those of highest scholastic ability as measured by school grades.

[1] Thomas C. McCormick, "Rural Intelligence and College Achievement," *Sociology and Social Research*, vol. 16, pp. 259–266, January-February, 1932.

[2] Amy A. Gessner, "Selective Factors in Migration from a New York Rural Community," *Cornell Agricultural Experiment Station Bulletin* 736, Ithaca, N. Y., 1940.

[3] Noel P. Gist, C. T. Pihlblad and Cecil L. Gregory, "Selective Aspects of Rural Migration," *Rural Sociology*, vol. 6, pp. 3–15, March, 1941. See also "Selective Factors in Migration and Occupation," *The University of Missouri Studies*, vol. 7, University of Missouri, Columbia, 1943.

In checking the relationship of scholastic standing to distance of migration, they found that those who made the lowest school records tended to remain at the same address as that in which they went to school. Those who stayed in in the same county had a lower school record than those who went to adjoining counties and those who went to more distant Missouri counties had the highest scholastic ratings of the entire group, although there were no statistically significant differences between their rating and those of persons going out of the state.

Marked sex differences in school achievement were observed, but the differential selective processes operating in migration seemed to operate in the same direction with both sexes.

A study[1] of almost 17,000 youth at the State College of Washington leaves no doubt as to the educational selectivity of migrants to towns and cities, even in the state of Washington, where 95 per cent of young people of high school age enter high school and where approximately 70 per cent graduate. Measures of selectivity employed were age at leaving school, years of schooling, and type of schooling. A much higher proportion of those going to towns and cities continued schooling beyond 18 years of age than of those who remained behind. Those leaving for towns and cities had completed more schooling that those who remained behind. In fact the differences in educational attainments were extreme, considering that both groups had a fairly high level of education. Of those moving to cities less than half as many had only an eighth-grade education and almost twice as many had 13 years or more. More than twice as many young men of those who went to towns and cities as those who remained behind had attended college or normal school, and approximately twice as many had attended some other special school such as business or vocational school. Even with this high level of educational attainment of rural migrants, however, their education was less than that of the urban group with which they had to compete on arrival in the city.

Differences were less extreme measured between rural girls migrating and those remaining behind by these three criteria. But of those migrating almost twice as many had training in special skills, such as beauty, business, and vocational school training. Much of this special training no doubt was obtained after migration. Rural young women moving to towns and cities were inferior to the urban young women with whom they had to compete, as measured by proportion having normal school and college training.

The number of urban youth moving ruralward was a much smaller group than that moving urbanward, but was also selective. Urban young men moving to rural areas were only slightly superior in their education, as measured by

[1] Paul H. Landis, "Educational Selectivity of Rural-urban Migration and Its Bearing on Wage and Occupational Adjustments," (Scientific Paper No. 673, Washington Agricultural Experiment Stations). Published in *Rural Sociology*, vol. 11, pp. 218–232, September, 1946.

age at leaving school, to the rural group moving to cities. This group was, however, much better educated than the rural group with which it had to compete in the country, although inferior to the urban-reared group remaining in cities. Young women moving from towns and cities to the country were a less select group than young men moving to the rural areas. They, in fact, had far less education than the stable urban group and somewhat less education than rural girls who moved to cities. They were, however, better educated in terms of years in schooling than the stable rural group with which they had to compete. Urban young men moving to rural areas were inferior in educational achievement, as measured by grades of schooling completed, to the urban group remaining in cities. In spite of this selectivity, the average education of this group was about the same as that of the rural group which went to cities and far above that of the stable rural group with which they had to compete.

Urban young men moving to rural areas were an inferior group compared to the urban group which they left. They were also slightly inferior to the group which left rural areas for cities, although superior in educational qualifications to the rural group with which they had to compete.

The educational preparation of urban young women moving to rural areas was considerably superior to that of rural young women moving to towns and cities if one bases the comparison on college and normal school training. In fact, by this measure the urban group moving to the country was also superior to the stable urban group. This group was small and was influenced by the migration of urban young women to rural areas to accept their first jobs in teaching.

An extremely low proportion of young women moving from urban areas to rural areas had training in special skills that pointed directly to a vocation. This is as would be expected because of the lack of opportunity for those with business training, nurses' training, beauty school training, etc., in rural areas.

It is clear from the above analysis that in the case of this sample of youth, the rural migration of urban youth fell far short of compensating for the loss of rural youth to the city. The city youth gained were generally no better educated than the group the rural community lost, but the principal loss lay in the fact that the country sent its best trained to the city and got few of the urban-trained in return.

In the exchange of migrants between the rural South and the industrialized North between 1905 and 1940, Shryock and Eldridge report[1] that the South gained more college-trained than it lost. In this exchange the Northeastern and North Central states made a net gain of those with less than a seventh-grade education.

[1] Henry S. Shryock, Jr. and Hope Tisdale Eldridge, "Internal Migration in Peace and War," *American Sociological Review*, vol. 12, pp. 27–39, February, 1947.

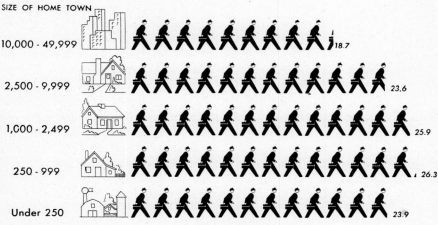

Per Cent of Young Men from Places of Sizes Shown Lost to Places of 100,000 or More Population at the Time of Taking Their First Job

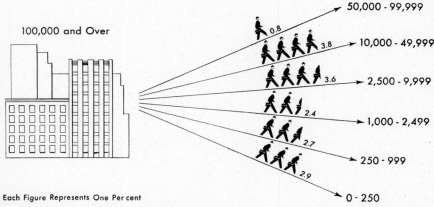

Per Cent of Young Men from Metropolitan Centers Lost to Smaller Places at the Time of Taking Their First Job

Even if the quality of the exchange between metropolis and smaller places were equal, the rural community in losing a greater volume of its trained youth would be shortchanged. (Data are for approximately 2,000 civilian young men. Migration is at the time of taking first job. Paul H. Landis, "The Territorial and Occupational Mobility of Washington Youth," *Washington Agricultural Experiment Stations Bulletin* 449, July, 1944.)

This whole question of quality of migrants from the farm involves matters of social definition which are tied up with so many cultural factors, as has been shown in Chapter 8, that it is not possible to arrive at a conclusive answer that would apply to the nation as a whole. Rural people and sociologists alike have often observed that many communities, with the movement of leading families to town or city for the purpose of educating their children or for other reasons, have been robbed of local leadership. Undoubtedly in numerous farming areas the loss of even one family deals a heavy blow to local institutions, for in many neighborhoods leadership centers in one or a few influential families. Whether or not the movement of families of this type is more common than that of families of poor quality who go to the city because they are dissatisfied with farm life, are unsuccessful, or feel too much restrained in the primary group, would be hard to say. It certainly is true that often the most intelligent family goes to the town or city to obtain the advantages offered there. In such cases, of course, the country's loss is the city's gain, and frequently the family's and the nation's gain also.

The farm community gains in the long run through the depletion of numbers in its population. Farm life has improved in part because it has become more mechanized and more commercialized, because fewer people are able to do more work. It is unfortunate that rural people must bear the burden of rearing children for the city and yet it is obvious that the American farm under present conditions cannot use this surplus.[1] As long as the farm continues to rear an excess of children, high standards of living on the farm can be maintained better with an exodus of youth. The damming up of young in many communities during the early thirties resulted not only in economic and social maladjustments but also in psychological frustration among youths who found country life uncongenial and themselves out of tune with the whole tenor of farm life to which they were sentenced.[2]

The Financial Loss.—Movement to the city is expensive for the rural community. O. E. Baker observes:

The cost of the contribution which the farming people have made to the productivity and prosperity of the cities, suburbs, and villages is greater than is commonly recognized. If it costs $2,000 to $2,500 (at pre-depression prices) to rear and educate the average child on American farms to the age of 15, when he may be assumed to be self-supporting,—and $150 a year does not seem an excessive estimate of the cost of food, clothing, medical services, education, and all the incidental expenses—then the 6,300,000 net migration from the farms during the decade 1920–1930 represents a contribution of about $14,000,000,000. This contribution is almost equal to the value of the wheat crops plus half that of the cotton crops during these years.

Nor is this all. When the farmer and his wife grow old and die, the estate is divided among the children. During the decade 1920–1930, about one-fifth of the farmers and their wives died, and their estates were distributed among the children. One-third or more of the children had moved to town, and many of those children who remained

---

[1] T. W. Schultz rates the excess labor supply of agriculture a basic problem of the national economy in chap. 4 of his *Agriculture in an Unstable Economy*, McGraw-Hill Book Company, Inc., New York, 1945.

[2] Bruce L. Melvin and E. N. Smith, *op. cit.*

on the farm had to mortgage it in many cases to pay the brothers and sisters who lived in the cities their share of the estate. A rough estimate indicates that between $3,000,-000,000 and $4,000,000,000 was drained from the farms to the cities and villages during the decade 1920–1930 incident to the settlement of estates.[1]

Farm Security Administration (Lee).

YOUTH TO EXPORT

Too many children for one farm to support. One important reason for the migration of farm youth is the relatively high farm birth rate.

According to a study of the inheritance of a small sample of Whitman County farms in Washington, about 82 per cent, or four-fifths, of the money went to towns and cities.[2] This wealth, accumulated through years of effort on the farm, had passed from the parents to children in the city. The county studied is given chiefly to large wheat farms operated by machinery and may

[1] O. E. Baker, "The Outlook for Rural Youth," *U.S. Department of Agriculture Extension Service Circular* 223, Washington, D. C., 1935.

[2] F. R. Yoder and A. A. Smick, "Migration of Farm Population and Flow of Farm Wealth," *Washington Agricultural Experiment Stations Bulletin* 315, Pullman, 1935.

represent an extreme situation. It may be that more than a normal percentage of young people in this area leave farms and that for this reason a high proportion of inheritances go to children living in towns or cities.

Tetreau,[1] studying Probate Court records for 400 Ohio and 1,100 Arizona farm estates and for 300 Ohio and 1,800 Arizona city estates, found significant differences in the flow of inherited wealth in urban and rural areas. The proportion of wealth from city estates flowing ruralward was much less than the flow of wealth from farm estates cityward. In Ohio counties, and in one of the two Arizona counties, 20 per cent of the value of farm estates went to city heirs, 80 per cent going to farm heirs.[2]

Loss of Experience.—Movement to the city is expensive because of the loss of accumulated experience. The average farm youth, as well as the older person, has a background that fits him for farming but is of little value in the city.

Psychic Effects of Loss of the Youth Group.—The migration of rural youth to the city probably reflects in the persistence of conservative traditions in the rural area; revolt, change, and innovation are chiefly engineered by youth. The city, because it draws a high proportion of youth, can be expected to manifest these traits more than the rural community, which is left chiefly with the very young and the old, the few youths who remain being perhaps of the less aggressive type.

POSSIBLE SOCIAL CONSEQUENCES OF THE PRESENCE OF RURAL PEOPLE IN THE AMERICAN CITY

It seems likely that the flow of rural people into the city may have hindered the process of stratification there, that the tendency to put on front and to be ostentatious is less developed in American cities than it would be were it not for the presence of a large group which maintains at least a few of its rural traditions. It is possible also that urban institutions may have been somewhat affected. Carpenter speaks of the rural church in the city,[3] and Kolb and Brunner suggest that urban institutions carry over the vestiges of a rural heritage.[4] It is even possible that a part of the average urban man's lack of interest in law enforcement may be a carry-over from rural tradition which

[1] E. D. Tetreau, "The Location of Heirs and the Value of Their Farm Inheritances; Farm and City Values," *Journal of Land and Public Utility Economics*, vol. 16, pp. 416–429, November, 1940.

[2] Another interesting finding in Tetreau's study is that heirs to farm estates are more numerous in Ohio than in Arizona, suggestion that mobility detaches owners of farm property from potential heirs, Arizona owners having more recently migrated to that state.

[3] Niles Carpenter, *The Sociology of City Life*, pp. 267 ff., Longmans, Green and Company, New York, 1931.

[4] J. H. Kolb and E. de S. Brunner, *A Study of Rural Society*, rev. and enlarged ed., pp. 174–179, Houghton Mifflin Company, Boston, 1940.

assumes that man can live without law. In any case, political machines in our great cities have depended for their power on immigrant groups fresh from other nations and for the most part unfamiliar with American democratic ideals. There are many factors involved in this situation of which rural mindedness leading to lack of public concern could be no more than one.

Most people in America today, even the ultra-urban, are not more than one or two generations removed from the soil; the most sophisticated urbanite in the largest city has rural antecedents. Perhaps it is because they are so recently removed from the farm that many of our urban people have an exaggerated sense of superiority over rural people. Much of the conflict between city and farm may be an outgrowth of this basic fact. A little city experience, like a little learning, may be a dangerous thing in that one may come to think more highly of himself than circumstances warrant.

Less tentative and speculative than the generalizations given above is the hypothesis that problems of social adjustment in the city are greatly intensified by the constant inflow of persons with a farm heritage. Inferences and some data concerning this problem are presented in the following paragraphs.

CULTURE SHOCK AS A PHENOMENON IN RURAL-URBAN MOVEMENT

The newcomer to the metropolitan community may be entirely unprepared for the cultural situation encountered there; until he adjusts himself, he is likely to experience mental and social conflicts of varying intensity. Carpenter, in studying the sociology of city life, makes much of this state which he calls "culture shock."[1] When the immigrant with old-world folkways comes to this country, he faces intense problems of social adjustment.[2] Rural youth, similarly, in going to the city may undergo extreme shock because of the difference between the rural world of primary-group patterns and the urban world of secondary-group relationships. The full extent of the adjustments of the average rural youth who goes to the city is unknown, but shock is undoubtedly common.

Culture shock is most intense for those individuals who have had little social experience or who have lived in extremely isolated environments where they have never had contact with diverse culture patterns or unfamiliar social forms, and is least intense for those who are already accustomed to problems of readjustment and social change.[3] This is convincingly shown in the adjustment of immigrants from foreign countries. Pauline V. Young comments:

The problems of the immigrant have their origin, for the most part, in the change he is making from a primary to a secondary society. It is not simply that a Pole or an

[1] Niles Carpenter, *op. cit.*, pp. 272–274.

[2] This was a major problem involved in the study by W. I. Thomas and F. Znaniecki of *The Polish Peasant in Europe and America*, 5 vols., Chapman & Grimes, Inc., Boston, 1920.

[3] Temperamental differences, of course, always enter into problems of adjustment.

Italian has come to America, but rather that a villager has come to the great city. Being of a different language and cultural group complicates the situation, it is true, but many of the Polish peasant's difficulties appear when he moves to an industrial city in Poland, and conversely he escapes many of the self-same difficulties if he moves to rural America and avoids the corroding urban influences. This observation is borne out by the behavior of rural Americans who go to the great city and by the relative ease with which the city-bred European fits into American urban life.

In short, in addition to the immigrant's strange language and customs we must recognize also the more significant changes which he is generally called upon to make when he sets out from an isolated, homogeneous small village community, where life is warm, personal, and intimate, and where he lives in a world having little specialization, few machines, little reliance upon individual initiative, and only a minimum of private property. Such communities exist in America, but it is rarely the good fortune of the immigrant to find them upon his arrival.[1]

The new-found personal liberty of a secondary-group environment often subjects the rural youth to stress; old controls are gone and he may not sense the new ones.[2] To the rural-bred individual the urban world may at first seem like a nonmoral, unfriendly world, in which men trample one another in their efforts to gain personal and selfish ends. But if he overcomes culture shock, he develops a more plastic personality; he becomes more versatile; personal idiosyncrasies which may have been suitable in the old setting are discarded in the new. Nervous and mental strain may continue, however, even though transition from rural to urban culture has been accomplished successfully.

VOCATIONAL ACCOMMODATION OF MIGRANTS TO THE CITY

It has already been suggested that a major motive impelling movement to the city under the American culture pattern is the desire to improve one's occupational status, to obtain success in a career not possible on the farm. Several studies throw light on the rural youth's vocational accommodation in the city.

Sorokin, Zimmerman, and Galpin[3] summarize evidence on this point, stating that the fields of art and business seem to be less accessible to farm migrants than the professions. Work in educational and religious organizations appeals to the idealistic farm child, especially since advancement in them requires no capital. For this reason he sometimes climbs far in these fields; also he many times succeeds in the professions of law and medicine. The Gee study[4] previously summarized (page 109) suggests that the rural-born are

[1] Pauline V. Young, "Social Problems in the Education of the Immigrant Child," *American Sociological Review*, pp. 419–429, June, 1936.

[2] W. I. Thomas and F. Znaniecki, *op. cit.*, offer extensive proof on this point.

[3] P. A. Sorokin, *et al.*, *op. cit.*, vol. 3, pp. 528–530.

[4] Wilson Gee, "Rural-urban Origin of Leaders in Education," *Rural Sociology*, vol 2, pp. 402–408, December, 1937.

relatively successful in achieving distinction as educational leaders in the city. But there seems to be evidence that the mass of migrants go into the lower classes in the city.

Reuss indicates that the occupation into which the individual goes when he migrates to the city is dependent largely on his social level in the rural community. According to his findings, upper-class rural migrants go predominantly into the professions and proprietary businesses, middle-class migrants enter clerical work, and lower-class migrants enter domestic and personal service and skilled and unskilled labor.[1]

Zimmerman studied certain aspects of the vocational adjustment of farm youths in Minnesota, most of whom left home between the ages of 18 and 25.[2] Forty per cent moved to other farms to become farmers; 60 per cent went to towns and cities, joining the "mighty struggle for social position within urban society." Of the youths who moved from farms to cities, 23 per cent became common laborers, 13.8 per cent artisans, 10.4 per cent clerks, 10.1 per cent entered business for themselves, and 2.6 per cent became owners of business or entrepreneurs. The handicaps in climbing the vocational ladder are probably greater for the farm youth than for one with a city background; though he frequently climbs high, he probably works harder to get there. Rural women appear to climb more easily than rural men. He concludes that at least rural migrants move up just as frequently and as quickly as people with an urban background, eventually finding their level in the city on the basis of their ability; if they do not, the second generation does.[3]

A survey of housing in Memphis, Tenn., shows that incomes of migrants to the city from rural areas tend to be low in the substandard residential areas studied, much lower than those of nonmigrants in the same areas. Workers who moved to the city from farms had poorer houses than those who had no farm experience.[4]

The State College of Washington study[5] of 16,732 youths, previously cited, showed that in spite of initial educational disadvantages, rural youth migrating to cities excelled urban youth with whom they competed in income. (See figures.) Urban youth, on the other hand, who moved to rural areas, excelled resident rural youth in income. Urban girls moving to rural areas were espe-

[1] Carl F. Reuss, *op. cit.*

[2] C. C. Zimmerman, "The Migration to Towns and Cities," *American Journal of Sociology*, vol. 32, pp. 450–455, November, 1926.

[3] For a summary of studies on the vertical circulation of rural migrants to the city, see P. A. Sorokin, *et al.*, *op. cit.*, vol. 3, pp. 520–534.

[4] L. M. Graves and Alfred H. Fletcher, *Slums: The Cause and Treatment* (mimeographed), City Health Department, Memphis, 1938.

[5] Paul H. Landis, "Educational Selectivity of Rural-urban Migration and Its Bearing on Wage and Occupational Adjustments," (Scientific Paper No. 673, Washington Agricultural Experiment Stations). Published in *Rural Sociology*, vol. 11, pp. 218–232, September, 1946.

cially successful as measured by economic criteria. From the standpoint of status-giving occupations, rural youth moving to cities seemed to be at a disadvantage, especially rural girls. They did however, achieve superior occupational and economic status to rural youth remaining behind. Urban

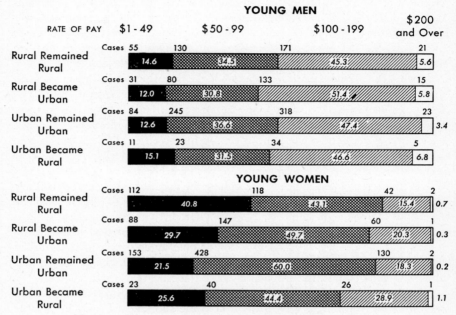

MONTHLY WAGE ON FIRST JOB BY MIGRATION-RESIDENCE GROUPS

Fewer of the migrating rural than of the stable rural group were in the lower income brackets and more were in the higher income brackets. Rural young men moving into cities exceeded their urban competitors in income. A far higher proportion of girls moving from rural to urban areas fell in the higher income brackets on their first job than of those remaining in rural areas. A higher proportion of the farm-to-city migrants also fell in the upper income brackets than that proportion of the urban group with which they competed.

youth, by contrast, migrating to rural areas, rated high in both financial and occupational success.

URBAN ACCOMMODATION AND THE BIRTH RATE

One of the most objective measures of the effect of urban adjustment on the rural person is the birth rate. The high birth rate of rural couples has been demonstrated adequately in Chapter 4. Do these high birth rates persist with urban residence?

A study by Kiser[1] of comparative births of urban-born and rural-born

[1] Clyde V. Kiser, "Birth Rates Among Rural Migrants in Cities," *The Milbank Memorial Fund Quarterly*, vol. 26, pp. 369–381, October, 1938.

living in cities, shows that rural migrants to cities have no higher birth rates than those born in cities. Findings are consistent for white samples in Syracuse and Columbus and for a Negro sample in Harlem. Although the samples are too small to be conclusive, they suggest either that urban migrants represent a selection of those from rural areas who lack interest in family life or that rural migrants in cities quickly assimilate urban reproductive mores.

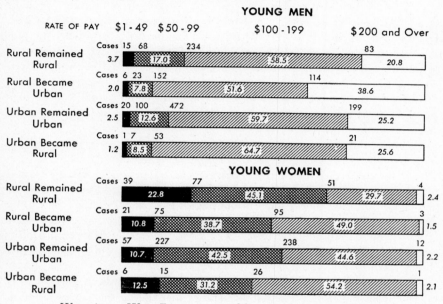

WAGE AFTER WORK EXPERIENCE BY MIGRATION-RESIDENCE GROUPS

Rural young men who moved to urban areas far surpassed in income young men who remained in rural areas. After experience on the job they also far excelled their urban-born and -reared competitors in earnings. In spite of the fact that the rural group had less schooling, young women moving to towns and cities far surpassed in income their rural sisters who stayed in the country. They also excelled their urban competitors in the proportion attaining more than $100 monthly incomes.

Notestein's study[1] of fertility in the East North Central States shows that "the proportions of Negro families childless were startlingly high," ranging from 30 per cent for a small sample of rural farm families to more than 50 per cent for families in large cities. The figure is nearly twice that for the native whites and two and a half times as large as that for foreign-born whites.

Urban settlement has an immediate and drastic effect on the Negro family. Kennedy,[2] in a study of the migration of Negroes from rural areas to urban

[1] Frank W. Notestein, "Differential Fertility in the East North Central States," *The Milbank Memorial Fund Quarterly*, vol. 16, pp. 184–185, April, 1938.

[2] Louise V. Kennedy, *The Negro Peasant Turns Cityward*, Columbia University Press, New York, 1930.

centers, shows that migration has thrown the sex ratio out of balance, thereby decreasing the marriage rate. Urbanism delays the age of marriage, and the general rise in the standard of living leads to smaller families. Sickness and health problems during times of major migration, due to poor housing, poverty, and maladjustment, inherent in their accommodation to urban living, have been acute and have contributed to a high mortality rate.

Kiser[1] traced the movement of a group of Negroes from the Negro colony of St. Helena Island to Harlem in New York City, and to other urban centers. He reports comparable results with regard to the difficulty of family life. Those Negroes who establish normal home life in the city make the best adjustments, but city migrants delay marriage. Their attitudes toward children change, since there is a consciousness of the difficulty of rearing children properly in the city. Problems of family life are complicated because four times as great a proportion of married Negro women as of married native white women work.

Fears of the disastrous effect of urban migration on the birth rate are of long standing. Charles Booth[2] at the beginning of the century expressed the view that cities use up the energy of newcomers so that by the third generation it has used up all their energy. "English London is kept up in bone and sinew and energy by the country element pouring in from above—afterwards to be transformed into waste." Gini,[3] Italian population authority, believes that cities use up the reproductive energies of the race. This tendency of urbanism toward race suicide is stressed by American rural sociologists Sorokin and Zimmerman.[4]

That urban living does rapidly reduce the fertility of rural newcomers is evident from the facts presented. It appears that during the first generation their birth rate may fall to a level lower than that of the urban-born.

URBAN ADJUSTMENT IN RELATION TO RURAL COMMUNITY BACKGROUND

Throughout Part II we stressed the relationship of experience to personality patterns. The hypothesis was advanced that, of individuals facing the problem of accommodation to the urban community, those from isolated areas would be expected to experience the greatest difficulty in adjustment. Leybourne[5] has made an interesting study of migrants from the southern Appa-

[1] Clyde V. Kiser, *Sea Island to City*, Columbia University Press, New York, 1932.

[2] Charles Booth, *Life and Labor of the People in London: First Series "Poverty,"* vol. 3, p. 75, London, 1902.

[3] Corrado Gini, *et al.*, *Population* (Lectures on the Harris Foundation 1929), University of Chicago Press, Chicago, 1930.

[4] P. A. Sorokin and C. C. Zimmerman, *Principles of Rural-urban Sociology*, part 5, Henry Holt and Company, Inc., New York, 1928.

[5] Grace F. Leybourne, "Urban Adjustments of Migrants from the Southern Appalachian Plateaus," *Social Forces*, pp. 238–246, December, 1937.

lachian plateau to the city of Cincinnati. Here are people who, because of the extreme geographical isolation of their former homes, have had little experience in social adjustment when they come to the city to find employment. Although their names are not found on relief rolls more frequently than those of their Cincinnati neighbors, they are able to obtain only poorly paid unskilled work. Most of the jobs they hold in industry are exceedingly insecure and few of their employers offer them employee participation in insurance or club membership, outdoor sports, or any of the socialized activities of more progressive industrial enterprises.

Cincinnati natives are hostile toward the "hillbilly" because of his ignorant beliefs and the unsanitary conditions under which he frequently lives. His ideas as to a desirable standard of living were formed in the circumstances of the mountain environment. Usually he knows little about handling money because he has never had much; he gives little heed to providing for the future, because he has never thought of his future in terms of an economic security which he personally must provide through cash savings; he seems possessed of a reckless, pioneer spirit, which does not protect him well from the hazards of unemployment; he carries over many of the pioneer ideas of self-defense and personal vengeance which characterize the primitive environment from which he came. Because of his intense loyalty to kin, barriers are set against his forming many connections in the city. With the increase of urban experience, however, there is evidence that he joins groups, casts off many of his individualistic traits, and even cooperates in trade-unions. Eventually he is accommodated to the city.

A more extensive study by Caldwell,[1] also dealing with the adjustments of mountaineers to an urban environment, takes 57 mountain families in Kentucky who moved to Lexington, a city of 60,000 population, and compares their adjustment problems with those of 57 families from nonmountain countries. Familial, health, educational, religious institutions, and court experience were used as adjustment indices. The mountain families had three times as many social maladjustments in the city as they had had in the mountains and twice as many in the city as the group coming from the Bluegrass region had in the city. Caldwell explains this by the fact that one who is well adjusted to mountain culture is almost certain to be a misfit in the city; for instance, one is not permitted to dump sewage in the garden in the city, although it is considered proper procedure in the mountains.

He reports a high rate of domestic disorder among mountain families in the city, which he is inclined to attribute to the strain of modern living so suddenly thrust upon them; domestic disorder, separation, desertion, divorce, and illegitimacy appear.

[1] Morris G. Caldwell, "The Adjustments of Mountain Families in an Urban Environment," *Social Forces*, vol. 16, pp. 389–395, March, 1938.

There is a high rate of economic maladjustment among the mountain families in the city as compared to the Bluegrass families, there being little work in Lexington for mountain people. Under the mountain culture they could eke out a living by raising the necessities of life, but under city conditions they have to depend on a cash income to survive; grocery bills, rent, and debts have to be paid and sometimes relief must be resorted to.

There is evidence of serious health maladjustment among mountain families in the city, for they have 25 times as many health difficulties there as in the country, and over twice as many as the Bluegrass families. The difference can be explained in part by the fact that their health problems more readily come to public attention in the city.

Educational difficulties also show up in the city, or rather are transferred from the country to the city. Mountain parents have had an average of less than five years of schooling of about six months per year, an educational handicap which, of course, affects their ideas of sanitation, domestic harmony, and child care.

Their religious maladjustments increase with city life, much more than those of the Bluegrass families. Their court and institutional experiences also multiply in the city, and much more rapidly than those of the Bluegrass families; in the mountain culture drunkenness, assault, cruelty, and nonsupport are largely individual matters, but not in the city.

Summarizing his results as measured, Caldwell reports 18.7 maladjustments for mountain families in the city and only 6.2 for them in the mountains. The Bluegrass families had only 11.2 maladjustments per family in the city. Part of this difference is explained by the fact that the Bluegrass persons had been in the city for a somewhat longer time; on the other hand, it seems that the mountain families probably face a much greater problem of adjustment to urban culture.

Intimate aspects of economic adjustment of rural families from the Ozark Mountain region in the city of St. Louis have thus been described by Huseman:

They said that they were so worried and confused by the pressing need for subsistence that they were numb to other things about them. The tension was released when they were employed and as long as they worked they were quite satisfied. But often "on the job" it was hard to receive orders and work under "hard-boiled bosses."

The majority of the women described their first weeks in the city as a "terrible" period during which they almost went mad. Long hours "cooped up" with a group of children, who had been accustomed to spend most of their time outside, was far from pleasant. The mothers were too frightened to allow them to leave the crowded rooms. The smoke and dirt were stifling and the noise confusing. Lonesomeness, homesickness, and futile attempts to make friends with the neighbors who lived under the same roof marked the efforts to adjust. The church, which played a big part in country life, failed in the city.

The men who found work had little trouble "gettin' along" but leisure time was far from a pleasure. One man spent each Sunday and holiday at the Zoo when he could afford carfare. Another family rushed off to the country at every opportunity.

Some of the children had difficulty when they started to school. Not only were they frightened at seeing so many other children but they were timid and backward in their actions. Their dialect did not contribute to their acceptance among their schoolmates. Some turned belligerent and fought while others merely withdrew. The children, however, naturally began to make friends and brought them home; they soon went to the public libraries for books; they were invited to the mission Sunday Schools and settlement houses, and soon the mothers and fathers were also becoming interested to a limited extent.[1]

Those more favored by education, social opportunity, and desirable rural environmental situations seem not to experience the extreme problem of adjustment described in the preceding studies. Further studies by Beers and Heflin[2] in Lexington indicate that there is a great deal of difference in adjustment problems, depending on background of families coming to the city. They find that although newcomers were somewhat at a disadvantage often they were only slightly so. Actually in most cases they achieved a higher status than they had prior to migration. Also the longer newcomers were situated in the city, the fewer the difficulties of adjustment that were evident. These studies do show, however, that rural migrants to the city experience more adjustment problems than their neighbors of urban origin.

These authors suggest that adequate preparation of migrants for social and economic adjustment in the city might become an important social objective.

Studies[3] at the State College of Washington of rural migrants to Spokane (population 150,000 during the period of industrial expansion in World War II) showed that, although certain problems of adjustment were serious, in general they were of short duration and were soon overcome to the point where the migrants preferred to remain in the city.

All of these studies would seem to point to the fact that decreasing rural isolation, improved education and other such influences work in the direction of decreasing problems of adjustment in migration from country to city.

Without doubt the extensive farm-to-city migration from disadvantaged rural areas of recent years has contributed heavily to certain pathological conditions of the city. Although the adjustment problems of those coming from isolated rural communities probably are atypical, it seems likely that the majority of those moving to cities from farms experience varying degrees of

[1] Elsie Huseman, "The Adjustment of Rural Families in St. Louis," 1932. Unpublished master's thesis at Washington University, quoted from S. A. Queen and L. F. Thomas, *The City*, p. 412, McGraw-Hill Book Company, Inc., New York, 1939.

[2] Howard Beers and Catherine Heflin, "Rural People in the City," and Heflin and Beers, "Urban Adjustment of Rural Migrants," *Kentucky Agricultural Experiment Station Bulletins* 478 and 487, respectively, Lexington, July, 1945 and June, 1946, respectively.

[3] Paul H. Landis and Katherine Day,"Farm and Small-town Workers in Metropolitan War Industry," *Washington Agricultural Experiment Stations Bulletin* 460, Pullman, March, 1945.

conflict in adjusting themselves to the anonymous atmosphere of a secondary group. In the adjustment process which ensues, some break under the strain. As a consequence individuals with farm backgrounds may constitute more than a normal proportion of suicide cases, of those who break under nervous strain and find their way to institutions for the mentally diseased, of those who experience such frustration that they turn to crime, or of those who fail economically and become dependent. Unfortunately, conclusive evidence demonstrating the validity of these assumptions is not available. Proof awaits further studies of the more intimate aspects of personality adjustment of peoples going from rural environments to the city.

It is recognized that the approaching similarity of rural and urban experience, especially in areas where consolidated schools have developed and where farm youths have considerable contact with town and city, has undoubtedly had an important influence in reducing culture shock of those who go to the city. As these newer trends in rural life affect the more remote hinterland, problems of social adjustment consequent to urbanward migration undoubtedly will decrease as a matter of course. However, there is a challenging need for more intensive study of adjustment experiences of those entering urban areas from various types of rural areas, relating problems of social and occupational adjustment to the rural community backgrounds of the persons involved. There is also need for educators, religious workers, welfare workers, and others to give increased attention both to preparing farm youth for problems of urban adjustment and to easing the shock of the adjustment process upon their arrival in the city. As long as the most isolated rural areas of the United States tend to contribute large numbers of youth to the metropolis, where they are faced with new social experience, problems of accommodation will be pronounced.

QUESTIONS FOR REVIEW AND DISCUSSION

1. Summarize evidence on the qualitative loss of the urbanward migration.
2. Does the migration to the farm offset this loss?
3. What economic loss to the farm is involved in the cityward drift? What gains are realized?
4. City possible consequences of the presence of large numbers of people with a farm background in the city.
5. Explain "culture shock." What type of person or group is most likely to experience it on entering the city?
6. Cite evidence that throws light on problems of vocational accommodation of rural migrants to the city.
7. Summarize findings demonstrating that rural people from isolated areas experience great difficulty in accommodating themselves to the city.
8. Are their adjustment difficulties typical of those of all migrants?
9. State reasons for believing that farm migrants have contributed to the pathologies of the city.

COLLATERAL READING

Baker, O. E.: "The Outlook for Rural Youth," *U.S. Department of Agriculture Extension Service Circular* 223, Washington, D. C., 1935.

Beers, Howard W. and Catherine Heflin: "Rural People in the City," *Kentucky Agricultural Experiment Station Bulletin* 478, University of Kentucky, Lexington, July, 1945.

Caldwell, Morris G.: "The Adjustments of Mountain Families in an Urban Environment," *Social Forces*, vol. 16, pp. 389–395, March, 1938.

Carpenter, Niles: *The Sociology of City Life*, pp. 267–274, Longmans, Green and Company, New York, 1931.

Gist, Noel P., C. T. Pihlblad, Cecil L. Gregory: "Selective Aspects of Rural Migration," *Rural Sociology*, vol. 6, pp. 3–15, March, 1941.

Heflin, Catherine P. and Howard W. Beers: "Urban Adjustment of Rural Migrants," *Kentucky Agricultural Experiment Station, Bulletin* 487, University of Kentucky, Lexington, June, 1946.

Kennedy, Louise V.: *The Negro Peasant Turns Cityward*, Columbia University Press, New York, 1930.

Kiser, Clyde V.: "Birth Rates Among Rural Migrants in Cities," *The Milbank Memorial Fund Quarterly*, vol. 16, No. 4, October, 1938.

————: *Sea Island to City*, Columbia University Press, New York, 1932.

Leybourne, Grace F.: "Urban Adjustments of Migrants from the Southern Appalachian Plateaus," *Social Forces*, pp. 238–246, December, 1937.

McCormick, Thomas C.: "Rural Intelligence and College Achievements," *Sociology and Social Research*, vol. 16, pp. 259–266, January–February, 1932.

Queen, S. A., and L. F. Thomas: *The City*, chap. 20, McGraw-Hill Book Company, Inc., New York, 1939.

Reuss, Carl F.: "A Qualitative Study of Depopulation in a Remote Rural District: 1900–1930," *Rural Sociology*, vol. 2, pp. 66–75, March, 1937.

Sorokin, P. A.: *Social Mobility*, chap. 21, Harper & Brothers, New York, 1927.

————, C. C. Zimmerman, and C. J. Galpin: *A Systematic Source Book in Rural Sociology*, vol. 3, chap. 22, University of Minnesota Press, Minneapolis, 1932.

CHAPTER 16

PROBLEMS OF ACCOMMODATION IN THE FARM-TO-FARM MOVEMENT

ACCOMMODATION IN INTERREGIONAL FARM-TO-FARM MIGRATION

THE interregional farm migrant is likely to face adjustment on several frontiers: (1) Habits of farm people who have lived in a stable environment are relatively fixed, so well fixed that they persist with tenacity under new conditions. (2) Adjustments to new machine techniques are involved especially when the farmer shifts to a new kind of agricultural area. (3) Adjustment to natural resources must be made. In the case of the farmer this adjustment is basic, for to know land and its husbandry is the preface to any successful agricultural practice. (4) Adjustment to culture which includes the whole realm of custom, tradition, and practice in the new area must be made. The attempt to project old customs and practices into the new situation leads to maladjustment. (5) There is the vital problem of attaining status in the new social group, of finding a place in its life. In a rural area one cannot very well live anonymously, concerned only with vocational interests. Ordinarily the farmer lives in a neighborhood where he is expected to function in at least a certain number of group relationships and to participate in some neighborhood institutions. Change from one region to another may involve him in a radically different set of customs and social relationships.

Generally speaking, the urban worker needs only his skills to break into a new community; he needs no capital and makes little or no investment in machinery. Community adjustments for the city-to-city migrant are few because the urbanite does not live in a neighborhood in any intimate sense. If he so desires, he needs to fit only into the work situation; if group social attachments are unimportant to him, he needs to make few adjustments. The migrating farm family usually expects and wants to become an intimate part of the new primary group.

SPECIAL PROBLEMS OF THE INTERREGIONAL FARM MIGRANT

Interregional migration involving long distances is not sufficiently attractive today to the well-established farmer to cause him to take part in it. Most of the present long-distance movement from farm to farm is of those who have been unable to find or hold a place in agriculture in the region where they are located, *i.e.*, the young, the unsuccessful, or the defeated.

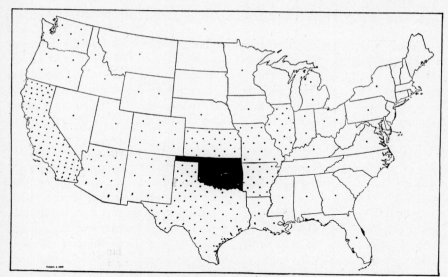

OUT-MIGRANTS FROM OKLAHOMA, 1935–1940, BY STATE OF DESTINATION (ONE DOT
EQUALS 1,000 MIGRANTS)

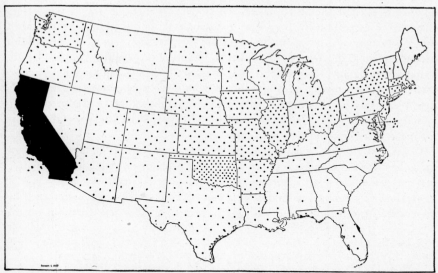

Henry S. Shryock, Jr., and Hope Tisdale Eldidge, "Internal Migration and the war," *American Sociological Review*
vol. 12, pp. 27–39, February, 1947.

IN-MIGRANTS TO CALIFORNIA, 1935 TO 1940, BY STATE OF ORIGIN (ONE DOT EQUALS 1,000)

California is characterized by a heavy in-migration from other states and regions;
Oklahoma is characterized by a heavy out-migration. The interregional migration of the
drought-depression period was deruralizing in effect, the war interregional migration even
more so. It is estimated that although 35 per cent or more of the 95,000 Oklahoma migrants
to California shown above came from farms, not more than 13 per cent settled on farms in
California. During the war period, Dec. 1, 1941, to March, 1945, intercounty migration of
11,810,000 persons 14 years of age and over resulted in net loss of 820,000 farm persons.

Much of interregional farm migration is motivated by compulsive forces—not by opportunities. Thus, the mass movement from the Great Plains during the 1930's was brought about chiefly by drought and accompanying hazardous conditions of living. Thus, also, the migration from the southern cotton belt westward was brought about by acreage reduction, soil depletion, tractor farming, and other influences which have decreased the number of agricultural opportunities in the South.[1]

Migration motivated by compulsive forces uproots a considerable proportion of people in the early middle years of life who ordinarily have family responsibilities, thus causing a serious problem of social accommodation, one which is of concern not only to the migrant but also to the territory into which he goes.[2] If he is driven from the old environment with few mortgageable assets, he must face adjustment in the new community without capital and without possibilities for borrowing. In this respect his situation is different from that on the early agricultural frontier because at that time speculators were willing to lend money at a high risk in the hope of making large interest gains.

The interregional migrant of today must enter areas where the best opportunities in agriculture have been taken. No area in the nation offers chances for expansion in agriculture for people without capital.[3] In several of the Western states, irrigation projects are opening new land for agricultural production, but the best of it probably will be occupied by people already living in the area. No interregional migrant of today, then, can expect to arrive in an unexploited area and match wits with nature alone, as was once the case; today he must match wits with an established residential population which ordinarily has a better economic and experiential background than he for making the most of new opportunities.

Thus, migratory groups that have been dispossessed in agriculture or industry can hardly be expected to solve their problems by individual initiative for they face well-nigh insurmountable difficulties. Guidance, public credit, or public assistance are essential for a considerable portion of those forced by impersonal, mechanistic, and climatic factors to seek a new foothold on the

[1] See Alma Holzschuh and Omer Mills, *A Study of 6,655 Migrant Households in California*, 1938, Farm Security Administration, San Francisco, 1939.

[2] More than three-fourths of the heads of 6,655 families entering California were between 20 and 44 years of age, the median age being 33.5 years. The most usual household was comprised of parents and a child under 5 years of age. *Ibid*.

[3] Probably the Pacific Northwest offers as many possibilities for expansion of agricultural lands as any other region, but even there opportunities are not awaiting the man without capital. See Pacific Northwest Regional Planning Commission, *Recent Migration into the Pacific Northwest*, Portland, 1938. Also *Migration and the Development of Economic Opportunity in the Pacific Northwest* (mimeographed), Pacific Northwest Regional Planning Commission, Portland, 1940.

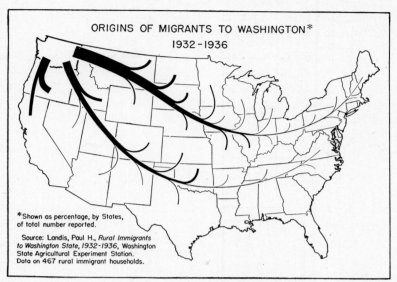

STATES OF ORIGIN OF 467 RURAL IMMIGRANT HOUSEHOLDS (ABOUT 2,300 PERSONS) ENTER-
ING THE STATE OF WASHINGTON, 1932–1936.

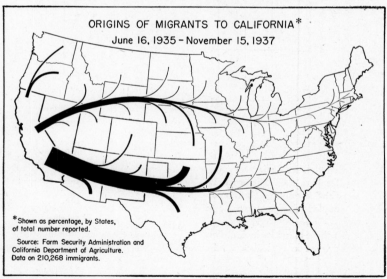

STATES OF ORIGIN OF 210,268 MIGRANTS ENTERING CALIFORNIA, 1935–1937

The upper chart indicates the source of migrants to Washington but is typical of interregional rural migration into all Pacific Northwest states—Washington, Oregon, and
Idaho. The lower chart shows source of interregional rural migration into California. The
dividing line for the migrants is the northern border of Oklahoma, those north of this line
usually moving to the Pacific Northwest, those south into California.

land. To obtain and retain a place in agriculture was difficult even during the days when homestead lands were free.

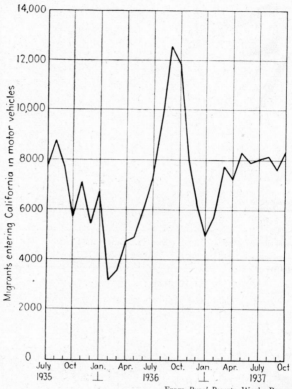

From *Rural Poverty*, Works Progress Administration.

MIGRANTS "IN NEED OF MANUAL EMPLOYMENT" ENTERING CALIFORNIA IN MOTOR
VEHICLES, BY MONTHS

"About seven thousand migratory workers per month motored into California from July, 1935, to October, 1937. The usual range was from a low point of three to five thousand in January and February up to eight thousand per month during the summer. Drought on the Great Plains, coupled with good crops on the coast, caused an unprecedented migration in 1936."

Observe that these migrants included only those in need of "manual employment." Many of them sought work in agriculture. Inherent in this situation were difficult problems of accommodation.

Social and psychological aspects of interregional farm migrations, past and present, have not been adequately studied and yet they are of first importance. Certain problems involved can best be illustrated by analyzing the movement of drought settlers from the northern Great Plains into the Pacific Northwest. The adjustments of this migrating group may not typify the experience of all such groups but with minor variations the same general principles apply to any people forced out of an old agricultural environment into a new one.[1]

Intimate case histories of drought migrants from the northern Great Plains were obtained from interviews with 381 drought migrants settling in rural areas in the state of Washington; letters written to real-estate agencies, chambers of commerce, and railroad companies by prospective migrants inquiring about the West were analyzed in an attempt to understand the motives for movement and problems of readjustment to be faced.[2] Briefly, the social and economic characteristics of the 381 settlers studied were as follows: The great majority had few assets on arrival in the West; 82 per cent no longer held assets in the state from which they had come. One-fourth had less than $100 on arrival; 65 per cent had less than $500; 80 per cent less than $1,000; and 90 per cent less than $3,000. Many entered the state destitute except for their automobile, trailer, and household goods, their cash having been exhausted by the expenses of the journey. The settlers had been a stable group in the past, one-third of them having lived in only one state previous to the time of migration and another one-half having lived in only two states. The families were larger than the average-sized family in the state of Washington but average size for families in the Great Plains. The average age of heads of families was younger than that of heads in the rural farm population of the northern Great Plains, or of the Pacific Northwest.

MOTIVES FOR MIGRATION AND PROBLEMS OF ECONOMIC ADJUSTMENT

Motives and Economic Goals.—The interregional rural migration from the Great Plains to the Coast was motivated by compulsive forces. The 381 families interviewed in the state of Washington gave the following reasons for leaving their former homes:[3]

[1] This migration has been into Oregon, Washington, Idaho, and western Montana. An even larger group has entered California from the Southern drought states and from the cotton states. The problem of accommodation there is much more severe than in the North. Thousands of drought migrants, share croppers, and farm laborers in California are living on irrigation ditch "banks" and taking to the road with the mass of migratory laborers who work at seasonal farm labor in that state and in other states on or near the Coast.

[2] Full results are published in Richard Wakefield and Paul H. Landis, "The Drought Farmer Adjusts to the West," *Washington Agricultural Experiment Stations Bulletin* 378, Pullman, 1939.

[3] Lack of work and drought were the two major reasons for migration reported by 6,655 migrant households studied in California. "Farm industrialization and mechanization, soil destruction, and the breakdown of tenancy, as well as lack of adequate local relief and high incidence of ill health during depression years are, other significant reasons for migration reported." Alma Holzschuh and Omer Mills, *op. cit.*

Reasons given	Number	Per cent of migrants giving reason
Drought and crop failure......................	201	52.7
Unemployment and low wages.................	93	24.4
Dissatisfaction and desire to change............	75	19.7
Unsatisfactory climate and ill health...........	75	19.7
Poor future outlook.........................	50	13.1
Influence of friends and relatives..............	17	4.5

The forces impelling migration led the group to seek conditions which would free them from drought, unfavorable climate, and general economic insecurity. This fact had a direct bearing on their selection of the area of settlement and on the success of their adjustment to it. Most of the Plains migrants entered timbered, cutover regions or settled in irrigated sections.[1] In timbered areas of the Coast free fuel was available, which was an important item to a plainsman who had always had to buy it, and there was abundant moisture for growing garden products. In the irrigated areas he could depend on an artificial water supply.

Economic Realizations.—Even though the group entering the Far West had practically no resources, more than 38 per cent acquired a tract of land, a number equal to the proportion of those who owned land in the Great Plains. Before the crisis experience which induced migration, 90 per cent of the farms owned were more than 80 acres in size; after moving only 28 per cent were of this size. Then over half of the settlers owned a half section (320 acres) or more; after migration only 1.5 per cent owned as much. On the Plains the value of farm property in a fourth of the cases exceeded $20,000, and in another fourth of the cases it was placed at $10,000 to $20,000.[2] In the West the total value of lands and improvements in over a third of the cases was under $1,000, in a total of 58 per cent of the cases under $2,000, and in 82.5 per cent of the cases under $5,000 (see figure).

In the ownership of small tracts of submarginal land[3] by a group which left home with few assets, one sees an expression of a supreme effort to acquire

[1] See *Recent Migration into the Pacific Northwest, op. cit.;* V. B. Stanbery, *Migration into Oregon,* part II, Oregon State Planning Board, Portland, 1938. Also, *Migration and the Development of Economic Opportunity in the Pacific Northwest, op. cit.*

[2] Inflated land values during pre-drought years on the Plains are undoubtedly reflected in some of these reported valuations, but even though these figures be discounted heavily to allow for this element, great differences still exist in value of property owned before and after migration.

[3] Studies in the region indicate that most lands settled are incapable of producing an adequate livelihood. See publications of the Pacific Northwest Regional Planning Commission previously cited. Also see Wakefield and Landis, *op. cit.*

security through individual initiative and enterprise. Many times, in order to purchase a small acreage on contract, the settler had to go on relief, seek employment with the Works Progress Administration, or obtain Farm Security Administration loans or grants. (Half the migrants studied had received relief

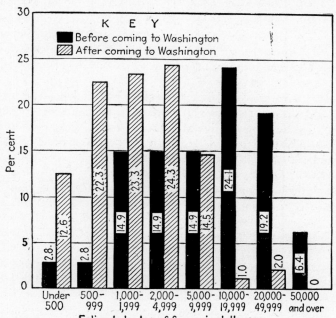

Richard Wakefield and Paul H. Landis, "The Drought Farmer Adjusts to the West," *Washington Agricultural Experiment Stations Bulletin* 378, Pullman, 1939.

COMPARATIVE WEALTH OF FARMERS BEFORE THE CRISIS INDUCING INTERREGIONAL MIGRATION AND AFTER SETTLING IN THE NEW REGION

Much of interregional farm migration today is induced by compulsive forces, since opportunities that attract settlers to new agricultural regions no longer are plentiful. Migration induced by compulsive economic forces is likely to be followed by difficulties of social and economic adjustment in the new area.

after moving to the Far West.) In the shift from one region to another a large group has lost tenure status. About 21 per cent were farm laborers in the Plains; in the West 41 per cent had become farm laborers.

Inadequacy of Past Farming Experience in the New Situation.—In his struggle to adjust to agriculture in the West, the drought farmer betrayed evidence of the inadequacy of his farming experience in the Great Plains to aid him in the new situation. Often wise, shrewd, hardheaded, able to drive a good bargain in a familiar environment in the West he was a gullible prospect for the exploiter. He was accustomed to a land with fertile soil which produced abundantly when moisture was sufficient. Arriving in the West he was uncritical of soil and ignorant of its importance to farming; often he entered a cutover region where large areas of wastelands are to be found. Seeing there huge stumps and verdant overgrowth with ferns higher than a man's head, seeing the black mulch of topsoil, experiencing the showers which fall on the western slope of the Cascades, he immediately concluded that he had found a paradise which waited only for a man with the courage to pull the stumps and clear the land. Those who are familiar with Western soils know that much of this land is not worth clearing, that many of these timbered areas are glaciated with gravel and rock underlying the surface soil, that on the slopes, even where there is good topsoil, it may be washed away if the ground is left bare in cultivation.

Sometimes even the critical were deceived. The fact that a fairly prosperous stump farm adjoins a vacant tract of wasteland is no assurance that the adjoining acreage will be as productive as the stump farm. Many of these soils are spotted, and only by a careful analysis can one know whether a particular piece of land can be profitably utilized for farming.

The Problem of Accommodation to New Farming Practices.—Since he knew nothing about the handling of water and little about many of the farming practices carried on in irrigated sections, the drought farmer experienced a new kind of farming. Fixed habits had to be discarded; old attitudes overcome. A man loses his dignity when he shifts from a quarter section, a half section, or a whole section to a 10-acre tract or a 5-acre garden. One settler who could not get his price for a three-bottom gang plow back in South Dakota brought it with him to western Washington, where he rented a fairly productive 20-acre tract. Finding that he could not use the gang plow, which required eight horses, he put it in his back yard to become a neighborhood curio, while he farmed with a team and walking plow. He said that the first day he plowed he went one round and then sat down and laughed at himself because he felt like a small boy playing with a toy. His only consolation was that none of the people who knew him when he really farmed could see him. He had been renting this tract for 2 years and could not make up his mind whether or not to buy because farming on a small scale did not seem like farming to him. Some drought migrants who had settled on small irrigated tracts reported that they were ashamed to be seen working with a shovel and wearing rubber boots while irrigating. It was a comedown to use a shovel after having steered a tractor down a long furrow. As a result, some felt like farm laborers rather than operators.

Most of the drought refugees, before they migrated West, thought they would be satisfied if only they could be secure. But soon an occasional plainsman who has established himself securely was dreaming longingly of the big crops back in Nebraska where he made more money in one or two seasons than he could expect to make in a lifetime on his small, fertile, well-watered tract in the Far West.

Farm Security Administration (Lange)

"A LITTLE FARM AND YOU ARE SAFE"

Farm migrants and others in quest of new lands where they can be secure are welcomed by those who boldly promise security for a profit.

There is a suggestion in these findings that interregional farm-to-farm migration, motivated by a desire for security, is hazardous under modern conditions. First, chances of finding the desired security are not good. Indeed the migrant is likely to find less security than he might have realized in his native region by a better adaptation of farming practices to natural conditions, it being easier to adopt new farming practices under known conditions than to adopt them under the unknown conditions of a new area. To make the point more specific, most of the Plains farmers in moving to the Pacific Northwest changed from a cash type of farming, from grain or corn or grain and livestock enterprises, to general or diversified farming, as the following data show:

Type of farm	Great Plains		Washington	
	Number	Per cent	Number	Per cent
Grain or corn..........................	59	32.3		
Grain and livestock.....................	46	25.1	1	1.1
Cattle...............................	22	12.0	3	3.4
Dairy................................	4	2.2	4	4.6
General and diversified..................	41	22.4	71	80.7
Specialized crops.......................	11	6.0	9	10.2
Total...............................	183	100.0	88	100.0

Might they not have stood a better chance of attaining security had they remained on the Plains and changed their practices to diversified farming, on their own land, where adaptations were possible, or on some other farm within the Plains that would lend itself to diversified farming where it was not possible on their own land? In becoming operators of general farms in the Far West they had to learn not only new techniques, but also all of the intricacies of new soils and climatic conditions.[1]

Second, the interregional migrant who found security at the expense of lowered economic and social status, was often dissatisfied on attaining it. Had he been guided toward adjustment in his native area and thus helped to avoid the financial and experience losses occasioned by selling out, moving, and resettling, he might have achieved security on a higher economic and social plane than was possible in a new area.

SOCIAL ADJUSTMENT

The drought migrants were highly cognizant of the general attitude of the new community toward them, both as individuals and as a group. The com-

---

[1] It is recognized that, from the standpoint of general economic adjustment, considerable reduction in farm population on the Plains may be desirable. The point made here is significant for individual adjustment.

munity concept of "drought folks" became stereotyped in many localities. Two factors generally seemed to determine the extent to which local communities were willing to accept the newcomers on friendly terms: (1) the comparative isolation of the area and (2) the extent to which local people found themselves in economic competition with the newcomers.

Culture Shock.—The drought migrants who came from an isolated area where neighborliness was characteristic and settled in a rural area closely adjoining a metropolitan community where anonymity prevailed were likely to be unhappy and dissatisfied; those who moved to a more isolated area, however, usually found the surroundings hospitable and the resident population friendly. In strictly farming communities there is little sense of economic competition among farmers and in some areas, especially where there are granges or rural churches, the newcomer was immediately welcomed into the local organizations. In rare cases the whole community, in a spirit of pioneer hospitality, turned out to assist him in establishing himself in his new home. Settlers in such areas characterized the new locality as one friendly toward newcomers.

Conflict.—In industrialized areas where the drought migrant entered the labor market in mills or other rural industries, he faced resentment of the laboring class already in the area. The entire community might consider him an intruder, with the exception of the employer, who secretly welcomed anyone who, having wearied of farming, thought that a $5 per day cash wage for a 7- or 8-hour day was a high rate of pay and was willing to work hard for it. In some communities the antilabor sentiments of the drought migrant excluded him from economic opportunities in rural industry and also, in case he voiced his sentiment against unions, from social participation. After a few years in the community he acquired prevailing mores and was as critical of the newcomer as the older residents once were of him.

Throughout all areas there was some resentment against the migrant who received relief, the assumption on the part of the resident relief recipient being that, inasmuch as funds were limited, he should not have to share them with the stranger, and on the part of the taxpayer that the state should not be held responsible for an out-of-state group, even if the group were unfortunate and deserving of sympathy and assistance.

Moral Shock.—In some communities, such as mill towns, where "lumber jack" mores carry over from a male, pioneer, nonmoral period, the moral shock to incoming groups was considerable. The migrant from a rural community with rigid moral standards felt as though he had been planted in a place of iniquity. Although wanting to be friendly in order to reestablish himself, he could not but condemn the moral practices of his neighbors.

Clash of Family Mores.—In communities where resident women customarily worked in canneries or picked hops or berries, there was a conflict of local patterns with family mores of the drought migrants, many of whom chose relief rather than permit their wives to work for wages.

Housing Adjustments.—One serious handicap to satisfactory social adjustment of the migrants was the general inadequacy of their housing facilities. Because they usually settled on undeveloped or deserted farms, they often lived in houses that were in a run-down condition or found it necessary to build their own shelters from any cheap material that was available. Families often were large and overcrowding was common. Nine per cent of the families lived in one-room dwellings and over half of them lived in three rooms or less. Only about one-fifth of them had five or more rooms in which to live.

More than one-sixth of the family dwellings were classified by the interviewer[1] as being in poor condition. A house to be classed in "poor condition" was one which did not provide adequate shelter from the elements. Either the wind blew freely through open cracks in the walls and broken window panes or the roof allowed a quantity of water to drip through whenever it rained. A slightly smaller percentage of the houses was classed as being in "good condition." This meant that they were of sound construction and in a good state of repair and that they were capable of being heated and of being kept clean. Size was no criterion. The remainder of the houses fell somewhere between these two divisions.

The same general condition existed with regard to household furnishings. Nearly one-fourth of the homes were classified as bare; that is, they did not contain furniture necessary for general use. A few houses did not contain a table and there were no chairs in many of them. Boxes, stools, and benches often were used as chairs and in some of the homes part of the family had to eat standing up or sitting on the bed, which often was placed beside the kitchen stove. Sixty per cent of the homes were classified as having adequate furnishings, which meant that they had enough furniture for all necessary purposes, even though often it was very rough and rickety. Only 15 per cent of the homes were furnished well enough to be considered comfortable. Curtains and other furnishings that brighten up homes were noticeably lacking.

Such living conditions are not only trying to family life, but they also restrict social adjustments with neighbors, because they have a depressing effect on entertainment within the home and contribute greatly to a feeling of social inferiority.

New Patterns.—A considerable number of migrants by force of circumstances were compelled to join the ranks of migratory workers during the agricultural harvest when jobs were available. It is probable that some of them, being unable to reestablish themselves on a secure basis, became a permanent part of this army of migratory laborers. This tendency was not as pronounced in the Pacific Northwest as in California where the preponderant number of

---

[1] The interviewer was invited into practically all the homes.

migrants from Southern drought states settled. Some of these stable plainsmen took to the road by choice. They did not know the world was so interesting, or that moving was so easy, until they made this first long trip. Now they wanted to take other trips. They became followers of the road.

A certain number of the newcomers to the West failed to make satisfactory social and economic adjustments and as a consequence suffered a degree of personal disorganization. A young man described the demoralization of a drought migrant family whom he employed on a berry ranch:

At one time Mr. Jones, the father of this family, had owned a large ranch in North Dakota but had lost everything except a few family belongings and his truck. He and his wife and five children came West in the truck to look for work. Finding no steady work and having too much pride to enroll on WPA, they traveled from one crop to the next, managing to make enough to carry them through the winter. The next summer they happened to come to me asking for work and, as I needed berry pickers, I hired them. The first year they all worked but the mother. They were out in the field every morning at six and stayed there until noon and then trotted off to their shack across the railroad tracks for lunch. They were always the first ones back from lunch and the last to leave the field at night. During the five and one-half weeks that they worked for me they earned about $225; they were very well pleased and so was I. When they left they promised to be around in time for next year's crop.

One year later, in June, I got word from the same family that they were ready to come to work any time that I was ready for them. When they arrived we talked for some time, and I was very interested in what had happened to them after they left me the summer before. They had gone from my place to the apple orchards and other fruit crops and after they had finished they went back to their old home to see their friends and then down into Florida. At frequent intervals they stopped long enough for the children to get some schooling. The children would obtain books and read and study for about two weeks and then take a test on the work that they had covered, after which the family would continue on its journey. In early spring they had returned to Everett, Washington, and the children entered school there. Their father finally decided he would join up with the WPA. He told me this with an expressive oath. Even though he finally did go on relief he still has faint hopes of getting a foothold and again owning a farm, although his hopes seem to be weakening.

Their first year they had been very industrious, but this year they seemed to be different. They were late to work in the mornings and ready to quit any time. They asked more favors than before and their entire attitude and outlook on life seemed to have changed. To me it is a pitiful sight to see people as ambitious as they were at one time, unable to adjust themselves in a new life.[1]

The experiences of social adjustment described in the preceding paragraphs were typical of those encountered in the Pacific Northwest region. Problems of adjustment in California and Arizona, where migration was largely from the western cotton states (refer again to the maps on pages 223

[1] From an account by James Richardson.

and 225), were far more severe. Of 6,655 cases studied in one sample, two of every five were from Oklahoma, and the majority were from the four states, Oklahoma, Texas, Arkansas, and Missouri.[1] This group, like those moving from the northern Great Plains, had a history of stability, half of the sample

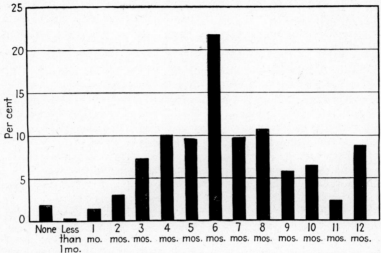

From Alma Holzschuh and Omer Mills, *A Study of 6,655 Migrant Households in California*, 1938, Farm Security Administration, San Francisco, 1939.

NUMBER OF MONTHS OF EMPLOYMENT DURING 1937 OF HEADS OF 6,655 RURAL MIGRANT HOUSEHOLDS IN CALIFORNIA, 1938

Indicative of the economic hazards of unguided interregional rural migration under modern conditions was this situation where more than half of the newcomers obtained six months or less employment a year.

having lived 20 years or longer in the state from which they came. They were not accustomed to making readjustments.

Most of them on entering the new region had to join the army of migratory laborers, living in tents or lean-tos on ditch banks or along the highways, subsisting on an average of six months' yearly employment at low wages (see chart). Disease, dire poverty, and social maladjustment were characteristic.

A dramatic account of the struggles of an Oklahoma farm family that had been "tractored out" by corporation farming in a cotton section and had taken to the road to work as wage hands in the crops of California was the basis of John Steinbeck's best-selling novel, *Grapes of Wrath*. This realistic narrative, although it exaggerated the hardships of adjustment of the average interregional farm migrant, has been called the *Uncle Tom's Cabin* of the migrant problem, and had the effect of arousing the attention of the nation to that problem in California.

[1] Alma Holzschuh and Omer Mills, *op. cit.*

COLONY SETTLEMENT AS A FACTOR IN ADJUSTMENT IN LONG-DISTANCE MIGRATION

The general tendency of interregional farm migrants is to take their community with then insofar as possible. Urban migration is a movement of individuals; interregional farm-to-farm movement tends to be a movement of groups—friends, relatives, and neighbors. In frontier days people traveled in caravans because of the need for mutual aid and protection on the road as well as in the new community; today, when hazards of the road have disappeared, people no longer travel in caravans but the movement of locality groups and of groups of relatives into new areas persists. Thus, the rural migrant is able to transplant a substantial part of the old primary group environment into the new location. Generally speaking, the more distinct the culture of the migrating group the more likely is it to settle in colonies and the longer is it able to maintain its unique characteristics.[1]

In the movement of drought refugees from one region to another, colony settlement in a modified form persisted, although, because of the automobile, travel was by families rather than by neighborhoods. Settlers from the home neighborhood kept drifting into the new region until a new neighborhood group was formed. Thus, in Washington in 1938, studies of drought migrants in seven different areas showed that well over one-half of them settled near other migrants from their home community. More reported having moved to the state because of the presence of friends or relatives there than for any other one reason, 55 per cent giving this as an important factor in the selection of their destination.[2]

In some cases group settlement was motivated by a community leader whose judgment was respected. In one rural area in Washington a group of 80 people was found to have once lived in or near a South Dakota town of 300

[1] Warren S. Thompson, "Research Memorandum on Internal Migration in the Depression," p. 4, *Social Science Research Council Bulletin* no. 30, New York, 1937.

[2] The relative importance of this factor is shown in the following table from Richard Wakefield and Paul H. Landis, *op. cit.*:

REASONS GIVEN BY 381 DROUGHT MIGRANTS FOR SETTLING IN WASHINGTON

Reasons given	Number	Per cent of migrants giving reason
Relatives and friends	211	55.4
Heard of opportunities there	80	21.0
Liked the country	76	19.9
Employment and high wages	68	17.8
Mild and healthful climate	36	9.5
Publicity and real-estate promotion	29	7.6

population; this group had been persuaded to move chiefly by the influence of a dynamic Baptist preacher.

From the standpoint of social adjustment in the new area, group movement is of great significance in that the migrants are enabled to encounter the new conditions with a united front. The stress of individual adjustment is lessened, for the formation of new neighborhood alignments is made unnecessary. Even where there is conflict with the resident group in the new area, the newcomers can maintain their own social and institutional life with some degree of satisfaction.

But although group settlement greatly eases the adjustment of the first generation of new settlers, it prolongs the entire adjustment process. Old family and neighborhood mores, religious philosophies, and in the case of nationality groups, language patterns, persist much longer than in the case of isolated settlement; but the new adjustment must eventually be made. The old group, because it has sufficient social life without making adjustments, clings to its patterns and passes them on to the children. The children, however, because they have broader contacts with the out-group, usually find it necessary to modify these patterns, although in some cases the children in the new group may dominate those in the resident group. For example, in 1938 in certain communities of Washington where people from Southern states had recently settled, residents complained that their children were acquiring the accent of the migrant children, who dominated the school and neighborhood situation. In the case of extreme culture difference, conflict between family and community patterns may cause the second generation to face difficult problems of adjustment. Eventually, however, the adjustment is made, the second or third generation absorbing many of the patterns of the new locality.[1]

THE LONG-TIME ADJUSTMENT OF INTERREGIONAL FARM-TO-FARM MIGRANTS

The initial adjustments of a group of interregional farm-to-farm migrants, especially in a time of economic crisis such as the drought-depression period which affected the Great Plain states so critically, may not be indicative of the ultimate outcome of their venture into a new section of the country. In the state of Washington three years after the initial study of the drought migration summarized in the previous pages, as many of the original settlers were reinterviewed as could be located.[2] Field workers returned to the initial

---

[1] For interesting studies of the problems involved in the settlement of various nationality groups in a rural setting, see John P. Johansen, "Immigrant Settlements and Social Organization in South Dakota," and "Immigrants and Their Children in South Dakota," *South Dakota, Agricultural Experiment Station Bulletin* 313, 1937, and *Bulletin* 202, 1936, respectively.

[2] Paul H. Landis, "After Three Years: A Restudy of the Social Economic Adjustment of a Group of Drought Migrants," *Washington Agricultural Experiment Stations Bulletin* 407, Pullman, October, 1941.

areas of study and succeeded in locating 129 of the original 227 families in four of the areas covered.[1] At that time all of the drought settlers had been in the state a period of three to eight years.

At the time of these interviews economic assets of the group had almost doubled as compared to the time of their arrival. However, half of the group still had assets worth less than $750. The assets acquired depended a great deal upon the character of the area in which they settled. The worst situation was in an irrigated section in which settlement had been promoted by a transcontinental railroad and in which the water supply for irrigation was inadequate; the best situation, in a cutover area that offered some potentialities for the development of farm land.

An analysis of the character of the group's assets showed that their net worth had been increased primarily by buying small acreages on a contract basis. This increase in value represented primarily their output of labor in erecting a small dwelling and in improving the land.

Change in tenure status was marked; 56.6 per cent were still in the same tenure status; 13.3 per cent had decreased their status by becoming tenants rather than owners; 12 per cent had left farming for other private occupations; 7.3 per cent had left farming for urban employment; 8.4 had increased their tenure status by becoming owners, and 2.4 had retired because of incapacity to work.

At the time of the second interview problems of social adjustment had largely disappeared. The newcomers had already lost the characteristics of strangers and were feeling themselves a part of the common life of the community. Registration for voting had increased from 14.7 per cent to 70.5 per cent. In general, the group that had remained were satisfied with the new life they had adopted, and planned to remain in the state.

At the time of the second interview in 1941 the economic outlook still was far from bright in many parts of the state. Already, however, those on the coastal areas were beginning to get WPA employment in shipyards at relatively high wages.

Public relief in the form of Work Projects Administration wages, general assistance, and Farm Security Administration grants played an important part in the permanent settlement of the group reinterviewed. Sixty-one per cent had, according to records in relief offices in the respective counties, received public assistance at some time after their arrival in Washington. According to statements made by families interviewed, the certain income which WPA pro-

---

[1] In the original study five areas were covered. One, the Yakima Valley, an irrigated area, is so highly mobile in population that no attempt was made to restudy specific settlers in that area. A study was, however, made during the same period of the progress of drought settlers generally in the Yakima Valley. See Carl F. Reuss and Lloyd H. Fisher, "The Adjustment of New Settlers in the Yakima Valley, Washington," *Washington Agricultural Experiment Stations Bulletin* 397, Pullman, February, 1941.

vided in some cases made it possible for them to purchase their farm, work stock, and machinery. Of the total group, 24 stated that at one or more periods since settlement in the state they could not have kept alive without relief.

A higher proportion of the group remaining than of the group leaving received relief in the state of origin, and in Washington as well. Although the sample is small, with one exception the results are consistent for the three counties for which data were obtained.

This probably indicates that the group receiving relief in the previous state has been somewhat less mobile in the new area. It may mean also that a proportion of the group that received public assistance in Washington had remained because of the public assistance. This interpretation seems likely, since much of the public assistance was in the form of a WPA cash wage that may have been used in part toward the purchase of real estate. If this interpretation is the correct one, it should not be accepted as prima-facie evidence that the more stable group lacked initiative and thrift. Many of them may have been making the best of a bad situation which they saw no way to improve. The group that remained was, on the average, older and had larger families than those that moved on. These two factors tend to have a stabilizing effect on any group and also have a direct bearing on receipt of public assistance. Numerous studies of rural families on relief have shown that size of family is directly associated with relief recipiency, the large family tending to be on relief in a much higher proportion of cases than the small family.[1]

The war period brought to the interregional farm migrant of the drought period opportunity which could not have been anticipated even in 1940–1941 when the restudy was made. Not only in Washington, but throughout the entire coastal area, the war years brought unlimited opportunities for employment. Those settlers in the vicinity of metropolitan areas were strategically located. Their small farming venture offered them a place to live. They abandoned the farming enterprise and became war workers. In the vicinity of shipyards, shipyard busses went out as far as 75 miles and transported workers to their jobs daily.

Soon their identity as "Oakies," "Arkies," "drought migrants," and strangers was lost as they became a part of the old group with the influx of hoards of war workers, many of whom came from the rural areas in which the drought migrants originated.

THE WAR MIGRATION

World War II, with its unprecedented demand for workers, drew from small-town and farming areas large numbers of migrants, many of whom

[1] A number of these studies for the nation and for various states have been summarized in Paul H. Landis, "Relief Data as a Criteria of Submarginality," *Journal of Farm Economics*, vol. 20, pp. 488–494, May, 1938.

moved long distances. The map shows the state of origin of 580 rural families migrating to Spokane war industries.[1] It will be seen that much interregional migration was involved.

Similar maps for California and Oregon would show similar flows of rural population westward during the period of World War II, most of it to war

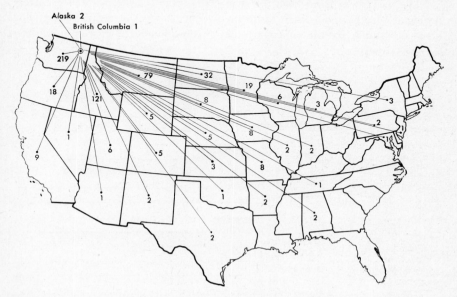

STATES OF ORIGIN OF 580 RURAL FAMILIES WORKING IN SPOKANE WAR INDUSTRY IN 1944

industries. The California migration, as during the drought period, would show Southern Plains states, principally Oklahoma, contributing large numbers of rural migrants.

The war migration not only uprooted the more mobile farm population, but also a substantial number of those long rooted in the soil. (See chart on p. 242.)[2] It will be seen that many had lived in their former community 10 years or longer.

The immediate postwar years have not shown the hasty retreat to farms that was anticipated, nor has the return migration to home counties been great. The census found[3] that 17,310,000 nonveteran civilians still lived in a different county in February, 1946, than that of their April, 1940 residence, whereas

[1] From Paul H. Landis and Katherine H. Day, "Farm and Small-town Workers in Metropolitan War Industry," *Washington Agricultural Experiment Stations Bulletin* 460, March, 1945.

[2] *Ibid.*, p. 16.

[3] *Internal Migration in the United States: April, 1940, to February, 1946, Population*, Series P-S, No. 11, U.S. Bureau of the Census, Washington, D.C., Dec. 6, 1946.

only 1,200,000 returned to their home counties between August, 1945, when war ended, and February, 1946. Veterans were returning to their home counties in 75 per cent of cases.

ACCOMMODATION IN INTERCOMMUNITY FARM MIGRATION

The movement from farm to farm in the same region creates less severe problems of adjustment than those involved in long-distance movement, but many of them are of the same type, and intercommunity migration implicates

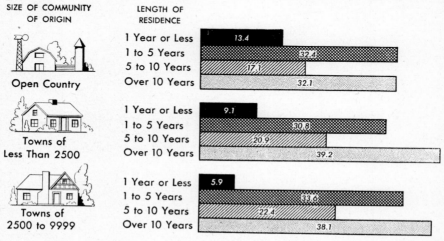

YEARS RESIDENCE IN HOME COUNTY PRIOR TO MOVING TO SPOKANE WAR INDUSTRY

much larger numbers. Tenants move often; many change farms every two or three years; about one out of three changes farms every year.[1] Associated conditions vary somewhat from section to section. In most sections they move in the early spring, usually the first of March, but in the wheat section, moving is done in the late fall, about the first of November. At either time the children must change schools and adjust to a new social group and to new institutional relationships.

The problems of accommodation are not confined to the children. Every change of community creates similar problems for all members of the household; every move increases the possibility that the adult will lose institutional attachments. The mobile tenant as a rule has scant loyalty to such institutions as church, grange, or even school and political organizations.[2] These and other aspects of tenancy are discussed more fully in a later chapter. Similar problems of accommodation are faced by owners when they move to a new community, but, generally speaking, owners move less often.

[1] *Farm Tenancy*, p. iv., Report of President's Committee, National Resources Planning Board, February, 1937.
[2] *Ibid.*, pp. 54–68.

One should not assume that the necessity of making readjustments is entirely a liability. There are often advantages to be gained from moving— economic, social, psychological. It is likely that the children of farm families who have moved at least once are better prepared to meet the new elements of city culture than the children of families who have always remained in one place, provided the two groups are on the same economic and educational level.

QUESTIONS FOR REVIEW AND DISCUSSION

1. In what realms of experience does the interregional farm-to-farm migrant encounter problems of adjustment?

2. What factors (*a*) entering into his motivation and (*b*) existing in the environment he enters, complicate the problems of adjustment of the interregional farm migrant?

3. Compare problems of accommodation within primary and within secondary groups.

4. In what ways do modern problems of adjustment differ from those which existed on the early frontier?

5. What economic group is involved in the migration from the drought area to the West Coast? Cite evidence.

6. What reasons did drought migrants give for leaving? How did these compulsive forces affect goals sought by the migrants?

7. How did economic resources attained during the early days of their adjustment to the West compare with predrought assets in the Plains?

8. Illustrate difficulties of adjustment induced by the persistence of past habits and attitudes, using plainsmen in the Far West as examples.

9. Are people who move in quest of security likely to be content with security when they realize it?

10. Illustrate culture shock consequent to farm-to-farm movement.

11. What problems of social adjustment may arise in the case of long-distance farm migration?

12. Explain the effect of colony settlement on (*a*) early social adjustments, (*b*) long-time adjustments.

13. Discuss interregional migration during the war.

14. Discuss adjustment problems of intercommunity farm migration.

COLLATERAL READING

Holzschuh, Alma, and Omer Mills: *A Study of 6,655 Migrant Households in California,* 1938 (mimeographed), Farm Security Administration, San Francisco, 1939.

Johansen, John P.: "Immigrant Settlements and Social Organization in South Dakota," *South Dakota Agricultural Experiment Station Bulletin* 313, Brookings, 1937.

Kraenzel, Carl F.: "Farm Population Mobility in Selected Montana Communities," *Montana Agricultural Experiment Station Bulletin* 371, Bozeman, 1939.

Landis, Paul H., and Katherine H. Day, "Farm and Small-town Workers in Metropolitan War Industry," *Washington Agricultural Experiment Stations Bulletin* 460, March, 1945.

Steinbeck, John: *Grapes of Wrath* (a novel), The Viking Press, Inc., New York, 1939.

Wakefield, Richard, and Paul H. Landis: "The Drought Farmer Adjusts to the West," *Washington Agricultural Experiment Stations Bulletin* 378, Pullman, 1939.

CHAPTER 17

CITY-TO-FARM MOVEMENT, MOTIVES AND IMPLICATIONS TO ADJUSTMENT

THE PRECEDING chapters emphasized the drift to the city and its implications. But data on the movement from farms to towns and cities also show a counter movement. (Refer again to the figure on page 183). From a half million to more than two and a half million people move from towns and cities to farms each year. In times of extreme depression, as we have seen, this movement to farms usually approximately balances the movement from farms to towns and cities; during the year 1932, it actually exceeded the latter movement. Periodically it is of major proportions.

This ruralward migration is of great significance, even though it has not been publicized as extensively as the movement cityward. It involves those people economically dispossessed by the city who seek subsistence on the farm, those who have small or average means and want to increase their sense of security by owning land, those of all the higher income classes who want something the city has been unable to give them, and many others.

The ruralward movement from the city is most often motivated by a desire for *subsistence* rather than for *status* as is the urbanward drift. The belief is generally held that the farm will provide at least the essentials for existence, if not a cash income and a high social position. That this belief is in part an illusion, relief data demonstrate; one out of eight of the total rural population was on relief during May, 1935, as compared to one out of six of the urban population.[1] Of course, a considerable part of this group was composed of villagers but, in many areas, relief among farmers was widespread. It is quite evident that the farm can no longer be depended upon to provide security for the urban backwash of a depression period. Nonetheless, as long as the illusion persists, the unsuccessful urbanite will drift toward the farm whenever economic conditions force him to adjust his ambitions to making merely a living.

The revolt against the city has been most prominent on the Eastern seaboard where congestion makes it difficult to move freely from the metropolis to the country on week ends and where cities have developed to such a size that they seem as prisons to some. The great increase in population in small towns adjoining cities and the growth of the part-time farming movement during the years 1930–1940 are suggestive of some of the characteristics of

[1] Corrington Gill, *On Relief*, Graphic Unit, Research Section, Federal Emergency Relief Administration, 1935.

the ruralward movement. The depression phenomenon of crowded homes in backward farming areas such as the Appalachian and Ozark Mountain regions indicates that great numbers of farm-born youth returned home. During the years 1930–1935 the largest increase in farm population was in suburban areas; the next greatest increase was in submarginal land areas, despite the fact that good land-use adjustment requires population decrease in regions of sub-marginal land.[1]

The back-to-the-land movement, then, includes a conglomerate group of rich and poor and middle class, of former farm residents and metropolitan born. Individual motives are as many as are the destinations of movement.

SPONSORS OF THE BACK-TO-THE-LAND MOVEMENT

The back-to-the-land movement has been widely advocated. During the depression of the early thirties, it was one of the most talked-of programs in government circles, the extreme crisis in urban industry, which expanded relief rolls to unprecedented proportions, having led many to believe that the way out was through the resettlement of great numbers of urban residents on the land. Certain industrial magnates felt that this program was desirable. The late Henry Ford, who was an avid believer in the virtues of the industrial worker living on the land as a part-time, gardener-farmer, was a leader in encouraging land settlement among his employees. "With one foot on the land and the other in industry, the country and every family in it are soundly based," he said. The Alabama Fuel and Iron Company workers were urged during the depression to raise their own meat, fruits, and vegetables.[2] Mrs. Franklin D. Roosevelt developed an interest in the resettlement of people living in the coal towns of West Virginia, where mines had closed down and the future outlook for a great number of families in the community was practically hopeless. Resettlement of inhabitants of these areas abandoned by industry on small tracts and the providing of part-time industry through the establishment of factories producing goods for government use were a part of the original plan. Franklin D. Roosevelt, soon after coming to the Presidency, was responsi-ble for the establishment of the Division of Subsistence Homesteads in the Department of interior to make loans for the purchase of subsistence homesteads.

One of the most interesting of the developments sponsored by the Resettle-ment Administration (now the Farmers' Home Administration) was the establishment of the Greenbelt towns, three having been built in the vicinity of large cities as Federal experimental demonstration projects. The first town to be constructed was Greenbelt, Md., a modern planned suburban community,

[1] Carl C. Taylor and Conrad Taeuber, "Wanted: Population Adjustment, Too," *Land Policy Review*, vol. 2, pp. 20–26, March–April, 1939.

[2] M. Emery, "School in Self-reliance," *National Business*, vol. 25, p. 71, December, 1937.

with over 12,000 acres of land and designed to take care of 3,000 families. The objectives of the Greenbelt towns as outlined by the sponsoring agency were as follows:

To obtain a large tract of land, and thus avoid the complications ordinarily due to diverse ownerships; in this tract to create a community, protected by an encircling green belt; the community to be designed primarily for families of modest income, and arranged and managed so as to encourage a family and community life which will be better than they now enjoy, but which will not involve subjecting them to coercion or theoretical and untested discipline; the dwellings and the land upon which they are located to be held in one ownership, preferably a local public agency to which the Federal government will transfer title, and which agency will rent or lease the dwellings but will not sell them; a municipal government to be set up, in character with such governments now existing or possible in that region; coordination to be established, in relation to the local and state governments, so that there may be provided those public services of educational and other character which the community will require; and, finally, to accomplish these purposes in such a way that the community may be a taxpaying participant in the region, that extravagant outlays from the individual family income will not be a necessity, and that the rents will be suitable to families of modest income.

To develop a land-use plan for the entire tract; to devise a system of rural economy coordinated with the land-use plan for the rural portions of the tract surrounding the suburban community; and to integrate both the physical plans and the economies of the rural area and the suburban community.[1]

A few projects have been carried out by private individuals. For instance, Benjamin Brown, a wealthy Jew, established 100 families on the Jersey Home-steads, a 1,200-acre cooperative settlement project.[2] Father Ligutti's Home-stead at Granger, Iowa, another such project, was sponsored by a Catholic priest.[3] Fifty homes were plotted on a 224-acre tract, home ownership to be acquired by the settlers through long-time payments.

Much of the movement back to the land, however, was and is without sponsorship. Impersonal pressures of a hazardous economic order drive many to seek refuge in the suburbs or in their parental homes back on the farm.

THE PART-TIME FARMING DEVELOPMENT

Certainly one of the major phases of the drift ruralward, especially during the past three decades, has been the marked tendency of urbanites to engage in part-time farming. Their farms are concentrated in industrial areas in the

[1] *Greenbelt Towns*, The Resettlement Administration, Washington, D. C., September, 1936.

[2] R. F. Armstrong, "Four-million-dollar Village," *Saturday Evening Post*, vol. 210, pp. 5–7 *ff*., Feb. 5, 1938.

[3] W. C. Taylor, "Father Ligutti's Homestead (at Granger, near Des Moines)," *Christian Century*, vol. 56, pp. 56–58, Jan. 11, 1939.

eastern part of the nation and about the metropolitan centers on the West Coast (see map). Baker estimates that about 2,000,000 back-to-the-land people were still living on farms in January, 1935, when the Census of Agriculture was taken, and that another 2,000,000 youths were backed up on farms because of a lack of industrial opportunity. In 1934, about 2,000,000 farm operators (almost a third of the nation's farmers) had "work for pay or income

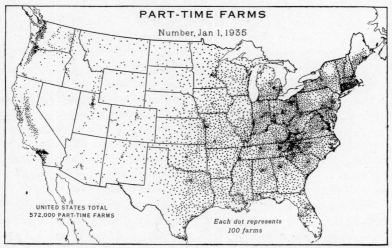

PART-TIME FARMS

Number, Jan 1, 1935

UNITED STATES TOTAL
572,000 PART-TIME FARMS

Each dot represents
100 farms

U.S. Bureau of Agricultural Economics.

Part-time farms are one index of city-to-farm movement. They are concentrated in the hinterland of industrial centers. This is a picture of a depression period when part-time farming was popular.

at jobs, business, or professions, not connected with the farm."[1] Outside revenue averaged $573 per year.[2]

The part-time farming group has been studied more extensively than any other large group of ruralward migrants. In many respects this group is typical of some of the other groups that have moved from town to country but are not engaged in part-time farming; for this reason, a fairly comprehensive summary of the characteristics, interests, and adjustment problems of the part-time farming group is given.[3] The data are for the 1930's, but are significant because

[1] O. E. Baker, *A Graphic Summary of the Number, Size, and Type of Farm, and Value of Products*, U. S. Department of Agriculture Miscellaneous Publication 266, p. 2, Washington, D. C., 1937.

[2] Associated Press release.

[3] A part-time farm is defined here as one that contributes to the family living and whose operator normally derives a substantial part of his total income from an occupation other than farming or from some nonoccupational source.

Wakeley has identified four types of part-time farmers in Iowa: (1) the part-time general farmer who ordinarily farms ten acres or more, has a team of horses and other livestock,

they are more typical of the future than the gasless years of the early 1940's when the suburban trend was checked.

CHARACTERISTICS OF THE PART-TIME FARMING POPULATION

The part-time farming population is composed predominately of middle-aged, middle-income people with large families, according to the findings of several part-time farming studies in widely scattered states.[1] Undoubtedly the preponderance of people with large families is explained in part by the desire of parents to rear their children in the open country. In many areas skilled and semiskilled classes make up an abnormally high proportion of the group. Common laborers and professional people are also numerous, but there seems to be a rather low proportion of the proprietary classes represented. Near large urban industrial areas the majority of part-time farmers are industrial workers, many of them retired or unemployed. In Connecticut 40 per cent were found to be in these two categories.[2] In areas where rural industries such as lumbering and mining predominate, most part-time farmers are people who have always lived in rural areas but have supplemented their income from agriculture by industrial earnings. In the Appalachian and Ozark Mountain regions, in the Lake states cutover timber region and the cutover timber regions of the West Coast, in coal fields in the Eastern states, and in other such areas, part-time farming has been characteristic.[3] Frequently in better farming sections the old farmer who is ready to retire, rather than moving to town, moves to a small part-time farm in the immediate neighborhood of a town or city.[4]

---

and produces farm crops, mostly for food but occasionally for sale; (2) the garden farmer who grows garden products and small fruits primarily for home use; (3) the specialist who concentrates on one enterprise and produces his speciality primarily for the market, but sometimes purchases farm products for resale; (4) the person who lives in the country, but is not particularly concerned about agricultural production and generally has less than a single acre of land. Ray E. Wakeley, "Part-time and Garden Farming in Iowa," *Iowa Agricultural Experiment Station Bulletin* 340, pp. 22–23, Ames, 1935.

[1] For substantiating data, see Carl F. Reuss, "Social Characteristics of Part-time Farmers in Washington," *Washington Agricultural Experiment Stations Bulletin* 380, Pullman, 1939; Ray E. Wakeley, *op. cit.*; R. L. Adams and J. L. Wann, "Part-time Farming for Income," *California Agricultural Experiment Station Bulletin* 581, Berkeley, 1934; M. E. John, "Part-time Farming in Six Industrial Areas in Pennsylvania," *Pennsylvania State College Bulletin* 361, State College, 1938.

[2] I. G. Davis and L. A. Salter, Jr., "Part-time Farming in Connecticut," *Connecticut Agricultural Experiment Station Bulletin* 201, Storrs, 1935.

[3] For a study of the problems of some of these groups, see P. G. Beck and M. C. Forster, *Six Rural Problem Areas*, pp. 58–59, 65–66, 95, 96, Federal Emergency Relief Administration, Washington, D. C., 1935.

[4] Ray E. Wakeley, *op. cit.*, finds that one in twelve part-time farmers in Iowa are in this group.

Hummel and Hummel, summarizing the findings of various part-time farming studies and comparing the results with their own study in Virginia, found that from 50 to 75 per cent of part-time farmers throughout the country had had farming experience before beginning their part-time farming enterprises.[1] A study of part-time farmers in metropolitan areas of New York state showed that almost 60 per cent were reared in the country.[2] These and several other studies suggest that the group, in a majority of cases, has had some farming experience before taking up part-time farming.

MOTIVES FOR ENGAGING IN PART-TIME FARMING

Chief among the motives for entering part-time farming are the desires to supplement the family income, to provide a better environment for children, and to escape city life. In Iowa two-thirds of the farm families studied took up part-time farming to increase their income or to reduce the cost of living; one in every seven turned to the rural environment as a better one in which to rear children; and one in 12 moved to the country because of a preference for it as a place to live or because of dislike of the city.[3]

Adams and Wann tabulated the reasons given by part-time farmers in California for entering agriculture, dividing them into economic and personal.[4] About an equal number gave as their chief economic reason the need to supplement their income and to provide for their old age. The chief personal reason given was love of country life, more citing this than any other reason. The reason of second importance was to improve or safeguard health; of third importance, to provide a better environment for children. Other personal reasons mentioned were the wish to indulge in a hobby and to find recreational outlets.

Reuss, summarizing factors involved in the part-time farming movement in Washington, found the quest for security on part-time farms heightened in times when families felt economic pressure. Unemployment, layoffs, and limited work schedules led them to seek residence on the land as a way of conserving limited cash income through saving rent and raising produce for home use. Facilitating the movement to the land during periods of industrial depression were the lowered prices for small plots which were offered by real estate dealers on small monthly payment terms. Supplementing this movement were the desires to live away from the city, to indulge in a hobby, to cultivate gardens, and in general to indulge in "gentleman farming."[5]

[1] B. L. Hummel and R. B. Hummel, *Part-time Farming in Virginia*, Virginia Polytechnic Institute, Blacksburg, and Division of Rural Research, Works Progress Administration, Washington, D. C., 1938.

[2] Kenneth Hood, "An Economic Study of Part-time Farming in the Elmira and Albany Areas of New York, 1932 and 1933," *Cornell Agricultural Experiment Station*, Ithaca, 1936.

[3] Ray E. Wakeley, *op. cit.*

[4] R. L. Adams and J. L. Wann, *op. cit.*

[5] Carl F. Reuss, *op. cit.*

ECONOMIC RETURNS FROM PART-TIME FARMING

A study of part-time farming in the state of Washington indicated that the gross value of farm products produced was on the average about $250 and the net value slightly under $150.[1] Supplementing this income the average nonfarm income of part-time farmers was around $700 per year. Whether the total income was sufficient to assure economic security is somewhat doubtful; probably many families spent the $150 saved on food for transportation.

A large proportion of the part-time farmers were home owners; in fact, over 90 per cent, which would seem to indicate that part of the reason for entering the rural area was to acquire a family homestead.[2]

Hummel and Hummel found that part-time farming families in Virginia made an average saving of $58.08 per year through the use of home-produced foods.[3] They concluded that the family with a half-acre garden, a cow, two hogs, and a flock of chickens could be almost self-sufficing as far as food supply was concerned.

A study of part-time farmers in six industrial areas of Pennsylvania showed that they received 45 cents an hour for the time spent in industry but a return of only about 13 cents an hour for labor on their farms. In spite of this differential, well over half of the group had no criticisms to make of part-time farming.[4]

Wakely found that one out of five of the part-time farm families studied in Iowa was receiving relief.[5] This proportion was much higher than that among all farmers and higher than among people in the cities around which the part-time farms are located. He found also that three out of four of the families were without adequate supplemental employment and that they often failed to make the anticipated contribution to the family income. Many of the economic difficulties of the part-time farmers, he reported, were due to the fact that a certain proportion of them had no background of farming experience and no agency existed to assist them in an educational way to become farmers.[6]

Hood found that part-time farmers in New York state sold on the average $80 worth of products per year.[7] However, over half of the group studied sold nothing during the year of study; less than a fourth of the annual food needs of the group was produced on the farm.

---

[1] *Ibid.*

[2] In addition to the city folks who enter part-time farming is a group of farmers who supplement their small farming enterprise by industrial employment, thus becoming part-time farmers. This latter group is not considered in the present discussion.

[3] B. L. Hummel and R. B. Hummel, *op. cit.*

[4] M. E. John, *op. cit.*

[5] Ray E. Wakeley, *op. cit.*

[6] An interesting satire by an ex-farmer on an attempt to farm without a background of experience is found in "To Hell with Farming," *American Mercury*, vol. 42, pp. 313–318, November, 1937.

[7] Kenneth Hood, *op. cit.*

In Connecticut, part-time farmers were found to sell less than 3 per cent of all products marketed by the farmers of that state, even though 60 per cent of the farms there are operated on a part-time basis.[1]

These instances, taken from widely scattered sections of the country, show that the economic returns from part-time farming are not high and that security is not always achieved. There are, however, in some cases compensating advantages of a noneconomic nature.

ECONOMIC IMPLICATIONS OF SUBSISTENCE FARMING

The economic effects of the increase in subsistence living are far-reaching and complicated—too complicated to permit extensive discussion here. Suffice it to say that today the urban and the rural community alike thrive on expenditures for consumable products. Any increase in subsistence living is likely to reduce automatically the amount of money spent for agricultural products and also for the goods of many types of industry. Many who see in the return to the soil a utopia of security certainly have not gone deeply into the full implications of such a move. Any movement that brings security to some, that increases a people's delight in living, and that enriches the experience of children is worth economic sacrifices, but there is always a price to pay for a lowered standard of living.

Pollard, in a fascinating article in which he described the possible future of Grainger County, Tenn., which was severely afflicted by the depression, showed the ultimate effect of completely self-sufficient living on the farm.[2] Beginning with an affirmation that Grainger County could meet its problems by a "bitter-ender" solution, this to consist in the barring of all luxury goods purchased with cash, he then pointed to some of the far-reaching consequences of such action.

This is unquestionable, because it means only the adoption of methods by which agricultural communities have lived since the dawn of history. Grainger County can save some $70,000 on clothing. It can go back to the spindle and distaff, to home cobbling, and to home weaving, and in these ways can possibly save more than $70,000. It can also save at least $42,000 on food. It can use chicory instead of coffee and it can use sorghum instead of sugar. And then, Grainger County can do away with automobiles entirely. There is absolutely no doubt that this solution is possible for this county. History teaches us nothing more thoroughly. This is the solution advocated by many estimable gentlemen who sit in armchairs, and worry about other people's extravagances. It is entirely feasible, entirely possible, and it is the solution which has been adopted through necessity and has actually been undertaken. But if Grainger

[1] I. G. Davis and L. A. Salter, *op. cit.*

[2] A. L. Pollard, "What a County Trade Balance through Agricultural-Industrial Companionship Will Mean," excerpt from the *Proceedings of the Third Conference on Companionship of Agriculture and Industry*, held at the University of Tennessee, November, 1933.

County adopts this solution, what about the world outside. If, for example, Grainger County goes without automobiles, what about Detroit? Grainger County, it is true, may be saved from reverting to wilderness by such a solution, but can Detroit be saved from reverting to jungle? Personally, I believe that it would be definitely more desirable that Grainger County should revert to wilderness than that Detroit should revert to jungle. The wilderness of Grainger might be peopled by bobcats, but the jungle of Detroit would be peopled by creatures far more ferocious.[1]

Continuing his analysis, Pollard described a trip through Grainger County, where he saw more homemade sledges in use in one hour than during the previous 10 years and saw a house built without materials from the outside except a few nails, four hinges, two latches, and eight sash. Rude handicraft was reviving in the face of stark necessity. He concluded that the best solution for Grainger County was a combination of part-time farming and industry.

Although dealing with an extreme situation, this article suggests possible economic implications to the city if increasing numbers of people should find it possible to draw a considerable amount of their subsistence from farm living. The same effects would be felt by commercial agriculture, which must depend for a market for its goods upon those who purchase rather than raise food-stuffs. There is a compensating factor which should not be overlooked, however. Many families, by living on the farm, have probably improved their diet and are actually eating many foods that they would have been unable to buy had they lived in the city. Their expenditures for processed agricultural products do not necessarily decrease proportionately to their consumption of home-grown products.

NONECONOMIC VALUES OF RURAL LIVING FOR URBAN WORKERS

Numerous popular articles testify to the fact that many urban people find great satisfaction in living on a farm, either living there full time or commuting to work in the city. Although some of these accounts are written for journalistic effect and may be lacking in sincerity, they no doubt in most instances reflect genuine appreciation gained at first hand, just as the sarcastic, critical indictments of rural living by other individuals probably reveal actual experience.

Some of these persons report that the depression drove them toward a quieter form of life, thereby giving them a chance to live as they chose, a thing they had not dared to contemplate before. They find the simple life most satisfying.[2]

[1] *Ibid.*, p. 6.
[2] P. Curtiss, "They Are Moving to the Country," *Harpers*, vol. 171, pp. 67–79, June, 1935.

One writer states that farming is for him a religious experience, a form of religious art.[1] A New England woman, upon returning to her isolated farm after losing her job in the city, found the experience a pleasant one; great equanimity and peace of mind have come to her through close contact with elemental things.[2]

A noted writer reports that she finds more time and strength for her work when living in the country, that she likes her fellow men better when she is not forced to associate with them too often.[3] A city couple who bought a dairy in New England say that "after seven years of tinkering and digging, we are still joyously going back to the old place whenever we can spare a week end."[4] Another author, retreating to a cabin in the Berkshires, found health, vigor, sleep, and zest for life.[5] A New York City couple, after the crash of 1929, moved to a farm and found complete release. They no longer felt compelled to do things, but found that on the farm there is always something to do.[6] One writer cites values to his children for which there is no dollar and cents compensation;[7] another states that farm life provides an ideal combination of physical and mental work.[8]

Equally vigorous, on the other hand, are the protests of those who were much too busy on the farm to spend the summer watching the cows crop the grass while they dreamed the days away.[9]

A comprehensive study of part-time farmers in the vicinity of metropolitan centers of New York state by Hood showed that while well over half of them considered that there was an economic advantage in living in the country,[10] over a third felt that one of the big assets of country living lies in the fact that they like it; others mentioned improved health and "better place to rear children." Almost half of this group saw disadvantages in living in the country as compared to the city, among them being the need for transportation, the lack of conveniences, and bad roads. The majority of the group studied, however,

[1] R. L. Burgess, "Farming: A Variety of Religious Experience," *American Review*, vol. 3, pp. 591–607, October, 1934.

[2] Lucile Grebenc, "I Come Home," *Forum*, vol. 91, pp. 40–45, January, 1934.

[3] Dorothy Canfield Fisher, "Why I Live Where I Live," *Golden Book*, vol. 16, pp. 540–542, December, 1932.

[4] R. Haley, "Week-end Pioneers," *Forum*, vol. 99, pp. 328–332, June, 1938.

[5] C. W. Whittemore, "I Am Rich: Life in a Cabin in the Berkshires," *Scribner's*, vol. 97, pp. 375–378, June, 1935.

[6] D. Taylor, "City Fellow Goes Rustic," *American Magazine*, vol. 118, pp. 52–53 *ff.*, July, 1934.

[7] T. H. Alexander, "So I Bought a Farm," *American Magazine*, vol. 120, pp. 70 *ff.*, December, 1935.

[8] L. Owen, "Escape from Babylon," *American Mercury*, vol. 26, pp. 477–486, August, 1932.

[9] "To Hell with Farming," *op. cit.*

[10] Kenneth Hood, *op. cit.*, pp. 128–134.

felt that the country was more desirable than the city as far as they personally were concerned. In a total of less than 5 per cent of the cases were both husband and wife dissatisfied with rural life; in only 2 per cent of the cases was one of them alone dissatisfied. Another 12 per cent, while not disappointed with country life as such, were dissatisfied with their location. In four out of five cases both part-time farmers and their wives were contented not only with country living but with their location. A great number took a keen interest in their work on the place, and gardens, flowers, crops, and livestock became hobbies.

SOCIAL ADJUSTMENT OF CITY-TO-FARM MIGRANTS

The reception which the urban person moving to the country receives there seems to depend in considerable part upon the personal characteristics of the newcomer. Although conditions no doubt differ in various sections, the findings of Hood for areas in the vicinity of metropolitan communities in New York are suggestive of several of the possible reactions of the community to strangers from the city. The financial status and occupation of the newcomer affect his adjustment problems, the community naturally resenting the coming of destitute families who plan to make a living from a few acres of barren soil. Natives object to the coming of the poorer laboring classes because of their low standard of living; they oppose also the influx of those with a standard of living higher than the prevailing standard of the community, *e.g.*, salaried professional people. The objection to the latter group arises from the fact that they immediately demand better roads, better schools, and more community services, and the full-time farmers feel they cannot afford these luxuries. Communities usually object to the entrance of foreign-born families, also.

For several reasons, Hood reports, the rural community often welcomes newcomers from the city. Most of them produce few competitive crops and, in fact, most of them sell very little farm produce; they are available as a labor supply in busy seasons; they help share the tax burden for the support of local institutions; the denser settlement of the neighborhood makes possible new services—telephones, electricity; a market is created for real estate; a larger membership is made possible for local organizations as well as more adequate financial support.

In many communities this ruralward movement probably has had the effect of entirely changing the complexion of social life, calling for institutional adjustments and for extensive revisions in land-use patterns, increasing the burden upon routes of transportation, and greatly intensifying the problem of commuting between farm and city.

In some areas of the East the whole countryside and all the small villages surrounding the city had been taken over by commuters. For example, Leland B. Tate, in studying the commuter movement in the vicinity of Rochester,

N. Y., found that 21.7 per cent of the regular dwellings in the area surveyed were commuter dwellings; in one township near the city almost 50 per cent of all homes were commuter-owned.[1]

A series of studies[2] dealing with suburbanization in Connecticut by Whetten and his colleagues suggests various problems of adjustment experienced by certain communities that have been invaded by former city residents. They describe conflict between old-time residents and the suburban families in Windsor whose points of view toward civic affairs clash. The newcomers "are not so much interested in preserving the charm of antiquity as they are in having all the familiar conveniences in their country homes. They want electric lights, sewers, sidewalks, water, and roads. They want modern schools and modern homes. They want progress and growth."[3] The older residents, wishing to preserve the historic charm of their New England village, resent the intrusion of the outsiders with their new-fangled ideas and also the increased expenditure for various public services.

Bayne, describing the trend of rural settlement of city people in Dutchess County, N. Y., stated that already eight out of every ten dwellings were occupied by nonfarm families, much to the concern of local farm residents.[4] He found that numerous problems were created for the local community by the newcomers. Many of the new families were barely able to raise their subsistence; most of them could not afford the best stock or even care for the stock they had. Taxes and gasoline came high. Social contacts in the area described between the newcomers and the residents were very few.

The greatest obstacles to the successful settlement on the land of city people for farming purposes are the finding of a suitable piece of land at a reasonable price, the financing of the purchase of a tract, and the building of a homestead. If the family is not concerned about farming income, the situation is, of course, different. In the vicinity of some of the larger metropolitan centers of the East, an individual can purchase a rural homestead of 100 acres of land and a house cheaper than he can buy space and build a home in the city. This is because much of the soil in the countryside has been depleted and is too unproductive to support a family dependent on full-time farming. The decline

---

[1] Leland B. Tate, "The Rural Homes of City Workers and the Urban-rural Migration," *Cornell Agricultural Experiment Station Bulletin* 595, Ithaca, 1934.

[2] Nathan L. Whetten and E. C. Devereux, Jr., "Studies of Suburbanization in Connecticut," no. 1, *Connecticut Agricultural Experiment Station Bulletin* 212, Storrs, 1936; Nathan L. Whetten and R. F. Field, "Studies of Suburbanization in Connecticut," no. 2, *Connecticut Agricultural Experiment Station Bulletin* 226, Storrs, 1938; and Nathan L. Whetten, "Studies of Suburbanization in Connecticut," no. 3, *Connecticut Agricultural Experiment Station Bulletin* 230, Storrs, 1939.

[3] Nathan L. Whetten and E. C. Devereaux, Jr., *op. cit.*, p. 135.

[4] M. C. Bayne, "Middle Country," *Survey Graphic*, vol. 27, pp. 458–462 *ff.*, September, 1938.

in land values has made it comparatively easy for city people who desire to commute to obtain farmsteads.

In the shift from industry to part-time farming the urbanite probably faces less severe problems of social adjustment than in cases where he turns completely to farming. This is true because the part-time farmer is able to continue many of his previous social and economic habits. On the other hand, he is not without his problems of adaptation. Studies indicate, however, that well over 50 per cent of part-time farmers are satisfied with the change.[1] Wakeley found that nine out of ten of the group studied in Iowa preferred to live on farms, in spite of the fact that many of them had not made a successful economic adjustment, one out of five being on relief.[2] He concluded that even though financial necessity drove many of this group to the farm, an improvement in economic conditions will not draw all of them back to the city.

Adams and Wann found that a majority of both the part-time farmers and their wives felt that their farming venture was a good idea, most of them answering "yes" to the question, "Would you do it again?" These authors also studied reasons for failure among those who had quit, and found that lack of finances, production of commodities at too high a cost, extravagance of family members, purchase of an automobile without sufficient income, wives unable or unwilling to assume part-time farming duties, buying the homestead at too high a price, no experience in the type of work demanded, sickness in the family, laziness, too much time spent away from the farm, and similar economic and personal factors were involved in their failure.[3]

Popular articles written by more sophisticated suburban farmers indicate some of the problems of adjustment faced by these types. Some with a propensity for individualistic behavior cannot adjust to the social controls of the smaller community. The people seem to them to live "unnecessarily in chains bound by small fears, conventions, social pressures, and petty prudences."[4]

Some are too idealistic when they enter into the new venture to be practical. They may invest lifetime savings in poor land because of a lack of understanding of the limitations under which a farmer necessarily operates, and as a consequence may lose everything and end on relief.[5] Others who have gone back to the soil as an escape from unemployment may find adequate compensations for a time but eventually become restless and dissatisfied with the new

[1] M. E. John, *op. cit.*, finds that 63 per cent of a sample of 887 part-time farmers had no adverse criticisms to make of their part-time farming experience. Those who had objections state that their main difficulties were expense of transportation, inconvenience of transportation facilities, and lack of household conveniences. See also Kenneth Hood, *op. cit.*

[2] Ray E. Wakeley, *op. cit.*

[3] These authors list 23 reasons which are sometimes given for failure.

[4] F. Crowder, "Farewell Suburbia," *Forum*, vol. 98, pp. 134–137, September, 1937.

[5] An interesting account of such a case is given in Mrs. C. H. Dirlam's "We Sowed Plans and Reaped Relief," *Saturday Evening Post*, vol. 207, pp. 38 *ff.*, May 25, 1935.

situation; they return to the city centers as soon as opportunities open to them.[1]

Undoubtedly in many instances a higher standard of living prevails among the urban people who move to farms than among farmers of the region. Luxuries and conveniences tend to be prominent among them, though their income may be very modest. In a study in the state of Washington, many more homes of part-time farmers than of full-time farmers were found to have running water, bathrooms, automobiles, and radios.[2] Also a much higher proportion of part-time than of other farms were found to be situated on good roads and close to a school. On the other hand, rural slums have developed in the vicinity of many cities where poverty is as dire as in the tenements.

For some years much was heard about the decentralization of industry, and there has actually been considerable movement in this direction. During the decade 1920–1930, the population in intermediate-sized cities and in satellite cities increased more rapidly than in the central metropolis.[3] Certain industries moved out into the fringes of cities and some even into open-country and small-town areas. With the shift of industry then went labor. From a social viewpoint this movement has frequently been disastrous because one of the motives of industry has been to escape labor-union control and to hire workers in small-town and country areas at low wages. Some of the early subsistence programs led in this same direction; in fact, subsistence resettlement was curbed in part because of the danger of exploitation by industry of part-time farm workers.[4]

SOCIAL AND PSYCHOLOGICAL EFFECTS OF THE RURALWARD MOVEMENT

The commuter movement has no doubt hastened the "rurban" trend, i.e., the blending of rural and urban cultures and psychological traits. Probably the predominant effect has been to diffuse the culture of the metropolis into the hinterland, for people moving from an urban community into a rural area are likely to carry with them many urban traits. On the other hand, in certain cases at least, the tendency has been to ruralize somewhat the urban group. As Tate comments:

The movement into rural homes is pushing the periphery of the city beyond its corporate limits and extending its zone of influence. It is bringing about the establishment of business centers on the edge of the city and the extension of delivery services,

[1] For a popular account, see C. M. Simon's "Retreat to the Land; Experience in Poverty in the Ozarks," *Scribner's*, vol. 93, pp. 309–312, May, 1933.

[2] Reuss, *op. cit.*

[3] R. D. McKenzie, *The Rise of Metropolitan Communities*, McGraw-Hill Book Company, Inc., New York, 1933.

[4] J. Mitchell, "Low-cost Paradise," *New Republic*, vol. 84, pp. 152–155, Sept. 18, 1935.

and therefore an expansion of the trade area. At the same time it is bringing the rural area into a new relationship with the city and breaking down the old idea that a rural area is one of isolation and a minimum of conveniences.[1]

There is a growing consciousness that the metropolis is too stimulating, that life has become too complex, that the pace is too strenuous for the human nervous system, that the metropolis makes too many mental demands and too few physical ones. Many urbanites, through country living, are beginning once more to emulate the virtue of working with one's hands, of keeping occupied, of using time profitably, to emulate many of the elemental values which have always characterized rural life. Living in the simple atmosphere of the country tends automatically to reduce superficiality. There is an unusually high proportion of children among urban people moving to rural areas. Children make for neighborhoods by forcing contact between adults, thus introducing a closer-knit type of living than is characteristic in the densely settled areas of the metropolis.

Often the city person who returns to the farm is greatly hindered in adjustment because of the persistence of habits which have been well established in the urban community. Habits of work, thrift, social tastes, and recreation developed in the city may be incompatible with the requirements in the rural community into which he moves, depending somewhat on his character and the patterns of the area into which he goes. If he has an urban income on which to draw, he may be able to fulfill all the desires to which he is habituated; if he must depend upon the farm for a living, there is a strong possibility that he will be unable to conform to the requirements of farm life. Success or failure will depend, of course, on amount of capital and capacity to modify established habits.

SOCIAL ADJUSTMENT OF URBAN MIGRANTS TO THE DISTANT HINTERLAND

The commuter and part-time farming movements in the vicinity of metropolitan cities represent quite a different problem of adjustment from that of urban peoples who move to a distant hinterland to engage in full-time farming.

It is probably a safe assumption that most of those who return to the farm are among the misfits of the city, incapable of making an adjustment there. The question is often raised as to whether or not this backwash group is inferior. Certainly it is not necessarily so. Failure to adapt to city living is not an absolute index of ability or capacity to adapt successfully to life in the farm community. In any case, however, there has been a loss of time and experience by this backwash group so that its return probably represents some general disadvantage to the farm community. The influx in times of depression of

---

[1] Leland B. Tate, *op. cit.*, p. 47.

people who during past periods of prosperity have contributed only to the city puts a heavy burden on the farm community. In many rural areas their return during the last great depression led to overcrowding of homes, serious exploitation of land in submarginal areas, and an increase in human misery. Many return to the rural community because of a need to escape intolerable conditions in the city rather than from any fundamental desire to live on a farm. Some are misfits in the rural community as well as in the city. Often their coming aggravates local institutional problems by increasing school enrollments, by swelling relief rolls beyond all normal proportions, and by causing the exploitation of natural resources, through the intensive use of land which otherwise might have been employed in a more reasonable manner.

Individual problems of this returning group are numerous and intense. Many feel frustrated and disappointed in life, some have no aptitude for or interest in farming, and even those who do possess these qualities usually are lacking in financial resources.

Of course, there are some who are neither a problem to the community nor to themselves. Among them are young people who have always wanted to farm and have, by work in other lines, accumulated enough funds to begin a farming enterprise. Even those who were driven to the farm by industrial crisis are often able to make satisfactory adjustments. At least, they were an object lesson to youth on the farm, many of whom, during the depression, came to regard agriculture more highly because they learned that the city, like the farm, had its hazards.

As to the occupational adjustment of urban-born young men moving ruralward, the charts on page 214 and 215 show that an undue proportion falls in both extremes as compared to the stable urban group. As compared to the stable rural group, more were in the lowest income class, but more also were in the two upper income levels. After work experience, urban young men who had moved to rural areas gained some advantage over urban-reared young men who remained in cities. Urban-reared young women who moved to rural areas achieved a higher income level after experience on the job than any other residence-mobility group. However, the number of cases involved (48) in this group was too small to be conclusive. As to finding a place in preferred occupations, urban youth moving to rural areas excelled other groups in obtaining positions of high status.

In summary, this brief review of the city-to-farm movement shows that people of diverse personality types, and with varied experience backgrounds and motives are seeking rural areas. Many are motivated by a desire for economic security, having been disillusioned in their struggle for status in the urban community. Others no doubt have revived in late middle life or in old age the sentimental attachments of their youth to land and rural scenery and seek a quiet atmosphere away from the highly competitive urban environment.

Among them are the defeated who have been forced to realize that they cannot find a secure place in the city's life, can achieve neither recognition nor the economic reward and perhaps not even the satisfaction that they had hoped urban life would bring them.

The movement is most significant because it is one more representation of the major tendency for rural and urban life to merge in the highly fluid society of today. Significant also from the personal viewpoint is the meaning of the adjustment struggle that ensues in the change from an urban to a rural habitat. The data at hand based on the experience of part-time farmers and of commuters indicate that various economic and social problems are involved both for individuals and for the communities into which they go. Much more study of this aspect of urban-rural movement is needed if we are to understand all its implications. But even in the absence of this desirable information, it is obvious that the trend from urban to rural living in the vicinity of the metropolis is a major one in modern life and that the quest for a place on the land by defeated economic groups during times of industrial depression is likely to continue even though we live in a commercial agricultural age when the farm does not necessarily offer greater security than town or city.

QUESTIONS FOR REVIEW AND DISCUSSION

1. What seems to be the dominant motive of the city-to-farm movement? How does it compare with the dominant motive of urbanward migration?

2. In what areas has the back-to-the-land movement been most prominent?

3. What various groups sponsored the back-to-the-land movement during the early thirties?

4. Analyze the social characteristics of the part-time farming population.

5. What reasons do people give for having entered part-time farming?

6. Is part-time farming profitable financially? Summarize the evidence.

7. What are some possible economic implications of subsistence farming?

8. Do urban people who enter part-time farming seem to be satisfied with their venture? Summarize the findings.

9. Discuss the adjustment problems incident to city-to-farm movement, (*a*) as they involve the person moving to the country, (*b*) as they affect the community in which the urban migrant settles.

10. Mention the factors that hinder the accommodation of urban people to country life.

11. What are some of the broad social implications of the city-to-farm movement?

12. What problems, not experienced by those settling within the metropolitan fringe, may be involved in the accommodation of urban people moving to the distant hinterland?

COLLATERAL READING

Adams, R. L., and J. L. Wann: "Part-time Farming for Income," *California Agricultural Experiment Station Bulletin* 581, Berkeley, 1934.

Allen, R. H., L. S. Cottrell, Jr., W. W. Troxell, H. L. Herring, and A. D. Edwards: *Part-time Farming in the Southeast*, Research Monograph IX, Division of Social Research, Works Progress Administration, Washington, D. C., 1937.

Davis, I. G., and L. A. Salter: "Part-time Farming in Connecticut," *Connecticut Agricultural Experiment Station Bulletin* 201, Storrs, 1935.

Farm Security Administration: *Greenbelt Towns*, Washington, D. C., 1936.

Hood, Kenneth: "An Economic Study of Part-time Farming in the Elmira and Albany Areas of New York, 1932 and 1933," *Cornell Agricultural Experiment Station Bulletin* 647, Ithaca, 1936.

John M. E.: "Part-time Farming in Six Industrial Areas in Pennsylvania," *Pennsylvania State College Bulletin* 361, State College, 1938.

Reuss, Carl F.: "Social Characteristics of Part-time Farmers in Washington," *Washington Agricultural Experiment Stations Bulletin* 380, Pullman, 1939.

Tate, Leland B.: "The Rural Homes of City Workers and the Urban-rural Migration," *Cornell Agricultural Experiment Station Bulletin* 595, Ithaca, 1934.

Wakeley, Ray E.: "Part-time and Garden Farming in Iowa," *Iowa Agricultural Experiment Station Bulletin* 340, Ames, 1935.

Whetten, Nathan L.: "Studies of Suburbanization in Connecticut," no. 3, *Connecticut Agricultural Experiment Station Bulletin* 230, Storrs, 1939.

———, and E. C. Devereux, Jr.: "Studies of Suburbanization in Connecticut," no. 1, *Connecticut Agricultural Experiment Station Bulletin* 212, Storrs, 1936.

———, and R. F. Field: "Studies of Suburbanization in Connecticut," no. 2, *Connecticut Agricultural Experiment Station Bulletin* 226, Storrs, 1938.

CHAPTER 18

SOCIAL DIFFERENTIATION AND THE PROCESS OF STRATIFICATION

THE PRINCIPLE OF SOCIAL DIFFERENTIATION

GROUPS living in established societies develop a sense of social difference, which usually involves fictions of inferiority and superiority, with certain groups, races, or classes set apart. Social barriers are erected to protect the rights and interests of the favored classes, hindering those who aspire to coveted positions, and, at the same time, affording some guarantee that those who have already attained access to the better things of the society will retain them.

In many societies the numerous artificial barriers which fence men off into different grades and qualities require that a man find his vocation within his own classification in the hierarchy of status. Because his limitations are fixed and permanent, he ordinarily lives the life to which the social system assigns him with a fair degree of satisfaction. Of course, even under the most rigid of social systems, there are always those who have ambitions greater than can be satisfied by their opportunities. But in a caste system where there is nothing the individual can do to mitigate his frustration, he may as well develop an attitude of resignation. These artificial barriers, which exist only in the minds and customs of men, become the deterministic factors in experience, establishing the universe of action for any man born in the society. In our society social differentiation is based primarily on differences in occupations and incomes, for here social esteem and self-respect are closely related to kind of work engaged in and to income.[1]

STRATIFICATION AND THE AMERICAN CULTURE PATTERN

The tendency of the frontier of the American West was to destroy class lines, to dispense with the symbols of stratification which existed in English society. There is little place for stratification on an agricultural frontier where one is accepted chiefly on the basis of achievement, rather than on his past. Whatever the cause may be, every vocation was opened to every man. Thus was created a restless urge to climb for the highest place one could achieve. No caste lines were drawn and the lines between the social classes were ill-defined. This notion of equal opportunity for all was a contribution of our

[1] For an extensive treatment of social differentiation, see C. C. North, *Social Differentiation*, part 1, University of North Carolina Press, Chapel Hill, 1926.

nation of boundless resources, and it was on the frontier, where a man's grasp often equaled his reach, that such a philosophy, through realization, was nourished.

American society, in holding out to man unlimited rewards, creates a situation in which few individuals are ever satisfied with possessing temporary goals because they seldom represent all that is desired. Thus, they habituate themselves to eternal striving and in this striving find satisfaction or disappointment. The farm laborer wants to be a tenant; the tenant, an owner; and the owner of an 80-acre tract wants a quarter section; when he has that, he wants a half section.

Though this striving for distant goals makes the attainment of happiness difficult for many, it releases human energy and individual initiative in a way not possible under a rigidly stratified social system. With all the differences between the rural and urban environments, the step from farm to town or city vocation can be made by an aspiring farm youth of ability, and the channels for vertical movement are sufficiently free in the city for a farm youth to climb to the pinnacle.

H. G. Wells, observing some years ago the freedom for social climbing offered by the American culture pattern, considered it astonishing that the European immigrant from a down-trodden or even oppressed class on entering America so soon caught this spirit of equality, throwing off his sense of inferiority and acquiring the feeling that he was as good as anyone. This spirit still characterizes the American way of life and can be clearly seen in operation in the farm community.[1]

THE LEVELING EFFECT OF RURAL ASSOCIATION

There are certain factors in the community where the family-sized farm is maintained that strongly resist tendencies toward stratification. Neighbors in many sections still exchange work, and owner and tenant alike are drawn in on this exchange, associating not only in work but at meals. The women are drawn together by the exchange of work in cooking for harvest hands. Under such conditions there is little opportunity for a system of stratification to form; a snobbish housewife might soon find herself without friends; a farmer who is too "exclusive" might find that neighbors are unwilling to help him when he needs them.

Moreover, to the extent that an open-country community maintains its institutions—school, church, grange, farm bureau—one who would participate in community life must associate with all members. Universal participation is the motto of most farm organizations, which means that a high degree of

[1] H. G. Wells, *Social Forces in England and America*, pp. 324–340, Harper & Brothers, New York, 1914. See also Harry Elmer Barnes, *Society in Transition*, pp. 559 *ff*., Prentice-Hall, Inc., New York, 1939.

democracy must exist. Farm people usually accept a man on a personal basis; not that farmers accept all men as equal, but they accept all men for what they have proved themselves to be. Today those rural aristocrats who fail to appreciate the plebeian tastes of their neighbors can get into the car and go to the city; but there are still many social pressures that make it easy to be a "good fellow" in the community and to participate in the common life. The way of the snob is hard in the primary-group environment.

In American small towns one finds a differentiation in social function and occupation, and also the beginning of social stratification. The bankers and a few of the leading businessmen of the town may form the nucleus of a new elite group; or it may draw its membership from townspeople who want desperately to let the rest of the town know that they are important.[1] Such are among those who loaf in the town drugstore rather than in the pool hall.

Social stratification as exhibited in the attitudes and behavior patterns of small-town residents in the West is well illustrated in the following account:

In my home town the townspeople definitely do not consider the lumber workers their equals. The farmers are given a status superior to the lumber workers. The attitude seems to be this: that the farmer is slow and plodding, but at least his morals are decent and his mores similar. The lumber workers' free and easy attitude toward drinking, marriage, religion, and life in general, conflicts with that of the average church-going townsman who is conservative and prudent. Drought migrants are automatically classed with the rest of the lumberjacks if they work in the mills or the woods. They may be just as strongly religious and just as strict in their morals as the farmers, but they are put in the "lower class" by the stigma of their economic position. This, of course, increases their problem of adjustment. They are misfits and have to change established ideas or remain "square pegs in round holes."

An "elite" group has been formed in my town which considers itself very modern and tolerates the liberalism of the workers. But since the members are from the higher income group, they think of themselves as superior, deploring the crudity of the other townspeople, the farmers, and the lumbermen. The professional men and women and some business owners make up this group, but it seems to be maintained by the efforts of the women, who "ape" the big city and try to pattern themselves and their activities after urban ideals. Pleasure and cultural activities occupy their time, whereas work and institutional interests occupy the other people. This same group has its dancing club and holds dancing parties frequently. Everyone dresses as if he were going to the Waldorf-Astoria, and the affairs are very formal for a small town. It is positively social suicide to offend a member of this group and "reputational" suicide also as they are

[1] J. M. Williams makes much of the village's place in developing class differences. See his *Our Rural Heritage* and *The Expansion of Rural Life*, Alfred A. Knopf, Inc., New York, 1926. C. C. Zimmerman, in *The Changing Community*, pp. 447–448 (Harper & Brothers, New York, 1938), gives an interesting case history of a village and the influence of its "leading families." J. F. Steiner, in his *The American Community in Action*, gives several instances of community stratification; see especially pp. 33–36, 95–100, Henry Holt and Company, Inc., New York, 1928.

the most avid gossipers in town. Most of the women of this group have time to spare and when they are not playing bridge they often go to Seattle or Aberdeen for concerts, lectures, or other social events. They see to it that their husbands find time to go also.

The middle class, containing the church-going citizens, the "Babbitts," and the average inhabitants, is dominated by church leaders. Not all of this class are ardently religious, but they at least profess some faith and are conservative in their ideas. The "goings on" of the lumberjacks and the worldliness of the elite both meet their disapproval. They are characteristically self-centered and interested in developing their town into a city. In spite of the fact that the farmers and lumberjacks provide the trade, these townsmen continue to regard themselves as superior and "citified." However, there are a few prosperous farmers and their wives who are leaders in this group because of their economic standing and because they are college educated. Superior education raises their status, as education is highly regarded in rural areas.[1]

Brunner, Hughes, and Patten find in the large towns evidences of social differentiation and the beginnings of stratification.[2] They describe a county seat in which the Baptists live on one side of the street and the Methodists on the other; a Far Western town with a population of 2,000 in which poor people and employees in the fruit-packing industry live on the west side of the track and have their own school and churches, the churches being of the sectarian type. Members of the older denominations reside on the east side of the track in the wealthier part of the town. The division affects local politics, association, and social relationships.

They find that not only does the railroad track often divide communities with different status, but natural divisions such as geographical obstacles, a river or a lake, may mark lines of social stratification. They indicate that in almost all of the villages studied there was some tendency toward segregation into social groups. The most noticeable instances were in the South and Southwest where Negroes and Mexicans were segregated in separate parts of the village. But in most Northern towns the well-to-do have built beautiful homes in certain parts of the town and have developed quality hills not much different from the gold coasts of the city.

Bell[3] also has called attention to the beginnings of social stratification in the small town where one finds some differentiation of occupation and social function. Studying Shellstone, Iowa, an agricultural community with a farm trade center, he finds at first no stratification. At one time the aristocrats of the town went to the Baptist Church, but this mark of distinction has disappeared. However, on closer study he finds that certain types of occupations tend to bring different degrees of distinction. The banker and those who work in the

[1] From a student paper.

[2] E. de S. Brunner, G. S. Hughes, and M. Patten, *American Agricultural Villages*, p. 71, Doubleday & Company, Inc., New York, 1927.

[3] E. H. Bell, "Social Stratification in a Small Community," *Scientific Monthly*, vol. 38, pp. 157–164, February, 1934.

bank rank highest; the businessmen and professional men rank second; the landowner, third; the renter, fourth; and the occasional laborer, fifth. The lines of distinction, however, are rather superficial since the children of all groups may play together and since individuals of any class may by personal qualities transcend class lines.

The small town seems to hold a unique place in its ability to create a sense of social difference, as compared to either farm community or city. On the farm, in most communities, there is still enough equality of situation, occupation, and wealth to make it impossible for much of a sense of difference to exist. Likewise, in the large city, there can be little distinction within the mediocre masses or the great lower class. Only a few can achieve eminence at the high apex of the city's social pyramid. But in the small town minor differences can easily be exaggerated into distinctions of importance. These are quickly fortified by custom. Thus, those with a few distinctive traits may effectively assume an air of snobbishness and be recognized as a distinct social class.

One of the most convincing studies[1] of stratification in rural towns is that of a farm trade center only two generations away from the frontier, "Prairieton, South Dakota." The researchers find three distinct strata in this trade center of some 3,500 people. (1) The low status groups consist of ex-farmers, farm hands and unskilled laborers, (2) the middle class of store-keepers, craftsmen, retired farmers and professional people, and (3) the successful entrepreneurs and large land holders who constitute the elite class.

For their analysis of stratification, which is made within the conceptual framework of Howard Becker's constructive typology, they compare the elite group, in colloquial term known as the "Tops," who live on the bluff on the east side of town, with the lowest status group, who are colloquially known as the "Bottoms," and who live in the lower area of the town. The two groups are markedly differentiated in terms of family backgrounds, associations, occupational and residential history, forms of speech, relief history, secularism, family type, educational attainments, vital statistics, as reflected in length of life, infant mortality and sickness. Dietary habits differ. The "Tops" are interested in preserving the girlish figure; the "Bottoms" are not.

The two groups have stereotyped attitudes toward themselves and toward the other group. The elite feel that they have arrived by personal merit and by the law of "survival of the fittest." They are sure that the "Bottoms" are explained by innate shiftlessness, laziness, and lack of intelligence. The "Bottoms" think that the "Tops" are there because of luck, "pull," inherited wealth, and educational opportunities not available to others. The classes are mutually exclusive; each prefers to associate within its own circle. Class dis-

[1] John Useem, Pierre Tangent, and Ruth Useem, "Stratification in a Prairie Town," *American Sociological Review*, vol. 7, pp. 331–342, June, 1942.

tinction affects community cooperation and civic administration. Different social organizations, including churches, attract different strata.

In older communities, settled for three or more generations, it is possible that considerable stratification exists. This is suggested by Kaufman's study,[1] "Prestige Classes in a New York Rural Community," where not only the researchers who lived in the community but also residents of the community

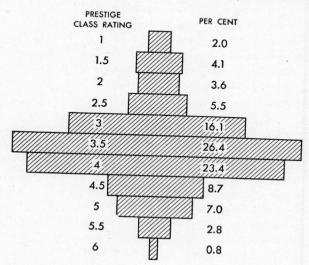

Kaufman, *op. cit.*

THE CLASS STRUCTURE OF THE MACON COMMUNITY

were able clearly to distinguish prestige classes. The class structure, as represented by prestige groups, is depicted in the accompanying chart which differentiates 11 prestige groups varying considerably in social status.

A further study of social class in New York State shows that different patterns of family behavior can be differentiated within the various social classes.[2]

OCCUPATIONAL HOMOGENEITY AS A LEVELING INFLUENCE IN THE FARM COMMUNITY

The homogeneity of occupation of the farming group is a factor in reducing stratification in farm communities. All farmers are manual laborers except, of course, the few large-scale operators who act chiefly as managers of their enterprises. Work differs from farm to farm but, generally speaking, manual

[1] Harold F. Kaufman, "Prestige Classes in a New York Rural Community," *Cornell University Agricultural Experiment Station, Memoir 260*, Ithaca, New York, March, 1944.

[2] Edith Jeffers Freeman, *Social Class as a Factor in the Family Group Relations of Certain New York Farm Families*, Cornell University Press, Ithaca, N.Y., 1943.

labor predominates and the operator and his family do much of the work. Most jobs on the farm and in farming areas are of the "overalls" variety. It may matter slightly whether one wears the common blue denim overalls or the more clean-looking, more sophisticated, white-striped ones, but not greatly. Even one who climbs from tenancy to ownership does not expect to do less work or a different kind of work. Such a condition is not conducive to the development of consciousness of differences in status.

One reason for the intense struggle for status in the urban community lies in the fact that a considerable part of the gainful workers there are occupied in nonmanual occupations. In these occupations chiefly people today achieve honor and become the object of envy and emulation; status is increased as one progresses in some one of the professions, in administrative work, and to a lesser extent in clerical work, which is given white-collar status.

Effective systems of social stratification usually have at the top of the social pyramid a place of greatest distinction. In rural society there is no pinnacle in the social hierarchy. In the city one finds the center of most systems of social organization, the controlling bodies of most nation-wide institutions, the seat of most political authority; here the social elevators lead to great heights; and it is for this reason that aspiring youths who wish to achieve distinction are attracted urbanward. Others who for some reason cannot go to the city but yet nourish high ambitions feel frustrated on the farm.

Democracy is essentially a trait of those who do common things in a common way, living in an environment where there is natural equality. Aristocratic ideas come with opportunity for extreme forms of distinction. There probably can be no real democracy in a highly specialized society. The most democratic areas in America are located at the outlying fringes of social isolation; the least democratic areas, in the metropolis. The leisure to engage in specialized artistic tasks, to achieve superficial refinements, to build social traditions is essential to the crusting over of a social system such as is necessary for the development of stratification. These processes seem to be more urban than rural.[1]

ECONOMIC HINDRANCES TO SOCIAL STRATIFICATION IN THE FARM COMMUNITY

In our society wealth most often forms the groundwork of social differentiation, its possession providing a basis for exclusiveness.[2] In a self-sufficient

[1] This is not denying the fact that the proletarian classes of the city also may be a powerful influence in working toward democracy and keeping alive the open-class principle in American society.

[2] E. A. Ross shows that those who acquire wealth convert it into social power. See his *Foundations of Sociology*, pp. 218–219, The Macmillan Company, New York, 1905. This idea is prominent also in Thorstein Veblen's *Theory of the Leisure Class*, The Macmillan Company, New York, 1905.

agricultural community where the primary concern is subsistence, differences in wealth are never extensive for in a semibarter, subsistence economy great wealth cannot be accumulated. Though rural America has gradually shifted away from a pioneer economy, farmers have been for the most part middle-class folk. There has been dire poverty in some communities, but there have seldom been great riches in these same communities as is so common in the metropolis, where slums and gold coast almost join at their backdoors.[1]

As agriculture enters the urban market and becomes increasingly com-mercialized, the accumulation of wealth becomes the basis of a consciousness of superiority in the farm community as in the city. Indications of milder forms of stratification are appearing; for example, in areas where agriculture is most commercialized, social differences between farm operators and farm laborers are becoming marked. On the West Coast, where large commercial farms are most numerous, the terms "fruit tramps," "rubber tramps," "hop pickers," "automobile gypsies," "migs," commonly applied to the migratory workers carry an opprobrious connotation, implying inferiority. In California and Arizona, the dispossessed share croppers and farm owners who have moved in from the cotton states lying eastward are classified as "Oakies," or "Arkies," which terms are brands for a new and undesirable rural class. Certain types of labor, such as pea picking and hop picking, have come to be regarded as the work of this class of people, so that in many communities the "better" local people will no longer engage in such work. The children of the farm workers are stigmatized and sometimes persecuted in the schools, and the entire family is unwanted in the community after the crops are harvested. The migrant from the northern Great Plains who had been accustomed to working on the family-sized farm of the Plains, obtaining bed and board with the family, experienced severe shock when he became a laborer in such areas and learned that he must take his dinner pail to work and furnish his own bed. More important still was the shock to his pride when he realized that he was not considered on the same level of social respectability as the man for whom he worked. Drought mi-grants to irrigated sections of the West Coast described this experience as the one that hurt them most.

Of much longer standing is the semi-caste system of the deep South where the highly commercialized cotton system with plantation management provides for vast differences in social status. Such terms as "poor white," "planter," and "cracker" imply recognized social differences. Reuss,[2] study-ing a community in Virginia, is conscious of recognized class differences which grow out of social and economic differences, with family traditions and

---

[1] For an interesting study depicting a situation of this character see Harvey W. Zorbaugh, *The Gold Coast and the Slum,* University of Chicago Press, Chicago, 1929.

[2] Carl Frederick Reuss, "A Qualitative Study of Depopulation in a Remote Rural District: 1900–1930," *Rural Sociology,* vol. 2, p. 67, March, 1937.

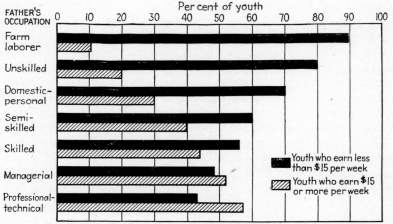

Based on data from Howard M. Bell, *Youth Tell Their Story*, American Council on Education

WHEN VERTICAL MOBILITY CEASES STRATIFICATION BEGINS

This chart shows the relation of the father's occupation to wages his employed children received. In many parts of the nation it is becoming difficult for the farm laborer to climb to a position of ownership, and the low economic status of the parent is beginning to be passed on to his children. The great mass of farm laborers' children in Maryland, as this study of the depression revealed, were in the lowest paid occupation. It was also found that the farm laborers' children received the least schooling of any group studied.

PER CENT IN INCOME CLASS

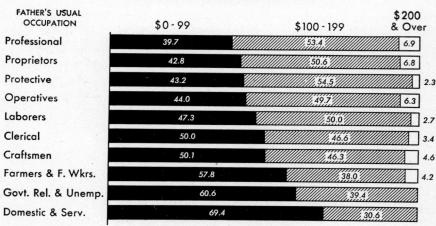

From Paul H. Landis, "The Territorial and Occupational Migration of Washington Youth," Youth Series, No. 3, *Washington Agricultural Experiment Stations Bulletin* 449. July, 1944.

WHERE 2,224 YOUNG MEN STARTED ON THE ECONOMIC LADDER, CLASSIFIED BY FATHER'S USUAL OCCUPATION

Data were obtained in 1942 for this group of young men who entered the work world during the previous decade. Income is the monthly wage received on the first job. Only civilian jobs are included.

community worth playing a vital part. " . . . whatever may be the case elsewhere, in many sections of the South it is possible with a marked degree of exactitude to sort the population of the community into an upper, a middle, and a lower class. Each person's station is somehow known and recognized by everyone in the community, including the individual himself."

Schuler, finding marked differences in social stratification in the corn belt as compared to the cotton South, seeks a satisfactory explanation. He concludes:

In the first place, the corn belt is a region more recently settled than much of the cotton belt. Social stratification in the North in a few generations may become much more significant than it appears to be at the present time.

Second, there are much larger proportions of "owners-in-prospect," to use Galpin's apt expression, among Northern than among Southern tenants. This factor tends to modify seriously the significance of sociological tenure class comparisons both within the North and when Northern tenure differences are compared with those in other regions. Tenancy does not exist in a social vacuum, but is powerfully influenced by the nature of the social bonds, the relationships of tenant to landlord, other than those of a purely economic or legal nature. This is particularly obvious in the case of large-scale forms of agriculture. As the third factor, then, may be pointed out the early appearance of the plantation in the South and its subsequent diffusion to suitable areas throughout the region.

Closely related to the plantation there is, finally, the system of mores and folkways characterizing the biracial Southern population, a system which amounts practically to the caste form of social organization. Its functioning has apparently served not only to depress the height of the social pyramid among Negro farmers and to intensify the competition between lower tenure class members of both castes, but to emphasize tenure class differences among white farmers in the South.[1]

Certain rather specific factors seem to be providing a new basis for stratification in farm life. The widespread giving of relief in farming areas, which originated during the drought-depression period of the early thirties, in some communities undoubtedly led to stratification. In many areas the "reliefers" associated almost entirely with other "reliefers," sometimes going so far as to form their own clubs and organizations. Even among those on relief there was a difference in status, the WPA workers being the aristocrats of the group.

Corporation farming has played a part in making for social differences, not only between operator and laborer, but also between the corporation management and the family-farm operator. Where carried out extensively it introduces industrial patterns into the farm community in a wholesale manner. In a mild way this type of influence can be seen operating in many farming communities that have become highly mechanized. The following account by a student is illustrative of the problem:

[1] Edgar A. Schuler, "The Present Social Status of American Farm Tenants," *Rural Sociology*, vol. 3, pp. 20–23, March, 1938.

The community feeling in this part of the state is practically nil. The small farmers are always angry with the large farmers. One large farmer bought a farm last year and put off a family who had no place to go. Some of the people criticized him but he just said, "He has to look out for himself; I'm looking out for myself." The fact that he has only one son to take over his property causes hard feelings among his neighbors who have large families. The general feeling is against ownership of large tracts by one person. There is one man in the community who makes a hobby of farming; he has the latest machinery and rents all the land around him and farms it efficiently, but he is very unpopular with his neighbors. He put a family off a farm last fall for no other reason than that he wanted to farm it himself. Later a fire got away from him and ran up on a butte near his place. His neighbors did not care whether they helped him put it out or not because they didn't feel that he showed them any consideration.

Holmes expresses the view that with the stabilization of American society the farmer will come to have a lower status in the social system of the nation than he has had in the past. Considering the fact of extensive relief loads in the 1930's in many rural areas, the national publicity given to problems of rural poverty and inadequate standards of living, and the expressed fears of some that an American farm-peasant class will come into being unless objectives of an effective national agricultural program are realized, his view, although perhaps extreme, is not without support. He says,

From the standpoint of rural sociology, the chief significance in this process of growing social stability is the probability that the farming population, which in America has been predominantly of middle-class status, is being transformed into a lower-class group. There is good reason to believe that, irrespective of whether the family-unit system prevails indefinitely in agriculture or not, the men and women who do the manual labor essential to the raising of farm produce will more and more come to be considered, and will so consider themselves, a part of the great American lower class. The farmer's traditional independence, so largely a product of governmental grant, is being lessened. An increasing proportion of American farmers are renters and laborers, who are thus individually responsible to landlords or employers; and of those who are owner-managers, an increasing proportion are in debt and thus to some extent responsible to creditors.

With the increasing numbers of native-born in urban industry, due to immigration restriction, the farmer's traditional contempt for city factory hands is sure to decrease. With the old easy paths toward success in the fields of business and the professions so largely blocked, even highly capable young people from the farms are no longer demeaning themselves when they take lower-class city jobs. The nonfarm relatives and friends of farming people will more and more be located near the bottom of the industrial ladder. In other words, if the process of transformation so hurriedly sketched has been correctly described, it in part involves the lowering of the status of the typical American farmer from that of middle-class rank to one appreciably lower in the scale.[1]

[1] Roy H. Holmes, *Rural Sociology*, pp. 73–74, McGraw-Hill Book Company, Inc., New York, 1932.

SOCIAL DIFFERENTIATION AND THE FARMER'S PLACE IN THE SUN

The lack of marked gradations in rural life seems to have some bearing on many problems of farm life especially as they affect youth. Because it is difficult to attain a high place in the social sun through farming, many ambitious and aspiring youths, who might be as well off in most respects on the farm, are

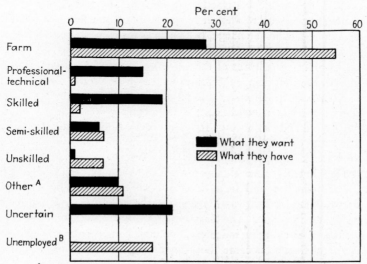

A Includes managerial, office-sales, domestic-personal, and federal project
B Includes those in school

Based on data from Lister and Kirkpatrick, *Rural Youth Speak*, American Youth Commission

DESIRES VS. REALIZATIONS IN THE VOCATIONAL FIELD

This chart compares the jobs that farm boys want with those they have. Frustration begins where realizations fail to meet desires. In our open-class system a far greater proportion of farm youth want to enter those vocations which bring recognition than can possibly do so. Farming for them means daily frustration. A new emphasis on the importance of farming might be an alternative to tightening of class lines. The appeal of the professions seems far to exceed the need for professional people; at least proportionately few farm youth who have professional ambitions are realizing them. Based on a study of 2,846 male farm youth in Maryland. This, of course, is a depression picture.

led to enter town and city vocations. The lack of a hierarchy of status in the farm community, therefore, probably decreases its holding power over youth at a time when contacts with people beyond the farm community inspire them with visions of possibilities for entering nonfarm vocations. The professions seem to attract an abnormal proportion, probably because they offer high status (see figure). The frustrating influence of this situation is apparent. Many are forced to farm or to enter the unskilled labor classes. The youth who remains in farming has little choice of social position regardless of his social ambitions. The very lack of social difference in the farm community probably makes for a keener striving on the part of a certain number of ambitious youths to get out of the community into the city, where social distinctions are clearly recognized and where social honors are more or less conspicuously bestowed on the successful.

It is possible that if we had more "gentlemen" farmers in America, farming as a vocation might achieve a place in the sun and, in so doing, come to a new professional dignity with room in it for those who crave emulation. Something would be gained by such a change, but much that is fundamental to democratic tradition would be lost.

In the established cultures of the Old World and the Orient, land ownership is a mark of aristocracy; the acquisition of great estates a road to superior status. The American colonies, true to the tradition of a landed aristocracy, made land ownership a condition for exercising the franchise; but as men moved westward and as cheap or free land was made available to all, it eventually lost some of its social meaning. What anyone can have for the taking cannot be a mark of superiority. It may be for this reason mainly that in this nation land ownership, since the opening of the West, has not been a conspicuous mark of distinction and the agricultural classes have not been given a high social status. Manufacturing and business early stole the show and have since remained in the limelight. The East was soon not only protecting its infant industries but worshiping its industrial Babbitts. Men who controlled industry, commerce, and finance became the aristocrats of the new order and remain so today.

Only in one region, and only for a period preceding the Civil War, has any large group of agriculturalists in America attained refinement and prestige. This group was composed of the rural aristocracy of the Old South. Here semifeudal landlords owned great estates operated by large retinues of slaves, found time for reflection, entertainment, and refinement, and sent their children abroad to pursue their education. Odum describes the better elements of their culture thus:

Inherent in the glory that was the traditional South were qualities often estimated to be the most distinctive and glamorous in the American picture: a way of living, zestful and colorful; a humanism over and above the basic puritanism of the early fathers; a setting of classical architecture, classical libraries, elegant furnishings, in the midst of groves and gardens and feudal settlements; dignity, polish, respect for form and amenities, pride of family, hospitality with merriment and conviviality abounding.

Among the basic factors capable of contributing to excellence, therefore, are certain cumulative composite qualities of the Southern people and their culture: a certain heritage abounding in the concepts and experience of good living, strong loyalties, spiritual energy, personal distinctions, and strong individuality; a certain distinctiveness in manners and customs; a certain poignancy and power of cultural tradition, with the promise of considerable distinctive achievement in many avenues of individual and institutional endeavor; evidences of capacity for romantic realism; a certain reserve of social resources as well as of physical wealth; a certain youthful buoyancy and stirring which gives promise of new reaches in economic achievement, creative effort, in the utilization of a certain sort of institutional genius for politics, religion, education, literature, and social science; a certain power arising from the abundance of reserve in human and physical resources, coupled with the first fruits of beginning accomplishments and a growing faith and confidence; a better preparation for larger gains in the future; and a certain drawing power for the rest of the country.[1]

After the Civil War, and especially after 1900, industrialists who came into the South to exploit raw materials and to build factories gradually captured the leading role in the financial drama and are attaining to a lesser extent the place of prestige in the social drama. In the heyday of the Old South's landed aristocracy, there were at the base of the social pyramid, as there must always be where social distinctions are great, the masses who had no share in the social distinctions of the favored few—the blacks in semifeudal servitude to the plantation owner, the "poor whites" of about equal status, and the independent operators of small tracts who competed with the plantation agriculturists.

Evidence of this chapter indicates that social stratification has never been particularly prominent in rural society in the United States, tendencies for social groups to become crusted into stratified forms having been blocked by migration, frontier conditions, and by a general situation in which universal opportunity was characteristic. As out society ages, as opportunities in rural areas become less plentiful, as the economic struggle becomes more intense, vertical social movement may be hindered; to the extent that it is hindered by economic or other factors, it seems likely that lines of stratification will be somewhat more rigidly drawn. Moreover, in the rural community of today, as conspicuous consumption of goods comes to be characteristic with the rise in standards of living, as urbanization continues, as intimate primary-group ties break with increased individualization, as a pleasure-leisure philosophy becomes more prominent and means for display more numerous, a greater range of social difference may come to exist and a consequent greater recognition of social class. Since economic success seems to be the basis for social distinction in the more competitive phases of our open-class society, it seems likely that the increased commercialization of agriculture will lead to an exaggeration of the mercenary motive and therefore to greater stratification. The rise of a dependent class could hasten this process.

[1] Howard W. Odum, *Southern Regions of the United States*, pp. 23–25, University of North Carolina Press, Chapel Hill, 1936.

Questions for Review and Discussion

1. What is social differentiation? How does it arise? How does it relate to social stratification?

2. Explain the relationship between the open-class principle of social organization and stratification.

3. What did the rural frontier contribute to American democratic tradition?

4. What factors in farm life hinder stratification?

5. Contrast the small town and open country in terms of degree of social stratification.

6. How does occupation affect tendencies toward stratification? How do these principles apply to farm life?

7. Show how changes in basic economic philosophies are affecting rural stratification.

8. Compare the corn belt with the cotton South in terms of degrees of stratification.

9. In what way are relief programs in rural areas affecting the sense of social equality? In what ways is corporation farming affecting it?

10. How might a greater degree of stratification in farming communities affect the farmer's social status? affect the drift to cities?

11. What price must a society always pay for granting great distinction to a few?

Collateral Reading

Bell, E. H.: "Social Stratification in a Small Community," *Scientific Monthly*, vol. 38, pp. 157–164, February, 1934.

Dollard, John: *Caste and Class in a Southern Town*, Publications of the Institute of Human Relations, Yale University Press, New Haven, 1937.

Holmes, Roy H.: *Rural Sociology*, chap. 5, McGraw-Hill Book Company, Inc., New York, 1932.

Kaufman, Harold F.: "Prestige Classes in a New York Rural Community," *Cornell Agricultural Experiment Station Memoir* 260, Ithaca, N.Y., March, 1944.

Moore, Wilbert and Robin M. Williams: "Stratification in the Ante-bellum South," *American Sociological Review*, vol. 7, pp. 343–351, June, 1942.

North, C. C.: *Social Differentiation*, University of North Carolina Press, Chapel Hill, 1926.

Schuler, Edgar A.: "The Present Status of American Farm Tenants," *Rural Sociology*, vol. 3, pp. 20–23, March, 1938.

Smith, T. Lynn: *The Sociology of Rural Life*, rev. ed., chap. 15, Harper & Brothers, New York, 1947.

Sorokin, P. A., C. C. Zimmerman, and C. J. Galpin: *A Systematic Source Book in Rural Sociology*, vol. 1, chap. 6, University of Minnesota Press, Minneapolis, 1930.

Steiner, J. F.: *The American Community in Action*, chap. 1 and pp. 95–100, Henry Holt and Company, Inc., New York, 1928.

Useem, John, Pierre Tangent and Ruth Useem: "Stratification in a Prairie Town," *American Sociological Review*, vol. 7, pp. 331–342, June, 1942.

Williams, J. M.: *The Expansion of Rural Life*, chap. 2, Alfred A. Knopf, Inc., New York, 1926.

Zimmerman, C. C.: *The Changing Community*, chap. 19, Harper & Brothers, New York, 1938.

CHAPTER 19

CULTURAL CHANGE

FEW TOPICS have been more popular in sociological literature than that of cultural change since about 1925, when sociologists began to become culture conscious. Considerable information has accumulated on the general subject, and evidence as to how the process comes about is not wanting.[1] It is generally recognized that cultural change is produced primarily by two other social processes—invention and borrowing. Invention is the process by which new ideas and new devices are brought into being; borrowing is the process by which traits from outside cultures are taken over and introduced into the native culture. Both invention and borrowing are stimulated by contact. An individual who has multiple contacts is able to assimilate a wealth of ideas which may provide the basis for new inventions. A people in contact with people of another culture has an opportunity to borrow extensively of those cultural elements that it does not possess by virtue of invention.

It has been discovered that, in a machine age, change occurs more rapidly in material aspects of the culture than in non-material aspects. Machine techniques change more rapidly than family codes, religious beliefs, and legal traditions. Scientific procedures spring up in the realm of mechanics, whereas in the nonmaterial realm old ideologies, outworn assumptions, and customary habits of thought which fail to prepare people for the implications of the new technology persist. A people may be modern-minded with regard to machines but in sentiments may still cling to social codes that belong to an isolated primary-group culture.

Such in brief are the outstanding findings of students of culture with regard to cultural change. It is our part here to analyze in some detail this process as it takes place in the rural environment. But first, let it be said that the writer assumes that cultural change and social change are different. Social change consists of changes in group composition and in interaction processes. The changes in population, in contact, adjustment, accommodation, and differentiation that have been discussed are the essence of the process of social change. The discussion of cultural change which follows, therefore, is confined entirely

[1] See such works as W. F. Ogburn, *Social Change*, The Viking Press, Inc., New York, 1922; F. S. Chapin, *Cultural Change*, D. Appleton-Century Company, Inc., New York, 1928; Paul H. Landis, *Three Iron Mining Towns: A Study in Cultural Change*, Edwards Bros., Inc., Ann Arbor, Mich., 1938.

to a consideration of the man-made superstructure which we think of as the cultural environment.[1]

THE RELATION OF MATERIAL CULTURAL CHANGE TO THE WORLD OF RURAL ENTERPRISE

Since the agricultural enterprise is closely identified with nature and with basic natural processes, it is inherent in the situation that there will be little change in rural culture as long as agriculture remains on an elemental level with the family winning its food supply from the soil. Nature's laws are relatively permanent and unchanging; once a people has worked out a farming technique which is fairly successful in a given geographical environment, they practice it from year to year with little modification. Settled agricultural peoples in the past experienced few contacts that would lead to the borrowing of new techniques; consequently, major changes in basic techniques came only when groups migrated into new territory where it was necessary for them to accommodate themselves to different geographical circumstances. Often migration itself was forced by war or natural catastrophe. The pronounced tendency of migrating peoples was, as it is today, to reconstruct their old culture in the new environment; but invariably some major changes in the cultural architecture had to be made if the colony was to survive in the new area. If an agricultural people was already established in the new area, the incoming group took over elements of the established culture and blended them with their own, or if a warring group came in and subdued the established group there was an exchange of cultural practices. If no agricultural people lived in the new habitat, the incoming group was forced to invent adaptive techniques or fail in conquering the environment. Obviously then, in a self-sufficient agricultural civilization, change even in material culture proceeds very slowly.

Rapid change in material culture is a function of urban industrial culture. In an urban regime the social group is surrounded by a human rather than a natural environment. Even though manufacturing utilizes the raw materials of a natural world, it is a complex of man-made processes. Because human inventions are susceptible to all kinds and degrees of modification and improvement, material progress in the urban enterprise is dependent chiefly on changes in culture. One invention leads to another, and men find themselves in a world of man-made tools rather than in a world of soil and seasons and immutable natural laws.

[1] For a discussion of the importance of differentiating social change and cultural change, which terms are often used interchangeably, and an attempt at demonstrating the validity of a distinction along the lines discussed above, see the writer's "Social Change and Social Interaction as Factors in Cultural Change," *American Journal of Sociology*, pp. 52–58, July, 1935; or his *Three Iron Mining Towns: A Study in Cultural Change, op. cit.*, chap. 16.

The ingenuity displayed in urban inventiveness is amazing and there can be no stopping place if the urban community is to grow and prosper. Once the market is saturated with a gadget, new ones not only are invented but must be invented and a desire for them created or industry must slow its pace and factories close. Since urban manufactured goods cater to created rather than natural wants, the expansion of the urban market (granted a stationary population) is dependent entirely on the creation of new products to meet wants of the consuming public, or on the creation of new wants. Thus inventiveness both in material and in nonmaterial culture is stimulated. Thus also the need of industry for an expanding market explains in considerable part the rapid shifts of fashion, the rise of fads, and the change of conventions that characterize urban life and the rapid evolutionary process that characterizes the life history of material inventions. Quickly they pass from the first crude stages to the refined stages of practical utility and then to the artistic stages. The bathtub was first a plain, even ugly-looking tub, then a beautiful corrosion-proof affair of immaculate white porcelain; now it has become a work of art in porcelains of a variety of tints. In the case of much of our material culture, new models are constantly being designed to extend the industrial market by stimulating desire. There is no boundary hindering the expansion of desire for the luxury goods which are produced by urban industry. The marketable goods of the rural community, on the other hand, for the most part cater to actual wants and hence the market for them cannot be indefinitely expanded; people will use only about so many potatoes, and so much wheat and corn.

It is not ordinarily practical to put many artistic touches on farm produce or to streamline farm livestock. But a commercial agriculture may become so closely identified with the urban market that its prosperity is more dependent upon artificial than upon natural wants. In the hinterland of the city especially, there has been a considerable development of types of agriculture catering to unseasonable urban wants, e.g., greenhouse farming. In a commercial agriculture, invention is much more prominent than in agriculture generally.

The urban market itself in introducing new forms of consumable goods produces widespread changes in custom and habits that affect agriculture profoundly. Consider food habits. Industry, in its attempt to capitalize on the facts and fads of science and pseudo science, has created an abnormal demand for certain processed products and in this way crowded others out; thus, the consumption of milk products and of vegetables and fruits (vitamin givers) has greatly increased, whereas the consumption of starchy foods has declined. Consider changes in style which likewise are initiated chiefly by urban industry. Sometimes skirts are short, sometimes long, as fashion dictates; cotton garments are replaced by rayon and silk to the advantage of the urban-industrial inventor of the rayon process or the importer of raw silk. Back of some of these changes in habits are, however, fashions in beauty. The quest for a slender feminine figure has helped immensely to curtail the demand for starchy cereals.

Regarding the effect of changes in the American diet on agriculture, Baker concludes,

> The outstanding fact in the development of the American diet since the beginning of the 20th century, which is as far back as statistical data permit safe conclusions, is the shift from the cereals toward the more expensive animal foods, particularly from corn and wheat toward milk and poultry products and pork. In addition, there was the notable increase in consumption of sugar after the prohibition amendment went into effect and the greater use, at least in the cities, of green vegetables. These shifts in diet have had profound regional influences. The 30 per cent increase, more or less, in per capita consumption of milk and dairy products, for example, has promoted the prosperity of the dairy states.[1]

The increased demand for tailor-made cigarettes, pipe-cut smoking tobacco, and sweetened plug-cut tobacco to replace "roll-your-own" cigarettes and long-green has undoubtedly had an effect on the market of the tobacco grower. The automobile industry alone in an average year uses 25 million pounds of wool, the product of 3 million sheep. The significant fact from the inventive standpoint is that the expanded market is primarily a result of the factory process, urban advertising, and urban distribution, not of any new invention at the agricultural end.

Although agriculture is not so dependent as industry upon inventiveness, it has been forced to change its practices with reference to the new in order to meet changes in demand of the urban market. There is considerable lag at this point in agriculture and probably there always will be, because farmers are so far removed from many of the fads of urban consumption that they fail to realize their significance to them until it is too late to make changes. Moreover, agriculture is a way of life to the farmer, and to change his enterprise radically is to change his personality; his particular type of enterprise in his world, and to modify it is to make necessary a major personal adjustment for him and for his entire household. In urban industry, in contrast, the making of a new device is but an item in the day's work, calling merely for new dies and perhaps an additional craftsman on the pay roll. Few if any personal adjustments are required.

---

[1] O. E. Baker, *The Future Need for Farm Land*, p. 6, mimeographed, U.S. Department of Agriculture, Washington, D. C., 1934.

Fashions in diet and in dress are not the only factors affecting agriculture. Economic conditions in the nation have a great deal to do with diet. When masses of the people are forced to live on restricted emergency diets, the consumption of cereals increases and that of meat, milk, fruits, and vegetables decreases. See Hazel K. Stiebeling and Medora M. Ward, "Diets at Four Levels of Nutrition Content and Cost," *U.S. Department of Agriculture, Circular* 296, Washington, D. C., 1933.

There may be other reasons for the lag in agriculture. Commenting on the resistance of the cotton farmer to change, the National Resources Planning Board suggests that perhaps it is due to the lack of facilities for demonstrating the effectiveness of new techniques in rural areas.[1]

It would not be true to reality to leave the impression that agriculture has shared only incidentally in the dynamic processes of contemporary culture. Improved techniques have reduced the need for manpower, increased production, and diversified the farming enterprise; new and better crop varieties and breeds of livestock have been developed, *e.g.*, hybrid corn; extensive research by agricultural colleges and by the U.S. Department of Agriculture has resulted in the introduction of many new techniques. Agriculture has been greatly improved by the inventive process, but even so, it depends less upon inventions for survival than does urban industry.

The future expansion of commercial agriculture may, however, depend on inventive processes. It is possible that the solution for the nation's farm problem may be found through the invention of techniques to divert surplus agricultural products into industrial rather than into food channels. Much is being said of late of the possible contribution of chemistry and other sciences which are experimenting with the industrial utilization of farm products. Considerable progress has already been made in the use of agricultural products for the making of fuels, ethyl alcohol, and various synthetic and cellulose goods.[2] Waste products also are being extensively utilized; cottonseed, for example, due to chemical research, now has an annual value of $200,000,000 to the farmer.[3]

PREREQUISITES TO RAPID CULTURAL CHANGE LACKING IN THE RURAL COMMUNITY

Rapidity of mechanical change and, to some extent, of change in group custom and individual habit is dependent upon efficient methods of diffusion. The natural tendency of habit is to persist, of culture to remain inert to change,[4] and only as high-pressure methods of diffusion are employed is the rate of change speeded up and cultural inertia overcome. These methods wait on (1) the development of techniques for rapid contact and (2) the formation of groups with motives for using these techniques in the interest of changes in habit and custom. Until very recently the rural community lacked the first

---

[1] *Technological Trends and National Policy*, p. 127, National Resources Planning Board, Washington, D. C., June, 1937.

[2] For a brief discussion of possibilities along this line, see *ibid.*, pp. 130–133, which deals with the industrial utilization of farm products.

[3] For a popular summary of significant developments, see L. F. Livingston, "Science Remakes the Farm," condensed from *The Magazine of Wall Street*, Jan. 18, 1936, in the *Reader's Digest*, pp. 92–94, March, 1936.

[4] See W. F. Ogburn, *op. cit.*, part 4, for a discussion of cultural inertia.

prerequisite, and in many areas it still lacks some of the devices for rapid contact. All farming areas tend to be less fully supplied with the media of contact than urban areas—to be removed somewhat from the influence of the metropolitan daily paper, effective radio communication, and constant experience with city advertising. The rural community is lacking also in the second essential to speedy change, *i.e.*, groups with a desire to promote; but it is being invaded by urban-industrial groups with motives for using the devices of contact—chiefly the advertisers of products of urban technology and groups who have utopias or other fabrications of the mind to sell in the interest of votes, converts, or reform. Advertising and propaganda—the tools of high-pressure diffusion—have until rather recently, however, been restricted in their effectivenessin rural areas.

Not only are the devices of salesmanship less developed and less practiced in the rural community, but the range of possible appeals is more restricted there. Such appeals as those to desire for beauty, to fear of social error, to desire for luxury and status, find less response in rural primary-group society than among many urban groups whose members struggle more intently for status and refinement. Nonetheless, as tools for diffusion extend their reach, high-pressure sales methods are employed to speed up change in rural life also; thus, fads and fashions in phrases, clothes, models, diets, even though they strike the city first and reach their climax there, tend to reverberate in the remote rural hinterland.

PSYCHOLOGICAL HANDICAPS TO CULTURAL CHANGE IN THE RURAL ENVIRONMENT

The countryman, as we have seen (Chapter 5), is accustomed to the inexorability of natural forces, they rhythmic change of the seasons, and the regular processes of life and growth. These experiences sometimes make him skeptical of what may be achieved by man's tinkering and often lead him to resist innovations. Farm people are passive in the face of change in part because of their long experience with traditional phenomena; much that they have learned regarding agriculture has come by way of father-to-son tradition, rather than by scientific training. Rural communities are still loaded with folklore in regard to agricultural processes, despite the fact that science has made heavy inroads in this field and has demonstrated its superiority. It is natural, therefore, that the rural man would tend to respect tradition and folklore.

As has been pointed out elsewhere, there is much more social pressure toward the maintenance of the *status quo* in the rural community than in the urban. A person living in a primary group, because he tends always to be conscious of the reactions of others to his behavior, finds it easier to conform to existing patterns than to seek new ones.

Resistance to new nonmaterial traits is greater in the rural community than in the urban, possibly because the rural community has more at stake in case of change. The authority of the rural system of control resides chiefly in established usage, that of the urban chiefly in law; a new pattern that rocks tradition costs a community or an individual more in the way of adjustment than a change necessitating only a modification of the law. Rural peoples still revere the past. Habit becomes fixed and permanent in a slowly changing order, elastic in a rapidly changing one. The spirit of change has become identical with the spirit of progress in the metropolis; the hinterland has felt the rate of change increase but is not geared fully to its pace.

The large urban community is, to a considerable extent, the product of science and technology. Man is most receptive to change where machines and other products of science and invention are most numerous, for these may be improved and perfected by change. Change is safest there for the new may be tested and tried on a small scale in the laboratory and, if it works safely, be applied to actual life. In rural communities where men live by folklore and tradition rather than by technic-ways, change involves risk; the trustworthy is the tried and tested as represented by long-established custom.

LACK OF STANDARDIZATION OF PRACTICE HINDERS DIFFUSION OF TECHNICAL CULTURE

Being chiefly of urban origin, inventions often have no utility or adaptability to rural activities, and even those which are designed for use in farming areas may not diffuse widely because agricultural techniques are not standardized as are industrial techniques but differ according to natural conditions, custom, and level of development. This fundamental difference will always exist, for hills and plains cannot be standardized; climate cannot be made uniform. Locally adapted varieties of crops and livestock breeds call for particular types of tools and care; screws and bolts can be standardized to fit all styles of cars of all nations, but many of the tools of a commercial agriculture cannot be standardized even on a national scale.

THE INCREASING RATE OF CULTURAL CHANGE IN THE RURAL ENVIRONMENT

We have discussed at considerable length the reasons for the less rapid change in rural culture than in urban in contemporary society, but another aspect of the problem is yet to be considered. The same inventive techniques that provided the basis for the growth of urban-industrial civilization provided also the basis for the agricultural revolution. Machine agriculture, no less than machine industry, has transformed man's mode of living. New machines, household conveniences, and other inventions of urban industry have found their way into the domestic and farm economy of the rural dweller. The modern farmer cannot fail to note that change and progress are often the same; in his memory he can visualize the dirt road that once passed his farmhouse; thirty years ago he could not have conceived of it, but today this dirt road has been converted into a modern paved highway open the year around. He can remember his first car and when he compares it with his present automobile he finds it less easy to believe that "they don't make machines of high quality any more."

The focus of invention is still in the city where it has, in many respects, become a profession, subsidized by educational institutions and by large industries, many of which have trained personnel and laboratories devoted to research, but the rate of assimilation of culture traits in rural society has obviously increased greatly and the assimilation of the new in itself makes for change and frequently for progress.

Despite considerable inertia, rural people in America are much more favorable to change and the notion of progress than most peoples in the past have been; the new, the sensuous, the comic, the aesthetic, the dramatic, the fastidious, may not make the "hit" in the rural community that they do in the urban, but they have some patrons there, at least among the youth. Also, we are beginning to live in a world where the new is more adaptable to the rural community than it has been previously. The rural community and the urban are beginning to approach each other with regard to many phases of standard of living, life philosophy, and modes of behavior.

M. L. Wilson, director of the U.S. Extension Service, has said,

Thirty-five or forty years ago, most farmers in my home section of Iowa thought that to go to an agricultural college was a waste of time. And they were still pretty contemptuous of most scientific farming. The county agent in my old home county tells me now that most farmers use hog cholera serum, balanced rations, scientific soil-conserving practices, and so on, as a matter of course. Hybrid seed corn is spreading rapidly. I have asked hundreds of county agents all over the country about the practical acceptance of science among their local farmers, and the answer is always about the same.[1]

He believes this trend is due to a considerable extent to the fact that experiment stations and extension services have propagated scientific agriculture until the day of scientific agriculture has actually come. There are in America about 8,000 people engaged in scientific research in agriculture; about $40,000,000 is spent annually for work in this field. In addition, there are 15 or 20 thousand teachers of scientific farming employed in colleges of agriculture, in the extension service, and in Smith-Hughes work in high schools.[2] The U.S. Department of Agriculture in Washington and the colleges of agriculture in the various states circulate millions of copies of their publications

[1] M. L. Wilson, op. cit., p. 5.
[2] Ibid., pp. 5–6.

among farm peoples of the nation, diffusing research findings and giving information concerning techniques and procedures.[1]

TECHNOLOGICAL CULTURE AS A FOCAL POINT OF CULTURAL CHANGE

The technological revolution in agriculture has been as significant in its way in changing life on the American farm as was the industrial revolution in transforming urban life. America is a land of large-scale machinery, where large investments in farm equipment are typical. The machine revolution in agriculture, although important for its effect on the development and expansion of commercial agriculture and the extension of our markets to all parts of the world, has had equally momentous results of a sociological nature.

One cannot look beneath the surface of the great changes which have taken place in nonmaterial phases of rural culture without seeing the far-flung influence of machine technology. The disappearance of the working "bee" as a type of rural recreation, the gradual breakdown of the work-exchange system that once characterized most rural communities, the decline in economic usefulness of the child to the farm enterprise, the breakdown of extreme conservatism, the waning importance of the neighborhood, the increased education of farm youth, the urbanization of farm people, their increased susceptibility to change—these and a thousand other changes which have taken place in the farm community must be credited in part to the influence of agricultural machinery.

Between 1910 and 1930, output per worker increased 39 per cent in manufacturing but 41 per cent in agriculture.[2] The wheat farmer with a combine can thresh 64 times as much wheat in a day as he formerly could with a flail.[3] By 1946, 33.3 per cent of all farms in the United States had tractors.

Sales of farm equipment for use in the nation rose from $222,907,764 in 1922 to $507,146,913 in 1937; the value of tractors sold increased from $53,860,771 in 1922 to $214,192,212 in 1937. The number of tractors on farms rose from 246,000 in 1920 to 2,000,000 in 1946. At the same time the number of horses and mules declined from 25,200,000 in 1920 to 14,937,000 in 1940. Farmers pay annually one dollar out of eight for farm power.[4] Thousands of farmers cannot break an inch of ground without first buying gasoline, kerosene, and fuel oil.

---

[1] Carl Taylor reports that 32 million copies of publications were circulated by the U.S. Department of Agriculture in 1931 and estimates that colleges of agriculture in the states probably circulated an equal number. *Rural Sociology*, rev. ed., p. 227, Harper & Brothers, New York, 1933.

[2] *Technological Trends and National Policy*, *op. cit.*, p. 99.

[3] *Building America*, p. 8, Columbia University Press, New York, November, 1935.

[4] M. L. Wilson, *op. cit.*, p. 7.

Mechanization is altering the whole nature of farming in the fruit and vegetable districts of the Pacific Coast, the wheat fields of the Great Plains, the corn belt, and even in large areas of the cotton country.

Farming in these parts of the United States is ceasing to be a way of life and is becoming a new kind of highly organized industry. The dominant type of farm in some of these areas no longer is a family-sized homestead; it is a great outdoor factory, built around labor-saving machinery which can be operated by gangs of seasonal workers.[1]

Here is a description of the urban-industrial extreme to which farming has gone in certain instances, an example of the effect of extensive change in material culture.

NEW AGENCIES PRODUCING CHANGE IN BEHAVIOR PATTERNS

The Radio.—No invention of the last century, except the automobile which extended movement and increased direct contacts, has had so much potentiality for producing change in the farm community as has the radio. As an educational medium making for uniform stimuli at all social levels and in all occupational classes, regardless of degree of spatial isolation, it has no equal. Inasmuch as most important programs are heard over nation-wide hookups, national advertising, and national and world events become a part of the thinking stock of those who have the instrument for tuning in. Ideas, interests, tastes in music, drama, and material culture are certain to be modified. Into the same home can come the lonely wail of a cowboy range song and the majestic strains of a Beethoven symphony, the practical home talk of the agricultural college experiment station specialist on how to plant, cultivate, or prune, and the weighty political and economic discussion of the learned professors on the Chicago Round Table, the news of the latest forest fire, and the details of the most recent holocaust in China. Rural and urban homes may now tune in to the same stations or to the same programs.

Exposure to the airwaves is limited only by the distribution of radio sets and the use to which they are put by their owners. A nation-wide study of radio service and rural people's attitudes toward it was made by the Bureau of Agricultural Economics, Department of Agriculture, in 1945.[2] The table on page 288 shows that 83 per cent of farm and 87 per cent of nonfarm households had radios. It must be remembered that these data were taken at a time when new radios and storage batteries had not been on the market for a long period. Therefore, the fact that 11 per cent of the farm and 8 per cent of the nonfarm households had been former owners is significant. This leaves but 6 per cent of

[1] "Rural Relief Needs," from a press release covering the statement by former Secretary of Agriculture Henry A. Wallace, before the Hearings of the Special Senate Committee to Investigate Unemployment and Relief, pp. 8–9, Jan. 11, 1938.

[2] *Attitudes of Rural People toward Radio Service*, Washington, D. C., January, 1946.

International Harvester Company

ONE HUNDRED YEARS FROM CRADLE TO COMBINE
Technological culture is a focal point of culture change.

farm and 5 per cent of nonfarm households that have been entirely without radios.

This study suggests that the extreme regional differences in radio ownership shown are due to economic conditions and not to a lack of interest in radio. Rural people in all regions and in both farm and nonfarm areas valued radio very highly. In the nation, 72 per cent of the total rural group, 66 per cent of rural men and 77 per cent of rural women, felt that it would make a great deal of difference to them if they did not have a radio.

News and other information rated highest in importance as far as programs were concerned, with entertainment the other major interest. Men placed a greater value on the former; women, on the latter. The news programs were emphasized as being more important by farm than nonfarm people.

PER CENT OF RURAL FARM AND RURAL NONFARM HOUSEHOLDS OWNING RADIOS IN 1945

	North Central			South			West			Entire country*		
	Farm	Non-farm	All	Farm	Non-farm	All	Farm	Non-farm	All	Farm	Non-farm	All
Radio owners.....	83	87	85	51	69	58	84	89	87	66	80	73
Former owners....	11	8	10	20	14	17	10	8	9	16	11	13
Nonowners.......	6	5	5	29	17	25	6	3	4	18	9	14
	100	100	100	100	100	100	100	100	100	100	100	100
Number of households studied....	422	408	830	567	405	972	241	302	543	1,317	1,218	2,535

* Including the Northeast, which is not shown separately.

Serious programs were rated as more important among farm people than the lighter entertainment programs—news and markets, weather, hymns and religious music, sermons and religious services, and farm talks. Oldtime music rated highest in the "purely entertainment" field. They liked least daytime serials ("soap operas"), dance music, and classical music. Interestingly enough, although they liked the "soap operas" least of all programs, these programs stood second to news only as items which farm women said they would miss most. This may be because "soap operas" take up most of the time in the day when farm women are alone and want some form of entertainment, however bad.

By contrast, rural nonfarm people, in addition to news programs, liked quiz programs, entertainment programs, such as staged by comedians and popular singers, dance music, and sports. In general, they preferred a lighter type of radio program than that preferred by farmers.

Without doubt the radio is doing much to modify the tastes, thought patterns, and interests of farm people, the advertisements and programs creating new desires and leading to the formation of new habits.

The Motion Picture.—Of great importance also is the motion picture, which among farmers somewhat less than city folk, but increasingly among all classes, is a medium for introducing new patterns in dress, song, phrase, convention, folkways, and morals. The motion picture bridges for many the long gap between their life and that of the various social classes of the city. Through it they become acquainted with the diverse social forms that characterize the different social classes. They see the luxury of the rich, the degradation of the poor, and come to realize in a measure the great gulf that separates social classes of the urban world. They become aware of differences in occupational activities and daily routine of other farm folk and of urban folk of the various occupations.[1]

Because of conservative religious traditions and because morality has been anchored deeply in certain past traditions, many farm people have stood out against the movie as an evil, and farm parents have not always been willing to allow their children to attend.[2] But in spite of this fact and of the fact that farm people have many times been shocked by the presentations of the movie, they have no doubt also learned new codes and developed greater tolerance for diverse ways of behavior. Influences in changing basic philosophies have probably been much more effective with the young than with the old, but all age groups have no doubt been affected. In addition to the commercialized entertainment film, the educational film of the county agent and the newsreel of the commercial movie have had their effect in producing change.

The Daily Paper and Magazine.—The metropolitan daily paper with its diversified news and advertising, and its emphasis on national and international affairs is an educational medium of pervasive influence. The number of farm people reading daily papers varies greatly throughout the nation, but everywhere the proportion is on the increase, millions of copies entering farm homes each day. To the extent that reading of the city daily becomes common in the farm community, to that extent farmer and urbanite are exposed to uniform stimuli.

Among the informal printed media of educational significance in the farm home, the magazine is probably of first importance. In its advertising of national products lie great potentialities for changing rural habits and folkways. It is probable that in the average farm home, magazines have tended to replace the mail-order catalogues as style sheets, although these latter, which for over a half century have been so influential in showing farmers the new product and enticing them to buy it, still are standard purchasing guides in many farm and village homes.

[1] Samuel R. McKelvie, "What the Movies Mean to the Farmer," *The Annals of the American Academy of Political and Social Science*, vol. 128, pp. 131–132, November, 1926.

[2] B. H. Hibbard, "The Movies and the Farm People," chap. 6 in *The Movies on Trial*, compiled and edited by W. J. Perlman, The Macmillan Company, New York, 1936.

POSSIBLE ADVANTAGES OF CULTURAL INERTIA

There are undoubtedly social advantages to be gained from a speeding up of cultural change; on the other hand, there are disadvantages. In many respects modern life has been greatly disturbed by the transformation in culture forms. A rapid rate of change may produce widespread personal demoralization and may even lead to such disorganization of culture patterns that social controls break down and society disintegrates. Speed of change in parts of the city is so great that there is serious question whether the human organism can long tolerate the pace. For this reason it may be desirable to live in an area in which change is slower and community life is more stable. There are advantages to personality in the equanimity of such a community. Some authors go so far as to look with great pessimism on the worth of urbanization to personality and social institutions, especially to such fundamental institutions as the family; others with equal conviction are inclined to favor the more isolated form of rural life because of the stable standards it establishes in the person and because of the persistence of fundamental cultural values in isolated rural areas. Many are apprehensive regarding the future of the family in the highly metropolitan area, most population authorities recognizing that least under our present mores the birth rate of the large city is not and will not in the future be sufficient to maintain present population. There is much objective evidence to the effect that the family does not function well as a complete institution in the urban community.[1] Somewhere between extreme geographical isolation and metropolitan congestion lies a happy medium for cultural growth.

QUESTIONS FOR REVIEW AND DISCUSSION

1. By what processes is cultural change brought about? Does it come more rapidly in material or nonmaterial culture?

2. Explain the relationship between contact and cultural change.

3. What factors inherent in agriculture historically have tended to hinder extensive change?

4. What essential elements in urban-industrial culture predispose it to frequent change?

5. Explain why urban-industrial expansion is dependent fundamentally on cultural change.

6. Explain why agriculture can respond less quickly to changing fashion than can industry.

7. Show how change in fashion affects agriculture.

8. What are the two prerequisites to rapid cultural change? How do the metropolis and the farm community compare in the prominence of these factors in their pattern?

9. What psychological factors have a bearing on the rate of cultural change in the farm community? what natural factors?

10. How does the rate of cultural change in the farm community today compare with that of the past?

11. Explain how changes in technology have led the way in producing extensive changes in agrarian culture.

[1] See Chapter 21 for evidence.

12. Explain the role of (*a*) the radio, (*b*) the moving picture, (*c*) newspaper advertising, in producing change in rural culture.

13. What are some possible advantages inherent in a degree of cultural inertia?

COLLATERAL READING

Barnes, Harry Elmer: *Society in Transition*, Prentice-Hall, Inc., New York, 1939.

Chapin, F. S.: *Cultural Change*, D. Appleton-Century Company, Inc., New York, 1928.

Cressey, Paul G.: "The Motion Picture Experience as Modified by Social Background and Personality," *American Sociological Review*, vol. 3, pp. 516–525, August, 1938.

Hibbard, B. H.: "The Movies and the Farm People," chap. 6 in *The Movies on Trial*, compiled and edited by William J. Perlman, The Macmillan Company, New York, 1936.

The Joint Committee Study of Rural Radio Ownership and Use in the United States, Section 4, Columbia Broadcasting System and the National Broadcasting Company, New York, February, 1939.

Landis, Paul H.: *Three Iron Mining Towns, A Study in Cultural Change*, Edwards Bros., Ann Arbor, Mich., 1938.

MacIver, R. M.: *Society*, chap. 25, Farrar & Rinehart, Inc., New York, 1937.

McKelvie, S. R.: "What the Movies Mean to the Farmer," *The Annals of the American Academy of Political and Social Science*, vol. 128, pp. 131–132, November, 1926.

Ogburn, W. F.: *Social Change*, The Viking Press, Inc., New York, 1923.

U.S. Department of Agriculture, *Attitudes of Rural People toward Radio Service*, Washington, D. C., January, 1946.

Winston, Sanford: *Culture and Human Behavior*, chaps. 6 and 7, The Ronald Press Company, New York, 1933.

CHAPTER 20

SOCIAL CONTROL

THE OPERATION OF SOCIAL CONTROL IN THE PRIMARY GROUP—A CASE STUDY

In June Kitty Smith graduates from the University of Michigan, thanks to a generous professor who at the last minute concedes her a D-minus in The Psychology and Technic of Teaching Spelling. In July, when her true love takes back his Sigma Chi pin, she enters her name at a teachers' agency. Early in September she arrives at Caribou, Nebraska, and is assigned the fifth grade at the Henry Wadsworth Longfellow school.

Two weeks later Kitty spends a hot Sunday morning taking a sun bath in a backless bathing suit on the lawn in front of her rooming house; before noon on Monday the principal of Longfellow school reprimands her for dressing immodestly and suggests that she spend her Sunday mornings in church. A month later the principal informs her that she may not smoke publicly in Caribou. On Armistice Day, pleasantly recalling the handsome face of John Strachey, who lectured at Michigan last year, she refuses to buy a poppy from a buddy; the fervor thus reawakened leads her to tell the fifth grade that world peace would be wonderful, information which reaches the adjutant of the American Legion post through a son who is doing badly in arithmetic. The superintendent of the Caribou schools now summons Kitty and forbids her to preach communism; he also instructs her not to wear chiffon stockings to school. . . . By February she is nervously aware that the whole Eastern Star is gossiping about her; wherefore, asked by Mrs. Robinson, its corresponding secretary, what kind of party she went to in Kearney last week end, she tells Mrs. Robinson that it is none of her . . . business. Six weeks later, just as the fires of spring are lighted, the Robinson car stops for gas at a combination hot-dog stand and dance hall some miles out of town, and it is unquestionably Kitty whom Mrs. Robinson sees necking with the Jones boy (from the hardware store) in a parked car under the cottonwoods. The superintendent has already heard . . . about Kitty's probable cocktails in Kearney. So now he discharges Kitty for immoral behavior.[1]

SOCIAL CONTROL DEFINED

Social control, the process by which order is established and maintained in society, consists essentially in the building of human nature so that it conforms to social definitions. Resident in the social group are the traditions of ages of human social experience, which surround the child from infancy. By absorbing

[1] Bernard DeVoto, "Tyranny at Longfellow School," *Harper's Magazine*, p. 221, January, 1937.

the group definitions he comes to fit the society of which he is to be a part. It is in this system of regular patterns that the individual finds meaning in life. Approached from this viewpoint, social control is not merely a matter of making the individual behave, but of making him a social creature. The directive or training element is always of first importance, but on the other hand, there are means of coercion or enforcement. If the nonconforming Kitty Smiths fail to observe social rules, the group has disciplinary measures by which they may be directed or coerced into line or forced out of the group.

Through social control all communities attempt to regulate behavior according to a set of standards. Regulative processes are designed to curb individualism and to reduce innovation; through them stability and order are maintained. In a rapidly changing society order is much more difficult to achieve than in a static society; in a highly individualistic society than in one which allows the individual little freedom of choice; in a mobile society than in an immobile one. It is much easier to regulate the individual in the intimate primary group, where he is conscious of the surveillance of others and interested in what they think of him, than in the secondary group of the anonymous community, where he cares little about their opinions. It is against this general background of principles that one must approach an analysis of social control in the rural neighborhood.

THE PRIMARY GROUP AS A UNIT OF CONTROL IN ALL RURAL SOCIETIES

In relatively static primary-group societies systems of social control are highly effective in the regulation of the individual. The life patterns of one generation are passed on to the next with little change, and few innovative tendencies are expressed by the new generation. Such has been the character of human society back to antiquity.

The ancient agricultural village, in which kinship groups lived close together, has been the chief controlling agency in the long experience of humanity. Law in its formal sense is a relatively recent development, but custom is as ancient as civilization, having dictated long before law appeared on the human scene.

W. I. Thomas and Florian Znaniecki in their famous treatise, *The Polish Peasant in Europe and America*, show with what complete effectiveness the old peasant neighborhood dominates the experiences of the individual and the extent to which he becomes disorganized and a problem to society when he is cast into the culture of the great city, where he is largely independent of the old family and neighborhood connections—a free man in an urban world with law as the chief guide to conduct.

The primary group in America probably has never been so homogeneous as in European countries, where stability characterizes rura llife and where for centuries people of similar nationality and cultural background have resided together. Rural America was settled by diverse peoples of different nationalities and customs. The result was that there never was a complete uniformity of social definition in many neighborhoods. It is in the communities settled by people of similar nationality and religious background that one finds the most persistent neighborhood patterns in the United States.[1] Nonetheless, rural groups in America have been sufficiently integrated so that fairly effective control has been realized.[2]

The neighborhood group is undoubtedly much less effective now as a unit of control in the nation than it has been in the past. Mobility has weakened attachments to the locality group for, if it is easy for the individual to divorce himself from the local group, he becomes less concerned about maintaining its standards. Also, as he becomes more mobile, he contacts new values and comes to understand that there are many codes beside his own, ranging all the way from those of the professional criminal gang, who make it their life's business to plunder, to those at the other extreme of people whose saintly nature is expressed in lifelong altruistic endeavor.

Mobility decreases attachment to primary groups and increases contact with secondary groups of diverse patterns, thus weakening the bonds which provide the basis for social control among members of local groups. Nonetheless many of the principles of control applicable to primary-group societies of the past still operate in the rural neighborhood even though contact has made for greater individualization and brought frequent innovation.

EFFECTIVENESS OF CONTROL IN THE PRIMARY GROUP

Students of the subject of social control generally recognize that an environment of intimate face-to-face relationships provides an ideal condition for the effective regulation of the person in relation to standards of the social group. As the member of such a group matures, he becomes increasingly conscious that his conduct always is scrutinized by others, and consequently habituates himself to thinking in terms of the response that his behavior elicits from them. Fear of gossip, a desire for praise, and, above all, avoidance of censure come to motivate him. To one who is highly sensitive to group opinion nothing is more painful than the lash of ridicule; nothing has a deeper sting than unfavorable group judgment. "What will the neighbors think?" always looms large in his consciousness.

[1] See J. H. Kolb and E. de S. Brunner, *A Study of Rural Society*, rev. ed., pp. 58–59, Houghton Mifflin Company, Boston, 1940.

[2] The kinship group remains an important factor in control in many rural communities of the United States. For an account of community control through the kinship group, see J. F. Steiner, *The American Community in Action*, pp. 82–85, Henry Holt and Company, Inc., New York, 1928.

The isolated primary group upholds a system of rigid discipline. Since its standards are well established and well understood by every member, behavior is predictable in terms of these standards. Social pressure in the form of group expectancy operates effectively because every members know what is expected of him. Anyone who falls short, like Hawthorne's character, Hester Prynne, must thereafter bear the mark of public disfavor. The scarlet letter on the front of her garment needed no label, for everyone in the primary group understood its significance. She had violated a well-understood rule of the group and so could expect neither sympathy nor forgiveness.

In a primary-group society there is little conflict over social definition; the family and the neighborhood agree. At every step of his development the child has impressed upon him the same uniform concepts of the good and the bad. Because the group is small and everyone is known, offenders are readily apprehended, and as readily and certainly punished. Habits become rigidly fixed because only one general set of habits is acceptable; innovators with undesirable patterns are quickly stamped out. Group disapproval is a painful and effective goad. For example, wheat allotment control under the Agricultural Adjustment Act has been placed in the hands of committees of local farmers, whose business it is to see that all conform to their agreements as to acreage. Supervisors report that farmers who violate their contracts often are made to feel the resentment of the entire community. One migrant interviewed in the state of Washington stated that he left Colorado because he had failed to keep his agreement and could not face humiliation among his neighbors.

SENTIMENT AND REPUTATION AS FACTORS IN PRIMARY-GROUP CONTROL

Since the primary group is one of intimate relationships, experience is heightened by emotion; teaching is flavored with affection or at times with wrath; even the ordering and forbidding technique is not impersonal, but often emphatic and pointed. In such a situation the tentacles of the group take strong hold of the individual, binding him well.

The child soon learns that disobedience will be taken personally, that the parent will feel hurt as though disobedience were an injury to him and not just a violation of his precepts. Throughout the range of primary-group contacts he learns to think of the effect of his conduct on others and in turn of how their reactions will affect him. Sentiment is always present. College students who have left the primary group still think of conduct in terms of the way their parents would react and avoid what to them would be pleasant experiences were it not for the fear of hurting their parents.[1]

[1] The author has frequently had occasion to notice this reaction in the autobiographies of college freshmen written in introductory sociology classes. See student papers published in Paul H. Landis, *Social Control: Social Organization and Disorganization in Process*, chaps. 20 and 21, J. B. Lippincott Company, Philadelphia, 1939.

Reputation is an important aspect of primary-group control, it being confined to the primary group in the case of most individuals. Essentially, reputation is the name one has established for himself by having behaved in a consistent manner among permanent acquaintances. The individual, in acquiring a reputation for himself in the primary group, sets a standard of social expectancy to which he thereafter feels obliged to conform. If he is known for his honesty, justice, goodness, and generosity, he behaves consistently in accord with these recognized qualities. Similarly, if he has established the reputation of being the community drone, in Rip Van Winkle fashion, he plays that role. If he has come to be known as the town reprobate, he finds it easy to maintain his reputation and to exaggerate this proclivity. One tends to play up to the picture of self reflected by his social group.[1] This tendency is especially noticeable in the child who, having obtained the reputation of being the bad boy of the neighborhood, proceeds to live up to it.

SOCIAL CONTINUITY AS A FACTOR IN RURAL PRIMARY-GROUP CONTROL

Many rural neighborhoods have a conscious past. Their leading families, having lived in them for two generations or more, have accumulated a wealth of background concerning local traditions. They act as jealous guardians of local standards, conserving the *status quo*, and have a powerful influence in determining whether the community will respond favorably or unfavorably to progressive movements and constructive changes.

Few rural areas experience the rapid changes of transitional areas of the city; few city areas have the long-time perspective that the average rural community possesses. Its past is both an asset and a liability, depending on one's point of view and purpose. It is a stabilizing influence but at the same time it may make for stagnation; it conserves the finer traditions, but also may keep the community anchored to ancient landmarks. It makes life easy, rhythmic, and safe for those who can conform; monotonous and repressive for those who have experienced a more stimulating way of life.

INFORMAL AND NONLEGAL CHARACTER OF SOCIAL CONTROL IN RURAL AMERICA

Problems of discipline in rural areas are lessened in that the strength and weakness of every man are common knowledge. If a misdeed is committed, it is usually known whom to suspect, for past behavior is recorded, not in case histories in a juvenile court nor in a relief office, but in the memories of citizens of the neighborhood.

The older generation in more stable rural groups have observed the young

---

[1] See Charles H. Cooley's idea of the "looking glass self." *Human Nature and the Social Order*, pp. 184–185, Charles Scribner's Sons, New York, 1922.

person from the time he was born. They remember the steps in his character development, the difficulties he encountered as he grew up, the times he strayed from the marked path, and the methods by which he was brought back; they know his deeds, his institutional connections, the reputation of his family.

Tradition, custom, gossip, local mores, and moral standards accomplish in the farm community everything that is accomplished by law, police, courts, and penal institutions in the great city. These informal devices work not only more effectively but also with less friction to the subject being controlled and with less cost to social organization than formal ones.

WORK AS A FACTOR IN SOCIAL CONTROL IN THE RURAL SETTING

One of the primary factors in the maintenance of regular and orderly behavior in rural areas is the work routine. One whose time is occupied with socially sanctioned work activities is not likely to engage in antisocial behavior. It is those who have much leisure on their hands who have come to constitute a major problem of control in the contemporary world. Realizing this, the city community has gone to great expense to provide recreational programs as antidotes for juvenile delinquency, crime, and other pathological forms of behavior which are prominent among those who have no socially approved way to spend time. Even in times of agricultural depression when crops do not bring profitable returns, even in times of drought when there are no crops, there is work for the farmer. For this reason rural people face less personal frustration as an outgrowth of economic adversity than urban people. When the urban man loses his business or his job, he loses all opportunity to express himself through work channels. Many forms of delinquency are but an expression of revolt against forced idleness, against being shut in with one's feelings of frustration. Moreover, the social experience of a rural man in not necessarily injured by economic adversity; he may have no crop and yet keep the respect of his neighbors, because his failure has usually been produced by some natural phenomenon that is inherent in the situation of every farmer.

In the urban community the job represents the only road to status for many, for one who is out of funds may be out of society. Unable to function in a normal way among friends, feeling himself excluded from the social group, the jobless individual may be led to revolt against controls and soon find himself beyond the pale of socially sanctioned activity.

ACCOMMODATION AS A FACTOR IN SOCIAL CONTROL

The more static rural communities, because they are removed from the crosscurrents of social influence, permit the individual to become more accommodated to his status than most people can be in the city. Indeed he may become too completely accommodated, not for purposes of personality integration and of control, but for purposes of individualization.

Accommodation develops a sense of smugness, of being satisfied with life, of fitting into situations that make up the world of the commonplace. Therefore, if we assume the fairly complete accommodation of the rural person, we can assume that one of the basic problems of social control is already solved. It cannot of course be inferred that every farmer is accommodated to his life; some, though they spend all their years on the farm, remain discontented misfits, having no taste for farming, finding the life drab and uninteresting, and only to be endured because circumstances offer no way out.

Those who are not accommodated create the friction points at which social upheaval takes place. Only rarely in rural society is there a sufficiently large group of like-minded individuals to provide a nucleus for revolt, revolution, or radical social action. The exception is in times of economic crisis when the state of accommodation may be destroyed and violent action initiated. Such was the case of the Farmer's Holiday movement which developed in the southeastern part of South Dakota and the northwestern part of Iowa during the darker part of the depression of the early thirties. Radical movements, however, usually develop in the urban rather than the rural community; most members of the Communist party are found among the industrial downtrodden of the large cities.

GOSSIP AS A DEVICE FOR CONTROL IN THE RURAL PRIMARY GROUP

One cannot read Sinclair Lewis' *Main Street* without obtaining a fairly realistic picture of what he has already observed in the small town or open-country neighborhood, *i.e.*, the effectiveness with which gossip controls behavior. One also sees operating in this book the social pressure of a primary group upon an innovator. Carol of St. Paul marries Dr. Kennewick of Main Street. For some years she tries to get innovations accepted in the community but with little success. Revolting first against the townspeople and finally against her husband, she returns to the city to recover the freedom that she had once had in the secondary group. In the end she returns to her husband and to Main Street, has a baby, and settles down to find herself at last accommodated to Main Street's pace, Main Street's gossip, and Main Street's standards. One who has never been in St. Paul, who has always lived in the rural neighborhood, seldom feels irked by the restraints of the primary group, taking them for granted because he has never known anything different.

Blumenthal, in his study, *Small Town Stuff*, shows how people in a small town are wittingly or unwittingly affected by their fear of gossip. This is so much the case that they learn to analyze their every action in terms of how other people will regard it. A reputation may be ruined by malicious or idle chatter. Whispers such as "Don't breathe a word of this" are uttered and even in formal meetings someone may propose, "We had better watch our step or the whole town will be on our necks before we adjourn." Most small-town inhabitants know they are being talked about and can only hope that what is said is more favorable than unfavorable.[1]

Everyone knows the other person's business, private and public, and does not hesitate to give his opinion on it. The women play bridge and gossip and have their "cat sessions." One is always aware that what he does will be known and discussed and is always concerned with what people will think. A reputation is something valuable and not to be thrown away by a careless act. Because my aunt and uncle with whom I live hold an enviable position in the town, I have had to watch my step all the more carefully, there being plenty of jealous people who would enjoy tearing down the reputation I have made for being at least fairly decent.[2]

RURAL SOCIAL CONTROL AND INDIVIDUATION

Sanderson, discussing the rural community historically, observes that to the primitive man the group is "all"; the individual as a personality does not exist.[3] It is only at the higher levels of social development that the individual comes to exercise controlling forces within himself, and social control in terms of his own thought and conscience becomes important.

Park observes that a relatively high proportion of the early more individualistic immigrants to the United States[4] were lodged in almshouses, whereas the later immigrants, who have been lacking in individualism and have clung to the simple village organization with its provisions for mutual aid that characterized their foreign culture, have maintained a great degree of economic independence. It has also been observed that among the Jews and Japanese in this country, who have retained close-knit familistic patterns, there have been few commitments to institutions for the socially inadequate.

The room given for individuation varies greatly from society to society, but none ever completely smothers it. On the other hand, few social orders dare give much place to the rebel. The static rural societies of yesterday never worshiped the reformer and never boasted of free speech or a free press. These are notions of a highly individualistic order; in fact, of one in which regulation is weak.

The secondary group challenges the person with choice, freedom, and opportunity such as encourage individuation. Self-control is essential if he is not to exercise his individualism in such a manner that he will not destroy

---

[1] Another interesting account is that by Kennethe Leslie, "Smaller Town Stuff," *Studies in Sociology*, vol. 1, pp. 25–26, 1936.

[2] From a student paper.

[3] Dwight Sanderson, *The Rural Community*, chap. 16, Ginn and Company, Boston, 1932.

[4] Robert E. Park, *et al.*, *The City*, pp. 120–121, University of Chicago Press, Chicago, 1925.

himself nor endanger the patterns of social organization that prevail in his society. It is partly for this reason that the system of social control of the city is often less effective and less meaningful than that of the rural primary group, for a close relationship exists between inefficient control and personal disorganization.[1] A well-knit system of social organization seems to be essential not only to effective group regulation but equally to the development of an integrated and stable personality.

SOCIAL CONTROL AND PROBLEMS OF PERSONAL ADJUSTMENT

The ideal system of social control would strike a delicate balance between individual freedom and social restraint. Social discipline may smother individuality and destroy creativeness; it may allow considerable liberty but give so little room for personality expression that frustration results; it may permit liberty that becomes license, the person injuring himself or becoming a nuisance to his neighbors. There is a happy medium where the individual has sufficient opportunity to develop his personal traits but at the same time is made to conform in things essential to group welfare. Is this ideal more nearly attained in rural society in America than in urban? The question cannot be answered dogmatically.

AN EVALUATION OF PRIMARY-GROUP CONTROL

We may start with the following theoretical premise—that the individual, if his personality is to be integrated and if he is to be successful in life adjustments, must feel himself a part of community life; only then does he feel psychologically and sociologically complete. Lacking this sense of unity with the group, personality suffers a degree of disorganization. We have already seen that pathological conditions are at their worst in parts of the city where the system of social regulation is least effective. From this standpoint it would seem that most rural areas approach nearer the ideal situation than most urban areas.

Many of the strong customary controls of the ancient agricultural village were transferred to the American rural neighborhood, especially where it was

[1] See Ruth S. Cavan, *Suicide*, University of Chicago Press, Chicago, 1928; C. Shaw, et al., *Delinquency Areas*, University of Chicago Press, Chicago, 1929; F. Thrasher, *The Gang*, University of Chicago Press, Chicago, 1927. See Robert E. L. Faris, "Cultural Isolation and the Schizophrenic Personality," *American Journal of Sociology*, vol. 33, pp. 784–795, March, 1928; H. Warren Dunham, "The Ecology of the Functional Psychoses in Chicago," *American Sociological Review*, vol. 2, pp. 467–479, August, 1937, for data on schizophrenia. See also P. A. Sorokin, C. C. Zimmerman, and C. J. Galpin, *A Systematic Source Book in Rural Sociology*, vol. 2, chap. 13 and vol. 3, chap. 19, University of Minnesota Press, Minneapolis, 1931, for a discussion of pathologies as evidence of ineffective social control. Also, see Paul H. Landis, *op. cit.*, chaps. 22, 23, and 24.

composed of near relatives or of homogeneous religious groups, but even here individualization has been increased by the development of devices for communication and transportation.[1] Probably the more progressive rural community, which has facilities for the enrichment of experience but at the same time maintains fairly rigid codes, represents, from many viewpoints, a near ideal situation for social control. However, there are undoubtedly stable areas in the city which also approach ideal conditions. It is possible too that the more objective approach to problems of control in the urban community may eventually develop a superior environment in which human beings not only will have greater personal freedom but will be well regulated by ideals applicable to secondary group circumstances. Until that time comes, and it seems not to have arrived, the system of social control in primary groups, where members have a personal interest in one another, is more effective.[2]

The greatest threat to social control in any society is rapid change, for change makes a mock of custom and tradition, the cornerstones of social organization. The influence of custom in the metropolis has all but disappeared in the face of new technic-ways; national stability is in part dependent on the more conservative and more stable rural hinterland. The breakdown of the family, the conflict of social classes, the disregard of moral sanction, and the growth of social pathologies have been in considerable part an outgrowth of a disintegrating system of social regulation which has been unable to withstand the tide of urban change.

THE PRIMARY GROUP AND INDIVIDUAL JUSTICE

Cooley called the primary group the nursery of human nature and commented at length on the finer human traits nourished there—honor, honesty, love, justice, and sympathy.[3] In too much of our sociological study we have been inclined to let the matter rest at this point. It is true that the primary group develops some noble traits; it also may develop some not so desirable. Whether loyalty is a virtue or not depends upon the primary group to which one is loyal; whether high ethical standards or their opposite are upheld depends upon the standards of one's primary group. Studies of the urban gang have robbed us of any illusion that primary-group patterns are always ideal from the standpoint of society at large.[4] The gang builds loyalty to itself but the codes are often in direct opposition to those of society.

Frequently patterns are perpetuated in isolated rural communities that are

---

[1] Dwight Sanderson, *op. cit.*, chap. 14.

[2] This problem has been discussed more fully in the writer's *Social Control: Social Organization and Disorganization in Process, op. cit.*, chaps. 10 and 11.

[3] Charles H. Cooley, *Social Organization*, chaps. 3 and 4, Charles Scribner's Sons, New York, 1909.

[4] See, for example, Frederic Thrasher, *op. cit.*

entirely out of step with the more progressive patterns of the national culture. Fiction, moving pictures, and the comics describe the patterns of the mountain hillbillies and feature characters have grown up with the stamp of "feudin' " upon them. Although greatly exaggerated, they suggest a tangible problem.

From the standpoint of individual adjustment viewed from a larger perspective, the primary group frequently is very unjust in its judgments of persons, for in a setting where everyone knows everyone else, the reputation which a person develops may stay with him much longer than the character traits which were originally responsible for that reputation. A single delinquent act in childhood or youth may brand a person as long as he stays in the community. It is in the primary group that the sins of parents are passed on to their children through social heritage. A lazy good-for-nothing father transmits his reputation in the neighborhood to his children and with rare exceptions the neighborhood accepts the children at the face value of their father. This being the case, children of socially inadequate parents are sometimes cruelly treated by the rural group

The Iowa study cites several instances of rural children suffering because of the stigma of their family's status in the neighborhood, and cases of radical improvement in personality when a new teacher, unwilling to accept the neighborhood's evaluation, helped the child to an appreciation of his worth.[1]

PRIMARY-GROUP CONTROLS IN TRANSITION

All of American society not long since was regulated in large part by the simple ordering and forbidding techniques of primary groups. In them informal social control devices were usually sufficient for the maintenance of order. The city has outgrown primary-group experience in considerable part and also the control devices it employed. The transition of rural society toward a less integrated local life, but a more diversified and stimulating one, calls for a readjustment of the pattern of social control. Less effective have become the informal control devices of the neighborhood as the automobile has taken youth beyond the critical eyes of neighbors. Under such conditions the breach between youth and age widens, the old fearful because the young are escaping their restrictions and the young glorying in secret rebellion. Rural youths, like urban youths, are beginning to sense the power of youth groups, free from the domination of elders, and are planning their courses along new lines. Rural parents, unlike urban parents, do not worship at youth's shrine or imitate their ways and often find in the new situation cause for alarm.

But for better or for worse greater freedom has come to youth and the rural community, finding them breaking away, is at a loss to know what to do about it. In rural communities, as in the urban, there are now appearing con-

[1] Bird T. Baldwin, *et al.*, *Farm Children*, pp. 163–168, D. Appleton-Century Company, Inc., New York, 1930.

flicting definitions of "right" and "wrong." Diversity of experience and a multiplicity of contacts inevitably introduce a heterogeneity of life patterns. As standards multiply, it becomes necessary to challenge some of them; in challenging, some youth may challenge all. We are approaching a time in the rural community when effective control cannot be realized as a matter of course, but must be achieved as in urban society by the conscious exercise of a body of restraints, not that control will need to be achieved as fully by the conscious exercise of restraining forces as in the city, but much more so than in most static rural orders.

QUESTIONS FOR REVIEW AND DISCUSSION

1. What is social control and what does it accomplish?
2. Explain how social control operates within primary groups.
3. Why is social control of an informal sort more effective in primary than in secondary groups?
4. Show the effect of sentiment in making effective control devices of the primary group.
5. How does group continuity make for effective control?
6. How does an abundance of work affect problems of social regulation?
7. Show how accommodation or lack of it bears on the process of social regulation.
8. Explain how gossip acts as a control device within the primary group.
9. How does individualization bear on problems of social control?
10. Discuss the superiority of social control in the farm community as compared to that in the city.
11. Are primary groups always just in the patterns imposed and the judgments passed upon the individual? Explain.
12. At what points may one see primary-group controls breaking down?

COLLATERAL READING

Bernard, L. L.: *Social Control*, The Macmillan Company, New York, 1939.
Blumenthal, Albert: *Small-town Stuff*, University of Chicago Press, Chicago, 1932.
Landis, Paul H.: *Social Control: Social Organization and Disorganization in Process*, J. B. Lippincott Company, Philadelphia, 1939.
Lewis, Sinclair: *Main Street* (a novel), Harcourt, Brace and Company, New York, 1931.
Sanderson, Dwight: *The Rural Community*, chap. 16, Ginn and Company, Boston, 1932.
Sorokin, P. A., C. C. Zimmerman, and C. J. Galpin: *A Systematic Source Book in Rural Sociology*, vol. 2, pp. 261–266, University of Minnesota Press, Minneapolis, 1931.
Thomas, W. I., and F. Znaniecki: *The Polish Peasant in Europe and America*, vol. 1, vol. 2, and vol. 5, chap. 2, Chapman & Grimes, Inc., Boston, 1918, 1919, and 1920, respectively.

Part IV

SOCIAL INSTITUTIONS IN A CHANGING CULTURE

UNIVERSAL as are the needs that lead to their development, institutions are never perfect and never fully able to meet the needs for which they are established. In more static societies where people are relatively immobile and where culture changes slowly, institutions over periods of centuries may come to meet in a near ideal way the recognized needs of a social group; in a dynamic society where culture changes at a rapid rate and where men move freely both upward and outward, institutions are seldom adequate. The institutional structure with its symbolic forms and its emotional hold may change far too slowly to meet new conditions and, even when most intelligently directed, usually fails to anticipate conditions of the future.

We have just completed a review of some of the dynamic aspects of rural life as affected by mobility and change. Are the institutions that serve farm life today adequate for the exigencies of this society or are they still adapted to the older more static situations of yesterday? What problems do they face and how are these problems being met? Can the finer elements that some of these institutions once stood for be maintained in an age when many of the older institutional values and practices are passing and when even more of them must pass?

No institution is self-sufficient or in itself complete. It is but a sector of social experience and must therefore adapt itself to other institutions and to major changes in the total culture pattern of a society. The adaptations may come too slowly, but forces of change bring them in spite of emotional resistance. Where do our rural social institutions stand in the dynamic culture setting of the nation?

CHAPTER 21

THE FARM FAMILY IN A CHANGING CULTURE

SOCIAL institutions never exist in a vacuum; they are always a part of a total situation. One can understand the nature of the family and changes affecting it only as he understands the culture setting in which it functions. If the modern farm family is unique, it is due in part to factors outside the family; if the farm family is different from the urban family, it is because of the different total situation in which the farm family operates. Everywhere the basic functions of the family are the same but there is a wide variation in the manner of their execution and in the extent to which the family discharges them or leaves them to other institutions.

THREE MAJOR FUNCTIONS OF THE FAMILY

The family is a basic institution in all societies: (1) in passing on the biological heritage, (2) in transmitting the cultural heritage, and (3) in providing a primary agency for socialization.[1]

Transmitting the Biological Heritage.—In passing on the biological heritage through the normal processes of birth and child rearing, the farm family functions more completely than either the urban or village family. It has more offspring than either and it not only replenishes its own numbers but provides a surplus, whereas the population of the great city does not even reproduce itself, the urban birth rate being extremely low. For years the size of the urban family has declined. Data for the city of Chicago show that the average size of the family in 1900 was 3.22 persons as compared to 2.85 persons in 1930. In small towns the family dropped during this period from 3.82 members to 3.72, but in farming areas families increases from 4.21 to 4.32.[2]

Marked contrasts are shown in the extent to which various residential and regional groups have children (see charts). The relatively large number of children in farm families and in the rural South as of 1940 is immediately apparent.

More significant still from the standpoint of transmitting the biological heritage is the fact that many persons in the city never marry. It has been observed that cities of over 2,500 population deter marriage about 10 per cent;

[1] Compare W. F. Ogburn, writing in *Recent Social Trends in the United States*, p. 683, McGraw-Hill Book Company, Inc., New York, 1933.

[2] W. F. Ogburn, *op. cit.*, p. 683.

that is, about 10 per cent fewer people marry there than if they were in rural areas.[1] More extreme would be the reduction in marriage rate in large cities. Many of those who marry in the large metropolis have no children; a study in 1930 showed that almost half of the families in the metropolis are without children. In cities generally one in three, in small towns one in four, and on the farm only one in six is without children.[2] Where there are no children, there can be no transmission of the biological heritage of the race.

AVERAGE PERSONS PER FAMILY BY RACE, RESIDENCE, AND REGION, 1940

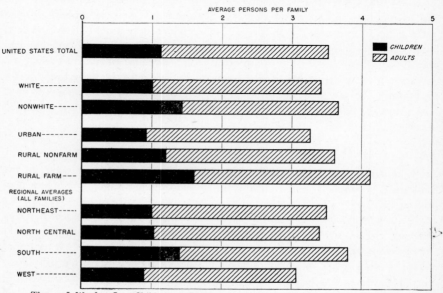

Thomas J. Woofter, Jr., "Children and Family Income," *Social Security Bulletin*, vol. 8, January, 1945.

A COMPARISON OF THE NATION'S FAMILIES BY RURAL-URBAN RESIDENCE AND BY REGIONS
The large families are rural farm families, the small families for the most part urban.

Passing on the Cultural Heritage.—The transmission of the cultural heritage presupposes the presence of children in the home; in homes with children the family remains the most influential single agency passing on the more vital of our traditions, standards, and attitudes.

Since the farm family has children more often than the urban, it more often is concerned with the transmission of culture. The general opinion among

---

[1] *Ibid.*, p. 681.

[2] *Ibid.*, p. 687. Data deal only with unbroken families. W. A. Anderson finds farm families in New York state more complete than rural nonfarm families; that is, there are fewer broken families on the farms, "The Composition of Rural Households," p. 23, *Cornell Agricultural Experiment Station Bulletin* 713, Ithaca, 1939.

observers is that the family heritage is more effectively transmitted to children in the rural community than in the urban; the child is subject to fewer distracting influences in the total environment and the parent, because of his dominant position, can pass on exactly that philosophy of life, exactly those attitudes and behavior traits that seem most important to him. As an agency for the transmission of culture, the farm family has weak points, however, in that culture base is, as we have seen, often narrow and restricted.[1]

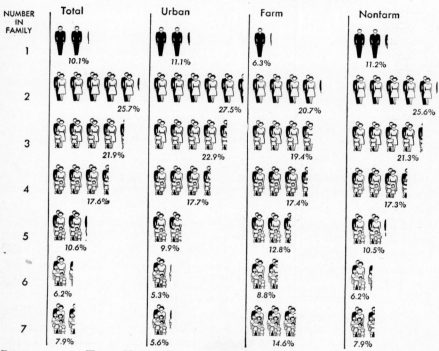

DISTRIBUTION OF TOTAL, URBAN, FARM, AND NONFARM FAMILIES IN THE UNITED STATES BY SIZE, 1940

Families of five or more are more common in farm areas.

Socializing the Individual.—Because the child has his first social contacts within the family, the interaction patterns of the family group have great influence in determining his general approach to life. His first ideals, whatever he knows of love, justice, brotherhood, affection, honesty, honor, in fact, all ideals ordinarily considered important to character, if acquired at all, are usually acquired in the family group. The family is the incubator[2] of primary-group values.

[1] Chap. 9 especially.

[2] See C. H. Cooley, *Social Organization*, chap. 4, Charles Scribner's Sons, New York, 1909.

As an agency for socialization the farm family is effective since there are usually children in the home close enough together in age to constitute a play group within the family, thus creating a situation which by some is assumed to be superior to the "only child" family situation so common in urban areas.

But often outside contacts are limited; the range of stimuli is circumscribed; the child absorbs the family pattern thoroughly, but it may be a pattern that has comparatively little value outside the local setting. This increases problems of adjustment and frequently makes for personality conflict when the young person is compelled to leave the intimate world of his childhood. The certainty and security, the conviction, the moral sense that is double enforced because the rural neighborhood often supplements family training, develop a smugness and rigidness of personality which sometimes is ill adapted for life in a larger setting. As a result the rural family is likely to fail in preparing the child for change. This topic has been discussed fully in other sections.

THE DISINTEGRATION OF FAMILY BONDS

Ogburn stresses the fact that the traditional American family has been held together by seven bonds—economic, educational, recreational, religious, social status, protective, and affectional.[1] In a factual analysis he indicates that these bonds have tended to disintegrate in the modern family, especially in the urban family. The economic function of the home has gradually been lost as factory, store, laundry, and bakery have encroached upon the domain once preempted by the family; recreational bonds have loosened their hold as civic, commercial, and school recreational activities have increased; religious bonds have been severed as religion has been taken outside the home or abandoned altogether. Social status once was transmitted through the family, but in urban society today the youth can escape the reputation of his family, whether it be good or bad, and be rated on the basis of his own qualities. Education has gradually shifted to include younger and younger ages, kindergarten and nursery schools lessening home responsibilities. Protection has increased outside the family—a police force shields one from physical violence; life insurance and accident insurance offer economic security independent of the primary group. Ogburn concludes that affection remains the one chief bond of the modern family.

This analysis may be applied to the farm family. There is no doubt but that in the more progressive areas many of the same forces which have acted as disintegrating agents in the urban family have also influenced the rural; on the other hand, the disintegration process has not gone nearly so far. Most of the bonds which were once important in holding the family together are still important in farming areas. Although the farm family is no longer so much an

[1] W. F. Ogburn, *op. cit.*, pp. 664–679.

economic unit from the standpoint of home manufacture of goods and home processing as it once was, nevertheless, the man, wife, and children, all have a part in the productive enterprise of the farm; they no longer card their wool and spin their clothing and in many cases no longer churn their butter or bake their bread, but they still each share in the work of producing a living on the farm—the children with chores, the wife with household work, and often with the care of chickens and garden, and the household head with heavier farm work.

Home recreation on the farm has given way in a considerable degree under the influence of the automobile and open road. Even so the rural child today spends many evenings at home within the family circle;[1] he attends many more recreational events in the community in the company of his parents than does the average urban child.[2] As to the family religious function, family prayers, reading of the Bible, and grace at meals are much more frequently found in the rural home than in the urban, although there is no doubt but that they are decreasing in both.[3]

As to the protective function and that of transmitting social status, the youth who remains in the rural community still inherits the social status of his family through social transmission. The protective function is still important in the rural family; women and children on the farm feel a need of the physical protection of the male[4] and of protection by him from economic hazards since life insurance, accident insurance, and various forms of social security are less prevalent among farmers than among many urban classes. Dinkle finds that the obligation of children to support the aged parents is no longer well established in the mores, although rural youth generally are more inclined to feel that children should support aged parents than urban youth. The difference is not as striking as one might expect.[5]

The affectional function, which Ogburn concludes is the principal tie of

[1] See *The Adolescent in the Family*, pp. 20 *ff*., White House Conference on Child Health and Protection, D. Appleton-Century Company, Inc., New York, 1934.

[2] *Ibid*. Leland H. Stott in "The Relation of Certain Factors in Farm Family Life to Personality Development in Adolescents," *Nebraska Agricultural Experiment Station Bulletin* 106, 1938, a study of 695 farm youths ranging in ages from 11 to 22 years, finds that 53 per cent of the boys and 66 per cent of the girls reported that they often went with their family on trips, picnics, visits, and to church gatherings, shows, and other entertainments.

[3] W. F. Ogburn, *op. cit.*, p. 674. These data are summarized in chap. 20.

[4] Groves suggests that in some areas in the South, because of race friction, both husband and wife are afraid on the isolated homestead, their fear at times amounting to terror. It is doubtful whether such a situation exists in many sections of the country. There are more city people, no doubt, who fear physical attack than rural people, although a sense of isolation and danger does exist in some farm homes. See his *The Rural Mind and Social Welfare*, University of Chicago Press, Chicago, 1922.

[5] Robert M. Dinkle, "Attitudes of Children Toward Supporting Aged Parents," *American Sociological Review*, vol. 9, pp. 370–379, August, 1944.

the modern family, is still supplemented and perhaps even outweighed by other important bonds among farm families. These other bonds have no doubt weakened under modern influences and romance may have become more prominent as a factor in farm marriage.

EMOTIONAL PATTERNS IN THE FARM FAMILY

The Romantic Pattern in Marriage.—Courtship and marriage in America have become highly individualistic. Romance rather than traditional institutional factors plays a major part in both marriage and family life. The romantic emphasis no doubt has contributed to family instability, but also perhaps to an increase in marital happiness where ideal relationships are achieved.

Although it is difficult to compare various social and occupational classes with regard to prominence of individualistic-romantic and traditional-institutional patterns, it seems that the metropolitan family has tended to approach the romantic extreme whereas the farm family represents a carry-over in many respects of the traditional-institutional type of family emotional relationship. This carry-over is inherent to some extent in the situation in which the farm family develops. Farm youth, until very recently, chose their associates from among the opposite sex and carried on their courtship under the scrutiny of the primary group. Consequently, adults—parents, neighbors, and relatives— were inclined to pass judgment on the pair and check romance by criticism. To some extent still, adult judgments in the farm community are projected upon the courtship behavior of youth. In the farm community also courtship is somewhat more likely to be among those who have known each other since childhood.[1] This probably tempers romance because the interested individuals always know each other's past, their family heritage, and general traits and capabilities.

In the metropolitan situation courtship may be undirected by adult supervision; in fact, it is likely to be so. Young people are involved in courtship and marriage who know practically nothing of each other's background, family traditions, or general social status. Strangeness probably lends to romance. Youthful inexperience results in a taking into account of individualistic interests primarily, neglecting institutional factors essential to the establishment of a permanent family.

In the past the farm family has probably gone to a utilitarian extreme, and in some communities still tends in a direction that stifles normal romantic interest. Another hazard to desirable family life, and perhaps also to romantic interest, exists in isolated rural areas with high fertility rates. Relatives are

[1] It is recognized that many marriages among rural youth occur outside the friendship circle of childhood. It is also admitted that marriage of childhood friends is possible and perhaps frequent in the metropolis. In the majority of cases, however, the situation described holds true.

more likely to marry here than in an urban situation.[1] In the marriage of distant relatives or even of neighbors in the local community there is an inbreeding of cultural tradition that probably makes for narrow-mindedness within the family. Contributing to this danger in the farm community is the fact that many times the young man who wishes to marry and remain on the farm has little choice as to whom he will marry, there being few eligible girls interested in farm life. This situation has its biological counterpart in the large city where many women cannot marry because of a lack of males of marriageable age.[2]

There is little doubt that today the romantic philosophy of marriage and family is permeating the farm community through the youth group. Duvall and Motz[3] found little difference in the attitudes of 403 rural and urban girls 14 to 24 years of age in the Middle West, with regard to marriage and its aims, wives working, and desire for children.

Emotional Patterns within the Family.—Because the urban family is experiencing a multitude of problems of a crisis nature, and because divorce and family discord are prominent in the city, psychological aspects of urban family relations have been made the subject of much study by family life counselors, psychiatrists, and clinicians. Even the more intimate phases of adjustment have been investigated, physical, psychological, and emotional factors involved in sex relationships, case histories of divorce, and factors lending to divorce having been studied extensively[4]. These studies reveal factors in family conflict that are seldom introduced in the divorce court, proving that the real reasons for family maladjustment are ordinarily quite different from the legal reasons. Comparatively little information is available on the more intimate aspects of farm family life. This being the case, what is written in the following paragraphs is drawn from scattered bits of evidence and is of a hypothetical nature. The subject is one meriting further investigation.

Affections in the farm home are less likely to be centered on one child than in the urban home because of the larger number of children in the rural family. Overattention to an "only" child often leads to a delay in psychological

[1] N. Carpenter, "Courtship Practices and Contemporary Social Change in America," *Annals of American Academy of Political and Social Science*, vol. 160, pp. 34–44, March, 1932.

[2] In the age group 20 to 24 there were 126 males to 100 females in the rural farm population in 1940; in the urban population there were only 89 males per 100 females. Of single women 20 to 34 years of age in 1930, 66 per cent lived in the city, whereas of single men of the same age, only 59 per cent lived there.

For a more extensive analysis of this problem, see *Recent Social Trends in the United States*, p. 681; also Paul Popenoe, "Where Are the Marriageable Men?" *Social Forces*, vol. 14, pp. 257–262, 1935; also Paul H. Landis, *Population Problems*, American Book Co., New York, 1943.

[3] Evelyn Millis Duvall and Anabelle Bender Motz, "Are Country Girls so Different," *Rural Sociology*, vol. 10, pp. 263–274, September, 1945.

[4] The studies of Ernest R. Mowrer are prominent in this field.

weaning, hindering the growth of self-reliance.[1] Therefore, there may be many more spoiled children, proportionately, in the city than in the country.[2] Studies show also that children of small families are more variable, more of them becoming successes and also more becoming failures.[3] It is likewise apparent that neurotic tendencies are more frequently found among only children.[4] Ogburn cautions us, however, that these traits and tendencies may not be due entirely to size of family.[5]

Farm parents may be inclined to display less affection toward their children than urban parents and to deal with them on a more mature level. There is perhaps less danger of emotional fixation because the entire family, including the mother, is absorbed in work interests. Many urban women who have little in the way of productive activities to take up their time, and no normal outlet for their energy, express it in maternal affection. The fact that the farm child has pets toward which he can direct some of his affection may have a bearing on the situation. Also, where there are several children in the family, affections tend to be diffused over the whole group and not fixed on any one member. There is some evidence that farm children are more critical of their parents than urban children, that they demonstrate their affection less, and confide in parents less than do city children.[6]

The problem of projection is frequently encountered in family relationships, parents tending to impose their desires on their children. By subtle means and sometimes unconsciously on their part, they attempt to influence the child's future in a way that will bring satisfaction to themselves. The future which would be most pleasing to the parent may not interest the child, although this is not always the case.

Kimball Young suggests that projection occurs most often in connection with vocational choice.[7] Certainly there is much projection of this type in the rural community. Sometimes it takes the form of wishing the child to enter a vocation which the parent has always idealized or wished to enter. In many cases such projection is desirable because the parent aids his child to receive the education or training necessary in the desired field. On the other hand,

---

[1] W. F. Ogburn, *op. cit.*, pp. 697–698. This is in line with the theory that the hysterical person reverts to infantile behavior because of having been pampered in childhood.

[2] L. L. Thurstone and R. L. Jenkins, *Order of Birth, Parent-age, and Intelligence*, p. 120, University of Chicago Press, Chicago, 1931. See also Ray E. Baber, *Marriage and the Family*, pp. 304–307, McGraw-Hill Book Company, Inc., New York, 1939.

[3] W. F. Ogburn, *op. cit.*, p. 698.

[4] L. L. Thurstone and R. L. Jenkins, *op. cit.*, p. 121.

[5] W. F. Ogburn, *op. cit.*, p. 698.

[6] National Council of Parent Education, Ernest W. Burgess, "Family Relationships and Personality Adjustment," in *Papers on Parent Education Presented at the Biennial Conference*, p. 24, New York, 1931.

[7] "Parent-child Relationships: Projection of Ambition," *The Family*, vol. 8, pp. 67–73, 1927.

there are some parents who try to project farming upon the child who has no interest in it, occasionally with tragic results.

If undesirable, projection in the farm family is probably more fatalistic than in the city family for the farm child has less varied experience and therefore less chance to learn what his interests are. A domineering parent can almost force his son into farming because he can limit his opportunity for acquiring experience in, and his contact with, other types of vocations. In the city the child is likely to see various alternatives because of a more complex community environment. If frustrated by his parents, the urban child may more readily find an alternative outlet.

Little study has been made of the sexual adjustment of husband and wife in the farm setting, most such studies having been confined to the urban environment. The entire environment about the farm family suggests the normality of sex, reproduction, and other life processes. Whether the farm family approaches the matter of human sex relations and life processes with the same objectivity that it approaches these matters in the natural world about it is doubtful. Prudishness, religious taboos, and other such factors probably are more prominent among farm families than among urban families; hence, it would be expected that a certain amount of sexual maladjustment would exist. But even if this is so, sexual maladjustment probably is not recognized as such and emotional complexes that develop are not treated with the same degree of frankness and objectivity on the farm as in the city, and therefore do not lead to the breakdown of the family. There is a degree of stoicism and seriousness centering about matters of sex and reproduction in the farm family. Children are taken for granted,[1] most married people expecting to have them. On the other hand, many overworked farm women live in fear of repeated pregnancies.

Sometimes perhaps there is too much stoicism in the relations of the farm parent and child; in cases there may be a lack of normal emotional manifestations. Stolidness and bluntness may come to characterize family relations, and there may be instances when interest shown in livestock is greater than that shown in children. Although the latter criticism is open to question, it is sometimes made of farm families. Groves suggests that rural people have a

---

[1] Change in attitudes toward having children are in the making in farm communities. A study of 13,528 youths in Maryland, contrasts the attitudes of farm and village, town, and city youth in regard to children. It shows that a somewhat higher proportion of village, town, and city than of farm youth desire no children. The difference is not extreme, however. There is another point in their findings which seems highly significant, namely, that the great majority of farm youth want only two children. This apparently reflects the influence of an urban-industrial pattern diffusing into rural communities. Undoubtedly the situation described is more extreme than exists in more isolated rural sections, since Maryland is in a metropolitan area. J. J. Lister and E. L. Kirkpatrick, *Rural Youth Speak*, p. 71, American Youth Commission, Washington, D. C., Feb. 1, 1939. Similar results are reported by Duvall and Motz, *op. cit.*

stoical philosophy which leads them to cover their emotions lest they be accused of sentimentality. He also indicates that the farm environment furnishes many opportunities in which anger may be aroused.[1]

The farmer, accustomed to venting his anger upon livestock, may express temper also in the home, there being little social restraint to inhibit its expression. Hawthorn says that primitive man and more backward farmers compare well in certain emotional traits, brooding over grudges, concealing envies.[2] Pent-up passions smolder in the rural breast, yielding little to the lapse of time. Support for Hawthorn's view is found in the survival of family feuds of long standing in isolated mountainous regions. Caldwell, describing the experience of the mountain family, indicates that a tendency freely to express extreme anger and other violent emotions retards its adjustment when it moves to the city and comes under the social restraints imposed there.[3]

AUTHORITY PATTERNS IN THE FARM FAMILY

Patriarchal

The farm family is generally assumed to be more patriarchal then the urban. Certainly it is no more patriarchal, and likely much less so, than great numbers of immigrant families in the city (there are many more foreign-born in the American city than in farming areas), but on the farm the man is generally recognized as head of the household.[4] This is in part an outgrowth of the fact that physical strength and endurance are essential in the world of rural activity. Recognizing her inferiority in terms of farm work, which calls for heavy physical exertion, the woman readily accepts the man as head of the family. The children likewise accept this system of family organization, at least until they are of high school age, because no other is presented to them. Usually a benevolent patriarchy is maintained, although not always. Domination may be more extreme than is consistent with American notions of equality, but ordinarily farm women are accommodated to their position of lesser authority, accepting it as a matter of course. The freedom of woman and her desire to be recognized as the equal of man is largely an urban phenomenon because only in the city has she had an opportunity to match mental ability with man in many fields of professional activity.

[1] E. R. Groves, *op. cit.*, pp. 93 *ff*.

[2] Horace B. Hawthorn, *The Sociology of Rural Life*, p. 257, D. Appleton-Century Company, Inc., New York, 1926.

[3] Morris G. Caldwell, "The Adjustments of Mountain Families in an Urban Environment," *Social Forces*, vol. 16, pp. 389–395, March, 1938.

[4] W. I. Thomas and Florian Znaniecki, in *The Polish Peasant in Europe and America* (vols. 1–3, 1918, and vols. 4–5, 1920, Chapman & Grimes, Inc., Boston), show the extent to which the authoritative pattern of the immigrant home is characteristic. Similarly, R. E. Park and H. A. Miller in their *Old World Traits Transplanted* (Harper & Brothers, New York, 1921), show how the patriarchal pattern can become a part of a social milieu and the extent to which it can dominate familial relationships.

Williams, describing the parent-child and husband-wife relationships in the early American family, shows that the traditional pattern of parental authority and filial obedience was strictly enforced in rural areas.[1] This pattern, transported mainly from the Old World, has been deeply ingrained in the religious mores and general consciousness of American rural society. Male jealousy was an important influence in holding the early family together and in limiting the social relationships of the wife.[2] Because of male dominance, modesty was prominent in the behavior of both mother and daughter. Comradeship, as we know it today among boys and girls, did not exist.

The subservience of wife and children to the male and the tendency for family relationships to be patriarchal in the early American family have been observed by many writers. Calhoun states that among the Puritan settlers marriage was considered essential, bachelors and single women being regarded with suspicion.[3] Chivalry was prominent but, he believes, it was only a disguise for male superciliousness. Remarriage was frequent because the abundant fatherhood of the old worthies tended to wear out a succession of wives.

Benedict observes the tendency of some farm parents today to maintain too rigid control over their children.[4] Because the farmer is more or less isolated with no close neighbors to act as a check on parental authority, and no standards by which he can compare his discipline of his children with the practices of others, he may become unduly authoritative more or less unconsciously. She observes also that usually in the farm home family interests predominate over individual interests.

Miller finds that many farm girls who have finished school but still live in the parental home feel unhappy and dissatisfied because parents refuse requests for new clothes and because they think they have a hard role generally, parents tending to be unsympathetic and lacking in understanding.[5] The father, she observes, does not hesitate to disapprove of a vocation which he dislikes, usually with the result that the girl has to abandon the idea of entering it. Lively finds that the husband's relatives are more often a part of the farm household than are those of the wife.[6]

[1] J. M. Williams, *Our Rural Heritage*, pp. 56–77, Alfred A. Knopf, Inc., New York, 1925.

[2] J. M. Williams, *The Expansion of Rural Life*, pp. 57–58, Alfred A. Knopf, Inc., New York, 1926.

[3] W. A. Calhoun, *A Social History of the American Family from Colonial Times to the Present*, Arthur H. Clark Company, Glendale, Calif., 1917.

[4] Agnes Benedict, *Children at the Crossroads*, reprinted in C. E. Lively, *Readings in Rural Sociology*, book 1, part D, pp. 51–55, H. L. Hedrick, Columbus, Ohio, 1932.

[5] N. Miller, "Out-of-school Girls in a Rural County," *Journal of Home Economics*, vol. 25, pp. 463–467, July, 1933. For more evidence on this and similar points turn to Chap. 23.

[6] C. E. Lively, "The Life Cycle of the Farm Family," Ohio State Agricultural Experiment Station, mimeographed bulletin, 1932.

Stott[1] found in his Nebraska studies that rural parents are more authoritarian in their attitudes toward their children than are urban parents.

Duvall and Motz,[2] in studying attitudes of 403 native-born girls 14 to 24 years of age, in the Middle West, found the home training of the rural girls much more strict than that of the urban girls. In 75.9 per cent of cases rural girls reported strict and firm training, whereas only 59.9 per cent of urban girls did so. Discipline in rural homes was also much more consistent (see chart).

These varied sources of evidence seem to bear out the point that the farm home is somewhat patriarchal, both wife and children tending to be dominated

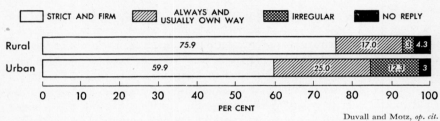

Duvall and Motz, *op. cit.*

TYPE OF HOME TRAINING RECEIVED BY 403 ADOLESCENT GIRLS BY PLACE OF RESIDENCE

by the male. It seems probable that this pattern is more prominent in farm homes than in homes of the American-born in the city. Sorokin, Zimmerman, and Galpin, however, suggest an important point which is significant in this connection: although the wife in the rural family is more subordinate to her husband than the urban wife, the husband in turn is more responsible to the wife, the parents to the children, the children to the parents, and the children to one another, the close relationships between members of the family not necessarily indicating repression.[3]

Of recent years many new factors have broken into the paternalistic system, such as the mingling of the sexes on a companionship or occupational basis, the repudiation of a rigid morality, the decline of family religion in which the father acted as priest, the earlier age of marriage of young folk,[4] and their greater freedom. Woman in America has been freed by various influences—

[1] L. H. Stott, "Parental Attitudes of Farm, Town, and City Parents in Relation to Certain Personality Adjustments in Their Children," *Journal of Social Psychology*, vol. 11, pp. 325–339, 1940.

[2] Evelyn Millis Duvall and Anabelle Bender Motz, "Are Country Girls so Different?" *Rural Sociology*, vol. 10, pp. 263–274, September, 1945.

[3] P. A. Sorokin, C. C. Zimmerman, and C. J. Galpin, *A Source Book for Rural Sociology*, vol. 3, p. 467, University of Minnesota Press, Minneapolis, 1932.

[4] The average age of marriage in the nation, contrary to popular opinion, has declined somewhat during the century. *Recent Social Trends in the United States*, p. 680; also Paul H. Landis, *Population Problems*, p. 65, American Book Co., New York, 1943.

the industrial revolution has taken her out of the home; education and economic independence have made her unwilling to submit to male domination; antipathy toward the notion of the superiority of the male is pervading American culture.[1] These influences are somewhat indirect in the farm home, but have had the effect of modifying rural attitudes.

Numerous forces have made for a greater individualization of family members and new opportunities have arisen both in city and country for the seeking of individual ends. The fact that many tasks once always carried out as a family enterprise are now done individually[2] has a definite bearing on authoritative patterns.[3]

In general still, however, the authority pattern of the farm family is aimed at making the child an economically productive, useful member of the household at as early an age as possible, as compared to the individualist family of urban society in which the child's development is an end in itself.

RURAL MORES AND FAMILY STABILITY

The stability of the rural family is a universally accepted fact. The number of divorces is the most simple index of stability, although not all family discord can be measured by such statistics. In many rural homes conflict continues for years without resulting in legal action, whereas with much less irritation the urban family may, because of differences in custom, resort to divorce. Nonetheless, divorce is a significant index of family stability.

The number of broken homes, *i.e.*, broken by divorce, death, or desertion, varies greatly with the size of the community. In cities of over 100,000 population, 16.7 per cent of homes are broken, in villages 14.7 per cent, and in farming areas only 8.1 per cent.[4]

Ogburn observes that there are about 2.5 times as many unbroken families without children living at home in Chicago as on surrounding farms.[5] Since children lend to family stability, it is significant that in Chicago only 6 per cent of the husbands and wives living together have more than two children, whereas in the rural areas 35 per cent have more than two children. Husbands living alone and wives living alone combined are 3.5 times as numerous in the metropolis as on the farm; wives living alone are five times as numerous (see table on page 320).

---

[1] Compare Lawrence K. Frank's "Social Change and the Family," *Annals of the American Academy of Political and Social Science*, vol. 160, pp. 94–102; Dwight Sanderson, "Changes in the Farm Family," *Religious Education*, February, 1924. See also Sanderson and Foster, *The Sociology of the Family*, mimeographed, Cornell Agricultural Experiment Station, 1929.

[2] J. M. Williams, *Our Rural Heritage*, pp. 76–77.

[3] Refer to Chap. 10 for a discussion of individuation.

[4] W. F. Ogburn, *op. cit.*, p. 690. Data are for 1930.

[5] *Ibid.*, pp. 684–685.

During the stress of World War II, the farm family suffered much less from the separation of husband and wife because of war labor migration and service in the Armed Forces (see table opposite). In 1945, in only 8.5 per cent

THE DISTRIBUTION PER THOUSAND OF THE DIFFERENT TYPES OF FAMILIES IN CHICAGO AND ON FARMS, 1930*

Type of family†	Metropolis	Farms‡
Husband and wife only..........................	398	163
Husband, wife, and 1 child......................	229	205
Husband, wife, and 2 children...................	122	202
Husband, wife, and 3 children..................	42	135
Husband, wife, and 4 children or more...........	19	214
Husband only.................................	63	25
Husband and 1 child...........................	5	6
Husband and 2 children	2	5
Husband and 3 children or more.................	1	5
Wife only....................................	72	14
Wife and 1 child..............................	31	12
Wife and 2 children...........................	11	6
Wife and 3 children or more...................	5	8
Total of all types of family...................	1,000	1,000

* Original schedules of the U.S. Bureau of the Census. Data from *Recent Social Trends in the United States*, p. 684, McGraw-Hill Book Company, Inc., New York.

† There the wife is under 45 years of age and the husband when listed without a wife is under 50 years; in a sample of native whites of native parents in the East North Central states.

‡ When the farms have the same age distribution as the metropolis, the frequencies of the different types of families on the farms are affected only very slightly.

This table shows about two and a half times as many unbroken families without children living at home in the metropolis (Chicago) as on the surrounding farms. In the large city only 6 per cent of the husbands and wives living together have more than two children, while in the rural area 35 per cent have more than two children. Husbands living alone and wives living alone added together are about three and a half times as numerous in the metropolis as on the farms and wives living alone are five times as numerous. The family structures for the town and for the cities of 100,000 inhabitants are intermediate between those of the farms and of the metropolis.[1]

of rural farm families were the men absent, whereas in urban families the proportion was 26.1. A part of this difference is explained by the fact that widows rarely remain on the farm is case of the husband's death. On the other hand, census data for 1940 show that, in 1940, 7.8 per cent of rural farm families

[1] *Ibid.*, pp. 684–685.

had female heads, as compared to the 8.5 per cent in 1945, indicating that the war situation affected the farm family very little. In urban families by contrast the proportion of female heads increased from 18.3 per cent in 1940 to 26.1 per cent in 1945.

Three other indices of completeness of the family are shown in the additional three columns of the table. The median size of the rural family was considerably greater than that of urban families. This means that there were on the average more children present, and although the data do not show it specifically, there were also more grandparents or other adults present in the

A COMPARISON OF FAMILIES IN THE UNITED STATES AS OF MAY 1945 BY PLACE OF RESIDENCE

Place of residence	Female head	Median no. persons	7 or more persons	Per cent with 3 or more children under 18
United States	21.9	2.87	5.0	14.2
Urban	26.1	2.72	3.2	10.9
Rural nonfarm	19.6	2.92	5.3	16.0
Rural farm	8.5	3.43	11.2	24.6

"Composition of Families in the United States at the End of the War in Europe: May, 1945," *Population-Special Reports*, Series P-46, No. 8, Sept. 6, 1946.

The war period of the 1940's exaggerated disadvantages of the urban family over the rural as far as its being a complete entity is concerned. In three times as high a proportion of cases the father was absent and a female head in charge, the difference in median number of persons in the home was considerable, and the proportion with dependent children under 18 more than twice as great.

rural farm family. Where grandparents are present there is the pressure of the preceding generation to add cohesiveness and permanence to the marriage of the parent generation.

The rural farm family has more dependents. Dependents are always a factor in making for family stability. It will be seen that families with seven or more persons were more than three times as numerous in the rural farm population as in the urban population. Also the proportion of families with young children was much greater in rural farm areas than in other areas, as is shown in the column at the extreme right. Only 10.9 per cent of urban families had children under 18; 24.6 per cent, of rural farm families.

The greater stability of the rural farm family is therefore in considerable part a product of these unique sociocultural situations in which the rural farm family is established.

The fact that the rural family is inclined to be patriarchal means that there is less likely to be an open conflict of two dominant wills than in a democratic family. The fact that the rural home has many functions to perform, that it still exists as an economic institution, and that all its members are occupied with home functions has a decided bearing.[1] Economically speaking, in many cases an urban marriage is a mistake, the old adage "two can live as cheaply as one" being almost true on the farm but not in the city. Many urban homes, since they have come to be set up in congested quarters, are simply places to sleep.[2] A rural home is always something more. Sex taboos, divorce taboos, more surveillance of group opinion, greater uniformity of standards, a lack of contacts that would stimulate sex interests, these also are favorable to the stability of the rural home. Even with less affection and with more conflict it is probable that the rural family will remain together. The very fact that contacts are limited means that there is less temptation to find a way out of an unhappy situation if it arises.

A study of 250 successful farm and professional families shows some fundamental contrasts in the purpose of the home as viewed by women in each group.[3] The women in the professional class stress the importance of the recognition of individuality and of opportunity for personal development and for the growth of broad common interests; the farm women emphasize happiness, peace, comfort, security, and integrity. Only 2 per cent of the farm women list any items having to do with husband and wife relationships; either they do not feel free to mention them or they regard the family as a unit in which the individual as such is relatively unimportant. The idea of individual freedom seems almost nonexistent among them. The limiting of the size of families according to the level of income, considered important by the professional group, is not mentioned by the farm women. This study, then, indicates that although certain elements are common to successful family living any-

---

[1] A study by Hildegarde Kneeland of the U.S. Bureau of Home Economics shows that care of children takes 28 per cent of women's time in city homes but only 10 per cent in farm homes. She suggests that it is doubtful whether the comparison is fully valid, however, because the city homes studied had more children under three years. On the other hand, there were more children in the farm homes, which should compensate somewhat. It seems likely that city women do spend more time in caring for their children because they have less other household work. In city homes 23 per cent of the women do their washing at home as compared to 70 per cent of the women in rural homes. Rural women also spend twice as much time tending fires. In the case of both rural and urban samples the families are those employing no outside help. "Woman's Economic Contribution to the Home," *Annals of the American Academy of Political and Social Science*, vol. 143, pp. 33 ff., May, 1929.

[2] W. F. Ogburn observes that since the First World War the number of multiple family dwellings in cities has increased rapidly until in recent years (he is writing of the condition in about the year 1929) approximately half of all Chicago building permits issued are for apartment buildings and only about one-third are for one-family houses. *Recent Social Trends in the United States*, p. 667.

[3] C. C. Woodhouse, "A Study of 250 Successful Families," *Social Forces*, vol. 8, pp. 511–532.

where, there are essential differences in the values of family life stressed by the two groups. The gist of the matter seems to be that in the farm home the family unit is considered of most importance; in the professional home a greater amount of emphasis is placed on individual interests and their expression.

A nation-wide Gallup Poll on the chief faults of wives and husbands, which covered 3,100 men and women from coast to coast in 1946, showed that farm couples find less fault with each other than others.[1] A third of farm men felt

MARITAL ADJUSTMENT

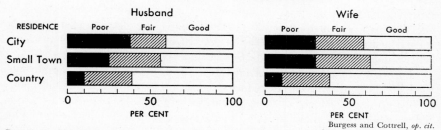

Burgess and Cottrell, *op. cit.*

Rural or Urban Residence in Childhood and Adolence and Martial Adjustment

that their wives had no faults. Of the total group of men polled only 8 per cent felt that their wives had no faults. Not a single farmer mentioned "poor housekeeping" as a fault of his wife. These data suggest that vast differences in evaluative standards of husbands and wives toward each other still characterize urban and rural couples.

These differences in values apparently carry over into the marriages of the next generation. For example, Burgess and Cottrell in their *Predicting Success or Failure in Marriage*,[2] present data showing that country rearing, in the case of both husband and wife, has a high positive relationship to success in marital adjustment (see chart). Urban rearing is a decided disadvantage to the husband but is less disadvantageous for the wife than small-town rearing.

Girls in the Duvall and Motz study,[3] reporting on the happiness of their parents' marriages, show marked difference by residence. More rural girls than urban girls considered their parents' marriages very happy, and happy. At the unhappiness end of the scale, rural girls placed only 2.9 per cent of their parents, whereas 15.9 per cent of the urban girls did so. These data are especially significant since rural girls in the study held attitudes toward marriage, courtship, and family life generally similar to the urban girls. By these values,

[1] William A. Lydgate, "The Chief Faults of Wives—and Husbands," *Redbook*, vol. 87, pp. 28–29, 121–122, 126, June, 1946. Condensed in *Reader's Digest*, vol. 49, pp. 88–90, July, 1946.

[2] Prentice-Hall, Inc., New York, 1939.

[3] *Op. cit.*

which presumably were predominately of the individualistic rather than of the institutional-patriarchal type, they considered their parents' marriages happy.

THE FARM FAMILY AND THE NATION'S FUTURE

Many have been apprehensive of the urban trend of family life in America, for it means individualization at the expense of the institution;[1] it means a smaller family; it means a decline in national population if carried beyond a certain point, and eventually the decline of the city. More important than the numerical aspect of the situation, however, in the eyes of many students of our national culture, is the decline in effectiveness of the family as an influence in social control, the breakdown of moral standards, the disintegration of fundamental primary-group virtues, the decline of religion, and the loss of many other values that are considered of great importance to society.

But there are compensating factors, for although something is lost through the individualization of family members, something is also gained. In this highly mobile age independence of thought and deliberate choice of action are essential to a functional morality. The maintenance of a high standard of living demands a more rational type of mores than prevails in backward areas where the full power of fecundity is exercised because birth control is taboo.[2] Something has been added to the quality of farm life by the new trend. Many of the urbanizing influences that affect the farm family are undesirable from a broad social viewpoint, but certainly not all of them. There no doubt is a happy middle ground where will be maintained some of the essentials of the stable farm family, but where some of the freedom of the new emancipated urban family will also be allowed.

1. In order to understand the family or other social institutions what general approach is essential?

2. Outline the major functions of the family and compare the farm with the metropolitan family as to extent to which these functions are exercised by them.

3. How do farm and urban families compare with regard to the strength of traditional bonds?

4. Does it seem that the farm family emphasizes institutional rather than romantic aspects of family life more than the urban family?

[1] See P. A. Sorokin and C. C. Zimmerman, *Principles of Rural-urban Sociology*, chaps. 15 and 27, Henry Holt and Company, Inc., New York, 1929; also O. E. Baker and T. B. Manny, *Population Trends and the National Welfare*, mimeographed, U. S. Department of Agriculture, Washington, D. C., 1935; and C. C. Zimmerman and Merle Frampton, *Family and Society: A Study of the Sociology of Reconstruction*, D. Van Nostrand Company, Inc., New York, 1935.

[2] For an interesting statement of this problem see O. E. Baker, "The Effect of Recent Public Policies on the Future Population Prospect," *Rural Sociology*, vol. 2, pp. 123–141, June, 1937, and the discussion on pp. 141–142.

5. Compare the farm family with the urban family with regard to emotional patterns; with regard to projection of parental ambitions upon children.

6. Characterize the farm family with regard to authority patterns; to the place of woman; to the place of children.

7. What general factors act as stabilizing factors in rural marriage?

8. Compare the attitudes of wives in successful farm families with those of wives in successful professional families.

9. Explain why the future trend of population growth of the nation may depend upon the farm family.

COLLATERAL READING

Baldwin, Bird T., Eva A. Fillmore, and Lora Hadley: *Farm Children*, chap. 3, D. Appleton-Century Company, Inc., New York, 1930.

Burgess, E. W., and Leonard S. Cottrell: *Predicting Success or Failure in Marriage*, pp. 85 *ff.*, Prentice-Hall, Inc., New York, 1938.

Dinkle, Robert M.:"Attitudes of Children Toward Supporting Aged Parents," *American Sociological Review*, vol. 9, pp. 370–379, August, 1944.

Green, Arnold W.: "The Middle Class Male Child and Neurosis," *American Sociological Review*, vol. 11, pp. 31–41, February, 1946.

Kolb, J. H., and E. de S. Brunner: *A Study of Rural Society*, 3d ed., chap. 11, Houghton Mifflin Co., Boston, 1946.

Landis, Paul H.: *Adolescence and Youth: The Process of Maturing*, part III, McGraw-Hill Book Co., Inc., New York, 1945.

————: *Social Policies in the Making: A Dynamic View of Social Problems*, part III, D. C. Heath and Company, Boston, 1947.

Lydgate, William A.: "The Chief Faults of Wives—and Husbands," *Redbook*, vol. 87, pp. 28–29; 121–122; 126, June, 1946. (Condensed in *Reader's Digest*, vol. 49, pp. 88–90, July, 1946.)

Sanderson, Dwight: *Rural Sociology and Rural Social Organization*, chap. 10, John Wiley & Sons, Inc., New York, 1942.

Sorokin, P. A., C. C. Zimmerman, and C. J. Galpin: *A Systematic Source Book in Rural Sociology*, vol. 2, chap. 10, University of Minnesota Press, Minneapolis, 1931.

White House Conference on Child Health and Protection: *The Adolescent in the Family*, pp. 8–29, D. Appleton-Century Company, Inc., New York, 1934.

CHAPTER 22

THE RURAL SCHOOL IN A DYNAMIC SOCIETY

EDUCATIONAL institutions in contemporary society are among the most influential agencies in making for progress and enlightenment. Yet educational institutions like all others are afflicted with culture lags. Old patterns, old systems of organization, persist in the face of widespread social changes. Older institutional forms are maintained long after conditions which led to their creation have disappeared and their practices and services may be ill adapted to the new conditions.

PERSISTENCE OF THE ONE-ROOM SCHOOL

The rural school as a pioneer institution is a credit to the foresight, self-sacrifice, and enterprise of the American settler. Almost before his own log cabin or sod house was completed, he and his neighbors built a school and hired a teacher, lest their children should grow up in ignorance. The one-room rural school developed throughout the entire nation as the most universal neighborhood institution aside from the family. That it filled a need in the rural society of yesterday no one can question. Although the one-room school, immortalized in literature and poetry, earned its reputation, its persistence into out time is a culture lag of no mean proportions.

The surfaced highway and automobile have made the one-room school obsolete in most communities, whereas the increased efficiency of the larger school system and the development of secondary education have made a more serviceable educational unit indispensable if farm youth are to share in the benefits of the best of modern educational training.

PROBLEMS OF THE ONE-ROOM SCHOOL

Even though more than half of the population of the nation is found in urban areas, about half (51 per cent) of the children to be educated are found in rural areas, i.e., small towns and open country.[1] There are in the United States approximately 100,000 one-room schools, and about three-fourths of the rural school buildings in the nation are one- and two-room schools. If the one-room school has all eight grades, the teacher must conduct 40 to 60 classes per day in the one room where the pupils study and recite. In some classes there will be

[1] See *Biennial Surveys of Education in the United States*, published biennially by the U.S. Department of the Interior, Washington, D. C.

IMPROVING LIBRARY SERVICE

The traveling bookmobile, now used in several states, makes library books accessible to people in hamlets and open country and to isolated one-room schools, which usually have poor library facilities and often none at all.

only one to three pupils, and seldom over five in any class. Her success depends in considerable part on her ability to maintain discipline and to tend fires. If she keeps an orderly room and does not burn the grate out of the stove, all too often she is considered a good teacher. In some districts the maintenance of discipline is a major problem, and some farm parents would as soon have their children disciplined as motivated. Probably half the country schools have no library facilities whatever; only in rare instances do they have well-stocked libraries.

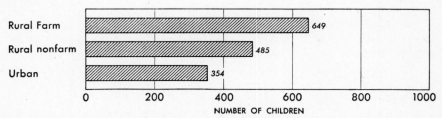

NUMBER OF CHILDREN 5 TO 17 YEARS OF AGE PER 1,000 ADULTS 24 TO 64 YEARS OF AGE, BY SIZE OF COMMUNITY, 1940
The burden of educating their children falls most heavily on the farm population.

There are often compensating factors in the program of the one-room school. The child learns to work with little direction, to concentrate in a noisy room; also, the long walk to school in various kinds of weather has its disciplinary benefits. Many beginning teachers have a zeal and enthusiasm that may be lacking among more experienced educators. But these factors do not outweigh the disadvantages of the one-room school and do not make up to the child for the inadequacy of his training.

The financial burden of the small district school may be extremely heavy, making the school not only inefficient but also insecure. Thousands of district schools during the depression of the early thirties had to close their doors. In Kansas the closing of schools became so extensive that it was made a political issue in the 1936 presidential campaign. World War II and the period following found teacher-training standards lowered, teachers scarce, and many rural schools without qualified teachers. In January, 1943 at least 7,000 rural schools were closed for lack of teachers.

Renne makes the following generalization, supported by data on school finance:

. . . the support of schools is local, personal, and direct, and it is a sociological fact that the more direct and easily traceable the route of the tax dollar from the taxpayer's pocket to the support of the particular governmental enterprise, the more likely is that enterprise to be criticized or curtailed when economic conditions pinch ever so lightly.[1]

[1] Roland R. Renne, "Rural Educational Institutions and Social Lag," *Rural Sociology*, vol. 1, p. 314, September, 1936.

The problem of rural school finance is a matter not altogether of the inadequacy of local taxation, but partly of a lack of taxable resources. Even though they have the most children, rural states usually have the least wealth. Big business and industrial corporations are centered primarily in large cities, where much of the nation's taxable assets are found, whereas rural districts with an army of children to educate may be relatively poor.[1] A comparison is often made in terms of values of school property per pupil enrolled, which for city schools in 1941–1942 was $429 and for rural schools, $200.[2] Many rural areas have had to be satisfied with inexperienced teachers, poorly equipped buildings, short terms, the average number of days in the rural school session for 1941–1942 being 167 days compared to 181 days in urban schools. The average teacher in the United States during 1941–1942 was paid $1,507; the rate for city teachers was $2,013 whereas that for rural teachers was only $1,018.

The solutions most often cited for problems of the open-country school include plans for increasing the size of the school district, the creation of a more stable economic base by setting up larger units of taxation, and state and national support of education, so that opportunity can be equalized between the more wealthy urban-industrial areas which have few children and the prolific rural states which have little natural wealth but immense human resources.[3] (See chart on page 330.)

INEQUALITIES OF EDUCATION ON THE SECONDARY SCHOOL LEVEL

That youth on farms in the United States attend school in smaller numbers proportionately than those in towns and cities no doubt reflects inequalities in rural and urban educational facilities. At the time of the taking of the 1940 census, 75.6 per cent of urban youth 16 and 17 years of age, representing the upper level of high school education, were in school, whereas but 61.3 per cent of the total rural youth group were in school (see table on page 331). However, only 56.8 per cent of farm youth were attending school, whereas 67.6 per cent of rural nonfarm youth, living in villages and in open-country areas but not engaged in farming, were attending. More farm girls than farm boys were in attendance, 60.9 per cent as compared to 53 per cent. In the age group 18 to 20

[1] Leslie L. Chisholm, *The Economic Ability of the States to Finance Public Schools*, Teachers College, Columbia University, New York, 1936.

[2] *The Biennial Survey of Education in the United States*, Circular No. 231, 1945, U.S. Office of Education.

[3] See for instance, R. R. Renne, *op. cit.*, vol. 1, no. 3; "A Survey of the Common School System of Washington," by the Washington State Planning Council, September, 1938; Leslie L. Chisholm, *op. cit.*; also Leslie L. Chisholm, *The Shifting of Federal Taxes and Its Implication for the Public Schools*, Journal of Experimental Education, Research Monograph, No. 1, Madison Wis., 1939.

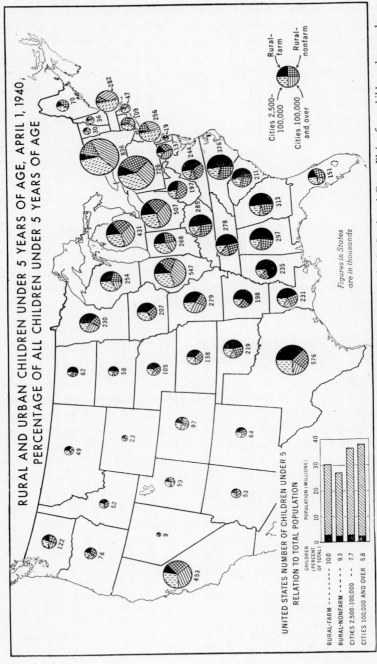

RURAL AND URBAN CHILDREN UNDER 5 YEARS OF AGE, APRIL 1, 1940; PERCENTAGE OF ALL CHILDREN UNDER 5 YEARS OF AGE

Cities 2,500-100,000

Cities 100,000 and over

Rural-farm

Rural-nonfarm

Figures in States are in thousands

UNITED STATES NUMBER OF CHILDREN UNDER 5 RELATION TO TOTAL POPULATION

CHILDREN (PERCENT OF TOTAL)

POPULATION (MILLIONS)

RURAL-FARM - - - - - - 10.0
RURAL-NONFARM - - - - 9.3
CITIES 2,500-100,000 - - 7.7
CITIES 100,000 AND OVER 5.8

In most states rural children make up three-fourths of all children under 5; in the South and Great Plains farm children alone make up half or nearly so. Note from the small chart at the lower left the high ratio of children to population in rural-farm areas. Children under 5 are an index of a state's future educational burden.

an even greater contrast existed, the percentage of urban youth attending school being much higher. Great differences exist among the states. (Study maps on the following page.)

SCHOOL ATTENDANCE OF YOUTH 16 THROUGH 20 YEARS OF AGE, BY RESIDENCE AND SEX,* 1939–1940

Residence and sex	Per cent attending school	
	16 to 17 years of age	18 to 20 years of age
Total urban.................	75.6	26.1
Male.....................	77.1	30.0
Female...................	74.3	22.5
Total rural.................	61.3	20.6
Male.....................	59.2	20.9
Female...................	63.5	20.4
Rural-farm.................	56.8	19.4
Male.....................	53.0	18.4
Female...................	60.9	20.6
Rural-nonfarm..............	67.6	22.2
Male.....................	68.2	24.3
Female...................	67.0	20.1

* From *Population*, vol. 2, pp. 35–37, Bureau of the Census, U.S. Department of Commerce, Washington, D. C.

Various studies indicate that where high schools are made more accessible to rural youth, the proportion attending increases.[1] Many farm youth are near no high school which they could attend and often have to enter a distant district school as tuition pupils. Consider, for example, Michigan's rural school system.[2] Approximately three-fourths of the farm boys and girls receive their elementary education in the state's 4,800 one-room schools. If they wish to continue beyond the elementary grades they must enter, as nonresident tuition pupils, a high school located in some one of 533 villages and cities. High school districts in lower Michigan are on the average only 13 square miles in size but they draw pupils from an area of about 88 square miles. In Upper Michigan districts the situation is even more extreme. In almost half (43 per cent) of the high schools nonresident pupils outnumbered resident pupils during the years 1920 to 1931. But, as would be expected, a much

[1] For a summary of a number of these studies see Bruce L. Melvin and Elna N. Smith, *Rural Youth: Their Situation and Prospects*, p. 44, Research Monograph XV, Division of Social Research, Works Progress Administration, Washington, D. C., 1938.

[2] J. F. Thaden and Eben Mumford, "High School Communities in Michigan," pp. 34–35, *Michigan Agricultural Experiment Station Special Bulletin* 289, East Lansing, 1938.

PER CENT RURAL FARM

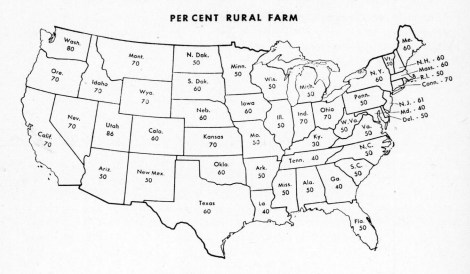

PER CENT RURAL NONFARM

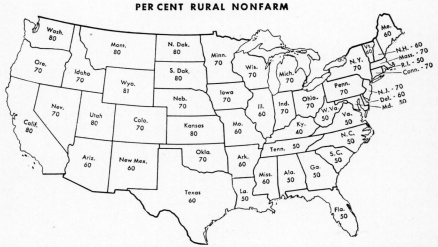

U.S. Census Data

Per Cent of Rural Farm and Rural Nonfarm Youth Ages 16 to 17 in School,
1940

School attendance of those 16 to 17 years of age is much lower for farm than for nonfarm rural youth in most states. In many states 50 per cent or less of farm youth of this age are in school.

higher percentage of urban than of farm children of upper ages attend school.

Pollard makes the following observation with regard to cultural expenditures in an isolated rural county in Tennessee:

The cultural expenditures of Grainger County are not important, but their very insignificance is one of the most significant facts of the entire county situation. For higher education the county spends about $2,000 which, put into human terms, means that of the 1,150 boys and girls of the county between the ages of 18 and 23 there are just seven able to attend college. By no application of laws of probability is the ability to profit by education so rare as this. A daily newspaper is received by one family out of every four and a cheap farm paper, or woman's magazine, by one family out of five[1].

These deficiencies in the educational training of farm youth cannot be said to be solely the result of inefficient school facilities. There are undoubtedly many farm youth who quit school because they have no liking for it, but whether this group is greater than among village and town pupils is doubtful. It is possible that work and handicaps of living on the farm while going to school tend to discourage persistence. Studies among rural boys in New York state reveal that 51.6 per cent of farm boys quit school to work, whereas only one-third of village boys quit for this reason. In many areas the work values of parents or of the youth himself interfere with his schooling.[2] In all areas lack of funds is a factor.

Community attitudes toward education are extremely important in affecting the educational attainments of farm youth for they constitute social pressures that influence both parents and youth. Matthews quotes the attitude of a local leader in an isolated mountain community toward education:

After the school has teached 'em all it knows, they ain't fittin' for nothin' any more. You couldn't git one of 'em in twenty feet of a plow. And if you did, they wouldn't know "gee" from "haw." They won't tech nothin' but easy jobs, and there ain't none of them any more. All they want to do is play basketball an' chase up an' down the road yander. I'll tell you what the school does to them. It makes 'em plum p'int blank lazy![3]

The judgment expressed here was common in many farm areas twenty years ago. In more progressive sections opinion has gradually come to favor high school and even college education. This change in attitude may explain in considerable part the increased enrollment of farm youth in high schools and colleges, for an appreciation of the worth of education goes a long way in determining the sacrifice a family will make to help or to permit a child to

[1] A. L. Pollard, "What a County Trade Balance through Agricultural-industrial Companionship Will Mean," p. 3, excerpt from the *Proceedings of the Third Conference on Companionship of Agriculture and Industry*, held at the University of Tennessee, November, 1933.

[2] W. A. Anderson, and Willis Kerns, "Interests, Activities, and Problems of Rural Young Folk," Table 3, p. 7, *Cornell University Agricultural Experiment Station Bulletin* 631, Ithaca, 1937.

[3] M. Taylor Matthews, *Experience Worlds of Mountain People*, p. 19, Columbia University Press, New York, 1937.

continue his schooling. It also helps determine whether the youth includes high school or college training in his life ambitions.[1]

That attitudes and values of rural people may be an important factor in the differential schooling of youth, where tuition and transportation obstacles

PER CENT IN EDUCATIONAL CLASS

SIZE OF HOME TOWN	BOYS (8,750 Cases) Less Than H. S. Graduation	H. S. Graduation	Above H. S.
Under 250	47.5	43.5	9.0
250 - 999	39.0	50.5	10.5
1,000 - 2,499	37.1	52.3	10.6
2,500 - 9,999	35.1	50.5	14.4
10,000 - 99,999	36.2	47.9	15.9
100,000 & Over	28.3	52.3	19.4

SIZE OF HOME TOWN	GIRLS (7,559 Cases) Less Than H. S. Graduation	H. S. Graduation	Above H. S.
Under 250	33.3	56.0	10.7
250 - 999	30.3	57.1	12.6
1,000 - 2,499	27.8	59.4	12.8
2,500 - 9,999	26.1	58.0	15.9
10,000 - 99,999	27.7	52.8	19.5
100,000 & Over	20.9	60.6	18.5

DISTRIBUTION OF YOUTH IN WASHINGTON BY SIZE OF PLACE AND SCHOOLING

The sample deals with those who have completed their schooling. Farm youth are included in school population of all places but naturally predominate in the schools in the smaller towns. Generally, the smaller the place, the less the schooling for both young men and women. Data are for a state in which parity of opportunity is about as near to realization as can be expected. Other data show that youth in the smaller places terminate their schooling at an earlier age.

to school attendance are removed, is suggested by the current situation in the state of Washington where consolidation is practically universal, where there is no tuition for farm pupils, and where transportation to the consolidated school is provided. Under these rather ideal conditions fewer youths from small

[1] Indirect evidence on this point is found in studies of urban youth. A greater proportion of children of professional families complete high school than of children of any other occupational group. The tradition of learning in the family is probably a dominant factor in this situation. See *Youth in the Labor Market*, a series of mimeographed releases by the Division of Social Research, Works Progress Administration, Washington, D. C., 1939.

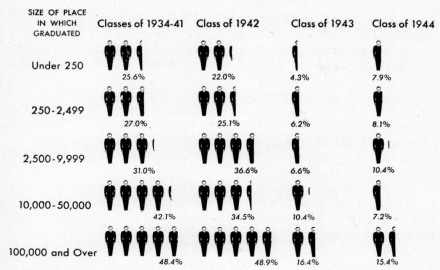

SIZE OF PLACE IN WHICH GRADUATED	Classes of 1934-41	Class of 1942	Class of 1943	Class of 1944
Under 250	25.6%	22.0%	4.3%	7.9%
250-2,499	27.0%	25.1%	6.2%	8.1%
2,500-9,999	31.0%	36.6%	6.6%	10.4%
10,000-50,000	42.1%	34.5%	10.4%	7.2%
100,000 and Over	48.4%	48.9%	16.4%	15.4%

PROPORTION OF YOUNG MEN CONTINUING THEIR SCHOOLING AFTER HIGH SCHOOL GRADUATION IN WASHINGTON BY SIZE OF PLACE IN WHICH GRADUATED

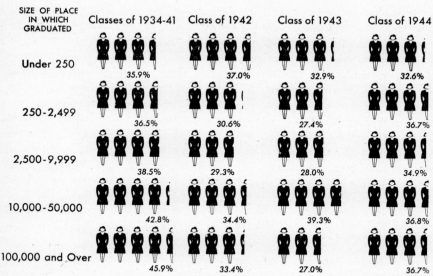

SIZE OF PLACE IN WHICH GRADUATED	Classes of 1934-41	Class of 1942	Class of 1943	Class of 1944
Under 250	35.9%	37.0%	32.9%	32.6%
250-2,499	36.5%	30.6%	27.4%	36.7%
2,500-9,999	38.5%	29.3%	28.0%	34.9%
10,000-50,000	42.8%	34.4%	39.3%	36.8%
100,000 and Over	45.9%	33.4%	27.0%	36.7%

PROPORTION OF YOUNG WOMEN CONTINUING THEIR SCHOOLING AFTER HIGH SCHOOL GRADUATION IN WASHINGTON, BY SIZE OF PLACE IN WHICH GRADUATED

places complete high school or go beyond (see chart, p. 334).[1] After high school marked differences in attendance appear, as is shown in the chart.

The two pictographic charts[2] show the situation for a larger sample, over 180,000 youth, for the period 1934 to 1944. It will be seen that, whereas almost half of Washington young men in places of 100,000 or more continued their schooling beyond high school graduation, only about a fourth of those in places of under 250, where the school population is predominately of farm youth, did so. During the war years the contrasts were even greater, but fewer of both groups were in school. The larger the place, the fewer the farm youth represented in the school population, and the fewer the proportion continuing their schooling.

The situation for young women was similar but not so extreme during the depression and immediate pre-war years. During the early war period work opportunities in larger places apparently drew urban girls from school, whereas girls in the small places continued schooling before entering the work world. In depression, in peace, and in war the education of rural youth suffers.

RESISTANCE TO PROGRESSIVE FORCES

In the face of demonstrable facts concerning the inequalities in farm, village, and urban education, why has the one-room school survived? There are many explanations, not the least of which is that of emotional attachment. The farmer has always been proud of his school. Often it is his only neighborhood institution outside the family and is the focus of community life. Fearing the school in the village or city and mistrusting what his children may learn there, he wants to keep the school within the neighborhood under his scrutiny and supervision. He is skeptical of the town school's curriculum and extra-curricular program, and fearful as to the expense of education in the larger district where he cannot control costs. The fact that the longer school term in town and its extracurricular activities, such as athletics, interfere with work, the child having less time to assist on the farm, is another cause for misgivings. He frequently is satisfied with the institution he already has, thinking in some

[1] Paul H. Landis, "The Territorial and Occupational Mobility of Washington Youth," *Washington Agricultural Experiment Stations Bulletin* 449, Pullman, July, 1944.

[2] Paul H. Landis, "Washington High School Graduates in Depression and in War Years," *Washington Agricultural Experiment Stations Bulletin* 463, Pullman, May, 1945. Also preceding studies in this series, "Six Months after Commencement, An Analysis of the Activity Roles of 135,651 Graduates of Washington High Schools, Classes of 1934 through 1941," *Bulletin* 420, September, 1942; "High School Graduates in the War Year: A Study of the After-commencement Activities of 15,277 Graduates from Washington High Schools in 1942," *Bulletin* 438, March, 1944; "Washington High School Graduates in the Second War Year," *Bulletin* 454, October, 1944, all of the Washington Agricultural Experiment Stations, Pullman.

cases that it cannot be improved upon, in others that it need not be improved upon, that "it was good enough for me, so it's good enough for Susie and Johnnie."

He has a sense of ethnocentrism; he sometimes feels that the rural values which his community maintains are to be protected from the urban values which permeate the consolidated school, especially if it is located in town, failing to realize that youth today need to be oriented to a complex social world, that perhaps half of them will have to live in such a world, that there is not sufficient room for all youth on the farm, that maybe his own son or daughter will find their way into some urban vocation, and that perhaps their interests can best be met off the farm. He may fail to recognize the value of breadth of contact in the molding of youth and to appreciate the fact that the consolidated school offers a much better apprenticeship to modern society than the one-room school of the closely-knit local group, that it may be desirable for the child to come in contact and perhaps to absorb to a degree patterns somewhat in conflict with family and neighborhood patterns, that through such experience he is becoming better prepared for the life he will have to live than if he is hide-bound in the customary patterns of one group. Some, fearing that if their children are well educated they will go to the city, wish to hinder their schooling for this reason.

Compensating for farmers with such attitudes as are described above, there are, in all progressive farming areas, an increasing number who want their children to have the best education available and who consider the consolidated school the way forward. Many of these parents want their children to find a place in the world beyond the local community, and want them to have a better education than they themselves were able to obtain. The progressive group is often hindered in attaining its ends, but consolidation will nonetheless continue.

SPECIAL PROBLEMS OF CONSOLIDATION

Cost.—The first, last, and most vigorous objection made to consolidation is cost. The farmer fears any movement that will place an increased burden of taxation upon his property. What does consolidation experience show? There is no simple answer. Consolidation may be expensive or it may be economical, depending a great deal upon the effectiveness with which the plan of consolidation is carried out. Even when done on an economical basis, it may mean increased cost for some areas. It may increase cost in some one-room school districts and decrease cost in others within the same area, depending upon the character and cost of the educational program being supported.

A basic problem is that of the cost of the school building. Some of the early consolidations were made in boom times; communities erected expensive buildings, loading themselves with debt, whereas they might have built less lavishly, avoided the burden of heavy taxes, and yet achieved the same benefits as far as the quality of education was concerned. Reasonable expenditures for a new building and equipment are necessary if costs are to be kept within a desirable limit.

Fear of increased maintenance costs may be more important in retarding consolidation than a high initial cost. The farmer recognizes that when the school is placed under the control of a larger district, either rural, or town and rural combined, his immediate locality loses its grip on the purse strings. Even

TYPICAL SCHOOL DISTRICT BOUNDARIES

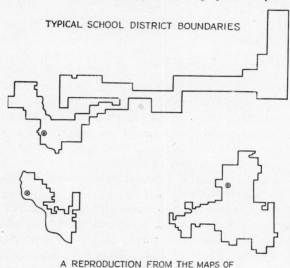

A REPRODUCTION FROM THE MAPS OF
WASHINGTON SCHOOL DISTRICTS

Note: Observe not only the helter-skelter boundaries,
but the worse than accidental location of the
schools. In each case marked by the symbol ◎

Washington State Planning Council

CONSOLIDATED BUT WITHOUT PLAN
Visualize the problem of transporting pupils in the district shown in the upper figure.

though costs may be low at the time of consolidation, there is always the chance that they will be raised and he will be powerless to interfere. This is the basis for much of the opposition to consolidation.

Services.—More important than the cost of school consolidation from the idealistic standpoint are its benefits. Many school districts could well afford to pay more for education provided it was of a better quality. We have already called attention to the weaknesses of one-room district schools with small enrollments, inexperienced teachers, short terms, scant equipment, and inadequate buildings. Although most of these districts are not rich, some of them could afford to pay more for an educational system that increased their children's opportunities by providing an enriched curriculum, better teachers, and broader social experience.

Organization.—Often consolidated districts are poorly designed, consolidation usually being carried out by various local districts voting themselves into the larger district. The consequences of this method of organizing are strikingly illustrated in the accompanying figure which sketches sample school districts in the state of Washington.[1] Obviously such districts are not economical nor practical. Problems of transportation, for example, are made extremely difficult and costly. Commenting on this situation, a Washington State Planning Council report recommends a state-wide reorganization of district boundaries, which would take into account a number of relevant factors, and concludes with the following statement:

. . . we recognize that wise redistricting does not mean that we should go on making ever larger districts, merely in order to abolish under-financed schools. Some of our districts may be found to be already too large. It rather means that each county should so determine the boundaries of its districts that greater economies of administration, a closer approach toward equality of taxable wealth, a wiser adjustment of transportation routes, and better educational services may result.[2]

Transportation.—The Washington State Planning Council study shows that transportation is one of the major issues affecting the cost of consolidation. During the year ending June, 1936, the transportation of 80,000 pupils required 2,000 busses at a total cost in excess of $1,600,000, all of this cost being borne by the rural consolidated school district in addition to necessary expenses for instruction and the school plant operations. The study shows that some districts actually spent over half of their revenues for transportation. It concludes that under such conditions it is extremely difficult to equalize rural and urban educational opportunity when urban revenues may be spent entirely on teaching staff and plant operations. Where transportation has been none too carefully planned, the cost is unnecessarily wasteful, as can be seen from the diagrams previously cited. The only way to simplify transportation in such cases is to revise transportation routes and reorganize districts.[3]

The Washington State College Agricultural Extension Service has summarized comments on problems of school consolidation as expressed by farmers in districts affected. These comments show that for the farmer also one of the major issues is transportation and related problems. In group conferences where consolidation is discussed, farmers complain that where chil-

[1] Consolidation has progressed rapidly in the state of Washington, school districts having decreased in number from 2,733 in 1909, to 1,856 in 1930, to 1,491 in 1938. Consolidated districts increased from 92 in 1909, to 415 in 1938. From reports to the author by the State Department of Education.

[2] *A Survey of the Common School System of Washington*, p. 23, Washington State Planning Council, Olympia, Sept. 24, 1936.

[3] *Ibid.*, p. 21.

dren must be transported to school the entire day is often consumed, leaving the child little time to help with the chores or other activities or to participate in community or 4-H Club work. In cases where the younger children travel on the same bus with high school children, they have to leave and return at the same time as the older children although their school day is shorter than that of the others. This means that they must spend a couple of hours a day on the streets of the small town or on the school grounds in unsupervised play. Risks to health are involved as children without supervision often fail to wear their rubbers and wraps while at play.[1]

The Curriculum.—If the consolidated school is located in town, townspeople often have control of curriculum making, a disproportionately high percentage of them being on the school board. They quite naturally may favor the adoption of a curriculum that is more fitted to the needs of the town than the farm child. Evidence on this point is presented by Kumlien in his study of high school education in South Dakota. In that state, at a time when 65 per cent of all gainfully employed men were engaged in agriculture, only 7.1 per cent of the high schools offered vocational training in agriculture. On the other hand, 36.8 per cent offered training in commerce, at a time when only 7.8 per cent of gainfully employed men were engaged in commerce.[2] By 1934, only 40 per cent of the rural high schools in the United States were teaching vocational agriculture, and it is estimated that only 14 per cent of farm boys 14 to 20 years of age were trained in agriculture.[3] However, it must be recognized that there is some logic in this discrimination. A high percentage of farm youth will be employed in urban commerce;[4] for this reason it is desirable that rural schools teach such subjects as commerce and secretarial training, but on the other hand it is highly desirable that they also teach vocational agriculture.

Takes Youth Away from the Farm.—No doubt the farmer who believes that education will send his children to the city is sound in his judgment. Experience has demonstrated the point over and over again. If the youth through the consolidated school program discovers that he has special talents or special interests, it is only natural that he will want to go where he can exercise them. Few rural communities have a place for those gifted in music, art,

[1] F. E. Balmer, *Social and Educational Problems of Rural Communities*, Memorandum 23, Agricultural Extension Service, Pullman, Feb. 23, 1939. Data used are based on a report of M. Elmina White, Assistant Director of the Agricultural Extension Service.

[2] W. F. Kumlien, "The High School Education of Farm Boys and Girls in South Dakota," p. 15, *South Dakota Agricultural Experiment Station Bulletin* 250, Brookings, 1930.

[3] Office of Education, "Vocational Education and Changing Conditions," p. 106, *Bulletin* 174, U.S. Department of the Interior, Washington, D. C., 1934. See also H. M. Hamlin, "Our Dual System of Rural Education," *School Review*, vol. 44, p. 181, 1936.

[4] Kumlien in the study cited above finds that three-fourths of farm pupils attending South Dakota high schools do not return to the farm. However, a higher proportion of those trained in agriculture and home economics than others do go back.

oratory, or writing, or for those with special skill in mechanics, drafting, or mathematics. Education increases the youth's perspective, widens his horizon, and gives him a greater range for intelligent choice. It also helps him to learn the nature of his capabilities. For these reasons chiefly, it has had the effect of sending rural young people away from the farm.

Training in agriculture offers no guarantee that a youth will be interested in farming as a life work. Evidence on the college level is presented by E. C. Johnson, Dean of the College of Agriculture at the State College of Washington.[1] Of a sample of 556 graduates in agriculture studied, only 14 per cent were operating farms, 20 per cent were employed in some form of government service in the U.S. Department of Agriculture or in state departments of agriculture, and 13 per cent were engaged in business enterprises, some of which, however, had a direct relation to agricultural life.

ADVANTAGES OF CONSOLIDATION

We have discussed at some length the problems involved in the consolidated school movement. Because any progressive program is bound to face considerable opposition, these difficulties might well be recognized in advance and frankly considered. Many of them can be avoided by an intelligent approach, the success of consolidation depending in large part upon the way it is carried out.

There are many decided advantages to consolidation, most of which can be summed up under two general headings—socializing benefits and benefits in broadening the scope of rural community life.

More Effective Socialization.—The one-room rural school in far too many cases still clings to the old philosophy that the purpose of the school is to teach subject matter. In contrast is the purpose of the modern progressive school system, which is to modify the lives of the learners, to develop their personality. Subject matter is one of the tools by which personality is shaped.

In previous sections we have dealt extensively with the problem of socialization in rural areas, noting the handicaps to the rural child resulting from the isolation of the rural neighborhood, the lack of rural play groups, and the restrictive atmosphere of the one-room school. Shyness, play handicaps, speech difficulties, and other problems of conditioning were discussed.[2] Limited social participation is characteristic of rural children. The meagerness of rural library facilities means that they do not have stimulating contacts with a wide range of books. Baldwin and his coworkers in the Iowa study show that no provision is made for the upkeep of rural school libraries and that very few books are

[1] "The Work of the Agriculturally Trained," mimeographed radio address over station KWSC, Mar. 14, 1939.

[2] Refer to Chap. 9.

available.[1] This same study indicates that the socializing facilities of the consolidated school are superior to those of the one-room school.[2]

Studies of drought settlers in an irrigated area of Washington showed that school children who came to the area from one-room schools had great difficulty in maintaining their grade level; those from consolidated schools seldom faced such difficulty. Of the one-room school children only one had been advanced beyond his normal grade, 40 per cent were retarded one or more grades, and 11 per cent were retarded two or more grades.[3]

The consolidated school can provide the needed break between primary and secondary group for many farm children, giving them experience in making the more superficial contacts called for in secondary-group participation. But even it is limited in its power to socialize farm youth for the reason that many of them, because school busses leave immediately after school, are unable to participate in anything except regular curricular activities. This is unfortunate because in many instances extracurricular functions are known to have a more important influence in the broadening of personality, the prevention of frustration, and the testing of character than the curriculum.

New and Broader Community Life.—In many rural neighborhoods of yesterday the one-room school was recognized as the center of the neighborhood and the focus of interest. We have indicated that the old neighborhood has tended to break down with the development of modern means of communication and transportation, and that where it still persists new interests beyond the scope of neighborhood life are developing. Students of rural life believe that the new consolidated school unit, if properly designed, will become a focus of the larger community. It actually has become that in many localities today.[4]

The late Dwight Sanderson, authority on rural community organization in the United States, believed the larger school attendance unit automatically developed a community consciousness, and that it might either impair or strengthen community life, depending on the extent to which communities were intelligently organized.[5]

Because the interests of parents tend to follow those of their children, the consolidated school is a broadening influence in the neighborhood; more and more the interests of children and youth are being focused in the school system and its extracurricular activities—music, athletics, clubs, and special days.

[1] Bird T. Baldwin *et al.*, *Farm Children*, p. 91, D. Appleton-Century Company, Inc., New York, 1930.

[2] *Ibid.*

[3] Carl F. Reuss and Lloyd H. Fisher, "Adjustments of New Settlers in the Yakima Valley," *Washington Agricultural Experiment Stations Bulletin* 397, Pullman, February, 1941.

[4] See E. de S. Brunner and I. Lorge, *Rural Trends in Depression Years*, p. 86, Columbia University Press, New York, 1938.

[5] Dwight Sanderson, "Criteria of Rural Community Formation," *Rural Sociology*, vol. 3, pp. 373–384, December, 1938.

Thus it has possibilities for becoming one of the most constructive of rural institutions in building and making meaningful a new rural life.

SPECIAL PROGRAMS AND PROBLEMS BEYOND THE SCOPE OF THE CONSOLIDATION MOVEMENT

Although the school consolidation movement represents the greatest single step in the advance of rural education in recent years, it does not present a universal solution for the rural school problem, there being areas in America which are so sparsely settled and which always will be because of the nature of their economic enterprise (for instance, cattle ranching in mountainous or dry plains areas), that there is no practical way to consolidate their schools.

Moreover, in many instances the consolidated school does not solve the basic difficulty of educational finance. In some sections children are too numerous and resources too scarce to make an effective educational program possible. As Renne observes, after summarizing the progress in education achieved through the consolidation of schools and the reductions in transportation costs: "Similar progress has not yet been made . . . in the method of financing schools by more diversified taxes and increased federal aid."[1]

In those areas where the one-room school for one reason or another must persist, for a time at least, better financing could do much to improve school standards by providing necessary equipment, by permitting employment of better trained teachers, by providing library facilities, and by otherwise creating an environment conducive to effective learning.

Perhaps new and untried methods of meeting the needs of rural areas need to be developed. A plan of unusual merit for schooling on the high school level originated in South Dakota during the drought-depression period of 1930–1936. In order to make it possible for children of relief families and others on the economic margin to attend high school, dormitories not unlike those of the old church academy were organized throughout the state by the State Emergency Relief Administration. Buildings were rented and proctors, preceptors, cooks, and janitors hired to care for the pupils. The cost of food per pupil during the school year 1934–1935 was only $34, and it was estimated that one-fifth more young people in the state were in high school than could otherwise have been. The dormitories were an excellent adaptation to the needs of the Great Plains states where distance often makes boarding in town necessary.

GENERAL OBJECTIVES FOR THE RURAL SCHOOL IN A DYNAMIC SOCIETY

Although farm communities still rarely recognize the fact, the schools they support are training youth who will live not only in the rural community but

[1] R. R. Renne, *op. cit.*

also in town and city areas, who will enter not only the agricultural occupation but also any one of the thousands of other vocations that exist in our highly complex society. Rather than preparing youth to be lifelong members of fairly static neighborhoods, they should be preparing youth to participate as mobile members of a complex social order. An awareness of this problem has developed in more progressive rural communities and the newer consolidated school probably prepares the youth for living in this kind of world. Whether or not he is prepared for it by the one-room school, and he seldom is, he is likely to make the transition to more dynamic phases of society during some period of his life. The failure of the school to fit him for it probably leaves him without adequate preparation.

Even the best rural schools can only partially prepare the child for adult life. Financial limitations will always keep most consolidated schools from achieving the level of vocational training and guidance that the great city school system is able to attain. But the training of the well-equipped rural consolidated school is immeasurably more effective in terms of preparing the modern youth for life than is that of the one-room neighborhood school.

This inequality of rural education affects both personality adjustment and vocational placement. On the former, the findings of Stott[1] are suggestive. He reports that children in one-room schools had lower adjustment scores on personality ratings than children in village schools.

On the matter of economic adjustment, the New York Regents Inquiry[2] comment on the readiness of pupils from various school systems for vocational responsibility is highly significant:

Boys and girls trained in rural schools are less frequently recommended by their teachers as ready for vocational responsibilities than are those prepared in city school systems. For withdrawing boys the percentage of unendorsed pupils increased from 29.9 in New York City to 58.2 in communities of less than 2,500, and for girls from 32.3 to 41.4. Less than 4 per cent of both the boy and girl graduates in New York City schools were judged unfit for job responsibilities, while 15 per cent of the boys and 19 per cent of the girls in rural communities were judged unfit. It would appear that to the previously indicated academic handicaps of many country students must be added the teachers' judgment that they possess an inability to face work problems with reasonable expectation of success.

Considering the fact that so many farm youth must adjust to new work situations for which family heritage has failed to give them an apprenticeship, this indictment of the school's failure is a challenge.

[1] L. H. Stott, "Some Environmental Factors in Relation to the Personality Adjustment of Rural Children," *Rural Sociology*, vol. 10, pp. 394–403, December, 1945.

[2] Ruth E. Eckert and Thomas O. Marshall, *When Youth Leave School*, p. 11, The Regents' Inquiry, McGraw-Hill Book Company, Inc., New York, 1938.

Questions for Review and Discussion

1. Does the rural one-room school represent a lag in education?
2. Summarize the problems of the one-room school.
3. What financial difficulties handicap the one-room school?
4. Do farm youth compare well with urban youth in the proportion receiving high school training? Cite evidence.
5. How does accessibility of high schools to farm youth affect their entering high school?
6. Show how rural attitudes may affect the schooling of youth.
7. Summarize rural attitudes that have hindered the progressive development of rural educational institutions.
8. What problems arise in connection with the consolidation of schools?
9. Explain the relationship between district organization and transportation problems.
10. What arguments are advanced against consolidation?
11. Summarize the advantages of consolidation.
12. Why cannot consolidation be considered a universal means of rural school improvement? Suggest other needed programs.
13. Toward what general objectives should the rural school aim in a dynamic society?

Collateral Reading

The Advisory Committee on Education: *Report of the Committee*, U.S. Government Printing Office, 1938.

Brunner, E. de S., and I. Lorge: *Rural Trends in Depression Years*, chap. 7, Columbia University Press, New York, 1937.

Cook, L. A.: *Community Backgrounds of Education*, chaps. 2 and 3, McGraw-Hill Book Company, Inc., New York, 1938.

Gillette, J. M.: *Rural Sociology*, 3d ed., chaps. 18 and 19. The Macmillan Company, New York, 1936.

Kolb, J. A., and E. de S. Brunner: *A Study of Rural Society*, rev. and enlarged ed., chaps. 17 and 18, Houghton Mifflin Company, Boston, 1940.

Landis, Paul H.: *Adolescence and Youth*, part V, McGraw-Hill Book Company, Inc., New York, 1945.

Renne, Roland R.: "Rural Educational Institutions and Social Lag," *Rural Sociology*, vol. 1, pp. 306–321, September, 1936.

Sanderson, Dwight: *Rural Sociology and Rural Social Organization*, chaps. 16–18, John Wiley & Sons, Inc., New York, 1942.

Smith, T. Lynn: *The Sociology of Rural Life*, rev. ed. chap. 17, Harper & Brothers, New York, 1947.

Sorokin, P. A., C. C. Zimmerman, and J. C. Galpin: *A Systematic Source Book in Rural Sociology*, vol. 2, chap. 12, University of Minnesota Press, Minneapolis, 1931.

Still Sits the Schoolhouse by the Road, Committee on Rural Education, Sponsored by the Farm Foundation, Chicago, 1943.

CHAPTER 23

TRENDS IN RURAL RELIGION AND THE FARMER'S CHURCH

THE QUALITY OF RURAL RELIGION

RELIGION is rarely an isolated part of life but, by its very nature, embraces many aspects of personality. Religious philosophy may be closely related to the economic and social codes of a people. One who is closely identified with nature phenomena, who often feels alone, or who is introverted, views life and human destiny differently than does one who lives in congested social space.[1]

The religion of the American farmer is likely to be more personal and less social than that of the urbanite,[2] more conservative, more local in its application, less missionary in spirit, more static, clinging to old emotional values,[3] less intellectual, more supernatural and less humanistic, looking toward the ultimate outcome of life rather than toward the socializing values obtainable through religion in this present one. It is frequently more contemplative and self-centered and less dynamic in social action.[4]

It seems probable that the rural religious attitude is less critical, skeptical, and inquiring than the urban; that the rural man is more inclined to accept absolutes, to hold more firmly to the view that the Bible is the final word of truth, that sin and righteousness, good and bad, truth and falsehood are always clear-cut and distinct, that the good way is clearly marked for anyone who wills to find it. Such views are the products of limited experience. Urbanization, by increasing the complexity of social relations, has eliminated many clear-cut definitions, for they survive best in a relatively stable world. With the decline of clear-cut definitions are likely to arise doubt, skepticism, cynicism, and also greater tolerance. But with these attitudes may also come greater freedom from conviction, release from the sense of duty, and escape from the influence of religious controls.

The natural phenomena with which the farmer deals inspire more confidence in God than do the artificial phenomena so prominent in the city. The

[1] Compare H. B. Hawthorn, *The Sociology of Rural Life*, p. 256, D. Appleton-Century Company, Inc., New York, 1926.

[2] See L. L. Bernard, "A Theory of Rural Attitudes," *American Journal of Sociology*, pp. 648 *ff*., March, 1917.

[3] Compare J. M. Williams, *Our Rural Heritage*, pp. 151–152, 248, Alfred A. Knopf, Inc., New York, 1925.

[4] *Ibid.*

rural man is constantly reminded that the powers controlling his life are natural—the seasons, the weather, growth, life.[1] The urban man seldom faces these processes and most of his troubles are not induced by nature, but by fellow beings. If he is unemployed, it is not because the Lord or Providence was unkind but rather because the employer closed down a factory or the city council ruled that his business was not legitimate. There is often a cure for his problem, but it is usually a human cure. Urbanites, therefore, do not project their troubles on the Lord or Satan as often as does the rural man, rather blaming some individual or individuals or some aspect of civilization. Instead of seeking consolation in religion the city man joins a labor union or the political gang in his ward. Although these urban patterns are diffusing into rural areas, something of the grasp of the supernatural still survives there.

SECULARIZATION IN RURAL AND URBAN LIFE

The effect of the urbanization processes of the last two centuries, according to Frank Hankins, sociologist, has been not only to remove man from close dependence upon nature, but to reduce the chance element in life to the extent that he no longer looks on nature as a mysterious supernatural force.[2] Rather the play of human forces which he sees on every hand suggests to him that man controls his own destiny. The city environment releases the individual from many social pressures, and at the same time multiplies opportunities for indulgence in selfish morbid pleasures. Religion is dependent upon constant communication and fellowship among believers. City life has destroyed much of this fellowship and with it much of religious faith. It is isolated people—farmers, herdsmen, villagers—who believe in supernatural sanctions and cling to dogmatic emotional attitudes growing out of customary folkways and mores.

An age of machine technology, materialism, and excessive social life, Williams believes, has taken the mystery out of life for many people; the new interest in objectivity has "sapped the sense of mystery of the early days and weakened the attitude of reverence."[3]

The conflict between science and faith has no doubt made great inroads on the farmer's religion. It is difficult to pray for rain in the face of weather predictions based on scientific fact, even though faith may supersede all obstacles, and to trust the Lord to produce events in direct contradiction to known scientific laws. The U.S. Weather Bureau has probably been more influential in silencing prayers for rain than all the teachings of evolution.

Tracing the trend of the first thirty years of this century, Fry describes

[1] Refer to Chap. 5.

[2] Frank Hankins, *An Introduction to the Study of Society*, pp. 524–526, 532, The Macmillan Company, New York, 1935.

[3] J. M. Williams, *The Expansion of Rural Life*, pp. 234–235, Alfred A. Knopf, Inc., New York, 1926.

secularizing influences affecting both rural and urban religious life.[1] Pleasure seeking has usually been considered the antithesis of devoutness, but the automobile has destroyed Sabbath pleasure taboos, the Sunday joy ride having become an almost universal pastime, and the moving picture now competes with church services.

Evidence suggests that these secularizing influences have not as yet weakened traditional religious functions in the farm family so much as in the city family. Concerning family religious practices, a study reported in *Recent Social Trends in the United States*, shows that in the matter of church attendance, 85 per cent of the rural children attend with their families, whereas in the large city only 40 per cent go with their families. Family reading of the Bible is reported in 22 per cent of the homes of rural white children, but in only 10 per cent of the homes of city white children. Grace at meals is a practice in 30 per cent of the city homes and 38 per cent of the rural homes, and a considerably higher percentage of the children in the rural areas than in the large city participate in family prayers.[2]

More recent data of Duvall and Motz[3] show that rural young people are still brought up under a more strict religious training than urban youth, and that they are more regular in their attendance at church.

PERSISTENCE OF PRIMITIVE FORMS OF RELIGIOUS EXPRESSION

The appeal of religion in the recent past has been to the supernatural. Eternal life, retribution in the hereafter, and similar themes have always been prominent in evangelistic messages. Revivals and camp meetings, which are typically rural institutions, are evidences of the survival of more primitive forms of religious expression in rural areas.[4]

Much satisfaction is obtained by people living in isolated areas from the emotional debauchery which sometimes accompanies extreme types of religious expression. Cralle comments on the tendency of people in the Ozark Mountains to withdraw from the church as soon as it abandons emotionalism and creates a paid ministry.[5] Evidently the mountaineers derive little satisfaction for their

[1] C. Luther Fry in *Recent Social Trends in the United States*, pp. 1012–1013, McGraw-Hill Book Company, Inc., New York, 1933.

[2] See the section by W. F. Ogburn on "The Family," *Recent Social Trends in the United States*, p. 674. Data taken from a study by E. W. Burgess made in connection with the White House Conference on Child Health and Protection.

[3] Evelyn Millis Duvall and Annabelle Bender Motz, "Are Country Girls so Different?" *Rural Sociology*, vol. 10, pp. 263–274, September, 1945.

[4] For an extensive discussion of revival practices see Frederick M. Davenport, *Primitive Traits in the Religious Revival*, The Macmillan Company, New York, 1905.

[5] W. O. Cralle, "Social Change and Isolation in the Ozark Mountain Region of Missouri," *American Journal of Sociology*, vol. 41, pp. 435–446, January, 1936.

undernourished emotional life from the formal type of church service. Among them the Pentecostal Church, which conducts services with an intense emotional fervor reminiscent of the "canebrake revival" days, finds ready reception. The Pentecostal preacher comes into the community as a holy man, demanding no salary and willing to subsist on whatever may be given him in way of the foodstuffs. This gesture is gratifying to the mountaineer who is unaccustomed to paying his minister in cash.

Similarly, one finds among the migratory workers of the Pacific Coast the Pentecostal Church and other revivalistic branches of the Protestant faith making a strong appeal. Here again the evangelist is willing to meet his converts on their own level, often traveling with the migratory group, living in an old trailer, preaching in the camps, demanding little compensation, and offering much to the workers in the way of emotional satisfaction.

The more sordid life is, the greater the chance element encountered; the more culturally dispossessed the group, the greater the attraction of emotional religion. But today, sordidness of life seems not to be primarily a rural phenomenon. Some of the greatest revivalistic movements of modern times have taken place in the cities; but there, as in the country, they appeal to the culturally dispossessed at the lower end of the economic and social scale. Billy Sunday, the Raders, Aimee Semple McPherson, and other less spectacular evangelists appeal to the metropolitan masses in much the same manner as the revivalist of yesterday appealed to the rural man. There is some difference, however, in the appeal. The exaggerated fear of the world to come seems to be less prominent in the modern urban revival, faith healing being the major keynote. But the religious service is no less emotional and no less primitive than among isolated rural groups.

The growth in American cities of astrology, numerology, fortune telling, and other practices that border the magical suggests that great numbers of city people who have forsaken orthodox religion feel highly insecure. Urban life has not robbed them of their belief in the supernatural; it has merely changed their approach to it. Redfield, discussing Yucatan society, states that religion and ritual are of decreasing importance in modern cities there, but are still important in rural areas.[1] In these cities black magic and sorcery have come to supplant among the more illiterate groups the authority of ritual and religion.

Emotional substitutes for religion, such as have appeared in the city, are not yet prominent among rural groups. The more radical type of labor union, which calls for near-religious self-sacrifice, furnishes great masses of devotees in the city a channel for emotional expression. It is interesting to observe that union officials working among migratory farm workers on the West Coast consider that emotional religions interfere decidedly with union activities,

[1] Robert Redfield, "Culture Changes in Yucatan," *American Anthropologist*, vol. 36, pp. 64–68, January and March, 1934.

people who have found an outlet through religion not being likely to devote themselves to the union. There is probably the additional element that those who seek the early reward in heaven promised by the emotional religions, are resigned to conditions as they exist and are not greatly interested in the reforms which the unions advocate.

Among the upper classes of the city new faiths of a metaphysical nature have replaced old orthodox beliefs, but they are designed to meet the same psychological needs that orthodox religion meets for rural people. For example, the Christian Science movement[1] involves chiefly the middle classes in the nation's largest cities.[2]

THE RURAL CHURCH

General Characteristics.—There are in the United States approximately 128,097 rural churches, *i.e.*, churches located in towns of under 2,500 population and in the open country.[3] The great majority of rural churches are Protestant,[4] Catholic churches being centered primarily in the city. This can be explained by the fact that most of the immigrants to this country who settled in cities were from the predominantly Catholic southern European countries, whereas those who settled in rural areas were chiefly from northern Europe, where the population is largely Protestant.[5] As a rural institution the church has ranked third in importance. Immigrant and pioneer groups, once their homes and schools were built, set about to establish local churches. In thousands of rural neighborhoods these churches were an important focus of life.[6]

The Life Cycle of the Church in the Rural Settlement of America.—Hollingshead, studying churches in rural Nebraska, finds four phases in the regular sequence of a church's life history.[7] First is the organization of the congregation in the newly settled area; second, the erection of the edifice after the

[1] Another such development is "psychiana," sponsored by Dr. Frank B. Robinson, conducted almost entirely by mail and radio advertising, and claiming 600,000 to 1,000,000 followers.

[2] J. K. Johnson, *Christian Science: A Case Study of a Religion as a Form of Adjustment Behavior*, Washington University Doctoral Dissertations, St. Louis, June, 1937.

[3] Based on data from the 1936 *Census of Religious Bodies*. Data for the 1936 census are not available at the time of this writing.

[4] *Ibid.*

[5] P. A. Sorokin suggests that the "native" religion of an area persists among rural people and cities data from various nations in support of the idea. He considers Protestantism the "native" religion of the United States. See his discussion of this point in "Rural-urban Differences in Religious Culture, Beliefs and Behavior," *Publications of the American Sociological Society*, vol. 23, p. 299, 1928.

[6] For an interesting example, see Vernon J. Parenton, "Notes on the Social Organization of a French Village in South Louisiana," *Social Forces*, vol. 17, pp. 79–80, October, 1938.

[7] A. B. Hollingshead, "The Life Cycle of Nebraska Rural Churches," *Rural Sociology*, vol. 2, pp. 180–191, June, 1937.

neighborhood has developed a degree of economic stability. During the third phase maintenance of the congregation, payment for the edifice, and support of the pastor are characteristic. The final phase is one of gradual decline in membership, followed by the loss of the minister, and finally the abandonment of services and the death of the church. Two groups of denominations are distinguishable: those interested in saving souls and those interested mainly in the establishment of an ecclesiastical organization. The first group sends evangelists to the pioneer with the idea of converting him; the second, because it is interested in making the church the center of community life, establishes churches only where communicants form colonies. The ecclesiastical church, its original members drawn from an immigrant group which was land hungry and deeply interested in permanent land ownership, has survived in spite of the extensive changes that have taken place during the last fifty years, whereas evangelical churches founded among the old American stock, whose interest in land was only casual and who settled cheap land to sell it, have gradually died.

Churches located in focal trade centers on railroad lines have the greatest chance of survival; those in the open country the least.[1] Generally speaking, the larger the town the greater the chance the church has to survive; vice versa. the smaller the town the smaller the chance to survive, the church in the open country being even less likely to live than the church in the small town.

The Trend of the Rural Church.—The rapid decline of the rural church in many areas is a phenomenon which has been observed for some years. Lively's study in 1921 which located and mapped 1,058 abandoned rural churches in Ohio is widely known.[2] In numerous areas the church has shifted from the open country to the village. Kolb and Brunner in their study of American villages find that in the open country two churches die for every one that is organized.[3] In the village the number appearing and the number disappearing approximately balance. Undoubtedly, however, the changes are much more profound in nature than mere changes in numbers reveal.

It would be interesting to know the characteristics of the churches that appear and of those that decline. General observation would lead one to believe that the older, conservative denominations disappear, their place being taken by newer aggressive sects. Pentecostal, Nazarene, Four Square Gospel, and in larger towns Christian Science churches probably are springing up in fields abandoned by Christian, Baptist, Presbyterian, Methodist, Congregational, and other long-established religious bodies.

[1] A. B. Hollingshead, "Ecological Factors in Rural Church Integration," *Sociology and Social Research*, vol. 23, pp. 144–156, November–December, 1938.

[2] C. E. Lively, "Some Rural Social Agencies in Ohio, 1922–23," p. 17, *Ohio State University Agricultural Extension Service Bulletin*, Columbus, 1924.

[3] J. H. Kolb and E. de S. Brunner, *A Study of Rural Society*, rev. and enlarged ed., p. 464, Houghton Mifflin Company, Boston, 1940.

The historical and logical factors involved in the decline of the country church and ways of meeting the problem are summarized in an article by Thomas A. Tripp, part of which follows:

There is a popular notion that the rural church is "dying out." Some people seem to take a fiendish delight in telling how fast country churches are passing out of existence. Others utter dark lamentations about it. But there are not many who know just what the situation is and fewer still who seem to be doing anything about it.

The truth is, many country churches have been closed. Some have died which should have done so, many should never have been born, a few now living should probably cease to exist, and others which appear alive are already dead without knowing it.

Some parishes have died which should have lived and many that are expiring should be saved from annihilation. Some died a natural death, many died by violence through bad overhead administration, and others simply committed suicide by factional disputes and indifference.

In the first place too many churches have been organized. As the frontier was settled there was a strong tendency to overexpansion by every institution, including the churches. Sectarianism and competition prevailed, particularly during the "denominational era" from about 1865 to 1910 when each communion sought to get into every community.

New parishes are still being formed and, in spite of losses, numerous localities have several competing congregations. The situation must now be viewed with common sense. . . . After overchurching, the most serious cause for the closing of country churches is the shifting of farm populations and the concomitant trend of rural people and institutions to towns and cities. The loss of farms by their operators in recent years has resulted in a higher percentage of tenant farmers. Tenants move from farm to farm and from community to community making for a more unstable country community.

When the tenancy rate exceeds 20 per cent in a given locality the church begins to decline. Old people retire from the farm, settle in town and join the church there. Younger people go to the towns and cities to work leaving the country church behind.

And many of the more prosperous farmers, not to be outdone by the city-bound Joneses, have joined the church in a near-by town. All this takes so much strength from the crossroads church that it is often starved out.

When a country parish becomes seriously weakened by such forces as those mentioned above it is often yoked or consolidated with one in town. Or it may die and the members who have sufficient religious interest join a town church.

Due to modern developments the crossroads church, like the country store and district school, follows the villageward trend. However, the church is the last of the three to die out in the farm neighborhood.

The most disturbing factor in the situation, though, is the fact that when the church goes to town it does not take its constituency with it to nearly as high a degree as other institutions. Hence, many farmers are left without religious services.

It should add greatly to the zeal and religious spirit of town churches if their official boards would seriously undertake to bring their farm neighbors into their fellowship and if, when they enlist them, they would give country men and women equal representation in the leadership of the parish.[1]

The villageward shift of the open-country church may have far-reaching implications to rural religion. The centralized church that draws its membership from a large area provides more in the way of facilities, ministry, and symbolism than can the isolated neighborhood church, but its religious controls are frequently less effective. Farm people are likely to be less loyal to and less willing to sacrifice for a village or town church than for a neighborhood one. They may feel less obligation to attend regularly because there is not the same degree of group surveillance, friends and neighbors observing one's absence less readily and bringing less pressure to bear to persuade one to renew attendance. Once a person who has been strictly disciplined in religion tastes freedom, he seldom returns to the fold. That no doubt has been the experience of thousands of rural people who have broken away by steps. They left the neighborhood church for the advantages of a larger church and eventually broke away from all church attachments. On the other hand, in many villages farm leaders become pillars of the church.

Town and city churches tend to be more social-minded and less God-centered than the open-country church and, consequently, many farm people do not obtain so much emotional satisfaction in the urban as in the neighborhood church, which conforms more to their notions of orthodoxy. These losses are partly compensated for by social gains but, from the standpoint of the church and organized religion, they have had serious results.

Forces Affecting the Open-country Church.—Rural ministers are inclined to bemoan the loss of interest in their churches, the diminishing size of their congregations, the futility of their situation, often failing to realize that social forces beyond control of the church are in operation. The breakdown of the neighborhood and the declining influence of local institutions are phases of social change which no single institution can long resist. In many cases the struggle of the open-country church for survival is futile. The problem of the rural ministry is not to maintain the rural church as an institution, except as it can supply a need which cannot be met better in other ways, but to make it serve a vital need in the modern age for, as in the case of all institutions, churches will survive if they serve a useful function in the community.

SPECIAL PROBLEMS OF THE NEIGHBORHOOD CHURCH

The church in the open country faces issues which have a definite bearing on its survival or failure to survive. Frequently it has an irregular ministry.

[1] Thomas A. Tripp, "Is the Country Church Dying?" *The Missionary Herald*, vol. 134, pp. 489–491, November, 1938.

The Census of Religious Bodies of 1916 showed that one-third of the ministers in open country and small towns devoted only a part of their time to church duties. In many rural sections, especially in the South, the minister depends, as on the early frontier, on a secular occupation engaged in during the week for all or part of his income. Another problem is that presented by the itinerate minister. The old circuit rider of the pioneer period has largely disappeared, but many preachers today fill the pulpits of two to five different charges, alternating Sundays between them. A study in Missouri[1] describes the three-hour-a-month minister. In one county it was found that 80 per cent of the open-country churches and nearly half of the village churches were without a resident minister.

Melvin W. Sneed and Douglas Ensminger in the study *The Rural Church in Missouri* (1935), which covers 2,561 rural churches in the open country and in places of up to 2,500 people, find that only 21 per cent of open-country churches have a resident pastor as compared to 72 per cent in places of 1,500 to 2,500 population. Their findings indicate that the larger the town the greater is the likelihood of its having a resident minister. They find that the open-country churches only 10 per cent have a full-time minister; whereas of places of 1,500 to 2,500, two-thirds have a full-time pastor. The larger the village, the greater the likelihood of its having a full-time minister.

In many cases the salary of the minister in the neighborhood church is extremely low, yet the cost of his services is a heavy burden to the community. Often he has been poorly trained, the chief prerequisite to entering the ministry in some churches being a "call" to preach. His lack of education no doubt has had some bearing on the decline of the neighborhood church, it being extremely difficult for a preacher to interest people who excel him in the use of English grammar.

Rural churches have been slow to adopt the modern pleasure philosophy, and many are yet Puritanical in their attitude toward play. Rural ministers lament the fact that their congregations have lost all interest in truth and righteousness, that people seek only pleasure and are careless about their souls, and it is true that movies, radios, pleasure riding, and numerous "worldly" attractions are strong competing influences in our time. The urban church, with the increase in leisure time, has come to look upon recreational activities as constructive rather than destructive, making for good rather than being tools of the devil, and has even taken the initiative in sponsoring recreation as part of its youth program. Farm young people contacting the town and city church absorb these patterns and lose interest in the local church with its narrow views and its condemnation of pleasure and worldliness.

[1] *A Rural Survey in Missouri*, p. 34, Department of Church and Country Life of the Board of Home Missions of the Presbyterian Church in the United States of America. Other studies in this same series deal with rural church problems in Pennsylvania, Arkansas, southeastern Ohio, Illinois, and Kentucky.

CONSTRUCTIVE TRENDS IN THE RURAL CHURCH FIELD

The Larger Parish Movement.—"The most promising means of bringing new life to the rural church seems to be through the larger parish."[1] As Rich defines it, the larger parish "is a group of churches in a larger rural community, or a potential religious community, working together through a larger-parish

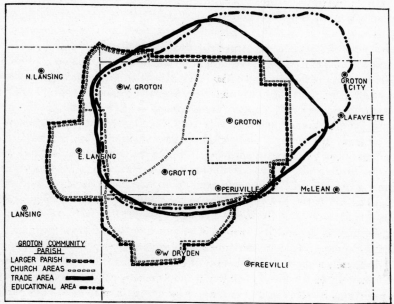

Mark Rich, "The Larger Parish," *Cornell Extension Bulletin* 408, Ithaca, 1939

THE GROTON, NEW YORK, LARGER PARISH

"At the center of the area is a village with a population of 2000 inhabitants. In the village are four Protestant churches. In the surrounding area there are four, small, open-country churches that naturally belong with the village, educationally, socially, economically, and politically. Therefore, the larger parish maintains that all of these churches have a common relationship. If the open-country churches begin to decline, it is the concern of the village church, because the adjacent church is a part of the community of which the village is the center. Without closing any of the churches, or doing away with the individual church programs, the larger parish proposes a plan whereby all the churches can work together to serve the whole community."

council and a larger-parish staff to serve the people of the area with a diversified ministry."[2]

The larger parish makes for cooperation between churches and makes

[1] Dwight Sanderson in the foreword to Mark Rich, "The Larger Parish," *Cornell Extension Bulletin*, Ithaca, 1939.

[2] Mark Rich, *ibid.*, p. 4.

possible a specialized ministry because organization is based on a comparatively large unit of service (see the figure on page 355). The staff ordinarily consists of the pastors of the individual churches and of specialists employed by the larger parish. These latter include at least two full-time paid workers; *e.g.*, pastor and associate pastor, or pastor and director of religious education, or pastor and director of women's work. This plan permits specialization within the staff, different members giving attention to the work for which they are particularly fitted. The direction of functions of interest throughout the parish is in the hands of a council comparable to a church board. Rich estimates that there are approximately 100 larger parishes in the United States.[1]

Consolidation of Churches.—Another movement that has grown considerably in certain areas is that to consolidate churches (the larger parish represents a kind of consolidation). Various plans have been developed and put into practice for consolidation in areas where overchurching exists. The *union church*, which is most common in the Far West, is formed when one or more churches of one denomination are merged with another denomination. The *federated church* is a union of two or more organized churches of different denominations which unite for local work, each body maintaining its affiliations with its own denomination. Under the *undenominational plan*, no denominational connections are held by either the new unit or any of the bodies uniting. This plan is commonly found in the Middle West. The *affiliated church* is free to form its own constitution and control its own local affairs like the undenominational, but maintains connections with denominational bodies for specific purposes such as ministerial supply and distribution of benevolences.[2]

Closely allied to this consolidation movement is the tendency of modern denominations to cooperate in entering new areas. Instead of the old practice whereby leading denominations rushed into new territory on a competitive basis, new areas are divided up among the home missions societies of the churches, so that only one church enters a field.

Rural Ministers' Institutes.—An educational program for rural ministers is sponsored by many leading Protestant denominations. The Town-country Department of these denominations, in cooperation with the Federal Council of Churches of Christ in America, has worked out jointly with a number of the agricultural colleges a program of summer institutes for small-town and country pastors. These institutes are designed to put the minister in touch with influences affecting farm life and with the general trend of social events in the rural community. The purposes as stated by the sponsors are to provide opportunity to discuss special problems of the church under the guidance of

---

[1] *Ibid.*, p. 3.

[2] Elizabeth R. Hooker, *United Churches*, pp. 35, 36, 80, 100–101, Doubleday & Company, Inc., New York, 1926; H. W. McLaughlin, *The Country Church and Public Affairs*, chap. 8, The Macmillan Company, New York, 1930.

national authorities on the topic, to make available to rural leaders facilities and research findings that will be of practical value to them in their daily work with small-town and farm people, and to provide an opportunity for fellowship on an interdenominational basis. In these schools, which usually last for a period of two weeks, courses in rural sociology, farm economics, social psychology, mental hygiene, recreation, rural church leadership, and other such subjects are taught.

THE CONTRIBUTION OF THE RURAL CHURCH TO THE URBAN CHURCH

Although many urban churches do not recognize the fact, a considerable proportion of their members have received their early religious training in a rural church, and it is likely that this same situation will prevail in the future because of the normal movement of youth from open country and town to city. The home missions activities of many of the more prosperous urban churches in support of weak congregations in isolated rural areas are, for this reason, logical as well as necessary. Unfortunately, in some cases home missions funds are used to keep alive a church in a competitive situation which should be allowed to die.

THE CHALLENGE OF A MOBILE SOCIETY TO THE CHURCH

One of the major problems in modern society from the standpoint of personality adjustment is the shock that is often experienced when the person shifts from one rural community to another or from the rural environment to the urban. It would seem that an opportunity is presented at this point for the church to perform a major social service in helping to ease the shock of readjustment of the individual entering a new community. Some clergymen are alive to this problem as is evidenced by the example of Lutheran ministers in the Great Plains who have been following the movement of their people to the Pacific Northwest with interest, helping them to get in contact with a minister in the new area so that he may aid them in getting settled and in finding a place in the life of the new community.

Much more important probably than the problem offered by the intercommunity migrant is that involving the crisis adjustment of youth who enter the city from rural areas. Here is offered an opportunity for an exchange system between churches by which young people might be kept in contact with institutional agencies as one step in easing the shock of adjustment to the new social situation. The impersonality of the city, the lack of intimate contacts, the sense of strangeness, and the loneliness of farm youth in the city create within him a need for contacts with those who would take an unselfish interest in him. It would seem that the church should shift its emphasis toward some of these newer problems of adjustment that are so prominent in a highly mobile society. If this new service function were more effectively performed, the church in this way might accomplish more toward maintaining its prestige as a fundamental social institution than by too much emphasis on traditional services.

QUESTIONS FOR REVIEW AND DISCUSSION

1. Characterize the farmer's religious attitudes and suggest factors conditioning them.
2. Show how the process of secularization has affected rural religious attitudes and practices.
3. Compare religious practices of rural with those of urban families.
4. Are emotional expressions of religion primarily rural phenomena at the present time? Explain.
5. Compare the life cycle of the ecclesiastical rural church with that of the evangelical type.
6. Why do rural churches die? Summarize the important reasons.
7. What are some of the losses that may result from the shift of a church from open country to town?
8. Summarize the special problems experienced by the open-country church.
9. What is the larger-parish movement and what does it aim to achieve?
10. Outline four methods of consolidating churches.
11. In what ways does the rural church contribute to the urban church?
12. Along what lines might the rural church supply a needed service?

COLLATERAL READING

Cain, B. H.: *The Church Ministering to Rural Life*, United Brethren, Dayton, Ohio, 1941.
Chapman, Stanley H.: "The Minister: Professional Man of the Church," *Social Forces*, vol. 23, pp. 202–206, December, 1944.
Hollingshead, A. B.: "The Life Cycle of Nebraska Rural Churches," *Rural Sociology*, vol. 2, pp. 180–191, June, 1927.
———: "Ecological Factors in Rural Church Integration," *Sociology and Social Research*, vol. 23, pp. 144–156, November–December, 1938.
Kolb, J. H., and E. de S. Brunner: *A Study of Rural Society*, 3d ed., chap. 21, Houghton Mifflin Company, Boston, 1946.
Lindstrom, David: *Rural Life and the Church*, The Girard Press, Champaign, Ill., 1946.
Recent Social Trends in the United States, chap. 20, McGraw-Hill Book Company, Inc., New York, 1933.
Rich, Mark: "The Larger Parish," *Cornell Extension Bulletin* 408, Ithaca, 1939.
Sims, N. L.: *Elements of Rural Sociology*, 3d ed., chaps. 24 and 25, The Thomas Y. Crowell Company, New York, 1940.
Smith, T. Lynn: *The Sociology of Rural Life*, rev. ed. chap. 18, Harper & Brothers, New York, 1946.
Sorokin, P. A.: "Rural-urban Differences in Religious Culture, Beliefs and Behavior," *Publications of the American Sociological Society*, vol. 23, pp. 229 ff., 1928.
Taylor, C. C.: *Rural Sociology*, rev. ed., chap. 19, Harper & Brothers, New York, 1930.

CHAPTER 24

RURAL GOVERNMENT IN A CHANGING ENVIRONMENT

RURAL GOVERNMENT AND SOCIAL CONTROL

SOCIAL control in rural life is maintained without the elaboration of formal control devices. Police, courts, and laws are multiplied a hundredfold in more complex forms of social life but in rural culture the legal structure is far from imposing it. It deals more with service functions than with discipline, more with administration than with regulation.

Most of the government of the county seat, which is the only government with which the average farmer has to deal, provides for collecting taxes, recording titles and land deeds, clearing estates, making legal records, and supervising local institutions. The urban man, hedged in by regulative law, is law conscious; the farmer, as far as forces of control are concerned, is neighborhood and God conscious. Rarely does delinquency become so serious in rural areas that it must be handled on a legal basis.

Baldwin and his coworkers in their study of Iowa farm children found that there were occasional cases of petty theft, trespassing, and boisterous conduct among the older children; that these offenses were dealt with by the admonitions of parents, friends, and relatives; that juvenile delinquency, unless extremely flagrant in character, did not reach juvenile authorities.[1] The general tendency was to minimize misdeeds and to protect the offender. In the rural communities studied no serious crimes were committed and controversies such as would lead to legal entanglements were usually avoided.[2] Consideration for the rights of one another seemed to be a more pertinent factor in maintaining harmonious relationships than respect for law as such. In contrast, urban children in congested areas see the uniformed policeman almost daily and encounter prohibitions which carry penalties almost hourly; rare indeed is the slum child who has never been reprimanded by an officer of the law.

Because there are comparatively few laws in the rural child's environment, he develops neither an attitude of respect, nor one of disrespect, for law. He simply lives in a world where other means more effective than law are in force; he is regulated, not in terms of what is legal or illegal, but of what is

[1] Bird T. Baldwin *et al.*, *Farm Children*, p. 146, D. Appleton-Century Company, Inc., New York, 1930.
[2] *Ibid.*, p. 48.

right or wrong. He is guided for the most part by a moral conscience, whereas the urban child is guided for the most part by a legal conscience.

One should not imply that there are never legal disputes among rural people; usually they hesitate before taking a matter to a lawyer, trying to work out an adjustment without resorting to law. Such legal suits as arise are more likely to center about disputes involving real property. Williams, characterizing the old-fashioned country lawyer, observed that he was more learned in human nature than in law.[1] The successful rural attorney grasped the facts of his case as they would appear to a typical farmer, and then built a rule of law under which he could obtain the justice sought. He was interested in deciding a case "justly," in accordance with law, and particularly with custom. Laws, to the farmer and the lawyer alike, were to be enforced and not to be changed. Both resisted the making of new laws.

In modern times government has increasingly entered the service field, supervising, standardizing, and guiding the course of many institutional and noninstitutional aspects of human behavior, but this trend has characterized more especially the great society, rather than rural society. In fact, there has been a serious lag in the growth of service functions of rural government. Ordinarily the county employs few specialized officers to deal with problem cases. Even public-health services have lagged seriously and professional services on an efficient level have always been at a minimum in rural institutional fields.[2] Actually, the rural community does not need the highly specialized institutions that the city maintains, and could not afford them if a need existed. The most vicious problem areas are urban; the great diversity of behavior problems are urban.

EXTENT AND COST OF LOCAL GOVERNMENT

There are in the United States 3,072 county governments, 3,165 city governments (governments of places of above 2,500 population), and 13,433 town and village governments (governments of incorporated places with less than 2,500 population). In addition, there are numerous townships, school districts, and other local units that perform some governmental function.

According to a study by *Fortune Magazine* there are over 175,000 overlapping taxing units in the nation.[3] The state of Illinois leads with 17,336 distinct taxing agencies. By no means are all these small taxing units rural, but many of them are.

An Illinois study shows that in Kane County, which was created in 1836,

[1] J. M. Williams, *Our Rural Heritage*, pp. 108–109, Alfred A. Knopf, Inc., New York, 1925.

[2] For a more complete presentation of service aspects of county administration in rural areas, see Chaps. 28–30.

[3] "U. S. Taxes," *Fortune Magazine*, pp. 107–109 ff , December, 1937.

the county was at first the only governmental unit.[1] During the century that has since elapsed, the number of minor political subdivisions has grown until there are now 179 units performing some public function. These units of government are classified as follows:

County	1
Townships	16
Road-building districts	16
Elementary school districts	107
High school districts	16
Non-high school districts	1
Cities and villages	16
Park districts	3
Sanitary districts	2
Forest preserve	1

The cost of local government is tremendous.[2] People are inclined to scrutinize tax rates of national and state governments very carefully, forgetting the excessive cost of their own local government.[3] Actually, 8 per cent of our national income goes to Federal taxes whereas, according to the *Fortune Magazine* article previously cited, 12 per cent goes to state and local governments, chiefly counties, cities, towns, and school districts.

ABUSES OF LOCAL GOVERNMENT

Much attention has been focused upon the problem of local government, especially of the county since it is the chief governmental unit in most rural areas. Numerous studies have called attention to the colossal inefficiency and waste in local government, a waste that has continued so long that public apathy concerning it prevails.[4] Local officers are chosen for personal popularity and influence, not knowledge of their work. There being no central executive on whom to fix responsibility, it is shifted about. Conspicuous waste exists in many phases of county administration and often it is legally sanctioned. In some rural areas it is assumed that anyone can fill a public office satisfactorily, and little criticism is offered of the way county affairs are handled.

The widespread use of the fee system encourages inefficiency.[5] Fees for

[1] H. S. Hicks, *The Wasteful System in Local Government*, p. 3, published jointly by the Illinois Chamber of Commerce, the Aurora Chamber of Commerce, and the Elgin Association of Commerce.

[2] J. T. Askew, "County Consolidation and the Cost of County Government," *The American City*, vol. 49, pp. 56–57, February, 1934.

[3] S. Crowther, "Our Extravagant Counties; Program for Taxation Economy," *Ladies' Home Journal*, vol. 49, pp. 8–9 *ff.*, May, 1932.

[4] A. Shaw, "County Reform in Demand," *Review of Reviews*, vol. 90, p. 49, August, 1934.

[5] Conrad H. Hammar and Glen T. Barton, "The Farmer and the Cost of Local Rural Government in Missouri," p. 46, *Missouri Agricultural Experiment Station Bulletin* 385, 1937.

such things as marriage licenses, the recording of land transfers, contracts, leases, wills, and, in the case of sheriffs or justices of the peace, fees for making arrests, are often allowed.[1]

Much misuse of political power is tolerated by the public. Probably nepotism, *i.e.*, the employment by public officials of relatives to work in their offices, is nowhere more prevalent than in county seats. Flagrant examples of the practice can be observed in local courthouses of many rural counties. One county treasurer employs six of his seven children in his own office; an auditor, elected year after year, always appoints his feeble-minded son as deputy. Time and time again in county offices, one finds an elected officer appointing his wife or daughter as secretary. Usually no one seems concerned, but the taxpayers of the county become greatly excited about problems of government and taxation in the National Capitol.

Wager believes that the lack of centralized authority is more responsible for the deficiencies in county administration than any other single factor.[2] Responsibility is divided; weak men are tempted to be dishonest or encouraged to be extravagant;[3] mistakes are easily concealed;[4] blame is shifted to the innocent. The whole system paralyzes ambition. Often the lack of official headship leaves the way open for a county boss to become entrenched. With offices distributed among his henchmen, the treasury is easily opened for plunder.

Cordell and Cordell suggest that in the average county the taxpayer does not know what to expect from officials whose duties he cannot define.[5] Therefore, when voting, he considers only the personalities of the candidates, not their training or experience.

It is interesting to note that in many counties the same inefficient family has been in office year after year, often unopposed by other candidates. In cases where the law confines the term of office to a limited consecutive period, two families have alternated in office for as many as two generations. Sometimes the families agree that whichever one is elected will appoint the other deputy to the office. In some communities this has come to be ironically called the "crown prince system."

An exhaustive study of a specific system of county government, its per-

[1] H. C. Bradshaw and L. P. Gabbard, "Possible Savings through Changes in Local Government," p. 16, *Texas Agricultural Experiment Station Bulletin* 540, College Station, 1937.

[2] P. W. Wager, "Needed for Every County," *The American City*, vol. 41, pp. 160–161, September, 1929.

[3] H. S. Curtis, "There Is Hope Even for the County," *The American City*, vol. 49, pp. 74–75, September, 1934.

[4] H. P. Jones, "Rural Municipalities of Tomorrow," *Survey*, vol. 67, pp. 37 *ff*., Oct. 1, 1931.

[5] W. and K. Cordell, "Taxpayer, Meet Your County," *Survey Graphic*, vol. 25, pp. 463–466 *ff*., August, 1936.

sonnel, qualifications for office, and expenditures, is that made by Renne for the state of Montana.[1] The situation described is no doubt typical of many counties throughout the nation. He finds that counties with a high property evaluation have comparatively low expenses. There is great variation in the cost per unit of work for various county offices, but almost without exception those counties which have the most experienced and well-qualified personnel show the lowest unit cost. Some counties have high costs because there is not enough work to keep the officers employed. Training and experience of officers are far below a desirable standard. Renne concludes that the greatest weaknesses in Montana county government are: (1) the absence of any effective coordinating agency; (2) the many independent, elective, administrative offices; (3) the lack of special qualifications or training to hold county office, with minor exceptions; (4) the short terms of office; and (5) the numerous counties with small valuation.

QUALIFICATIONS FOR OFFICE

A study of local government in Texas, where there are more than 8,300 governmental units performing one or more services, outlines the qualifications for county office in that state.[2] The authors, commenting on the state constitution, say, "Evidently the framers of the Constitution of 1876 were in full accord with the doctrine that anyone was capable of administering a public office."[3] Although according to the constitution 27 separate offices are required in a county, qualifications are mentioned for only two of these. The county judge is supposed to be informed in the law; the county justice must be a lawyer. No mention is made of experience.

Renne draws similar conclusions for Montana. With the exception of the offices of county attorney, surveyor, and superintendent of schools, the only requirements for county office are that the candidate be 21 years of age, a citizen of the state, and a voter in the county.[4] Concerning the educational qualifications of men holding county offices he finds that approximately half had finished high school but only 16 per cent had had four years in college.[5] The average length of time during which they hold office is five years.

A survey in Michigan revealed that 80 per cent of 295 justices of the peace had no special knowledge of the law and most of them had had only a common school education.[6] Only 21 of these officers exercised any judicial function

[1] R. R. Renne, "Montana County Organization, Services and Costs," *Montana Agricultural Experiment Station Bulletin* 298, Bozeman, 1935.

[2] H. C. Bradshaw and L. P. Gabbard, *op. cit.*

[3] *Ibid.*, p. 13.

[4] R. R. Renne, *op. cit.*

[5] *Ibid.*, p. 18.

[6] E. M. Barrows, "Mosquito District, There She Stands," *New Outlook*, vol. 164, pp. 42–46, August, 1934.

during the year 1932; yet the law requires that the taxpayers go to the expense of electing and installing them.

It must be admitted that there is little training for public office anywhere in American life. Government is not considered a field for professional service; there are no professional standards by which people who hold office can be guided, and the ethics of government are political rather than social. Rural conditions are in many respects worse than urban. As Lancaster remarks,

Conditions in rural areas do not at present favor the building up of a corps of permanent civil servants. Most officers in the county and other typical rural districts continue to be chosen by popular election, as a rule upon a party ballot, and for relatively short terms of office. The only other feasible method of choice would be appointment under some sort of merit system, designed to test the fitness of applicants. But the fact must be faced that the merit system has made little progress outside the urban sections of the country. Generally speaking, the agricultural population has shown little or no interest, if not active hostility, toward proposals to build up a permanent staff of administrators on *any* level of government. The states which have adopted the merit system for filling offices are in the urban and industrial sections of the country, and those counties where it has been introduced are for the most part highly urbanized. "The appointment of officials has seemed to the rural voter one way of enabling a little oligarchy to appoint its favorites and then extend its power, as indeed has often happened." In his own local area the farmer has felt more or less consciously that the retention of the long ballot has increased his control over his local officials. This has perhaps been true in many cases, although in practice it has meant lowered efficiency by removing the barriers between the official and various crude popular notions as to the conduct of the public business. Moreover, the long ballot has often had the effect of turning over the local government to a small group usually referred to as the "courthouse gang" and owing no responsibility anywhere. However, the introduction of the short ballot and the merit system would involve nothing short of a revolution in rural political mores. The average farmer or villager can see no adequate reason why offices should not be "passed around." County, township, and village offices strike him as rather "soft jobs" and after their holders have occupied them for a term or two, the general feeling is likely to be they have had them "long enough," and that someone else should "have a chance" at them.[1]

What can be done to improve rural government?

CONSOLIDATION OF GOVERNMENT UNITS

In many circles there is universal agreement as to the desirability of consolidating local units of government, of enlarging the unit of taxation, and of governmental regulation as a means of increasing efficiency and reducing cost.[2]

[1] Lane W. Lancaster, *Government in Rural America*, pp. 109–110. By permission of D. Van Nostrand Company, Inc., New York, 1937.

[2] *Local Government in New Jersey*, Princeton Local Government Survey, Pocket Report Series, vol. 2, no. 3, July, 1937.

This has been one of the most needed reforms since the automobile and the highway came into general use, perhaps for twenty years; yet by 1937 in only five counties in the nation, two in Tennessee[1] and three in Georgia,[2] had consolidation been adopted.[3]

If one considers the manner in which most of our counties came into existence he begins to understand why it is difficult to consolidate. Counties were divided into small units partly in response to demands of towns that wanted to be county seats. Also, the establishment of new units was a part of the ethos of expansion. Of course, there was some logic in having small counties in the day of horse-and-buggy travel; land changed hands frequently and settlers had need for a county seat close at hand.

Much resistance to county consolidation today comes from small towns that want to retain their position as county seats.[4] An instance in the Far West in 1936–1937 illustrates the vigor with which a county-seat town will fight to avoid relinquishing its status. In a county with only 8,000 population, the courthouse located in a town of 700 population was destroyed by fire. Six miles away is a town of 3,000 population which has long wanted the courthouse. Residents of the county-seat town accused those of the larger town of having deliberately burned the courthouse. The election which followed to decide where the new building was to be located was a militant affair with each side doing its best to rally enough votes from the countryside to obtain the new courthouse.

As would be expected, whenever problems of consolidation arise the most vigorous opponents are the politicians and their friends who have vested interests in retaining their offices and white-collar jobs. Emotional and other more substantial obstacles appear. Most people take pride in their county and do not want to see it lose its identity. Also, there is the problem of disposing of the old courthouse. In some states there are other decided handicaps; for example, in Texas under present laws each county receives the first $50,000 of automobile license fees.[5] If two counties were consolidated half these fees would be lost.

Most authorities agree that the township unit of government should be abolished. The article in *Fortune Magazine* previously cited recommends a central taxing authority so that numerous taxing districts may be made obso-

[1] "Bigger and Cheaper Counties," *Literary Digest*, vol. 107, p. 13, Oct. 18, 1930.

[2] E. H. Bradley, "Merger of Three Counties Shows Tangible Results," *Public Management*, vol. 19, pp. 215–216, July, 1937.

[3] James E. Pate, "Trends in County Government," *Social Forces*, vol. 16, pp. 418–426, March, 1938.

[4] L. G. Harvey, "In the Name of Local Pride," *Catholic World*, vol. 140, pp. 673–676, March, 1935.

[5] H. C. Bradshaw and L. P. Gabbard, *op. cit.*, p. 89.

lete. Some go so far as to suggest that town and county should be consolidated, thus doing away with the separate government for the small town.[1]

Manny advocates the "rural municipality," a unit which in some cases would consist of a trade center and its surrounding territory, and in others of an open-country neighborhood centering about a school, church, or crossroads hamlet.[2] Under this form of organization the county would become but an administrative unit of the state with few powers of local self-government, whereas the incorporated rural municipality would possess broad powers of local self-government. He sees in this plan an ideal method by which an effective type of rural social organization might be achieved.

CHANGES IN THE FORM OF COUNTY GOVERNMENT

Many have been the recommendations for a change in form of local government. Usually these call for the centralization of authority in a county manager or county executive who would be made responsible for all the activities of the county. The few cases where this plan has been put into practice show that it results in increased services and decreased costs.[3] However, by 1937, only a few counties in the nation had any form of local organization with fixed executive responsibility.

In a number of states there are legal obstructions to reform in that many elective county offices are specifically mentioned in the state constitution, which means that it is difficult to make changes without a change in law.[4] Moreover, there is a deep-rooted resistance to the development of centralized administration of the county. Rural people do not trust centralized authority and oppose changes that they do not understand.

More efficient systems of bookkeeping may require greater initial investments in machinery than rural counties can afford; even where they could be afforded the outlay of a large sum for equipment in the speculative hope of future economy does not appeal to taxpayers. Demands for funds to be spent on reforms are likely to be resisted, whereas customary waste goes on year after year unnoticed.

In addition to centralization of authority, the creation of a merit system for certain county offices, the removal from the partisan ballot of offices such as that of the county superintendent of schools, the lengthening of terms of office, and the decreasing of the number of elective offices by the short ballot are possible reforms.

[1] W. and K. Cordell, *op. cit.*

[2] T. B. Manny, *Rural Municipalities*, chap. 26, D. Appleton-Century Company, Inc., New York, 1930.

[3] James E. Pate, *op. cit.*

[4] H. P. Jones, "Model Law for County Manager Government Now Available," *The American City*, vol. 43, p. 118. August, 1930.

Summarizing, among the solutions suggested for problems of rural government are the enlargement of governmental areas through the consolidation of counties, or towns and counties, reorganizing boundaries to fit the scheme of modern transportation and communication;[1] the shifting of functions from the

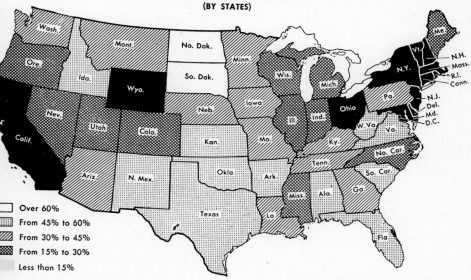

PER CENT OF TOTAL POPULATION
WITHOUT PUBLIC LIBRARY SERVICE, 1943
(BY STATES)

Over 60%
From 45% to 60%
From 30% to 45%
From 15% to 30%
Less than 15%

American Library Association

In many states more than 30 per cent of the population is without public library service. Rural people are usually the ones without library service in any state.

local area to the larger governmental unit for the sake of economy and efficiency, and the abolition of units of government, notably the township; improvement in administrative methods and in personnel by raising the requirements for office; the lengthening of tenure of office; and the adoption of the merit system.[2]

EXTENDING SERVICE FUNCTIONS THROUGH COUNTY COOPERATION

Most of the attention given county government in recent years has dealt with the problem of decreasing expenditures rather than of increasing services,

[1] H. C. Bradshaw suggests that each Texas county should have a minimum of 20,000 pouplation if county government is to be efficiently administered. "Reorganization of Counties," *Journal of Farm Economics*, vol. 19, pp. 741–749, August, 1937.

[2] For a critical summary of difficulties likely to be encountered in various approaches to reform in county government, see Lane W. Lancaster, *op. cit.*, chap. 15.

due to the fact that all counties during the depression period of the early thirties bore an excess burden of taxation. Most of them were forced to appeal to state and Federal governments for carrying on needed public functions and some were threatened with bankruptcy. Nonetheless there is definite need for an expansion of county services in rural areas of the nation, for in many cases the county is the ideal base for library service, public health service, hospitals, government agricultural programs, welfare and relief units, and community organization work in a variety of fields. Where the county is not sufficiently large to support efficient programs of the above character, a group of counties may be made the unit for such services.

Take the matter of rural libraries, for example. Of the 3,072 counties in the United States only about 600 have county-wide library systems serving both open-country and village inhabitants.[1] The American Library Association reports that in 1943 more than 600 counties—roughly one in five—were without a single public library within their boundaries. Some 35,000,000 persons in the nation were without library service, almost 90 per cent of whom were living in rural areas. A graphic summary of states showing the proportions of their populations without library service is given on the map on page 362. The Dakotas had over 60 per cent of their people outside public library service areas. Wyoming, with an equally sparse population, however, by a different system of library administration, had placed more than 85 per cent of its people in library districts.

Obviously here is a striking example of a vital need for expanded government service in the rural community. But many individual counties cannot finance an adequate central library with convenient branch stations. But a group of counties consolidating into a region for this particular purpose could do so. Branch libraries conveniently scattered throughout the region or district could make available to each neighborhood the full resources of the library system without excessive cost to any county.

Similarly in many fields such a district or regional grouping of counties for specific services is a practical way of meeting new needs. In many sparsely populated counties public health, public welfare, hospitalization, and other services could thus be provided; they can never be provided by any one county acting alone.

A TRANSFER OF FUNCTION TO LARGER UNITS OF GOVERNMENT

In spite of the fact that consolidation of counties has not made much progress, many functions of local government have been transferred to larger

---

[1] *The Equal Chance, American Library Association*, Chicago, 1943. For an earlier study, see Louis R. Wilson, *The Geography of Reading*, American Library Association and University of Chicago Press, Chicago, 1938.

units.[1] The shift was forced in many cases because of lack of funds. During the depression the state or the nation stepped in to finance and therefore to control many functions, such as road building, relief,[2] health supervision, the development of parks and playgrounds and airports, flood control, and housing, which were once handled almost exclusively by local units. The county commissioners, having exhausted their funds early in the depression, had to sit back and watch the emergency relief units take charge; the county engineer likewise gave way to the relief organization's project man; the county highway department shifted road building to relief agencies, as did the village street commissioners. The private charities—Red Cross, Salvation Army, sisterhoods, brotherhoods, and churches—declined in importance as relief units. There were jealousies and bitter words between the old and the emergency groups, but since the organization with the money held the whip hand, established organizations had to hibernate.[3]

Several states have stepped in to put limitations on local government or to set standards, sometimes by law and sometimes by requiring that the local unit comply with state regulations in order to receive grants in aid. These requirements pertain to such matters as supervision of schools, roads, and health, limitations on the amount of debt that can be acquired, and uniform methods of accounting. The principle of centralized government has been applied in many new relationships with counties.

Some recommendations have called for extensive reform. The New York State Planning Board suggests that certain submarginal land areas be turned into state administrative units and that local governments be done away with entirely there.[4] No doubt many sparsely populated areas could be handled successfully as state administrative units by setting up a state commission to manage all matters pertaining to them.

Zimmerman has traced the changing functions of local government in rural communities in England and America, observing the tendency of functions to pass from local community control to centralized control, from diversified adaptation to local conditions to standardized practices of urban control.[5] He believes that, although a pathological situation may exist with too much

[1] R. H. Tucker, "Virginia Improves Its County Government," *Review of Reviews*, vol. 86, pp. 45–46, September, 1932.

[2] For a detailed study of the problem of public welfare as it has affected county finance in rural areas, see Herman Kehili, *Receipts and Expenditures of Oregon Counties, 1928–1937,* Bureau of Municipal Research, University of Oregon, October, 1938.

[3] See the writer's "The New Deal and Rural Life," *American Sociological Review*, vol. 1, pp. 592–603, August, 1936.

[4] *Annual Report of the State Planning Council for the Division of State Planning*, 1936, p. 81, Albany, 1937. T. B. Manny, *op. cit.*, chap. 16, suggests this possibility also.

[5] C. C. Zimmerman, *The Changing Community*, pp. 8–10, 50–51, 391–395, 649, Harper & Brothers, New York, 1938.

localization, too much centralization is also a disease and that it is now developing in much of Western civilization. This process of decay of local self-government starts with state and Federal aid which is a preface to standardization. The new agencies of larger units of government become institutionalized in the local community and become a permanent structure. The local communities yield because they find outside assistance the best short-time way out of difficulties. Soon local initiative and inventiveness disappear and local, county, and regional administrative bodies become more and more subservient to central orders.

This is a point of view well worth considering in the transfer of certain kinds of local functions to state or Federal jurisdiction. Sometimes greater efficiency of administration may be gained at the expense of local initiative and pride in self-sufficiency.[1] In the long run this aspect of social cost may far outweigh the gain.

GOVERNMENT AS A TOOL FOR SOCIAL MANIPULATION

In the attitude of rural people toward local government one sees at many points a lack of appreciation of the power of control a man may exercise through his government. In urban-industrial relationships consciousness of political power is highly developed as exhibited in the effective use of lobbies, the sponsoring of legislation in favor of vested interest groups, and in many other aspects of behavior. The individual urbanite is much more likely to resort to law as a device for getting what he wants than is the ruralist.

An account of an automobile insurance adjuster suggests the nature of this difference in the use of law as a technique for gaining personal ends. His experience has been that the rural person is much less likely to claim damages in case of an accident than the urban person. The latter is likely to be familiar with his rights as an insurance claimant and to take full advantage of them, even pushing his claims on weak evidence if he thinks he can gain by it in court. In farming areas attitudes of dependability, honesty, and fair dealing predominate, with the result that suits for damages are few. He concludes,

Claim adjusting, I believe it may rightly be said, is fundamentally an urban business. Not only is the overwhelming majority of the personnel engaged in it of urban extraction, but the great percentage of the persons with whom the adjuster deals are residents of urban communities. This is true for the reason that the larger number of automobile accidents occur within the limits of cities. . . . Added to that is the fact that the urban mind is much more claim-conscious than the rural; urban people are much more aware of the possibility of extracting money from the mere having of an accident, while the rural person is more disposed to pay for his own damage and forget about it. Particu-

[1] Some of the writer's observations along this line are recorded in his "On the Evolution of Dependency Mores in the Primary Group under Federal Relief Agencies," *Social Forces*, pp. 556–559, May, 1935.

larly is this true in cases other than those involving automobiles. If Mrs. Jones of the farm or small town high-dives ungracefully over some merchant's poorly-lighted display, she is likely to brush herself hurriedly and hope nobody saw her, but if Mrs. Smith of X city turns her ankle and falls on a dry sidewalk, she promptly begins speculating as to whom she can most successfully sue: the city, the property owner, or the tenant. She usually winds up by suing all three.[1]

More and more in large-scale social relationships, the processes of law are being recognized as devices for protection, for regulation, and for realization of desired objectives on the part of special groups. Observations seem to indicate that throughout our society urban people much more than rural people are taking advantage of the law as a device for manipulating social affairs in line with their own personal or class interests. Increasingly, however, farmers are being forced to resort to politico-legal devices for realization of objectives.

Throughout the course of our national history various farmers' organizations have sought basic reforms and in so doing have at times developed programs designed to obtain class objectives.[2] Farmers have, however, been much less interested in the broader aspects of government than certain other vested interest groups in American society. It seems likely that in the future farmers as an occupational class will increasingly look toward government as a means for achieving desired ends. The New Deal epoch, probably more than any other similar period in our history, drove home to the average farmer on the family farm the consciousness of the power he might realize through the use of governmental channels. At that time he became accustomed to direct contact with the Federal government and learned something of the importance of politics in the affairs of the average man's life, of the importance of governmental manipulation of production and prices to his own economic well-being. He saw government activities in operation in his own locality in the conservation of resources, in the adjustment of complicated production schedules, in the extension of relief to the dependent, and in the resettlement of those who had been defeated by nature. This extension of a free hand by the Federal government into the intimate circles of their own personal interests no doubt created an awareness of political power among farmers in America such as they have not previously had.

Not only did these humanitarian programs of the government touch prosperous citizens of the rural community but in the form of socialized medicine, recreational activities sponsored by relief agencies, adult education by these same agencies, relief to the hungry, relief to distressed school districts, and various other such activities, they brought to the underprivileged

---

[1] This class paper was written by a man who for some years had been engaged in insurance adjusting work in rural and urban territories of the state of Montana.

[2] For a study of farmer movements see C. C. Taylor, *Rural Sociology*, rev. ed., chap. 28, Harper & Brothers, New York, 1933.

of rural areas a taste of some of the privileges that American democracy has always stood for but not always realized. Many of these programs introduced into rural areas added tone to life and will not soon be forgotten even though they were superimposed from the outside rather than conceived locally. Certain of these services will continue to be demanded and probably will have to be supplied through state, Federal, or local agencies. Many of them probably can be adequately supported and directed only by a Federal agency. The tendency of rural groups to look to the Federal government for one service or another and for protection of their interests and promotion of their programs will undoubtedly increase.

The full implications of these newer movements of a centralized government to social life on the farm, to future political action of farmers, and to local autonomy cannot as yet be fully conceived. Certainly they are of considerable significance in the contemporary scene.

QUESTIONS FOR REVIEW AND DISCUSSION

1. What seems to be the primary purpose of rural government? How does this compare with the purpose of urban government?
2. Contrast rural and urban attitudes toward law.
3. Show how local administrative units have multiplied.
4. Summarize the abuses of local government. Cite reasons why they are tolerated.
5. What are the usual qualifications for county office?
6. Is the consolidation of counties a practical approach to problems of county government? Justify your answer.
7. Why do small counties persist in a day of rapid travel?
8. What changes in form of county government have been recommended?
9. Illustrate the means by which counties could improve their public services by cooperation.
10. Trace the effect of the depression in shifting governmental functions from local to state and Federal government.
11. Discuss the merits and the demerits of centralized government.
12. Explain how various groups use government to achieve class objectives. Might the farmer exercise greater power through government if he sensed the possibilities as some other groups do?

COLLATERAL READING

Cole, W. E., and H. P. Crowe: *Recent Trends in Rural Planning*, chaps. 9 and 15, Prentice-Hall, Inc., New York, 1937.

Lancaster, Lane W.: *Government in Rural America*, D. Van Nostrand Company, Inc., New York, 1937.

Loomis, C. P., E. de S. Brunner, and D. M. Davidson, Jr.: "What the Farmer Is Thinking About," *Rural Sociology*, vol. 3, pp. 84–88, March, 1938.

Manny, T. B.: *Rural Municipalities*, D. Appleton-Century Company, Inc., New York, 1930.

Nelson, Lowry: "National Policies and Rural Organization," *Rural Sociology*, vol. 1, pp. 73–89, March, 1936.

Pate, James E.: "Trends in County Government," *Social Forces*, vol. 16, pp. 418–426, March, 1938.

Renne, Roland R.: "Montana County Organization, Services and Costs," *Montana Agricultural Experiment Station Bulletin* 298, Bozeman, 1935.

Sanderson, Dwight: *Rural Sociology and Rural Social Organization*, chap. 19, John Wiley & Sons, Inc., New York, 1942.

Sorokin, P. A., C. C. Zimmerman, and C. J. Galpin: *A Systematic Source Book in Rural Sociology*, vol. 2, chap. 16, University of Minnesota Press, Minneapolis, 1931.

Wilson, Louis R.: *The Geography of Reading*, American Library Association and University of Chicago Press, Chicago, 1938.

Zimmerman, C. C.: *The Changing Community*, pp. 8–10, 50–51, 391–395, 649, Harper & Brothers, New York, 1938.

CHAPTER 25

ECONOMIC VALUES IN THE NEW STANDARD OF LIVING

HYPOTHESIS

ECONOMIC factors always play an important role in the life of a social group, but their relative importance to the standard of living depends upon the system of values that the group places foremost. Economic factors mean most to a people when they pave the way to the attainment of a large number of the total satisfactions that enter into their standard of living. In some societies many life objectives may be realized without the individual's having attained even average economic success as defined by his own culture. Pre-westernized Oriental cultures were in distinct contrast to Occidental culture on this point. In them religious, philosophical, speculative, and other subjective values were placed above economic goods in the realm of coveted values, as contrasted to Western societies where life goals have been built so completely about pecuniary values that economic factors have been pivotal in attaining most life objectives.

In Occidental culture, status, success, achievement, and emulation—values which our competitive society ranks first—are attained most certainly through the accumulation of economic goods. Through economic goods in turn, numerous secondary values are attainable such as leisure, luxury, display, health, and comfort. Pecuniary values thus have come to represent many values of a more fundamental sort.

American culture is in a broad sense a unit, with both urban and rural phases of it rating pecuniary factors very high in their life schemes. It seems, however, that economic factors have been somewhat more evident in the urban scheme and that they have paved the way to a realization of more life values there than in rural culture. Rural culture is none the less strongly motivated by economic forces, and there, as in urban culture, they have a direct bearing on the standard of living maintained and the status that the individual achieves in his social setting. But basic and significant differences have existed in the direction that economic interest has taken in the traditional rural and in the urban scheme.

In the rural scheme the emphasis commonly has been on production and on the accumulation of the means for production. Farm land, machinery, and livestock—these have been foremost in the social economy as contrasted to consumption in the urban scheme.

These traditional differences have for all practical purposes made economic factors mean something quite different in rural and in urban society. In the farm community one achieves status primarily by what he acquires in the way of flocks and herds, land and buildings. From the time of the Hebrew patriarchs to the present this has been true. In urban society status is achieved only in part by production; more important is the front maintained by conspicuous consumption in clothes, food, home, furniture, automobiles, distinctive amusements, philanthropy, employment at tasks that do not involve making money. Under such a regime the standard of living comes to be measured chiefly in terms of the consumable goods that a family can buy.

The general thesis to be demonstrated in this chapter is that the recent trend of farm culture has been toward an emphasis on consumption as the important factor in the standard of living; that the drift in this direction has been so prominent that we seem to be rapidly approaching a situation in which economic resources available to the average family on the farm are not sufficient for realizing the objectives of the new standard of living; that such values are attainable only through cash income, not through work, thrift, and simple living; and that, therefore, if the farmer is to attain them, devices for improving his cash income must be employed. Having developed this thesis briefly, we shall summarize some recent programs and projects in the economic field that are designed to increase the amount of income the farmer can expend for consumable goods.

THE INCREASING EMPHASIS ON CONSUMPTION IN FARM CULTURE

A basic reason for the emphasis on production in the rural economic enterprise in the past has been that farmers consumed a considerable part of that which they produced. Today, with the increase in consumption of merchandised goods, they seek a money income to purchase these goods.

One important index of consumption tendencies in the farm community is the trend of merchandising in the small town. The many studies in this field[1] leave no doubt that farm people in the more prosperous areas of the country are participating more and more in the luxuries of urban living. The

[1] For studies of merchandising trends in farm trade centers see C. R. Hoffer,"Changes in the Retail and Service Facilities of Rural Trade Centers in Michigan, 1900 and 1930," *Michigan Agricultural Experiment Station Special Bulleten* 261, East Lansing, 1935; H. B. Price and C. R. Hoffer, "Services of Rural Trade Centers in Distribution of Farm Supplies," *Minnesota Agricultural Experiment Station Bulletin* 249, St. Paul, 1928; C. C. Zimmerman, "Farm Trade Centers in Minnesota, 1905 to 1929," *Minnesota Agricultural Experiment Station Bulletin* 269, St. Paul, 1930; J. H. Kolb, "Service Relations of Town and Country," *Wisconsin Agricultural Experiment Station Bulletin* 58, Madison, 1923; Paul H. Landis, "South Dakota Town-country Trade Relations, 1901–1931," *South Dakota Agricultural Experiment Station Bulletin* 264, Brookings, 1932.

number of functions performed in the home has declined and the farmer, like the urbanite, has come to depend more fully upon stores for food and clothing.

One need only to glance at merchandising trends of the farm trade center during the period of this century to sense the extent of change. As we saw in an earlier chapter, general stores which sold everything from nursing bottles to spectacles have greatly declined, and in their place, in the larger towns, have come urban department stores which serve the same needs on a much more elaborate scale. Millinery stores, dry-goods stores, and tailor shops have declined in number as ready-to-wear clothing stores have come to take their place. In the small town the luxuriant growth of bakeries, grocery stores, butcher shops (most of which now get their meat from a national distributor) testify that the baker's loaf, the butcher's cut, and the store's factory-canned, boxed, ready-to-eat foods have gained in popularity among farm people.

These merchandising trends, reflected in all farm trade centers, indicate the shifting of home enterprise on the farm to factory, wholesale house and store; the growth of creameries, bakeries, and the like mark the passing of what were once arts of the home. In many farm homes, as in city homes, the pantry has disappeared as trips to town have become easier and more frequent and farmers have become accustomed to making larger cash expenditures for food.

With all this luxury of living has come the new high standard of dying. The farmer's small town now also boasts of a lavish funeral home, and often has two or three in competition for the trade, and the larger trade center has its shop distributing ornately polished tombstones.

The old hitching posts, watering troughs, harness shops, livery stables, and blacksmith shops have gone. On almost every corner stands a modernized brick or stucco cubicle with staff waiting to serve the farmer-owner of a new streamlined automobile with free water, air, windshield and headlight wash, to sell him gasoline, oil, grease, accessories, and antifreeze; and in the middle of almost every block are salesrooms and garages where dealers sell and mechanics fix the respective makes of cars, and where every November new models are introduced to the once slow-moving, slow-changing town and countryside.

Another important index of consumption tendencies is the trend in installment buying. Farmers have always carried considerable debt, but this debt has centered first of all in land and secondly in other factors of production—machinery, livestock, and other chattels, and not in items for personal and family consumption. While no extensive data are at hand, it seems that farmers are participating increasingly in installment buying of consumable goods. A few years ago two large mail-order houses, that have always depended on farmers and people of small towns for most of their business, began offering a number of their items on installment terms. Education of farm people and increased contact with advertising media are no doubt factors in increasing desire to the extent that it leads to mortgaging future income for the purchase of consumable goods.[1]

There is little doubt but that farmers are spending an increasing proportion of their income for consumable items and that they are consuming an increasing quantity of manufactured goods. How much income do they have to spend?

INCOME OF THE FARM FAMILY

In a culture where satisfactions depend to a considerable degree on consumption, relative amount of income is of prime importance. Briefly what is the situation with regard to the farmer's income as compared to that of other groups in the United States?

Income varies greatly with the size of the community. The modal income of a sample of people in a metropolitan community was between $1,000 and $1,500. At the other extreme was the farm group with a modal income of $500 to $1,000. The farm group had the largest proportion of incomes of under $500 and the smallest proportion of over $5,000 (see page 378).[2]

A more significant comparison can be made in terms of occupational groups. The pictographic description on page 379 of median incomes of these various groups shows that the farmer was lowest both in median and mean income. The farm group had the highest proportion with incomes under $1,000 of the occupational classes listed and, excepting the wage-earning class, the lowest proportion with incomes of over $5,000. Since all these comparisons exclude the relief group, they show a somewhat better condition than actually existed during the 1930's. The situation, of course, varied markedly in all factors from region to region.[3]

The total value of products raised on farms varies greatly from farm to farm. An analysis based on total gross produce both for sale and home use in 1929 gives a striking picture of the range in values (see page 380). Observe that over one-fourth of the farmers in the United States at that time produced

[1] See Lowry Nelson and N. I. Burt, "Influence of Formal Schooling on Consumption Tendencies in Two Rural Communities," *Publications of the American Sociological Society*, vol. 23, pp. 255–260, 1929.

[2] This series of charts by the National Resources Planning Board is based on a nation-wide study of 300,000 families. The income is that received from all sources, "from the net earnings of different members, from profits, dividends, interest, and rent, from pensions, annuities, and benefits, from gifts used for current living expenses, from the occupancy of owned homes, and—for rural families—from home-grown food and other farm products used by the family." Income was measured before payment of income taxes.

[3] For a comparison of incomes by regions see *Consumer Incomes in the United States*, pp. 22–23, National Resources Planning Board, Washington, D. C. For a comparison of Negro and white incomes by regions, see pp. 28–29.

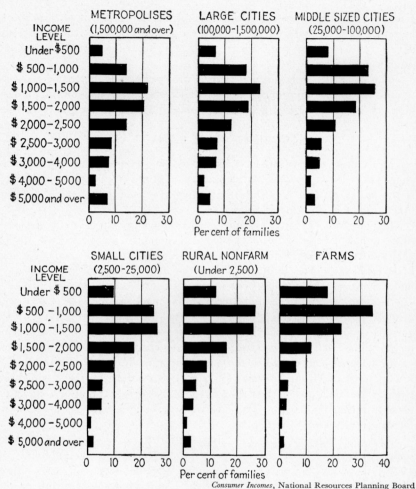

Consumer Incomes, National Resources Planning Board

INCOME DISTRIBUTION OF NONRELIEF FAMILIES IN SIX TYPES OF COMMUNITIES

Average incomes increase with an increase in urbanization. The largest incomes are found in the metropolis; the smallest on farms. Seven per cent of metropolitan families receive incomes of $5,000 and over as compared to slightly over one per cent of farm families. The median for farm families is $965, for those in metropolises $1,730. There is a graduation downward in family income from the metropolis through each of the smaller classes of cities. A conspicuously large number of farm families are massed in the low-income brackets, 52 per cent receiving below $1,000.

These comparisons are for 1935–1936, when incomes for all groups were low. The ratios shown are probably typical of the chronically low farm income. (See p. 381 for comparative incomes for nonfarm and farm groups to 1946.)

each less than $601 worth of products. Over 400,000 farmers produced each less than $251 worth. The modal group produced $601 to $1,000 worth. A total of over one-half of the farmers produced under $1,001 worth, four of every five under $2,501 worth, and only 15 in 1,000 reported more than $10,000 worth of products. Commenting on this chart the authors quote a

AVERAGE INCOMES OF NONRELIEF FAMILIES
IN SEVEN OCCUPATIONAL GROUPS
1935-36

EACH DISC REPRESENTS $1,000 OF INCOME FOR THE YEAR

Consumer Incomes, National Resources Planning Board

Farming brings the lowest average economic returns of any of the major occupations in the United States. The median income of farmers is $965, the mean income $1,259. At the opposite extreme is the independent professional occupation with a median income of $3,540 and a mean income of $6,734. More than 85 per cent of the farm families fall below $2,000 in annual income.

publication of the U.S. Department of Agriculture to the effect that "more than a million farming people in the United States have a level of living probably little if any better than that of the average Chinese farmer in the Yangtze Valley."[1]

The Brookings Institution compared the incomes of the farm population in various regions as of 1929 in terms of per capita income.[2] For the farm

[1] *Miscellaneous Publication 266*, p. 70, U.S. Department of Agriculture, Washington, D. C.

[2] M. Leven, H. G. Moulton, and C. Warburton, *America's Capacity to Consume*, p. 173, Brookings Institution, Washington, D. C., 1934.

population of the continental United States in that year it was $273 as compared to an average of $750 for the total population. The contrast between incomes of farmers in the various regions was equally striking. Regions ranked as follows:[1]

Region	Per Capita Farm Income
Pacific	$945
Mountain	489
Middle Atlantic	401
East North Central	290
Southwest	281
West North Central	256
Southeast	163
Continental United States	273

U.S. Department of Agriculture

DISTRIBUTION OF FARMS IN THE UNITED STATES BY VALUE OF PRODUCTS SOLD AND CONSUMED IN 1929

More than one-fourth of the farmers reported a gross production of less than $601 worth of products for sale and for home use. Four out of five reported less than $2,501 worth of products. Some 400,000 farmers produced $250 worth, or less, of products during the year.

The long-time trend of farm income in ratio to nonfarm income is shown (opposite page) in terms of the actual per capita income of farm and nonfarm groups, and of a parity index. Even though the parity ratio is based on marked

[1] *Ibid.*

FARM AND NONFARM PER CAPITA NET INCOME, 1910 TO 1946, PER CENT FARM PER CAPITA
NET INCOME IS OF NONFARM AND PARITY RATIO OF FARM AND NONFARM INCOME*

Year	Per capita net income			
	Income of farm persons	Income of non-farm persons	Income of farm persons, per cent nonfarm	Parity income ratio, 1910–1914 = 100
1910.......	$139	$ 482	29	105
1911.......	122	468	26	95
1912.......	135	483	28	101
1913.......	136	521	26	95
1914.......	140	484	29	105
1915.......	135	502	27	97
1916.......	155	580	27	97
1917.......	258	640	40	146
1918.......	304	671	45	164
1919.......	319	762	42	152
1920.......	265	878	30	109
1921.......	119	720	17	60
1922.......	153	718	21	77
1923.......	180	815	22	80
1924.......	180	792	23	82
1925.......	223	812	27	100
1926.......	216	858	25	91
1927.......	209	820	25	92
1928.......	222	830	27	97
1929.......	223	871	26	93
1930.......	170	761	22	81
1931.......	114	605	19	68
1932.......	74	442	17	61
1933.......	93	419	22	81
1934.......	111	488	23	83
1935.......	159	540	29	107
1936.......	171	626	27	99
1937.......	197	671	29	107
1938.......	165	622	26	96
1939.......	173	663	26	95
1940.......	177	721	25	88
1941.......	258	853	30	109
1942.......	389	1,060	37	132
1943.......	530	1,259	42	151
1944.......	530	1,326	40	144
1945.......	544	1,314	41	149
1946.......	620	1,326	47	168

*Harry C. Norcross, "Net Income Per Person on Farms," *The Agricultural Situation* vol. 31, pp. 5–6, October, 1947.

At only a few periods have farmers achieved anywhere near parity of income with non-farm people, as parity is defined here, *i.e.*, the ratio prevailing in 1910–1914. Rarely, except in wartime, have farmers exceeded this parity index. During the years 1916–1920, the farmers were far above parity. Then came the crash of 1920 when they dropped to 60 per cent of parity. World War II again placed farmers far above the 1910–1914 parity level. In 1946, farmers had the highest parity index in the history of American agriculture, 168. The early months of 1948 brought a rapid decline in the price of agricultural commodities probably indicating that the farmer's income will drop before that of other elements in the population, as was the case following World War I.

In actual dollars, the per capita income of farm people has always been low. Compare the actual differences for the period on which the index is based. Even in 1948, the farmer's per capita income was only $620, or 47 per cent of that of nonfarm people who had a per capita income of $1,326.

difference in actual income (1910–1914 per capita farm income was less than 30 per cent of per capita nonfarm income), only during war have farmers consistently achieved even the parity ratio. In 1946, when farm prices were near the peak of the World War II period, farmers had a parity index of 168, which was unusually favorable, but their actual per capita income was only 47 per cent that of the nonfarm person, $620 compared to $1,326.

For a period of almost twenty years problems of farm income have been made matters of national concern to the extent that the income of the farmer is manipulated by government policy which attempts to maintain a parity between farm prices and the prices of those industrial goods and services which farmers in a market economy must purchase.

Since it appears likely that national agricultural policy will have more to do with real farm income in the years immediately ahead, and no doubt into the long-time future as well, these policies and their social implication deserve attention here, even though they are primarily in the field of economics rather than sociology.

THE DEVELOPMENT OF NATIONAL AGRICULTURAL POLICY

Farming has been and still is to a large extent a familistic rather than a corporation enterprise; the farm is the home and the home is the farm. The family head is proprietor, marketing agent, and husbandman; the family is identified with the work enterprise. Such a system of organization is ineffective in a world where production has become less important to income than the regulation of production with reference to market demands. Corporate organization is much more efficient than familistic organization in the manipulation of production and the control of marketing. For this reason agriculture tends to operate at near full capacity regardless of economic conditions. Whether prosperity or depression prevails, the number of acres of farm land in operation and the volume of production varies comparatively little. Approximately six million farm operators each plans and carries out his own economic enterprise. Control of production is, therefore, impossible on a national scale as far as farmers themselves are concerned. Moreover, the attempts of any one farmer to affect the national output of a particular crop is ineffective because he represents at best such a small part of the total number of operators.

In the past industry has been able to regulate its productive output in relation to consumer demands. The United States Steel Corporation, for example, during the depression of the 1930's reduced steel production to one fourth of the 1929 level, and correspondingly reduced its overhead costs. The price of steel fluctuated scarcely at all while farm crops dropped to a fraction of their former value. Centralized control in the steel industry makes this possible, a small board of directors controlling the operation of great steel empires such as the United States Steel Corporation. A few leading steel companies dominate the productive output of the entire nation.

In order to regulate agricultural production and thereby affect price, the Federal government has entered the field as coordinator, thereby superimposing upon the highly individualistic private enterprises of farming a system of government supervision centering in the United States Department of Agriculture. Depression activities of the 1930's culminated in the creation of the Agricultural Adjustment Administration which worked at the problem of agricultural adjustment through trying to reduce crop surpluses, and thereby raising prices. It operated through establishing national quotas for leading crops, second state quotas, third county quotas, and finally quotas for each individual farm. In order to reduce the surplus of foods and thereby increase prices of the main crops each operator who signed up was expected to reduce his acreage by the required ratio. The amount of land he was allotted for a particular crop was determined by his previous record of crop acreage. The government achieved his cooperation through offering incentive payments which rewarded him for not planting certain acreages in the crops of which there was a surplus.

Leading economists now look upon production control as an undesirable method of bringing about agricultural adjustment.[1] They point out that the depression program of the Agricultural Adjustment Administration for the most part failed to achieve the goal of decreased production. Data developed by Schultz, presented in the table on page 384, show that while acreage reductions were brought about, the reduction of production was actually not achieved, except in the case of cotton. Farmers put their better acreage in the crop of which there was a surplus, thereby compensating for the loss of acreage, Major benefits went to large operators.

The AAA during the depression decade did accomplish something for soil conservation, and viewed from a sociological and psychological angle, the AAA program was and is a remarkable achievement, bringing the farmer, as a class, for the first time directly to grips with the problem of social manipulation of the market to his advantage. The AAA is of further significance in that it has achieved a level of farmer cooperation never before realized in the nation. Farmers not only help plan national policy, but in every local community are the agents defining their problem and enforcing programs adopted through their local committees.

During the war the emphasis in agricultural adjustment gradually shifted toward increasing production, especially of certain crops which were needed

---

[1] *Postwar Agricultural Policy*, Report of the Committee on Postwar Agricultural Policy of the Association of Land-grant Colleges and Universities, (Distributed by most state agricultural experiment stations) October, 1944; also Theodore W. Schultz, *Agriculture In An Unstable Economy*, McGraw-Hill Book Company, Inc., New York, 1945.

to provide deficient foods and fibers. These goals were readily achieved by price supports which in advance guaranteed the farmer a minimum price for the products. As a part of the incentive the government also pledged itself to continue price supports for a two-year period following January 1 after the official declaration of the cessation of hostilities. This became, by presidential declaration, Jan. 1, 1947.

PER CENT CHANGE IN ACREAGES AND IN PRODUCTION UNDER AAA POLICIES, 1931–1933 AND 1940–1942*

Crop	Per cent reduction in acreage	Per cent change in production
Corn	20	+ 5
Wheat	13	+21
Cotton	38	−17
Tobacco	18	+ 4
Total	21	

* Data from Theodore W. Schultz, *Agriculture in an Unstable Economy*, pp. 171–172, McGraw-Hill Book Company, Inc., New York, 1945.

Leading economists, looking ahead, believe that the emphasis in the future in agricultural policy should be placed upon full production and let price seek whatever level it will. They recognize that farmers cannot live under such a regime in a depression period so recommend measures whereby the farmer can operate through reimbursements from the public treasury. Some recommend that the farmer be reimbursed merely for the difference between sale price of products and the cost of producing them.[1] Others suggest that the farmer be reimbursed for the difference between the sale price and the pre-depression price for particular products.[2] They believe that full production is desirable since it will provide cheap food for consumers during depression. The approach of the 1930's, *i.e.*, limiting production and attempting thereby to raise prices, if successful, penalizes all classes by maintaining a higher price for food, thus limiting the food supply for the masses and threatening the national diet.

Along with full production they stress the importance of measures to stimulate the consumption of agricultural products. Subsidized consumption would take the form of free-school and in-factory lunches, food-stamp plans, and other such measures designed to improve the diet of the American public and at the same time to stimulate the use of food products.

There will be a great deal of discussion in the future of what is a desirable

[1] *Postwar Agricultural Policy, op. cit.*
[2] Schultz, *op. cit.*

agricultural policy with regard to production, prices, and incentives to consumption. Whether the views expressed above will be followed, or whether the nation will revert to an economy of scarcity remains to be seen. Of this much, however, we may be certain, there will be agricultural policies federally designed and federally administrated, whereby agriculture will receive centralized supervision provided by the government. This is true because there is no other way by which supervision can be provided, and supervision is inevitably necessary.

AGRICULTURAL POLICY IN THE WORLD SETTING

The Malthusian fear of overpopulation has long since passed from the Western World. All Western European nations in the center of urban-industrial influences are either experiencing or are on the verge of population decline. The birth rate has been brought so completely under control that the threat of food shortage, except in wartime, no longer exists. The perfection of agricultural equipment, the improvement of soil fertility, crop development, and improved livestock breeds have placed the Western World in a position where huge surpluses of food and fibre will continue to be produced. The Western World will, therefore, face the necessity of some kind of adjustment in the field of agriculture.

It is true that great areas in the Orient face chronic food shortage and famine and will continue to do so. If economic machinery and social policies could be developed whereby agricultural surpluses of the Western World could find a market there, problems of agricultural adjustment would disappear, but there is in sight no economic machinery which would make this kind of distribution of agricultural surpluses possible except on a strictly relief basis.

It is doubtful that it would be wise to distribute food wholesale, on a relief basis, to the great areas of the Oriental World, where millions are chronically undernourished, until these nations are ready to adopt Western ideas of birth control. Death rates would be temporarily reduced, making for the survival of more child bearers for the next generation, thus aggravating further problems of misery and want. Any policy for extensive food distribution in Oriental nations which lack a philosophy for controlled population growth must be accompanied by medical information which will help break down the folklore and customs which support the practice of unlimited reproduction.[1]

AGRICULTURAL POLICY AND THE LOWER THIRD

Agricultural policy to date has for the most part been ineffective in meeting the needs of the lower third of the farming population. The Agricultural

[1] For studies of population policy see W. S. Thompson, *Population Problems*, 3d ed., chaps. 1, 25–26, McGraw-Hill Book Company, Inc., New York, 1942; Paul H. Landis, *Population Problems*, chaps. 10 and 25, American Book Company, New York, 1943.

Adjustment Act, with its emphasis on compensating farmers for taking certain acreages out of production, did comparatively little to increase the incomes of small farmers. In most cases it was the large operator who could take his poorer, least profitable acreages out of production and, by concentrating on his better land, raise as large or even a larger crop and at the same time receive a large subsidy from the AAA for acres not farmed. If agriculture takes the road of subsidizing farmers for cost of production, or even of guaranteeing the difference between the price levels of depression and the pre-depression price levels, it will do little to help the great masses of farmers who never produce enough for a decent living.

Such groups will have to come under the supervision of welfare policies designed for such groups. During the depression decade the Farm Security Administration program was designed for this group, that and various relief and welfare policies. These are discussed in a later chapter.

LAND SETTLEMENT IN AGRICULTURAL POLICY

After World War I this country and many European countries resorted to land settlement as a device for meeting the needs of soldiers.[1] There has been a great deal of talk by the uninformed in favor of such a policy for veterans of World War II. Farm economists, knowing the cost of such activities at the close of the last war and the record of failure of such ventures, and, also knowing the situation that is likely to prevail in agriculture once European agriculture goes back into production, strongly condemn any such policy. They do not believe such a venture to be economically sound or in the best interests of human welfare. They also believe such land settlement is almost certain to fail. They know that the settlement of soldiers is likely to be on subsistance-sized tracts. Subsistance farming everywhere in the United States is associated with a low level of living, poor health conditions, lack of social facilities, poor education, and extreme economic hazards. We live in a competitive agricultural economy and those without adequate acreages, machine efficiency, and a reasonable orientation to the demands of the market cannot hope to make a decent living.

During the depression of the 1930's many recommended subsistance farms as a relief measure. At that time any venture which took people off relief rolls even in part had some benefits, but as a general welfare approach, especially in times of prosperity, subsistance farming offers no satisfactory substitute for employment in industry. We should not encourage, by national policy, the kind of living which has failed to approach any of the standards of a reasonable level of living for the masses of our citizens.

[1] For an evaluation of the outcome of one of these ventures see Roy J. Smith, "The California State Land Settlements at Durham and Delhi," *Hilgardia*, vol. 15, pp. 399–492, University of California, Berkeley, October, 1943.

LAND DEVELOPMENT IN NATIONAL POLICY

Considering new land development as a relief measure, we must recognize certain economic forces which should at least be taken into account even if ignored. Except in war, we have had too much land in operation from the standpoint of needed agricultural production. To bring in more land only increases the problem of overproduction which is the chronic problem of American agriculture. New areas, even when much more productive than old areas, compete with other areas and increase problems there.

One cannot, however, place the development of new land entirely on such an economic basis. Many of the new lands seeking development are in the Far West where irrigation offers possibilities for great expansion. The drift of population over many decades has been toward the West. The drift is likely to continue. Many of these areas with productive farm land for development offer superior opportunity from the standpoint of potential social advantages. They also offer to the individual in many cases superior economic and climatic advantages to any he has previously found elsewhere. Personal, local, and even regional interests may in many cases not be identical with the national interests from the standpoint of over-all agricultural production needs. It is likely, therefore, that pressures for the bringing in of new land will continue, and that new lands will be brought into production. This will be done even though it may seriously complicate problems of adjustment in older or marginal land areas.

SUBSIDY OF RURAL EDUCATION AS A MEASURE FOR AGRICULTURAL ADJUSTMENT

We have described elsewhere the large stream of migrants that move from rural to urban areas. The volume of this migration should be increased rather than diminished in the interest of better levels of living in agricultural areas. The volume of migration should be increased most in those areas which offer the least in the way of social and economic opportunity, which have the least in actual and potential agricultural and other natural resources.

The stream of migration can be increased and the migrants be made a greater asset to the cities which receive them. As an incentive there should be launched an aggressive program of education in backward rural areas designed not only to increase the level of education but also to orient youth to opportunities beyond the local community. Impoverished areas produce the largest crop of children—children who need to be introduced to the requirements of urban-industrial life before migrating. This would motivate migration and prepare young people for the opportunities, responsibilities, and adjustments which will face them there. Considered from this viewpoint, urban communities and large urban states which constantly receive rural migrants have an opportunity to invest in their own future through federal subsidies to education in rural areal lacking economic opportunities.

In conclusion, if trends of the times are tokens of the future, farmers in the more prosperous sections seem to be on the way to enjoying many more of the material goods and services that we have come to consider essential elements of the "new standard of living." Rapid expansion of rural electrification, which will make available to many farm homes most of the luxurious mechanical devices the city now has, is probably the most significant omen of the better things in rural material culture just at hand.

A vital problem of farmers in the future is likely to be that of securing sufficient income to share in the consumption of luxury goods that are available to all who can pay the price. With an increase of contact, desires are sure to increase and with them frustrations if the new desires cannot be satisfied. It is at this point that the rich meaning of a simple life may be lost to those who cannot afford to live on the new level, for it is at this point that the older values of rural culture and the new values meet. The striking contrast breeds desire to participate in the new standards, and to be unable to afford to do so breeds inferiority feeling. The new material standard comes to be the measure of a man and of his satisfactions in the modern culture milieu.

QUESTIONS FOR REVIEW AND DISCUSSION

1. Explain how cultural values determine the meaning of material goods to life satisfactions.

2. What values have been basic in traditional rural cultures? How do these compare with urban values?

3. What seems to be the trend of rural values? Cite evidence.

4. How does the income of farmers as a class compare with that of other groups?

5. Compare agricultural income by regions.

6. Show how a higher income may be attained through class organization. What is the government doing along this line?

7. In what respect was the depression agricultural policy comparable in philosophy to the practices and policies of industrial corporations?

8. Describe attempts to increase farm income through national policy.

9. Discuss the social significance of the AAA.

10. Discuss national agricultural policy in relation to world food needs.

11. Has agricultural policy as such met needs of the lower third in agriculture?

12. Discuss land settlement as a device of national policy; land development.

13. How might aid to rural education become a vital plank in national agricultural policy?

14. Why has income as such become of increasing importance to farmers?

COLLATERAL READING

Baker, O. E., Ralph Borsodi, and M. L. Wilson: *Agriculture in Modern Life*, chap. 5, Harper & Brothers, New York, 1939.

Consumer Incomes in the United States, National Resources Planning Board, Washington, D.C., 1938.

Dummeier, Edwin F., and Richard B. Heflebower: *Economics with Applications to Agriculture*, rev. ed., McGraw-Hill Book Company, Inc., New York, 1940.

Kolb, J. H., and E. de S. Brunner: *A Study of Rural Society*, 3d ed., chap. 10, Houghton Mifflin Company, Boston, 1946.

Landis, Paul H.: *Population Problems*, chaps. 10 and 25, American Book Company, New York, 1943.

Larson, Olaf F.: "Lessons from Rural Rehabilitation Experience," *Land Policy Review*, vol. 9, pp. 13–18, Fall, 1946.

Leevy, J. Roy: "Contrasts in Urban and Rural Family Life," *American Sociological Review*, vol. 5, pp. 948–953, December, 1940.

Leven, M., H. G. Moulton, and C. Warburton: *America's Capacity to Consume*, Brookings Institution, Washington, D. C., 1934.

Postwar Agricultural Policy, Report of the Committee on Postwar Agricultural Policy of the Association of Land Grant Colleges and Universities, October, 1944. (Distributed by most state agricultural experiment stations.)

Schultz, T. W.: *Agriculture in an Unstable Economy*, McGraw-Hill Book Company, Inc., New York, 1945.

Smith, T. Lynn: *The Sociology of Rural Life*, chap. 2, rev. ed., Harper & Brothers, New York, 1947.

Thompson, Warren S.: *Population Problems*, 3d ed., chaps. 1, 25, 26, McGraw-Hill Book Company, Inc., New York, 1942.

What Peace Can Mean to American Farmers, Miscellaneous Publication No. 582, U.S. Department of Agriculture, Washington, D. C., 1945.

Woofter, T. J., and Ellen Winston: *Seven Lean Years*, University of North Carolina Press, Chapel Hill, 1939.

Zimmerman, C. C.: *Consumption and Standards of Living*, D. Van Nostrand Company, Inc., New York, 1936.

Part V

EMERGING PROBLEMS OF A DYNAMIC SOCIETY

PROBLEMS are perpetual in human experience. They appear in every form of human relationship; they are prominent in every social institution; they are inherent in every type of social situation; they enter the experience of every person. But problems, though perpetual, also change, manifesting themselves in new forms, the old problems taking on new face. New trends in culture building may intensify certain problems and lessen others. New forms of social experience may alleviate distress at one point but aggravate it at another. The same old problems inherent in youth becoming adults, in tenants becoming owners, in farm laborers becoming tenants; of keeping the wolf from the door, of defeating disease, of making a living and, at the same time, enjoying life— these and many more of the old problems persist. In many respects they are the same; in other respects they are new and, therefore, must always be approached with the understanding that they are a part of the total interactive pattern of modern life rather than sore thumbs set apart, divorced from the total body.

CHAPTER 26

PROBLEMS OF FARM YOUTH[1]

AN APPROACH TO YOUTH PROBLEMS

VIEWED from sociological perspective, youth is that period in life when the individual is in the process of transfer from the dependent, irresponsible age of childhood to the self-reliant, responsible age of adulthood, the uncertain period when parents begin to relax their hold and to shift responsibility from their own shoulders to those of their offspring, and during which the maturing child seeks new freedom and, in finding it, becomes accountable to society. The importance of youth as a sociological period depends largely upon the conditions of a particular society. Youth may be prolonged or scarcely exist, the child being ushered hastily into adulthood. It may be a period of social crisis—a prolonged seige of agonizing adjustment, which tests the mettle of the initiate, sometimes leaving him broken and defeated; or conversely, it may introduce the individual to no major decisions and challenge him with few problems of social adjustment.

The period of youth in our society has long been considered one of crisis, from either a common-sense or a scientific viewpoint. That it is an age of important physiological change is common knowledge growing out of universal experience. That it is an age calling for major psychological and emotional adjustments, under conditions established by our culture pattern, is also common knowledge.[2] Whether the problems of psychological character so commonly observed among American youth arise from within because of physiological, emotional, and psychological maturation or from without because of the complexity of the social system which youth encounters is an interesting subject for speculation.[3] Suffice it to say that the sociologist can see enough in the external environment of contemporary youth to find adequate explanation for much of youth's turmoil. Substantiating this view is the striking evidence that the psychological crises which are supposedly a counterpart of organic

[1] Acknowledgement is made to the journal *Social Forces* for permission to reproduce in this chapter a considerable portion of an article previously published therein.

[2] G. Stanley Hall made much of the psychological crisis of adolescence. See his *Adolescence* and his *Youth: Its Education, Regimen, and Hygiene*, D. Appleton-Century Company, Inc., New York, 1905 and 1906, respectively.

[3] The American Medical Association's official organ, *Hygeia*, vol. 16, p. 824, September, 1938, in a healthogram states that "There does not appear to be any more reason for regarding adolescence as a period of turmoil physically than for so regarding any other period of growth."

changes during the period of physiological adolescence do not appear in some societies with a different culture pattern.[1] In fact, the evidence for the social origin of adolescent crises is sufficient to justify an hypothesis to the effect that if one wants to understand youth problems, he should first analyze the social experience of youth under the culture pattern of their time.

Accepting this as a valid approach it is assumed that farm youth of today experience unusual problems, and problems differing from those of farm youth in our earlier rural society and from those of urban youth, because of the changing social and cultural milieu in which the modern farm youth matures.

THE YOUTH AGE GROUP IN OUR SOCIETY

Societies that introduce the child directly into adult responsibility do not have a youth group in the modern sense. Today we define youth as that group between 16 and 24 years of age. (This is the group described in this chapter and in most current literature on youth.) Our forefathers on the frontier of yesterday expected the child to shoulder adult responsibilities by the time he reached 16 years of age and often before. Not more than three centuries ago the average life expectancy at birth was less than 30 years of age; under such conditions to have deferred independent status so many years would have been to waste most of life. We have lengthened the life span until the average expectancy of life at birth is about 63 years, and have prolonged the age of infancy and projected youth far into maturity. Compulsory education laws ordinarily require 8 years of schooling and custom dictates further training for those who can afford it. The age when the youth may become a free, self-supporting member of society has been extended, and law and custom carefully regulate the age of marriage to make sure that family responsibilities will not be assumed too early in life. There is no longer the almost direct passing from childhood to adulthood, but a prolonged period of social adolescence which has come to extend far beyond physical adolescence.

The substance of the matter is that we now have in the United States over 20 million youth 16 to 24 years of age, young people who are in no sense children, and yet many of whom are in no true sense adults, not having come to full moral, economic, and familial responsibilities. Urban-industrial society has delayed maturity for the sake of education, health, economic security, and more complete sophistication.

SIGNIFICANCE OF THE WIDENED GAP BETWEEN CHILDHOOD AND ADULTHOOD IN CREATING INDEPENDENT YOUTH GROUPS

Much social significance is connected with the prolongation of youth in modern society. In primitive agricultural societies, as Winslow observes, there

[1] This has been adequately demonstrated in Margaret Mead's study, *Coming of Age in Samoa*, William Morrow & Co., Inc., New York, 1928.

are no youth problems and youth is not set apart as a separate group.[1] But today numerous groups consisting entirely of youth have developed; in them youth exercise control, formulating codes, practices, and patterns for life fairly independent of adults. In most societies adults have been the conservers of tradition and have been able to pass these traditions on to their offspring. The independent youth groups of our society make possible escape from adult patterns, and more rapid change in mores, traditions, and customs. Youth consequently have come to play a part in social change such as ordinarily has been denied them. Many implications to family, church, and state are involved, but these are more applicable to the urban than to the rural community, because as yet most youth groups are urban.

But many farm youth are members of at least the high school group, which is perhaps the most important youth group in our society and which in its informal functioning is relatively independent of adult control. The entrance of farm youth into the high school has probably done more to break down patriarchal patterns in the rural home and to divorce youth from parental domination than any other single influence. Many high school values come to supersede those of the home, the farm child making haste to conceal family codes and to take on liberalizing influences. The new generation seeks greater freedom; the old hesitates to give it, fearing the demoralization that the new freedom might engender.

In one respect at least they (rural youth) are agreed with urban youth: whatever it is that troubles them and whatever it is they are after in life, they no longer expect to find their way by listening to their elders. In fact, so certain are they that they live in another world, they do not intend even to reveal themselves to the older generations.

They are beginning to sense in a vague way that science implies new values and meanings for life. This frightens their elders who thought they were living in a scientific age, because they used gasoline engines and allowed their sons to attend agricultural colleges.[2]

MAJOR PROBLEMS OF YOUTH IN OUR SOCIETY

According to present standards the most important decisions facing youth are (1) moral, (2) economic, (3) marital. During the early period of American history, religious decision would have been placed at the head of the list and many would place it there today, although in actual practice it does not seem to come first. Moral decision as here conceived, involves the adjustment of youth to the system of social control, rather than the narrower concept of morality. On this decision hinges the civic freedom and social usefulness of the adult. Economic decision has to do with the choice of a vocation and initiation

[1] W. Thatcher Winslow, "International Aspects of Modern Youth Problems," *Annals of the American Academy of Political and Social Science*, vol. 194, pp. 165–173, November, 1937.

[2] "Rural Youth," *New Republic*, vol. 49, pp. 57–58, Dec. 8, 1926.

into it, the process by which means the dependent child becomes the self-supporting adult, contributing his share to the accumulation of society's capital of economic goods. Marital decision involves on the part of young women the choice of marriage or career, and on the part of all who decide to marry the selection of a mate and the establishment of a home, which marks biological adulthood. The following paragraphs outline some of the difficulties that farm youth face in the transition to adulthood in these three phases of experience

FATHER'S USUAL OCCUPATION	YOUTH'S PRESENT OCCUPATION	
	Same	Different
Professional	10.8	89.2
Farmers & F. Wkrs.	79.0	21.0
Proprietors	27.0	73.0
Clerical	12.1	87.9
Craftsmen	35.7	64.3
Operatives	17.5	82.5
Domestic & Serv.	8.5	91.5
Protective	←2.5	97.5
Laborers	29.6	70.4
All Occupations	26.3	73.7

From Paul H. Landis, "The Territorial and Occupational Mobility of Washington Youth," *Washington Agricultural Experiment Stations Bulletin* 449, July, 1944.

A FARM HERITAGE IS THE USUAL GATEWAY TO FARMING

These data compare the occupational backgrounds of youths in various vocations. Data are for 7,218 young men. Note that 79 per cent of youth in farming came from farm families.

under current conditions, certain comparisons being made between the situation of farm and that of urban youth. Later other special problems of farm youth are discussed.

INITIATION TO THE WORK WORLD

Apprenticeship to work is the natural experience of childhood in primary-group societies where people of all ages mingle in the common activities of life. Thus the child comes to a realistic understanding of what adult life holds for him, and also learns the work folkways of his elders. Some vestiges of this kind of social experience carry over in contemporary farm life in spite of the encroaching influence of outside agencies, especially the school with its daily routine of study and its many extracurricular activities. The transfer to maturity comes more slowly even on the farm than it once did, although farm youth as compared to urban youth become habituated to work at a relatively early age.[1] Urban-industrial society has developed to the point where there is

[1] J. J. Lister and E. L. Kirkpatrick, studying the age at which farm as compared to other youth in Maryland took their first full-time job, found that one-fifth of the farm boys

no natural bridge between the play activities of childhood and the work activities of adulthood, so that any apprenticeship that is to be obtained must come through the school curriculum or after the young person is on the job. Town and city youth ordinarily have no contact with the parent's work and no way of acquiring intimate knowledge of it. This undoubtedly has created problems of far-reaching consequence to youth in town and city; an even more serious problem is inherent in the situation of the farm-reared youth who would enter an urban vocation, for not only does he lack contact and experience with it, but ordinarily he must enter a strange environment and undergo possible culture shock while becoming accommodated to the new life. The social waste, the futile trials and errors, the frustrations, the disappointments of farm youth in selecting, experimenting with, and mastering nonagricultural vocations no doubt would make an interesting story, one which has never been adequately told. Since no concrete evidence is available, one can only guess that the problem is of major importance in the experience of thousands, perhaps even millions, of farm youth. A surprising proportion of farm youth today have no intention of farming, and probably a great majority would prefer some other vocation if given a choice.[1]

A study of occupational preferences of high school pupils in Missouri shows that only about 22 per cent of the farm boys wished to farm; about 12 per cent wanted to be aviators; 11.6 per cent, engineers (figure on p. 398). The situation among farm girls was even more extreme, only about 1 per cent expressing a preference for farming as compared to 24 per cent who preferred stenography and 22 per cent who preferred teaching (figure on p. 399). Several similar studies are available and, though differing in detail, they show somewhat comparable results.[2] (Compare the results for Maryland shown in the pictograph on page 273 in Chapter 18.) The external difficulties all youth experience in seeking a satisfactory place in the vocations are imposing. Barton expressed the problem succinctly, as it existed in a depression decade:[3]

Opportunity has narrowed for thousands of rural youth. The gilded doors of urban life and work no longer stand wide open. The ladder of farm ownership has wider

took their first full-time job at the age of 14. Less than one-half as many took a full-time job so early in village, town, and city. They also found a much higher proportion of farm youth employed than of other groups. *Rural Youth Speak*, pp. 29–30, American Youth Commission, Washington, D. C., 1939.

[1] See David Cushman Coyle, *Rural Youth*, pp. 10–11, Social Problems, No. 2, National Youth Administration, Washington, D. C., 1939.

[2] Mildred B. Thurow, "Interests, Activities, and Problems of Rural Girls," *Cornell University Agricultural Experiment Station Bulletin* 617, Ithaca, 1934; W. A. Anderson and Willis Kerns, "Interests, Activities, and Problems of Rural Young Folk," *Cornell Agricultural Experiment Station Bulletin* 631, Ithaca, 1935; J. J. Lister and E. L. Kirkpatrick, *op. cit.*

[3] J. R. Barton, "Rural Youth: Problems and Possibilities," p. 2, *University of Wisconsin Extension Service Stencil Circular* No. 195, March, 1938.

rungs in it, the angle is steeper, and it has too often become a two-way climb. The farm owner-operator is still in the majority but the long-time trend has been against him.

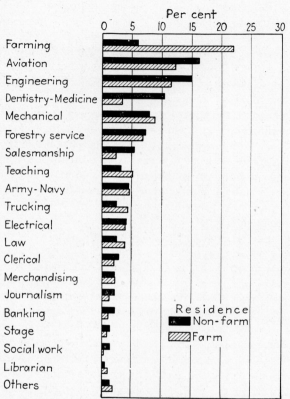

E. L. Morgan and M. W. Sneed, "The Activities of Rural Young People in Missouri," *Missouri Agricultural Experiment Station Bulletin* 269, Columbia, 1937.

PER CENT OF FARM AND NONFARM YOUNG MEN PREFERRING OCCUPATIONS LISTED

Only 22 per cent of this group of high school farm boys preferred farming. Many and varied careers were desired by both the farm and nonfarm groups.

Again, many who are actually engaged in farming feel thwarted and unhappy. A study[1] of Oregon youth, ages 16 to 25, made in 1936, shows that 72.6 per cent of a group of 124 rural young men out of school were farming, but only 46 per cent preferred farming as an occupation. Of a group of 88 young rural women out of school, 85.2 per cent were engaged in homemaking

[1] B. D. Joy and J. R. Beck, "Situations, Problems, and Interests of Unmarried Rural Young People 16 to 25 Years of Age," Table 3, p. 13, *Oregon Agricultural College Extension Service Circular* 277, December, 1937.

or housework, but only 20.5 per cent preferred such work, meaning that over three-fourths had not entered their desired vocation.[1]

Equal difficulty lies in the fact that many farm youth want to farm and are better fitted for farming than any other occupation, but, being unable to do so, turn to urban work as an alternative.[2] Each year between 150,000 and 200,000

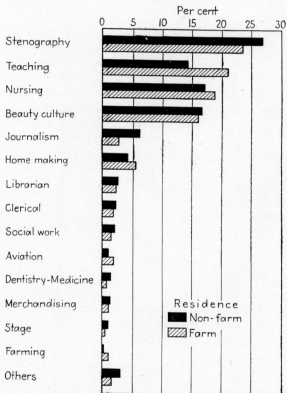

E. L. Morgan and M. W. Sneed, "The Activities of Rural Young People in Missouri," *Missouri Agricultural Experiment Station Bulletin* 269, Columbia, 1937.

PER CENT OF FARM AND NONFARM YOUNG WOMEN PREFERRING OCCUPATIONS LISTED

Many of this group of high school girls wished to be stenographers, teachers, nurses, and beauty culturists, whereas practically none preferred farming.

farm people reach the age of 18 with no prospect of farming because no farms are available. For example, in 1920, 160,000 farmers died or passed the age of 65; during that year, 337,000 farm boys reached the age of 18, a surplus of

[1] *Ibid.*, Table 4, p. 14.

[2] Interesting evidence on this point is presented in J. J. Lister and E. L. Kirkpatrick, *op. cit.* They find that a large number of Maryland youth who express a desire to live in the city say they would prefer farming if conditions of farming were more satisfactory.

177,000. Likewise, in 1930, the surplus of farm boys coming to maturity was 201,000. [1]

During the years 1940 to 1950, 1,824,000 men 25 to 69 years of age in the rural farm population will die or reach retirement age (70 years).[2] To replace them 3,039,000 youth will reach their 25th birthday, a ratio of 167 young men to every 100 operators leaving agriculture. The situation varies considerably for states and regions, as is graphically shown in map.

Delay in entering lifework is prominent in both urban and rural society because of the limited opportunities. Often there is a period of waiting between school and employment, there being more or less blind stumbling about of many youth who are unfitted to enter the occupational world or who can find no opening. Many maladjustments are inherent in this situation. Those who are thwarted occupationally are likely to be thwarted in marriage because marriage, as well as social status, group association, and general happiness, is very much conditioned by economic factors. For example, home demonstration workers, making a study in 1930 of rural girls in North Carolina who had left school but who had not entered any definite occupation, found them generally dissatisfied and unhappy. This situation seemed to prevail regardless of the social level of the families. Associated with their inability to become self-supporting and to find a new status were conflicts with parents over clothes and spending money. Most of the girls thought their role was hard and wanted to see a new side of life. Frequently their parents had no sympathy with this desire, fearing that it might involve them in financial obligations. These girls seemed to be developing a dislike of country life because of social disadvantages, loneliness, and lack of chance for self-improvement, and because they had little opportunity to meet new people or to express social and recreational desires. Many were unhappy because of unfamiliarity with social conventions.[3]

An excellent summary of the vocational problems of rural youth is given by Melvin and Smith.

Guidance toward occupations is almost entirely lacking in rural areas. Youth commonly pass through the rural school curriculum with the hazy assumption that they are being prepared to enter adult life. But the preparation they receive other than that core of knowledge recognized as general fundamental training too often has only indirect relation to their future work. Most youth enter adult occupations by chance. Giving them greater opportunities for both general and specific occupational training and for learning more about occupational openings is a special need facing rural America.

[1] David Cushman Coyle, *op. cit.*, pp. 7–10.

[2] Conrad Taeuber, *Replacement Rates for Rural-farm Males Aged 25 to 69 Years by Counties, 1940–1950* (mimeographed), United States Department of Agriculture, Washington, D. C., December, 1944.

[3] N. Miller, "Out-of-school Girls in a Rural County," *Journal of Home Economics*, vol. 25, pp. 463–467, July, 1933.

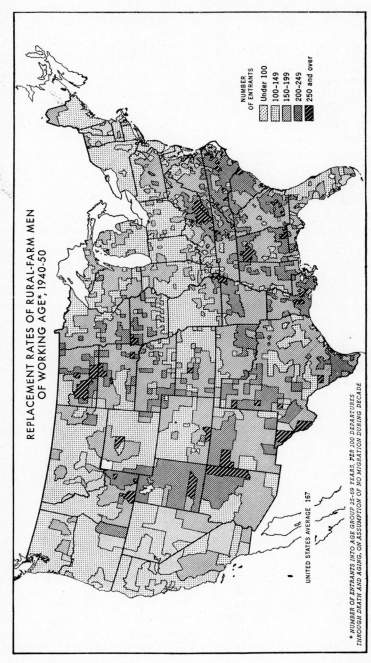

REPLACEMENT RATES OF RURAL-FARM MEN
OF WORKING AGE*, 1940-50

NUMBER
OF ENTRANTS
Under 100
100-149
150-199
200-249
250 and over

UNITED STATES AVERAGE 167

* NUMBER OF ENTRANTS INTO AGE GROUP 25-69 YEARS, PER 100 DEPARTURES
THROUGH DEATH AND AGING, ON ASSUMPTION OF NO MIGRATION DURING DECADE

In most farming areas young men come to working age in greater numbers than old men pass the working age. In some areas over 250 enter the working years for each 100 leaving by reason of death and old age. This requires a heavy migration of youth to other areas.

Rural schools are responsible for the training and guidance of three broad groups of pupils: those who will go into commercial agriculture; those who will enter non-agricultural occupations in either rural or urban areas; and a third large group comprising those who under present circumstances are destined to remain in rural territory living on the land on a more or less self-sufficing basis. It is being increasingly recog-

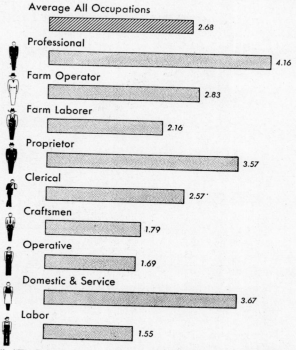

Average All Occupations 2.68

Professional 4.16

Farm Operator 2.83

Farm Laborer 2.16

Proprietor 3.57

Clerical 2.57

Craftsmen 1.79

Operative 1.69

Domestic & Service 3.67

Labor 1.55

From Paul H. Landis, "The Territorial and Occupational Mobility of Washington Youth," *Washington Agricultural Experiment Stations Bulletin* 449, July, 1944.

An Index of Occupational Heredity

Father to son is less likely in farming than in several other occupations. This is explained in part by the fact that the relatively high birth rate of the farm family and the relatively few farm opportunities make transfer of the majority of farm youth to some other occupation necessary. Also important is the fact that many farm youth prefer other occupations. An index of 1.00 in the chart would indicate that youth are as likely to enter their father's occupation as any other, of more than 1.00 that they are more likely to enter it. (Data are for 7,703 young men and compare their occupation after an average period of 5 years out of school with those of their father.)

nized that one of the first duties of the school is the discovery of the particular potentialities and aptitudes of the developing pupil so that on reaching the youth age the individual has some idea of the vocation or vocations in which he or she could reasonably expect to succeed if given additional and proper training. It is, of course, not to be expected that every rural high school can be equipped to train youth in a wide variety of skills, but there are certain fields in which they must provide training if a large proportion of rural young people are to have any vocational training at all. Vocational training in agriculture is doing much to prepare youth for farming, but with all the efforts in this direction it is doubtful if at present enough youth are being trained in high schools and colleges to provide an adequate number of farmers to raise the agricultural products needed for market at the highest possible level of efficiency and at the same time to operate their farms in accordance with the best principles of soil conservation.[1]

INITIATION TO FAMILY RESPONSIBILITIES

If the farm youth remains in the home neighborhood, the assumption of marital and family responsibilities comes as a matter of course and involves few radical readjustments. In more static communities marriages are among those who have known each other over a period of years and whose families have established their reputations. Difficulties are anticipated by parents in advance; advice is volunteered. Youth, during the period of courtship previous to marriage, encounter again and again the attitudes of the community toward their romance. Courtship is not the individualistic matter that it is in the anonymous society of a great city.

The economic foundation of the new family often is laid by parents who are willing to share their farm, to donate the tenant house, or perhaps even to retire to town and relinquish the entire farm to the new couple. Even if they cannot go this far, they often help by lending machinery and work stock, or by giving them a start in other ways. In rural America today, with all the inroads that change and mobility have made on older patterns, the passing of farms from father to son is still common.[2]

Further evidence of the greater ease of establishing the family as an economic unit in farming areas than in town and city is shown by the fact that although the depression of the thirties slowed down the marriage rate among all youth groups in America, its effect on the marriage rate among farm youth was negligible. Melvin and Smith observe that "it is doubtful if depression conditions have any marked effect in causing farm youth to postpone marriage."[3]

Undoubtedly the more sound economic foundation[4] of the rural family and the guidance of adults who project adult values onto courtship and marital

[1] Bruce L. Melvin and E. N. Smith, *Rural Youth: Their Situation and Prospects*, p. 119, Research Monograph XV, Division of Social Research, Works Progress Administration, Washington, D. C., 1938.

[2] Almost 20 per cent of farm tenants in the United States in 1930 were, according to the census, related to their landlords.

[3] Bruce L. Melvin and E. N. Smith, *op. cit.*, p. xvii. It is possible that this situation is indicative of a lower standard of living on the farm.

[4] Sound in the sense that the family operates as an economic unit, not in the sense that it is more likely to acquire wealth or succeed in reaching a comfort level of living.

relationships have been important factors in stabilizing the rural family, reducing marital maladjustment and divorce. Of course, sometimes this guidance proves disadvantageous. Much friction is caused because too great an interest is shown on the part of the neighborhood and relatives in the affairs of the newly married couple. But by and large the effect in this interest has been to stabilize the new family and to make the new couple conscious of social pressures and controls, so that there is less tendency for rural youth to view marriage as an individualistic gesture and more of a tendency to regard it as a social institution which concerns others as well as oneself.

PER CENT MARRIED OF TOTAL YOUTH POPULATION, BY AGE, RESIDENCE, AND SEX 1940*

Age	Urban		Rural farm		Rural nonfarm	
	Male	Female	Male	Female	Male	Female
16 years.................	0.3	2.3	0.4	5.7	0.3	5.0
17 years.................	0.5	6.0	0.9	12.2	0.7	11.8
18 years.................	1.6	12.7	2.8	2.32	2.4	23.1
19 years.................	4.2	20.6	6.5	33.9	6.4	35.3
20 years.................	8.9	29.7	12.6	44.9	13.4	46.8
21 years.................	16.0	38.0	20.8	53.4	23.3	55.4
22 years.................	23.8	46.3	28.9	61.1	32.6	62.5
23 years...	33.5	54.0	37.7	67.9	43.3	68.8
24 years.................	42.4	59.9	45.3	72.8	51.9	73.5

* *Population*, vol. 4, part 1, pp. 22–24, Bureau of the Census, U.S. Department of Commerce, Washington, D. C., 1943.

Rural youth marry young and thus gain certain psychological advantages that are inherent in marrying during the early years of maturity. It will be observed (see table) that at all ages a much higher proportion of rural than of urban youth are married.[1] Women marry at a younger age than men and, as may be seen, the marriage rate among rural girls is especially high.

Adding to family stability, if youth remain on the farm, is the absence of any necessity to make new community adjustments. Disorganizing influences in the external environment often project themselves onto the family, as is evidenced by high divorce rates as well as other forms of family pathology in disorganized urban areas.[2]

On the other hand, undoubtedly a considerable part of the marital conflict so prevalent in the city involves youth with a rural background who are trying

[1] This group includes the rural nonfarm group, who also marry young.

[2] The studies of E. R. Mowrer and of other urban sociologists reveal these relationships. See, for example, Mowrer's *Family Disorganization*, University of Chicago Press, Chicago, 1932.

to adjust themselves to an urban marriage partner or to urban institutional life, social and economic.

Today young people living on farms frequently date, court, and marry village or city youngp eople. Miss Thurow found that of a group of farm girls, age 15 to 29, in Genesee County, New York, who "dated," 21.2 per cent dated boys on farms, 32.3 per cent boys in villages, and 20.2 per cent boys in cities.[1] The remaining 26.3 per cent dated boys in two or more of the above areas. Almost equally difficult may be the adjustment to urban living of young couples both members of which have a farm background.

INITIATION TO ADULT MORALITY

We are inclined to talk about youth as a period for sowing wild oats, and such it often is. Because childhood controls are released during adolescence, it is logical to assume that new, divergent, and often delinquent patterns will appear when youth is brought face-to-face with the multiple patterns of a complex society. An undue proportion of crime is committed by young people between the ages of 16 and 25, as shown by the high rate of commitment of those in this age span to institutions for delinquents; it is equally true that religious confessions and great moral decisions are made during this same period. Both rebellion and reform may be expected to originate with youth where youth have many patterns from which to choose.

The farm youth, if he remains within the primary-group atmosphere of the family and neighborhood, never makes moral choices in an urban sense. Parents, relatives, and neighbors dominate until they die, and by that time usually the youth has become a mature man, with habits well fixed, often in fact with a family of his own, so that he has himself become a conserver of tradition, concerned with passing on to his children the regulations which he received from his forebears.

These are some of the influences that have made for stability in rural life in the past and have made the rural primary group an effective agency in social control. Throughout antiquity, and in much of the rural life of modern times, the masses of individuals did not choose. They obeyed. They did not even desire to rebel because they were immobile, having few contacts with new or varied ways of life. One who knows but one way considers it the right way; but modern rural society, with its increasing heterogeneity of patterns and multiplicity of contacts, presents most youth with the problem of choice, thrusting upon them the necessity of deciding for themselves whether this or that way will be their way of life. Therefore, in many contemporary rural communities there exists conflict between the old generation and the new: the old generation stoutly upholding the values of the integrated neighborhood,

[1] Mildred B. Thurow, *op. cit.*, Table 22, p. 34.

the new generation absorbing the life philosophies of town and city; the old generation clinging to old ideals and threadbare religious creeds, the new generation reaching out for new experience and threatening to exterminate the old.

In communities near the city, this struggle between the old and the new took place a generation ago, so that adults living there have come to accept the freedom of modern urban life as a rightful heritage of youth. Communities less closely in touch with the city face the struggle in the present generation. Isolated communities have not yet experienced it fully, but will as means of communication and transportation are projected into the more remote hinterlands. World War II brought some of it to most areas.

Farm youth in the more mobile parts of rural society, like urban youth with their experience in secondary groups and in youth groups, often by the time they have reached 20 years of age have made more moral decisions than the adult in static rural societies of the past made, or than youth in the remote hinterland of today make in the course of a lifetime. Moral choice and moral maturity are thrust upon them to a greater extent than they have ever been in societies consisting chiefly of primary groups under the domination of the elders. Obviously problems of personal adjustment have been greatly increased for youth, and problems of social control for society. The fact that farm youth in going to the city often experience a distinct break between the old surveillance of primary-group control and the relatively complete freedom of the urban secondary-group world often no doubt subjects them to moral strain which urban youth, who have always known this freedom, do not experience.[1]

FRUSTRATION OF FARM YOUTH

In a rural society completely isolated from contacts with town and city youth absorb the ways of their parents and neighborhood so fully that there is relatively little friction or sense of frustration. Of course, even in an isolated society there are always individuals whose interests do not fully conform to those of the family, neighborhood, or community, but by and large people who know only one philosophy of life absorb it and live a fairly well-accommodated life under it.

But conditions of absolute geographical isolation do not characterize our time. Even the isolated youth gets glimpses of a different kind of life from that which he and his parents live. In the movies, for instance, he sees pictured other ways of life, often far more romantic and enticing than anything he has known. If the family has an automobile, he probably takes an occasional trip

[1] W. I. Thomas and F. Znaniecki's study of the Polish peasant youth's adjustments substantiates this point of view. See their *The Polish Peasant in Europe and America*, 5 vols., Chapman & Grimes, Inc., Boston, 1918–1920.

to the city,[1] where he sees displays of wealth and luxury and evidences of leisure and pleasure, strange and fascinating patterns of human behavior, elaborate forms of human culture, such as create a fairyland of romance for him. He reads in newspapers, magazines,[2] and school textbooks, and if he is fortunate enough to have a radio, hears over it things indicating that many people live by a set of codes far different from those which he has known. In such a situation the ambitious person who is compelled to stay on the farm because of lack of finances or of educational or social opportunities may develop an intense sense of frustration, feeling himself entirely out of joint with his community, his family, and the ideals which his family holds for him. Frequently the only solution is to find some way of entering the live of the city,[3] but many could be satisfied by a better community environment.

Melvin and Smith feel that the government has a definite obligation to improve the situation of rural youth and cite four lines along which it might be expected to act:

(1) Assisting to equalize and to broaden educational opportunity; (2) helping young people find work for which they are fitted by training or aptitude; (3) providing work when private employment is not available; and (4) making provision by which youth can develop their full potentialities through wholesome leisure-time activities.[4]

Special problems of farm youth have been made the subject of extensive research by rural sociologists and a considerable volume of literature has accumulated.[5] Problems which farm youth seem to consider the most critical center around vocational choice, opportunity and adjustment, and family participation. Selecting a mate, planning for a home, providing an economic foundation for a home, developing personality, finding a greater range for

[1] E. L. Morgan and M. W. Sneed, *op. cit.*, in Table 26, p. 42, show that 75 per cent of the 2,297 farm youth in high school studied had traveled outside the state. About 86 per cent of nonfarm youth (living in the open country and in places of under 5,000 population) had traveled outside the state.

Mildred B. Thurow's study, *op. cit.*, Table 18, p. 31, dealing with girls in the age group 15 to 29, shows that 60 per cent had been outside the state on trips 50 miles or more away from home.

[2] The above studies examine the nature and range of newspapers and magazines in rural farm and rural nonfarm homes. E. L. Morgan and M. W. Sneed, *op. cit.*, Fig. 4, p. 37, also compare farm and nonfarm groups on the basis of newspaper subscriptions.

[3] Bird T. Baldwin and his colleagues believe that the restricted environment of rural youth often provides such limited opportunities that it affords sterile soil for the growth of great ambitions. The individual may be unable to find a way into the larger world, may remain on the farm but always feel frustrated there, finding many of the patterns of the rural neighborhood uncongenial. *Farm Children*, p. 149, D. Appleton-Century Company, Inc., New York, 1930.

[4] Bruce L. Melvin and E. N. Smith, *op. cit.*, p. 131.

[5] See A. F. Wileden, "Neglected Youth—What About Them?" *Rural America*, vol. 12, pp. 10–11, May, 1934. See also, W. Thatcher Winslow, *op. cit.*

self-expression and more opportunity for social participation are important issues. Many farm youth are unable to continue their education but cannot find satisfactory work. Some feel that they could find work if they had the opportunity to acquire the skills. Some feel that they might have a happier social life if they could learn how to fit into it. Vocational and social adjustment problems are revealed by practically all studies of youth.

A questionnaire canvass by E. L. Kirkpatrick, of the Youth Section, American Country Life Association, conducted among 2,000 members of rural clubs, mostly in colleges and universities, in 1936, showed that the outstanding needs of these youth in their home communities fell in the fields of recreation, organization, education, religion, health, standards of living, and employment.[1] Only one person in three felt that informal educational facilities were meeting local needs adequately.

No doubt many of these frustrations along recreational, social, educational, and aesthetic lines seem unreasonable to parents and would have appeared so to anyone in our society of a generation ago. To a considerable extent they reflect the breadth of contact of modern youth and the great diversity of desires stimulated by this contact. Rural life is much improved over what it was a generation or two ago and the level of farm living is undoubtedly much higher, but desires are regulated primarily by the extent of the things one knows rather than by absolute need. Rural youth today see many things that their grandfathers could not have wanted because these things were not within the compass of their experience. Many of the things that farm youth want today urban youth also want, but urban youth want many things that farm youth do not want. It is hard to compare groups in terms of satisfaction or frustration, because these qualities are in the realm of values and are conditioned by past experience. It would be unfair to create a picture showing farm youth more dissatisfied than other groups. They may or may not be. Many of their dissatisfactions may be unreasonable; many of them may want things which the average young person cannot expect to have, even in an open-class system which gives every man a certain freedom of choice as to what he will have in life. Perhaps farm youth in America are more unhappy and experience frustration more than farm youth in other countries of the world. This would seem logical in view of the greater enrichment of our life, the greater breadth of our contacts, and also the greater scope in our economic system for the exercise of individual initiative. The masses of people do not expect much under a caste system where vocations are well defined by virtue of birth. Most people under such an order undoubtedly are quite happy and satisfied with the lot which birth brings them.

In considering the American youth problem one must, therefore, always

[1] E. L. Kirkpatrick, "2,000 Prospective Leaders Look at Their Home Communities," *Rural America*, vol. 16, no. 2, pp. 3–4, April, 1938.

take into account the fact that the ideals of our society offer every man much more than he can possibly grasp, creating a situation in which frustration is more or less inevitable. Even many of those who bemoan the dearth of recreational and leisure-time activities in the farm community in so doing are projecting urban values on the rural scene. Youth feel the lack of these activities only inasmuch as they have had contact with an urbanized school philosophy and with urban recreation facilities. Their feeling the lack does not necessarily mean that conditions are worse than they were in the past nor that they are worse in rural America than they are in other nations; it merely indicates that there is a dearth of entertainment in the farm community of the kind that an urbanized individual has come to like. The degree to which the farm neighborhood can develop facilities to supply such entertainment is a matter of speculation; perhaps even the degree to which they should be developed is open to question.

A frustrating factor of great social concern in the experience of farm youth is their limited educational opportunities. Often they do not have the training necessary to cope with the complexities of modern life and, therefore, feel thwarted and inferior. Melvin and Smith, commenting on this point, observe that those who will leave farms receive little special consideration in the educational system. Too often the high school curriculum is built on the assumption that the youth who finish high school will go on to college. Many communities have no high school readily accessible. They conclude that "because inadequacies and inequalities in educational opportunity do exist, there are thousands of out-of-school rural youth poorly prepared to cope with modern life."[1]

Melvin's study of youth in relief households of the nation, made in October, 1935, showed that few of those both in open country and in villages who had completed their schooling had had more than an eighth-grade education and a high proportion had had far less (see figure, page 410).[2] Less than one in five of the open-country group had had any high school work and one in three had not gone beyond the sixth grade. The condition was much worse than average in the South where almost half of the white youth and three out of five Negro youth had completed only six grades or less of schooling. Other studies show that rural youth on relief had much lower educational attainments than youth in neighboring households not on relief.[3] More young women than young men were found on relief in rural areas, probably because the depression had blocked vocational outlets which ordinarily were open to them in the

[1] Bruce L. Melvin and E. N. Smith, *op. cit.*, p. 120.

[2] Bruce L. Melvin, *Rural Youth on Relief*, pp. 31–34, Division of Social Research, Works Progress Administration, Washington, D. C., 1937.

[3] T. C. McCormick, *Rural Households, Relief and Non-relief*, pp. 32 *ff.*, summarizes the results of a study which sampled areas throughout the nation. Research Monograph II, Works Progress Administration, Washington, D. C., 1935.

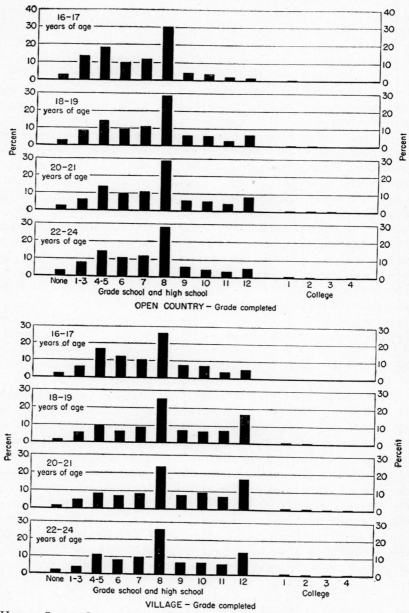

HIGHEST SCHOOL GRADE COMPLETED BY OUT-OF-SCHOOL OPEN-COUNTRY AND VILLAGE
YOUTH ON RELIEF IN THE UNITED STATES (EXCLUDING NEW ENGLAND) BY AGE
AS OF OCTOBER, 1935

A surprising proportion had not gone beyond fifth grade and comparatively few had
gone to high school. Open-country youth were not so well educated as the village group.

city.[1] Out-of-school rural girls seemed to be less certain of their future than boys.[2]

FARM YOUTH AS A CULTURALLY MARGINAL GROUP

The term "marginal man" has been used to designate individuals who bridge two fairly distinct cultures, *e.g.*, the immigrant child, who bridges the Old World culture of the parental home and the new American culture.[3] In a greater or less degree many farm youth find themselves in the position of the marginal man, since those coming into contact with urban society and required to assimilate urban culture often possess few patterns that are appropriate to urban living.

As Baldwin and his colleagues observe, the social limitations placed upon children in the rural community both in the school and in the home frequently are a decided disadvantage because their lives are so closely interwoven with the prevailing practices of the neighborhood that there is little chance for personal expansion or the enrichment of personality patterns.[4] Although lacking practice in social adjustment, most of them must bridge the gap between rural and urban cultures, some facing the issue when they enter the consolidated high school where town and rural cultures meet, some on reaching a college campus where rural and urban meet but where urban standards dominate, some on going to the city to enter an urban occupation.

The effects of the farm youth's marginal position are evidenced at many points. The persistence of mild patriarchial domination in the home means that the parent is unwilling to release his hold on youth; yet farm youth, in contacting the town and city high school group which experiences greater freedom from parental domination, come to resent their own lack of it and, even though there may be no open conflict, an undercurrent of dissatisfaction is present. Such parental domination is often at the basis of the child's leaving home and may even explain in large part his dislike for farming. The domination of parent may take the form of refusing to give the youth a return for his labor,[5] of restricting his social freedom, of insisting on too rigid discipline. This becomes especially serious today when farm youth sense the extreme freedom that prevails in town and city.

The projection of work values from parent to child may be of critical import in the farm home. Duty and responsibility may bear heavily, too

---

[1] Bruce L. Melvin, *op. cit.*, p. xvi.

[2] C. E. Lively and L. J. Miller, "Rural Young People 16 to 24 Years of Age," *Ohio Agricultural Experiment Station, Mimeographed Bulletin* 73, Columbus, 1934.

[3] See, for example, E. V. Stonequist, *The Marginal Man*, Charles Scribner's Sons, New York, 1937.

[4] Bird T. Baldwin, *et al.*, *op. cit.*, pp. 30–31.

[5] C. E. Lively and L. J. Miller, *op. cit.*, pp. 6–8. For data see p. 214.

heavily, on the farm youth, until he sees no escape except through revolt.[1] Work and more work may come to make up the daily ritual of life until it becomes almost a religion to the older generation and a plague to the new.

In immigrant communities the projection of Old World patterns in religion, work, language, or custom may be at the basis of conflict between the young and the old. This situation has been most prominent in the past but survivals of it still exist.

The breach between youth and maturity, noticeable in every neighborhood in Homeland, was nowhere more apparent than in the attitude toward religion. The self-contained spirituality of the older generation left little opportunity for a sympathetic understanding of the ideals of adolescence. The young, on the other hand, were impatient with the crystallized dogmas of their elders. Some expressed themselves as uninterested in the things the minister talked about, and showed indifference toward religion as it was being presented to them. The education of these young people was too limited to permit them to analyze the generally accepted creeds, but their education was sometimes more extensive than that of the ministers. Revolts of adolescent idealism were apt to languish into spiritual indifference, for the young people were emotionally too healthy to enter into sectarian conflicts.[2]

There has been a sharp clash between the modern urban pleasure philosophy and the semipuritanic, work-duty philosophy of the farm community. Where communities have been in contact with the stream of culture change for a generation, this conflict was met by the last generation, who have since become recreation-pleasure minded; in many communities the new philosophy is permeating today by way of the high school, where farm youth invariably develop some interest in the recreation-pleasure activities fostered for town and city youth, thus incurring neighborhood condemnation for spending time and money on "foolishness."

At the basis of all these conflicts which reflect the adjustments of two generations is the carry-over among the old of serious interest in family, progeny, land, security, and independence—values and ideals that make little appeal to more sophisticated farm youth who have learned to desire the superficial values of urban culture. Though this conflict between the old and new generations is never wanting in any environment, it seems to have been greatly reduced in urban culture, where people of all ages emulate youth and imitate their behavior. In the city today almost everyone wants to appear young; consequently, youth receive relatively little condemnation. But in the farm community people still grow old and once a person begins to age psycho-

---

[1] This thesis is advanced in the White House Conference Report, *The Adolescent in the Family*, pp. 158–162, D. Appleton-Century Company, Inc., New York, 1934.

[2] Bird T. Baldwin, Eva A. Fillmore, and Lora Hadley, *Farm Children*, pp. 30–31. By permission of D. Appleton-Century Company, Inc.

logically, inelastic habits and attitudes crystallize and more plastic youth appears rebellious, frivolous, reckless, wordly, and godless.

Youth today has adjustments to make because of the instability of the social group caused by changing standards, loosening of home control, because of more economic activities outside of the home, weakened control of the church, and increased freedom without adequate education in the use of freedom.

It is true that difficult situations confront every farm boy and girl, but it is also true that difficult situations often hold valuable compensations. Emphasis in every program should be on the opportunities to be capitalized, rather than on the problems to be met.[1]

In conclusion, farm youth in many communities are in that interesting transitional stage between a rigidly controlled rural social order and a freedom-giving emancipated urban social order, struggling to make the step from an intimate locality group, in which group purposes dominate individual action, to a nonlocal, impersonal secondary group in which individualization has become highly developed; wrestling with the moral decisions the new freedom brings; fighting the economic problems one necessarily faces if he leaves the traditional family occupation to enter one that is beyond the scope of his cultural heritage; gradually making the break from the old primary-group system of courtship with its practical emphasis to the new and more enticing romantic pattern of highly individualized urban society; fighting the habits of an old established rural order; experimenting with the heterogeneous patterns of a new pleasure-motivated, luxury-scaled urban pattern; moving more rapidly toward the goals of an urbanized social order than the parent generation in most areas; often bringing the parent generation along although not without great effort, but in far too many cases leaving the older generation behind after a period of struggle and conflict during which the new freedom has been gained. This seems to be the essence of the youth problem in the farm community of today.

QUESTIONS FOR REVIEW AND DISCUSSION

1. Define youth as a social experience. What age group is involved?

2. What is significant about the fact that our society has a distinct youth group?

3. Compare the initiation of farm and urban youth to the work world. What special difficulties do farm youth face?

4. How do population numbers relate to the vocational problems of youth?

5. In what ways is the problem of assuming family responsibility different in the farm community from what it is in the urban community?

6. Contrast the differences in moral restraints imposed upon youth in primary and in secondary groups.

7. Point out factors leading to frustration in the experiences of farm youth.

[1] G. L. Warren, "Programs for Farm Youth Based on Social and Economic Conditions," *Journal of Home Economics*, vol. 24, pp. 605–607, July, 1932.

8. What cultural factors may intensify feelings of frustration?
9. In what sense is farm youth a "marginal" group?
10. At what points do values of the older and the younger generations clash?

COLLATERAL READING

Anderson, W. A., and Willis Kerns: "Interests, Activities, and Problems of Rural Young Folk," *Cornell Agricultural Experiment Station Bulletin* 631, Ithaca, 1935.

Bell, Howard M.: *Youth Tell Their Story*, American Council on Education, Washington, D. C., 1938.

Hoffer, C. R.: *Introduction to Rural Sociology*, rev. ed., chap. 6, Farrar & Rinehart, Inc., New York, 1934.

Landis, Paul: *Adolescence and Youth: The Process of Maturing*, McGraw-Hill Book Company, Inc., New York 1945.

Lister, J. J., and E. L. Kirkpatrick: *Rural Youth Speak*, American Youth Commission, Washington, D. C., 1939.

Melvin, Bruce L.: *Rural Youth on Relief*, Research Monograph XI, Division of Social Research, Works Progress Administration, Washington, D. C., 1937.

————, and Elna N. Smith: *Rural Youth: Their Situation and Prospects*, Research Monograph XV, Division of Social Research, Works Progress Administration, Washington, D. C., 1938.

Morgan, E. L., and M. W. Sneed: "The Activities of Rural Young People in Missouri," *Missouri State Agricultural Experiment Station Bulletin* 269, Columbia, 1937.

Thurow, Mildred B.: "Interests, Activities, and Problems of Rural Girls," *Cornell Agricultural Experiment Station Bulletin* 617, Ithaca, 1934.

White House Conference on Child Health and Protection: *The Adolescent in the Family*, pp. 8–29, 158–178, D. Appleton-Century Company, Inc., New York, 1934.

Williams, Robin M.: "Rural Youth Studies in the United States," *Rural Sociology*, vol. 4, pp. 166–178, June, 1939.

Woofter, T. J., and Ellen Winston: *Seven Lean Years*, chap. 5, University of North Carolina Press, Chapel Hill, 1934.

CHAPTER 27

SOCIAL ASPECTS OF FARM TENURE[1]

THE PROBLEM IN PERSPECTIVE

ABOUT FARM tenancy centers not one social problem, but a whole complex of them. In fact, tenancy has a bearing on almost every problem that the farm community experiences, bears directly on the functioning of all rural social institutions, and plays a vital part in many economic considerations affecting American agriculture. Farm tenancy as such is not necessarily pathological. Many of its features are desirable; others are undesirable. Some are tenants by choice; many by necessity. At its best farm tenancy may represent a fairly ideal kind of life; at its worst it creates many undesirable social situations.

Farm tenancy is not new but there is a new interest in its social implications. Abuses of the tenant system have been so common in American agriculture that the public has gradually come to view it as something undesirable, and in recent years there has been a growing feeling that something should be done about it. The American Institute of Public Opinion found that 83 per cent of the American public favored a government program to help tenants to become farm owners.[2]

WHY FARM TENANCY?

Basically, we have farm tenancy because many people want to own land but do not want to farm it, and there are many others who want to farm land but cannot own it. This is only a partial explanation. It has been traditional in America for a young man to start at the bottom and work up. (Evidence of this social climbing is found in differences in age of owners and tenants. The 1930 census showed that only about one-third of farm owners were under 45 years of age as compared to two-thirds of farm tenants.) Climbing is a part of the open-class tradition at the basis of our democracy. The youth starts as a farm hand; through saving his wages he gradually accumulates enough capital to buy the necessary livestock and equipment and to rent a piece of land. If he is ambitious he looks beyond this, hoping someday to become an owner of land after having acquired sufficient resources as a tenant to purchase a tract. Sociologists and

---

[1] Acknowledgment is made to the journal *Rural Sociology*, in which a portion of this chapter was previously published.

[2] Reported by Henry A. Wallace, former Secretary of Agriculture, in an address on farm tenancy over the Columbia Broadcasting System, Jan. 22, 1937.

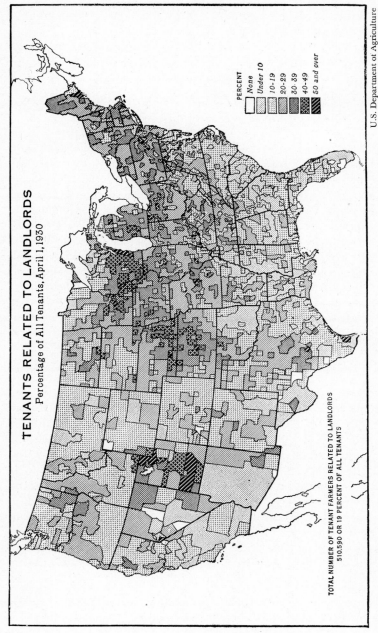

TENANTS RELATED TO LANDLORDS
Percentage of All Tenants, April 1, 1930

PERCENT
None
Under 10
10-19
20-29
30-39
40-49
50 and over

TOTAL NUMBER OF TENANT FARMERS RELATED TO LANDLORDS
510,590 OR 19 PERCENT OF ALL TENANTS

U.S. Department of Agriculture

Almost one-fifth of the tenant farmers of the United States in 1930 were related to their landlords—were brothers, sisters, children, or grandchildren—or had married a brother, sister, child, or grandchild. The percentage related is comparatively low in the South and in the more arid parts of the Great Plains region, but is very high in the states of the Northeast and northern part of the Middle West. In some counties of Wisconsin, Minnesota, Nebraska, Kansas, and Utah two of every five tenants are related to their landlords.

economists, therefore, always have talked of an agricultural ladder in which tenancy has been recognized as one of the essential steps.

In the tenant group are not only those who are struggling upward toward ownership, but also a large number who expect to become owners through inheritance. Many tenants in this country are related to the owners either as

EACH FIGURE REPRESENTS 100,000 PERSONS

SOURCE. UNITED STATES CENSUS OF AGRICULTURE

Rural Poverty , Works Progress Administration

TENURE DISTRIBUTION BY RACE OF MALES ENGAGED IN AGRICULTURE IN SEVEN SOUTH-
EASTERN COTTON STATES, 1860, 1910, 1930

"The number of males engaged in agriculture in these Eastern Cotton States doubled between 1860 and 1930. This was an increase of whites, who were four times as numerous in 1930, while the number of Negroes increased hardly at all. Most of the increase consisted of tenants and laborers. Thus, the relatively simple situation of 1860, when nearly all whites of age were owners and nearly all Negroes were laborers, has changed to one in which tenants predominate. At present large numbers of whites compete with Negroes for a place on the land, and are in most respects equally disadvantaged.

"While present Negro tenants and owners are children and grandchildren of laborers, the white tenants and laborers are the children and grandchildren of former owners. Large gains in the helpless sharecropper class are fixing the institution of tenancy, with its accompanying limitations, more firmly in the Southern agricultural organization."

sons or sons-in-law, or more distant relatives (see figure, opposite). A considerable proportion of these are young people who have taken their parents' place on the farm and expect to inherit it when the retired parents die.

Tenancy is prominent in some parts of the country because investors consider land a good speculative investment; in other parts a secure, if not too remunerative, investment. Tenancy in the cotton South is explained in part by the breakup of the plantation system and the resulting transfer from a slave economy, which was virtually a hired-labor economy, to a share-cropper tenant economy (see sociograph, above).

More significant than these rather long-time factors in explaining why tenancy has become so extensive, was the recruiting of the tenant class during the years prior to World War II from above rather than from beneath. During the crises which agriculture experienced between the two wars, the tenant

FARM MORTGAGE DEBT, REAL ESTATE TAXES, AND REAL ESTATE VALUE, 1910-44

INDEX NUMBERS OF AMOUNTS PER ACRE

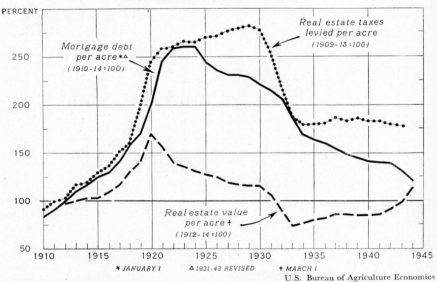

*JANUARY I   △ 1931-43 REVISED   + MARCH I

U.S. Bureau of Agriculture Economics

"Farm-mortgage indebtedness more than doubled from 1910 to 1920. Despite a sharp drop in land values, indebtedness continued to increase until about 1928. Taxes on farm real estate also increased at a rapid rate, adding to the heavy load of fixed charges borne by farmers in the 1920's. Since 1930 there has been a substantial reduction in indebtedness" at first because of the liquidation of debt through foreclosure and assignment; during World War II, because of debt payment. Debt is the straw that breaks the camel's back.

class was recruited increasingly from the ranks of farm owners. During the postwar depression and again during the great depression of the early thirties, thousands of farmers lost their land to insurance companies, mortgage companies, lending agencies, as well as to private mortgage holders. Thus, not only were many owner-operators deprived of their farms but many investors and investment corporations became owners of land they did not want, but, having come by it, they rented it to others to farm. These two depressions brought to focus a number of social and economic trends which produced a crisis for the farm owner. The high price of land, excessive mortgage debt, and heavy expenditures for machine equipment, combined with the low prices in a cash-market economy, were principal factors involved.

Contributing also to the pyramiding of tenancy during those years was, first, our system of inheritance. A relatively high birth rate on the farm combined with migration means that farms are usually taken over by one child of the family who then must buy out other heirs, part of whom may live in town or city. The child who takes over the home farm is loaded with mortgage debt. Because of this debt many family estates fall into the hands of large lending corporations or private mortgage holders in times of crisis. Second, the nation experienced, during those two decades, the culminating effect of the earlier period of land speculation which involved not only urban investors but many farmers who increased their land acreages by mortgaging their farms. A large number of this group bought during the prevailing high prices of the war period, and the debt which they contracted more than exceeded the value of the land during the depression period. Third, this period brought to a climax the aftereffects of an earlier epoch of cheap or free land, land which had been obtained with little capital outlay by people many of whom in the crisis demonstrated themselves unable to maintain it. Fourth, this period, and especially the years of the early thirties, produced an almost unparalleled credit stringency, which not only hindered the climb of tenants upward but also contributed heavily to the failure of farm owners, reducing many of them to a tenant status.

Another cause for alarm was the effect of the events of this period in crowding many tenants to the level of farm laborers. Large numbers had mortgaged chattels—work stock and machinery—to the point where they finally lost all their assets and were reduced either to the status of the unemployed or that of farm laborers. In the South, crop acreage reductions under the Agricultural Adjustment Act and in many sections the more extensive use of machinery, which increased the amount of land that could be operated by one man, reduced the number of farmers needed, setting many farm tenants adrift as laborers.[1]

During these years public leaders suddenly began to appreciate the fact that the difficulty of climbing the agricultural ladder was increasing and that the danger of moving downward was becoming more imminent; that new economic and social forces were threatening the essential democratic traditions of rural society, striking heavily at the family-farm ideal.

CLASSES OF FARM TENANTS

The tenant class is made up of those who operate land which others own; beyond this there is little similarity among various tenant classes. Three general groups of tenants are found in American agriculture—cash tenants, share tenants, and croppers. What are their basic differences?

---

[1] An interesting series of studies on labor displacement in agriculture has been made by the Works Progress Administration, under the general title, "Studies in Changing Techniques and Employment in Agriculture." See also Paul S. Taylor, "Power Farming and Labor Displacement in the Cotton Belt, 1937," *Monthly Labor Review*, pp. 595–607, March, 1938.

The Cash Tenant.—The cash tenant pays a fixed cash rent for the land and the risk of operation is entirely his since he pays his rent regardless of the out-

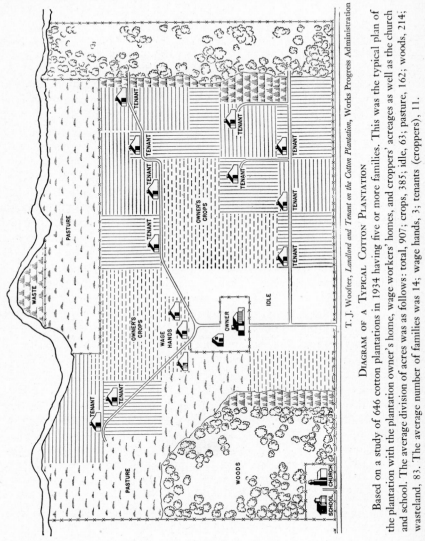

T. J. Woofter, *Landlord and Tenant on the Cotton Plantation*, Works Progress Administration

DIAGRAM OF A TYPICAL COTTON PLANTATION

Based on a study of 646 cotton plantations in 1934 having five or more families. This was the typical plan of the plantation with the plantation owner's home, wage workers' homes, and croppers' acreages as well as the church and school. The average division of acres was as follows: total, 907; crops, 385; idle, 63; pasture, 162; woods, 214; wasteland, 83. The average number of families was 14; wage hands, 3; tenants (croppers), 11.

come of the crop. Cash tenants are relatively few in the United States and are sparsely scattered throughout the nation,[1] share renting being generally preferred. In the state of Iowa especially, and in immediately surrounding areas in bordering states, desirable farms are rented for cash to a highly responsible

[1] See H. A. Turner, "A Graphic Summary of Farm Tenure," Fig. 21, p. 18, *Miscellaneous Publication* 261, U.S. Department of Agriculture, Washington, D. C., 1936.

tenant class. In Alabama and in other regions in the South, especially along the lower Mississippi River, there are renters who are defined as cash tenants, but usually they are located on very small farms and are so poor that each year they have to borrow money to pay their rent.

The Share Tenant.—The share tenant is one who operates independently, furnishing his own equipment, and giving part of the crop as rent. This is the

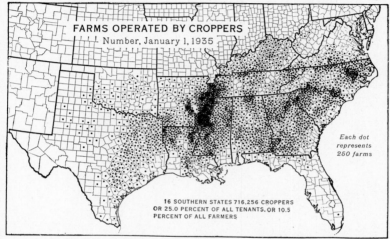

FARMS OPERATED BY CROPPERS
Number, January 1, 1935

Each dot represents 250 farms

16 SOUTHERN STATES 716,256 CROPPERS OR 25.0 PERCENT OF ALL TENANTS. OR 10.5 PERCENT OF ALL FARMERS

U.S. Bureau of Agricultural Economics

"In the South there are many farm workers classed as tenants because they are paid with a share of the crop, yet they have little, if any, more capital than a farm laborer. These workers, who have to be supplied with their work stock by the landowner, and commonly advanced a loan to provide food and living expenses, are called croppers. They are most numerous in the rich river bottom lands of western Mississippi and eastern Arkansas, where cotton dominates; also in the adjacent delta counties of Missouri, which are not shown on the map. Recently the tendency is to convert the croppers in this area into ordinary wage laborers, the landowner taking all the risk and all the profit, if any. More than three-fourths of all croppers in the Nation grow cotton, and about a tenth, tobacco—note Kentucky and Virginia in the map above."

most common type of tenant. From the standpoint of social and economic status share tenancy, in the Northern states, is almost the equivalent of ownership.

Croppers.—The cropper system is confined almost entirely to cotton farms in the South (see figure). Its unique feature is that work animals and tools are furnished by the landlord, the cropper paying rent with a share of the crop. He is little more than a farm laborer who receives his pay in kind rather than in cash. In this system reside the most serious problems of agricultural tenancy in the nation.

Part Owners.—A large group of tenants, who may be either share tenants or cash tenants, are part owners; that is, they own part of the land they farm but operate additional rented land. This system is most common in the northern

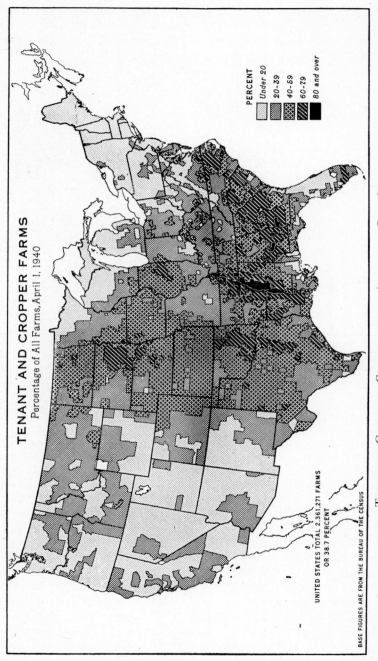

TENANT AND CROPPER FARMS

Percentage of All Farms, April 1, 1940

PERCENT

Under 20
20-39
40-59
60-79
80 and over

UNITED STATES TOTAL 2,361,271 FARMS
OR 38.7 PERCENT

BASE FIGURES ARE FROM THE BUREAU OF THE CENSUS

Tenancy is Generally Concentrated in Areas with Good Soil.

Great Plains wheat-growing and cattle-raising sections, where land held by absentee landlords is usually available.[1]

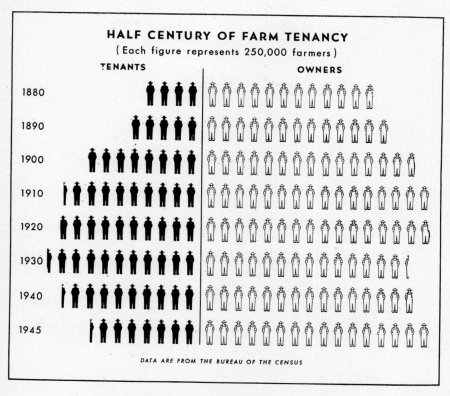

HALF CENTURY OF FARM TENANCY
(Each figure represents 250,000 farmers)

TENANTS   OWNERS

1880

1890

1900

1910

1920

1930

1940

1945

DATA ARE FROM THE BUREAU OF THE CENSUS

THE TREND OF FARM TENANCY

Between 1880 and 1930 there was a constant increase in percentage of farms operated by tenants. It has declined since 1930. The U.S. Census of Agriculture shows the following trend:

Year	Per cent of farms operated by tenants
1880	25.6
1890	28.4
1900	35.3
1910	37.0
1920	38.1
1930	42.4
1940	38.7
1945	31.7

[1] *Ibid.*, Fig. 20, p. 17.

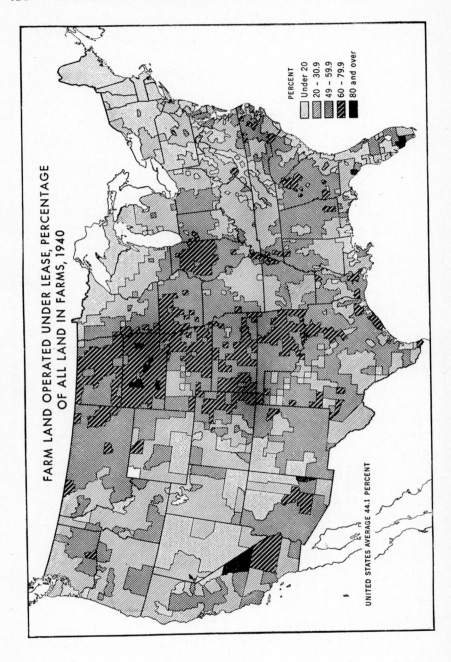

FARM LAND OPERATED UNDER LEASE, PERCENTAGE OF ALL LAND IN FARMS, 1940

PERCENT
Under 20
20 – 30.9
49 – 59.9
60 – 79.9
80 and over

UNITED STATES AVERAGE 44.1 PERCENT

The proportion of all farm land under lease to operators is more significant than the per cent of farms operated by tenants. It will be seen from the map

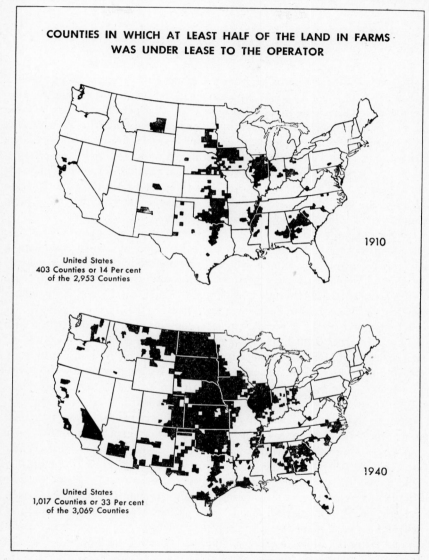

COUNTIES IN WHICH AT LEAST HALF OF THE LAND IN FARMS WAS UNDER LEASE TO THE OPERATOR

1910

United States
403 Counties or 14 Per cent
of the 2,953 Counties

1940

United States
1,017 Counties or 33 Per cent
of the 3,069 Counties

opposite that in the nation in 1940, 44.1 per cent of all land was so operated. The areas of greatest density were the Great Plains, parts of Iowa and Illinois, the deep South and parts of California and Arizona.

The trend toward the operation of farms by tenants over a 30-year period is strikingly shown by the maps of page 425, which compare 1910 with 1940 by showing areas where at least half of the land is under lease to the operator. The black area of the map has increased greatly.

THE EFFECT OF TENANCY ON LAND AND ON FARM IMPROVEMENTS

Tenancy has been expensive from the standpoint of waste of our natural resources.[1] It has long been known that tenancy leads to the mining of soils. The tenant tends to scale his enterprise to a one-year period, whereas, in order to rotate crops properly, one must think in terms of a three- or four-year cycle. Many soil conservation projects are expensive to maintain; men who operate a farm for only a short time cannot afford to maintain them. Usually soil-building and soil-conserving crops are less profitable than cash crops which deplete the soil. It is to be expected that a man who is to be on a farm for a short period will raise the crop that is most profitable at that particular time. Why build up the soil if another is going to reap the benefit?

The problem of soil waste in American agriculture is, however, not to be blamed entirely to the tenant. Many owners have bought land for speculation, expecting to farm it only temporarily. Other owners have carried such a heavy mortgage debt that they have been forced to mine the soil in order to earn interest payments and retain their equity in the land. But by and large, conditions tend to be worse on tenant-operated farms.

One major reason for the nation-wide consideration of problems of farm tenancy during the drought-depression period of the early New Deal epoch, when newspapers, forums, and discussion groups, as well as scientists in many fields first became concerned, was that the nation for the first time in its history had become conservation-minded. Wind-driven soils of the Great Plains powdered cities lying eastward to the Atlantic seaboard; floods took unprecedented tolls in life and property in metropolitan districts of the East. Punctuating as they did the message of soil-conservation experts, foresters, and geographers, these acts of nature made the public lend a receptive ear. People were ready to believe that the restoration of forests and grass to the uplands would reduce the havoc of floods and conserve moisture, that the restoration of the Plains to proper use by planting drought-resistant grasses would hinder wind erosion. A reduction in tenancy offered one way to improve land use.

Under the customary American short-term lease, farm property on tenant-operated farms deteriorates rapidly. This is so because the owner is less concerned about improving the property when he does not live on it, and the tenant has no motive for maintaining improvements on a farm which he does

[1] See *Farm Tenancy*, part I, Report of the President's Committee, National Resources Planning Board, Washington, D. C., 1937.

not own and does not expect to operate for any length of time. Houses and barns, wells and fences fall into disrepair; orchards and groves decay or die out and new ones are not planted. Thus not only is there an individual loss but a loss to the community and to the public. These difficulties to land use and improvements on farm property are not necessarily inherent in all tenancy but they are inherent in tenancy as practiced on the average farm in our nation where about one tenant in three remains on a farm only one year, where a considerable proportion of farms change hands every two or three years,[1] and where most leases are for one year and in 80 per cent of the cases are mere verbal agreements.[2]

Under a better type of lease, which would ensure long tenure to the tenant guaranteeing him certain rewards for building up the soil and improving farm property and which would assure him that his rent would not be raised, he would have a motive for improving the property on which he lives; at the present time, if he makes any improvements, like as not he will be asked to pay a higher rent the following year. Adequate leases would bind the landlord and the tenant to certain obligations which would protect both and at the same time conserve the public's heritage of natural resources.

TENANCY AND COMMUNITY INSTITUTIONS

Tenants are not concerned to the extent that owners are with the development, support, and maintenance of modern rural institutions—schools, churches, roads, recreational and health organizations, and government. Perhaps even more significant is the fact that the absentee landlord is not willing to carry a heavy tax burden for the support of local institutions which he and his family do not use.

Most local institutions, in order to function effectively, need to be built about a stable population that can be depended upon year after year, because effective leadership and a continuing program of activities are possible only when the community contains a nucleus of stable residents. This is especially true of voluntary social and recreational organizations in farming areas which depend upon unpaid leaders who must make personal sacrifices if their programs are to succeed. A man who knows that he and his children are going to live in a community until they grow up is usually more willing to assume responsibility and to give attention to local problems than is one who knows he will soon move on. Urban communities differ in that they are able to maintain paid professional leadership for many of their social and recreational organizations.

[1] *Ibid.*, p. iv.

[2] *The Flexible Farm Lease*, U.S. Department of Agriculture, Washington, D.C. (undated, but 1938 or 1939).

Educational problems are numerous in communities with a highly mobile tenant class. A rural school may be overcrowded for a time; then, with a shift

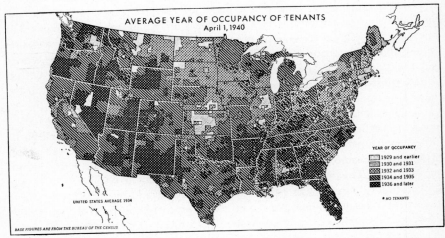

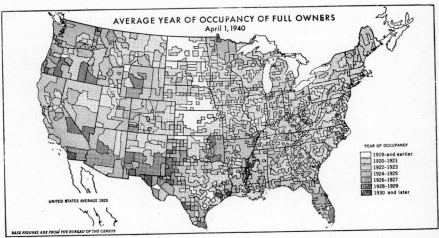

To live on the same farm a lifetime or for succeeding generations has never been an American ideal, but even so owners are much more stable than tenants, as a glance at these two maps shows clearly. Short tenure on land is associated with soil waste and deterioration of farm property.

in families, the district loses most of its pupils. Movement during the school year means a change in schools and often the retardation of the pupil. The problem of readjusting to a new school often is a factor in causing the child to drop out when he reaches the age when attendance is no longer compulsory.

Poor school attendance characterized the tenant family, especially in the South. Poverty among share croppers there has contributed to low educational achievements and illiteracy.[1]

The burden for the support of schools, like that for all local institutions, in any community falls to a large extent on the owner, tax-paying group. The interest of the owner group in improving community institutions is usually at a low ebb if the farms are mostly in the hands of tenants, for the absentee land-lord is seldom motivated by sufficient altruistic sentiments to cause him to boost for better local functions for the other person when they will cost him money. Schools are, therefore, poor in areas with a high rate of tenancy. The absentee landlord has little interest in replacing the little frame schoolhouse with a new building of good construction when it will mean high taxes on his land for a period of fifteen or twenty years. An owner who has children to educate may be willing to carry that burden.

The decline of the rural church is blamed in part to tenancy, for where rates of tenancy are high, country churches cannot survive. In shifting from com-munity to community the tenant loses interest in and contact with the church; therefore, church memberships are fewer and attendance is less frequent among tenants than among owners.[2] When a tenant enters a neighborhood as a stranger, few social pressures exist to lead him to continue his interest in the support of the church. In regions of low tenant income the inability of the tenant to support the church financially has a definite bearing on its disap-pearance, for generally, farm owners bear the major burden for the financial support of local churches.[3] In many Southern areas the lack of proper clothing among share croppers practically excludes them from attendance at church or participation in its activities.

Tenancy creates one of the major problems of rural electrification now faced by power companies and by the Rural Electrification Administration. In areas where the tenancy rate is high, the mobility of the farm operators is high. One renter may take advantage of electricity; the next may not use it. Because a company must be sure of a certain sale of power over a period of years, it cannot afford to finance construction in such communities. The situation pre-sents an equally difficult problem to the tenant, who hesitates to buy electrical equipment because there are so few farms where he can use it. There is another aspect to the problem. The owner usually is not interested in the electrifica-

[1] *Farm Tenancy, op. cit.,* pp. 59–60.

[2] *Ohio Rural Life Survey,* pp. 40–42, reports that only 13.4 per cent of tenants were members of churches in the community as compared to 86.8 per cent of owners. Department of Church and Country Life, Presbyterian Church, New York. See also *Farm Tenancy, op. cit.,* pp. 60–61.

[3] A survey in Johnson County, Missouri, showed that owners contributed 2.9 times as much per person as did tenants. O. R. Johnson and W. E. Ford, "Land Tenure," *Missouri Agricultural Experiment Station Bulletin* 212, Columbia, 1917.

tion of a tenant-operated farm or in the installation of other conveniences, which return nothing to him from the economic standpoint and cost him heavily.

THE TENANT'S STANDARD OF LIVING

The standard of living of tenants as measured by such criteria as food, housing, household equipment, and health expenditures, varies greatly from section to section of the country. In many Northern states the living standard

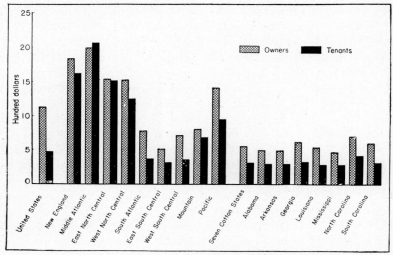

Works Progress Administration, based on Census data

MEDIAN VALUE OF FARM DWELLING, BY TENURE, 1930

The median value of tenant dwellings in the United States is less than half that of owner dwellings. In all sections except the Middle Atlantic States tenant dwellings have a lower value than those of owners. The most extreme situation is found in the seven cotton states shown on the graph. The value of farm dwellings is generally recognized as one of the best measures of the material aspects of the standard of living.

of the tenant, while not on a par with that of his owner neighbor, is not far below it. At the other extreme, throughout the area where share cropping predominates, tenancy is closely associated with poverty, ignorance, degradation, ill health, and misery. Many houses are windowless shacks, without screens, with leaky roofs, with no flyproof privy, and often with no privy of any kind (refer to the chart on page 489). Many of the people subsist on fatback pork, corn bread, sorghum molasses, and sweet potatoes. Pellagra and rickets, diseases caused by undernourishment, are common. Croppers own no tools or livestock and often are dependent upon the owner for even food and clothing, which he advances to them on credit, at interest rates which run as high as from 20 to 50 per cent per year.[1] Though the tenant's home and diet and health in the North and West may not equal those of his landlord, they seldom reach the low level found in the South. There are, however, throughout the nation tenant families living in dire poverty, poverty as severe, as enervating, and as destructive as the poverty found in our widely publicized city slums. Numerous studies of rural relief made during the depression period of the early thirties show that the proportion of tenants on relief was much higher than that of owners.[2]

Compensating somewhat for this darker side of the picture, many tenants are able to maintain a relatively high standard of living.[3] Under the ordinary cash-rent and share-tenant systems they enjoy a great deal of independence, more than do most workers in industry, and many of them are able to obtain for themselves and their children more of the essentials of good living than the urban masses.

Some tenants are large-scale operators who are tenants by choice, some of them feeling that they can earn more by renting than they could by owning, for as tenants they can invest all their capital in equipment rather than in land and handle larger acreages.[4] Others who are not so well off may prefer tenancy to mortgaged ownership; no doubt many of them can maintain a better standard of living as renters than they could as owners, for all their income can be spent for consumable goods rather than for land. On the average, however, the tenant's standard of living is lower than that of the owner in all sections.

The 1940 agricultural census assembled information concerning conveniences in owner and tenant homes for the various states (table, page 432). Note the marked contrast in percentages in the two groups. More than twice as many owners as tenants in the nation had four rooms or more; over twice as many, electric lights; over twice as many, water piped into dwellings; and three times as many, water piped into bath. Striking differences are shown in comparing region with region and state with state for both owner and tenant classes.

---

[1] *Farm Tenancy, op. cit.*, p. 46. See a so Charles S. Johnson, E. R. Embree, and W. W. Alexander, *The Collapse of Cotton Tenancy*, University of North Carolina Press, Chapel Hill, 1935; T. J.Woofter, *Landlord and Tenant on the Cotton Plantation*, Research Monograph X, Division of Social Research, Works Progress Administration, Washington, D. C.,1936.

[2] The findings of a great number of these studies have been summarized in the writer's "Relief Data as Criteria of Submarginality," *Journal of Farm Economics*, vol. 20, pp. 488–494, May, 1938. Refer also to chap. 27.

[3] Numerous studies have been made comparing the level of living of owners and tenants residing in the same community under similar conditions. Fifty of these studies, all but one of which have been made since 1922, are summarized by Edgar A. Schuler in his "The Present Social Status of American Farm Tenants," *Rural Sociology*, vol. 3, pp. 20–33, March, 1938.

[4] Carl C. Taylor, Helen W.Wheeler, and E. L. Kirkpatrick, *Disadvantaged Classes in American Agriculture*, pp. 37–40, Social Research Report 8, Farm Security Administration, Washington, D. C., 1938.

SIGNIFICANT INDEXES REGARDING THE HOMES OF FARM OPERATORS, BY TENURE OF OPERATOR BY STATES, 1940*

Percentage of owner-occupied and tenant-occupied dwellings having specific characteristics

State and region	3 rooms or less		Needing major repairs		Running water in dwelling		Private bathtub or shower		Electric lighting	
	Owner	Tenant	Owner	Tenant	Owner	Tenant	Owner	Tenant	Owner	Tenant
Maine	5.1	16.9	34.6	46.9	35.7	27.7	18.7	11.4	54.3	48.9
New Hampshire	4.0	12.9	18.6	22.4	60.2	59.9	35.5	32.2	66.8	65.5
Vermont	2.2	9.3	29.0	39.3	76.7	64.7	38.5	27.0	56.8	50.9
Massachusetts	3.5	17.9	16.2	18.3	73.4	69.5	55.1	48.4	83.8	80.0
Rhode Island	3.7	14.1	16.9	21.7	59.0	57.7	41.2	40.6	80.0	79.6
Connecticut	3.8	15.4	15.1	17.5	68.1	72.0	53.3	52.3	80.9	83.6
New York	2.1	8.4	22.9	29.9	47.5	38.0	33.6	23.2	71.4	66.3
New Jersey	3.8	14.6	21.4	27.2	67.6	53.2	52.4	35.6	85.3	75.2
Pennsylvania	3.1	13.1	26.8	32.0	41.2	32.1	24.8	15.5	61.0	52.2
Ohio	4.4	8.8	22.5	31.3	28.1	14.9	20.8	9.3	64.8	52.2
Indiana	8.5	12.0	21.8	27.7	21.7	12.3	15.4	6.6	54.1	43.3
Illinois	9.6	11.0	27.2	32.4	21.2	11.7	18.1	9.0	44.7	33.9
Michigan	8.3	13.6	25.9	34.6	32.2	20.5	18.7	10.0	73.4	63.1
Wisconsin	9.7	11.6	28.8	32.1	21.4	15.2	13.3	8.2	53.3	44.8
Minnesota	16.5	14.5	23.7	30.3	15.1	7.9	10.0	4.2	35.4	21.8
Iowa	4.0	5.8	20.4	27.1	29.3	15.5	22.7	9.4	50.3	31.4
Missouri	21.9	33.9	30.8	41.0	8.7	3.6	6.9	2.3	20.7	11.1
North Dakota	19.9	21.7	35.5	47.7	8.0	4.8	4.9	11.8	21.5	11.5
South Dakota	17.6	12.7	29.4	34.4	14.9	11.0	8.5	3.5	27.1	13.6
Nebraska	7.1	10.5	22.0	29.2	33.2	17.1	23.4	8.9	42.1	22.1
Kansas	7.6	11.2	29.7	40.0	22.7	10.6	17.7	6.7	36.5	21.1
The North	8.9	13.9	25.5	33.0	28.5	15.5	19.5	9.0	52.3	34.6

Delaware	4.0	12.0	20.0	29.3	32.5	16.8	23.8	10.0	53.3	27.6
Maryland	4.1	13.3	24.4	31.8	36.9	20.2	28.3	11.9	51.6	30.9
Virginia	13.1	33.1	27.7	38.2	15.8	6.9	11.6	4.1	30.5	13.9
West Virginia	14.0	35.3	33.3	44.4	13.1	6.0	7.7	2.9	29.1	16.5
North Carolina	15.0	35.4	32.3	46.3	11.6	2.3	7.2	1.1	34.7	13.4
South Carolina	15.4	37.0	23.0	30.9	12.5	1.9	9.7	1.0	32.9	9.4
Georgia	15.2	43.8	28.1	41.4	12.1	2.1	8.5	.9	34.3	9.1
Florida	20.6	50.8	35.0	41.2	25.5	12.0	21.3	7.4	30.4	13.6
Kentucky	24.7	48.3	34.4	44.6	5.4	2.6	4.2	1.3	19.3	9.5
Tennessee	23.8	55.4	32.7	45.7	9.1	2.3	6.1	1.1	22.0	8.4
Alabama	22.3	55.8	36.3	51.1	7.6	1.4	5.3	.7	25.6	6.6
Mississippi	19.3	58.4	35.3	38.0	7.6	1.4	6.0	.9	18.5	4.4
Arkansas	30.6	55.2	40.6	48.4	5.1	1.3	3.7	.8	14.7	4.1
Louisiana	23.7	56.6	29.2	40.1	12.1	2.7	9.9	1.8	19.2	5.0
Oklahoma	30.3	50.7	39.8	56.9	13.8	4.6	9.7	2.4	23.7	9.2
Texas	21.6	45.6	26.4	37.9	32.1	13.5	21.2	5.4	30.8	12.3
The South	20.4	47.9	31.9	42.9	14.1	4.5	9.9	2.2	26.8	9.2
Montana	34.6	46.1	23.9	31.2	19.5	10.7	12.6	5.5	34.3	24.9
Idaho	27.7	42.6	29.4	36.5	38.6	23.0	24.1	10.0	63.8	59.3
Wyoming	36.2	54.6	30.6	34.4	20.2	12.4	13.4	6.9	36.1	28.6
Colorado	24.3	36.7	29.4	39.9	30.7	16.2	19.8	7.5	45.4	30.8
New Mexico	56.1	64.4	27.9	38.3	15.6	14.3	10.4	7.1	19.5	19.3
Arizona	64.9	70.7	17.1	26.2	30.4	30.4	23.1	17.7	30.4	41.8
Utah	28.2	54.0	29.2	40.8	57.5	36.1	36.2	14.9	80.5	68.6
Nevada	30.3	49.9	23.4	26.9	49.8	38.1	35.9	23.5	53.4	50.9
Washington	18.8	32.0	21.7	31.8	61.9	49.2	43.1	27.4	75.8	65.2
Oregon	17.5	31.0	24.3	32.4	57.6	45.9	40.7	25.9	64.6	55.3
California	15.7	42.4	15.5	24.8	87.4	70.7	74.3	47.2	85.4	80.0
The West	25.9	42.6	22.8	31.2	53.9	42.6	40.5	25.8	63.0	56.4
United States	15.5	36.5	28.0	38.9	25.0	10.6	17.6	6.0	42.6	20.6

* Bureau of Human Nutrition and Home Economics. Compiled from the Sixteenth Census of the United States (1940), *Housing*, Bureau of the Census.

Take the matter of having water piped into the house, which probably saves the farm housewife more labor than any other single convenience. (The average farm housewife carries several dozen buckets of water from a pump in the yard into the house every week.) In a few states, mostly located on the North-

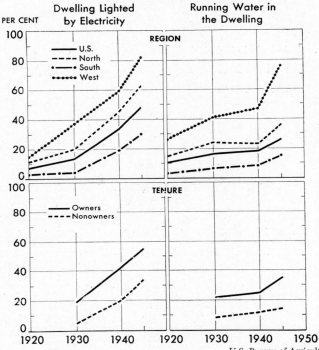

TRENDS IN ELECTRICITY AND RUNNING WATER
IN FARM DWELLINGS, 1920-45

U.S. Bureau of Agricultural Economics

Thanks primarily to the Rural Electrification Administration, rural electrification has showed marked gains over 25 years. The mountainous West with abundant waterpower leads. In the nation over a third more owners than tenants have electricity. Except for the Far West, few farmers have running water. Even in 1945 only about 17 per cent of tenant's homes had running water; only about 38 per cent of owner's homes.

eastern seaboard, more than half the landlords and tenants had water piped into the dwelling. The proportion of tenants was somewhat lower than that of the landlords but not strikingly so. Westward, even in the Northern states, the proportions of tenants having water piped into the house decreased and the difference between landlord and tenant became greater. Iowa, in some ways the most favored agricultural state in the Union, had comparatively few homes with running water. In 1945 one-third of the landlords (35 per cent) had water piped into the dwelling and less than one-fifth of the tenants (17 per cent). (See chart on page 434.)

The situation with regard to electric lights has changed considerably in recent years, thanks to the Rural Electrification Administration, but differ-

TRENDS IN TELEPHONE AND RADIO
IN FARM DWELLINGS, 1920-45

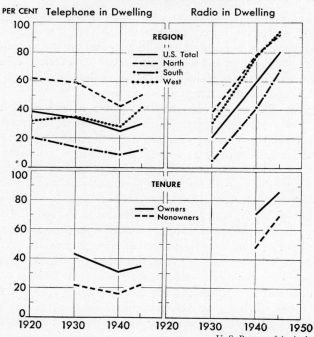

U. S. Bureau of Agricultural Economics

With the coming of the automobile, telephone use in farm homes declined. There is a differential between owners and tenants in ownership of a telephone. The radio has become a nearly universal possession of farm homes in the North and West. Of tenants in the nation 70 per cent have radios; of owners, over 85 per cent.

ences between owners and tenants are still considerable. In 1945, some 68 per cent of owners had electricity, but only 54 per cent of tenants (chart; page 434).

The automobile has made the telephone less essential, but considerable difference in telephone ownership between owners and tenants exists. Both owners and tenants have shared in the rapid growth of radio use, but only 70 per cent of tenants, as compared to 86 per cent of owners, had radios in April, 1945, when the Census of Agriculture was taken (chart above).

McMillan, in a recent paper,[1] has rightly raised the question of whether

[1] Robert T. McMillan, "Are Tenure Differences Due to Tenure?" *Journal of Farm Economics*, vol. 28, pp. 1029–1036, November, 1946

tenure differences such as those discussed in this section are actually due to tenure. In his critical analysis he shows that differences in age of tenants and operators, size of farm operated, differences in family history with regard to having acquired an original homestead, and other such factors actually account in part for some of the marked differences in the tenure classes.

SOCIAL POSITION OF THE FARM TENANT

Schuler, in a study designed to uncover the effect of tenancy on social status, chose two regions for comparison, the corn belt and the cotton South.[1] The high points of his findings are as follows: Farm owners in both the North and the South, both blacks and whites, feel better off as owners than they did before they became owners. Tenants in the South think that they would rather become mortgaged owners than remain tenants. On the other hand, of the Northern group the majority feel they are better off as tenants than if they were owners of a mortgaged place. Southern nonowners feel certain that they would be much better off as owners, but Northern landowners are not so sure.

These different reactions, no doubt, represent to a considerable extent a difference in the status of tenants in the corn belt of the North and in the Southern cotton belt. In the corn belt of Iowa, a number of tenants who pay cash rent feel themselves equal to owners in every way, and many of them actually make as much money as do the owners. In the South, the owner has much more prestige than the tenant. Farmer attitudes as to status are reflected in their choice of a vocation for their children. Most Negro farmers in the South would rather their sons would choose some occupation other than farming, and not even half of the Southern white owners and tenant farmers would prefer their sons to be farmers. Northern farmers express little preference as to what their sons become, feeling that the son should decide for himself; but of those who express a preference, the majority name farming as first choice. In all sections, farmers who hope that their sons will become farmers hope that they will become owners.

More subtle aspects of social status may be measured by the prevalence of intermarriage between farm owner and tenant classes. Schuler finds that the tendency of all groups is to marry in their own class, but this tendency is most pronounced in the South, where caste lines are more rigidly drawn. Social visiting also takes place in all sections chiefly within a particular tenure class. He is inclined to explain the difference in social stratification in the North and South, as reflected in attitudes of owners and tenants, by the fact that, in the North, settlement has taken place so recently that stratification has had little time to develop. Also, in the North a much larger proportion of tenants can look forward to becoming owners. Plantations appeared early in the Southern

[1] E. A. Schuler, *op. cit.* For a more extensive account see his *Social Status and Farm Tenure—Attitudes and Social Conditions of Corn Belt and Cotton Belt Farmers*, Social Research Report 4, U.S. Department of Agriculture, Washington, D. C., 1938.

system of agriculture, and difference of social status led to the development of a virtual caste system. The status of the Negro probably has affected unfavorably the status of the white tenant, both tending to be given a low caste position.

TENANCY AND PROBLEMS OF PERSONAL ADJUSTMENT

The principles and problems involved in social adjustment have been discussed extensively in other chapters. It has been demonstrated many times that mobility, which takes the person from community to community, involves him in a series of new adjustment processes that constitute for him a crisis in personality development. As a highly mobile group in American agriculture, tenants are faced repeatedly with situations demanding readjustment. Adult, youth, and child, meeting new situations, must either learn to fit into them or fail in adjustment. The problems of the child in fitting into a new school environment, of the entire family in maintaining harmonious relations with neighbors in a new primary group, of the head of the household in working under the supervision of a new landlord, the need to learn the capacities of the new farm to produce, these and numerous other problems of vital import to personality are involved in the shifting of several hundred thousands of tenants from one farm to another and from one community to another each year.

In most communities there is not much discrimination shown against the tenant, often none at all, except in the Southeast and to a lesser extent in the Southwest; nevertheless, he does not feel that he is a part of the community life, he does not remain in one place long enough to develop a sense of identification with the group and its interests, and he may move too often even to feel at home in the community. Adjustment is doubly difficult for his children, because they continually are being taken out of one school and placed in another in the middle of the term; in the corn-hog country the move comes in early spring, about March, and in the wheat country it comes in the fall after school is in session. Little wonder that the numerous studies of farm tenancy show that tenants have fewer social contacts than owners, participate in fewer social organizations, and in general play a small part in the organized social and institutional life of the community.[1]

REDUCING TENANCY

During recent years social action of two principal kinds has been contemplated in meeting the problem of tenancy: (1) measures designed to reduce farm tenancy by promoting ownership; (2) measures designed to improve the conditions of tenancy.

[1] For a typical study, see W. V. Dennis, "Social Activities of the Families in the Unionville District," Chester County, Pennsylvania, *Pennsylvania Agricultural Experiment Station Bulletin* 286, State College, 1933.

To offset the various handicaps, such as high land prices, small profits in agriculture, and credit stringencies, which in recent decades have hindered tenants from climbing to the status of ownership, two major governmental programs have been designed to assist the tenant in becoming an owner. The Farm Credit Administration, created in 1933, makes loans to owners in danger of losing their land and makes loans to tenants and laborers who want to buy farms. Such loans were in great demand during the thirties. In 1938 more than 2,000 applicants a month were obtaining farms through them.[1] During 1945, when credit was less in demand, applications averaged over 1,000 monthly.

More recent is the Bankhead-Jones Farm Tenancy Act, first administered by the Farm Security Administration, which made available $10,000,000 for the fiscal year ending June 30, 1938, to competent tenants, share croppers, and farm workers desiring to purchase farms; $25,000,000 for the fiscal year ending June 30, 1939; and $40,000,000 for 1940. This program is now under the Farmers' Home Administration.

Loans are made for a 40-year period at a $3\frac{1}{2}$ per cent interest rate. Full payment can be made at any time after five years. Loans have been in such great demand that the program has had to be limited each year to a few counties. In each county, committees consisting of three farmers certify all applicants eligible to receive loans. The applicant must purchase a family-sized farm that can be operated chiefly with family labor; the price of land purchased must be in accordance with values determined by the county committee and the FHA. Loans may include not only the cost of the farm but cost of repairs to buildings and of improving the land. In the amended act of 1946, veterans are given preference for tenant purchase loans. Loans to veterans and others are to be granted only if the farm unit is of such a size and type as to assure an efficient family-type farm-management unit.

We have hardly yet begun to realize developments that might be possible through a well-directed program for financing farm purchase. Denmark has made a record in this respect that is unrivaled. In 1875 a system of land credit banks was established in that country to help tenants and others to the ownership of small farms. This movement as it developed, along with the growth of cooperative credit unions and cooperative marketing associations, made Denmark, within a period of about fifty years, a nation of farm owners, a nation in which almost half of the farming population had been poor, illiterate tenants.

It is generally recognized that helping people to buy farms is not sufficient. Henry Wallace, in an address over the Columbia Broadcasting System, called attention to the fact that in the history of the nation we have given away 200,000,000 acres of land to homesteaders, but that a high percentage of this same land is today operated by tenants. Plans must be formulated for keeping

[1] *The Agricultural Situation*, vol. 22, No. 8, Bureau of Agricultural Economics, U.S. Department of Agriculture, Washington, D. C., August, 1938.

the owner from losing his farm through speculation and excessive mortgage debt. Many tenants have developed habits of waste and are lacking in the capacity to manage; it is highly questionable whether such persons should be put on farms. In the light of these facts the activities of the Farmers Home Administration in trying to educate and rehabilitate people of tenant status assume great significance.

IMPROVING TENANCY

Many problems of tenancy center about the relation of the tenant to the landlord. Difficulties here are due primarily to the short-time lease, most leases in America being made on a year-to-year basis, and, as we have seen, 80 per

PLANTATIONS MAKING SUBSISTENCE ADVANCES: AMOUNT, DURATION, AND ANNUAL RATE OF INTEREST, BY AREAS, 1934*
(Cotton Plantation Enumeration)

Area	Total plantations reporting	Amount of advances	Average months duration	Annual rate of interest
Total..........................	535	$634,980	3.6	37.1
Atlantic Coast Plain..............	44	29,924	4.3	19.0
Upper Piedmont..................	33	8,436	3.4	18.7
Black Belt (A)....................	88	39,424	3.8	19.5
Black Belt (B)....................	81	22,449	3.4	22.9
Upper Delta......................	119	280,274	3.3	40.6
Lower Delta......................	34	25,031	3.0	44.8
Muscle Shoals....................	16	8,147	3.4	14.9
Interior Plain....................	29	42,818	3.6	36.3
Mississippi Bluffs.................	45	46,061	3.1	40.3
Red River........................	20	43,154	3.7	30.0
Arkansas River...................	26	89,262	2.9	55.0

* From T. J. Woofter, *Landlord and Tenant on the Cotton Plantation*, p. 63, Works Progress Administration, Washington, D. C., 1936.

About the furnishing system center many of the worst evils of cotton tenancy. The cropper is advanced varying amounts to carry him through until the next crop is harvested. These advances are made by landlords and merchants. The average annual interest rate, it will be observed, is 37 per cent. It ranges in various sections from 15 to 55 per cent. Woofter comments: "It is evident . . . that landlords and merchants are taking care to keep the interest rate well above any possibility of loss from defaulting tenants. . . . Since landlord and merchant credit continue to be relatively easy to obtain, there is no decided incentive for prompt payment of debts. Moreover, the hard terms and the knowledge gained by experience that the store bill will eventually take a large proportion of the crop anyway, often cause the tenant to become discontented, to produce poor crops, and to be indifferent toward repayment."

cent of them being oral only.[1] The tenant is uninterested in making improvements for which he receives no return; the landlord complains of the run-down condition of his farm and buildings. Much attention has been given in recent years to the improvement of the farm contract, the aim being to design one which will guarantee a long-time lease, make obligatory upon both owner and tenant certain responsibilities, and assure the tenant of reasonable compensation provided he meets a set standard in the management of the farm.

It is recognized, of course, that there is little hope of the great majority of farm tenants (1,858,421 in 1945) becoming owners. This being the case, measures for improving tenancy as a system of life offer great promise for immediate action. A study of tenancy systems in certain foreign countries, Scotland, New Zealand, and Australia among them, indicates that tenancy is not necessarily bad.[2] Fairly effective tenancy systems can be worked out and made to function satisfactorily. In Scotland, boards have been provided by law to determine farm rental rates, and laws have been passed guaranteeing the tenant that he will be paid for making improvements on buildings and fences and for restoring soil fertiliy. Rental contracts are for long periods and can be broken only for legal cause. Courts have been set up for adjusting differences between landlords and tenants. The entire system is designed to preserve the land, to increase the value of tenant-operated farms, and to stabilize the tenant farmer.

In this country much study is being given to new forms of lease contracts and, no doubt, in the near future new forms of legislation will come into being, having to do with the improvement of tenancy in the interest of conserving both our natural and human resources in agriculture.[3]

In the South a focal point for attack is the "furnishing system" whereby the landlord provides the tenant with credit at the plantation commissary as a part of the contract, or arranges for credit to be extended him at a local store or bank. Frequently high prices are charged and exorbitant interest rates prevail (table on p. 439). The system is fundamentally unsound in that it not only creates an impossible situation for the tenant but involves great risks to the creditor. Here it would seem that some general system of production credit at reasonable interest rates is essential.[4]

[1] *The Flexible Farm Lease, op. cit.*

[2] See Erich Kraemer, *Tenure of New Agricultural Holdings in Several European Countries*, Social Research Report No. II, U.S. Department of Agriculture, Washington, D. C., 1937; Marshall Harris and Douglas F. Schepmoes, "Scotland's Activity in Improving Farm Tenancy," *Land Policy Circular*, p. 10, February, 1936; Elizabeth R. Hooker, *Recent Policies Designed to Promote Farm Ownership in Denmark*, Land Use Planning Publication No. 15, U.S. Department of Agriculture, Washington, D. C., 1937.

[3] For an excellent summary of the tenancy problem and possibilities for improvement, see Dover P. Trent, *The Nation's Soil and Human Resources*, mimeographed, U.S. Department of Agriculture, Washington, D. C., not dated.

[4] *Ibid.*, pp. 11–12. See also Charles S. Johnson, *et al.*, *op. cit.*

OTHER MEASURES

During the years since 1930 many measures of far-reaching importance have been aimed at increasing the security of the farm owner and at helping him maintain his equity in the land. These measures bear directly on problems of tenancy since tenants, as we have seen, have been recruited from above as well as from beneath. Not only do farm laborers work up to tenancy, but farm

ESTIMATED EQUITY OF FARM OPERATORS IN FARM REAL ESTATE, 1880-1940
(BASED ON THE CENSUS)

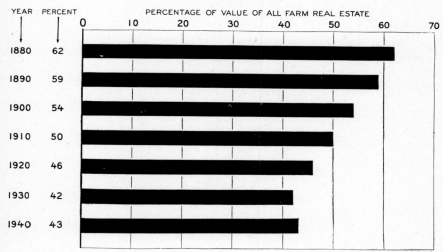

U.S. Bureau of Agricultural Economics

In 1880 the equity of farm operators in farm real estate, that is, the proportion remaining after the value of farms operated by tenants and the mortgage debt on farms operated by owners has been subtracted from the value of all farms, was over 62 per cent. Each decade thereafter, in periods of prosperity as well as of depression, the percentage declined about four points, until in 1930 it was only 42 per cent. An increasing proportion of farm operators has been sharing the income from the land with landlords or mortgage holders. But the percentage of farms mortgaged declined between 1920 and 1940, doubtless owing in large measure to foreclosures.

Because many farm owners have a small equity in their land, the tenant class is recruited from above in times of economic adversity. World War II lightened the farm dept.

owners, many of them with years of experience as owner-operators, drop to the rank of tenants.

A high proportion of farm owners in America own only a small equity in their land, it being heavily encumbered with indebtedness. Between 1910 and 1928 the percentage of farms that were mortgaged steadily increased. In 1930, 41 per cent of them were mortgaged, the debt amounting to over 40 per cent of the value of the mortgaged farms. According to an estimate made in 1932, based on 17,000 reporting farms, 5 per cent of all mortgaged farms were mortgaged for more than their total value, 16 per cent for over three-fourths of their value, and 38 per cent for over half their value.[1] The chart on page 441 shows the equity of farmers in their land at census periods from 1880 to 1940. As a consequence during times of financial stress when prices are low and credit is difficult to obtain, a large number of these individuals forfeit ownership. This situation was so prominent throughout the nation during the depression of the early thirties that the government greatly expanded credit facilities, extended its lending activities, reduced interest rates, and gradually assumed an increasing proportion of farm debt, shifting it from private to public agencies.

During this period special measures were taken to hinder foreclosures on farms. Moratorium provisions were established by law, giving creditors two years of grace in which to redeem their assets after foreclosure proceedings had been instituted. Debt conciliation committees were appointed throughout the nation to try to work out a new standard of values between creditors and debtors and to redraw mortgage contracts. During two and one-half years beginning Sept. 1, 1935, these committees adjusted debts of 68,948 individual farmers by an average of 25 per cent. Debts of 229 million dollars were scaled down to 171 million dollars.[2]

It was during this period also that long-time programs of economic adjustment were greatly expanded. Land retirement programs were aimed at returning submarginal lands to the public domain, at reducing human failure and the waste of our soil resources; land classification and land zoning activities were developed to protect the land and to guide the individual in making his adjustments to the land. Soil conservation became the national motto; erosion control, a national program. The nation became aware, as at no previous time in our history, of the relationship between waste and human risk, between natural resources and human welfare, between unproductive land and unproductive lives.

The objectives of a more stable agriculture, a more permanent type of land ownership, and adequate programs for helping those who wish to become owners to climb normally and independently toward this status are still far from realization.

QUESTIONS FOR REVIEW AND DISCUSSION

1. What factors have been responsible for the increasing rate of tenancy?
2. Trace the trend of farm tenancy in the nation; in your state.
3. Distinguish between three classes of tenants.
4. Suggest points at which problems of conservation and farm upkeep are affected by tenancy.

[1] E. F. Dummeier and R. B. Heflebower, *Economics with Applications to Agriculture*, pp. 514–515, McGraw-Hill Book Company, Inc., New York, 1934.

[2] *Helping the Farmer Adjust his Debts*, Farm Security Administration, U.S. Department of Agriculture (undated but about 1938).

5. Show how tenancy affects community institutions—schools, churches, voluntary organizations, and rural electrification projects.

6. How does the tenant's standard of living compare with that of the owner in different regions of the nation?

7. Does tenancy increase health, relief, and welfare problems? Cite evidence.

8. How does the social status of the tenant compare with that of the owner in the South? in the North?

9. Explain the problems of personal adjustment faced by the average tenant family.

10. What factors in the tenant situation are likely to lead to greater stratification in rural life unless they are corrected?

11. Outline recent measures designed to increase farm ownership.

12. Might a more satisfactory system of farm tenancy be developed? Explain.

13. Show how measures designed to strengthen the position of the farm owner will help check an increase in farm tenancy.

14. How may long-time adjustments in agriculture affect problems of tenancy?

COLLATERAL READING

Anderson, C. Arnold and Bruce Ryan: "Social Participation Differences Among Farm Tenure Classes in a Prosperous Commercial Farming Area," *Rural Sociology*, vol. 8, pp. 281–290, September, 1943.

Gillette, J. M.: *Rural Sociology*, 3d ed., chap. 25, The Macmillan Company, New York, 1936.

Hoffsommer, Harold: "The AAA and the Cropper," *Social Forces*, vol. 13, pp. 494–502, May, 1935.

Johnson, C. S., E. R. Embree, and W. W. Alexander: *The Collapse of Cotton Tenancy*. University of North Carolina Press, Chapel Hill, 1935.

"Let's Talk About Farm Leases and How They Can Be Improved," United States Department of Agriculture, Washington, D. C., 1945.

McMillan, Robert T. and Otis Durant Duncan: "Social Factors of Farm Ownership," *Oklahoma Agricultural Experiment Station Bulletin* B-289, November, 1945.

McMillan, Robert T.: "Are Tenure Differences Due to Tenure? *Journal of Farm Economics*, vol. 28, pp. 1029–1036, November, 1946.

Raper, Arthur F.: *Tenants of the Almighty*, The Macmillan Company New York, 1943.

Report of the President's Committee: *Farm Tenancy*, National Resources Planning Board, Washington, D. C., 1937.

Roberts, Harry W.: "Effects of Farm Ownership on Rural Family Life," *Social Forces*, vol. 24, pp. 185–194, December, 1945.

Schuler, Edgar A.: *Social Status and Farm Tenure—Attitudes and Social Conditions of Corn Belt and Cotton Belt Farmers*, Social Research Report No. 4, U.S. Department of Agriculture, Washington, D. C., 1938.

Taylor, Paul S.: "Power Farming and Labor Displacement in the Cotton Belt, 1937," *Monthly Labor Review*, pp. 595–706, March, 1938.

Turner, H. A.: "A Graphic Summary of Farm Tenure," *Miscellaneous Publication* 261, U.S. Department of Agriculture, Washington, D. C., 1936.

Woofter, T. J.: *Landlord and Tenant on the Cotton Plantation*, Research Monograph X, Division of Social Research, Works Progress Administration, Washington, D. C., 1936.

CHAPTER 28

SOCIAL ASPECTS OF FARM LABOR

At few points in the agricultural enterprise is the confusion caused by the disorganizing forces of a transitional age more apparent than in the farm labor situation. The farm labor group has drawn the castaways of mechanized farming areas as well as of urban industrial culture. To this group, at the bottom of the social pyramid in rural society, drift not only the tenant farmers and share croppers who have been crowded out of farming by the newer trends but also former farm owners who have lost their farm property through speculation, mortgage debt, or failure induced by natural hazards. Here also one finds youth who want to farm but have been unable to establish themselves as farm operators, and those who do not want to farm but have been balked in seeking other work outlets. Among farm laborers one finds the least in the way of income and security that agriculture affords. Many of them are so completely grounded that they can never hope to climb the rungs of the agriculture ladder to reach a better social and economic position.

In this problem, as it manifests itself in some sections, one sees the confusion caused by the older philosophy of a family-farm paternalistic type of agriculture in which farmer and laborer were close together, the laborer being treated as a member of the family, and that of a large-scale commercial agriculture in which industrial patterns are beginning to characterize relationships between operator and worker.

The widespread belief, now largely a myth in certain regions, that the farm laborer is a coworker with the farm family, persists in the face of the fact that in many sections agricultural labor has become a semiindustrial group working in certain cases on large commercial farms which are not far different from outdoor factories.

It is in the farm labor field that the clash between capital and labor is becoming apparent in the agricultural situation. On the one hand are large-scale producers on corporate farms, well organized to dominate the labor group; on the other hand, a mobile fly-by-night group of laborers trying to attain sufficient force to stage organized combat through strikes and sabotage. To the extent that organizations of farm laborers and of farm employers have developed they have been built along industrial lines, imitating the laborer-employer patterns of urban-industrial organization. It is in this situation that some of the newer aspects of the farm labor problem have developed.

NUMBER OF FARM LABORERS

The Federal Census of 1940 showed that during the last week in March there were 7,940,727 family workers on farms in the United States and during the last week in September, 8,128,770. The number of hired workers at the March period was 1,753,441 persons and for the September period, 3,121,482. Since the number of workers fluctuates from month to month, an invoice of labor employed at other months would have been quite different. The number of family workers employed is at its peak in June, the low point in farm employment, January. With hired labor, the peak month for the nation is July, the low months January and February.

An index of seasonal variation in agricultural employment for the period 1925 to 1936 in the United States shows the following with regard to fluctuations in workers employed:[1]

	All workers	Family workers	Hired workers
12 months' average...............	100	100	100
January........................	81	84	70
February.......................	84	87	72
March..........................	88	90	80
April...........................	96	98	94
May............................	107	107	108
June............................	116	115	119
July............................	113	111	120
August.........................	104	102	111
September......................	106	104	111
October........................	114	111	122
November......................	103	102	107
December......................	88	89	84

In various regions the monthly cycle of employment on farms varies according to crops raised. Some crop areas demand large numbers of workers for short periods, others few workers, but require them for longer periods.

Although the family labor group is the largest group of workers, the major part of this discussion centers about the hired labor group, since this is the group about which problems of income, migration, social security legislation, and other issues of social policy center.

CLASSES OF HIRED FARM LABORERS

It is in the hired farm labor group that one finds many unique rural problems. It is this group that is the most conglomerate culturally, racially, and

[1] From Witt Bowden, *Three Decades of Farm Labor*, Table 5, p. 11, U.S. Department of Labor, Washington, D. C., 1939.

socially of the farm population. Attitudes and characteristics vary according to past conditions of living. A worker's economic status and his social outlook are determined in part by the length of time he has been a farm laborer; by whether he is a regular farm laborer or an industrial worker filling in a period of industrial unemployment or a farm owner bridging a period of drought; by whether he is a white man who has known a better way of life or a member of a racial group that has never experienced what the American considers the comfort level of living; by whether he is one of the roving migrants who for many years have been divorced from all local ties or one who stays in the same community and knows that he is of it even though he lives "beyond the tracks"; by whether he is a part of a family group that travels in quest of work or a foot-loose single worker who either is unmarried, is divorced, or left home without the formalities of a divorce. To describe adequately social and economic types of farm laborers is in some respects as difficult as to describe types of Chicago industrial workers. There are many kinds of folk who work at farm labor. Nonetheless, a crude kind of classification is essential to any degree of understanding.

The Hired Man.—We ordinarily think of the hired man as one who works for long periods on one farm, sharing in the life of the family. Often he is a capable, stable, experienced, intelligent worker who looks forward to acquiring enough assets to become a tenant and eventually an owner. Like the hired girl, he is usually employed on a monthly basis. His number has greatly decreased in most sections of the country.

This group is not ordinarily a problem group although it does create difficulties. The character of the average hired man sometimes is far from ideal, and his influence on the children in the family is not always a wholesome one. Often the farm laborer has little place in the social life of the neighborhood, being forced to seek recreation in the town.[1]

The Resident Seasonal Worker.—The resident farm laborer ordinarily lives in the small town. Often he is a married man with a family. Eking out a miserable existence, his lot in some respects is as bad as that of the migratory laborer. During depression periods he and his family are on relief rolls, for usually he finds little employment in the small town during the six months of the year when no agricultural work is available.[2]

---

[1] Carl C. Taylor, *Rural Sociology*, rev. ed., pp. 106–108, Harper & Brothers, New York, 1933.

[2] Studies in the Yakima Valley, Washington, show that the earnings of resident laborers are little more than those of transients. Usually resident laborers have less than six months of employment per year. Wage rates are usually low in agriculture. Resident farm labor families are likely to live in the poorest shacks in the community. See Paul H. Landis, "Seasonal Agricultural Labor in the Yakima Valley," *Monthly Labor Review*, pp. 1–11, August, 1937; also Paul H. Landis and Melvin S. Brooks, "Farm Labor in the Yakima Valley, Washington," *Washington Agricultural Experiment Stations Bulletin* 343, Pullman,

The Casual Farm Laborer.—The casual farm laborer is one whose usual occupation is outside agriculture. He is found engaged chiefly in the harvest of seasonal crops, working at jobs that require little skill or training and often comparatively little vigor, such as picking fruits, vegetables, or hops. The number of casual workers in agriculture depends considerably on conditions of employment in urban centers, for at times of unemployment great masses flock from the city to the hinterlands in search of farm work.

The Hobo or Bindle Tramp.—The migratory single worker, the "bindle tramp," who carries his worldly possessions in a bed roll and travels from section to section by freight, is a common type in many agricultural sections. He is seen loafing in the city park, cooking in the "jungle," and riding the box car. He works and wanders by turn. The amount of time spent at work depends on the availability of jobs and the mood of the hobo.

The Migratory Family Worker.—Large numbers of migratory family workers are a comparatively new phenomenon in agriculture, made possible by the cheap secondhand automobile. In a car about ten years old[1] the migratory family moves from job to job. Their migration habits are somewhat different from those of single workers because they are more restricted by transportation costs, and they seek jobs at which the whole family can work— such as picking berries, peas, hops, and cotton. These migratory families usually find only short-time employment in any locality and, instead of settling down as many had once hoped to do, they have to keep moving in quest of work.

The migratory farm laborers' occupation offers but a scanty hand-to-mouth existence as they drift from job to job, often with a lapse of months between periods of employment.

THE MIGRATORY WORKER A PRODUCT OF SEASONAL AGRICULTURE

The migratory worker exists because of the seasonal demand for labor in intensive crop areas where the supply of local help is insufficient. California has the greatest need for migrant seasonal workers of any state, but the citrus and vegetable areas of Florida, the irrigated areas of the Pacific Northwest where apples, hops, and berries are grown, the pea fields of Idaho, and the berry fields of Arkansas, all demand the migrant for short periods. Intensive crop districts in the vicinity of eastern metropolitan centers also use large numbers of seasonal workers.

1936; Paul H. Landis and Richard Wakefield, "The Annual Employment Cycle of Farm Labor Households," Washington Agricultural Experiment Stations, mimeographed, Pullman, 1938.

[1] See Carl F. Reuss, Paul H. Landis, and Richard Wakefield, "Migratory Farm Labor and the Hop Industry on the Pacific Coast," *Washington Agricultural Experiment Stations Bulletin* 363, Pullman, 1938.

The situation in the Yakima Valley, Washington, is typical of the fluctuating seasonal demand for labor that characterizes many crop areas. Before the mechanization of World War II, 32,000 full-time workers working ten hours a day, six days a week, were needed during the second week in September to pick hops (figure below). Two weeks later the hop season was practically over. Although the apple-picking season started soon afterward, even at its

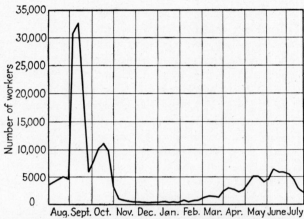

Paul H. Landis, "The Hop Industry, A Social and Economic Problem," *Economic Geography*, vol. 15, p. 89, 1939.

ESTIMATED NUMBER OF HIRED WORKERS NEEDED EACH WEEK OF THE YEAR FOR AGRICULTURAL WORK IN THE YAKIMA VALLEY, WASHINGTON

Hops were chiefly responsible for the transient labor problem in the Yakima Valley, Washington, because the hop acreages required over 32,000 full-time workers during the early September harvest. In comparison, the apple harvest a month later required only around 12,000 hired laborers and the summer harvest of soft fruits only 4,000 to 6,000 from week to week. During winter months only 400 to 500 full-time workers were needed. Mechanization during World War II greatly reduced these peak loads, lessening the need for extensive farm labor migration.

peak, which was not reached until the middle of October, only about 12,000 workers were required. By midwinter the demand for farm laborers in the Yakima Valley had shrunk to about 500 workers per week. Thus the number needed at the peak period was about seventy times that of the period of low demand.[1]

Many agricultural areas in irrigated sections of the West experience a similar fluctuation in demand for farm labor. With the development of mechanized farming in cotton and sugar production in the South, the tendency is for labor to be employed chiefly in the harvest, causing violent seasonal fluctua-

[1] Paul H. Landis and Melvin Brooks, *op. cit.*, Table 8, p. 29. For an analysis of the situation in Arizona's irrigated areas see E. D. Tetreau, "Hired Labor Requirements on Arizona Irrigated Farms," *Arizona Agricultural Experiment Station Bulletin* 160, Tucson, 1938.

tions in demand for it.[1] In Florida thousands of tenants periodically seek casual jobs as agricultural workers.[2] In this situation lies the making of a transient labor problem there.

The South may yet come to have the most critical farm labor problem in the

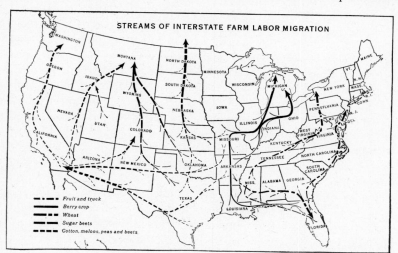

STREAMS OF INTERSTATE FARM LABOR MIGRATION

Fruit and truck
Berry crop
Wheat
Sugar beets
Cotton, melons, peas and beets

U. S. Bureau of Agricultural Economics

The Main Lines of Movement of the Nation's 200,000 to 350,000 Mobile Agricultural Laborers

(Estimates of number of migrants are by Paul S. Taylor, "Migratory Farm Labor in the United States," *Monthly Labor Review*, March, 1937, p. 10.)

nation if thousands more share croppers should be dispossessed by machine agriculture and changes in farm management.[3] In this case many sections of the nation would feel the effects of an increase in foot-loose wanderers seeking employment in the only field they know—agricultural labor. The general tendency of the machine in agriculture has been to replace the regular farm worker, to reduce the total volume of need for farm labor, and to increase greatly the seasonal fluctuation in demand for labor.[4]

[1] Harold Hoffsommer cites data showing that on 27 large cotton plantations in Louisiana six hired laborers per plantation are employed during the slack season (January), and 40 during the busiest season (September). He also shows that on larger Louisiana cane farms three times as much labor is employed during the busy season as during the slack season. "Social Aspects of Farm Labor in the South," *Rural Sociology*, vol. 3, pp. 434–445, December, 1938.

[2] N. A. Tolles, "A Survey of Labor Migration between States," *Monthly Labor Review*, vol. 45, p. 12, July, 1937.

[3] The Southeast now has a relatively high proportion of hired labor if one includes the share cropper. See Harold Hoffsommer, *op. cit.*, pp. 435–436.

[4] C. Horace Hamilton, in his, "The Social Effects of Recent Trends in the Mechanization

THE FARM LABOR PROBLEM BY GENERAL REGIONS

The highest proportion of farm laborers is concentrated in the specialized crop areas of the East Coast, Florida, along the southern border of the nation, in Nevada, in beet-growing areas of other Mountain states, and on the West Coast. California has the largest proportion of farm laborers in its total farm population of any state in the nation, more than half of the people engaged in agriculture there being employed as farm laborers.[1]

The great interior belt of the continent employs comparatively little farm labor and so does not have a serious farm labor problem except in times of manpower shortage, such as during World War II when government recruiting, even of hired-man labor, was common. The hired man previously described, who lives with the family and works on a monthly basis, is still characteristic of much of the Middle West. The demand for numbers of seasonal labor there has been greatly reduced by the machine, and such seasonal jobs as exist are filled largely by the migratory bindle tramp.

The most serious farm labor problems in depression times are found in the irrigated sections of the West, where thousands of migratory laborers, the number sometimes estimated to mount as high as 150,000 or 200,000, wander from crop to crop. Oversupply of labor leaves the worker in depression times open to many types of exploitation.[2]

Equally serious is the problem in the deep South, where there are now comparatively few migratory laborers but where there is the promise of an increasing number of them as share croppers become dispossessed. The problem of the cropper, who has a status as low as that of farm laborers in any section of the country, is of great concern in the South. The problem of unpaid family labor on the farm is also serious there. Unpaid family workers are proportionately more numerous there than in other sections of the country and the amount of family labor expended on farms is much higher.[3]

The problem of the South, reflecting depression conditions but probably prophetic of a longer future, has been concisely summarized by Tolles:

The greatest potential source of future migration in the United States is to be found among the tenant farmers of the southeastern cotton belt. The thousands of former

---

of Agriculture," *Rural Sociology*, vol. 4, March, 1939, summarizes various studies showing the marked decrease in the number of workers needed with the increased use of machinery on plantations in Texas and in the Southeastern states. The future of the displaced laborers is also considered.

[1] This is according to the 1930 census. If one counted casual laborers, no doubt the proportion would be much higher.

[2] Paul S. Taylor, "Migratory Farm Labor in the United States," *Monthly Labor Review*, p. 546, March, 1937.

[3] Harold Hoffsommer, *op. cit.*

tenants now to be found seeking casual jobs in Florida may be only the forerunners of much greater numbers of both white and Negro migrants.

Tenancy in the old South is the successor to the slave system. Both institutions were, in different ways, devices for holding on the land, on a subsistence basis, sufficient labor to meet the maximum seasonal requirements of agriculture. As a result, the

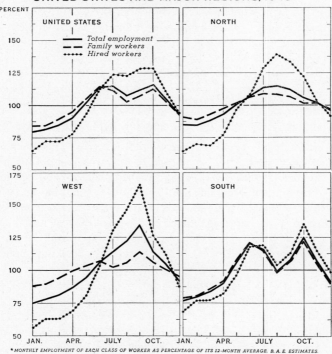

SEASONAL PATTERN OF FARM EMPLOYMENT,
UNITED STATES AND MAJOR REGIONS, 1943*

*MONTHLY EMPLOYMENT OF EACH CLASS OF WORKER AS PERCENTAGE OF ITS 12-MONTH AVERAGE. B. A. E. ESTIMATES.

U.S. Bureau of Agricultural Economics

In all sections of the nation, those who depend on farm labor for a living must expect to be unemployed a third to one-half of the year. The late summer and fall peak in farm labor demand is highest in the West. This requires a great deal of seasonal migration.

Southeast is now drenched with labor and is therefore especially vulnerable to all forces which may cause the displacement of workers. The depression, followed by the crop-restriction program, has already forced some displacement of tenants. Much greater displacements may be caused in the near future as a result of technical developments. If the mechanical cotton picker is perfected, most of the demand for tenants and wage workers in the eastern cotton belt may be eliminated. But apart from the cotton picker, the spread of improved methods already in use is likely to cause considerable displacement. Mechanical equipment and the use of check-row planting are capable of eliminating much of the labor requirement for cotton raising, except in the picking season. It is questionable whether the landowner of the old South will continue to provide sub-sistence the year round for workers who are needed only during a brief season. To compete with the rapidly developing areas of the West and of foreign countries, the plantation of the old South may be forced to adopt its competitors' method of hiring workers only during the season when their labor is required. In that case a large frac-tion of the one million tenants of the old cotton belt may be converted into constant migrants from job to job or displaced from agriculture altogether.[1]

Periodically, farm labor in the metropolitan regions of both the East and the West has its unique aspects. Hundreds of families in the vicinity of eastern cities move out to truck-farming areas each spring, some moving in March when asparagus is ready to be cut and bunched, and some staying until Novem-ber when the cranberries are picked. Beans, peas, tomatoes, strawberries, respberries, onions, beets, and carrots all call for migratory workers during the harvest.

THE FARM LABOR PROBLEM IN DEPRESSION AND IN WAR

During the depression period of the thirties the crisis in farm labor centered about problems of welfare. That decade of research and agitation was cli-maxed by Steinbeck's *Grapes of Wrath*, a realistic and moving fictional drama that reached millions of Americans through the novel and its screen presenta-tion. This was followed by the investigations of the Tolan Committee of the National Congress on interstate migration. Testimonies of this investigation filled more than 13,000 pages and totaled some eight and one-half million words.[2] These investigations were being brought to a close at the outset of the war.

The problems of a huge surplus of agricultural labor, of their futile and unguided migration, poverty, disease, suffering and deprivation, ill health and neglect vanished with World War II, and a scarcity of workers, high wages, government-guided and even subsidized migration, government sponsored health, welfare, and housing programs became characteristic.

Maximum agricultural production became the national goal of agriculture. As early as 1942 there was a nation-wide cry from American farmers for workers. It seemed evident to those in the Department of Agriculture that providing workers to harvest the crops was a key factor in reaching full-pro-duction goals in agriculture. The Tidings' Amendment to the Selective Service Act provided for the deferment of essential farm workers, and the Federal government in 1942 began on a large scale, not only to direct labor migration, but actually to transport workers from population pockets in isolated mountain regions and in the deep South to areas of great scarcity. This was supplemented

[1] N. A. Tolles, *op. cit.*, pp. 1–14.

[2] Report of the Select Committee to Investigate the Interstate Migration of Destitute Citizens, U.S. House of Representatives, 24 vols., Washington, D. C., 76th and 77th Congress, 1940–1941.

by an even more extensive program for transporting foreign workers into the country to act as a farm labor battalion to be shifted from one specialized crop area to another as the peak work seasons in specialized crops required.

By the first of May, 1943, the Office of Labor of the War Food Administration in the Department of Agriculture had transported 14,124 domestic workers across state lines, had imported 52,098 Mexican Nationals, 8,828 Jamaicans and 4,698 Bahamans. These numbers were greatly increased in 1944, when the number of foreign workers imported was increased by more than a third.

For the purpose of operating the farm labor program, Congress appropriated $26,100,000 in 1943 and $30,000,000 in 1944. Half of this money went to mobilized local and intrastate labor, the other half to finance interstate and foreign phases of the labor program.[1]

WAGE RATES IN DEPRESSION AND IN WAR

There are few types of employment on which one finds less satisfactory data concerning wages than that of farm labor. Often, in addition to the cash wage, perquisites are given in the way of housing, camping space, or garden produce.[2] Hours, conditions of work, and perquisites given are so diverse that figures on wages are almost useless for comparative purposes.[3] Rates of pay vary greatly from crop to crop in the same area and between regions.[4] Like other phases of the American economy, they fluctuate violently. A comparison of the 1930's with the 1940's is, therefore, made. Reports on the income of Negro farm laborers in the Louisiana Delta indicate that the average total cash income for the year 1936 was $178, including income of the entire family from all sources.[5] Cash incomes of laborers interviewed during the sugar-cane harvest averaged around $240 per year.[6]

The cash income of those who worked at farm labor on the West Coast, where wages were highest during the depression decade, usually fell between

[1] George W. Hill, "Wartime and Postwar Farm Labor in the West," (mimeographed), read before the Western Farm Economics Association, Los Gatos, Calif., June 29, 1944.

[2] See J. C. Folsom, "Perquisites and Wages of Hired Farm Laborers," *Technical Bulletin* 213, U.S. Department of Agriculture, Washington, D. C., 1931.

[3] For example, in Washington during the season when apple pickers averaged $2.56 per day, hop pickers in the same area averaged $1.25 per day. The difference is explained in part by the fact that the earnings of children employed in hops are included in the averages, but even adult earnings are much less for hops than for apples. Paul H. Landis and Melvin Brooks, *op. cit.*, Fig. 11, p. 25.

[4] The most comprehensive statistical summary of wages known to the author is *Wages Paid in Agricultural Occupations, All Counties, State of California, Year 1938*, mimeographed, U.S. Farm Placement Service, Los Angeles, Calif., 1939. Wages are given by crops and type of activity for all California counties.

[5] Harold Hoffsommer, *op. cit.*, p. 443.

[6] *Ibid.*, p. 444.

$200 and $400 per year.[1] The worker was employed less than six months of the year at all types of labor, and his daily earnings, when he was employed,

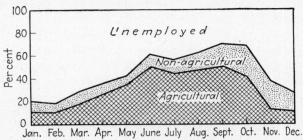

PER CENT OF TIME RESIDENT AGRICULTURAL WORKERS WERE EMPLOYED IN A DEPRESSION YEAR

The percentage distribution of the time each month spent by family heads and single workers who reside in the Yakima Valley, Washington, at agricultural and nonagricultural work and without employment. Data are for the year 1935.

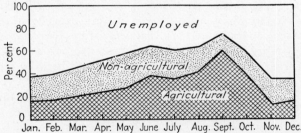

Paul H. Landis and Richard Wakefield, "The Annual Employment Cycle of Farm Labor Households," Washington Agricultural Experiment Stations, mimeographed, Pullman, 1938.

PER CENT OF TIME MIGRATORY AGRICULTURAL WORKERS WERE EMPLOYED IN A DEPRESSION YEAR

The percentage distribution of the time each month spent by transient family heads and single workers who visited the Yakima Valley, Washington, at agricultural and nonagricultural work and without employment. Data are for the year 1935.

1. Observe the proportion of time each group was employed.
2. Compare residents and transients with regard to:
    a. Proportion of time employed,
    b. Months when employment was received.

were low as compared to those received by other types of unskilled workers. Most farms employing transients gave little in the way of perquisites although free fuel might be supplied, a patch of potatoes might be made available, and, in

[1] Paul S. Taylor, "Synopsis of Survey of Migratory Labor Problems in California," Farm Security Administration, San Francisco; Paul H. Landis, *op. cit.*

Data for a sample of farm laborers, obtained in the Yakima Valley, Wash., but including many who work up and down the West Coast during the course of the year, show that almost one-fourth of them earned less than $100 a year and 47 per cent under $200 a year,

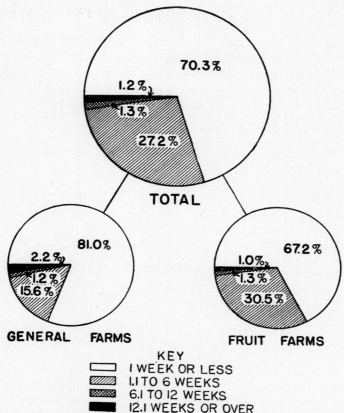

Paul H. Landis and Melvin S. Brooks, "Farm Labor in the Yakima Valley, Washington," *Washington Agricultural Experiment Stations Bulletin* 343, Pullman, 1936.

DURATION OF JOBS ON FRUIT FARMS AND GENERAL FARMS

This chart is based on a study of more than 5,500 jobs in the Yakima Valley, Washington, during the years 1935 and 1936, and illustrates the brevity of most jobs in farm labor. More than 70 per cent last only a week or less and slightly more than 1 per cent last three months.

1. Consider the time lost in seeking jobs under such conditions.
2. Consider travel expense involved in seeking work from farm to farm.

some types of work, housing in the form of frame shelters or tents might be furnished.

Summarizing a number of studies, Tolles found that adult men, among

whereas only one-fourth earned over $400 a year. The average cash income of heads of families was approximately $200. A comparison of a group of relief with a group of non-relief farm labor families showed that the total income of those families on relief was approximately $270 a year, whereas that of households not in receipt of relief averaged $465. These figures represent the combined earnings of all members of the family but do not include perquisites. Paul H. Landis, *ibid.*

these seasonal migrants, averaged about $300 per year and that migrant families averaged about $400 per year.[1]

Most of the jobs at which the migratory laborer worked were of short duration, which meant that he had to shift constantly from job to job and from locality to locality; that is, unless camping facilities were provided near the

WAGE INCOMES OF INDUSTRIAL WORKERS AND OF HIRED FARM
WORKERS AND NET FARM INCOME OF FAMILY WORKERS, ADJUSTED
FOR CHANGES IN LIVING COSTS*, UNITED STATES,
ANNUAL AVERAGES PER WORKER 1910-43

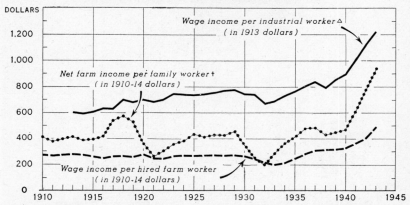

*INCOME PER INDUSTRIAL WORKER ADJUSTED BY THE BUREAU OF LABOR STATISTICS INDEX OF COST OF LIVING;
INCOME PER HIRED FARM WORKER AND PER FARM FAMILY WORKER ADJUSTED BY THE BUREAU OF AGRICULTURAL
ECONOMICS INDEX OF PRICES PAID BY FARMERS FOR COMMODITIES USED IN FAMILY LIVING.
△INCLUDES FACTORY, MINING, AND RAILROAD EMPLOYEES   ESTIMATES FOR 1943 ARE PRELIMINARY
†INCLUDES FARM OPERATORS AND UNPAID FAMILY WORKERS

The wages of hired farm workers are always very low compared to those of industrial workers and even compared to the net income of family workers. Oversupply of workers is one reason.

center of a community where there was work over a period of months. During 40 to 60 per cent of the year the migrant worker was unemployed. Often his quest for work brought him to a community before the crop was ready, so that he might be idle even during the busy season.[2]

During the early part of war, farm labor wages lagged considerably behind industrial wages, but eventually in some crop areas competitive bidding between growers for the harvest of perishable crops led to extremely high wages. Also, labor spent a great deal of time jumping jobs in response to these bids.

This eventually led to the establishing of wage ceilings in agriculture. These ceilings were established at $2,400 for the year, which in seasonal crop areas in the West was interpreted to be 85 cents an hour.[3]

[1] N. A. Tolles, op. cit., p. 14.

[2] Ibid., p. 13; Paul H. Landis and Melvin Brooks, op. cit., pp. 47–54.

[3] William H. Metzler, Two Years of Farm Wage Stabilization in California, U.S. Department of Agriculture, Bureau of Agricultural Economics, Berkeley, Calif., February, 1946.

Perhaps more significant than the wage stabilization program itself was that in most communities wages were determined by wage boards on which labor was represented. Bringing together growers, workers, and interested public agency representatives was a step in cooperation between employees of seasonal labor and workers. This may well have significant implications to future employer-employee relations, which in areas hiring large groups of seasonal workers have always been highly unsatisfactory.

ANNUAL AVERAGE MONTHLY IN A WAR YEAR, FARM WAGE RATES, UNITED STATES AND MAJOR GEOGRAPHIC DIVISIONS, 1943

Area	Per month		Per day	
	With board	Without board	With board	Without board
United States............................	$ 61.91	$ 72.85	$2.87	$3.27
New England...........................	69.54	103.65	3.55	4.56
Middle Atlantic........................	60.09	89.81	3.34	4.26
East North Central.....................	58.25	79.25	3.24	4.04
West North Central.....................	66.25	85.75	3.63	4.56
South Atlantic.........................	31.91	45.36	1.72	2.20
East South Central.....................	30.61	42.16	1.58	2.02
West South Central.....................	42.75	58.70	2.27	2.74
Mountain..............................	80.14	107.57	3.86	4.77
Pacific................................	112.89	148.10	5.23	6.57

Source: Louis J. Ducoff, *Wages of Agricultural Labor in the United States.* Table 14, p. 50, Washington, D. C.: Bureau of Agricultural Economics, U.S. Department of Agriculture, September, 1944.

HOUSING FOR FARM LABOR

Research of the depression period of the 1930's called attention of the nation to the low level of living of migratory farm workers, to the lack of sanitary facilities surrounding camp sites, and to the disadvantageous conditions for schooling of children. The Farm Security Administration during that decade was the government agency which was responsible for the development, at government expense, of housing projects for migratory workers. These projects, known as farm labor camps, up to the beginning of the war, when the program was terminated, had provided 97 camps capable of housing 30,000 migratory workers, either in cabins or on tent platforms. Plans were ready for 150 more camps but wartime restrictions prohibited their completion.

During the war period, however, the War Food Administration did acquire, through lease of tourist cabins, hotels, and other quarters, homes and barracks for additional migratory workers. These camps proved invaluable in obtaining workers during the war period and many communities which had before the war objected to camps for fear they would hold undesirable elements in the community, found them an asset at a time when the loss of crop could have

Farm Security Administration (Photograph by Art Commercial Studio and Lange)

A GOVERNMENT CAMP FOR MIGRATORY FARM LABORERS

Above: Airview of Yamhill Migratory Camp at Dayton, Oregon. Notice cottages, central buildings for bathing and laundering, clinics, and, at the extreme left, tent platforms.

Below: The Automobile clinic provided by the United States Department of Agriculture in one of the mobile farm camps for migratory laborers.

been a major catastrophe to the community.

Other benefits of wartime housing of labor will undoubtedly affect living conditions in the future. Before interstate workers or other nationals were moved into a community, housing and sanitary facilities were inspected by those responsible for the farm labor program. This was true of family-farm tenant housing as well as of housing of large-scale operators. There is little doubt that many farm communities for the first time saw the farm workers as human beings deserving of consideration.

The housing of labor in pools at housing centers also placed on the farmer certain responsibilities to which he had not been previously accustomed. Workers transported to a community had to be guaranteed employment 75 per cent of the time at an agreed wage. Also the farmer was responsible for transporting his labor daily from the central labor pool to the farm. The farmer, in some cases, had to assume the responsibility for training labor to do a particular job. He used not only foreign nationals who were new to the job, but German and Italian war prisoners and in many cases youth from the cities who were housed in special labor camps and made available for farm labor during the summer months.[1]

All of these innovations have no doubt favorably modified farm employer attitudes and may have created a social climate in which the extreme distress of farm workers of the thirties cannot recur.

THE FUTURE OF THE FARM LABOR PROBLEM

We have spent most of our attention here in discussing the hired labor force of the American farm. This group is the group that is most often the problem group, at least in public consciousness. Actually, however, it accounts for only approximately one-fourth of the labor force of the American farm. This particular group, a considerable proportion of which is seasonal, will tend to be increasingly replaced by mechanization. During recent years the cotton picker, the hop picker, the cranberry picker, the corn picker, and numerous other such devices have reached the stage of practical operation where they will inevitably reduce the big demand for transient seasonal labor. To the extent that they do so, they reduce the farmer's labor bill, his problem of housing and supervising transient workers, and the community's problem of absorbing the migrant group.

The unpaid workers on the farm periodically constitute a major problem of an entirely different character and one for which a solution in times other than of peak industrial production seems remote. Schultz,[2] analyzing the economic problems of agriculture in the contemporary economy, believes the surplus of labor on the American farm is the major problem of agriculture. He feels that agriculture is trying to support more people than it can support at an adequate level of living. Certainly this is true in depression periods

[1] W. A. Anderson and Irving A. Spaulding, "Farm Labor Camps and City Youth," *Agricultural Experiment Station Bulletin* 819, Cornell University, Ithaca, N. Y., April, 1945.

[2] Theodore W. Schultz, *Agriculture in an Unstable Economy*, McGraw-Hill Book Company, Inc., New York, 1945.

when millions of farm youth, who would like an outlet in urban industry, are held on farms with too little to do and practically no reward for the things they are forced to do.

Oversupply of labor on the farm means underemployment of workers who are there. It means a low economic reward, a low standard of living. Schultz believes that migration out of agriculture, particularly in poor farming areas, is ordinarily not more than one-third to one-half enough to produce a level of farm income equal to that of labor in other occupations. He believes that the success of agriculture in large part is dependent upon creating job opportunities in other occupations, industry, service jobs, and the like, which will be available to both men and women from farm localities.

The efficiency of farm production is increasing. Fewer can produce more. As the carry-over problems of the war emergency passes, the demand for agricultural products will decrease. Better farm practices and better farm techniques will demand fewer workers. Agriculture will continue to produce more manpower than is needed on the farm.

In summary, it has been shown that approximately four million persons work for wages on farms during some part of the year. During the long period preceding World War II, when agriculture experienced critical conditions as far as income was concerned, farm laborers were a group whose income and welfare were, for the most part, at a very low level and public policy for the most part ignored their problems. This situation, which was just coming to public attention at the close of the 1930's, became a major problem during World War II when the War Food Administration was forced to take the position that farm labor was a key factor in agricultural production and made the recruiting, transportation, living and working conditions of farm workers a major interest in farm policy.

The welfare of farm workers in the future will be closely identified with the conditions of employment in industry and the level of prosperity of agriculture. Farm laborers are, for the most part, an unskilled group. The overflow of underemployed family workers on farms, unemployed industrial workers, farm operators who are underemployed and who have a low level of income, young people on college vacations, and many others in times of slack urban employment, will find in farm labor a way to occupy their time at a low wage. This will force the level of farm wages down and tend to make farm operators careless about living and working conditions.

But the vicious cycle is even a more extensive one; masses of farmers in periods of industrial unemployment and low agricultural prices are themselves in no position to pay high wages. Stabilizing of the entire economy at a level of full employment or near full employment offers the only constructive approach to the farm labor problem. At best, placing farm labor under the provisions of the Social Security Act, establishing minimum wage regulations, and regulating working conditions are but palliative measures, even though necessary and desirable ones.[1]

QUESTIONS FOR REVIEW AND DISCUSSION

1. Contrast the traditional views about the farm labor problem with newer developments in this field.

2. Distinguish between various classes of hired farm laborers.

3. What factor in agriculture is responsible in large part for the existence of migratory farm labor?

4. Describe the newer aspects of the farm labor problem in different regions of the nation.

5. In what region is unpaid family labor most extensively used? Mention reasons why this should be so.

6. Compare depression and wartime earnings of hired farm workers.

7. About what per cent of the time were the migratory worker on the West Coast employed during the depression decade?

8. Describe social conditions associated with the farm labor group.

9. Has the farm employer become "social minded" in dealing with hired labor? Discuss.

10. Discuss progress in housing farm workers.

11. Why is family labor often a major problem of agriculture?

COLLATERAL READING

Anderson, W. A. and Irwin A. Spaulding: "Farm Labor Camps and City Youth," *Cornell Agricultural Experiment Station Bulletin* 819, April, 1945.

Bowden, Witt: *Three Decades of Farm Labor*, U.S. Department of Labor Serial No. R 976, Washington, D. C., 1939.

Brown, Malcolm, and Orin Cassmore: *Migratory Cotton Pickers in Arizona*, Division of Social Research, Works Progress Administration, Washington, D. C., 1939.

Collins, Henry Hill Jr.: *America's Own Refugees*, Princeton University Press, Princeton, 1941.

Ducoff, Louis J.: *Wages of Agricultural Labor in the United States*, U.S. Bureau of Agricultural Economics, Washington, D. C., 1944.

Ham, William T.: "Wage Stabilization in Agriculture," *Journal of Farm Economics*, vol. 27, pp. 104–120, February, 1945.

Hamilton, C. Horace: "The Social Effects of Recent Trends in the Mechanization of Agriculture," *Rural Sociology*, vol. 4, pp. 3–19, March, 1939.

Hoffsommer, Harold: "Social Aspects of Farm Labor in the South," *Rural Sociology*, vol. 3, pp. 434–445, December, 1938.

Landis, Paul H.: "Seasonal Agricultural Labor in the Yakima Valley," *Monthly Labor Review*, pp. 1–11, August, 1937.

———: "Social Aspects of Farm Labor in the Pacific States," *Rural Sociology*, vol. 3, pp. 421–433, December, 1938.

———: "Men for the Farm," *Survey Graphic*, vol. 32, pp. 256 ff., June, 1943.

McWilliams, Carey: *Factories in the Fields*, Little, Brown & Company, Boston, 1939.

———: *Ill Fares the Land, Migrants and Migrant Labor in the United States*, Little, Brown & Company, Boston, 1942.

[1] For a discussion of Social Security for farm workers see Chap. 30.

Metzler, William H.: *Two Years of Farm Wage Stabilization in California*, U.S. Bureau of Agricultural Economics, Berkeley, Calif., February, 1946.

Report of Select Committee to Investigate the Interstate Migration of Destitute Citizens, U.S. House of Representatives, 24 parts, Washington, D. C., 76th and 77th Congress, 1940–1941.

Taylor, Paul S.: "Migratory Agricultural Workers on the Pacific Coast," *American Sociological Review*, vol. 3, pp. 225–232, April, 1938.

———: "Migratory Farm Labor in the United States," *Monthly Labor Review*, pp. 537–549, March, 1937.

———: "Patterns of Agricultural Labor Migration within California," *Monthly Labor Review*, vol. 47, pp. 980–990, November, 1938.

———: "Refugee Labor Migration to California, 1937," *Monthly Labor Review*, vol. 47, pp. 240–250, August, 1938.

Tolles, N. A.: "A Survey of Labor Migration between States," *Monthly Labor Review*, vol. 45, pp. 1–14, July, 1937.

Wage and Wage Rates of Hired Farm Workers, United States and Major Regions March, 1945, Report No. 4, Bureau of Agricultural Economics, Washington, D. C., October, 1945.

CHAPTER 29

RURAL PATHOLOGY AND WELFARE INSTITUTIONS
A POINT OF VIEW

THE MODERN concept of social problems is primarily a product of urban-industrial civilization, as is the modern approach to social welfare. Under the individualistic economy of an agricultural society, few social problems are recognized as such; they are considered individual or neighborhood problems rather than social problems in the broader sense. Why worry about contagious diseases when one lives miles from neighbors? Or poverty if it is isolated so that it does not inspire the pity of others? Or family conflict if it does not grate upon the nerves of irate neighbors who think the police should interfere? Or security if one has land? Or child welfare as long as most children work under their own father on the family farm? All the above situations may, in an isolated farming economy, concern relatives or neighbors, but not the state or society at large.

In the city an individual or neighborhood problem becomes a social problem because people live under a regime in which private acts are of social concern. The contagious disease of one is a threat to the entire city. The conflicts of a family are soon projected into other social relationships and the family becomes a problem case for those who live next door. Security becomes a major issue where almost everybody works for someone else and depends upon the pay check as the only source of income. Increasingly, as the nation has become urban-industrial in character we have had to underwrite personal risks by social legislation and social insurance. With the expansion of urban-industrial culture and of secondary-group relationships has come the need to shift blame for individual weakness from the person to the group. The old rural philosophy is that every man, and the natural providence which attends him, is responsible for his own success or failure, but the mechanization of industry has driven those who are in close touch with social trends to conclude that few people are entirely to blame for their failures. In an urban-industrial civilization it is recognized that forces operate in the lives of most individuals that are beyond their control; that even with the best exercise of foresight and thrift, persons are sometimes caught in the grip of circumstances that bring them to failure.

Increasingly, the experiences of an urban-industrial order have led the masses to place the blame for their troubles upon social factors—the employer, the political gang, the government, the business cycle, industry, or any one of a thousand factors of social nature—and increasingly many have had to admit through trying experience that their own best efforts are not sufficient to protect them from these forces. Farmers are still able to blame a considerable part of their frustrations and defeats on providence or the weather, although social factors are coming to be recognized as of secondary importance.

Parallel with the growth of urban-industrial civilization has been the growth of man's power of manipulation, which gives him courage and confidence in coping with natural forces; with it also the power of the few to control the destinies of the many has been greatly increased. The economic stratification of the urban occupational pyramid brings those at the top a sense of social power for they regulate not only wealth but men. There creeps over the masses of the proletariat a sense of futility because of dominating social and economic forces put into operation by manipulations of the powerful few. Economic control, for example, has become centered in the hands of a group that holds in its hands the destiny of many thousands. Whether or not twenty thousand men will work tomorrow depends not on the weather, but on the counsel of a board of five directors of a great corporation. Whether another several thousand stockholders will receive their next dividend depends also upon the deliberations of this board.

It is equally true that at the Board of Trade in a distant city the price the farmer will receive for wheat may be determined, but the farmer does not recognize himself as being in the grip of such social forces to quite the extent that industrial workers do. Actually, the farmer is becoming increasingly entwined in the web of commercial-industrial culture; he is much more subject to the influence of social forces than he himself recognizes. But because it is in the city that critical social problems originate, and there that they are first recognized, protective social legislation begins in the city and applies first to industrial workers. It cannot long be confined to urban-industrial circumstances, however, in a nation where agriculture is becoming closely connected with the market.

THE SOCIAL WORK APPROACH AS A PRODUCT OF URBAN-INDUSTRIAL CULTURE

In a strictly rural economy where primary groups prevail, each kinship group or neighborhood carries the responsibility for its own social inadequates. Their needs are met on a personal basis with a case history understanding of all circumstances. In urban culture the misfortune of the individual becomes the problem of the state. No interested kinship or neighborhood group has recorded in memory the case history of the socially inadequate person; as a consequence social work has had to be developed to meet the exigencies of a secondary-group society. Social work is a technique for seeking a solution to the individual's need in an anonymous world, comparable to that of neighbors in primary groups. Each case is handled on its individual merit after all contributing factors are understood. It is doubtful, however, whether even the most careful social work investigation ever reveals as completely the background experience of clients as does the memory of older people in stable rural neighborhoods.

The techniques of the social worker are scientifically designed and may be more intelligently used than primary-group devices simply because the trained worker, although making a personal approach to the case, handles it on an impersonal basis. The social worker in the rural community builds a case history which is already commonplace to the local group. Neighbors have little sympathy with his quest for background information about the client and consider it prying into other folks' affairs. They immediately sense any mistakes in diagnosis because they themselves have already formed an opinion of the client and of how he should be dealt with. This opinion may not agree with that of the social worker; and even the scientific handling of the case may violate neighborhood judgments. The social worker, because he does not know the true character of a local good-for-nothing, may treat him as though he were an important person, in that way making more of him than the community conceives possible.[1]

SCARCITY OF RURAL INSTITUTIONS FOR THE SOCIALLY INADEQUATE

Institutions for social welfare have never been particularly prominent in rural areas. The county poor farm was maintained by many counties to care for the indigent old. Most of these were a disgrace to the community and a humiliation to the old, but it was the best type of institution rural counties were willing or able to support. The county commissioners, or comparable bodies, administered a county poor fund made available through taxation to care for indigent persons not living at the poor farm. Miserable county jails provided for the offender who failed to conform to local laws.

Most rural welfare institutions have been operated with little professional vision; many studies have exposed objectionable conditions in them. In places these institutions of a self-reliant community persist in the old forms, and where they are no longer in existence, much of the old philosophy that led to their creation and maintenance still holds sway.

There are few engineering, health, or welfare problems encountered within the limits of the typical small rural area sufficiently large to constitute a challenge to those trained to get results in such fields. Here and there in the state and Federal services and in the largest cities may be found administrators of the first order of ability, but such is seldom or never the case in smaller areas. Even if public servants were released

[1] See Bird T. Baldwin, *et al., Farm Children*, pp. 163–168, D. Appleton-Century Company, Inc., New York, 1930.

from their present bondage to the "courthouse gang," the prospect before them would not be attractive. . . .

In the second place, administration in the typical rural area is carried on much closer to those affected so that officials act under the direct impact of popular ideas and prejudices.[1]

We are beginning today to see specialization in social welfare in many progressive rural communities. Rural social work is being established on a professional basis in the field of public assistance, trained workers dispensing relief among those who are needy. Specialized forms of social welfare institutions and practices such as are common in the city, however,—free clinics, free hospitals for the poor, nursing services, child guidance services, juvenile courts, child welfare agencies, provisions for probation, and similar modern procedures—have not been highly developed.

INERTIA IN RURAL SOCIAL WELFARE PROGRAMS

There is little question but that rural social welfare programs within such fields as rehabilitation of juvenile delinquents, treatment of criminals, and abolition of child labor, have lagged behind those of the city. It is natural that they should have done so.

Take the field of dependency. The city has for years stressed change, comfort, luxury, and status rather than stability, thrift, and security, and has become increasingly insecure; as a consequence the group has increasingly had to assume risk for individuals who fail economically. In the city it has long been recognized that many cannot hope to acquire a surplus for emergency or old age. It has also long been known that many urban industries either cannot or will not assure a man an income at times when they themselves are not making a profit. In rural society it has been assumed that the farm will at least provide subsistence. Rural mores sanctioned the quest for security and self-sufficiency, rating these values above comfort and luxury.

But rural subsistence practices have changed more radically than have rural mores and rural welfare programs. Subsistence living on the farm represents a pioneer rather than a contemporary plane of living and farm people, like others in American society, have long been seeking more than the security of subsistence living. The average farmer in his attempt to participate in commercial markets now gives little attention to the production of items that will make for self-sufficiency on the farm. He cannot afford to do so and, besides, he wants processed goods which demand a cash expenditure. Unless he finds a place for his produce in the commercial market, he may have as little income as the unemployed urban laborer. And even those who operate farms which produce the minimum essentials of food, must have cash to buy clothing,

[1] Lane W. Lancaster, *Government in Rural America*, pp. 112–113. By permission of D. Van Nostrand Company, Inc., New York, 1937.

school books, gasoline, automobiles—all of which items the American farmer considers necessary.

The field of child labor, also, illustrates the serious lag in social welfare attitudes and practices in farming areas. Child labor in the United States has for many years been chiefly an agricultural problem. In fact, the defeat of all efforts to pass the Child Labor Amendment is directly chargeable to agricultural interests in the predominantly rural states. The census of 1940 showed that 52 per cent of 14 to 17 year olds gainfully employed were employed in agriculture; of those 14 years of age 71 per cent were employed in agriculture.[1] It is generally recognized that some child labor on the farm under the direction of parents is healthful, teaches the child discipline and thrift, and develops a sense of responsibility. But there is much exploitation of childhood in branches of agricultural labor, in truck gardening and berry-producing areas, in fruit areas, in areas growing hops, and in cotton areas. Even though the child is under the supervision of parents, the family may be so pressed by economic necessity that they dare not be lenient. In any section, child labor may interfere with education, health, or other aspects of his development.

In some areas the child's schooling is seriously interrupted and his health jeopardized. Among transient agricultural laborers, for instance, thousands of children follow the road with their parents, poorly housed, poorly fed, and exposed to unsanitary conditions.[2] They may live in a tent with practically no household equipment, may be ravaged by dysentery, and exposed to typhoid. In many camps where they work and in most camps on the road, there is little protection from flies and mosquitoes, no adequate sewage disposal facilities, and usually no bathing facilities. Water supplies are often of questionable purity. Health hazards are numerous in the life of the child of the transient and the occasional farm laborer, and moral hazards are equally great.[3] Throughout the South under the share-cropper system many children are compelled by necessity to work long hours in the cotton fields in order to help their parents eke out a miserable existence. Living conditions are far below a desirable American standard; educational attainments are low; poverty and degradation are too frequently characteristic.[4]

[1] For a general discussion of children employed in agriculture see Katherine Lumpkin and Dorothy Douglass, *Child Workers in America*, Robert M. McBride & Company, New York, 1937.

[2] Refer again to Chap. 25.

[3] Carl F. Reuss, Paul H. Landis, Richard Wakefield, "Migratory Farm Labor and the Hop Industry on the Pacific Coast," *Washington Agricultural Experiment Stations Bulletin* 363, Pullman, 1938.

[4] See C. E. Allred and B. D. Roskopf, "Educational Status of Rural Relief Families in Tennessee," Tennessee Agricultural Experiment Station, November, 1936; and "Education of Persons in Rural Relief Households in Virginia," 1935, Virginia Polytechnic Institute, January, 1937.

True, this picture presents a decided contrast to the average situation on the general farm operated by the family. But those who idealize the work of children on the farm may well temper their views by a realistic look at both sides of the question, for exploitation of children is not, as many suppose, confined to urban industry.[1]

THE PATHOLOGICAL LOCALITY GROUP

We have long deplored the existence of urban slums and for some years, thanks to excellent studies of the city, there has been a widespread understanding of the fact that selected spatial areas in the city, because of peculiar culture patterns that develop in them, are conducive to abnormal behavior. Comparatively little attention has been given to similar factors in rural life, perhaps because our approach to rural life to date has been largely economic rather than social, largely in terms of fact rather than in terms of process, largely structural-economic rather than psycho-social. But a social-psychological approach to the rural community would no doubt reveal that there is a comparable phenomenon in rural areas, though it probably is not so extensive as in urban centers. Not only are there unique economic communities in rural areas, pockets where the entire population lives below a desirable standard, but also there are communities in which the processes of disintegration have been severe on the social, moral, and psychological level. In many neighborhoods social and moral disintegration are as group-wide as in degenerate urban areas.

In the primary group whatever pattern is accepted becomes a compulsive throughout the neighborhood unit. Only the defiant dare stand out against it. In the urban community birds of a feather may flock together for there are a great number of species; in the more isolated rural neighborhood there may be only one species from which to select associates. There are rural neighborhoods in America where drunkenness, vice, and thriftlessness have become community-wide, where almost everyone feels the compelling power of these patterns and participates in them.

Certain small towns as well as open-country communities become noted for the prevalence of sexual looseness and other forms of immoral behavior, and in them youth acquire standards that are probably not above the level of those found in the city slum, even though they may lack some of the slum's sophisticated expressions. The rural sociologist to date has little information concerning these conditions, but observation and experience would lead one to believe that the rural social worker is in many areas going to find that, in the field of general behavior problems, his task is as large as that of the urban worker.

We have not been alarmed about rural pathological patterns because they affect the neighborhood itself and the people living in it rather than the larger world outside. A passive degenerative pathology rather than an active diffusing

[1] See Katherine Lumpkin and Dorothy Douglass, *op. cit.*

type exists. For this reason in part study of rural pathology has been neglected by students of rural life.[1] In the city, because of the proximity of one group to another, because of the contact between the pathological situation and the normal, pathological conditions are more contagious, or if not more contagious at least they more readily come to the attention of a normal group which is concerned. In rural life degeneration may flourish in isolation without outside notice. The only local group to condemn it may be an uninfluential religious element that mourns the tendency of youth "to go to the dogs," heaping reproach upon the allies of Satan and pouring fervent prayers to the Lord, a group that has no knowledge of constructive social action, no idea that souls might better be saved by providing stimulating wholesome outlets for normal energy.

Rural neighborhoods may be pathological in the sense that their entire pattern of life is out of line with the larger society. Such a condition in a static society would be of no concern for such neighborhoods become abnormal and unwholesome only when youth leave them. In a community where there has been considerable inbreeding, local customs are more unified than in others, family customs having been superimposed upon community customs. Along with biological inbreeding has been such an inbreeding of ideas that little tolerance is felt for outsiders. Serious problems are created for welfare workers and community leaders who would attempt to instill in these neighborhoods a spirit of progress. There is a unity of experience that an outsider cannot even appreciate.

A rural worker, teacher, extension worker, welfare worker, or minister, who enters a pathological community with vision and a program of action, is sure to encounter more inertia than he would in most urban areas or normal rural areas, because there is no nucleus of local leadership to support a program of action. Even those good people who mourn the existing situation may not be sympathetic toward a program of rehabilitation for they lack the background to understand the welfare worker's approach. Only in progressive rural communities are modern procedures taken for granted.

THE PROJECTION OF URBAN PATHOLOGICAL PATTERNS INTO RURAL AREAS

The city not only projects its better commuter homes to rural districts and its finer types of recreation, but also its roadhouses and its cruder forms of barn dances. The population of the incorporated area thus takes advantage of

[1] One important reason why the pathological aspect of rural life has been neglected by the rural sociologist is that most rural sociologists do their research through agricultural experiment stations or in cooperation with Federal agencies. One can expose the city slum with little danger of a reaction from the slum; in the rural slum, because one immediately identifies and characterizes a small local area, it becomes the focus of attention in the state in which the work is carried out.

two things: the freedom and seclusion which the open country offers, and the release from the necessity of observing city ordinances.

The patrons of these establishments are usually of urban or village origin rather than from the farm, although occasionally people from the surrounding country, who mingle with the lower elements of the town and participate with them, are attracted. But the problem is in the rural area and must be handled there.

SPECIAL PROBLEMS OF RURAL WELFARE WORK

The social worker in rural areas cannot, as in the city, turn to a specialist for advice and assistance on special problems of delinquency, disease, feeble-mindedness, insanity, or psychopathic personality. He must be resourceful in handling many situations for which he is not specially trained. With rare exception he will find that the county system of government has not yet made provision for the handling of special cases. The law may leave their disposal in the hands of the local judge, who, very likely, is not fitted for the work and has no sympathy or insight into special problems. It will be some years before most rural counties reach the point that more progressive urban communities passed some ten or twenty years ago in the treatment of juvenile offenders and other problem cases.

Rehabilitation of the socially inadequate in rural areas is, at best, difficult. It is practically impossible for one to escape his reputation; even if he moves to an adjoining community his past follows him; relatives and friends of his family always learn of his weakness and they never forget. The ingenuity of the welfare worker will be taxed to avoid a tragic end in the case, for example, of youthful delinquents in farming and small-town areas.

The rural community, because it is not so competitive as the city and makes fewer economic demands upon the individual, is likely to be more tolerant toward the feeble-minded and less prone to institutionalize them. The feeble-minded member of a family is commonly sheltered in the home until some obvious delinquency forces action. For years it has been known that the feeble-minded girl in the rural area often bears an illegitimate child before local authorities become sufficiently incensed to interfere. Farmers have long been acquainted with the practical aspects of eugenics as applied to animal and plant breeding but are as a whole unconcerned about the practical implications of accepted eugenic procedures obviously applicable to the human race. Rural people, like the urban masses, are not acquainted with mental hygiene, psychiatry, and other devices for dealing with mental deficiency and mental disease.

Too often the rural welfare worker must be not only a "jack-of-all-trades" in his practice, but must spend a great deal of time and energy convincing family, friends, neighbors, and local officials that what he thinks should be done in a particular case is actually the thing to do.

In conclusion, as neighborhood and local institutions have disintegrated, new welfare agencies have had to be created. Interdependence in a close-knit neighborhood takes care of most welfare functions, but with increased mechanization and commercialization of agriculture and the disintegration of local ties, welfare agencies of a secondary group must necessarily be depended upon. Parallel with the decline of the neighborhood has been the decline of familistic tendencies; the degree of attachment to the family has decreased. Although commercialized agriculture has brought greater prosperity to the American farmer than he previously enjoyed, it also has brought him greater insecurity and need for relief. A commercial agriculture turns to the government, expecting it to underwrite personal risks. A highly specialized mechanical age demands specialization in professional services; therefore, our time is seeing the growth of specialized welfare agencies in rural life. These are still much less specialized than in the city and much less numerous, but the mere fact that they are demanded betrays the passing of an effective primary-group society and the coming of a rural society in which specialization, division of labor, and, consequently, insecurity, are prominent.

An interesting aspect of the newer social welfare programs in the farm community is that they have been superimposed on the local community from the outside. It is partly for this reason that they are often ill-adapted both as to procedures and personnel.

QUESTIONS FOR REVIEW AND DISCUSSION

1. Explain the difference in approach to a human problem in the primary and the secondary group. In what sense are "social" problems present only in secondary groups?

2. Why is the rural group gradually coming to consider problems of its members of concern to the great society, rather than to primary-group members only?

3. Explain basic differences in the prevailing attitudes of farmers as compared to industrial workers in placing blame for difficulties encountered.

4. Show why social work is essentially a product of urban-industrial society.

5. Compare the average rural with the average urban area as to prominence of modern welfare institutions.

6. Cite problems that are inadequately handled by rural welfare programs.

7. Explain why certain pathological patterns in the primary group tend to become community-wide.

8. Why have rural pathological groups been given little attention?

9. What difficulties are rural leaders likely to encounter in trying to institute reforms in such groups?

10. Why must the rural welfare worker be more versatile and resourceful than the urban worker?

COLLATERAL READING

Brown, Josephine C.: *Public Relief*, 1929–1931, Henry Holt and Company, Inc., New York, 1940.

Browning, Grace: *Rural Public Welfare*, University of Chicago Press, Chicago, 1941.

Kolb, J. H., and E. de S. Brunner: *A Study of Rural Society*, 3d ed., chap. 24, Houghton Mifflin Company, Boston, 1946.

Meriam, Lewis: *Relief and Social Security*, The Brookings Institution, Washington, D. C., 1946.

Myrdal, Alva: *Nation and Family*, Harper & Brothers, New York, 1941.

Pollack, Jack H.: "Wanted: A U.S. Department of Welfare," *Coronet*, vol. 20, pp. 1–8, May, 1946.

Woofter, T. J. Jr.: "Children and Family Income," *Social Security Bulletin*, vol. 8, pp. 1–6, Social Security Board, Washington, D. C., January, 1945.

——— and Ellen Winston: *Seven Lean Years*, chap. 2, University of North Carolina Press, Chapel Hill, 1939.

CHAPTER 30

RURAL WELFARE AND REHABILITATION

The DECLINE of economic security has been closely correlated with the disappearance of self-employment. The great depression of the 1930's showed

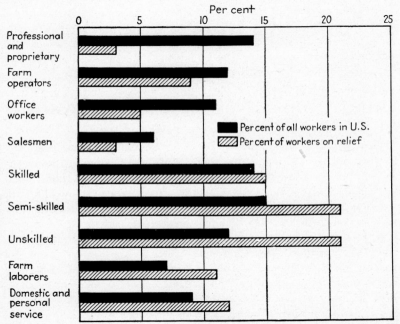

Per cent

Based on data from Corrington Gill, "Who are the Jobless? What Can They Do?" WPA reprint from *The New York Times*, November 24, 1935.

RELATIVE REPRESENTATION OF OCCUPATIONAL GROUPS ON RELIEF AS OF 1935

In May, 1935, every seventh worker in the nation was on relief, every sixth urban worker, every eighth rural worker. As will be observed above, farm operators were less often on relief than farm laborers, an abnormally high proportion of farm laborers being on relief. Other data show that a much higher percentage of tenants and croppers than of farm owners were on relief.

clearly, however, that even self employment is no longer a guarantee of economic security. May, 1935, found one in six urban workers on relief as compared to one in eight in the rural population. Even farm operators were not immune, as is so clearly shown by the chart above.

Factors leading to the economic collapse of farming is basic to the understanding of rural relief and rehabilitation problems. We therefore begin with the study of factors associated with rural relief.

It is assumed that at the outset that rehabilitation in farm communities requires a better use of resources or their restoration. It is not primarily a matter of getting a man a job, except in the case of the farm laborer, or of establishing different social relations, or of inspiring him with a will to work, as is often the case in the urban setting. In the rural community the welfare worker who would do the outstanding thing from a long-time viewpoint must work with those constructive agencies which look to the improvement of the foundations of agriculture as such.

Rehabilitation on the farm, if the individual is to remain there, must necessarily follow the approach of helping him to use more intelligently the resources, usually the land, of his immediate locality. For this reason, if welfare work in the rural community is to go beyond the point of alleviating distress, if it is to aim at rehabilitation of the able-bodied person, it must do so by teaching the better use of land and other resources.

THE RELATIONSHIP OF RURAL RELIEF TO NATURAL RESOURCES

Many studies,[1] since the severe depression days of the thirties, have demonstrated beyond doubt that there is a close relationship between rural relief and basic resources, relief loads being concentrated in submarginal land areas[2] or other areas where adjustments to basic resources have not been adequate. Take, for example, a nation-wide study conducted by the FERA in 1934 which studied basic factors explaining high relief loads in the six rural areas where conditions were most extreme.[3] The areas were: (1) the Lake States Cutover Area, which is characterized by poor soil, a short growing season, a relatively small percentage of land in farms, a decadent lumbering industry, woodworking and copper mining industries, and unemployment in iron mines and in industry generally, owing to technological improvements. (2) The Appalachian-Ozark Area, which has a mountainous terrain with little arable land but a large number of farms, some self-sufficing and others part-time.

[1] Rural sociologists have played the major role in the scientific analysis of rural relief data since the initiation of Federal relief and rehabilitation programs in 1933. For a more extensive history of rural sociological research refer to the Appendix that deals with the history of rural sociology.

[2] By submarginal land is meant land which is so poor that it cannot provide its present population with a decent standard of living under average conditions of management, even when employed in its most productive capacity.

[3] The results of the study are published as Research Monograph 1 of the FERA by P. G. Beck and M. C. Forster, entitled *Six Rural Problem Areas, Relief—Resources—Rehabilitation*, Division of Social Research, Works Progress Administration, Washington, D. C., 1935.

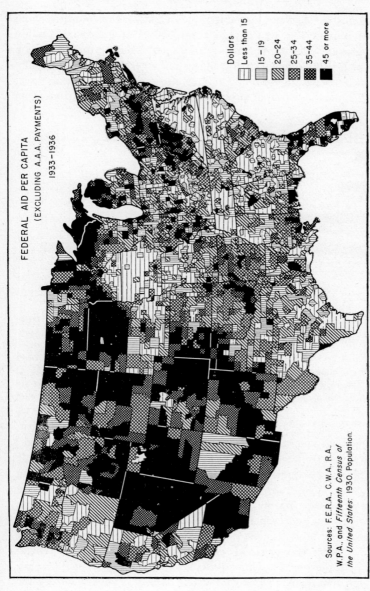

FEDERAL AID PER CAPITA
(EXCLUDING A.A.A. PAYMENTS)
1933–1936

Dollars

Less than 15
15 – 19
20 – 24
25 – 34
35 – 44
45 or more

Sources: F.E.R.A., C.W.A., R.A.,
W.P.A., and *Fifteenth Census of
the United States*: 1930. Population.

"The largest relief expenditures per person in the total population were concentrated during the 4-year period in the drought area of the Great Plains, in the Mountain States, in the Cut-over Area of Minnesota, Wisconsin, and Michigan and in the northern part of the Appalachian Highlands. The high ratios of relief expenditures to population in these rural areas reflect both high relief loads and relatively high payments, except in the Appalachian Highlands where the payments per case were relatively low."

The region has many decadent lumbering and woodworking industries and abandoned coal mines. The dense population had been increasing rapidly because of a high rate of natural increase and because, during the depression when there were no employment opportunities elsewhere, the excess population was dammed up in the area. (3) The Short-grass Spring-wheat Area, where there is low and variable precipitation, where wind erosion is an

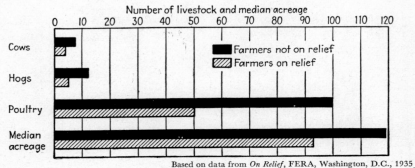

Based on data from *On Relief*, FERA, Washington, D.C., 1935.

A COMPARISON OF LIVESTOCK AND LAND ACREAGES OF FARMERS ON RELIEF AND THOSE NOT ON RELIEF

"Farmers on relief have smaller farms than farmers not on relief. Moreover, fewer farmers receiving relief own livestock. Only 69 per cent of farmers on relief owned cows, compared with 85 per cent of farmers not on relief; 58 per cent of the farmers on relief owned hogs, compared with 60 per cent of the farmers not on relief; and 85 per cent of the farmers on relief owned fowls, compared with 92 per cent of the farmers not on relief. Not only do fewer farmers on relief own livestock than their nonrelief neighbors, but those who do are also at a definite disadvantage in the number of stock owned. The chart shows that the relief farmer owning stock has only slightly over half as many cows, less than half as many hogs, and only half as many fowls as the average farmer who is not on relief."

imminent menace, and where the worst sections are periodically abandoned.[1] (4) The Short-grass Winter-wheat Area, a region with light and variable rainfall, characterized by arable agriculture on an extensive scale necessitating large investments in power machinery. (5) The Western Cotton Area, where there had been an overexpansion of cotton farming, a surplus of population because of immigration, and crop failure due to drought in the western part. (6) The Eastern Cotton Belt, where the plantation system of agriculture, originally based on Negro slavery, had persisted with the share cropper replacing the slave. The traditional system of agriculture had been disrupted because of loss of foreign markets, ravages of the boll weevil, and low prices for cotton.

[1] George W. Hill in "Rural Migration and Farm Abandonment," (mimeographed, Federal Emergency Relief Administration) dealing with Tripp County, South Dakota, indicates that in one township, which was once a fertile and productive area, more than half the families had moved out by 1934 and their farms had remained unoccupied.

Gordon W. Blackwell, studying certain rural localities in North Carolina with 20 per cent or more of their families on relief found evidences of maladjustment to the land.[1] Olaf F. Larson, studying areas of high relief loads in Colorado, concluded that the highest relief rates and the worst land areas went together.[2] He said,

> With few exceptions the counties which have had the highest relief rates have been the worst land areas as measured by agricultural income or plane of living indices. Areas with highest proportions of the population on relief appear to reflect chronic rather than temporary conditions of stress. . . . Poor or improperly used land and high relief rates go together.

Similar studies in South Dakota,[3] Wyoming,[4] Texas,[5] and Tennessee[6] indicated that relief rates were highest in least productive areas such as those characterized by wasteland, wind erosion, inadequate water supply, low soil fertility, or those in which maladjustments in man's relationship to the basic natural resources of the community were evident.[7]

THE RELATION OF RURAL RELIEF TO FARM MANAGEMENT PRACTICES

Evidence consistently supports the conclusion that during the depression of 1930–1935 those who operated smaller than average farms and who had less than the average number of work stock, milk cows, poultry, and who had no garden, tended to be on relief rolls[8] (see chart). Work stock proportioned to

[1] Gordon W. Blackwell, "Concentration of Rural Relief in Certain Localities in North Carolina," *Rural Sociology*, pp. 200–213, June, 1936.

[2] Olaf F. Larson, "Rural Relief and Agricultural Adjustment," *Proceedings of the Western Farm Economics Association*, pp. 50–63, 1936.

[3] H. L. Stewart, "The Agricultural Situation in the Intensive Livestock Production Area of Southeastern South Dakota," *Resettlement Administration Bulletin* K-11, Washington, D. C., December, 1935.

[4] H. L. Stewart, "Natural and Economic Factors Affecting Rural Rehabilitation in Southeastern Wyoming," *Resettlement Administration Bulletin* K-13, Washington, D. C., March, 1937.

[5] H. M. Pevehouse, "Natural and Economic Factors which Affect Rural Rehabilitation on the North Plains of Texas," *Resettlement Administration Bulletin* K-5, Washington, D. C., July, 1936.

[6] C. E. Allred, *et al.*, "Rural Relief and Rehabilitation Possibilities in Williamson County, Tennessee," *Cooperative Bulletin* 13, Washington, D. C., May 20, 1936.

[7] Paul H. Landis and Rachmael Forschmiedt, "Causes and Consequences, A Study of Rural Relief in Relation to County Backgrounds," mimeographed, Rural Sociology Research Laboratory, Pullman, Washington, 1936.

[8] Among works presenting evidence are T. C. McCormick, *Rural Households, Relief and Nonrelief*, p. 2, Monograph 2, Division of Social Research, WPA, Washington, D. C.; the K series published by the Resettlement Administration in cooperation with the U.S. Department of Agriculture and the WPA. Each of the following bulletins in the series

farm needs undoubtedly makes for efficiency in farm operation. The raising of cows and poultry and a garden makes for more effective self-maintenance. The farmer who failed to practice these principles of farm management, for whatever reason, tended to appear on relief rolls when the crisis came.

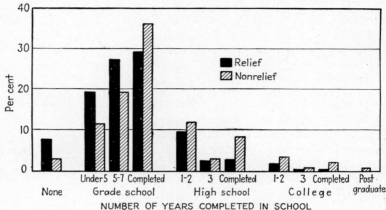

Rural Poverty, Works Progress Administration

COMPARISON OF THE EDUCATION OF HEADS OF RURAL RELIEF AND NON-RELIEF HOUSEHOLDS, OCTOBER, 1933

"The heads of rural households receiving relief had distinctly less schooling than their neighbors who were not on relief. More of those on relief had not completed grade school, while more of their nonrelief neighbors had completed grade school or even attended high school or college. More than twice as high a proportion of those on relief as of those not on relief had never attended school. Areas with large numbers of Negroes and Mexicans had higher illiteracy rates, but in all areas those not on relief had a decided advantage in educational attainment over those on relief." (Data cover villages and open country in a nation-wide sample.)

The question might well be investigated as to whether some of the farm management practices which help make farmers self-sufficient in times of crisis are not the better practices at all times. It is very likely that the opposite is true: that in normal times extreme specialization is more profitable than the types of diversification which seem to have kept farmers off relief during the depression.

presents data on size of farm and each supports the conclusion stated above: K-1, Sherman County, Nebraska; K-2, Hyde County, South Dakota; K-3, Perkins County, Nebraska; K-4, Hettinger County, North Dakota; K-7, Divide County, North Dakota; K-8, Sheridan County, North Dakota; K-10, Curry County, New Mexico; K-11, Moody County, South Dakota; K-12, Hale County, Texas; K-13, Goshen County, Wyoming. Another series by C. E. Allred and staff supporting this hypothesis was published during 1936 by the Tennessee Agricultural Experiment Station in cooperation with the WPA and the Tennessee Welfare Commission. Also Olaf F. Larson, *op. cit.*; Paul H. Landis, "Rural Relief in South Dakota," *South Dakota Agricultural Experiment Station Bulletin* 289, Brookings, 1934.

CHARACTERISTICS OF THE FARMER ON RELIEF

Studies comparing characteristics of rural relief and nonrelief groups in the same community almost without exception showed that relief families were below average in income and employment.[1] For instance, samples of relief and nonrelief farm operators and rural villagers in 47 counties in 19 states were compared. Study of their employment history revealed that during the first four years of the depression (Nov. 1, 1929, through Oct. 31, 1933) the male heads of relief households had faced unemployment 2.5 times as often as nonrelief heads in the same community. (These comparisons include villagers and part-time farmers who depended on employment earnings to supplement farm income.) Farm laborer families on relief in the Yakima Valley, Washington, averaged an annual income of $294, whereas the nonrelief group averaged $585. Relief groups faced longer periods of unemployment. Farm laborers in the Yakima Valley compared as follows: relief group, 24 weeks employment per year; nonrelief group, 44.7 weeks.[2]

The relief population was low in educational training. Both national and state studies showed that heads and wives of rural relief households had less schooling than their nonrelief neighbors. The older children of relief households who had completed their schooling also had less training than the children of their nonrelief neighbors.[3] Especially significant in its bearing on educational status of rural relief families is a study by Hummel, Eure, and Bennett made in the state of Virginia.[4] They found that 71 per cent of children of relief households, between the ages of 10 and 17, were retarded in school, and that a lower percentage of the relief than the nonrelief group were in school, especially after passing the age of compulsory attendance. Also among the relief group a higher percentage had never attended school. According to their report, retardation of the relief group was induced by delay in entering school, failure to pass grades, irregular attendance, and prolonged absences. A Tennessee study[5] reported similar findings. (For national data, see chart opposite.)

As would be expected the rural relief group was below average in standard of living. A comparison of a rural relief group with their nonrelief neighbors

[1] Chief among these is T. C. McCormick, *op. cit.*

[2] Paul H. Landis, Mae Pritchard, and Melvin Brooks, "Rural Emergency Relief in Washington," p. 34, *Washington Agricultural Experiment Stations Bulletin* 334, Pullman, 1936. See also Paul H. Landis and Melvin Brooks, "Farm Labor in the Yakima Valley, Washington," *Washington Agricultural Experiment Stations Bulletin* 343, Pullman, 1936.

[3] See T. C. McCormick, *op. cit.*, pp. 33–34; Paul H. Landis, Mae Pritchard, and Melvin Brooks, *op. cit.*, pp. 36–38; Paul H. Landis, *op. cit.*, pp. 25–26.

[4] B. L. Hummel, W. W. Eure, and C. G. Bennett, "Education of Persons in Rural Relief Households in Virginia, 1935," Virginia Polytechnic Institute, Blacksburg, January, 1937.

[5] C. E. Allred and B. D. Roskopf, "Educational Status of Rural Relief Families in Tennessee," Tennessee Agricultural Experiment Station, Knoxville, 1936.

in South Dakota in 1934 revealed that a much higher percentage of the non-relief group owned automobiles, radios, and telephones, and subscribed to daily and other newspapers and magazines.[1] Whether the differences were induced by the depression or whether they had existed before is unknown.

The relief group was below average in stability, clients tending in a relatively large proportion of cases to be "rolling stones," moving from community to community and changing from occupation to occupation more frequently than their nonrelief neighbors. Several state and Federal studies dealing with characteristics of rural relief households support this generalization.[2]

Evidence in a great number of state and Federal studies cited indicates that the relief families had more children of dependent ages than the nonrelief families, even though they were less able to support them.

This should be expected since our competitive economy takes no account of a man's economic responsibilities in connection with his economic reward. Children are an economic liability rather than an asset on the commercial farm and are as much of an economic handicap to the farm wage worker as to the industrial worker. Woofter[3] has shown strikingly the ratio between size of family and unit income per family member for wage and salary workers. Counting a child a half unit for this purpose he shows that for 14,750,000 families with wage and salary income in the nation, the unit income for a couple is $592; for a couple with one child $508; for a couple with two children $429; for a couple with three children $281. Data were for 1939.

Much the same ratio would hold for farm workers. Although the relationship would be somewhat less significant for farm operators, because farm children do still contribute something to income, the fact remains that the more children, the smaller the slices into which the economic pie is cut for members of the family. The large family is more likely to be the victim of depression. When one considers that the high birth-rate areas are those with poor natural resources, the likelihood of the large family being the one on relief is greater.

REHABILITATION

The activities of the Farm Security Administration over a period of more than ten years provides the most extensive lesson in what may be done to adjust a family to a natural environment and to a farming enterprise. The most extensive activities of the Farm Security program were in the field of making loans. These loans were used at the outset to replace cash relief which was widespread in farm communities; later as a program for rehabilitation.

The standard loan program of the Farm Security Administration involved

[1] Paul H. Landis, *op. cit.*, pp. 48–51.

[2] *Ibid.* Most previous citations present evidence on this topic.

[3] T. J. Woofter, Jr., "Children and Family Income," *Social Security Bulletin*, vol. 8, pp. 1–6, Social Security Board, Washington, D. C., January, 1945.

(1) the advancement of a loan to finance farm and home operation, (2) supervision of the loan including assisting the farm family to develop sound farm and home plans.

In addition, where the Farm Security Administration had a number of borrowers in a community, it developed various cooperatives such as those for the joint purchase of breeding sires, consumer and producer cooperatives, and group health plans.[1]

It is reported that between July 1, 1935, and the end of 1945, almost 770,000 farm families, one out of every eight farm operators reported by the census, had had a standard loan.[2]

It is not possible to fully evaluate the economic, educational, and social influences of this program. Its influence no doubt varied from section to section. Needless to say, few organizations of government have been more widely criticized and praised.[3] Few organizations have been so subjected to Congressional scrutiny and so often threatened with elimination. Actually, at the present writing the Farm Security Administration as such has disappeared as an organization, although certain features of the loan program are continued under the Farmers Home Administration.

One aspect of the program alone, the improvement of home living and diet in the deep South through the development of the garden-raising and home-canning program, and the introduction of the pressure cooker was a revolution of major proportions.

The financial experience of the loan program was unusually favorable considering the fact that most of the loans were granted to persons who were not considered good credit risks by other credit agencies, in fact, in many cases to people who, in the absence of the loan, would have required direct relief grants. A large proportion of this has been returned and a comparatively small per cent has had to be written off.[4] The fortuitous circumstances of high prices which the war brought, of course, may largely explain the fact that such a large proportion of the loans was repaid.

Certainly this much must be said for the standard-loan program of the

[1] For a good account of group health plans see Richard Hellman, "The Farmers Try Group Medicine," *Harper's,* December, 1940. Also Franz Goldmann, "Medical Care for Farmers," *Medical Care,* vol. 3, pp. 19–35, February, 1943. See also data presented in the chapter on rural health following.

[2] Olaf F. Larson, "Lessons From Rural Rehabilitation Experience," *Land Policy Review,* vol. 9, pp. 13–18, Fall, 1946.

[3] The most widely criticized phase of the FSA program was the rural resettlement program, especially group settlement on cooperative farms. This phase of the program is intentionally omitted here as by Jan. 1, 1947 some 8,500 of the 9,520 units had been sold to private owners and some 831,982 acres of project lands had been sold with only 111,035 acres remaining. The remainder of these lands and homes were being disposed of as quickly as possible.

[4] Larson, *loc. cit.*

Farm Security Administration. Through trying to improve farm and home management, through the wise use of credit to expand the farm enterprise, through the educational and supervisory features which were designed to improve not only the farm operations but the families living, health and community setting the program dealt with the kind of forces out of which improved rural life must be made. Through similar means future constructive welfare programs in the farm community must operate.

SOCIAL INSURANCE COVERAGE AND PROPOSALS*
(x indicates coverage)

Kind of insurance or benefit	Now in effect (only nonfarm wage workers are eligible)	Proposals to cover farm and other workers (By Social Security Board)	
		For hired farm laborers†	For farm operators‡
Old age and survivors§	x	x	x
Medical	—	x	x
Hospitalization	—	x	x
Maternity	—	x	x
Disability:			
Permanent§	—	x	x
Temporary	—	x	—
Public assistance for needy children and aged and blind adults	x	x	x
Unemployment compensation	x	x	—
Credits for service people:			
Old age and survivors	—	x	x
Unemployment compensation	—	x	x

* From Catherine Carmody, "Fact Sheet on Social Security for Farmers," U.S. Department of Agriculture, Washington, D. C., Nov. 6, 1944.

† Includes wage workers in other industries.

‡ Includes the self-employed in other industries.

§ Includes benefits for dependents.

The prepaid medical care program is also forward looking and sound in principle. The experience of the FSA demonstrated repeatedly that in many cases the farmer is defeated economically because of heavy medical expense in the family, and that health insurance along the lines of cooperative prepayment plans is the only way to protect a loan. It is true that many of these cooperative medical groups have not survived over a long period because the coverage was too limited for sound insurance. But with more comprehensive coverage, such principles, in the absence of tax-supported (socialized) medicine, seems to offer the only adequate means of providing rural medical care, a vital step toward economic security.

SOCIAL SECURITY FOR FARMERS

It is clear from the facts presented in this chapter that farming is no longer a secure and self-sufficient life. It is subjected to the vicissitudes of a market economy, and in times of low or uncertain markets fails to provide for the man who lives on the land.

The Federal Social Security Act, which was passed in 1935, had in view primarily the wage-earning group which is most seriously affected in times of industrial unemployment. In recent years there has been serious consideration of the need for more comprehensive social security legislation.

Of interest in this connection is the prospective coverage of farm workers and farm operators. Proposed measures would cover both, including farm operators under the category of the self-employed who would pay both the worker's and employer's shares of assessments for coverage assessed against employer and employee.

The tabulation opposite snows the three major categories of coverage now applicable to wage workers, and in the two columns at the right indicates the kinds of coverage that would be available under proposed social security legislation. Farm workers would share in all the benefits now available to industrial workers if this program were adopted, and farm operators would share in most of them.

The fact that such measures are being proposed is indicative of the insecure position of the farm population in the fields of health and welfare.

COMPLEMENTARY ASPECTS OF RURAL AND URBAN WELFARE PROBLEMS

We have commented in a previous chapter on the fact that the backwash from the urban community during times of industrial depression adds to the burden of relief in rural areas, the extra load of providing for urban castaways falling upon the farm community. But this is a two-sided problem. Periodically part of both the urban and the rural relief problem is due to changes in the agricultural enterprise which reflect directly in the displacement of farm laborers and share croppers, and the driving of youth from the farm because of a lack of economic opportunity there. Great armies of farm people are no longer able to find a place in the agricultural structure and many of them, both in times of depression and in times of prosperity, seek outlets in industrial employment of an unskilled character. In times of depression they flood the urban labor market. Others working at farm labor spend the winter on urban relief rations.

As long as agriculture tends toward commercialism, one can rest assured that social welfare programs, drafted more or less after urban patterns, must increase in rural areas, for in modern society any group unable to provide for its own security is protected by the state. If social security is a necessity in urban centers where man lives on cash wages under an economic system that does not always assure him those wages, then is not the time coming when we must recognize that the agriculturalist who subsists largely on a cash income must also be underwritten by some form of social insurance if he is to live in times when income is low? Although some kinds of farming permit a certain amount of subsistence living, most specialized types produce only cash crops. Thus, like miner and lumberman, many farmers of today are simply producing raw materials, few of which are to be used in the form in which they are produced. Subsistence agriculture has largely disappeared from most rural communities, and with its passing, rural welfare problems, in many respects comparable to urban welfare problems, must be met by social policy.

Looking at the problem of rural welfare from the rehabilitation viewpoint, such measures as soil conservation, improvement in farm management practices, crop insurance, health insurance, and other constructive programs, such as are foreshadowed in prospective social security legislation, seem to point the way forward.

QUESTIONS FOR REVIEW AND DISCUSSION

1. Trace the development of economic insecurity in rural areas.
2. What factors are unique in rural rehabilitation problems?
3. Cite evidence to prove that there is a close relationship between relief needs and natural conditions in farming areas; between relief needs and farm management practices.
4. In what areas was relief heaviest during the 1930's?
5. Present evidence showing the relationship between (1) rural poverty and natural resources; (2) farm management practices.
6. Point out characteristics of farm families that have to have some form of public assistance in depressions.
7. Discuss the relationship between size of family and poverty.
8. Discuss problems of and programs for rural rehabilitation.
9. Is land settlement a good device for economic readjustment? Defend your answer.
10. Show how urban and rural relief problems overlap.

COLLATERAL READING

Asch, Berta, and A. R. Mangus: *Farmers on Relief and Rehabilitation*, Research Monograph VIII, Division of Social Research, Works Progress Administration, Washington, D. C. 1937.

Beck, P. G., and M. C. Forster: *Six Rural Problem Areas, Relief-Resources-Rehabilitation*, Research Monograph I, Division of Social Research, Works Progress Administration, Washington, D. C., 1935.

Eaton, Joseph W.: *Exploring Tomorrow's Agriculture*, Harper & Brothers, New York, 1943.

Landis, Paul H.: *Toward Constructive Social Policy*, D. C. Heath and Company, Boston, 1947.

Larson, Olaf F.: "Lessons from Rural Rehabilitation Experience," *Land Policy Review*, vol. 9, pp. 13–18, Fall, 1946.

————: *Ten Years of Rural Rehabilitation in the United States*, Bureau of Agricultural Economics, Washington, 1947.

McCormick, T. C.: *Rural Households, Relief and Nonrelief*, Monograph II, Division of Social Research, Works Progress Administration, Washington, D. C., 1936.

Schultz, Theodore W.: *Agriculture in an Unstable Economy*, McGraw-Hill Book Company, Inc., New York, 1945.

Smick, A. A.: "Recent Trends in Rural Social Work," *Sociology and Social Research*, vol. 23, pp. 446–473, May–June, 1939.

————: "Training for Rural Social Work," *Sociology and Social Research*, vol. 22, pp. 538–544, July–August, 1938.

Smith, Roy J.: "The California State Land Settlements at Durham and Delhi," *Hilgardia*, vol. 15, pp. 399–492, University of California, Berkeley, October, 1943.

Woofter, T. J., and Ellen Winston: *Seven Lean Years*, University of North Carolina Press, Chapel Hill, 1939.

Yoder, Dale and Davies, George: *Depression and Recovery*, McGraw-Hill Book Company, Inc., New York, 1934.

Zimmerman, C. C., and N. L. Whetten: *Rural Families on Relief*, Research Monograph XVII, Division of Social Research, Works Progress Administration, Washington, D. C., 1938.

CHAPTER 31

THE PROBLEM OF RURAL HEALTH

HEALTH IN THE CONTEMPORARY CULTURAL SETTING

MEDICINE has made great advances in the last few decades—advances in scientific technique unparalleled in previous periods of history—becoming a highly specialized profession with many branches. Specialization has tremendously increased its efficiency. The general practitioner, a sort of jack-of-all-trades in the medical field, cannot possibly maintain the health of a community at the same level as could a staff of specialists; yet the isolated rural community is scaled to this type of practice.

As medical science has advanced, the tendency has been not only toward greater specialization, but also toward an increased use of mechanical devices. It would be impossible for a single individual to learn to operate them all. The trend will be increasingly in the direction of more elaborate equipment, more complex techniques, and more refined tools; hence it will be increasingly difficult for the individual practitioner to keep pace with the latest medical developments.

Doctors are shifting to clinics and hospitals where they can specialize, where modern devices are available to them, the equipment being provided usually on a group basis. Such units are as a rule found only in the urban centers where a large population aggregate can be drawn upon for clientele. On this point the Committee on the Costs of Medical Care observes that in many cities groups of from three to twenty physicians and dentists are utilizing joint office space, waiting rooms, scientific equipment, and technical and clerical personnel, sometimes employing younger practitioners as assistants on a salary basis. Some clinics have even built their own buildings.[1]

THE PROBLEM OF RURAL HEALTH

Many important studies have focused attention on rural health in the United States, the cost of medical care in rural areas, and the general lack of medical service.[2] Rural health problems in the Old South have for some years been attracting the attention of such philanthropical associations as the Rocke-

[1] I. S. Falk, C. Rufus Rorem, and Martha D. Ring, *The Cost of Medical Care*, chap. 23, Publication 27, Committee on the Costs of Medical Care, University of Chicago Press, Chicago, 1933.

[2] Several of the more important studies are cited in subsequent parts of this chapter and specific data are presented.

feller[1] and the Julius Rosenwald Foundations, the latter confining itself to the field of Negro health.[2]

That the Social Security Act made special provisions for the expansion of health projects in rural areas is striking testimony of the social lag in rural health facilities, especially in the field of public health service. Once the city was a place of plague, filth, and disease; today many cities excel the rural community in health facilities and sanitation and have lower disease rates, in spite of the supposed natural advantages to health in the country. The disadvantages to health have been overcome in our better cities by improvement of sanitation facilities, provision for pure water supplies, development of sewage disposal systems, and various health provisions—city zoning, health inspection, free clinics, and free hospitals. These, and numerous other services such as government inspection of food-packing plants and of milk and water supplies, have raised the standard of urban health and, to the extent that farmers consume processed goods, rural health also.

Community expenditures for medical care, according to the Committee on the Costs of Medical Care, vary greatly with the size of the community, ranging from $16 per capita per year in towns of under 5,000 population, and in the open country to $32 per capita per year in cities of 100,000 population and over. A series of eight community surveys showed a range in annual cost of from $6.45 per capita in a rural county in Tennessee to $54 per capita in the city of Philadelphia. These differences in costs reflect in part differences in personnel and in institutional facilities, in part differences in volume of service rendered, and in part differences in fees.[3]

LACK OF HEALTH CONSCIOUSNESS AMONG RURAL PEOPLE

Man has become health conscious and germ conscious primarily because he has become "citified." Fears of isolated rural peoples once centered on wild beasts and savage tribes; isolation made man fairly safe from germ diseases, which are carried mostly by foods, fingers, and flies. The situation is much different in modern times when the farmer's children attend town school, church, and movie.

Farm people in the past in America have been notorious for their neglect of health, their disregard for sanitary precautions, their lack of pure water supplies and sewage disposal systems.[4] They have given less attention than many urban classes to nutrition, balanced rations, vitamins, and newer ideas

[1] The Rockefeller Foundation has done a great deal toward hookworm and malaria control in the Southern states.

[2] See Edwin R. Embree, *Review for the Two-year Period*, 1936–1938, Julius Rosenwald Fund, Chicago, 1938.

[3] I. S. Falk, *et al.*, *op. cit.*, chap. 34.

[4] "Rural Medicine," pp. 222–236, *Proceedings* of the Conference Held at Cooperstown, N. Y., Oct. 7 and 8, 1938, Charles C. Thomas, Publisher, Springfield, Ill., 1939.

of an adequate diet. Farm women are often noted as good cooks but their good cooking may be along the lines of traditional food folkways rather than along the lines of the latest scientific knowledge. Because farmers are hard workers, they are in most cases much more concerned that an abundance of substantial food be provided than that their wives be guided by ideas of what constitutes a healthful diet.

The farmer's work philosophy has a direct bearing on his attitudes toward health. He takes price in his strength, in his ability to withstand hardships— cold, heat, exposure, ailments, minor accidents—and he has no time to be sick. Urban adults may boast of their operations and make long stories of their periods of convalescence, but not the average farmer. Because he is used to an active life, enforced idleness is extremely unpleasant to him; to admit sickness is to confess weakness. These attitudes are prevalent also among farm women, many of whom with heroic stoicism pay scant attention to minor cuts, bruises, and burns, trusting nature to heal them.

The farm child, and perhaps also children of the lower income classes in the city, are probably more stoical than the urban child of middle- and upper-class families to ordinary aches and pains, thinking little of sore toes or smashed finger-nails. The doctor is not called every time they have a stomach-ache or the dentist consulted when they have a toothache; their parents suffer little ills without medical attention and they expect their children to do likewise. There is a disciplinary influence here that would be desirable were it not for the health risk sometimes involved.

It is doubtful whether the neurotic symptoms that appear among women of the sophisticated urban classes are as prevalent among rural women who, burdened with housework and the care of children, are faced with a strenuous life of constant activity. The farm wife has less time to develop neurotic symptoms, to worry about inferiority complexes and snubs, or to conjure up imaginary situations to escape reality in the social world. There is a great deal of truth in the statement of Arthur E. Hertzler, in *The Horse and Buggy Doctor*, that "in those days (meaning during the early days of his practice thirty to fifty years ago) there were few 'female complaints' because women had no time for them."

And even in cases when the farm woman has neurotic symptoms or a real disease about which she does a great deal of talking, she is likely to go about her daily work year after year, perhaps complaining but never seeking skilled medical care, sometimes with disastrous results. Rural people tend to let illnesses go to the point where it is difficult to cure them, before seeking medical advice. Infected tonsils and decayed teeth, poor eyesight, dull hearing, and many seemingly minor defects are commonly neglected. Testimony to this effect is abundant regarding drought migrants and migrants from the Southern cotton states to the state of California, where the Farm Security Administration in 1938 initiated an elaborate program of socialized medicine for non-resident agricultural workers.[1] Examination proved that a considerable number of these people, representing the lower agricultural classes in most cases, especially those from the cotton states who were for the most part ex-share croppers, had allowed serious physical defects to proceed beyond the possibility of repair. There is little attention among these groups to diet; prenatal maternal

SCREENS AND SANITARY FACILITIES FOR FARM HOUSES IN SEVEN SOUTHEASTERN COTTON STATES 1934

T. J. Woofter, *Landlord and Tenant on the Cotton Plantation*, Works Progress Administration

All cotton states fare badly in screening and sanitation. Tenant homes are less adequately protected than those of owners. It is important to remember that these states have the highest birth rate and export more population to other parts of the nation than does any other group of states.

care is practically unknown; and modern notions of sanitation, and practical applications of the germ theory are nonexistent. These same people, before the socialized medical program was introduced, were carrying such diseases as smallpox, diphtheria, and typhoid fever from one valley to another in the course of following the harvest.

Dysentery has been widespread in most Western transient camps during each summer season.[2] Sanitary conditions in these camps, where they have not been rigidly supervised or built and maintained according to regulations of

[1] Based on copies of unpublished addresses provided the author by Omer Mills, Regional Economist, Farm Security Administration, with headquarters at San Francisco. This medical program is described on pp. 509–511.

[2] Carl F. Reuss, Paul H. Landis, and Richard Wakefield, "Migratory Farm Labor and the Hop Industry on the Pacific Coast," p. 20, *Washington Agricultural Experiment Stations Bulletin* 363, Pullman, August, 1938.

state health authorities, have been conducive to the development of ill health and to the spread of diseases.[1] The high mobility of the people and the close contacts in the camps make an ideal situation, one comparable to that found in urban slums, for the passing on of diseases from one family to another.

Bird T. Baldwin and his colleagues comment on the lack of medical care in connection with maternity cases in rural Iowa.[2] Child bearing is considered a natural function of women, requiring little curtailment of regular activities and a minimum of financial drain upon the family. Many farm women are willing to undergo personal sacrifice in order to save the expense of consulting a physician. It is possible that one sees here a carry-over of attitudes that have developed out of seeing birth as a normal process among livestock. Little medical care is given animals but the general outcome is usually natural, healthful, and without particular damage to them.

The attitude of farm parents toward illness in their children is also, in general, one of optimism.[3] Because they assume that many of the contagious diseases of childhood are inevitable, or practically so, and that the child might as well establish an immunity while he is young, frequently they make no attempt to keep him from being exposed to disease. Nor do they take any precaution to isolate the sick child in the family. As a consequence, farm children become an easy prey to any contagious disease that comes their way.

Such attitudes toward contagious diseases have largely disappeared among urban people of all classes because of the effective enforcement of quarantine in the city, and have disappeared in more progressive rural communities, but without doubt they are still widespread among farm people in many sections.[4]

[1] *Ibid.*, p. 18. See also John Steinbeck, *Their Blood is Strong*, Lubin Society, San Francisco, 1938; Edith Lowery, *They Starve that We May Eat*, Council of Women for Home Missions and Missionary Education Movement, New York, 1938.

[2] Bird T. Baldwin, *et al.*, *Farm Children*, p. 182, D. Appleton-Century Company, Inc., New York, 1930. Dr. T. J. Parran, the Surgeon General of the U. S. Public Health Service, estimates that every year there are a quarter of a million babies in the United States delivered by midwives, many of whom are ignorant and untrained. Some 40,000 mothers have no attendant at all during childbirth. Between 8,000 and 10,000 women die needlessly from causes connected with childbirth, and five times that number become invalids. It is estimated that each year 50,000 stillborn babies could be born alive. Of the 70,000 babies who die during the first month, one-half could be saved. Dr. Parran's figures are for the nation, but undoubtedly a considerable part of this neglect of maternal and infant care takes place in rural areas, since free medical service is usually available to the poor in the city. From the report of an interview with Dr. Parran, published by Carrol P. Streeter, "A Health Program for Rural America," *The Farmer's Wife Magazine*, March, 1938.

A study by the U.S. Children's Bureau revealed that one-third of the mothers in two counties in North Carolina were attended only by midwives at childbirth.

[3] Bird T. Baldwin, *et al.*, *op. cit.*, p. 184.

[4] See A. Withington, "Mountain Doctor," *Atlantic Monthly*, pp. 257–267, 469–477, 768–774, September, October, December, 1932, respectively; and H. A. Bigelow, "Maternity Care in Rural Areas by Public Health Nurses," *American Journal of Public Health*, No. 27, pp. 975–980, October, 1937.

It is still assumed in some sections that the child had better contract the contagious disease while he is nonproductive and can be taken care of by his parents; otherwise he might come down with it later in life when it would interfere with his work, or in the case of mumps or other so-called "children's" diseases, when it would be more serious to his health than in early childhood.

Frayser, studying preschool children in South Carolina in 1929, found that only a small percentage of them had a regular hour for going to bed and for arising, that tooth brushes were in little use, and that the need of attention to the first teeth by a dentist was not realized. Habits of personal cleanliness, however, were as good as could be expected, none of the white children reporting bathing less than once a week in cold weather. Only half of the white children had three meals a day at regular hours and half of them ate habitually between meals, many parents considering the appetite of the child the only important guide to food habits. Only 9 per cent of the white children received Grade A diets and only 16 per cent, Grade B diets. Milk consumption was inadequate, as was the amount of fruits and vegetables used in the diets.[1]

The White House Conference on Child Health and Protection reports that rural white children are very low in the percentage brushing their teeth, Italians and Mexicans being the only groups lower.[2]

In a study of 13,500 youths 16 to 24 years of age in Maryland, almost 3,000 of whom lived on farms, Lister and Kirkpatrick found that a much smaller percentage of village, town, and city than of farm youth had received no dental care during the preceding year,[3] 35 per cent of village, town, and city children as compared to 40 per cent of farm youth.

The Committee on Costs of Medical Care compared the nonfatal-illness rates of the rural and urban population. It found that rural areas had much less medical attention as measured by several indices (see the following table). Although the open country had the lowest illness rate, it will be seen that it had the smallest percentage of preventive vaccinations for smallpox, smallest rate of surgical operations, less attention to dental care, less attention to eye care, and fewer doctors' calls per 1,000 population per year.

The Farm Security Administration, working among farm clients with low incomes, found an average of 3.5 physical defects per person.[4] Sixty-nine per

[1] Mary E. Frayser, "Children of Preschool Age in Selected Areas of South Carolina," *South Carolina Agricultural Experiment Station Bulletin* 260, Clemson, 1929.

[2] *The Adolescent in the Family*, pp. 184–185, D. Appleton-Century Company, Inc., New York, 1934. See also Jessie Whitacre, "Dental Decay among Texas School Children," p. 30, *Texas Agricultural Experiment Station Bulletin* 491, College Station, 1934.

[3] J. J. Lister and E. L. Kirkpatrick, *Rural Youth Speak*, p. 74, The American Youth Commission, Washington, D. C., 1939.

[4] These are unpublished findings of Jesse F. Yankly of the Farm Security Administration reported by Dorn, *op. cit.*, p. 26. For a study of number and character of defects among farm laborers and farm tenants in southeast Missouri see "The Physical Status and Health of Farm Tenants and Farm Laborers in Southeast Missouri," a series of studies by C. E. Lively and Herbert F. Lionberger, published by the University of Missouri in 1942.

cent had one or more decayed teeth. Twenty-eight per cent of white and 68 per cent of Negroes had defective vision in both eyes, 55 per cent of whites and 62 per cent of Negroes had diseased tonsils. Nine per cent of the heads of white households had hernia. Six per cent of white children and 10 per cent of colored children under 15 years of age showed aftereffects of rickets.

INDICES OF MEDICAL CARE RECEIVED BY PERSONS LIVING IN DIFFERENT-SIZED COMMUNITIES*

Service	100,000 or more population	5,000 to 100,000 population	Towns with less than 5,000 population	Open country
Illness rates per 1,000 population......	809	906	937	787
Percentage of persons with a history of smallpox vaccination..............	73	54	49	39
Annual frequency of surgical operations per 1,000 population.............	76	73	64	49
Percentage of illnesses treated surgically	9.0	7.8	6.4	6.0
Annual dental cases per 1,000 population.........................	308	304	221	155
Annual number of eye refractions per 1,000 persons aged 5 years and over..	51	52	42	29
Doctors' calls per 1,000 population per year.........................	2,420	2,233	1,750	

* Tabulations prepared by Dr. S. D. Collins of the United States Public Health Service and published by Harold F. Dorn, "Rural Health and Public Health Programs," *Rural Sociology*, vol. 7, pp. 22–32, March, 1942.

One cannot explain all rural health difficulties either by rural philosophy or by rural carelessness. There are fundamental reasons why facilities for sanitation and sewage disposal, water and milk supplies, and food supplies, cannot be as carefully supervised on isolated farms as in the city. Utilities are expensive; the rural person must himself regulate activities which in the city would be regulated for him. Most city water is tested and analyzed at regular intervals during the day, and the milk supply is carefully guarded. The Public Health Service in the city is vigilant in shielding the public from diseases that might be contracted through food supplies on the market. Not only is the enforcement of quarantines much more rigid in cities than in the country, but immunization programs, tuberculosis testing, clinics for social diseases, publicity concerning special health problems, and many similar agencies and influences are more prominent. The extensive development of safety devices in modern industry, stimulated to a considerable extent by accident compensation, the instance of industry for its own protection upon first aid, upon sterilization of minor wounds and medicine for the sick, the growth of compulsory health insurance in industry, and numerous other such influences have made the adult in the urban community health conscious.

Moreover, the urban school exercises close supervision over the health of its children, usually employing a full-time nurse. Some of the better staffed schools even have a school dentist. Many rural counties maintain a school nurse, but as a rule she makes only infrequent periodic visits.

Rural physicians are general practitioners rather than specialists. The Committee on Costs of Medical Care found that 86 per cent of the physicians in places of 5,000 or less population called themselves practitioners; whereas in cities of 50,000 or more population, less than 40 per cent so classified themselves.[1]

The decline in the number of physicians per unit of population in rural areas, up to a point, is justified and even desirable because of the greater ease of movement of farm peoples who are now able to seek the service of specialists.

Several studies indicate that rural physicians are aging, being on the average older than those practicing in cities. Comparatively few recent graduates of medical schools enter rural areas.[2] Inasmuch as the practice of medicine requires a long training period in an urban situation and under conditions where equipment is adequate, it seems logical that young doctors would hesitate to begin work in small towns and rural communities where they would almost of necessity have to become general practitioners with little in the way of modern equipment to aid them in their work.

Dr. Williams summarizes the situation as follows:

During the past 30 years there has been a marked change in medical education in the United States. Educational requirements have been raised in an endeavor to furnish better trained physicians to serve the public. As a result, no person can now enter medical school who has had less than two years of college work. After completing the medical course, which requires 4 years, many graduates take as much as 4 or 5 years of interne or hospital training. This long, expensive, and rigorous procedure to attain qualifications in medicine of necessity restricts the number of physicians who settle in the rural areas. Because of his training, a recent medical graduate who enters practice is usually inclined to locate where hospital and laboratory facilities are available and where his opportunities for financial success are greater. As a result, most of the recent medical graduates locate in the larger cities or towns.

[1] Falk, Rorem and Ring, *op. cit.*

[2] Evidence on the age of rural physicians, their training, their mobility, and related points has been produced in the following studies: C. R. Hoffer, "Public Health and Educational Services in Michigan," *Michigan Agricultural Experiment Station Special Bulletin* 207, Lansing, 1928; W. F. Kumlien, "Rural Health Situation in South Dakota," *South Dakota Agricultural Experiment Station Bulletin* 258, Brookings, 1931; and Harold Maslow, "The Characteristics and Mobility of Rural Physicians: A Study of Six Wisconsin Counties," *Rural Sociology*, vol. 3, pp. 267–278, September, 1938. The latter article also contains a bibliography on medical services in rural areas.

It is by no means unusual in the rural districts to find that the physicians in a given county are all more than 50 years of age and that none of them have been graduated during the past 25 years. This seeming concentration of physicians in the larger towns and cities is an important factor to consider when approaching the medical care problem in rural areas.

The improvement of roads, the universal use of automobile, and improved methods of communication, have made it unnecessary for physicians to locate in strictly rural regions away from villages and towns. The concentration of physicians in the larger towns and cities has a tendency to improve the quality of service rendered and to increase the use of the hospital and clinic facilities of a community.[1]

Underlying this situation one sees the effect of basic changes in American civilization—specialization, individualization, the disintegration of primary-group influences, and other such factors. The practitioner cannot keep regular hours if he works in a primary-group setting, for all of his time belongs to his clients and they feel free to make many unreasonable demands upon it. Specialists, on the other hand, can usually order their lives much to suit themselves. The doctor who serves on the staff of a clinic or hospital can maintain fairly regular hours. The tendency toward greater individualization, along with the passing of a sense of primary-group responsibility characteristic of the anonymous atmosphere of the city, has probably led to the decline in importance in the medical profession of the service motive, once so prominent in the personality of the rural doctor. Desire for personal freedom, mercenary motives, need for higher fees to purchase desired equipment—all of these factors bear directly on the trend of medical practice in rural areas.

RURAL MEDICAL SERVICE

Study after study over many years has called attention to the serious lack in health facilities of rural communities. During the period 1934 to 1936 there were found to be 297 counties in 30 states that had more than 2,000 persons per physician. In 1934, 16 counties, scattered through eight states, had no physician; in 1936, 19 counties, six of them in Texas and four in Nebraska, were without a physician. The average number of persons per doctor in the nation was 780; in New York, 620; in California, 571. But in rural states, the situation was far different—1,431 persons for each doctor in South Carolina,[2] and 1,095 in South Dakota.[3] During recent years the situation has become more grave, and agitation more pointed for improvement of health conditions in rural areas.

[1] R. C. Williams, "Health and Medical Care through Planned Programs," mimeographed address, Farm Security Administration, Washington, D. C., Feb. 2, 1938.

[2] Preceding figures are from "Medical Service at Public Expense," by Dr. Joseph Slavit, cited in *Who Shall Pay the Doctor Bills* p. 5, mimeographed, Extension Service, University of Wisconsin, Madison, 1936.

[3] W. F. Kumlien, "Rural Health Situation in South Dakota," *South Dakota Agricultural Experiment Station Bulletin* 258, Brookings, 1931.

Just before the war the ratio of doctors to people in rural areas was one to 1,700; in urban areas one to 650. This situation was made even more acute during the war period.

The situation for nurses is equally bad. The Committee on Costs of Medical Care, reporting on the condition in regard to graduate nurses, showed that their number per 100,000 population increased from 16 to 240 between the years 1900 and 1929. But these nurses were not distributed evenly, rural areas and small towns having very few, whereas the urban nursing field was overcrowded.[1] In 1940, the state of Mississippi had 62 active nurses per 100,000 people, industrial Massachusetts, 403. Many rural hospitals do not have a single graduate nurse. During the war the ratios became even more critical although exact data are not available.

Of the 3,070 counties in the nation, 1,250 are without a general hospital. Over 700 of these counties have a population exceeding 10,000. Even an adequate Public Health Service program is lacking in many rural areas. The Public Health Service program is essentially a preventative one, and therefore a vital need in every community.

THE TOLL OF NEGLIGENCE

The experience of Selective Service brought home to the nation in a dramatic way the catastrophic toll of ill health to a nation with a presumed high standard of health and a high level of living. Of some 9,000,000 draftees examined, 43 out of every 100 were rejected, but, from farm areas, 53 out of every 100 were turned down. Part of the rejects were due to lack of education but on the basis of health alone, farm youth had a reject rate of 41 out of 100 compared to 38 out of 100 for the nation. Many of these rejects could have been prevented by proper health care in childhood.

Mayo,[2] in a study of preventable deaths in North Carolina, gives data indicating that approximately half of all deaths in that state are preventable under the terms of his definition. His definition assumes that North Carolina has physical-geographic conditions equal to those of other states and that the people are genetically as sound as those of other states. Believing this to be true, he feels that North Carolina could attain a death rate as low as that prevailing in the states with the lowest death rate.

Certainly in all sections of the country sickness and death take a heavy toll because of negligence which is due in large part to inadequate health facilities, medical and hospital care in rural areas.

[1] *The Economic Aspects of Medical Services, op. cit.*

[2] Selz C. Mayo, *Preventable Deaths in North Carolina*, Progress Report No. RS-6, North Carolina Agricultural Experiment Station, State College Station, Raleigh, N. C., September, 1945.

THE GROUP APPROACH TO MEDICAL PROGRAMS

Throughout the nation cooperative hospital and health plans have become increasingly popular. The Blue Cross has spread throughout urban communities of America. The success of such group insurance plans depends upon having a large number of subscribers. Group plans have been less numerous in rural areas and generally less successful because of few subscribers. The most extensive efforts in the field of group medical care were those sponsored by the Farm Security Administration among its borrowers. Its program goes back to 1936, when the FSA began formulating plans for medical care for low-income families in rural areas, not as a matter of charity primarily, but to

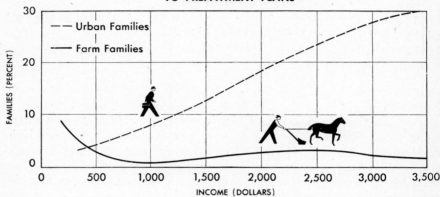

PERCENTAGE OF URBAN AND FARM FAMILIES SUBSCRIBING TO PREPAYMENT PLANS

U.S. Bureau of Agricultural Economics

Thanks to the Farmers Home Administration, formerly the Farm Security Administration, low-income farmers have participated extensively in group health plans; but farmers in general have the privilege of prepaid health care much less often than urban dwellers.

protect loans advanced. Experience had shown that many loan failures were caused by bad health.

In many communities health cooperatives were formed with the participation of local medical societies. To the trustee or treasurer subscribers paid a health fee averaging $15 to $45 per family per year, the amount depending on services contracted for by the group. The usual plan was for doctors to bill the health association on a regular charge basis and to collect in full where pooled funds were sufficient to cover the charges; where not sufficient each doctor received a pro-rata share. The county medical society passed on bills submitted, and approved charges. The FSA acted only as an organizing and supervising agency.

Before any plan was established a working understanding was reached with the State Medical Association or its component group. Similar working agreements were reached with local medical societies. The underlying principles were, (1) each family had a free choice of physicians among participating doctors; (2) fees were paid a year in advance by all participating families; (3) fees were based on the ability of the group of families to pay, this determination being based upon farm management plans and other records which FSA families were required to keep. Health associations were usually on a county or district basis. Up to the beginning of the war the Farm Security Administration had developed medical care programs in 1,000 counties, a third of the counties of the nation. Some 120,000 families representing approximately 630,000 persons were covered by group medical care units.

Success in this venture led to the organization of similar plans for dental care. More than 226 plans had been developed in 252 counties of 17 states with a membership of over 245,000 persons receiving at least limited dental care on a prepayment basis. More than a hundred of the general medical care plans discussed above covered limited dental care also.

The distribution of their group medical care plans is shown in the map on the next page.

In January, 1946, there were 706 medical units in operation which covered 1,029 counties. They served at that time some 52,503 families or 268,943 persons. Some of these plans provided only doctor's services, but others provided hospital and surgical services, and dental care. Fees ranged from $20 to $45 per family per year, depending on services contracted.

The experience of FSA plans, (now Farmers' Home Administration) has demonstrated the difficulty which a group faces in trying to carry an adequate health insurance program, with insurance coverage applicable to small groups. Most such groups eventually fail because sound insurance requires a large group. On the other hand, farm people generally like prepayment plans. The educational benefit of such plans no doubt has been far reaching.

Many studies[1] indicate clearly that farm people, as well as others, increasingly favor some type of group-administered health program.

This kind of public sentiment has paved the way for the legislation proposed in Congress over a period of years, such as is embodied in the Wagner-Murray-Dingle Bill, which would include within the Social Security program a nation-wide system of compulsory health insurance in which farmers, as a self-employed group, would share by paying both the employer's and employee's share of the health premium.

There is little doubt that the problem of health care is a major interest in

---

[1] Fortune Poll *Fortune*, p. 14, July, 1942; *Hearings Before the Committee on Education and Labor*, 79th Congress; C. F. Reuss, "Farmers View the Medical Situation," *Washington Agricultural Experiment Stations V Circular*, 20, Pullman, Wash., September, 1944.

Paul H. Landis, "Washington Farm Security Borrowers Weigh the Future," *Washington Agricultural Experiment Stations Bulletin* 472, Pullman, January, 1946.

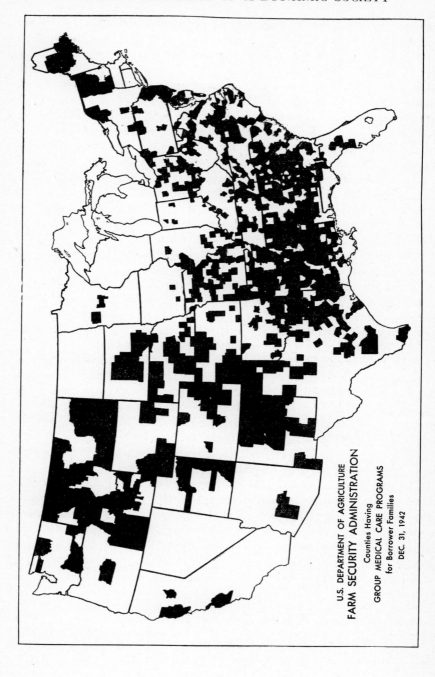

U.S. DEPARTMENT OF AGRICULTURE
FARM SECURITY ADMINISTRATION
Counties Having
GROUP MEDICAL CARE PROGRAMS
for Borrower Families
DEC. 31, 1942

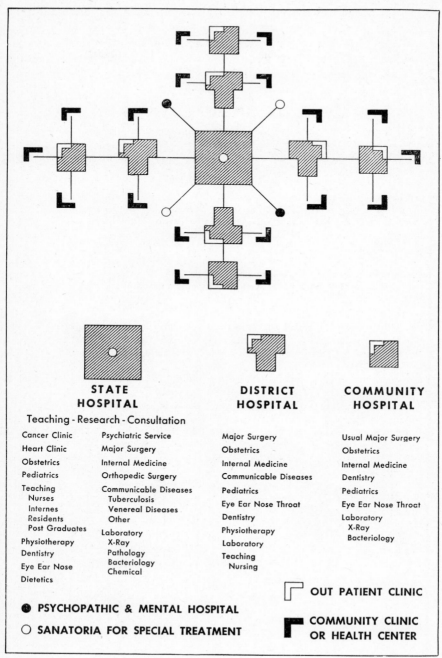

STATE
HOSPITAL

DISTRICT
HOSPITAL

COMMUNITY
HOSPITAL

Teaching - Research - Consultation

Cancer Clinic	Psychiatric Service
Heart Clinic	Major Surgery
Obstetrics	Internal Medicine
Pediatrics	Orthopedic Surgery
Teaching	Communicable Diseases
Nurses	Tuberculosis
Internes	Venereal Diseases
Residents	Other
Post Graduates	Laboratory
Physiotherapy	X-Ray
Dentistry	Pathology
Eye Ear Nose	Bacteriology
Dietetics	Chemical

Major Surgery
Obstetrics
Internal Medicine
Communicable Diseases
Pediatrics
Eye Ear Nose Throat
Dentistry
Physiotherapy
Laboratory
Teaching
  Nursing

Usual Major Surgery
Obstetrics
Internal Medicine
Dentistry
Pediatrics
Eye Ear Nose Throat
Laboratory
  X-Ray
  Bacteriology

⬤ PSYCHOPATHIC & MENTAL HOSPITAL

◯ SANATORIA FOR SPECIAL TREATMENT

OUT PATIENT CLINIC

COMMUNITY CLINIC
OR HEALTH CENTER

Farmers' Home Administration

AN ADMINISTRATIVE PLAN FOR A STATE-WIDE SYSTEM OF MEDICAL CARE

the minds of farmers today.[1] There is also little doubt that private medical care has failed to meet the challenge of this situation. Socialized medicine, that is, medical care on a tax-supported basis comparable to public education, or nation-wide health coverage through some sort of compulsory levy, such as proposed under the Federal Social Security Act, is the likely solution to rural people's vital health needs.

QUESTIONS FOR REVIEW AND DISCUSSION

1. What new factors in American culture, and in the practice of medicine in particular, have changed the nature of rural medical needs?

2. What essential physical differences help explain the greater progress of urban than of rural health during recent years?

3. Point out differences in health philosophy of rural and urban people, and give possible explanations for these differences in attitudes.

4. What factors in urban-industrial culture make man health-conscious?

5. Discuss inadequacies of medical service in rural areas of the nation.

6. What bearing has a weakening of the primary group had on the life philosophy of the medical practitioner?

7. Outline the essential features of the socialized medical program in Saskatchewan; of the Hospital Association in Oklahoma.

8. Along what lines is progress in medical programs for rural areas to be expected?

COLLATERAL READING

Better Health for Rural America, U.S. Department of Agriculture, MP-573, October, 1945.

Falk, I. S., C. Rufus Rorem, and Martha D. Ring: *The Cost of Medical Care*, chap. 23, Publication 27, Committee on the Costs of Medical Care, University of Chicago Press, Chicago, 1933.

Goldmann, Franz, M. D.: "Medical Care for Farmers," *Medical Care*, pp. 1–43, February, 1943.

Hellman, Richard: "The Farmers Try Group Medicine, Rural Public Health under the Farm Security Administration," *Harper's Magazine*, pp. 1–8, December, 1940.

Interdepartmental Committee to Coordinate Health and Welfare Activities: *A National Health Program*, U.S. Government Printing Office, Washington, D. C., 1938.

Need for Medical-care Insurance, Federal Security Agency, Bureau Memorandum no. 57, April, 1944.

"Rural Medicine," *Proceedings* of the Conference held at Cooperstown, N. Y., Oct. 7 and 8, 1938. (Includes an extensive bibliography of rural medicine.) Charles C. Thomas, Publisher, Springfield, Ill., 1939.

What Farmers Pay for Medical Care, U.S. Department of Agriculture, Miscellaneous Publications, No. 561, 1945.

Medical Care and Health Service for Rural People, A Study Prepared as a Result of a Conference held at Chicago, Ill., Farm Foundation, Chicago, Ill., Apr. 11–13, 1944.

[1] *Ibid.*

CHAPTER 32

IMPLICATIONS OF THE RURAL TREND

EXTENT OF RURAL CHANGE

THE TREND of rural life is inextricably tied in with the trend of American culture. Although rural life is unique, rural culture and rural conditioning processes distinctive, the rural community functions in the larger world and can never be divorced from its interactive processes. Even though the farmer is geographically isolated today as compared to the city person, few are so completely set apart as to be beyond the reach of the tentacles of the modern system of communication. No matter how conservative the individual, how out of contact he is with the stream of social change, it is almost impossible for him to escape completely the stimulating and challenging influences of modern technology that entice him to revise his methods. Though agriculture has remained for the most part a family enterprise, even it has become involved in the system of international relations in the world-wide chain of modern commerce. A change in the price of wheat on the London market is soon reflected in the price of wheat on the plains of the Dakotas and the Palouse country of eastern Washington.

Even though the rural mind, as compared with the urban mind, maintains considerable inertia in the face of new ideas, there are few minds so hedged by tradition or so channeled by stereotypes that they do not once in a while become jarred by a stirring radio message, the subtle thrust of a newspaper or magazine advertisement, or the appeal of an advertising poster by the roadside.

The personality-forming processes of the rural world are still very different from those of the urban world; nonetheless, modifications in American culture that have come during the years since 1910, in which the automobile and the highway have become universal, changes that have come since the late 1920's when the radio came into extensive use, changes induced by the influence of numerous media of impression, such as the cheap newspaper and magazine, changes made possible by extensive expenditures for advertising, have been and are producing further change in rural life. The processes of urbanization, mechanization, industrialization, and individualization are in progress in the rural community. An imitating of urban patterns, an absorbing of secondary-group customs, an accepting of the ways of urban-industrial society is the order of the day. This is evidenced in many phases of rural experience, both in the field of material culture and of ideas, but so far much more in the field of material culture.

What are some of the major aspects in these trends that are now observable in the rural environment? What also are some of the gains to be anticipated through these processes, and the losses? What bearing will change have on the rural personality and the rural community of tomorrow? What are the implications of change to problems of relief, rehabilitation, community rebuilding, community reorganization, and problems of social control?

A JUDGMENT OF THE NEW

Whether or not the trend of rural life away from the isolated, self-sufficient, self-reliant, familistic, neighborhood rural economy toward the individualistic, nonfamilistic economy of urban society is viewed as constructive or destructive depends on one's bias. That many problems are inherent in the disintegration of local patterns no one can question. No groups lose their old philosophies without facing a crisis in experience; disruptive tendencies always bring shock and call for readjustments. Old patterns of social control disintegrate before new ones are established; disillusionment follows until a new working philosophy can be acquired. Certain conflicts are inherent in this situation. Youth and age may become divided in sympathy and interests because youth makes the transition to the new quickly, while their elders hesitate or offer resistance.

The material aspects of this shift are usually looked upon as constructive. It is well for farmers to have automobiles, tractors, running water, electricity, modern household equipment, leisure, and recreation, but a part of the price any people must pay for an improvement in the material aspects of their civilization is change in their basic philosophies; machines have a strange way of transforming habits and life philosophies. New technic-ways appear to replace the old folkways and mores no less in rural society than in urban. Every institution is affected by man's adaptation to the machine.

Urban man has paid a tremendous price for the transfer from the old handicraft system to the new mechanized industrial order. Rural man is now making that transfer in America and is paying a price also. Much less has been said about the shift in rural areas, partly because it has been less obvious and perhaps less rapid, but more because problems that have appeared in the farmer's adjustment to the machine have not yet come to the consciousness of society at large.

Though there are those who lament the development of the factory system in industry and are fearful of the rapid rate of mechanical change in urban society, the preponderant opinion seems to be that the way forward is to be found through better adaptation to these. This same philosophy may come to dominate attitudes toward mechanistic trends in farm life. Through the channels of commercial agriculture we may come to realize a better social economy in which farm living will rise to a higher and more satisfactory level because farm people have been liberated from the drudgery of too much work.

With the passing of the open-country church, the one-room school, and other institutions that have been meaningful in the life of the farmer, comes the problem of trying to fit into the newer scheme as much as possible of the meaning of the older form of life. Inevitably, something will be lost but much will be gained. Many new government agencies and private developments look forward to a more stable farm economy. It may be a long time before the farmer will realize the security that subsistence living once brought, but in a world where most social classes want other things it is doubtful whether the farmer can seek security as a primary virtue and keep a high and respected place in society. Naturally, as he loses his old means of security in the interest of a higher standard of living, more luxuries, and greater participation in the affairs of the nation, other means of security must be provided. His risks, like those of other occupational groups, will have to be underwritten by various forms of social insurance.

SUBSISTENCE VS. SPECIALIZATION AS A GOAL

Our form of societal organization is built on the assumption that most people are willing to make great risks for the sake of economic rewards. A person who had never experienced other than subsistence living would probably be satisfied with "batching" in the mountains, living on hominy, corn pone, and sow belly, and wearing the products of his own handicraft. As a rule, American people would not because our culture is built on a different scale. It is likely that few of those who obtain only a bare subsistence on the land are satisfied with their lot in a democracy such as ours which preaches opportunity for all. Except under a caste system, in which opportunities are denied certain classes by long-established custom, such a philosophy is unsatisfactory even to the poorest. Only by the building of a rigid caste system and fortifying it by tradition over a long period of time could a return to subsistence living be made feasible in American agriculture.

It should not be implied that there is no virtue in subsistence programs. Educational and other efforts designed to encourage people to depend more fully on the soil in order to obtain a more healthful diet, especially in those areas where gardens can be raised easily and where chickens and cows can be conveniently kept, certainly should be sponsored but it must be remembered that subsistence activities only supplement a livelihood and do not provide a whole living, at least as America conceives a living. Few in American society, regardless of how rural they are, can live according to accepted standards without a fairly large cash income. Those dependent upon agriculture must raise agricultural produce that will find a place in a specialized cash market.

Under the new rural order, belief that the farm is a place of subsistence living is an illusion. It is as true as ever that a man can live from his fields, pounding corn into meal with a pair of stones and home-curing bacon, but the plain fact of American culture is that American man will not live this way. He has become habituated to a culture in which what were once luxuries have become commonplace necessities. To him subsistence wholly on the farm is not possible. The people who come the nearest to achieving it are those living on hill farms in backward mountain areas, people who have never known any of the luxuries that are common in most parts of America. Here are a few individuals who have maintained home industry, using the land as a means of subsistence. Rural America is not likely ever to return to this primitive mode of living. Rather it will continue to seek economic gain by producing marketable goods. If rural institutions are to be effective, they must have the support of a successful agricultural economy. Subsistence farming cannot support schools, churches, roads, and social organizations that minister to the needs of the more than half of our citizenry who come to maturity via rural institutions and social organizations; nor can it well support the cities' industry and trade.

Inasmuch as the trend of modern life is toward greater specialization, a factor in the success of agriculture will be specialization. Increasingly the farmer's success will depend on his ability to fit into the new regime, competing in a modern order of specialized vocations in which bargaining strength is the determining factor.

CHANGE AND PROBLEMS OF SOCIAL CONTROL

Resident in stable rural cultures are forces of custom and tradition which form the foundations of social order. In them one finds the cornerstones of family, religion, and government. Change destroys the ancient landmarks and removes trusted guideposts. The authority of the tried and tested is challenged when men toy with the new. In many phases of urban life people have escaped the grip of tradition and are experiencing the treacherous freedom of superficial law. As change pervades the rural hinterland at an increasing rate, one sees the same forces at work there with the same resulting problems of social control.

Closely allied to the problem of change, as it affects social control, is that of mobility. With comparative ease the youth of today escapes the surveillance of the group, and only his habits bind him to its definitions of the "right." In a new group with different definitions his habits change. Effective social discipline of the individual in the isolated hinterland is no guarantee that he will be prepared to function in the social order which he will encounter on moving out from the childhood nest. As automobiles and social stimulation make rural folk more mobile, residual forces for social control can be expected to weaken. Society must then resort to more rational education or the less desirable alternative of providing the necessary measures of law to meet the exigencies of the situation.

Underlying changes in rural philosophy have far-reaching implications to problems of social control of the immediate future. The traditional rural man has been nature-minded. Forces of providence have explained causation in much of his thinking, for he has conceived of his problems as originating in nature forces. But increasingly rural people, like urban people, have become conscious that they are in the grasp of man-made forces rather than forces of providence; that their problems are induced by the market, the economic order, the political regime, world conditions, and they too increasingly place the blame for their troubles upon social groups rather than upon nature or upon God. One who can blame God, providence, or nature for his troubles, tends to be resigned to them. One who blames other social groups is more likely to become militant, to challenge these forces, and to try to do something about them.

In the face of this changing rural philosophy, religious controls of the traditional church will be weakened because the traditional rural religious view has been built about the concept of nature causation rather than of social causation. Increasingly farmers will attempt class control through group action and class unity. Instead of seeking God's favor so that the elements will favor him and make his enterprise fruitful, the farmer is likely to seek the power that comes through united group action, for such power bears more observable fruit in regulating politicians, market exchanges, and prices than does the traditional religious approach to the God of the natural world.

POTENTIALITIES OF SOCIAL MANIPULATION

Much of human energy for centuries was dissipated in a vain attempt to manipulate magical forces that seemed to pervade the natural world. Natural science turned energy toward the manipulation of laws to which the natural universe responded. Achievement in all phases of applied natural science has been amazingly romantic. Its application to problems of plant and animal production has made it possible for the farmer to realize ends undreamed of a half century ago. So also, through the application of science to farm tools, the farmer's power to cultivate and produce has been increased.

As farm life has become more complex and more interwoven with the life of this nation and of all nations, we have begun to see that control through natural science is not enough. Forces that lie closest to the success of any large commercial venture today reside not in the realm of natural science but in the realm of social science. Any group that fails to learn how to manipulate social forces in the modern world is doomed to fail in attaining its objectives.

Farmers seem to be gradually awakening to the fact that what they realize in the way of economic returns from their enterprise depends more on their politico-social strength than on their ability to produce. For years great industries have exercised social power to achieve their ends, whereas each individual farmer has struggled with natural forces hoping that through their conquest he would succeed. In a complex social order intelligent manipulation of the enterprise in relation to social forces is essential. As farmers come to appreciate this fact, increased cooperative action in many fields may be expected; and greater political unity and a more effective class consciousness will certainly result. Not that class consciousness is desirable for the total social group but, in a society where the farmers have been the only large economic group not to exercise monopolistic power through class organization, this represents a method of acquiring a reasonable share of the material benefits offered by a competitive society.

THE RURAL PROSPECT

How far modernization processes will carry rural America cannot now be foreseen even in the field of material culture. It is possible that mechanization of the American farm has barely begun. The growth of rural electrification foreshadows further changes. Corn pickers, cotton pickers, hop pickers, and numerous other devices are encroaching on those jobs in agriculture which have always been considered hand work. How far industrialization of the farm labor class in America will proceed is again a matter for speculation. Paul Taylor, authority on farm labor in California, where industrialized farming is most extensive, has, as we have seen, described the farm labor group there as one composed in considerable part of a semiindustrialized proletariat. How far tractor farming or corporation farming will encroach upon the domain of the family-sized farm, so basic in American tradition, is yet to be seen, but that there has been a good start in this direction in certain types of agriculture is viewed by many with alarm.

How much further we can go toward a strictly commercial agriculture, specializing in the extreme and neglecting to grow for home consumption, no one can say as yet. How far we should go was a vital topic of debate during the 1930's when agricultural experts as well as politicians were preaching mixed doctrines and trying strange experiments, because they believed that the security of the old self-sustaining order ought to be restored somehow to an insecure commercial agriculture. Then programs varied from the planting of the economically dispossessed on subsistence tracts, to readjustments of production in the interests of price control for commercial advantage. There are still those who dream of building security into the new order by the old means of subsistence farming, but social forces move America forward toward still greater specialization and greater commercialization. In place of the old security have come newer forms of social insurance—government subsidies, crop insurance, relief, social security, the necessary devices of a cash economy.

Whether the conservative mores, the political inertia, the independent individualism of people who create their own opinion in rural solitude, the moral-religious convictions of people who believe in absolutes, can be relied upon tomorrow for purposes of social control to the extent they have been in the past is open to question. In a day of radio and television, automobile and air liner, the old faiths and certainties upon which personality was once based and about which the system of social regulation was built have a tendency to evaporate, leaving those who once felt most sure less certain of their foundations. When self-control, under the motivation of accepted principles, is weakened, external restraints imposed by the state or other institutions become more necessary.

Whether we shall see the complete passing of the rural primary group as a nursery of the majority of the nation's citizens no one can foresee. It seems unlikely that the neighborhood will fully disappear for a generation or two at least. As it decreases in importance, new efforts may be made to increase intimacy of contact, or we may learn to condition the individual to have less need of primary association than he has had in the past. Rural primary groups with their homely virtues and vices have not been a perfect medium for training. Primary groups, however, rest more responsibility on the social group for control, for the direction of personality formation, and for choice of a course for their members than do secondary groups where the individual must be more self-sufficient because he is less closely identified with the group.

If we are to anticipate a time when greater individualization along functional lines will be required, the individual will need to be taught how to choose as well as· how to obey; emotional self-dependence rather than emotional dependence; love of anonymity rather than of the pleasures of living intimately; social conscience rather than loyalty to a local in-group. That the tendency of social experience is in this general direction is apparent, but if such a goal is desirable it is as yet far from attainment.

To the pace of urban change is sometimes credited the high rate of nervous and mental disease and the general breakdown of personality so characteristic of the metropolis. The appropriate question, "Can the human organism stand the pace?" has not been asked,[1] and many would be inclined to answer that it cannot. That rural culture will ever reach the point where mechanization, speed, and other pressures break down the organism is doubtful, but the farm community, as long as it exports a considerable proportion of its youth to city and metropolis, shares in the expense of personal disorganization, and it is even possible that it pays an unusually heavy penalty, in proportion to its numbers that go urbanward, for having failed to prepare youth entering the city to adjust to a rapidly changing social order.

[1] See W. F. Ogburn, *Social Change*, part 5, The Viking Press, Inc., New York, 1923; William McDougall, *Outline of Abnormal Psychology*, pp. 215 *ff*., Charles Scribner's Sons, New York, 1926.

It would be futile speculation to predict the extent to which problems that we have always considered primarily urban will appear in farming areas during the next generation. But as the primary group becomes weaker, the sense of obligation to one's neighbor diminishes, and soon the person in trouble finds that he, like the man in the city, if he wants help, must pay for it, or, if unable to do so, seek the gratuities of a centralized paternalistic government through one or more of its specialized agencies. Equally significant, with the demise of the group's sense of responsibility for its members, is the weakening of the individual's sense of contact with and loyalty to the group and its traditions. The gate is thus opened to delinquency and crime and other forms of divergent behavior—*e.g.*, careless courtships, irresponsible marriages, hasty divorces. That family, neighborhood, and community will lose in influence in farming districts to the extent they have done so in many parts of the metropolis seems quite unlikely, but to the extent that the drift is in that direction, farm life will have its share of the newer forms of social pathologies now most typical of the metropolis. There is a degree of incompatibility between the old primary-group ideals and the new materialistic goals so rapidly being acquired by our rural culture;[1] between agricultural and industrial patterns; between rural folkways and industrial technicways.

Consciousness of rural pathologies and of local problem areas has grown immensely during the years since 1933 when the arms of the Federal government were being widely extended, when the cause of the culturally submarginal was sponsored with paternalistic benedictions, and when political-minded government agencies were employing the tools for publicity in spreading enlightening propaganda concerning the needs of these groups. A part of the net effect has been to expand the social consciousness and to draw rural needs into the general welfare perspective as never before; and also to create in every open-country community, hamlet, and town a sense of expectancy which anticipates further Federal benefits.[2] The far-reaching implications of these trends to government and to rural welfare cannot as yet be fully understood.

THE CHALLENGE OF A DYNAMIC RURAL SOCIETY

American farmers of today, and the leaders who work with them, face the interesting challenge of a dynamic rural society which holds the promise of a better rural life than peasant society has ever known, and the possibility, which as yet is far from being realized, of creating a civilization far more worth while in many respects than a predominately metropolitan civilization could become. Somewhere between the remotely isolated farm and the congested metropolis must be found the ideal life for America. Maybe it is not to be

[1] Compare Carl F. Kraenzel, "Standards of Living During the Period of Agricultural Adjustment," pp. 47–48, *Proceedings of Western Farm Economic Association*, Laramie, Wyo., 1936.

[2] For a more extensive discussion see Paul H. Landis, "The New Deal and Rural Life," *American Sociological Review*, vol. 1, pp. 592–603, August, 1936.

found wholly on the farm; maybe it is to be found in several places, perhaps in the small city, perhaps in the better residential areas of the large city, perhaps in the small town; but certainly part of that ideal life must be sought on the family farm not too far divorced from the influences of the city and yet not too closely identified with the superficial values and standards that our relatively new urban-industrial culture seems to have developed.

Urbanism has achieved much, but does not yet represent the ideal in social experience. As Lowie remarks:

> For seven centuries Western civilization has been none too efficiently struggling with the problem of urban life. The equilibrium reached by peasant communities was upset when men and women began to flock to the towns. The results were over-crowding, squalor, disease, gangs, insecurity. These have not prevented survival, but survival is on a lower level of social harmony than in ruder conditions.[1]

Although the city has not found the ideal life, it has found certain conveniences and a certain objectivity that are essential to it. Although the isolated farm has not achieved it, living there under primary-group influences has produced values rich with human meaning that should be incorporated to some extent in any satisfactory social system. Through some rational or accidental combination of the two ways of living, it is possible that a more wholesome and satisfying life may be realized.

QUESTIONS FOR REVIEW AND DISCUSSION

1. Show how newer forces in rural life have changed culture, personality, and rural economic orientation.

2. Do distinctive elements still exist in rural culture? In what direction is rural life tending?

3. In what respects are the new cultural elements considered desirable? undesirable?

4. What problems of adjustment are inevitable with changes in material culture?

5. Why can subsistence no longer be a major goal of farm culture? Can it be a minor goal in the experience of American people?

6. What factors make the problem of social control in rural areas different from what it was a generation or two ago?

7. Compare the farmer's progress in manipulating geographical forces and in manipulating social forces.

8. What factors in our culture make it desirable that farmers increase their politico-social strength?

9. What new problems will become more prominent as the trend of rural life toward urban, secondary-group characteristics progresses?

10. Is there hope for rural progress as a consequence of recent social trends? Explain.

COLLATERAL READING

Baker, O. E., Ralph Borsodi, and M. L. Wilson: *Agriculture in Modern Life*, Harper & Brothers, New York, 1939.

Cole, William E., and Hugh Price Crowe: *Recent Trends in Rural Planning*, Prentice-Hall, Inc., New York, 1937.

[1] Robert H. Lowie, *Are We Civilized?* p. 292, Harcourt, Brace and Company, New York, 1929.

Landis, Paul H.: *Social Policies in the Making: A Dynamic View of Social Problems*, D. C. Heath and Company, Boston, 1947.

National Resources Planning Board: *The Problems of a Changing Population*. U.S. Government Printing Office, Washington, D. C., 1938.

Prentice, E. Parmalee: *Hunger and History*, Harper & Brothers, New York, 1939.

Sanderson, Dwight, and Robert A. Polson: *Rural Community Organization*, chap. 14, John Wiley & Sons, Inc., New York, 1939.

————: *Rural Sociology and Rural Social Organization*, chap. 30, John Wiley & Sons, Inc., New York, 1942.

Appendix

DEVELOPMENT OF RURAL SOCIOLOGY IN THE UNITED STATES[1]

One event is usually cited as the beginning of a widespread interest in rural life problems in the United States, the appointment by Theodore Roosevelt of a Country Life Commission in 1907. The commission's report, dealing with problems of farm business and farm living, appeared in 1909 as a government bulletin and later was reprinted in booklet form by the Spokane Chamber of Commerce for free circulation. The work of the commission, according to C. J. Galpin,[2] "probably moved rural sociology ahead a generation."

Rural sociology as such has developed along three lines—research, teaching, and extension work—and at the present time faces the problem of rural social-work training. It was from the beginning and remains today primarily a research movement. I shall first trace its growth as such.

Rural Sociology as a Research Development.—In 1911 C. J. Galpin was given a half-time appointment at the University of Wisconsin by H. C. Taylor, Head of the Agricultural Economics Department, to study the rural life problem. Galpin's first research bulletin was published in 1915 under the title, *The Anatomy of the Rural Community*, and dealt with the patterns of social organization in Walworth County, Wisconsin.[3]

In 1919 H. C. Taylor was appointed chief of the Bureau of Agricultural Economics, U.S. Department of Agriculture. Immediately, through his influence, the Division of Farm Population and Rural Life was created within the bureau, and Galpin was put in charge. This gave rural sociology a dignified and permanent connection with Federal research.

In 1925 the Purnell Act was passed by Congress. It called for an appropriation of $20,000 the first year with an increase of $10,000 each year until $60,000 was reached as the annual appropriation for each agricultural experiment station to provide for "such economic and sociological investigations as have for their purpose the development and improvement of the rural home and rural life." This gave rural sociology a publication outlet and access to the Federal franking privilege. Research departments in rural sociology sprang up more rapidly than personnel warranted; so for a time, beginning in 1927, the Social Science Research Council granted fellowships for training workers. The growth of rural sociology, however, in the agricultural experiment stations has not been so rapid as one might expect. A study by Professor E. de S. Brunner[4] in 1930 indicated that 20 of the state colleges had failed to

[1] An abridgment of a paper read at the Ninth Annual Meeting of the Pacific Sociological Society, held at Pomona College, Dec. 28–30, 1937. Reprinted from *Sociology and Social Research*.

[2] "Rural Sociology," *Bulletin* 37, pp. 45–52, *U.S. Office of Education*, 1924.

[3] For a fascinating account of Galpin's part in the development of rural sociology, read "My Drift into Rural Sociology," *Rural Sociology*, pp. 115–122, June, 1937; pp. 299–309, September, 1937; pp. 415–428, December, 1937; or his *My Drift into Rural Sociology*, Rural Sociology Monographs, No. 1, University of Louisiana Press, University, 1938.

[4] "The Teaching of Rural Sociology and Rural Economics and Conduct of Rural Social Research in Teachers' Colleges, Schools of Religion, and Non-state Colleges," *Social Forces*, vol. 9, pp. 54–57, October, 1930.

use Purnell funds for social studies. All were using these funds for agricultural economics. Experiment stations, being staffed with men trained in natural science disciplines, did not take readily to the inexact and often questionable procedures of sociological research.

The experiment station connections of rural sociology have also tended toward narrowing the approach and the perspective of the research worker for his work is confined to state boundaries. It is for the most part aimed at answering specific questions of immediate practical import to farmers. Consequently, the contribution of rural sociology to the field of social theory has not been so great as might be desired.

The next great impetus, after the Purnell Act, to the growth of rural sociological research was given by the New Deal. The Federal Emergency Relief Administration was created in 1933. In August of that year, Dr. E. L. Kirkpatrick, of the Wisconsin Agricultural Experiment Station, joined the staff. He was responsible for bringing Dr. E. D. Tetreau and a group of other rural sociologists to Washington to carry on research. In July, 1934, Dr. Dwight Sanderson, Head of the Department of Rural Social Organization of Cornell University, was appointed first Coordinator of Rural Research in the Rural Section of the Division of Research and Statistics. At the close of the year Dr. Sanderson returned to his position at Cornell and Dr. J. H. Kolb, Head of the Department of Rural Sociology at the University of Wisconsin, took over the work. In the fall of 1935, Dr. Kolb returned to Wisconsin and Dr. T. J. Woofter became head of the Rural Unit. . . .

These men saw immediately the possibility of tying up the Rural Research Unit of the FERA with the Purnell workers in rural sociology in the agricultural experiment stations. Cooperation began late in 1933, but it was not until the fall of 1934 that a group, with both FERA and agricultural experiment station connections, formulated a cooperative plan,[1] the gist of which was as follows: that the FERA appoint a leading rural sociologist with experiment station connections in the state college as State Supervisor of Rural Research and provide a salary ranging from $125 to $180 per month for a full-time assistant who would assume major responsibility for field work. This plan, with few modifications, has been in operation since that time in states which adopted it. (Cooperative work terminated Sept. 1, 1939.)

Because of the possibilities of cooperation with relief agencies with their large budgets,[2] and because rural relief problems were acute, rural sociology was expanded in most of the land-grant colleges. During the fall of 1934, state supervisors of rural research were appointed in 23 states, and cooperative contracts were drawn up with the experiment stations. On Oct. 1, 1937, there were 41 research workers in rural sociology.[3]

This brief survey suggests the momentum rural sociological research has acquired. Into what fields have the rural research workers gone? Up to the depression period, community surveys; studies of rural groups, of local institutions, of rural problems; studies in popu-

[1] Some cooperative work was carried on with the colleges during the latter part of 1933 and early in the year 1934 under the Civil Works Administration, but it was in midsummer of 1934, at a meeting in Chicago, that the plan for cooperative research between the agricultural experiment stations and the FERA was formulated.

[2] The amount of funds made available to rural sociology was without precedent. Dwight Sanderson, at the close of the year 1934, estimated that expenditures for rural research during that year by the FERA probably equaled those of all state agricultural experiment stations under the Purnell Act for the preceding five years or those by the Division of Farm Population and Rural Life of the U.S. Department of Agriculture during the whole 15 years of its existence. See "Status of and Prospects for Research in Rural Life Under the New Deal," *American Journal of Sociology*, vol. 41, pp. 180–193, September, 1935.

[3] Based on the annual directory, *Personnel in Rural Sociology*, Division of Farm Population and Rural Life, Oct. 1, 1937.

lation; studies of the rural standard of living, the small town, town-country relations, and rural leadership predominated.

During the depression years, when so much supplemental money was available through relief agencies, most of the Purnell money was turned toward the study of pressing emergency problems. As a consequence, a great many publications have accumulated dealing with the characteristics of the rural relief population, the relation of the rural relief problem to rural resources, possibilities for rural rehabilitation, problems of farm tenancy, transient farm labor problems, rural planning problems, and population migration.

What of the future of research in rural sociology? C. E. Lively, rural sociologist at the University of Missouri,[1] thinks that rural sociology will continue to deal chiefly with problems of rural social organization. He conceives of the term "organization" as involving problems of disorganization.

Rural Sociology in the College Curriculum.—Rural sociology has found an important place in the college curriculum. Professor C. R. Henderson taught a course called Social Conditions in American Rural Life at the University of Chicago during the school year 1894–1895. The first textbook in the field, *Constructive Rural Sociology*, was published by John M. Gillette in 1913. There are now about a dozen systematic texts.

By 1916 there were at least 100 courses in rural sociology being taught in the United States.[2] During the fall of 1937 there were 634 teachers giving one or more courses in rural sociology.[3]

The epoch-making publication in the literature of rural sociology is the three-volume *A Systematic Source Book in Rural Sociology* by Sorokin, Zimmerman, and Galpin, which appeared in 1930 and which brings together the literature of many nations.

Although rural sociology is widely taught, there is not a very diversified curriculum in most schools since rural sociology simply tries to explain rural life by the theories of general sociology. After the general course, courses in community organization and rural institutions or rural surveys, rural research, the small town, the "rurban" community, and rural social movements are among others taught in certain larger departments. Now many of the state colleges are introducing courses in rural social welfare or rural social work.

Rural Sociology Extension.—Rural sociology findings have frequently been popularized in agricultural extension service publications, and gradually to many of the staffs of extension services has been added a rural sociology extension specialist who has given himself to such activities as the development of community recreation, the sponsoring of local dramatic groups, and a great range of other community building activities. There are now 69 rural sociologists engaged in agricultural extension work in the United States.[4]

Rural Case Work.—Rural social work was suddenly transformed from a dream to a bold reality during the years 1933–1935. And now rural sociology faces the problem of rural social welfare. To what extent the rural sociologist should become identified with rural social work is a question of considerable debate in a good many of the agricultural colleges at the present time. Should rural sociology departments develop a rural social work curriculum or leave rural case-work training to the urban-centered universities? Most of us in rural sociology are, as I suppose all sociologists are, in favor of divorcing social work from sociology. On the other hand, the rural sociologist has at his command at the present

[1] Lively's conclusions are based on letters from Purnell workers who answered his inquiry as to what they thought rural sociologists should do during the next ten years.

[2] "Teaching of Rural Sociology; Particularly in the Land-grant Colleges and Universities," *American Journal of Sociology*, vol. 22, pp. 433–460, January, 1917; also in the *Publications of the American Sociological Society*, vol. 11, pp. 181–214, 1916.

[3] *Personnel in Rural Sociology, op. cit.*

[4] *Loc. cit.*

time a greater wealth of knowledge concerning the rural relief problem than any other person.[1] He has given five years of intensive study to it and is perhaps in a better position than anyone else to give the prospective social worker a comprehensive description of the rural relief problem and of rural mores, attitudes, and psychology. This, in my opinion, is the fundamental grounding that the social worker must have if he is to succeed in the primary-group atmosphere of the rural community.[2]

Rural Sociology Comes of Age.—One index of maturity in a scientific field is the appearance of a permanent organization and a journal to give it expression. In 1916 a rural section was created within the American Sociological Society and has functioned since that date.

At the December meeting in 1935 the rural sociology section decided to publish a new journal. The University of Louisiana agreed to underwrite the publication during its infancy. *Rural Sociology* became the new quarterly journal.

At the December, 1936, meeting the rural sociologists seriously discussed the possibility of an American rural sociological society entirely independent of the parent organization. (The Rural Sociological Society was created as an independent body in December, 1937, and the journal *Rural Sociology* became the official publication of the new society.)

[1] See G. Vaile, "The Contribution of Rural Sociology to Family Social Work," *Family*, pp. 106–110, June, 1933; also J. F. Steiner, "Education for Social Work in Rural Communities; Rural Sociology Indispensable or Merely Desirable," *Social Forces*, pp. 41–46, September, 1927.

[2] See the author's discussion of conditions prevailing in the Great Plains states during 1934, in "If I Were a County Relief Director," *Survey*, July, 1935.

NAME INDEX

A

Abernathy, Thomas P., 20*n*.
Adams, R. L., 248*n*., 249, 256, 260
Adler, Alfred, 146*n*.
Alabama Fuel and Iron Company, 245
Alexander, T. H., 94*n*., 253*n*.
Alexander, W.W., 431, 443
Allen, R. H., 260
Allport, Gordon W., 88–90
Allred, C. E., 467*n*., 477*n*.,–479*n*.
Anderson, C. Arnold, 443
Anderson, Nels, 14*n*.
Anderson, W. A., 201, 202, 308*n*., 333*n*.,
    397*n*., 414, 459*n*., 461*n*.,
Aristotle, 151*n*.
Armstrong, R. F., 246*n*.
Asch, Berta, 484
Askew, J. T., 361*n*.

B

Baber, Ray E., 314*n*.
Bain, Read, 14*n*.
Baker, O. E., 57, 67*n*., 68*n*., 101, 168*n*.,
    172*n*., 208, 209, 221, 247, 280, 324*n*.,
    388, 509
Bakke, E. Wright, 69*n*.
Baldwin, Bird T., 39*n*., 83, 94, 95, 105, 117,
    135, 141, 142, 147, 152*n*., 302*n*., 325,
    341, 342*n*., 359, 407*n*., 411, 412*n*.,
    465*n*., 490
Balmer, F. E., 340*n*.
Barnes, Harry Elmer, 14, 263*n*., 291
Barrows, E. M., 363*n*.
Barton, Glen T., 361*n*.
Barton, J. R., 397–398
Bayne, M. C., 255
Beck, J. R., 398*n*.
Beck, P. G., 248, 474*n*., 484
Becker, Howard, 266

Beebe, G. W., 50*n*., 57
Beers, Howard, 219, 221
Bell, E. H., 265, 276
Bell, Howard M., 144, 188, 195, 270, 414
Bell, Hugh M., 126–127
Benedict, Agnes, 317
Bennett, C. G., 479
Bernard, L. L., 61*n*., 91*n*., 120*n*., 132, 133,
    303, 346*n*.
Bernert, Eleanor H., 169*n*.
Bigelow, H. A., 490*n*.
Blackwell, Gordon W., 477
Blumenthal, Albert, 298, 303
Boas, Franz, 71*n*.
Bogardus, Emory S., 156*n*.
Booth, Charles, 216
Borsodi, Ralph, 57, 101, 388, 509
Bossard, J. H. S., 31*n*., 163*n*., 173
Bowden, Witt, 445*n*., 461
Bradley, E. H., 365*n*.
Bradshaw, H. C., 362*n*., 363*n*., 365*n*., 367*n*.
Branson, E. C., 39*n*., 160
Brooks, Melvin S., 446*n*., 448*n*., 453*n*., 455,
    456*n*., 479*n*.
Brown, Benjamin, 246
Brown, Josephine C., 471
Brown, Malcolm, 461
Browning, Grace, 471
Brunner, E. de S., 15, 22*n*., 24*n*.–26*n*., 28,
    38*n*., 40, 63, 82, 84, 133, 143*n*., 158*n*.,
    186, 210, 265, 294*n*., 325, 342*n*., 345,
    351, 358, 372, 389, 471, 511
Burgess, E. W., 131*n*., 137*n*., 157*n*., 314*n*.,
    323, 325, 348*n*.
Burgess, R. L., 253
Burt, N. I., 99, 377

C

Cain, B. H., 358
Caldwell, Morris G., 217–218, 221, 316

SUBJECT INDEX

A

AAA (see Agricultural Adjustment Administration)
Absentee landlord, 427, 429
Acadians, French, 153–154
Accommodation, as a factor in social control, 297–298
  in farm-to-farm movement, 222–243
  problem of, 163–166
  vocational, 212–214
  (See also Adjustment)
Adjustment, of city-to-farm migrants, 254–260
  of farm tenants, 437
  of farm-to-city migrants, 211–220, 216, 357–358
  of farm-to-farm migrants, 222–243, 357–358
  of farm youth, 393–413
  marital, 319–324
  occupational, 259
  personal, 300, 302, 344
  in rural and urban cultures, 4–5
  (See also Accommodation; Rural conditioning)
Adolescence in modern society, 394
Advertising in farm and urban magazines, 87, 289
Affiliated church, 356
Age composition, 33–39
  and migration, 167–171
  significance of, 37–39
Agricultural Adjustment Administration, 131, 295, 383–386, 419
Agricultural ladder, 417, 419, 444
Agricultural policy, national, 382–388
Agricultural regions, 66
Agricultural revolution, 10–11, 21, 283, 285
Agricultural villages, 293, 300–301
  (See also Farm villages; Villages)

Agriculture, changes in, 278–281
  child labor in, 467–468
  commercialization of, 269, 444, 471, 483–484, 506
  customary folkways in, 86–87, 100
  economic returns in, 193–198
  government activities in, 382–388
  industrialization of, 444, 506
  labor displacement in, 419n., 449–451, 483, 506
  labor problem in, 444–461
  leaders in, 107–109
  persons engaged in, 10, 36
  research in, 87, 281, 284
  seasonal, 445–449, 451
  specialization in, 503–504
  subsidized, 384–386
  techniques of, 67, 286, 283
  tenure distribution in, 416–417
  tools of, 85–86
  training in, 341, 401–403
  (See also Farming)
Allport-Vernon scale, 88
Almanac, Dr. Miles', 70
Amana Colony, 18, 152–153
Ambivalence of the farmer, 123–124
America, stratification in, 262–263, 275
  (See also United States)
American Country Life Association, 408
American Institute of Public Opinion, 415
American Library Association, 368
Anatomy of the Rural Community, The, 511
Appalachian area, daily life in, 68
  language of, 93n.
  migrants from, 216–217
  migration back to, 245
  migration from, 168
  part-time farming in, 248
  relief loads in, 474–475
Arkansas, need for migrant workers in, 447
Army Alpha Test, 105